D077067

THE COMPLETE BOOK

of

20TH CENTURY MUSIC

THE
COMPLETE BOOK OF

20th Century Music

New and Revised Edition

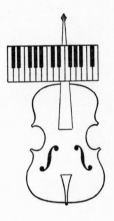

by David Ewen

Prentice-Hall, Inc.
Englewood Cliffs, N. J.

Books by DAVID EWEN

The Unfinished Symphony: The Life of Franz Schubert...From Bach to Stravinsky...Wine, Women and Waltz...The Man With the Baton...Composers of Today...Hebrew Music...Composers of Yesterday...Twentieth Century Composers...Musical Vienna (in collaboration with Frederic Ewen)...Men and Women Who Make Music...Pioneers in Music...Tales from the Vienna Woods: The Story of Johann Strauss, Father and Son...Haydn: A Good Life...Living Musicians...Music Comes to America...The Book of Modern Composers...Listen to the Mocking Words...Dictators of the Baton...Men of Popular Music...Songs of America...The Story of George Gershwin...Music for the Millions...American Composers Today...The Story of Irving Berlin...The Story of Arturo Toscanini...Fun with Musical Games and Quizzes (with Nicolas Slonimsky).

Preface

The Complete Book of 20th-Century Music is the first book in any language to analyze today's musical compositions in all the major forms.

The need for such a work is apparent. Modern music is no longer an esoteric field to be cultivated only by trained musicians. It is today heard so frequently in the concert hall, over the radio, and on phonograph records that the layman has learned to appreciate it as intelligently as he does the classics. But, for the most part, twentieth-century music is not so readily assimilable as the music of the past—certainly not on first hearing, at least. And analytical information on the major works of this century is not readily available.

The author has therefore felt that a convenient volume embracing at once the leading composers of our time and their most important works—and the major trends, movements, and techniques that influenced these composers and works—would be welcome. It should serve as a convenient help to the layman in better understanding contemporary works with which he is not yet familiar.

The plan of this book is simple. Composers are presented alphabetically, from Albéniz to Wolf-Ferrari. Each section begins with a critical analysis of the composer's style; and in certain cases where the composer initiated new techniques or movements, these are also clarified. (A convenient table of these techniques and movements, showing the sections where they are discussed, will be found at the end of the volume, beginning on page 473.) A brief biography of the composer follows. After that appear his major works, in chronological order, with such programmatic and analytical information as will help throw illumination on the music. Wherever possible, the author has utilized the programmatic analyses of the composers themselves, some of which were prepared by them expressly for this book. Discussions of operas and ballets include a succinct plot.

The attempt has always been to be informative without becoming technical, to avoid fastidiously terminologies that can be understood only by the conservatory graduate.

The greatest single problem facing the author has been the question of selection. Limitations of space have made impossible the inclusion of every functioning composer of the twentieth century; nor could every major work by composers represented be discussed. In general, the author has chosen those composers and those of their works about which the layman is most likely to seek information, by virtue of the frequency of their appearance on concert and radio programs and on records, and sometimes by virtue of their significance in influencing contemporary musical thinking. The most important composers—men like Ravel, Richard Strauss, Sibelius, Stravinsky, etc.—are discussed more or less exhaustively. Others are treated with greater selectivity.

The book includes more than a hundred composers who have produced music since January 1, 1900, and almost six hundred musical compositions. (For those interested in such detailed breakdowns, the book includes analyses of 77 concertos for solo instrument and orchestra; 118 symphonies; 59 orchestral suites; 11 orchestral rhapsodies; 117 other works for orchestra; 33 ballets; 47 operas; 30 major choral works; 57 works for chamber-music ensembles; 38 major works for the piano, and numerous smaller piano pieces; and 9 song cycles, as well as many songs.)

In cases where important works were written *before* 1900 by composers represented in this book, they are touched upon briefly in the biographical sections.

DAVID EWEN

Little Neck, N. Y.

Contents

SUPPLEMENT

Introduction

To a great many people, the term *modern music* implies much more than merely the music of our times. It signifies music that is discordant and disordered, as disrespectful of reason as it is of tradition; a twentieth-century phenomenon.

It is quite true that many composers today have gone in for unorthodox musical sounds and forms.

In an attempt to give music more *Lebensraum*, some composers have broken down the confining walls of structure and allowed their musical ideas to roam freely in unrestricted spaces. They have freed themselves from the so-called tyranny of the key center (or tonic) by writing atonally. They have opened up new avenues of musical expression by combining tonalities, rhythms, notes which never before have been joined.

Inevitably, perhaps, some composers have gone to extremes. They have written for "instruments" which never before have been called upon to make serious music. George Antheil included anvils, airplane propellers, electric bells, and automobile horns in his scoring of the *Ballet Mécanique*. An Italian modernist by the name of Luigi Russolo wrote a work for "thunderers," "whistlers," and even a "snorer." Nicolas Slonimsky has a composition calling for "a cat's meow" and another in which toy balloons are to be pricked by hairpins at a climactic moment. Ferde Grofé has a typewriter banging in *Tabloid,* and Richard Strauss invented wind and thunder machines for *Don Quixote* and *An Alpine Symphony.*

What must surely be the ultimate in outlandish instrumentation was achieved by Harold G. Davison in a work entitled *Auto Accident.* His score calls for the following equipment: "Two plate glasses, each resting on a wash bowl or crock, with a hammer or mallet, in readiness to smash them." These instructions follow: "On page nine, measure four, these plates are to be shattered with the hammer, one on the second count, and the other on the second half of the third count. In the next measure, the bowls containing the broken glass are to be emptied on a hard surface, table, or floor."

So much for eccentric instrumental effects.

Some composers, with no more regard for order and tradition, have tried to open up new horizons for melody. Mussorgsky's artistic success in molding the melodic line out of speech patterns was the starting point for those who would give birth to a new kind of recitative—the *Sprechstimme,* with its complete freedom from formal intervals. Others, not quite so ready to surrender the discipline of the interval, tried out intervals smaller than the half-tone. Alois Haba, a Czech, devoted himself exclusively to the writing of quarter-tone music. His opera, *Die Mutter,* required not only quarter-tone singing, but even quarter-tone instruments; for the première performance, a special quarter-tone piano, quarter-tone clarinets, and quarter-tone trumpets had to be invented. A quarter-tone piano was also constructed by an American, Hans Barth, who wrote a whole library of piano music for that instrument, performing it throughout the country.

New harmonic techniques were uncovered through the blending of unrelated tones. What is probably the final step in this direction is the tone clusters of Henry Cowell. (There are, however, examples of tone-cluster writing in the music of Charles Ives, who preceded Cowell.) Cowell used to write piano works calling for the banging of fists, elbows, and forearms on the keyboard. Whenever he gave this performance it was as much an exhibition of sheer physical stamina as of musical achievement. Accepting his playing in a spirit of fun, the managing editor of the *New York World-Telegram* once sent his sports editor to cover a Cowell concert, headlining the story "Battle between Kid Cowell and Kid Steinway."

Unusual experimentation with the piano was undertaken by another American, John Cage. Cage writes a new kind of piano music for an instrument called the "prepared piano." Cage "prepares" his pianos by stuffing dampers of metal, wood, rubber, felt, and other materials between the strings in carefully measured positions. This "preparing" gives the instrument percussive qualities unknown before; and each piece by Cage requires a different "prepared" piano.

Experiments in sonority have also yielded strange sounds. Few composers have gone as far as Edgar Varèse in this direction. Preferring to call music "organized sound," Varèse has utilized combinations of tones ranging from both extremes of the register, and fantastic percussive effects. Varèse's music, which defies all conventions, is characterized by what Paul Rosenfeld once described as "piercing, golden screams, sudden stops, extremely rapid crescendi and diminuendi."

To arrive at rhythmic freedom, composers like Erik Satie began writing barless music, while composers like Stravinsky and Ives exploited complicated polyrhythms and rapidly changing meters. But the greatest rhythmic complexity seems to have been achieved by the French composer, Olivier Messiaen, who has written a ten-movement symphony, *Turangalîla.* Rhythms are augmented, diminished, reversed; they are used canonically and combined contrapuntally. There are, in the awesome words of the composer, "nonreversible rhythms, asymmetric augmentations with several rhythmic identities, rhythmic modes, and the combinations of quantitative and sounding elements in reinforcing the values and the timbre of each percussion instrument by chords which form the resonance of these timbres."

In considering these extremes, it may be wise to recall that experimentation, even excessive experimentation, is no aberration of our times alone.

When the sixteenth-century *camerata* of Florence broke with poly-phony to produce the "new art" of homophony—a single melody with harmonic accompaniment, in place of several simultaneously sounded melo-dies—this was as much a break with the past as Schoenberg's desertion of tonality. To sixteenth-century ears, the sound produced by this new art seemed as strange and acrid as those of Schoenberg may seem to us. When Rameau (and Gluck after him) turned his back on the formalized opera of the Italians to produce the first music dramas, he was regarded by his con-temporaries with the same proportion of ridicule and anger that confronted Wagner a century ago, and Debussy and Alban Berg after him. The very learned Austrian *Kapellmeisters* of the eighteenth century went to their Emperor to denounce Haydn as a charlatan because he dared to tamper with (and thereby to amplify) existing symphonic forms. Haydn's successors—Mozart, Beethoven, Schubert, Schumann, Chopin, Liszt, and Wagner—all struck out for new paths. By doing so, they enriched the language of har-mony, changed existing concepts of melody, extended and sometimes created musical forms.

That most of the great composers of the past were adventurous in their thinking and impatient with tradition has made it possible for music to grow and change, as every living organism must. It is, however, not without some element of paradox that at least a few of the so-called "new" techniques, which have so horrified reactionary critics of our generation, can be found in the music of the masters. Dissonance is almost as old as consonance itself. There are unresolved discords even in Monteverdi (1567-1643), a fact that inspired the sixteenth-century theorist Artusi to remark acidly that music such as this could appeal to the senses but not to reason. Mozart's Quartet in C Major (K. 465) confused and astounded contempo-raries with its opening-bar discord; to this day the work is known as the "Dissonant Quartet." Even Haydn, who admired and loved Mozart without reservation, was puzzled by this strange music, and could only remark: "If Mozart wrote it, he must have had good reason to do so." Beethoven opened his First Symphony with a dominant seventh, and for doing this was accused by some critics of being downright stupid.

Nor is dissonance the only one of the much reviled twentieth-century practices to be found in the music of the past. Percy Scholes, in the *Oxford Companion to Music,* quotes an interesting canonic passage from one of Bach's works which is unmistakably polytonal. The whole-tone scale was used—before Debussy—by Mozart, Rossini, and Berlioz. The shifting tonali-ties and daring voice-leading in Beethoven's last quartets give a hint, and a strong one, of atonality. Polyrhythm can be found in Brahms, unorthodox intervals and harmonies in Chopin and Schumann.

Once, in analyzing a piece of music, Eric Blom pointed to several examples of so-called "modern" writing within the space of a few bars. He noted "a diminished seventh and a sweeping skip in the seventh bar, an unexpected transition to the tonic minor in the second, discordant suspensions in the next three, and a grinding false relation." It almost seems as if Blom were describing a piece of music by Bartók or some other twentieth-century rebel. Actually, he was discussing the ethereal slow movement of Mozart's C Major Piano Concerto (K. 467)!

Not everything modern, then, is new.

Nor is everything that is modern essentially "modern."

Iconoclasm is an intriguing facet of twentieth-century music. But it is by no means the only one, nor even the most important. For every composer who, like Bartók and Schoenberg, has fearlessly looked to the future, there have been others who have preferred to look to the past. The later Stravinsky, Casella, Respighi—even a younger American like Norman Dello Joio—have often gone to the seventeenth century for their forms and styles. (As did Debussy.) Hindemith has adopted the polyphonic style of the baroque age, though in a modernized version. Debussy and Paul Creston have at times returned to the melody of the Gregorian chant for their thematic material, and Roy Harris has often gone in for modal writing. Henry Cowell has recently utilized themes adapted from old American hymns.

If a Sessions or an Ives has gone in for excessive complexity, there have been others who have preferred the most stringent economy and directness of expression. Jean Françaix and Francis Poulenc have virtually made a fetish of simplicity in many of their works. Aaron Copland has consciously adopted a style that can be easily assimilated by unsophisticated audiences; others have done likewise, motivated by political or social considerations. Functional music also demands the most simple approach, and composers like Hindemith, Weill, and Copland have produced a kind of music that can serve an educational or utilitarian function.

For every Webern or Schoenberg who has gone in for cerebralism, and for every Reger and Busoni who has filled his work with intellectualism, there is an Elgar or a Glazunov who prefers the romantic and the emotional, the sensual and the passionate.

In other words, there are more approaches than one in the music of our day. The music of our time has been subjected to the same forces of action and reaction which have always produced opposing styles in the past.

In the last decades of the nineteenth century, German romanticism was perhaps the greatest single influence in music. The Wagnerian spell was irresistible. The younger men—under the enchantment of *Tristan* and the *Ring*—rivaled each other in the invention of gargantuan structures, elaborate orchestrations, overwritten harmonies and polyphony, and in producing gigantic climaxes, overpowering dramatic effects, passionate moods, sensuality. German composers not only spent their emotions lavishly within these musical superstructures; they sometimes translated philosophical concepts and

Faustian struggles into tones as well. With Mahler, Pfitzner, Reger, and Busoni this romantic approach was carried into the twentieth century.

Almost inevitably, forces were set into motion to counteract such excesses of romanticism. Erik Satie and Claude Debussy wrote miniatures, used subtlety of suggestion and delicacy of effect. Thus impressionism came into vogue. But impressionism also bred indiscretions, and music became overprecious and oversensual. Reaction came with the expressionist abstractions of Schoenberg and his disciples: music was now stripped of all emotion and feeling, reduced to the barest of essentials, and given the exactness of a mathematical formula. Others combated both romanticism and impressionism (and then the desiccated writing of the expressionists) by reverting to the classic forms and the simple expressions of the old composers, thereby bringing into being the neo-classic school.

To a great extent, the birth of the Russian national school in the latter part of the nineteenth century was also an open challenge to German art forms and concepts. By realizing an idiom and style derived from their own folk sources, Russian composers negated Germanic traditions. Out of the examples of the "Russian Five"—Mussorgsky, Rimsky-Korsakov, Cui, Balakirev, and Borodin—came the national schools that sprouted so richly in many parts of the twentieth-century world.

With many expressionist and neo-classic composers, music was becoming too much of an esoteric art appealing only to the intellectual few. A powerful movement away from this tendency was set into motion in different countries. In the Soviet Union the attempt was made to create a proletarian art speaking to and for the masses. In Germany of the 1920's, functional music for schools, radio, theater, and the movies was produced by men like Hindemith and Weill. In this country, composers like Copland, Blitzstein, Gershwin, and Morton Gould introduced the styles and techniques of popular and folk music into their major works.

In the last analysis, movements and countermovements, actions and reactions, are only incidental forces in the work of major composers. The most significant influence is still the creative one: the production of works of art that are honest, forceful, original. To the historian or critic throwing a coup d'oeil over the first fifty years of the twentieth century, it may be illuminating to remark that trends were crystallized with Debussy's *Pelléas et Mélisande,* Strauss's *Salome,* Stravinsky's *Rite of Spring* and *L'Histoire du Soldat,* Berg's *Wozzeck,* Falla's *El Amor Brujo,* Hindemith's *Mathis der Maler,* Ravel's *Daphnis et Chloé,* Scriabin's piano sonatas and symphonies, Gershwin's *Rhapsody in Blue,* and so forth. To the same historian, it may be important to point out that in these works new techniques were realized—in many cases made possible—by the excesses of the experimentalists. But to the lover of great music, the salient fact is only that these works are of major artistic importance, that this is music which brings esthetic pleasure and belongs with the significant creations of all time.

ISAAC ALBÉNIZ

Until Isaac Albéniz met and became a friend of his compatriot, Felipe Pedrell, he was a musician of great natural aptitude but with no apparent direction or purpose in his composing. He made a living as a pianist. As a composer, he produced mostly minor and unoriginal works.

Felipe Pedrell (1841-1922) was a Spanish scholar whose researches into old Spanish music were of great musicological importance. His definitive editions of Spanish church and organ music and his rediscovery of the folk music of Andalusia, Catalonia, and the Basque country brought into the light a rich but long-neglected heritage of music. These researches (together with his own passionate belief in Spanish folk music and dance as vital creative forces) pointed out a new goal for the composers of his native land. And his influence helped create a school of national Spanish composers. This school, of which Albéniz was destined to become the first major figure, and which was later to include Granados, Turina, and Falla, gave artistic distinction to Spanish music.

It was Pedrell who aroused Albéniz's thus-far latent ambition to become a serious composer; it was Pedrell who encouraged the younger man to turn to Spanish backgrounds and idioms for his inspiration and materials.

While Albéniz wrote operas, operettas (*zarzuelas*), and various works for the orchestra, his best and most inventive vein lay in music for the piano. In this field his work stemmed directly from Franz Liszt, both in his rhapsodic style and in his skillful exploitation of piano technique.

The predominating trait of Albéniz's music is its unmistakable Spanish personality. Inspired by Pedrell, he sought to interpret his native land: its people, geography, folklore; its sights, sounds, and smells. Though Catalan by birth, Albéniz brought to his music the sensuous texture of Andalusian music, which was sinuous in melodic line, flashing in rhythm, brilliant in color, warm in feeling, and volatile in its alternation between gaiety and melancholy.

Albéniz was born in Camprodón, in the province of Gerona, Spain, on May 29, 1860. His formal education, begun with Marmontel at the age of six and continued at the Madrid Conservatory two years later, was of brief duration. Albéniz ran away from school and home, and traveled aimlessly from one city to another, earning his living by playing the piano. A craving for musical knowledge eventually sent him to the Leipzig Conservatory, where he studied for a short period with Jadassohn and Reinecke. He then went to Brussels to study with François Gevaert. Subsequently he devoted himself seriously to the piano (this development was inspired by personal contacts with Liszt) and undertook a concert tour.

Settling in Madrid he met Pedrell, who turned his musical activity into more significant channels. In 1893, Albéniz went to Paris to concentrate on serious composition. A piano work, *Catalonia* (which he later orchestrated), was his first major attempt to write national music. It was also the first of his works to be performed by a major organization (the Société Nationale of Paris, 1899).

Serious illness induced Albéniz to return to his native land, where he spent the remaining years of his life. His own physical sufferings, the death of his daughter, and the chronic ailment of his wife all combined to make his closing years somber ones. It was during this period of mental depression and physical disability that he wrote what must be conceded to be his crowning masterpiece, the *Iberia* for piano.

Albéniz died in Cambo-les-Bains, in the Pyrenees, on May 18, 1909.

Besides *Iberia,* which is discussed below, Albéniz is best known for the following pieces for the piano: the nocturne, *"Córdoba,"* from his suite *Cantos de España; "Sevillana,"* from *Suite Española;* the Tango in D major, op. 164, no. 2, a prototype of all tango music; and *Navarra,* which was completed after the composer's death by Déodat de Séverac.

For *"Fête-Dieu à Seville"* (or *"El Corpus Christi en Sevilla"*), see *Iberia.*

IBERIA, for piano (1906-1909). Book I: 1. Evocación; 2. El Puerto; 3. Fête-Dieu à Seville or El Corpus Christi en Sevilla. Book II: 1. Rondeña; 2. Almería; 3. Triana. Book III: 1. El Albaicín; 2. El Polo; 3. Lavapiés. Book IV: 1. Málaga; 2. Jérez; 3. Eritaña.

Few tonal portraits of Spain penetrate so deeply into the heart of that country or reproduce its pulse and heartbeat so authentically as does this suite. The spirit and soul of Spain, in subtlest nuances and colors, are found in this music. Rich in imagery, varied in the use of colorful backgrounds suggesting the Orient, deft in projecting color and atmosphere, sensitive in evoking not only sounds but even smells, *Iberia* is, indeed, Spain set to music.

The first performances of the four books of *Iberia* were given by a young French pianist by the name of Blanche Selva between the years of 1906 and 1909, a single book being introduced at a time. But for the grace of this artist, the world of music would have been altogether robbed of this wonderful music. When Albéniz completed the first book, he was seized by a stifling mental depression. He was haunted by the fear that the music he had just composed was too difficult for performance. This fear grew so harrowing that he was determined to destroy his work rather than permit unplayable music to survive him. He might have yielded to this impulse. Fortunately, Blanche Selva learned of his fears. She prevailed on the composer to permit her to have the music before he destroyed it. In a few days' time she returned the music. But she also sat down to Albéniz' piano and played it for him from memory. Evidently the composer needed no further convincing, for he not only saved the work but also proceeded to write the three other books of the suite.

BOOK ONE: *"Evocación"* is a poignant Andalusian song whose sadness is contrasted with the gaiety of the *jota*. *"El Puerto"* describes the frenetic fiesta in a major Spanish resort. *"Fête-Dieu à Seville"* (or *"El Corpus Christi en Sevilla"*) dramatizes an ecclesiastical procession through the streets of Spain, with all its pomp and color, and with the majestic tolling of church bells. (This piece is often heard at orchestral concerts in the colorful transcription by Leopold Stokowski or in the more sober one by Enrique Fernández Arbós.)

BOOK TWO: *"Rondeña"* is a stately Spanish dance, a variant of the fandango. *"Almería"* portrays the Mediterranean seaport in the rhythm of the tarantas, a dance peculiar to that city, and with a jota-like melody. *"Triana"* depicts a suburb of Seville, famous for its gypsies, flashing castanets, and guitars.

BOOK THREE: *"El Albaicín"* captures the melancholia and excitement of a gypsy song heard in a Seville suburb. *"El Polo"* quotes a well-known Andalusian song of the same name, and is to be played, in the composer's own words, "with the spirit of a sob." *"Lavapiés"* interprets a popular quarter of Madrid.

BOOK FOUR: *"Málaga"* blends the flavor of a malagueña (the dance typical of Málaga) with a graceful theme. *"Jérez"* is patterned after a gypsy dance known as the *soleares,* and consists of a principal theme beautifully embellished with decorative filigree. *"Eritaña"* is a tavern on the outskirts of Seville, providing the background for this gaily rhythmic and at other moments highly poignant piece of music.

Arbós orchestrated five sections: *"Evocación," "El Puerto," "Fête-Dieu à Seville," "Triana,"* and *"El Albaicín."*

GEORGE ANTHEIL 1900—1959

Though long ago he abandoned the musical indiscretions that earned him the sobriquet of "bad boy of music," George Antheil will undoubtedly be permanently remembered for his notorious *Ballet Mécanique*. Scored for machines, anvils, bells, automobile horns, player pianos, percussion, the *Ballet Mécanique* created a mild sensation when introduced in Paris in June, 1926. On April 10, 1927, it was heard in Carnegie Hall, New York, under the direction of Eugene Goossens. The rather vulgar publicity campaign preceding this performance succeeded in converting a provocative musical event into something resembling a circus. The performance itself was further vulgarized by its indulgence in garish and sensational effects not called for in the score. The audience was demonstratively hostile (one wag, seated in the front row, attached a white handkerchief to his cane and rose, waving his symbol of surrender). The critics were equally vituperative.

The *Ballet Mécanique*—and the other iconoclastic works Antheil wrote during this period—are gone and forgotten; it is doubtful if they will ever be missed, even by the composer himself. Since then he has composed music in an entirely different vein. The day for experiment was over. He now sought to write expressive, dramatic music according to classical rules and within traditional forms. It is the music that Antheil has been writing since 1939 which is now represented on major concert programs and which has placed him among the more interesting American composers of our time.

Antheil was born in Trenton, New Jersey, on July 8, 1900. After an extended period of study with Constanin Sternberg and Ernest Bloch, he was admitted to the Settlement School of Philadelphia (precursor of the Curtis Institute) as a scholarship pupil. During this period, and while still under Bloch's influence, he wrote his first symphony.

In 1922, he toured Europe as a concert pianist, performing in leading cities and achieving more notoriety than fame through his passionate espousal of the most ultramodern examples of contemporary piano music. A performance of his First Symphony in Berlin convinced him that he preferred composition to playing the piano. He settled in Paris, where he wrote numerous works in the most advanced styles. They attracted considerable attention and considerable abuse. The high point of this phase in his artistic career was the performance of *Ballet Mécanique*.

After achieving substantial success with a jazz opera, *Transatlantic* (introduced in Frankfurt-am-Main in 1930), Antheil returned to the United States, settling in Hollywood. For a period of three years, from 1936 to 1939, he did no composing whatever. When he returned to writing music it was with a new romantic approach and a more orthodox style. He died in New York City on February 12, 1959.

The following works by Antheil (listed here in alphabetical order) are discussed below: Sonata No. 4 for Piano; Symphony No. 4, ("1942"); Symphony No. 6. For *Ballet Mécanique,* see biographical sketch above.

SYMPHONY NO. 4, "1942."

This is one of Antheil's most successful symphonic works. Written in 1942, it is a picture of World War II at that time. The composer explains: "In this symphony I attempted to strike out in a field which, in modern music, has been (I feel) rather neglected: the attempt to write a large symphony which, in its own modern way, attempts to be emotionally free, expressive of some large canvas of modern life. The symphony commences in chaos, fear, even war; but through suffering and pathos (in the second movement) and even brutal irony (in the Scherzo), finally leads to hope and future glory."

The symphony (which is played without interruption) comprises a strange mélange of many different styles and feelings: marching music, waltzes, thematic material suggesting Red Army choruses, dance tunes, jazz elements. But the predominating mood is martial. In organizing his material, Antheil resorted to the use of a march-like motto theme (somewhat similar to the one in Shostakovich's Seventh Symphony) which links the entire work, and is at times developed powerfully.

Two novel features distinguish the score. The second movement, traditionally slow in the classical symphony, here carries on the excitement and energy of the first movement, and does not lapse into repose until the development section. In the Scherzo, the traditional trio is replaced by a fugue.

Leopold Stokowski and the NBC Symphony introduced this symphony over the NBC network on February 13, 1944. It made such a favorable impression that it was greatly sought after by leading American orchestras. In a short period it was heard in San Francisco (Monteux), St. Louis (Golschmann), New York (Leinsdorf), and several other major cities.

SONATA No. 4 FOR PIANO (1948). I. Allegro giocoso-ironico. II. Andante. III. Vivo.

In this delightful sonata, one of Antheil's best works, the composer passes with flexibility from sentimental moods to ironic ones. The first movement burlesques salon piano playing; to make its point more obvious, it hastily quotes a few measures of Chopin, the darling of salon performers. In the slow movement, Antheil's lyrical vein grows tender. A powerful momentum gives the final movement drive, while sharp contrasts provide unflagging interest. Of the final movement, Virgil Thomson wrote in the *New York Herald Tribune:* "It is one of the few brilliantly conceived toccatas in the whole modern repertory."

The sonata received its première performance in New York City on November 21, 1948; Frederick Marvin was the performing artist.

SYMPHONY NO. 6 (1948). I. Allegretto. II. Larghetto. III. Allegro molto.

Antheil's Sixth Symphony was introduced in San Francisco by the San Francisco Symphony Orchestra under Pierre Monteux on February 10, 1949.

The first movement, in sonata form, was inspired by a reproduction of the Eugène Delacroix painting, *Liberty Leading the People.* There is here, the composer explained, "the smoke of battle, courage, despair, and hope, all marching into the future." In the Larghetto, the composer wished— as he noted—to "write an expanded lyric slow movement." He selected the song form with a trio of unconventional length. The composer described this movement as having the "breath of autumn, of sadness, and of optimism at once." The closing movement, a rondo, "means the triumph of joy and optimism over despair, war, annihilation." It is for the composer the natural follow-up to the "courage and hope-against-hope mood of the first movement."

KURT ATTERBERG   1887—

Though his name does not often appear on American concert programs, Kurt Atterberg is one of Sweden's major living composers. Probably no other Swedish composer of the twentieth century has been so extensively published, performed, and admired in his own country. He belongs with those conservative men who prefer self-expression to innovation. He fills classical and well-disciplined forms with music that is romantic, though Nordic in restraint. He achieves beauty with subdued colors and tight-lipped feelings and force through understatement. Some of his best works are national in feeling, drawing their materials from Swedish folk music.

Atterberg was born in Göteborg, Sweden, on December 12, 1887, and attended the University there. Deciding to become a civil engineer he went to Stockholm for further study. At the same time he took music lessons with Johann Andreas Hallén. From 1912 to 1914 he conducted a theater orchestra in Stockholm, holding at the same time an engineering post. Subsequently, a government subsidy enabled him to abandon engineering for music, and he then turned intensively to creative work, to conducting, and to writing musical criticism.

In 1928, Atterberg was subjected to considerable criticism and publicity. At that time, his Sixth Symphony won the first prize of ten thousand dollars in a world-wide competition sponsored by the Columbia Phonograph Company. The purpose of the competition was to honor the centenary of Franz Schubert's death with a work in the spirit of that master. Some of the critics, reviewing Atterberg's symphony, pointed out numerous borrowings from the works of other composers—Rimsky-Korsakov, Elgar, Dvořák, Granados. Ernest Newman suggested that these borrowings were deliberate. Early in 1929, Atterberg wrote an article called "How I Fooled the Music World" in which he confessed that this was so, that his symphony was intended as a satire on Schubert connoisseurs, and that by winning the grand prize he had perpetrated a successful hoax.

The following works by Atterberg are discussed below: Symphony No. 4 in G Minor; *A Värmland Rhapsody*.

SYMPHONY NO. 4 IN G MINOR (1918). I. Con forza. II. Andante III. Scherzo. IV. Finale.

This "little" symphony, as Atterberg once described it, freely utilizes thematic material derived from Swedish folk music. The two basic themes of the first movement (the first played, beginning in the third measure, by the first violins and violas; the second, by the oboe) have a distinct folk song character. A fermata leads to a beautiful slow movement in which a poignant melody for the clarinet is later subjected to variation. A gay dance tune, played by the first violins, sets the mood for the brief Scherzo. The finale is a spirited rondo vitalized by dance rhythms.

The Fourth Symphony was introduced in Stockholm in March, 1919.

A VÄRMLAND RHAPSODY, for orchestra, op. 36 (1933).

Atterberg wrote this rhapsody to honor the seventy-fifth birthday of Sweden's celebrated novelist, Selma Lagerlöf. For his musical ideas he went to the folk music indigenous to Värmland, the locale of Lagerlöf's masterpiece, *Gösta Berling's Saga*.

The work opens with a slow introduction. After a melody for violins, the tempo accelerates, then slackens; an eloquent melody for solo flute is now heard. The main section of the rhapsody then unfolds; the materials are two folk themes, the first played by the first violins, the second by the clarinet. After a climax is reached, the rhapsody ends with a soft, contemplative coda.

The Rhapsody was first heard over the Swedish Radio in Stockholm on November 20, 1933.

SAMUEL BARBER   1910—

As the nephew of Louise Homer, the celebrated contralto, Samuel Barber came into contact with and learned to appreciate great singing early. Subsequently, he himself studied the voice, and even gave several Lieder recitals.

His professional career as singer is now well behind him. But as a composer, Barber has never quite given up "singing." Of his many admirable qualities—his fine sense of musical design, the economy of his means, the inexorable logic of his thinking—the most significant is perhaps his highly developed lyricism. He has the gift of writing sustained melodies that flow easily and flexibly and have a high degree of expressiveness. This melodic gift was evident with his first apprentice efforts: the two songs he wrote when he was eighteen, and the excellent *Dover Beach* (after Matthew Arnold), for string quartet and voice, that came three years after that. As his talent ripened, he added poetic feeling to his lyricism. And, more recently, a growing intensity and strength of idiom have entered his writing. But his lyricism has remained on a high plane of eloquence; and the emotional factor has never been sacrificed.

Barber was born in West Chester, Pennsylvania, on March 9, 1910. Precocious in music, he was filling a post as organist when he was only twelve years old. His musical education took place principally at the Curtis Institute with Rosario Scalero (composition), Isabelle Vengerova (piano), and Emilio de Gogorza (voice). When he was eighteen, he began composing seriously; when he was twenty-three, one of his orchestral works was performed by the Philadelphia Orchestra—the overture, *The School for Scandal*.

Between 1935 and 1937, he won the Pulitzer Fellowship and the American Prix de Rome. In Rome, he wrote a symphony that was introduced there, and then performed at the Salzburg Festival. Soon after returning to this country he achieved additional prominence by being the first American composer whose work was performed by Arturo Toscanini and the NBC Symphony; on that occasion the *Adagio for Strings* and the Essay No. 1 were introduced. During World War II, Barber served in the Army Air Corps. In 1958 he received the Pulitzer Prize for his opera, *Vanessa* (see Supplement).

The following works by Barber are discussed below: *Adagio for Strings;* Concerto for Cello and Orchestra; Essays Nos. 1 and 2, for orchestra; *Medea;* Symphony No. 1 (in one movement); Symphony No. 2.

For *Cave of the Heart,* see *Medea.*

SYMPHONY NO. 1 (in one movement), op. 9 (1936).

While Barber was in Rome on the American Prix de Rome, he wrote the *Symphony in One Movement.* In December, 1936, it was introduced in Rome by the Augusteo Orchestra, Bernardino Molinari conducting. After Rodzinski had introduced the work in Cleveland the following year, he presented it with considerable success at the Salzburg Festival; this was the first time that an American composer had been represented there.

The composer has explained that the form of the symphony "is a synthetic treatment of the four-movement classical symphony. It is based on three themes of the initial Allegro non troppo, which retain throughout the work their fundamental character.... After a brief development of the three themes ... the first theme, in diminution, forms the basis of a Scherzo section (Vivace). The second theme then appears in augmentation in an extended Andante tranquillo. An intense crescendo introduces the finale, which is a short passacaglia based on the first theme."

Barber revised the symphony in 1944. The new version was heard for the first time on March 9, 1944, in New York City; Bruno Walter conducted the New York Philharmonic-Symphony Orchestra.

ADAGIO FOR STRINGS, op. 11 (1937).

This short work is noteworthy for its sustained melodic writing, and for the success with which it maintains a serene mood. The entire work is a development of a single melodic idea, which is given by the violins in the opening section. Written simply and romantically, it requires no analysis to be appreciated. On November 5, 1938, it was introduced by the NBC Symphony under Arturo Toscanini.

ESSAYS NOS. 1 AND 2, for orchestra, opp. 12 and 17 (1937; 1942).

Barber's choice of a literary rather than a musical form for these two short orchestral works is significant. Each composition bears a strong resemblance to an essay in that a thought is projected in the beginning, and then is allowed to develop to a logical conclusion in the way a central thought is elaborated by an essayist.

The first Essay is somewhat slighter in texture than the second. It is a Scherzo, comprising a series of simple themes (Andante sostenuto, Allegro molto, Scherzando) which are allowed freedom to develop along rather slight dimensions. The quiet mood established by the opening subject is restored at the close of the work, which ends in a questioning attitude. Midway there is a vigorous martial subject for the horns.

The second Essay has more proportion and stature. The three themes (the first announced by a solo flute; the second by the violas; the third by the brass) are developed dexterously in a fugal section reaching a dramatic climax. A repetition of the main theme, fortissimo, is followed by a coda in which the third theme is suggested by the basses.

The first Essay was introduced by the NBC Symphony under Toscanini on November 5, 1938. The second Essay was first heard on April 16, 1942, in a performance by the New York Philharmonic-Symphony Orchestra under Bruno Walter.

SYMPHONY NO. 2, op. 19 (1944). I. Allegro ma non troppo. II. Andante un poco mosso. III. Presto; Allegro risoluto; Allegro molto.

During World War II, Barber served as corporal in the Army at Fort Worth, Texas. There he wrote this symphony on commission for the Army Air Force. Though the composer insists that the work has no programmatic implications, it gives every indication of having been inspired by, and written as a tribute to, the Air Force. In the second movement, a climactic moment is suddenly interrupted by the voice of an electric instrument (manufactured especially for this composition) which simulates the sound of a radio beam giving a code message to a pilot instructing him on his course when he is flying "blind." Actually, this "theme" is given considerable prominence throughout the movement, being taken up rhythmically by the other instruments in the projection of the above and other code signals.

This symphony represents a departure from Barber's earlier preoccupation with the lyric element. Its dynamic power, rather than melodic content, is its great attraction. The first movement is in sonata form; the second has a nocturnal character; while the third is built around a set of variations and culminates in a fugue.

Serge Koussevitzky and the Boston Symphony Orchestra introduced this symphony in Boston on March 3, 1944. One week later, it was transmitted by short wave throughout the world by the OWI. In 1947, Barber revised the symphony extensively.

CONCERTO FOR CELLO AND ORCHESTRA, op. 22 (1945). I. Allegro moderato. II. Andante molto sostenuto. III. Molto allegro e appassionato.

On April 5, 1946, this concerto was introduced in Boston by Raya Garbousova and the Boston Symphony Orchestra under Koussevitzky. The

New York Music Critics Circle singled it out as the most important new American work of that season.

The main theme of the first movement is heard on the English horn after two introductory measures, and is later taken up by the solo instrument. A second subject is also shared between orchestra (the strings) and the cello. Following a cadenza for the cello, the original material returns and the movement ends with the two opening measures.

The slow movement is given up almost entirely to a sustained song which begins after a single introductory bar and which engages the attention of both the orchestra and the cello. Brilliant material appears in the closing movement, which has particularly effective virtuoso passages for the cello. But the movement does not concern itself exclusively with virtuosity; one of its finest pages is an emotional passage chanted by the cello.

MEDEA (CAVE OF THE HEART), ballet, op. 23 (1946).

This ballet score was commissioned by the Ditson Fund of Columbia University for Martha Graham. The subject of Medea and Jason was chosen, but (as the composer has explained), "neither Miss Graham nor the composer wished to use the Medea-Jason legend literally. These mythical characters served rather to project psychological states of jealousy and vengeance which are timeless."

The composer wrote further about this work:

"The choreography and the music were conceived, as it were, on two levels, the ancient mythical and the contemporary. Medea and Jason first appear as godlike, superhuman figures of the Greek tragedy. As the tension and conflict between them increase, they step out of their legendary roles from time to time to become the modern man and woman, caught in the nets of jealousy and destructive love; and at the end reassume their mythical quality. In both the dancing and the music, archaic and contemporary idioms are used. Medea, in her final scene after the denouement, becomes once more the descendant of the sun."

The ballet was introduced under the title *Serpent of the Heart* (somewhat later retitled *Cave of the Heart*), on May 10, 1946, in New York. Barber himself preferred the title *Medea*. When, in 1947, he prepared an orchestral suite drawn from the ballet score, the work bore the preferred name. The *Medea* suite was introduced by the Philadelphia Orchestra under Eugene Ormandy on December 5, 1947. The various sections of the suite are played without pause.

SONATA IN E-FLAT MINOR FOR PIANO, op. 26, (1949). I.
Allegro energico. II. Allegro vivace e leggero. III. Adagio mesto. IV. Fuga.

Barber's piano sonata is one of his most important works. He wrote it on a commission from the League of Composers with funds provided by Richard Rodgers and Irving Berlin.

In a modern idiom which has harmonic and rhythmic robustness, physical strength is combined with a fine-grained lyrical expression. This music, as Harriet Johnson remarked in her review in the *New York Post,* "encompasses realism and fantasy, conflict and resolution, poetry and power." Energy is set loose in the opening movement, whose interest is largely rhythmic. The third movement has poignancy and pathos: feelings deeply felt are voiced in expressive lyricism. The sonata closes with a monumentally conceived fugue, within whose formal construction majesty and grandeur find expression.

The sonata was introduced in New York by Vladimir Horowitz on January 23, 1950.

BÉLA BARTÓK   1881—1945

Béla Bartók first became attracted to Hungarian folk music in 1905. It is said that while vacationing in the interior of Hungary he overhead servants singing a strange, haunting melody, far different from any he had heard before. On investigation, he discovered that this tune and many others like it were indigenous to the district. His curiosity aroused, Bartók decided to travel throughout Hungary to discover whether other parts of that land had their own melodies. He visited remote corners, lived with the peasants, wrote down copious notes. The first adventure proved so fruitful that Bartók undertook several other extensive tours (some of them with his friend, Zoltán Kodály). He wandered from the Carpathian mountains to the Adriatic, from western Slovakia to the Black Sea. He unearthed several thousand folksongs and dances then completely unknown to the rest of the world, put them down on paper, and finally issued them in monumental publications.

The folk music that Bartók uncovered was far different from the sobbing, meretricious gypsy melodies that Brahms, Liszt, and other composers had up to then exploited as authentic Hungarian music. The real folk music was harder in texture, cruder in technique, more austere in spirit. The melodies, written in modal scales, had an exotic character. The rhythms were broken, abrupt.

Bartók's intensive study of this music greatly influenced his own creative writing. Previously he had written works derivative from Debussy and Richard Strauss. He now evolved an idiom of his own in which the harsh elements of Hungarian folk music—and its rugged spirit—were assimilated. His work become dissonant, severe, even grim—ultramodern in its avoidance of both consonance and tonality. It was music, however, that carried the pulse and heartbeat of Magyar culture.

The asperity of such works as the first three string quartets, the first two piano concertos, and the *Dance Suite* found but few enthusiasts among concertgoers. Despite the fact that in these works Bartók proved himself to be one of the most independent and original voices of our time, he was sadly neglected and his work was rarely performed.

In the works written by Bartók after he had settled in this country during World War II, simplification set in. His Third Piano Concerto and his Concerto for Orchestra—sometimes accepted as his greatest works—are more personal and warmer in feeling. As Bartók himself said: "With maturity comes the wish to economize—to be more simple. Maturity is the period when one finds just measure."

Bartók was born in Nagyszentmiklós, Hungary, on March 25, 1881. He began to study music early and showed unusual talent. He was only nine when he began composing piano pieces; in his tenth year he made public appearances as a pianist. Intensive study of music followed in Pressburg with Laszlo Erkel. After that, he attended the Royal Hungarian Academy, where he was a pupil of Stephen Thomán and Hans Koessler, and where he was appointed professor of piano in 1907. Meanwhile, in 1905, he had discovered the riches of Hungarian folk music.

A shy, modest, highly introverted artist, he lived his life in Budapest in virtual retirement, devoting himself to composition, teaching, and his research work in folk music.

In 1940, with Europe at war, he came to this country to settle (as he then thought) temporarily; actually he lived here for the last years of his life. In this country, where (sad to report) he lived in comparative poverty and neglect, he was unusually productive, and this in spite of the fact that he was often ill and in pain. He died in a hospital in New York City on September 26, 1945. Death, paradoxically enough, brought him that just measure of recognition and appreciation that life had denied him. Forty-eight major performances of his works took place within a few weeks of his death.

The following works by Bartók are discussed below: Concerto for Orchestra; Concerto for Violin and Orchestra; Concerto No. 2 for Piano and Orchestra; Concerto No. 3 for Piano and Orchestra; *Music for Strings, Percussion, and Celesta;* Quartet No. 2 in A Minor.

QUARTET NO. 2 IN A MINOR, for strings, op. 17 (1917). I. Moderato. II. Allegro molto capriccioso. III. Lento.

The six string quartets of Bartók are among the most significant in the entire repertory of present-day chamber music. For variety of idiom, contrast in sonority, daring invention, resourcefulness in writing for the four instruments, and independent thinking, these quartets are virtually unique. For the Bartók student they are particularly fascinating, for they epitomize the creative evolution of the composer.

In the first two quartets, brutal chords, broken rhythms, piercingly agonizing melodic thoughts, suggest the Bartók idiom in its first phases of development. Bartók wrote his First Quartet (op. 7) in 1908. The second came almost a decade later, begun in 1915 and completed two years after that.

The Second Quartet, which is often played, opens restlessly, the restlessness growing through the movement (despite an occasional moment of calm) until it develops into feverish excitement. The atmosphere lightens considerably in the movement that follows, a Scherzo which is playful and whimsical throughout. The quartet ends, however, in a depressing mood; the music is brooding and contemplative, plumbing profound emotional depths.

CONCERTO NO. 2 FOR PIANO AND ORCHESTRA (1931).
I. Allegro. II. Adagio; Presto; Adagio. III. Allegro molto.

Emil Haraszti has written that, in his opinion, this concerto represents "the highest pinnacle of pure music." It was written five years after the First Piano Concerto, and like other works of the same period is characterized by barbaric rhythmic force. The first movement (which dispenses with the strings) opens with an introductory motive for the trumpet. The solo piano then enters with the first theme, treated at some length. The second theme follows, also played by the solo instrument. Eight introductory bars in the piano preface the development section, in which the two major themes are developed with contrapuntal skill. The strings open the second movement with a chorale-like melody, after which the piano and tympani compete in percussive statements. The middle section erupts into an exciting Presto, based on a theme first heard in the piano. The Adagio returns, and with it the original tranquillity of the movement. In the final section, barbaric forces are set loose, with tympani and piano serving as the principal protagonists.

MUSIC FOR STRINGS, PERCUSSION, AND CELESTA (1936).
I. Andante tranquillo. II. Allegro. III. Adagio. IV. Allegro molto.

The ensemble for which this composition is written is two string quartets (merged in the first movement, but treated independently thereafter), the percussion, double-basses, and celesta. The violas are heard in the first theme, played pianissimo, with background embellishments by percussion; this theme is later taken up fugally by the other strings. The movement develops in sonority until it reaches a fortissimo; then it subsides. One principal theme of the second movement is heard pizzicato (second string group), while the first string group replies with the second subject. The third movement has been described by Lawrence Gilman as a "mystical nocturne," creating a hazy atmosphere of quiet and mystery. The work closes with an energetic Allegro molto, one of whose principal subjects is a peasant dance in the Lydian mode.

The composition was introduced in Basel, Switzerland, on January 21, 1937, by a chamber orchestra directed by Paul Sacher.

CONCERTO FOR VIOLIN AND ORCHESTRA (1938). I. Allegro non troppo. II. Andante tranquillo. III. Allegro molto.

One of Bartók's unqualified masterpieces, this concerto has (in the opinion of many authorities) now found a permanent place in the violin repertory. Bartók wrote it for Zoltan Szekely, who introduced it in Amsterdam with the Concertgebouw Orchestra under Willem Mengelberg, on April 23, 1939.

In the customary three movements, the concerto adopts more or less traditional forms. The first is in the pattern of the sonata-allegro form; the second is a theme with variations; the third, a rondo. One of the distinctive technical features of the composition is the utilization of the principal themes of the first movement in a freely varied form in the concluding rondo: one of these themes is passionately romantic, while another is in the twelve-tone technique. The middle movement consists of six variations on an expressive theme.

CONCERTO FOR ORCHESTRA (1943). I. Andante non troppo; Allegro vivace. II. Giuoco delle coppie; Allegro scherzando. III. Elegia: andante non troppo. IV. Intermezzo interrotto; Allegretto. V. Finale: presto.

Bartók explained that he gave his symphonic work the designation *concerto* because of its tendency to "treat the single instruments or instrument groups in concertante or soloistic manner."

The structures of the first and fifth movements are in recognizable sonata form. "Less traditional," wrote the composer, "are ... the second and third movements. The main part of the second consists of a chain of independent short sections, by wind instruments, consecutively introduced in five pairs.... Thematically, the five sections have nothing in common.... The structure of the fourth movement is likewise chain-like; three themes appear consecutively. These constitute the core of the movement. Most of the thematic material of this movement derives from the introduction of the first movement."

Bartók completed the Concerto for Orchestra after a serious illness. This fact may partially explain the lugubrious character of the music, which opens in a somber vein and maintains the mood for the greater part of the work; in the third movement a truly funereal atmosphere is projected. There is, however, occasional (though brief) respite from gloom—in the light-hearted pages of the second movement and in the closing portions of the concerto, which sound an optimistic note, as if in reaffirmation of life.

Commissioned by the Koussevitzky Foundation, the Concerto for

Orchestra was introduced in Boston by the Boston Symphony Orchestra, under Koussevitzky on December 1, 1944.

CONCERTO NO. 3 FOR PIANO AND ORCHESTRA (1945).
I. Allegretto. II. Adagio religioso. III. Allegro vivace.

When Bartók wrote his Third Piano Concerto, he knew that he did not have much longer to live. On the last bar of his sketches he wrote the Hungarian word *vege* ("the end")—the first time he had ever done so on a manuscript. He was writing finis not only to this composition, but to his entire creative life. Indeed, the composer did not live to complete the final measures. The last seventeen bars, for which he had left no notes, were developed and scored by his intimate friend, Tibor Serly.

Bartók had originally planned the work as a concerto for two unaccompanied pianos (he intended writing it for the duo-piano team of Bartlett and Robertson). As he realized that his days were growing fewer, he revamped the work as a loving and appreciative tribute to his wife, Ditta Pasztory Bartók, to whom he knew he could leave little except his creative works. The composition, therefore, became a deeply personal message from Bartók to his wife; and he felt that for such a message the proper medium was not two solo pianos but a single piano and orchestra.

While this concerto has virtuoso passages, and while it is often spiced with Bartok dissonances, it is essentially one of Bartok's most expressive works. It would be difficult to find among his compositions music of such serenity (occasionally jarred by the momentary invasion of turbulence, but serenity nevertheless) as that which appears in the second movement. These are the finest pages of the entire concerto; and they are among the most moving pages Bartók has written.

The first movement is in the conventional sonata form, with the main subject announced by the piano; the second theme is more decorative. In the second movement, the placidity of the principal subjects (an introduction for strings, followed by an almost Bach-like chorale for the piano) receives contrast from an agitated trio. The finale is an impulsive and fiery scherzo, in which the trio is a fugue.

The world première took place in Philadelphia on February 8, 1949. György Sándor was the soloist, and the Philadelphia Orchestra was directed by Eugene Ormandy.

ARNOLD BAX   1883—1953

Early in his career, Arnold Bax was sympathetically drawn to the works of the great Irish poets and to Celtic lore. In fantasies and legends of the Irish world of make-believe, Bax found room for his imagination to move freely.

Celtic influences—symbolism, mystery, dream-fantasy—asserted themselves in his music, together with the Celtic love for decoration and imagery. Bax's early tone-poems (*In the Faëry Hills, The Garden of Fand, Tintagel*) were directly inspired by Celtic lore; these were the works which first brought him to the attention of the music world. The romantic feelings and the poetic ideas of his later works are also heavily tinged with Celtic colors.

He was a romanticist whose artistic conscience compelled him to seek beauty and to capture it in his music. Sensitively projected, usually with restraint, this beauty is not always on the surface; nor, for that matter, is the full impact of Bax's subtle thinking apparent on first contact. What Julian Herbage said of Bax's symphonies applies to all of Bax's major works: "They demand from the listener the same clear intellect and austere sense of lyrical beauty that the composer himself possesses.... Bax himself thinks quickly and spontaneously, and expects the same quality from the listener."

Sir Arnold Trevor Bax was born in London on November 8, 1883. He entered the Royal Academy of Music when he was seventeen, and for several years was a pupil of Tobias Matthay and Frederick Corder. While still a student, he began composing and, by the time he was graduated, had quite a number of reputable works to his credit. With *In the Faëry Hills,* written in 1909, he achieved his first success; with *Tintagel,* which came eight years later, he established it firmly.

A man of exceptional modesty, he lived in complete retirement, avoiding the limelight fastidiously and never permitting publicity to invade his privacy. Bax was knighted in 1937, and in 1941 was named Master of the King's Musick. He died in Cork, Ireland, on October 3, 1953.

The following works by Bax are discussed below: *In the Faëry Hills; November Woods; Overture to a Picaresque Comedy;* Quintet for Oboe and Strings; Symphony No. 3; *Tintagel.*

IN THE FAËRY HILLS, tone-poem, for orchestra (1909).

Arnold Bax once noted that for him the problem of composition was one of translating ideas and impressions into music. Some of his best works are built around a definite program.

This beautiful tone-poem, based on an episode from *The Wanderings of Usheen,* is the first of Bax's works in which Celtic elements and colors, dreams and fantasies, are absorbed into his music. It was also the first of his works to bring him recognition.

The following program is followed literally: Lured by a fairy girl to an island where revelry prevails, the poet Usheen, invited to sing of pleasure, plucks from his harp a melancholy strain. The harp is snatched from his hands and thrown into a pool. The poet then hurls himself unreservedly into the dancing and the revels.

NOVEMBER WOODS, tone-poem for orchestra (1917).

Bax has often produced pictures of nature. *November Woods,* introduced by the Hallé Orchestra on November 18, 1920, describes a bleak autumnal day. A storm sweeps the leaves and creates an atmosphere of restlessness and struggle. There is a pervading feeling of loneliness.

TINTAGEL, tone-poem for orchestra (1917).

Tintagel contains the very breath and heartbeat of Celtic poetry and legend. The composer has noted: "Though detailing no definite program, this work is intended to evoke a tone picture of the castle-crowned cliff of Tintagel, and more particularly the wide distances of the Atlantic as seen from the cliffs of Cornwall on a sunny but not windless summer day. In the middle section of the piece it may be imagined that with the increasing tumult of the sea arise memories of the historical and legendary associations of the place, especially those connected with King Arthur, King Mark, and Tristram and Iseult. Regarding the last named, it will be noticed that at the climax of the more literary division of the work there is a brief reference to one of the subjects in the first act of *Tristan.*"

QUINTET FOR OBOE AND STRINGS (1923). I. Tempo molto moderato; Allegro moderato. II. Lento espressivo. III. Allegro giocoso.

This is one of Bax' finest chamber-music works. In the first movement, two subjects predominate: one for strings, the other (an oriental melody elaborately filigreed) for solo oboe. Both ideas are developed fully before the inclusion of further material.

Celtic flavors are prominent in the meditative second movement. An extended melody for violin opens this section and is its principal material. Throughout this movement there is a prevailing feeling of melancholy. But a more cheerful note is injected in the final movement, which comprises two bucolic themes, both introduced by the oboe.

SYMPHONY NO. 3 (1929). I. Lento moderato; Allegro moderato. II. Lento. III. Moderato; Epilogue: poco lento.

There are many reputable English critics who consider the symphonies of Arnold Bax as significant as those of Sibelius. They cover, wrote Wilfrid Mellers, "a wide and rapid emotional range, from the menacingly cruel to the lyrically beautiful, and each mood is conceived with the same dispassionate intensity."

Certain traits are common to all Bax symphonies. Though all utilize three movements, they are actually extended symphonic poems. An introduction is prominent in each, while all symphonies after the Second utilize a lyrical epilogue. Other qualities which identify them are their unusual color, their indulgence in Celtic moods and atmospheres, and their frequent use of motto themes.

The first two symphonies, written respectively in 1922 and 1924, are steeped in pessimism. The third—introduced in London under Sir Henry J. Wood, on March 14, 1930—avoids melancholy and is filled with what one annotator happily described as "benevolent grace." This is music gentle, rather than somber, in character, dominated by the spirit of the Northern legends which, Bax acknowledges, influenced him subconsciously.

The symphony opens with a tender melody for bassoon. This subject is repeated by other instruments, then is enriched and extended until a highly rhythmic passage arrives (Allegro moderato). An expressive idea for first violins induces tranquillity which, for the most part, the movement maintains until the end. The solo horn opens the second movement, which, according to Robert H. Hull, "stands out as a tranquil utterance of strange beauty." Two major melodies provide the essential material: one for trumpet solo, the other for first violins. The burst of energy released in the third movement is arrested in the highly effective Epilogue, which contains some of the best music of the entire symphony: a noble passage for trombones precedes music of exceptional poignancy and arresting beauty.

OVERTURE TO A PICARESQUE COMEDY, for orchestra (1931).

Successfully introduced by the Hallé Orchestra, in November, 1931, this overture (as the composer has written) "does not pretend to be the prelude to any particular play. It is simply a piece of music associated with some character as d'Artagnan or Casanova."

There are two principal themes: one is mocking and impudent; the other is more dignified. The overture sparkles with bright-faced gaiety from first bar to last, and has been described by one nameless critic as "a swaggering piece of music."

ALBAN BERG   1885—1935

In 1907, Alban Berg visited Berlin, where he came into contact with Arnold Schoenberg for the first time. It was not long before he succumbed completely not only to Schoenberg's personality but also to his theories on music. Schoenberg became Berg's teacher—the only teacher he was ever to have; and Berg became at once not only a devoted and conscientious pupil but also an ardent disciple and a passionate protagonist of the Schoenberg idiom.

He achieved significance as a composer with the twelve-tone technique of Schoenberg (*see* Schoenberg), which he utilized for the first time in the *Lyric Suite;* his command of that technique was second only to the master's. But Berg was by no means a stereotype of his teacher. He was much more human, much more expressive, much more emotional in his writing; he was successful in endowing the twelve-tone style with human values. As he wrote in the dedication of his *Chamber Concerto* (to Schoenberg), music to him was much more than mathematics; he always endeavored to fill it with the deepest emotional expressions and the most intimate feelings.

Berg was not a prolific composer; he left only a handful of works. He was always the painstaking composer who gave the most scrupulous attention to the slightest details of his compositions. If he was a consummate artist, he was also a consummate craftsman.

The son of a merchant, Berg was born in Vienna on February 9, 1885. Though he early showed a talent for music, and was encouraged by both his father and brother in his attempts at making music, he received virtually no formal instruction until he reached maturity. He did attempt some composition; by 1900 he had written a few songs in the formal tonal systems. A change of fortune compelled him to earn his living when he was twenty: he received employment in a government office. Two years after that, he went to Berlin and became associated with Schoenberg.

A piano sonata (op. 1), written in 1908, signified Berg's official emergence as a composer. A certain indebtedness to the postromanticism and chromaticism of Wagner is to be noted; but equally important was the absence of tonality. The sonata was followed by the String Quartet, op. 3 (1910), *Five Songs with Orchestra,* op. 4 (1912), *Four Pieces for Clarinet and Piano,* op. 5 (1913) and *Three Orchestral Pieces,* op. 6 (1913-14). In these works, the author showed he had arrived at atonal writing with complete mastery and flexibility.

Recognition was slow in coming. When Berg's first work to receive a performance was heard—two of the five songs from op. 4, in Vienna, on March 31, 1913—a riot broke out; police had to be called to restore order. Berg's music became the object of much vitriolic criticism, criticism that grew increasingly bitter and hostile with performances of subsequent works.

During World War I, Berg served in the Austrian Army. It was some years after the war's end before Berg returned to composition. Meanwhile, he was a crusader for modern music in Vienna, directing his energies to teaching, writing, and promoting public performances.

His major work following the war was the expressionistic opera *Wozzeck,* the writing of which had begun as far back as 1914. *Wozzeck* brought its composer international fame and international notoriety.

Alban Berg died in Vienna, on December 24, 1935, of blood poisoning caused by a carbuncle.

The following works by Berg are discussed below: *Chamber Concerto;* Concerto for Violin and Orchestra; *Lyric Suite; Wozzeck.*

WOZZECK, opera (1923).

Vienna of the early twentieth century rediscovered the dramas of Georg Büchner, written almost one hundred years earlier. It vibrated to their stark realism and acid indictment of social injustice. When Berg saw a performance of Büchner's *Wozzeck* in 1914 he recognized at once its potentialities as an opera. His first problem was to compress the twenty-five scenes of Büchner's play into a workable libretto of three acts, five scenes each. This he accomplished in 1917.

There is no appreciable change in plot in Berg's version of the play; it remains a somber tragedy. Wozzeck, a soldier, frequently the object of ridicule in his regiment, kills his sweetheart, Marie, in a violent fit of rage on discovering that she loves the drum major of the regimental band. He seeks escape in drink, but before stupefaction sets in he suddenly remembers that he has left the incriminating knife at the scene of the crime. He finds it, throws it angrily into the nearby pool, then jumps into the water to retrieve it. The pool seizes him and, helplessly, he drowns.

His libretto completed, Berg proceeded to adapt his unorthodox musical thinking to the demands of his play. Unorthodox, indeed, was the music that Berg produced! The three acts were planned along the general lines of an A-B-A song form. The first act, called "Exposition," utilizes such traditional musical forms as the passacaglia, rhapsody, suite, march, etc., to depict the various characters. The second act, *"Dénouement,"* was planned as a symphony in five movements (sonata, fantasia and fugue, largo, scherzo, and rondo martiale). Five inventions comprise the final act, the "Catastrophe."

Unorthodox, too, is the accompanying instrumental ensemble, including as it does a chamber orchestra, a military band, and a restaurant orchestra of high-pitched violins. Such unusual instruments as a bombardon, accordion, and an out-of-tune upright piano are utilized.

The traditional forms and unusual instrumentation serve Berg's atonal musical language—the stark, forbidding, free recitative (or *Sprechstimme*), in which melody (as we know it) has been replaced by a new kind of musical expression. The "lyric" line is often gruesome in its intensity, harrowing in its tension, shattering in its dramatic force. "It had become plain," wrote the composer, explaining his own brand of lyricism, "that this method of treating the voice in a music drama not only strengthened one of the best mediums for making such a work comprehensive—namely, words—but enriched the opera by the addition of a genuine means of artistic expression, created from the purest sources of music, ranging from a toneless whisper to the authentic *bel parlare* of far-reaching speech-melodies."

It took Berg six years to write his opera. He did not work uninterruptedly, of course, since there was the hiatus of his service in the Austrian Army. By 1921 he had completed the orchestration. In 1924, three excerpts were introduced at the Frankfurt Music Festival, creating a sensation—hysteria both in the praise and in the condemnation of the music. Indeed, so much attention did this performance attract that it was not long before an operatic presentation of *Wozzeck* was arranged, in spite of formidable production difficulties. On December 14, 1925 (after 137 arduous rehearsals), Erich Kleiber conducted the première of the opera at the Berlin State Opera. The event made musical history. There were those who considered it the most significant possible landmark in the evolution of contemporary opera, comparable in its importance to Debussy's *Pelléas et Mélisande*. Others saw neither logic or sanity in it. "I had the sensation of having been not in a public theatre but in an insane asylum. On the stage, in the orchestra, in the stalls—plain madmen." So wrote Paul Zschorlich in the *Deutsche Zeitung*. Indeed, so diverse were the critical opinions, and so excessive were they in the expression of their respective points of view, that a special booklet was published in Vienna analyzing the critical reaction to the opera.

But *Wozzeck*—admired and denounced as it was—demanded a hearing, for it was one of the most provocative works of our time. Throughout Europe, opera houses produced it. In approximately ten years it was given more than 150 times in twenty-eight cities. America saw it in 1931 when Leopold Stokowski introduced it both in Philadelphia and in New York.

Of the many remarkable features of this opera, the most extraordinary, perhaps, is the felicitous way in which music serves the drama, catching the subtlest inflections of the grim tragedy.

Wozzeck is occasionally heard on symphony programs through three excerpts entitled "Three Fragments." The first is taken from the close of Act I, Scene II, and includes the transition and the beginning of Scene III;

the second comes from the opening of Act III; and the third contains the end of Act III, Scene IV, and the closing music of the opera.

CHAMBER CONCERTO, for piano, violin, and thirteen wind instruments (1925). Epigraphe. I. Thema scherzoso con variationi. II. Adagio. III. Rondo ritmico con introduzione.

The key to understanding this twelve-tone chamber-music work is the number 3. Berg wrote this concerto as a birthday gift to his teacher and friend, Arnold Schoenberg. Conscious that the trinity of the twelve-tone technique consisted of Schoenberg, Webern, and himself, Berg constructed his music with fanatical mathematical precision with the number 3 in mind. There are three movements; the instrumental body comprises three groups (keyboard, strings, wind); the rhythmic and harmonic constructions carry out the pattern of threes.

In the Epigraphe that precedes the work, a kind of musical anagram is worked out, created out of those letters from the names of Schoenberg, Berg, and Webern that can be translated into musical notes (German notation); this anagram yields three themes which are utilized prominently throughout the work. The structure is also created out of the number 3 or its multiples. In the first movement there are six repetitions of the same idea (elaborated into a variation of thirty measures divided into three sections). The Adagio is in three-part song form. And in the concluding movement, material from the first and second movements is repeated in three combinations.

The Chamber Concerto was introduced at the Frankfurt Music Festival on July 2, 1927.

LYRIC SUITE, for string quartet (1926). I. Allegretto giovale. II. Andante amoroso. III. Allegro misterioso. IV. Adagio appassionato. V. Presto delirando. VI. Largo desolato.

In the *Lyric Suite* the twelve-tone technique is employed by Berg for the first time; and it is employed with such poetic insight and emotional feeling that the suite has become one of Berg's most popular works.

"Lyrical" is a happy description of the work; for, despite the twelve-tone technique, it is filled with graceful melodic ideas. The first movement, despite its occasional brusque harmonies, has a joyful character. The second carries strains reminiscent of the old Viennese waltz, and with it nostalgic recollections of the Vienna of old. There are emotional outbursts in the third section, but for the most part it is music of delicate suggestion. The fourth part was described by Erwin Stein as achieving "a summit of lyric expression" through "broad melody." The fifth movement is feverishly dissonant, but the sixth (in which Wagner's *Tristan and Isolde* is briefly quoted by the cello) is pervaded with a dark and brooding melancholy.

Concerning the formal construction of the *Lyric Suite*, Erwin Stein has written: "The sections are connected with each other in a peculiar manner. For instance, a theme, idea, or passage from one movement always reappears in the next."

In 1928, Berg arranged three movements from the *Lyric Suite* for chamber orchestra, in which form it has most frequently been heard. The three movements are: I. Andante amoroso. II. Allegro misterioso. III. Adagio appassionato.

CONCERTO FOR VIOLIN AND ORCHESTRA (1935). I. Andante; Allegro. II. Allegro; Adagio.

Berg's special gift for endowing atonalism in general, and the twelve-tone technique in particular, with vibrant human values is nowhere more evident than in this, his last work.

It was commissioned by the concert violinist Louis Krasner in 1934. But Berg did not receive an inspirational incentive for the writing of the music until one year later. At that time, one of his dear friends, a young girl who was the daughter of Gustav Mahler's widow by a second marriage, died suddenly. Berg now conceived the concerto as a requiem to the girl, whom he described in his dedication as "an angel."

Though written entirely in the twelve-tone system, the concerto is a personal document, deeply felt and profoundly moving. Indeed, when the work was first introduced in England, Constant Lambert (who has little sympathy for atonalism), described it as "the most beautiful and significant piece of music written since the War." Significance has sometimes been ascribed to works in the atonal idiom. But beauty! ...

The composer intended the first movement as a description of the girl; in it, her ingratiating personal qualities are delineated in several graceful themes, one of them reminiscent of an Alpine folksong, another suggesting the Viennese waltz. The second movement is a more dramatic pronouncement, for it speaks of the tragedy of death and culminates in the deliverance of the girl's soul. Here the strains of a Bach chorale (*"Es ist genug,"* from the cantata, *O Ewigkeit, du Donnerwort*) are introduced to suggest that the soul has, at last, found peace.

It is sad to contemplate that in writing a Requiem for someone else, Berg (like Mozart before him) was actually composing it for himself. This was his last work. When he was dying, Berg turned to his wife and remarked sadly: *"Es ist genug*—it is enough," quoting the title of the Bach chorale he had interpolated in his concerto.

Louis Krasner introduced the concerto on April 19, 1936, at Barcelona, during the fourteenth festival of the International Society for Contemporary Music.

LEONARD BERNSTEIN   1918—

Leonard Bernstein made his bow as a composer with the Sonata for Clarinet and Piano, written in 1941-42, the style of which was derived from Hindemith. That this was only a passing tendency became evident with a work completely different in character—the rhapsodic symphony, *Jeremiah,* completed in 1942. The spare and lean writing of the Sonata now gave way to romantic, even passionate, episodes. The second symphony, *The Age of Anxiety* (1949), is more restrained and economical than *Jeremiah,* but it, too, has intensity and ardor. In quite a different vein is the music for the ballet, *Fancy Free,* which draws its colors and vitality from popular sources.

Here, then, is a young composer who has yet to arrive at a definitive, identifiable style of his own. But what he has written is articulate, in good taste, admirably projected, and usually vital with dramatic thrusts. Generally speaking, Bernstein writes with broad sweeps of the pen, more concerned with the effect of the whole than with the subleties of its parts. He does not, as Irving Fine noted, "belong to the *note choisie* school. In the improvisational élan of his music, hiatuses in the harmony go unheeded, as do occasional lapses of taste. But . . . these defects seem insignificant in relation to the loftiness of the conception."

Bernstein was born in Lawrence, Massachusetts, on August 25, 1918. He attended Harvard University, where he took music courses with Walter Piston and Edward Burlingame Hill, revealing phenomenal talent. Following his graduation from Harvard in 1939, he studied at the Curtis Institute: conducting, with Fritz Reiner; orchestration, with Randall Thompson; and the piano, with Isabella Vengerova. Scholarships enabled him to attend the Berkshire Music Center, in Tanglewood, Massachusetts, in 1940 and 1941, where he was a pupil of Serge Koussevitzky. Koussevitzky made him his assistant in Tanglewood in 1942. One year later, Bernstein was appointed assistant conductor to Artur Rodzinski with the New York Philharmonic-Symphony Orchestra.

On November 14, 1943, Bernstein made his official debut as conductor when he appeared as a last-minute substitute for Bruno Walter with the New York Philharmonic. He created a sensation. Since then he has conducted the major orchestras of the world. In 1958 he was appointed music director of the New York Philharmonic. Bernstein has also distinguished himself as a composer for the Broadway stage.

The following works by Bernstein are discussed below: *The Age of Anxiety; Fancy Free; Jeremiah Symphony; Trouble in Tahiti.*

JEREMIAH SYMPHONY (1942). I. Prophecy. II. Profanation. III. Lamentation.

"In the summer of 1939," wrote the composer, "I made a sketch for a *Lamentation* for soprano and orchestra. This sketch lay forgotten for two years until, in the spring of 1942, I began a first movement of a symphony. I then realized that this new movement, and the Scherzo that I planned to follow it, made logical concomitants with the *Lamentation*. Thus the symphony came into being, with the *Lamentation* greatly changed, and the soprano supplanted by a mezzo-soprano.

"The symphony does not make use to any great extent of actual Hebrew thematic material. The first theme of the Scherzo is paraphrased from a traditional Hebrew chant, and the opening phrase of the vocal part in the *Lamentation* is based on a liturgical cadence still sung today in commemoration of the destruction of Jerusalem by Babylon. Other resemblances to Hebrew liturgical music are a matter of emotional quality rather than of the notes themselves.

"As for programmatic meanings, the intention is again not one of literalness, but of emotional quality. Thus the first movement aims only to parallel in feeling the intensity of the prophet's pleas with his people; and the Scherzo, to give a general sense of destruction and chaos brought on by the pagan corruption within the priesthood and the people. The third movement being a setting of a poetic text is naturally a more literary conception. It is the cry of Jeremiah as he mourns his beloved Jerusalem, ruined, pillaged, and dishonored after his desperate efforts to save it. The text is from the *Book of Lamentations*, I, 1, 2, 3, 4; IV, 14, 15; V, 20, 21."

Leonard Bernstein himself introduced the symphony with the Pittsburgh Symphony Orchestra on January 28, 1944. Jennie Tourel was the assisting artist. Since its première, the symphony has been performed by virtually every major American orchestra, and has been heard in several European cities. On May 16, 1944, the Music Critics Circle of New York selected it as the outstanding new American symphonic work of the preceding season.

FANCY FREE, ballet (1944).

Bernstein was commissioned by the Ballet Theatre to write the music for a ballet, *Fancy Free,* the choreography to be prepared by Jerome Robbins. In its predilection for modern American and South American popular idioms, *Fancy Free* is a sharp departure from the *Jeremiah Symphony,* composed two years earlier. It is excellent theater; the apt synchronization of the music to the action on the stage was one of the reasons for its unusual success.

The première took place on April 18, 1944, at the Metropolitan Opera

House, with Bernstein conducting. It was so well received that it was repeated almost two dozen times that spring by the Ballet Theatre.

The action begins with the sound of a juke box sounded offstage. The scene is a street corner near a bar. Three sailors are on leave, and they are "on the make." They meet one girl, then another; fight for them; lose them; then go in pursuit of a third.

An orchestral suite was prepared by Bernstein from the ballet score. It is in six sections: I. Dance of the Three Sailors. II. Scene at the Bar. III. Pas de deux. IV. Pantomime (Competition). V. Three Variations (Galop, Waltz, Danzon). VI. Finale.

THE AGE OF ANXIETY, Symphony No. 2, for piano and orchestra (1949). Part I: The Prologue; The Seven Ages (Variations I-VII); The Seven Stages (Variations VIII-XIV). Part II: The Dirge; The Masque; The Epilogue.

The inspiration for Bernstein's Second Symphony was W. H. Auden's poem, *The Age of Anxiety*. The poet's concern with the insecurity of our times, and his search for a faith that can be accepted, even if blindly, impressed the composer, who tried to carry over the poem's message in his music. He began his symphony in 1947. His feverish activity as a conductor, which brought him to the four corners of the world, compelled him to write the work by fits and starts—in hotel lobbies and airplanes, wherever and whenever he could find a free hour. He completed the final orchestration on March 20, 1949, while on a month's tour with the Pittsburgh Symphony. On April 8, 1949, it was introduced by the Boston Symphony Orchestra, under Serge Koussevitzky, with the composer playing the piano part. The critics acclaimed it as a major work; a month later it received the Hornblit Prize as the best new work heard that year in the programs of the Boston Symphony. The New York City Ballet presented it, with choreography by Jerome Robbins, on February 26, 1950.

The composer provided the following program for his music:

"Part I: (a) The Prologue finds four lonely characters, a girl and three men, in a Third Avenue bar, all of them insecure, and trying, through drink, to detach themselves from their conflicts, or, at best, to resolve them. They are drawn together by this common urge and begin a kind of symposium on the state of man....

"(b) The Seven Ages. The life of man is reviewed from the four personal points of view....

"(c) The Seven Stages.... The characters go on an inner and highly symbolic journey according to a geographical plan leading back to a point of comfort and security. The four try every means, going singly and in pairs, exchanging partners, and always missing the objective. When they awaken from this dream-odyssey, they are closely united through a common experience (and through alcohol) and begin to function as one organism....

"Part II: (a) The Dirge is sung by the four as they sit in a cab en route to the girl's apartment for a nightcap. They mourn the loss of the 'colossal Dad,' the great leader who can always give the right orders, find the right solution, shoulder the mass responsibility, and satisfy the universal need for a father-symbol....

"(b) The Masque finds the group in the girl's apartment, weary, guilty, determined to have a party, each one afraid of spoiling the others' fun by admitting that he should be home in bed.... The party ends in anti-climax, and the dispersal of the actors ... as the Epilogue begins. Thus a kind of separation of the self from the guilt of escapist living has been effected, and the protagonist is free again to examine what is left beneath the emptiness.

"(c) The Epilogue. What is left, it turns out, is faith.... Throughout the Epilogue the piano-protagonist has taken no part, but has observed it, as one observes such development on a movie screen, or in another human personality. At the very end he seizes upon it with one eager chord of confirmation, although he has not himself participated in the anxiety-experience leading to this fulfillment. The way is open; but, at the conclusion, is still stretching long before him."

TROUBLE IN TAHITI, opera (1952).

Bernstein wrote both the text and the music for this slight and witty little opera which is in seven scenes and takes under forty minutes for performance. The story centers around the bickerings and misunderstandings of a married couple in a characteristic suburb of an American city. It is treated with tongue-in-cheek humor and malice, which is carried over in the music, described by Howard Taubman as "gay, modern, and jazzy." Taubman continues: "Mr. Bernstein ... seeks to reach more deeply into the hearts of his principal characters, and in a long aria for the wife his music becomes searching and affecting.... The music does not have much variety. There is a brief jazz figure that keeps recurring and that keeps haunting one with its insistent banality long after the show is over. No doubt, the banality is deliberate, but Mr. Bernstein has failed, as a composer, to comment on it and thus to rescue it from the low standards of its genre. Where he does comment, as in the scene in which the wife tells us what she thinks of a film called *Trouble in Tahiti* she has just seen, Mr. Bernstein writes with delicious and irresistible vitality."

Trouble in Tahiti was introduced at the Festival of Creative Arts held at Brandeis University, in Waltham, Mass., on June 12, 1952.

ARTHUR BLISS   1891—

Bliss began composing seriously while he was still a student at the Royal College of Music in London. Some of his early works were performed, published, and praised. However, after World War I, he destroyed them all, feeling that they no longer represented him. Of the music he now wrote, the most interesting pieces were the *Rhapsody* (for soprano, tenor, flute, English horn, bass, and string quartet) and *Rout,* for voice and ten instruments. These two strangely contrasted works—the former tender and introspective; the latter riotous and satiric—were indicative of the composer's versatility of style, a versatility further emphasized with the highly percussive *Tempest Overture* and the *Colour Symphony,* with its imaginative association of color with musical ideas.

It was in the music Bliss wrote after 1925 that his style was finally crystallized. The striving for new media and effects was not over; his intelligence is too restless to be static. But experimentation was relegated to a relatively insignificant place in his thinking. Intensity of feeling, poetic moods, refinement of speech, were now the prevailing qualities of his writing. "If I were to define my musical goal," he once said, "it would be to try for an emotion truly and clearly felt, and caught forever in a formal perfection." In his best works he has achieved his musical goal with complete success.

Bliss was born in London on August 2, 1891, and received degrees from Pembroke College in Cambridge and the Royal College of Music in London. During World War I, he served as a commissioned officer, seeing heavy combat in France, where he was wounded at the Somme and gassed at Cambrai. For two years—from 1923 to 1925—he lived in the United States. In 1950 he was knighted, and in 1953 appointed Master of the Queen's Musick.

The following works by Bliss are discussed below: *Checkmate;* Concerto in B-flat Major for Piano and Orchestra; *Music for Strings.*

MUSIC FOR STRINGS (1935). I. Allegro moderato energico. II. Andante molto sostenuto. III. Allegro molto.

There is an intimate kinship between this work and Elgar's *Introduction and Allegro.* Both employ the string orchestra beautifully; both are romantic; both are built on solid foundations of English musical tradition.

The writing in Bliss's compositions is free of subjection to either form or program; the thematic ideas are allowed complete flexibility of movement.

This work is notable for the skill with which the thematic material is suggested, developed, changed, and distributed among different parts of the orchestra. No less admirable is the rich deployment of strings; now the players of one section are given different lyric parts, thereby enriching the musical texture; now striking contrast is achieved by elevating the first-desk men to the status of solo groups.

CHECKMATE, ballet (1937).

One of Bliss's greatest successes was achieved with a ballet written for the British Week of Music at the Paris International Exposition. On June 15, 1937, this ballet, *Checkmate*, was introduced by the Sadlers' Wells Ballet of London at the Théâtre des Champs Elysées in Paris. Constant Lambert conducted, and Ninette de Valois was responsible for the choreography.

The scenario was written by the composer himself. In the prologue, Love and Death, fighting for the lives of their subjects, play a game of chess. The ballet proper takes place on the chessboard. The struggle of the pawns, culminating in the murders of the Red Knight and the Red King by the Black Queen, is used by the composer as a symbol of the cruelty and lust of human beings in the game of life. This intriguing scenario draws from the composer a richly orchestrated score, dramatic, sensuous, and imaginatively picturesque.

The composer prepared an orchestral suite from the ballet score, comprising six sections: I. Dance of the Four Knights. II. Entry of the Black Queen. III. The Red Knight. IV. Ceremony of the Red Bishops. V. Death of the Red Knight. VI. Finale—Checkmate.

CONCERTO IN B-FLAT MAJOR FOR PIANO AND OR-CHESTRA (1939). I. Allegro con brio. II. Adagio. III. Andante maestoso; Molto vivo.

In 1939, the British Council commissioned Bliss to write a piano concerto for the New York World's Fair. Dedicated to "the people of the United States," this concerto was introduced in New York on June 10, 1939. Solomon was the soloist, and the orchestra was directed by Sir Adrian Boult.

The middle movement is one of Bliss's most poignant creations, a page of lyricism of rare sensitivity. It opens in an atmosphere of classic serenity before the first subject, a theme almost of waltz-like character is announced by the solo piano; the second subject is dreamy and diaphanous.

The first and third movements are virile. The first contains a great deal of bravura writing for the piano, together with some dramatic utterances for the orchestra. Extreme contrasts in rhythm and dynamics are found in the closing movement, which is in the nature of a scherzo. The highlight of this movement is an exquisite passage for solo cello, for which the piano provides a delicate background.

MARC BLITZSTEIN   1905—

It is not without significance that none of Blitzstein's theatrical works have thus far been introduced in the opera house. Two of them were first heard in Broadway theaters; a third, in a concert auditorium. This is, perhaps, as it should be. Blitzstein's operas belong in the theater, derive their significance from the theater. Music, for Blitzstein, is only the means to a theatrical end. It is used exclusively to serve the purposes of the stage; it is not intended to have independent artistic value. Consequently, Blitzstein is not to be dissuaded from using any musical means at his disposal, however questionable those means may be from an artistic point of view. When a cheap and cliché-ridden melody serves to heighten theatrical effect, when the stage business is improved by an obvious comic effect in the orchestra, or when a mood is best evoked with jazz, Blitzstein does not hesitate to employ these means. In all his operas there is a strange mélange of different styles, ranging from Handelian recitatives and formal arias to jazz, burlesque music, and comic or torch songs. It is not always excellent music, by any means, that one finds in his scores; but it always helps to make excellent theater. For this reason, the recent tendency on the part of Blitzstein to avoid the word *opera* in referring to his stage works is a wise one; they are essentially plays with music, or musical plays, in which actually the play—and not the music—is the thing.

Blitzstein was born in Philadelphia, on March 2, 1905. After attending public schools in Philadelphia, and the University of Pennsylvania, he took advanced courses in music at the Curtis Institute. Later he studied with Siloti in New York and Nadia Boulanger and Arnold Schoenberg in Europe.

His early works belong to the *Sturm und Drang* school of ultra-modern music, interesting as experiments in form, dynamics, tonality. Not until his growing social consciousness dominated his musical thinking did he succeed in evolving an identifiable personality. In his aim to reach large masses with social propaganda, he abandoned his earlier experiments and arrived at a greatly simplified idiom, derived from popular elements. His first major work in this direction was his opera *The Cradle Will Rock*, written in 1937, which made him famous.

Receiving a Guggenheim Fellowship in 1940, he wrote a second opera, *No for an Answer*, whose career was short-lived because the New York Commissioner of Licenses virtually censored the work by threatening the revocation of the auditorium's license on the specious grounds that it was unfit for operatic performances. (Since then, the auditorium has been often used for operatic presentations, without interference.)

During World War II, Blitzstein volunteered and served in the Eighth Air Force. He was given musical tasks, some of which resulted in major works. Following his separation from the armed forces, Blitzstein received a one-thousand dollar grant from the American Academy of Arts and Letters.

The following works by Blitzstein are discussed below:*The Cradle Will Rock; Regina; Symphony: The Airborne.*

THE CRADLE WILL ROCK, opera (1937).

The history of *The Cradle Will Rock* is surely one of the dramatic episodes in the American theater. It was scheduled as a production of the WPA Theatre, directed by Orson Welles, and produced by John Houseman. On June 15, 1937, it was seen in a dress rehearsal. Meanwhile, the left-wing libretto had been creating uneasiness in certain influential government circles, which used pressure on the Federal Theatre to have the production banned. The ban was not announced until virtually the zero hour of opening night (June 16), with the result that the audience began gathering at the Maxine Elliott Theatre, unaware that the show had been called off. Members of the cast proceeded to entertain the audience, while director, producer, and composer scouted the nearby vicinity for another auditorium. When the nearby Venice Theatre was found available, the audience was directed there. And—denied the use of scenery, costumes, or orchestra—the opera was presented in oratorio form: the actors and chorus went on the bare stage dressed in their regular street clothes; and the composer, also on the stage, played the score on the piano and informally explained to the audience, between scenes, what was taking place.

Thus, through accident, *The Cradle Will Rock* was presented in this unorthodox manner. The powerful impact it made on the audience was due not only to the intrinsic theatrical merits of the work but also to this unique manner of presentation.

Sam Grisman, a Broadway producer, attended that performance and, impressed by the dramatic appeal of the opera, offered to finance a Broadway run. Scenery, costumes, and orchestra were now dispensed with, not through necessity, but out of purely artistic considerations. In this unique presentation, *The Cradle Will Rock* became not only an outstanding artistic success, but a resounding box-office attraction. It ran for 124 performances. "The most versatile artistic triumph of the politically insurgent theatre," was the way Brooks Atkinson described it. Virgil Thomson called it the "most appealing operatic socialism since *Louise.*"

Ten years later, on November 24, 1947, the opera was revived by the New York City Symphony Orchestra, directed by Leonard Bernstein. In this performance it was heard with orchestra for the first time. The thunderous acclaim accorded the work after each of the two scheduled performances, and the chorus of approval by the critics (Olin Downes did not hesitate to describe it as a work of "genius") proved that it had lost little of its freshness and vitality. Once again an attempt was made to transfer the opera to the Broadway theater, with the hope of duplicating the success of a decade past; but this time the box-office appeal was negligible, and the opera "folded" after thirteen performances.

The text is by the composer himself. The plot unfolds in a night court, and is built around the attempt of steel workers to create a union, and the devious methods of their employers to frustrate the attempt. Capitalism is symbolized by Mr. Mister, who controls Steeltown, and who has the town judge, newspaper editor, college president, doctor, and clergy under his thumb. By bribery and coercion, Mr. Mister brings the leading citizens of Steeltown together into a "Liberty Committee" organized to smash the union, which, of course, it fails to do.

The score Blitzstein wrote carries great momentum. Through recitatives, arias, patter songs, parodies, chorales—all in a style that blends popular elements with the harmonic and contrapuntal devices of serious music—the composer evolved a new kind of musico-dramatic art form in which the music performs as important a part as the spoken word in projecting dramatic situations; at times the music even displaces the word. Sometimes the music appears in the background, contributing strokes of characterization, tonal comment, satirical asides. Sometimes it carries forth the dramatic sweep of the action with impulsive rhythms and dynamic chords. Sometimes it injects a note of mockery into very serious proceedings with parodies of blues songs, torch songs, etc.

SYMPHONY: THE AIRBORNE (1944). I. Theory of Flight; Ballad of History and Mythology; Kittyhawk; The Airborne. II. The Enemy; Threat of Approach; Ballad of the Cities; Morning Poem. III. Ballad of Hurry Up; Night Music; Ballad of the Bombardier; Recitative and Chorus of the Rendezvous; The Open Sky.

While serving with the Eighth Air Force in England, Blitzstein was commissioned to write a large symphonic work about the history of aviation. He wrote his own text, then composed the symphony. The orchestration was completed later, after the composer had been separated from the armed forces. On April 11, 1946, it was introduced in New York City by the New York City Symphony Orchestra under Leonard Bernstein.

The composer provided the following description:

"I call *The Airborne* a symphony (even though none of its three movements is strictly in sonata form) in the same way that Liszt named the *Faust Symphony* and Stravinsky the *Symphony of Psalms*.

"There are twelve more-or-less self-contained sections that occur as subdivisions of the three larger movements. The work is about fifty-five minutes in length; and is scored for a Speaker (I call him a Monitor, since nearly all his lines are couched in the imperative mood), male chorus, solo tenor (this part was conceived for Negro voice, because of what it might lend to the quality of the Ballad of History and Mythology), solo baritone, and full orchestra."

In his music and text, Blitzstein not only offers a vivid description of the evolution of aviation from Icarus to World War II, but also points up as a commentary the futility of war and destruction. The symphony culminates with a paean of praise to the open sky as a symbol of human freedom.

REGINA, musical play (1949).

Lillian Hellman's bitter play, *The Little Foxes,* about the predatory Hubbard family, whose members devour each other through hate, deceit, theft, and even murder, only to devour themselves as well, was recreated by Blitzstein into a musical play of great force. All of Hellman's vitriol is retained—her devastating characterizations have lost none of their knife-edged sharpness. But through his music, Blitzstein seems to have brought new dimensions and perspective to these ugly characters; and he did this—as Leonard Bernstein pointed out in an article in the *New York Times*—by bringing "sweetness and directness." Bernstein writes further: "Regina herself, perhaps one of the most ruthless characters in show business, sings melodies of enormous gentility and suaveness precisely at the moment when she is being most unscrupulous and heartless. There is a kind of urbanity involved in the musical treatment of this character which results in a theatrical coup.... I might say that this is the underlying technique of the whole piece: Coating the wormwood with sugar, and scenting with magnolia blossoms the cursed house in which these evils transpire."

To some of the drama critics, this contribution of softness to a hard play represents dilution. As Brooks Atkinson wrote, Blitzstein "softened a hard play.... What Blitzstein has added to it does not compensate for the loss in force, belligerence, and directness." But the music critics were more impressed by the results. Howard Taubman described the work as "exciting musical theatre," in which the composer has "intensified the sinister mood of the central theme by setting it against an atmosphere that is more wholesome."

As in his other operas, Blitzstein blends many different styles of writing in *Regina;* each situation dictates the style that best suits its interpretation. There is music derivative from spirituals, sung by the colored servants, and there is ragtime music for a colored band. Formal dances help to evoke the period. Some recitatives have Handelian majesty, while others are as austere and forbidding as *Sprechstimme.* There are lilting tunes and there are melodies of broad design. There are joyful choruses that in their bright-faced beauty make one think of madrigals; and there is a great deal of bitter music that brings up tonally the hatred and evil that permeate the entire household.

Among the most effective arias, or songs, are the two sung by Regina, in which she reminisces about her past and describes her sufferings, and one sung by Regina's daughter, Alexandra, at the end of the play.

The first performance of *Regina* took place in Boston on October 11, 1949. The New York run began on October 30, 1949. The principals included Jane Pickens as Regina and Brenda Lewis as Birdie.

ERNEST BLOCH 1880—

In or about 1915, after having written the Symphony in C-sharp Minor and the opera *Macbeth,* Ernest Bloch arrived at a new style and artistic mission. He now became conscious of his racial origins; what he wanted to do was to interpret his race in his music. His works began to mirror the "Jewish soul . . . the complex agitated soul that I feel vibrating through the Bible." Some of Bloch's most famous works were written during this period—notably *Schelomo, Baal Shem,* and the *Israel Symphony.* Without digging into the past of Hebrew music and reaching for authentic folk and religious materials (Bloch stated emphatically, "I am no archaeologist"), he created music that is Semitic in its colors and melodic contours, music whose racial identity emerges in its high-strung nerves, brooding emotion, and elegiac sadness.

After the *Sacred Service,* Bloch abandoned Hebraic programs and titles for his major works; but their stylistic traits remained for the most part recognizably Semitic. His writing has been rhapsodic; his forms, spacious; his speech, often savage, passionate, and intense. Yet in more introspective pages he is capable of giving expression to mysticism and poetry.

The son of a Swiss merchant, Bloch was born in Geneva on July 24, 1880. Early music study took place with Jacques Dalcroze and L. Rey in Geneva. After that, he studied with Eugene Ysaÿe and F. Rasse in Brussels, and Ivan Knorr and Ludwig Thuille in Germany.

In 1902, Bloch wrote his Symphony in C-sharp Minor. Disappointed by his inability to get it performed, and convinced that he could not make a living out of music, he became a businessman in Geneva. Music, however, was not abandoned: his spare time was devoted to composing and to conducting orchestral concerts.

His opera *Macbeth* was accepted for performance by the Paris Opéra Comique, and was introduced on November 30, 1910. Some critics did not like it at all. But others saw in it considerable power and talent: one of these was Romain Rolland, who made a special trip to Geneva to meet the composer and encourage him. It was largely due to Rolland that Bloch finally gave up business for music.

In 1916, Bloch visited the United States as the conductor of the Maud Allen troupe scheduled to tour this country. The troupe, however, went bankrupt, leaving Bloch stranded in a strange country without funds or friends. Several important musicians rallied to his aid by bringing about performances of his major works. The Philadelphia Orchestra, the Boston Symphony, and the Society of Friends of Music in New York devoted entire programs to his compositions. Through these performances—and through the winning, in 1919, of the Elizabeth Sprague Coolidge prize of one thousand dollars for his Suite for Viola and Piano—Bloch became comparatively famous.

From 1920 through 1925, Bloch served as director of the Cleveland Institute of Music. From Cleveland, he went to San Francisco to fill a teaching post and to write his epic rhapsody *America,* which won the first prize of three thousand dollars in a contest sponsored by the magazine *Musical America.* In 1931, several of San Francisco's art patrons created a special endowment to enable Bloch to give up teaching and devote himself entirely to creative work. For a few years he lived in retirement in a little village in Switzerland, working on his *Sacred Service.* When this work was finished, Bloch returned to America to direct its première in this country, on April 11, 1934.

Bloch now lives in Agate Beach, Oregon. Since 1950 Bloch has been exceptionally fertile. In 1953-1954 he became the first composer to receive top awards from the New York Music Critics Circle in two different categories, for his String Quartet No. 3 and Concerto Grosso No. 2 (see Supplement).

The following works by Bloch are discussed below: *Baal Shem;* Concerto for Violin and Orchestra; Concerto Grosso; *Concerto Symphonique; Israel Symphony;* Quartet No. 1; Quartet No. 2; Quintet for Piano and Strings; *Schelomo; A Voice in the Wilderness.*

ISRAEL SYMPHONY (1916).

In planning this symphony, Bloch intended to interpret the symbolic meaning of Jewish holidays. Romain Rolland induced Bloch to extend his objective to cover the entire Jewish race, and to change the original title of *Fêtes Juives* (Jewish Holidays) to *Israel Symphony*.

But the holiday idea persisted in Bloch's mind as he wrote his music. The first movement (Allegro agitato) is identified with the awesome Day of Atonement, and contains music of repentance. The moods are turbulent, disturbed by inner doubts and conflicts. Repose comes with contrition. The second movement (Andante moderato), which follows the first without interruption, brings peace to the repentant sinner. A climax is reached as human voices join the orchestra in intoning the phrases of a Hebrew prayer.

The symphony was introduced in New York, under the direction of the composer, at a concert of the Society of Friends of Music on May 3, 1917.

QUARTET NO. 1, for strings (1916). I. Andante moderato. II. Allegro frenetico. III. Andante molto moderato. IV. Finale: vivace.

The composer has confessed that this work was written during a period of double crisis. There was personal crisis: at this time (1916), Bloch was stranded in this country, penniless and friendless, faced with a difficult orientation to a new environment. There was crisis, too, in the world around him: Europe was in the midst of a war. Whatever unrest, uncertainty, or confusion Bloch felt is found in the nervous pages of this music, particularly in the cruel force of the last movement.

The composer has explained that the music of the quartet represented "a kind of synthesis of my vision of the world at that period." We have here a portrait of the world of serenity and dreams Bloch had known in his native Switzerland (third movement) as well as of the anguish of the dreamer who sees his reveries shattered by the cruel impact of reality (fourth movement).

While classical in form, the quartet is free in its rhythmic and harmonic writing. The first three movements were written while Bloch was still in Europe; the last movement was the first piece of music he wrote in this country. It was introduced in New York on December 29, 1916.

SCHELOMO, rhapsody for cello and orchestra (1916).

"Schelomo" is the Hebrew name for Solomon, the wise king of the Bible; and Bloch's rhapsody is a portrait of the king.

In 1915, the cellist Alexander Barjansky asked Bloch to write a work for his use. Steeped in the Bible at the time, Bloch decided to draw his inspiration from it. A figurine of Solomon, the work of Barjansky's wife, provided Bloch additional stimulation.

A solo cello speaks for Solomon and re-creates him in music that is, by turns, dramatic, rhapsodic, introspective, brilliant, devotional. The instrument is used much in the way a voice might be, as a kind of wordless singing obbligato. There are two principal melodic subjects, the first heard in the solo cello (Più animato), and the second played by the reeds (Allegro moderato).

The first performance of *Schelomo* took place in New York on May 3, 1917, at a concert of the Society of Friends of Music directed by the composer.

QUINTET FOR PIANO AND STRINGS (1923). I. Agitato. II. Andante mistico. III. Allegro energico.

Impressed by the potentialities of quarter-tone music for certain specific effects, Bloch conceived the idea of writing a sonata for cello and piano employing that technique. As he began planning the work, and as his thematic ideas grew, he realized a larger frame was called for. He finally decided on a piano quintet.

This quintet is not exclusively quarter-tone music by any means. But it does utilize quarter-tone intervals in passages calling for high tensions. Quarter-tone writing endows the melodic line with greater expressiveness. Novel colorings, barbaric rhythms, complex harmonic patterns, make further modern contributions. The form, however, remains classical.

Perhaps in no other of Bloch's works does he maintain so consistent a level of eloquence as here. The work opens in an atmosphere of mystery as the piano sounds a theme faintly suggestive of the *Dies Irae,* set against a quarter-tone background. This theme reappears throughout the work. Varied moods follow: primitive, passionate, intense, sensitive. Mystery and an all-pervading melancholy are sounded throughout the second movement: the unrelieved gloom at times develops into a kind of tortured despair. The poignancy is intensified until, toward the end of the movement—as the violins exclaim in piercing notes against the dark and brooding chords of the piano—it becomes virtually unbearable. The opening theme of the quintet returns in the beginning of the third movement; it is now strong and dramatic. Agitation persists, gaining momentum all the time, until the music becomes the chant of primitives, accompanied by percussive rhythms. Then the violence is over. The viola raises its voice in a poignant melody to restore serenity. (Bloch once described this last section as an "escape," a release of oneself from material considerations into spiritual values.)

On November 11, 1923, the Quintet was introduced in New York by the Lenox String Quartet and Harold Bauer; this performance took place at the inaugural concert of an organization then making its bow—the League of Composers.

BAAL SHEM, suite for violin and piano (1923). I. Vidui. II. Nigun. III. Simchas Torah.

One specific sect of the Hebrew religion is the inspiration of this suite: that known as Hasidism, founded by a mystic seer named Baal Shem, which developed and flourished in Poland in the late eighteenth century. The Hasids believed in goodness, joy, and pleasure. Religious worship was an occasion for feasting, revelry, and ecstatic music and dance. The Hasids believed that whatever God made is good. Consequently, even in evil there is some goodness; and there is no evil that is beyond redemption.

Hasidic folksongs and dances are as ecstatic and intense as the sect that gave them birth. Certain qualities of Hasidic music are found in this suite: its sense for improvisation (a carry-over from the synagogical chant); the intervaled construction; the throbbing rhythmic pulse.

The first movement, entitled "Contrition," is a mobile melody speaking of the return of a repentant sinner to the fold. In the second part, "Melody," an improvised song is heard, one such as a cantor develops as he intones his prayer in the synagogue. The music then passes from delicate and tender moods into a veritable orgiastic outburst of joy ("Simchas Torah"), as the Hasid celebrates his most joyous holiday—the commemoration of the handing down of the Torah to Moses and the Jewish people at Mount Sinai.

CONCERTO GROSSO, for piano and string orchestra (1925). I. Prelude. II. Dirge. III. Pastoral and Rustic Dances. IV. Fugue.

Many contemporary composers have reverted to the musical forms of the classical past; but in doing so they have usually endeavored to return to classic simplicity and objectivity. With Bloch, reversion to the concerto-grosso style of Corelli and Handel did not encourage classical writing. The resources of modern music were not abandoned. The esthetic aim here was to incorporate modern thinking and techniques within the framework of older forms. Bloch's composition pupils were given to writing rebellious works which ruthlessly swept aside all traditions. Bloch wished to prove to them that a composer can remain vibrantly contemporary in his speech without sacrificing classical structure.

Bloch wrote the Concerto Grosso in his last year as director of the Cleveland Institute of Music. It was introduced at the Institute on June 1, 1925.

The harsh sounds of the first movement (Allegro energico e pesante), with its massive sequence of strident chords, is an exercise in modern writing. This is music of ungovernable strength, whose effect is created through ponderous sonorities and bold rhythmic movement. Relief comes in the second movement (Andante moderato) with a threnody. A group of pleasing rustic dances follows (Assai lento); shifting meters provide a piquant contemporary flavor. A robust fugue (Allegro) filled with modern harmonies brings the work to a close.

A VOICE IN THE WILDERNESS, for orchestra and obbligato cello (1936).

This is Bloch's second major work for orchestra and obbligato cello, the first being *Schelomo*. But here the cello serves a different function. It is a kind of commentator, appearing between each of the six short movements, offering a terse discourse on the preceding section.

Bloch's original intention in writing this work was to present a group of short sketches for orchestra under the collective title of *Visions and Prophecies*. But as he began writing, contrapuntal solo melodies came to his mind, inspired by the music he was putting down on paper. Sensing the esthetic value of these melodies in the larger concept of the composition, Bloch decided to employ the rather unique idea of a "commentator" cello.

The composer has described the six movements (played uninterruptedly) as "meditations," and has explained that the work as a whole is descriptive of the "apparently unhappy destiny of man." The composer has stated further: "The various movements follow and link each other quite naturally. They are sometimes bound together by a barely perceptive thematic relationship or 'reminiscence,' but each has its own clearly defined character."

The suite was completed in Savoy and was successfully introduced in Los Angeles by the Los Angeles Philharmonic on January 21, 1937.

CONCERTO FOR VIOLIN AND ORCHESTRA (1938). I. Allegro deciso. II. Andante. III. Deciso.

American Indian music, which plays a role in the first movement of *America,* is also given some attention in the principal theme of the first movement of this concerto. But the music of the concerto is in no single style, just as it refuses to adhere to a single tonality. At times the writing has the rhapsodic character of Bloch's earlier Hebraic works; at times the music gives suggestions of impressionism, as in parts of the exquisite slow movement; at times it is severely modern in the freedom of its rhythmic movement and in the acerbity of its harmonies, as in the barbaric opening of the third movement.

The concerto was begun in 1930. At that time the composer wrote down some random ideas and sketches; these subsequently became the thematic materials for the concerto, which did not take actual shape until 1935, when Bloch wrote down the first part of the introduction. The necessity of completing other works delayed the writing of the concerto, and it was not finished until January, 1938. The world première took place in Cleveland on December 15, 1938. Joseph Szigeti was the soloist, and the Cleveland Orchestra was directed by Mitropoulos.

QUARTET NO. 2, for strings (1945). I. Moderato. II. Presto. III. Andante. IV. Finale.

Almost thirty years elapsed between the writing of Bloch's two string quartets. The second was completed in 1945, when Bloch was at the height of his creative powers. Less tortured in its struggle and less rebellious than its predecessor, the second quartet has an incandescence and spirituality of speech, a concentration and forcefulness of thinking that inspired Ernest Newman to compare it with the last quartets of Beethoven.

In reviewing the quartet for the *London Times,* Ernest Newman analyzed its unusual structure: "From an embryo in the second of the four movements, there comes into being an entity which from that point onward moulds the whole quartet from the inside into a single organic substance; differently accentuated or rhythmed as the work goes on, it assumes one personality after another till it expands in the finale into first of all the theme of a mighty passacaglia, then, re-rhythmed yet again, into the subject of a mighty fugue; while the whole work is rounded off in unexpected but inevitable rightness with a serene reminscence, in the final bars of a tiny melisma with which the first movement had opened."

The quartet was introduced in London by the Griller Quartet on October 9, 1946.

CONCERTO SYMPHONIQUE, for piano and orchestra (1948). I. Pesante. II. Allegro vivace. III. Allegro deciso.

Bloch's only piano concerto was introduced by Corinne Lacomble, under the composer's direction, at the Edinburgh Festival, on September 3, 1949. It is a powerful and intense work, large in dimension, restless in its questioning doubts, tragic in expression.

When the concerto received its first American performance over the NBC network (with the soloist who had introduced the work in Edinburgh, but with Ansermet conducting), Olin Downes described it as follows in the *New York Times:*

"The first two movements in particular made a strong impression. The piano alone, in the deep unisons and the swinging chords of the opening, without the orchestra, has the manner of deep tolling bells. When this unison motive is answered by the brass the mode of dark prophecy, as it were, is reinforced. The movement is almost monothematic, though there is a short lyrical counter-theme of a more tender nature. By far the greater part of the score hovers over the central theme, varies it, develops it with the aid of the solo instrument....

"The second movement has much of the scherzo quality, with rapid figurations and developments on the first part, and a long contrasting section with new melodic thoughts and a melancholy reflective mood.... Its contrast to the first movement only serves to accentuate the difference of mood within the frame of a unit that has its various facets of emotions and of thought.

"The third movement was ... given to the episodic and the sequential. But it may well be that the very mood of restlessness and inconclusiveness in this music necessitated just such fitful procedure on the part of the composer."

BENJAMIN BRITTEN 1913—

Though he was early attracted to the atonal music of Schoenberg and somewhat later was influenced by Mahler's postromanticism, Britten has adhered to no single style. He is essentially an eclectic composer whose manner of writing is influenced by the esthetic requirements of the work he is producing. He has written in many different veins—sometimes even in the same work—and always with a brilliant command of his technique, complete facility, and lack of inhibitions in his self-expression. At his best, he has engaging warmth and a fine poetic speech.

He has been especially successful in the writing of realistic music set to a definite verbal text, whether in song or in opera. His talent for re-creating atmospheric backgrounds in his music, for evoking the exact mood of his text, and for projecting dramatic climaxes has been exceptional. What F. Bonavia wrote about *Peter Grimes* might aptly apply to all of Britten's best works: "He has found the right symbol for every situation, and every page bears evidence of distinction and originality."

Britten was born in Lowestoft, Suffolk, England, on November 22, 1913. From earliest childhood he revealed phenomenal musical gifts. He began composing when he was five years old; before he was nine, he had written a string quartet; and by the time he was sixteen, his works included a symphony, a half-dozen quartets, ten piano sonatas, and some songs. In 1934, Britten published a *Simple Symphony,* for strings, which incorporated material from pieces he had written between the ages of nine and fourteen.

His academic study took place at Gresham's School, Holt, in Norfolk. At this time he took lessons in theory from Frank Bridge, whose influence on him was profound. In 1930, and for the next four years, Britten attended the Royal College of Music in London, where his teachers included John Ireland (composition), and Arthur Benjamin and Harold Samuel (piano).

He was only twenty-four years old when he first attracted public attention as a composer. His *Fantasy Quartet,* for oboe and strings, was performed at the 1934 festival of the International Society for Contemporary

Music at Florence, and was praised. The Society's 1936 festival, held in Barcelona, introduced another successful Britten work, the Suite for Violin and Piano. With the *Variations on a Theme of Frank Bridge,* introduced in London in 1938 and subsequently heard in many European and American cities, Britten became known internationally.

In the summer of 1939, Britten came to this country, remaining until 1942. In this country he wrote several major works which, performed widely in this country and abroad, increased his reputation further. After three and a half years here, Britten returned to his native land. A conscientious objector, he was exempted from war service; but he co-operated in maintaining morale by giving concerts in bombed areas.

His major undertaking was now the opera *Peter Grimes.* Its first performance was so successful that before long the major opera houses of the world included it in their repertory. *Peter Grimes* placed Britten among the major composers of England, a position he solidified with subsequent works.

The following works by Britten are discussed below: *A Ceremony of Carols; Albert Herring; Billy Budd;* Concerto No. 1 for Piano and Orchestra; *Les Illuminations; Peter Grimes;* Quartet No. 2; *The Rape of Lucretia;* Serenade; *Sinfonia da Requiem; Spring Symphony; Variations on a Theme of Frank Bridge; The Young Person's Guide to the Orchestra.*

VARIATIONS ON A THEME OF FRANK BRIDGE, for orchestra, op. 10 (1937).

For many years, Britten was a pupil of Frank Bridge, whom he greatly admired both as composer and as teacher. In 1937, Britten was inspired by a theme in the second of Bridge's *Three Idylls* to write a series of orchestral variations. Introduced at the Salzburg Festival in 1937 by the English String Orchestra under Boyd Neel, it was an immediate and unqualified success. One year later, it was repeated—and no less successfully—at the festival of the International Society for Contemporary Music held in London.

Following a brief introduction, in which certain elements of the Bridge theme are only suggested, the theme proper is introduced and then repeated without ornamentation. Ten variations follow, their subtitles giving us a clue to their musical or programmatic content: Adagio, March, Romance, Aria Italiana, Bourrée Classique, Wiener Waltz, Moto Perpetuo, Funeral March, Chant, and Fugue.

Though there are several undercurrents of sardonic humor (such as the suggestion of the goose step in the March, the tongue-in-cheek simulation of a Viennese waltz, and the parody of the operatic coloratura style in the Italian Aria), it is rather the deep emotional pages of this work that have made the most forceful impression upon listeners. The opening Adagio and the magnificent Funeral March are singularly moving. The closing fugue is treated in a somewhat unorthodox manner: the entire exposition is in unison.

CONCERTO NO. 1 FOR PIANO AND ORCHESTRA, op. 13 (1938). I. Toccata. II. Waltz. III. Impromptu. IV. March.

This concerto was originally written in 1938 and was introduced in London on August 18 of the same year, with the composer as soloist and an orchestra conducted by Sir Henry J. Wood. In 1945, Britten rewrote the concerto, making minor revisions in three of the movements and replacing one of them completely (the third movement, originally, was a Recitative and Aria). In June, 1946, the revised version of the concerto was heard at the Cheltenham Festival.

The composer has prepared the following descriptive notes:

"The pianoforte starts the first movement (Allegro molto e con brio) with an energetic leaping motif which sets the mood for its own side of the argument. This is the principal subject of the movement. The orchestra continues with a subsidiary phrase which reaches an angry climax in the alternation of two not very closely related chords—an idea which has however, significance throughout the work. After some discussion, the orchestra introduces hesitantly the second principal subject—a longer flowing tune on the woodwind. This the pianoforte mocks in brilliant fashion, and the orchestra tries to further its cause with the tune in the strings. The second section of the movement presents a grimmer aspect of this material.

"The second movement (Allegro, alla valse) is quiet throughout, as if overheard from the next room. The viola solo and clarinet suggest the first tune and the pianoforte adds the chordal motif from the first movement as a codetta. After a slightly more defined repetition the pianoforte starts a running theme, supported by waltz rhythms in the whole orchestra. This grows louder and louder and eventually the first waltz tune returns energetically and forte, as if the door had been slightly opened. But it is soon shut again, and to the end of the movement the mood is that of the beginning. The chordal motif is used again and again rather ominously.

"A set of variations on a theme first announced by the piano comprises the third movement (Andante; Lento). Suggestions of marching rhythms follow directly from the previous movement and lead to a series of march tunes played full of confidence by the pianoforte and then by the orchestra."

LES ILLUMINATIONS, song cycle for high voice and string orchestra, op. 18 (1939).

Britten's exceptional gift for writing songs that embrace a wide gamut of emotions with the greatest ingenuity of expression is nowhere more evident than in this cycle of ten decadent songs on prose poems by the French symbolist Rimbaud. Poetry and music achieve integration as Britten catches in tones the subtlest nuances and the most delicate imagery of Rimbaud's poetry. In the perfection of characterization of each song, and in the balance of the ten, Erwin Stein finds an example of Britten's gift for building large forms "by co-ordination rather than integration," as he concerns himself with "neatly fitting together a diversity of shapes" rather than "connecting and cementing them."

The cycle was written while Britten was in this country, and was introduced in London on January 30, 1940. It has been adapted into a ballet by Frederick Ashton, choreographer of the Sadler's Wells Ballet.

SINFONIA DA REQUIEM, op. 20 (1940). I. Lacrymosa. II. Dies Irae. III. Requiem Aeternam.

Though this symphony utilized the Latin titles of a Catholic Requiem Mass, its relation to the mass was intended by the composer to be emotional rather than liturgical.

The death of the composer's father was the inspiration for this strongly felt music. Britten wrote it in 1940 in the United States. On March 29, 1941, the New York Philharmonic-Symphony Orchestra under John Barbirolli introduced it.

Britten has provided the following analysis:

The first movement (Andante ben misurato) is a "slow marching lament. There are three main motives: (1) a syncopated, sequential theme announced by the cellos and answered by the solo bassoon; (2) a broad theme, based on the interval of the major seventh; (3) alternating chords on flute and trombones, outlined by piano and harps. The first section of the movement is quietly pulsating; the second, a long crescendo, leads to a climax based on the first cello theme."

Without a pause, the work proceeds to the second section (Allegro con fuoco), "a form of Dance of Death, with occasional moments of quiet marching rhythm. The dominating motif of this movement is announced at the start by the flutes and includes an important tremolando figure.... The scheme of the movement is a series of climaxes of which the last is the most powerful, causing the music to disintegrate and to lead directly to the final section."

The closing movement (Andante piacevole) begins "very quietly over a background of solo strings and harps," after which the flutes "announce the quiet ... tune which is the principal motif of the movement. There is a middle section in which the strings play a flowing melody. This grows to a short climax, but the opening tune is soon resumed and the work ends quietly in a long sustained clarinet note."

A CEREMONY OF CAROLS, for treble voices and harp obbligato, op. 28 (1942).

A Ceremony of Carols consists of an opening "Procession" (the choristers march up the church aisle chanting of Christ's birth), nine carols, and a "Recession" (a repetition of the opening "Procession," as the choristers march down the aisle again to leave the church). The carols are of medieval origin: five are of anonymous authorship; four are by James, John, and Robert Wedderburn; Robert Southwell; and William Cornish.

The music has a unanimity of style, even though there is contrast of mood from one carol to the next, as Britten recreates in modern terminology the style of the medieval plain chant. The simple and seemingly spontaneous music is filled with poetic beauty and religious feeling. The background of a single harp provides a remarkably effective accompaniment, and only on one occasion (between the two carols by Southwell) does it provide an instrumental interlude.

This work was introduced in London by the Fleet Street Choir, T. B. Lawrence conducting, on December 5, 1942.

SERENADE, for tenor solo, horn, and string orchestra, op. 31 (1943).

This delightful setting of English lyrics by Cotton, Tennyson, Blake, Ben Jonson, and Keats was introduced in London by Peter Pears, Dennis Brain, and an orchestra conducted by Walter Goehr, on October 15, 1943.

The Serenade opens with a prologue of a horn solo, which is repeated offstage at the conclusion of the work, the Epilogue.

Edward Sackville West, to whom this work is dedicated, described it as follows: "The subject is Night and its prestigia, the lengthening shadow, the distant haze at sunset, the Baroque panoply of the starry sky, the heavy angles of sleep; but also the cloak of evil—the worm in the heart of the rose, the sense of sin in the heart of man. The whole sequence forms an elegy or Nocturnal (as Donne would have called it) reviewing the thoughts and images suitable to the evening."

PETER GRIMES, opera (1944).

In 1941, the Koussevitzky Foundation commissioned Britten to write an opera, paying him a thousand dollars (two hundred dollars a month for five months). The composer selected for his text a poem entitled *The Borough* by George Crabbe.

In the poem, the fisherman, Peter Grimes, is an uncouth villain, turned hard and callow through the misunderstanding of his neighbors. Two apprentices work under him in slave conditions, and both die from maltreatment.

This subject appealed strongly to Britten, who saw in it a symbol of man's struggle against a narrow society: the conflict of the individual against unreasoning masses.

The subject of the Crabbe poem was amplified and changed by Britten's librettist, Montague Slater, to emphasize the helplessness of Grimes against the fury of the masses. Though he is innocent, he is doomed to inevitable disaster. Thus Grimes becomes—in spite of his cruelty, brusque manners, and explosive temper—a sympathetic character. As the opera opens, he is brought to trial for a crime he did not commit: the death of his apprentice. The trial absolves him of his guilt; but ugly suspicions persist. The antagonism between Grimes and society persists. Overwhelmed by this antagonism, Grimes becomes surly; even the one who would give him sympathy and unquestioning allegiance—Ellen Orford, with whom he is in love —is rewarded with blows as Grimes refuses to accept pity. Grimes acquires a second apprentice; the mob, wondering if another "murder" is about to take place, marches to Grimes' lonely hut to see what is happening. Grimes flees to his boat; the apprentice, who follows him, slips and falls. A few days later, the sweater of the apprentice is found on the beach, proof to the townspeople that Grimes has committed murder. With fear and anger tormenting him, Grimes loses his mind. Rather than face an angry mob, he takes to the sea, never to return.

The première of the opera took place at the Sadler's Wells Theatre in London on June 7, 1945. This was a gala event for more reasons than one. The theater was being reopened for the first time in five years, having been closed in 1940 by the Blitz. Besides, this was the first new opera heard in London in several years.

The opera proved to be a gripping emotional experience, and it scored a phenomenal success. There was a five-minute ovation for the composer. The critical reaction was equally enthusiastic. The correspondent of the *New York Times* called the event "a milestone in the history of British music." Ernest Newman described the opera as "a work of great originality.... The whole texture, musical and dramatic, of the opera is admirably unified, in spite of the many genres it employs, ranging from almost naked speech to music at its fullest power."

The success of *Peter Grimes* spread rapidly. In a short period, it was heard more than a hundred times in Sweden, Denmark, Switzerland, Italy, Germany, Holland, and Hungary, and was translated into eight languages. On August 6, 1946, it received its first American performance at Tanglewood, in Lenox, Massachusetts, under the direction of Leonard Bernstein. On February 12, 1948, it entered the repertory of the Metropolitan Opera Association.

With a variety of style—lyricism and piercing dissonance, simple jigs and complicated contrapuntal sea chanteys, polytonal duets, and starkly realistic tone-painting—Britten achieves a score of great dramatic force. The full strength of the implacable tragedy befalling Peter Grimes, and his psychological conflicts are subtly delineated in the music. With grim atmospheric verity the composer imaginatively catches the feeling of fatalism pervading the drama. The score has gripping tensions; but on occasion it also has tenderness.

The orchestral interludes, four in number, are sometimes heard independently on symphony programs. The *Four Interludes* were introduced on June 13, 1945, at the Cheltenham Festival, with the composer conducting the London Philharmonic Orchestra. They comprise the following sections:

I. "Dawn" (between the Prologue and Act I). As Ernest Newman wrote, this section is descriptive of the "gray atmosphere of the hard-bitten little fishing town." The fishermen quietly go about their respective tasks.

II. "Sunday Morning" (leading into Act II), a picture of the village streets on a peaceful Sunday as the church bells ring.

III. "Moonlight" (leading into Act III) depicting the street scene at night.

IV. "The Storm" (between Scenes 1 and 2 of Act I), a picturesque tonal setting of a storm as it rises and gathers force.

QUARTET NO. 2 for strings, op. 36 (1945). I. Allegro calmo senza rigore. II. Vivace. III. Chacony.

In 1945, musical England celebrated the 250th anniversary of the death of Henry Purcell. To honor Purcell, Britten wrote several commemorative works, one of which was this string quartet.

The quartet opens with the traditional sonata-allegro movement built around three themes, each of which is characterized by an interval of the tenth. The second movement is a lugubrious Scherzo for muted strings. It is in the third movement that Britten pays homage to Purcell by writing a "chacony," or chaconne, a form which the master utilized with great technical mastery. Britten's chaconne consists of a theme and twenty-one variations, divided into four distinct groups, each separated from the others by a cadenza.

THE YOUNG PERSON'S GUIDE TO THE ORCHESTRA, op. 34 (1945).

Commissioned by the Ministry of Education in England to write music for an educational film describing the various instruments of the orchestra, Britten hit upon the happy idea of writing a series of variations on a theme, each variation recruiting a different instrument (or group of instruments).

For his theme he selected a robust subject by Henry Purcell (taken from the Rondeau in the incidental music to *Abdelazar*). A set of thirteen variations follows, employing the following instruments: flutes and piccolo; oboes; clarinets; bassoons; violins; violas; cellos; double basses; harp; French horns; trumpets; trombones; percussion. The composition ends in a fugue in which the instruments enter, one by one, in the order in which they were heard in the variations; they then unite in a climactic enunciation of the Purcell theme.

THE RAPE OF LUCRETIA, opera (1946).

In contrast to the almost Wagnerian proportions of *Peter Grimes*, *The Rape of Lucretia* (which came one year later) is of chamber-music dimensions. The artistic expression becomes lean as the composer tries to penetrate to essentials. There are only six principals in the cast. The two "choruses" consist respectively of one man and one woman who, in the manner of the Greek chorus, explain and interpret the action of the play. The musical writing is most spare, too. Subdued atmospheric writing provides a background that is rarely assertive and allows the play on the stage to assume first importance. The writing for the voices is direct, usually melodic. Generally speaking, the opera is lyrical, though an occasional excursion into dissonance is allowed for the sake of dramatic effect.

The opera (based on a play by André Obey, *Le Viol de Lucrèce,* adapted for the composer by Ronald Duncan) is concerned with Lucretia, wife of the Roman general Collatinus, who is seduced by the Etruscan prince Tarquinius during the Etruscan domination of Rome.

The Rape of Lucretia was introduced at Glyndebourne on July 12, 1946. It was so successful that soon after the première it was performed about 130 times in England, before being heard in Holland, Belgium, Switzerland, and the United States. The American première took place in Chicago on June 1, 1947. On December 29, 1948, it was brought on the Broadway stage, where it enjoyed a brief run, though with considerably less success than it had known in the opera house.

Britten's talent for giving the precise musical setting required by a text and interpreting musically the psychological conflicts of his characters is as evident in this opera as in *Peter Grimes*. A memorable section is the interlude accompanying Tarquinius's ride. Here is not only the sweep of the horse's movement conjured with vivid strokes of sound, but the mental turmoil of Tarquinius, suggested in subtle overtones, as well.

ALBERT HERRING, opera (1947).

As an artistic (and possibly emotional) respite from the writing of such stark tragedies as *Peter Grimes* and *The Rape of Lucretia,* Britten wrote an opera buffa in the operatic project following these two works.

Albert Herring, written to launch the first independent season of the English Opera Company, was planned along economical lines to facilitate tours in England and Europe. The opera calls for a small cast and orchestra and limited scenery.

Eric Crozier wrote the libretto, adapting a story by Guy de Maupassant (*Le Rosier de Madame Husson*) and changing the locale from France to Suffolk, England. Madame Husson becomes Lady Billows, a lady with great reverence for virtue. Deciding to revive the May Day Festival, she offers a prize of twenty-five guineas for a May Queen of unquestionable morality. A search among local young ladies fails to uncover a single person capable of fulfilling the necessary qualifications. It is then decided to compromise on a May King, the choice falling on Albert Herring, a notoriously shy fellow. At the High Tea of the Festival, Albert Herring's friend, a practical joker, substitutes a glass of rum for Albert's glass of lemonade. Intoxication slowly sets in. Late that night, the young man's dormant emotions are stirred. He goes forth in search of debauchery and disappears into the night. The following day his whereabouts is a mystery. The wreath of orange blossoms which he had worn the day before is found crushed in the road, inspiring the belief that Albert is dead. His neighbors intone a moving dirge to his passing. Suddenly he appears—ill-kept, ragged, but proud of his new-found freedom.

The realism of *Peter Grimes* gives way in this opera to wit and lusty satire. In his utilization of arias, duets, and ensemble numbers, Britten remains true to the traditions of opera buffa; but the writing is ever piquantly modern. Broad comedy, as in Albert Herring's return in the final scene, is developed with a healthy respect for burlesque. Parody is occasionally indulged in, as, for example, in the sly quotation of the love-potion music from Wagner's *Tristan* when Herring drinks the rum.

Albert Herring was introduced in Glyndebourne, under the composer's direction, on June 20, 1947. Its American première took place at Tanglewood, in the summer of 1949, in a performance by the Berkshire Music Center Opera School.

SPRING SYMPHONY, for chorus, soloists, and orchestra, op. 44 (1949).

Britten's apotheosis of the vernal season is more in the nature of an elaborate suite than a symphony. While the four sections are intended to suggest the four movements of the symphony, the suggestion is more psychological than structural, and the similarity remains vague. There is none of the organic growth and development of ideas one expects in a symphonic work, and the essential forms of the symphony are not utilized.

The composer has here set fourteen English poems of springtime, both of the past and the present. His musical approach is a poetic one as well. He is concerned primarily in evoking the mood of each poem in atmospheric music. He draws his spirit from the old English madrigalists and, like them, has succeeded in bathing his music with radiant warmth, a joyousness of expression, and ebullient feelings.

Each section of the symphony comprises several poems sung without interruption. The introduction (Lento) is based on *Shine out, Fair Sun, with All Your Heat* (author unknown), sung by a mixed chorus. There then follow, in the first part, *The Merry Cuckoo, Messenger of Spring,* by Edmund Spenser (Vivace), for tenor solo and three muted trumpets; *Spring, the Sweet Spring,* by Thomas Nashe (Allegro con slanico) for mixed chorus, soloists, and full orchestra; *When as the Rye Reach to the Chin,* by George Peele; and *The Driving Boy,* by John Clare (Allegro molto), sung by soprano solo, a boys' chorus, and orchestra. John Milton's *The Morning Star* (Molto moderato ma giocoso), for mixed chorus, brass, and percussion, ends this section.

The second part opens with *Welcome Maids of Honour* (Allegretto moderato), by Robert Herrick, for alto solo, woodwinds, and divided strings.

The Shower, by Henry Vaughan (Molto moderato), for tenor solo and violins, and *Out on the Lawn,* by W. H. Auden (Adagio), for alto solo, chorus, winds, and percussion, complete this section.

In the third part we hear *When Will My May Come?* by Robert Barnfield (Allegro impetuoso), for tenor solo and strings; *Fair and Fair,* by George Peele (Allegro grazioso), a duet for soprano and tenor, accompanied by strings and woodwinds; and *Sound the Flute,* by William Blake (Allegretto), for chorus and full orchestra.

The symphony concludes with *London, to Thee I Present,* by Beaumont and Fletcher (Moderato alla valse), for full orchestra and chorus, and a single line from the famous round, *Sumer Is Icumen In* (Allegro pesante), interpolated into the preceding number.

Though the symphony was commissioned by the Koussevitzky Foundation, its world première took place not in this country but in Holland, on July 14, 1949, during the Holland Music Festival. The Concertgebouw Orchestra was directed by Eduard von Beinum. The work received an ovation; it was generally conceded that this performance was the most distinguished event of the entire festival. A few weeks later, on August 13, Serge Koussevitzky directed the American première at the Berkshire Music Festival at Tanglewood.

BILLY BUDD, opera (1951).

In *Billy Budd,* Britten returns to the sea, the setting of his first and, up to now, his most successful opera, *Peter Grimes.* There are other points of similarity between these two works. *Billy Budd* is the first of Britten's operas since *Peter Grimes* to revert to large structural dimensions, calling for large musical and stage forces; his other operas are both intimate and economical. And the central theme of *Billy Budd* is once again the brutality of injustice, of man's inhumanity to man. The source is a famous story of Herman Melville, adapted into a libretto by E. M. Forster and Eric Crozier. Billy Budd is a sailor compelled to serve in the British navy during the British-French wars in the 18th century. He is a lovable, happy-go-lucky lad, ready to do his duty. But he inspires the hate of the master-of-arms, John Claggart, who manufactures a false charge of treason against him. Aroused by this monstrous accusation, and too poor in words to defend himself against it, Budd loses his temper, strikes Claggart, and kills him. He is court-martialed and hanged. Captain Vere realizes the just provocation that led Budd to murder Claggart, but naval justice must be fulfilled.

If there are resemblances between *Billy Budd* and *Peter Grimes,* there are also differences. Indeed, these differences distinguish *Billy Budd* from most other operas. For one thing, *Budd* is scored entirely for men's voices (there is no love interest whatsoever). For another, it dispenses almost entirely with melodic arias and aurally pleasing ensemble numbers. Except for some sailor chanteys (and they represent some of the finest pages in the

score) and one or two lyrical pages, such as Billy's poignant resignation to
his sad fate in the final act, the vocal score is confined to dramatic recitatives
with the principal musical interest and variety found in the orchestration. It
is the drama, rather than the music, that is Britten's first concern; every
musical means at his command is employed to heighten and intensify that
drama. Thus a passage like the series of disconnected triads heard after
Budd has been condemned to die (the stage is empty) is of greater theatrical
interest than musical; so is the effective unaccompanied monologue of
Captain Vere, a discourse on good and evil, with which the opera ends.

   Billy Budd was commissioned by the Arts Council of Great Britain
for the Festival of Britain. It was introduced at Covent Garden, under the
composer's direction, on December 1, 1951. Most leading English critics
hailed it as one of Britten's most important (and most human) operas.
Scott Goddard described the score as "insidiously haunting"; Richard Capell
remarked that its "incidental felicities are innumerable and many things
are in the best vein"; and Stephen Williams referred to it as a "challenging,
stimulating work of art." On May 26, 1952, *Billy Budd* was introduced to
France as one of the major attractions of the Exposition of Masterpieces of
the 20th Century held in Paris.

FERRUCCIO BUSONI   1866—1924

   To composing, Busoni brought the same trenchant and restless intellect
which made him so fine a classical scholar, philosopher, poet, painter, essayist
—and one of the aristocratic interpreters of piano music of his generation. His
musical thinking was profound (sometimes even abstruse), as perhaps only
those who listened to his discussions on esthetics can best appreciate. Though
he was dissatisfied with the restrictions imposed on him by conventions and
academicism, he did not altogether break with the past in his indefatigable
search for new musical expression. He invented new scales, and new harmonic schemes growing out of these scales; he tried to evolve a new system
of musical notation; he experimented with quarter-tones. Frequently he
used composition as a kind of laboratory in which to test or prove his theories
or solve a specific technical problem. Since a great many creative theories
and problems occupied his mind, he did not achieve a single style, but went
from one manner to another, following the dictates of the musical problem
at hand. His music, consequently, is often an exercise in intellectual powers,

in which the form is dictated by the idea, in which emotion is avoided, and in which new musical resources are continually explored. It is not the kind of music that can have a wide and permanent appeal, and for this reason is not often heard; but it is the kind of music that exerts a far-reaching influence on musical development.

Busoni was born in Empoli, Tuscany, on April 1, 1866. The study of the piano was begun in childhood, and he made his public debut as pianist in Vienna at the age of nine, and as composer one year after that. An extensive concert tour, which brought him many honors, followed. For a while he settled in Leipzig to study composition. In 1889, he was appointed professor of the piano at the Helsingfors Conservatory. Other teaching posts brought him to the Moscow Conservatory and the New England Conservatory in Boston. All the while he continued playing the piano, but, dissatisfied with his performance, he decided to go into complete retirement and devote himself anew to piano study. From this extended period of study he emerged one of the greatest pianists of his time.

His first major works were written just before the beginning of the twentieth century: the Concerto for Violin and Orchestra (1896-97), the *Comedy Overture,* for orchestra (1897), and the Sonata in E minor for Violin and Piano (1898).

During World War I, Busoni settled in Switzerland, remaining there until 1920. He then transferred his home to Berlin, where he assumed a magisterial position in the city's musical life. He died there on July 27, 1924.

DOCTOR FAUST, opera (1924).

In this opera, for which Busoni wrote both the libretto and the music, he summed up his whole *Weltanschauung* and personality. It is a tremendous intellectual achievement which—despite its many pages of spiritual and noble beauty—can never achieve universal popularity because of its fastidious avoidance of emotion, love interest, or theatrical effect.

Busoni's designation of the opera as a "puppet-play" might suggest a work of limited dimensions. But *Doctor Faust* is nothing of the kind. It calls for live actors and is built along spacious lines. A work of formidable proportions, it utilizes a large cast of singers and instrumentalists and demands the fullest technical resources of the modern stage. What Busoni tried to emphasize was the opera's divorce from everyday reality and sentimentality; he attempted to project its monumental tragedy—an epic of disillusion and disenchantment, as F. Bonavia once described it—in a distant make-believe world. This also helped uncover the source of the opera, not the Goethe tragedy (which Busoni admired passionately), but an old German puppet-play.

Edward J. Dent has pointed out that Busoni identified himself completely with the character of Faust. Faust surrounded by his students was

Busoni surrounded by his disciples; Faust the magician, calling up visions of Solomon and Samson, was really Busoni the magical interpreter, calling up the spirit of Bach and Beethoven; Faust exclaiming, "Give me genius with all its sufferings," was articulating what Busoni felt all his life.

Musically, *Doctor Faust* represents (as Guido Pannain has noted) a synthesis of all of Busoni's stylistic methods. "It is the history of his musical soul."

Busoni died before he could complete the opera, and the task was left to Philip Jarnach, who worked from Busoni's sketches. The first performance took place in Dresden on May 21, 1925.

Busoni composed two orchestral studies for *Faust* which are sometimes performed at orchestral concerts: the *Sarabande* and *Cortège,* op. 51. The *Sarabande* accompanies Faust's last entrance and gives a premonition of his death. The *Cortège* is music for the procession of the guests at the wedding of the Duke and Duchess of Parma. These two studies were first heard in Berlin on January 13, 1921.

JOHN ALDEN CARPENTER   1876—1951

Carpenter was essentially a conservative composer who was satisfied with traditional forms and techniques which, nevertheless, he endowed with the imprint of his own personality. It is not easy to identify him with any one school or style, for he wrote in many different veins with equal success. His first important work was programmatic music spiced with wit and satire: the *Adventures in a Perambulator,* written in 1915. A change of style took place with the ballet *Krazy Kat* (1921), in which the influence of jazz is strongly felt; the jazz style found its culmination in the ballet *Skyscrapers.* In a work like *The Birthday of the Infanta* with its pronounced Spanish character, a new facet in Carpenter's creative idiom was uncovered. In the last decade and a half of his life, Carpenter turned to impressionistic writing. This manner identifies some of his finest works, notably *Sea-Drift* and parts of the Second Symphony.

Carpenter was born in Park Ridge, Illinois, on February 28, 1876, a descendant of the Aldens of colonial Plymouth. At Harvard University he took music courses with John Knowles Paine. After his graduation, he studied music privately with Sir Edward Elgar and Bernhard Ziehn.

For many years—until 1936—Carpenter successfully combined music with business. He was vice-president of the Chicago firm of George B. Carpenter and Co.; at the same time (in leisure hours) he composed numerous works that placed him with the foremost American composers. In 1947, the National Institute of Arts and Letters awarded him a Gold Medal (which, in music, is presented only once every nine years) in recognition of his "distinguished services." Carpenter died at his home in Chicago on April 26, 1951.

The following works by Carpenter are discussed below: *Adventures in a Perambulator; Sea-Drift; Skyscrapers.*

ADVENTURES IN A PERAMBULATOR, for orchestra (1915). I. En Voiture. II. The Policeman. III. The Hurdy-Gurdy. IV. The Lake. V. Dogs. VI. Dreams.

This work has a definite story to tell. Carpenter has stated that he tried to reproduce in music the varied impressions gathered by a child as he is being wheeled about in his carriage by his nurse. The detailed program, provided by Carpenter, follows in part:

"I. En Voiture. Every morning—after my second breakfast—if the wind and sun are favorable, I go out.... My nurse is appointed to take me. ...I am wrapped in a vacuum of wool, where there are no drafts. I am placed in my perambulator, a strap is buckled over my stomach, my nurse stands firmly behind me—and we are off!

"II. The Policeman. Out is wonderful! ...It is confusing, but it is Life! For instance, the Policeman.... He walks like Doom. My nurse feels it too. She becomes less firm, less powerful. My perambulator hurries, hesitates, and stops. They converse. They ask each other questions.... When I feel that they have gone far enough, I signal to my nurse, and the Policeman resumes his enormous Blue March. He is gone, but I feel him after he goes.

"III. The Hurdy-Gurdy. Then suddenly there is something else. I think it is a sound.... I find that the absorbing noise comes from a box— something like my music-box.... Suddenly, at the climax of our excitement, I feel the approach of a phenomenon that I remember. It is the Policeman. He has stopped the music.... Delightful forbidden music.

"IV. The Lake. My nurse firmly pushes me on.... The land comes to an end, and there at my feet is The Lake. I feel the quiver of the little waves as they escape the big ones and come rushing over the sand.

"V. Dogs. We pass on.... It is Dogs! We are coming upon them without warning.... They laugh, they fight, they run. At last, in order to hold my interest, the very littlest brigand starts a game of 'Follow the Leader,' followed by all the others. It is tremendous!

"VI. Dreams. My mind grows numb.... The wheels of my perambulator make a sound that quiets my nerves. I lie very still.... In order to think more clearly, I close my eyes. My thoughts are absorbing. I deliberate upon my mother.... I hear her voice quite plainly now, and feel the touch of her hand. It is pleasant to live over again the adventures of the day.... It is pleasant to lie quite still and close my eyes and listen to the wheels of my perambulator."

One of the interesting features of Carpenter's score is the amusing way in which he interpolates popular tunes. In the third section, "Hurdy-Gurdy," we hear strains of Irving Berlin's *Alexander's Ragtime Band,* while in the fifth part, snatches of *Ach, du lieber Augustin* and *Where, Oh Where Has My Little Dog Gone?* are skillfully woven into the musical fabric.

The *Adventures* was introduced by the Chicago Symphony Orchestra under Frederick Stock on March 19, 1915.

SKYSCRAPERS, ballet (1925).

In 1924, Diaghilev planned a tour of the United States with his Ballet Russe. For this visit he commissioned Carpenter to write music for a ballet about American life. Carpenter completed this assignment, but the tour never materialized. The première of Carpenter's ballet was not given by the Diaghilev troupe but by the Metropolitan Opera Ballet at the Metropolitan Opera House on February 19, 1926.

"*Skyscrapers*"—so runs a note in the published score—"is a ballet which seeks to reflect some of the many rhythmic movements and sounds of modern American life. It has no story, in the usually accepted sense, but proceeds on the simple fact that American life reduces itself to violent alternations of work and play, each with its own peculiar and distinctive character. The action of the ballet is merely a series of moving decorations reflecting some of the obvious external features of this life."

Skyscrapers is Carpenter's most modern score, often resorting to dissonance in interpreting the confusions and disorders of modern city life. But its principal attraction is its spicy use of jazz. This was not Carpenter's first utilization of jazz in a serious form—*Krazy Kat* preceded it. But it is unquestionably one of the most successful attempts to endow the popular jazz idiom with serious artistic purpose. The score is not only a realistic interpretation of a modern American city—its sounds and sights and smells—but it also conveys the feelings of a gentle irony and pity; the music, in short, is not only a portrait but a commentary.

In the first act, a skyscraper is in the process of construction. Coney Island is the scene of the second act, where frenetic merrymaking is succeeded by a brawl, the perpetrators of which are arrested. The stage empty, a Negro stretches out to sleep. He dreams of his Southland home, evoked for him in religious chants, then in a dance in which he joins. The scene returns to Coney Island as a factory whistle sounds. Once again the workmen are on the scaffold building the skyscraper.

An orchestral score developed from the ballet has been frequently represented at symphony concerts.

SEA-DRIFT, symphonic poem for orchestra (1933).

This orchestral poem, one of Carpenter's most sensitive works, derives its inspiration from the sea poems of Walt Whitman. It is particularly effective in its use of dynamics to suggest the roll and swell of the sea.

The composition is in two sections, each culminating in a dramatic climax. The opening of the piece (Lento tranquillo) beautifully suggests the shimmer and quiver of the waters as the first theme is heard in the lower strings. In the first section most of the principal thematic subjects are assigned to the horn. In the second section, the most effective subject is a *dolente* theme, heard in the English horn and then repeated by the strings.

Sea-Drift was introduced by the Chicago Symphony Orchestra under Stock on November 30, 1933.

ALFREDO CASELLA   1883—1947

Casella was one of the most trenchant minds, and one of the most influential forces, in contemporary Italian music. He worked indefatigibly for Italian music, old and new, and for the Italian composer. And he devoted himself with equal fervor to the cause of contemporary music. Every important new trend found him as its stout protagonist. He organized societies, concerts, festivals, periodicals to promote the interests of the present-day composer.

Never a highly original composer—though always writing with facility and skill—Casella too easily assimilated the styles of others. He began as an impressionist. Then he turned to polytonal music. After that, as his analytical mind absorbed and dissected the styles of his major contemporaries, he found himself writing in many different modern veins. Perhaps his most agreeable and effective music was produced in the neo-classical style. Here the scholar of old music and the ardent protagonist of new music found a common meeting ground.

Casella was born in Turin on July 25, 1883, and received his education at the Conservatory in Paris, principally with Gabriel Fauré. His musical education ended, he returned to his native land and became professor at the Santa Cecilia Academy in Rome. He assumed a dominating position in the musical life of his country, dividing his seemingly inexhaustible energies among piano-playing, conducting, composing, teaching, writing, editing, research, and the founding of musical societies. During World War II, he allied himself and his art to the cause of Fascism. He died in Rome on March 5, 1947, after a long illness.

The following works by Casella are discussed below: *La Giara; Italia; Partita.*

ITALIA, rhapsody for orchestra (1909).

Italia was one of Casella's first successful works, and has maintained its popularity. It was introduced in Paris on April 23, 1910, the composer conducting.

Though the rhapsody has no specific program, it was intended to reflect Sicilian and Neapolitan life. Sicilian life, we learn from a note in the published score, is "tragic, superstitious, passionate, as it is found under the scorching sun or in the inferno of the sulphur mines"; the life of Naples is a "turbulent, careless, frenetic existence which may be lived amid the magic of the Gulf of Naples."

For his melodic material, Casella drew copiously from Sicilian and Neapolitan melodies. The rhapsody opens (Lento) with a song heard in the province of Caltanissetta. Following some development, this song is succeeded by a tune popular in the Sicilian sulphur mines. An English horn then is heard chanting a hymn heard on Good Friday in religious processions in Caltanissetta. After a theme for the bassoon (based on a work song from the Catitu marble quarries) comes the finale, in which three popular melodies are heard: *Funiculi, Funiculà;* Costa's *Lariulà;* and Tosti's *Marechiare.*

LA GIARA, ballet (1924).

Casella composed the score of this, his best-known ballet, on a scenario based upon a Sicilian tale of Pirandello. It was presented with great success in Paris by the Swedish Ballet on November 19, 1924. The composer explains that the music "was composed in obedience to the fundamental idea of uniting in modern synthesis the old fundamental musical comedy of the Neapolitan school with the elements of Italian folklore, more particularly the Sicilian."

The text is an amusing one, and concerns the miser Don Lollo Zirafa, who is inordinately proud of a huge jar in his possession. Broken by a clumsy peasant (to the fury of Don Lollo) the jar is put into the hands of a local hunchback for repair. The hunchback enters the jar and repairs it, only to discover that now that his job is done he cannot get out. Don Lollo stoutly refuses to have his precious jar broken again. The hunchback takes the decision philosophically, sits placidly in the jar, smokes his pipe, watches the moon, and listens to a Sicilian song sung in the distance. A farmer's daughter enters the scene and dances around the jar. Peasants enter, make merry, and create such a hubbub that they awaken Don Lollo. In an uncontrolled fit of anger, Don Lollo sends the jar rolling down the hill until it smashes against an olive tree. The liberated hunchback is carried on the shoulders of the peasants in triumph.

An orchestral suite based on the ballet score is divided into two sections: I. Prelude (Andantino dolce quasi pastorale); Sicilian Dance (Allegro vivace). II. Nocturne (Lento; Calmissimo); Dance of Nela (Vivacissimo e leggiero); Entrance of Peasants and Brindisi (Allegro deciso); General Dance (Allegro rude e selvaggio); Finale.

PARTITA for piano and orchestra (1925). I. Sinfonia. II. Passacaglia. III. Burlesca.

This partita is one of Casella's successful efforts in fusing old classical forms with contemporary idioms. It was introduced by the composer in New York City on October 29, 1925, at a concert of the New York Philharmonic-Symphony Orchestra.

The composer has provided the following comments:

"I. Sinfonia. The ensemble results from fusion of the sonata form, bi-thematic, the suite of the Seventeenth Century, and the instrumental concerto and the concerto grosso. The chief themes are: the first given to the strings; one for the oboe with piano; and a subsidiary one.

"II. Passacaglia. While it evokes a more sombre atmosphere and is always loyally 'Spanish,' after the manner of the old varied dance form, it solves in a new and modern manner the problem of the varied theme. This reorientation of the old passacaglia is obtained by the successive introductions of contrasting rhythms, by the differing character given to the diverse instruments, and by a progressive variation of the persisting theme itself.... The eleventh variation is in the folk form of a Siciliana. The twelfth is a mysterious chorale of religious, distant solemnity. After some measures of piano and oboe, the clarinets bring back gently the first measure of the Passacaglia, which ends as it began.

"III. Burlesca. This is a frank and joyous rondo in which one can find a typical result of the influence beginning to be exercised in the field of pure music by Scarlatti, Rossini, and Verdi's *Falstaff*."

MARIO CASTELNUOVO-TEDESCO   1895—

Several important influences on Castelnuovo-Tedesco are reflected in his music. The first of these is his native city of Florence, described in some of his earlier works; indeed, no less an authority than Guido M. Gatti believes that the personality of the city has molded the composer's style. Another influence has been Shakespeare, whose plays and sonnets have inspired numerous songs, duets, and concert overtures. A third influence has been the Bible, reflected in such works as the Second Concerto for Violin and Orchestra (*The Prophets*). Finally, there has been the impact of the United States, resulting in such American works as the *American Rhapsody* and the *Indian Songs and Dances*.

But whatever the influence, Castelnuovo-Tedesco's music is always filled with romantic feelings and poetic concepts.

Castelnuovo-Tedesco was born in Florence on April 13, 1895. At the Cherubini Royal Institute he studied under Ildebrando Pizzetti, who made a profound and lasting impression on him. He began composing early. In 1926, he gained recognition with an opera, *La Mandragola,* which won the Italian Prize. During the next decade, his stature grew, and his reputation penetrated out of his own country. In the United States, performers like Toscanini, Scipione Guidi, Jascha Heifetz, and Gregor Piatigorsky introduced his major works, usually with considerable success.

After Italy embarked on its anti-Semitic program, inspired by its Axis partner, Castelnuovo-Tedesco, who was of Jewish birth, came to this country, settling permanently in California, where he wrote music for motion pictures. His opera, *The Merchant of Venice,* received the David Campari Prize in Italy in 1958.

The following works by Castelnuovo-Tedesco are discussed below: *Cipressi;* Concerto No. 2 for Piano and Orchestra; Overture to *Twelfth Night.*

OVERTURE TO *TWELFTH NIGHT,* for orchestra (1933).

Castelnuovo-Tedesco's passion for the plays of Shakespeare has inspired him to write concert overtures for many of them. The *Twelfth Night* overture received its first performance in Rome on January 6, 1935, with Vittorio Gui conducting the Augusteo Orchestra. In this overture, the characters, not the dramatic action, are of central interest. A slow introduction (Andantino malinconico) brings up Prince Orsino, while a mocking and gay passage for bassoon (Vivo e burlesco) evokes Malvolio. These two principal themes and several subsidiary ones (describing the heroine and the clown) are developed astutely. An ancient dance (galliard) provides rhythmic and atmospheric interest.

CONCERTO NO. 2 FOR PIANO AND ORCHESTRA (1937). I. Vivo. II. Romanza. III. Vivo e impetuoso.

This concerto was introduced in New York City on November 2, 1939. The composer was the soloist and the New York Philharmonic-Symphony Orchestra was conducted by John Barbirolli.

The music is direct in its appeal, making brilliant effects and containing a great deal of fine virtuoso writing for the piano. The first movement has graceful, sometimes sparkling, music; both principal themes are first introduced by the orchestra before being taken over by the soloist. A slow and dreamy Romanza follows. After a cadenza, the impetuous and headstrong closing movement arrives to provide excitement.

CIPRESSI, for orchestra, also for piano (1940).

Behind Castelnuovo-Tedesco's home in Florence there stood a row of majestic cypress trees, tracing the rise of a hill. Glancing out of his window, one day in 1920, the composer was so impressed by this vista that he decided to interpret it musically in a short piece for the piano. Twenty years later, he returned to it nostalgically—it reminded him of his lost home—and decided to give it orchestral dress. In this form it was introduced by the Boston Symphony Orchestra under Serge Koussevitzky on October 25, 1940.

CARLOS CHÁVEZ   1899—

From the native music of Mexico, particularly that of the Mexican-Indian, Chávez acquired some of his stylistic traits: the austerity and stark simplicity of melodic line; the percussive harshness of sounds; the primitive rhythmic force; the archaic idioms; the sudden, abrupt contrasts. Fusing such elements with the harmonic and instrumental techniques of the modern composer, Chávez arrived at a personal style that is unmistakably his—a style Mexican to the core.

Chávez was born in Mexico City on June 13, 1899, and was virtually self-taught in music. His early works revealed the influence of European composers. Immersion in the folk music of his native land brought him freedom from European influences: the first major work in which his Mexican style was evident was the ballet *New Fire*, written in 1921. After extensive travels in Europe and the United States, Chávez returned to his own country and became one of its most potent musical influences. He organized a symphony orchestra, the Symphony Orchestra of Mexico, which he has directed since 1928; he rehabilitated Mexico's educational system in music as director of the National Conservatory from 1928 to 1934; and he was director of the National Institute of Fine Arts from 1934 to 1953. His opera, *Panfilo and Lauretta*, received its world première in New York on May 9, 1957. Chávez has often appeared as guest conductor of leading American orchestras.

The following works by Chávez are discussed below: Concerto No. 1 for Piano and Orchestra; *Sinfonía de Antígona;* Toccata for Percussion Instruments.

SINFONÍA DE ANTÍGONA, for orchestra (1933).

A projected performance of Jean Cocteau's *Antigone* in Mexico City brought Chávez a commission from the Department of Fine Arts to write its incidental music. This music was adapted by Chávez into a "symphony," which he himself introduced in Mexico City on December 15, 1933.

This music mixes Indian styles with ancient Greek modes, thus acquiring a character all its own. The composer explains that this work is a "symphony, not a symphonic poem—that is, it is not subject to a program. Antigone, her self-confidence, defiance, heroism, and martyrdom are expressed by the music as a whole, not successively. The most elementary musical materials serve for this music, which could not be grandiloquent. Bare and elemental, it could not be expressed by laconic strength, just as what is primitive is reduced to its elements because it is primitive. The work has the basic structure of the sonata, and is strictly a symphony, though in one movement."

There are three major thematic ideas: the first is introduced by the solo oboe; the second is given by the violins; the third appears in the bass flute.

CONCERTO NO. 1 FOR PIANO AND ORCHESTRA (1940).
I. Allegro agitato. II. Molto lento. III. Allegro; Finale.

In this highly percussive and austere music, Chávez's style arrives at its fullest development. It is music of persuading power, original in its harmonic texture, varied in its acoustic effects. The piano and the orchestra are treated as an integrated musical body, neither part of which is subsidiary to the other. The composer has said that his intention was to write virtuoso music for both the piano and the orchestra; but rather than virtuosity, what impresses us is the personal character of Chávez's melodic ideas (some of them written modally), and the individual way he develops them rhythmically, acoustically, harmonically.

The first and third movements derive their force and strength from the rhythms of native Indian music. Between these two energetic movements comes a lyrical section, exotic in its use of archaic idioms.

On January 1, 1942, this concerto was introduced by Emanuel List, pianist, and the New York Philharmonic-Symphony Orchestra under Dimitri Mitropoulos.

TOCCATA FOR PERCUSSION INSTRUMENTS (1942).

This unusual work is scored for eleven types of percussion instruments (played by six performers), some of them indigenous to Mexico: Yaqui drums; tenor and side drums; bells; xylophone; cymbal; chimes; hardwood sound sticks; rattles; kettledrums; bass drum; gongs. Different groups of instruments are used in different movements: high and low drums predominate in the first; xylophone, chimes, cymbal, gongs, are heard in the second; and rattles, hardwood sound sticks, and the small Indian drum in the third.

The *Toccata* is in three movements played without interruption: Allegro sempre giusto; Largo; Allegro un poco marziale. The variety of dynamics, rhythm, and color provides continual interest.

This work was introduced in Mexico City on October 31, 1942, Eduardo Hernandez Moncada conducting.

AARON COPLAND   1900—

In the first of his works to attract attention—the *Music for the Theatre,* and the Concerto for Piano and Orchestra—Copland explored the potentialities of jazz as a serious medium for musical expression. This interest in jazz structure and style soon waned. In the music that followed—notably the *Dance Symphony,* the *Piano Variations,* the *Short Symphony,* and *Statements*—there can be heard the voice of a modernist whose skillful employment of advanced techniques of harmony, counterpoint, and rhythm was admired and praised by that esoteric circle of music lovers who went in for modern music. But the public at large failed to respond to this music.

Dissatisfied with his failure to please audiences, and feeling that he had been working in a sort of a vacuum, Copland now made a conscious effort to speak "in the simplest possible terms." Not only did he simplify his writing, but he also adopted a speech which he felt was more easily assimilable. He began writing functional music: music for school children (the opera, *The Second Hurricane*, and *The Outdoor Overture*, for orchestra), music for the movies (*Of Mice and Men, Our Town, The City, North Star, The Heiress, The Red Pony*), music for the theater (*Quiet City*), music for radio (*Music for Radio*). He adopted popular idioms even in his most serious efforts: that of Mexico in *El Salón México* and Cuba in *Danzón Cubano*. He drew inspiration for ballet music from the rich mine of American folk music: *Rodeo, Billy the Kid,* and *Appalachian Spring.* Even in a work like the Third Symphony, which made no attempt to absorb materials from outside sources, the tendency towards simplification is still present, and the influence of American folk music is continually suggested in subtle overtones of expression.

There has been no cheapening of style or artistic concession in this conscious effort to write music that can be appreciated by the many instead of the few. On the contrary, in his later works Copland has grown in artistic stature. His language has become personalized, his speech has acquired subtler emotional nuances. Two of his works—*Appalachian Spring* and the Third Symphony—were selected by the New York Music Critics Circle as the best new works produced by an American during the season in which they were introduced; and *Appalachian Spring,* in addition, was awarded the Pulitzer Prize in music. "Here is at last," as Arthur V. Berger wrote, "an American that we may place unapologetically beside the recognized figures of any other country."

Copland was born in Brooklyn on November 14, 1900. He began studying the piano when he was eleven and in 1917 took lessons in harmony with Rubin Goldmark. Subsequently, he attended the Fontainebleau School of Music in France, and from there he went on to Paris for three years of private lessons with Nadia Boulanger. Under her critical guidance, he composed his first works: a ballet, *Grohg,* and some smaller pieces for the piano, for chorus, and for string quartet.

Just before returning to the United States (in 1924), Copland was asked by Boulanger to write something that she could use during her forthcoming tour of the United States as organist. Copland wrote the *Symphony for Organ and Orchestra,* which Nadia Boulanger introduced early in 1925 with the New York Symphony Society, conducted by Walter Damrosch. One month later it was repeated in Boston by the Boston Symphony under Koussevitzky.

A generous patroness interested herself in Copland at this time. This, and the winning of a Guggenheim Fellowship in 1926 and 1927, relieved Copland of financial problems for several years and enabled him to devote himself intensively to composition. In 1929, he won a prize of five thousand dollars for his *Dance Symphony* in a competition sponsored by the RCA Victor Company. Since that time, he has been in the vanguard of American composers.

No résumé of Copland's career would be complete without a consideration of his many efforts on behalf of American composers. He has been instrumental in bringing about many performances of new American works through his organization of the Copland-Sessions Concerts, and the American Festival of Contemporary Music at Yaddo, in Saratoga Springs, New York. He has also distinguished himself with the League of Composers, of which he is now chairman, and with the American Composers Alliance, which he helped to create. His books, articles for the magazines, and lectures have also proved to be important instruments of propaganda for present-day American music.

The following works by Copland are discussed below: *Appalachian Spring; Billy the Kid; Concerto for Clarinet and String Orchestra; El Salón México; A Lincoln Portrait; Music for the Theatre;* Symphony No. 3.

MUSIC FOR THE THEATRE, for chamber orchestra (1925). I. Prologue. II. Dance. III. Interlude. IV. Burlesque. V. Epilogue.

Serge Koussevitzky was invited by the League of Composers to direct a concert of contemporary chamber-orchestral works in New York in 1925. For this concert, Koussevitzky asked young Copland (whose symphony he had recently performed in Boston) to write a new work. At that time, Copland was fascinated by the possibilities of jazz in serious composition. In planning a new work for Koussevitzky's use, he decided to explore jazz's artistic capabilities. *Music for the Theatre* was introduced by the Boston Symphony Orchestra under Koussevitzky in Boston on November 20, 1925, before receiving its New York performance at the League of Composers concert.

In writing this music Copland had no specific play in mind. The title was intended to convey the idea that the music has the dramatic and atmospheric qualities of the theater.

In the Prologue, a solo trumpet announces the first theme. After a second subject is heard in the oboe, there follows a development, rising to a dramatic climax, then subsiding into the serenity of the opening measures. The Dance is a nervous, highly rhythmic piece of music, and is followed by the lyric melody of the Interlude section. The Burlesque movement is in A-B-A-B form. In the closing Epilogue, material from the first and third sections is utilized. The entire work ends as it began, in an atmosphere of peace.

EL SALÓN MÉXICO, for orchestra (1936).

In the fall of 1932, Copland visited Mexico and carried away with him vivid impressions of its life and its music. One year after that, he came upon two scholarly works devoted to Mexican song which aroused in him the desire to write a work in Mexican style. Suddenly he recalled the impressions of his Mexican visit, particularly experiences in a popular dance hall called the "Salón México." He set to work on a musical composition about that dance hall which would portray the Mexico that the tourists saw and knew rather than the Mexico of ancient civilizations.

Adopting a form which was, as he put it, a "kind of modified potpourri in which Mexican themes and their extensions are sometimes inextricably mixed for use of conciseness and coherence," Copland created a vivid picture in which the smoke-filled and noisy dance hall is seen with all the exotic color of its background and clientele. The seductive rhythms of Mexican folk music pulse throughout the score and give it its greatest charm and appeal. Some authentic Mexican tunes are quoted, the most important being *El Mosco,* which is heard in the solo trumpet soon after the introductory measures.

The first performance of *El Salón México* took place in Mexico City on August 27, 1937; Carlos Chávez conducted the Orquesta Sinfónica de Mexico. The piece was heard in this country for the first time over the NBC network, on May 14, 1938, with Adrian Boult conducting the NBC Symphony.

BILLY THE KID, ballet (1938).

The composer's recent tendency to draw his subjects and melodic ideas from American folk-sources prevails in *Billy the Kid,* whose source is the cowboy. With his customary supple technique, the composer ingeniously incorporates into his score several familiar cowboy songs, notably *Git Along Little Dogie; Old Chisholm Trail; Goodbye, Old Paint; O Bury Me Not,* etc. Yet he never gives the impression that this music is just a potpourri of familiar tunes. The variety of mood and pace, the inventiveness of harmonic language, the picturesque re-creations of places and people bring to *Billy the Kid* both artistic scope and originality.

The action of the ballet, which begins and ends on an open prairie, has thus been summarized by the composer:

"The central portion of the ballet concerns itself with the significant moments in the life of Billy the Kid. The first scene is a frontier town. Familiar figures amble by. Cowboys saunter, some on horseback, others with their lassos. Some Mexican women do a Jarabo, which is interrupted by a fight between two drunks. Attracted by the gathering crowd, Billy is seen for the first time as a boy of twelve, with his mother. The brawl turns ugly, guns are drawn, and in some unaccountable way Billy's mother is killed. Without an instant's hesitation, in cold fury, Billy draws a knife from a cowhand's sheath and stabs his mother's slayers. His short but famous career has begun.

"In swift succession we see episodes of Billy's later life. At night, under the stars, in a quiet card game with his outlaw friends. Hunted by a posse led by his former friend Pat Garrett, Billy is pursued. A running gun battle ensues. Billy is captured. A drunken celebration takes place. Billy in prison is, of course, followed by one of Billy's legendary escapes. Tired and worn in the desert, Billy rests with his girl. Starting from a deep sleep, he senses movement in the shadows. The posse has finally caught up with him. It is the end."

Billy the Kid was commissioned by Lincoln Kirstein of the Ballet Caravan. It was written in the summer of 1938, and on October 16 of the same year it was successfully introduced by the Ballet Caravan in Chicago.

Most of the music of the ballet was subsequently incorporated by the composer into an orchestral suite. It includes the following sections: "The Open Prairie"; "Street in Frontier Town"; "Card Game at Night"; "Gun Battle"; "Celebration after Billy's Capture"; "The Open Prairie."

A LINCOLN PORTRAIT, for narrator and orchestra (1942).

Soon after the entrance of the United States into World War II, André Kostelanetz, the orchestra conductor, commissioned several American composers to write orchestral works descriptive of great Americans which "could be employed to mirror the magnificent spirit of our country." To Copland went the assignment of writing music about an American statesman, and—as the composer tells us—"the choice of Lincoln as my subject seemed inevitable."

The composer explains further:

"The composition is roughly divided into three main sections.

"In the opening section I wanted to suggest something of the mysterious sense of fatality that surrounds Lincoln's personality. Also near the end of that section, something of his gentleness and simplicity of spirit. The quick middle section briefly sketches in the background of the times he lived in. This merges into the concluding section where my sole purpose was to draw a simple but impressive frame about the words of Lincoln himself."

The text, read by a narrator, is drawn from the letters and speeches of Lincoln which "seemed particularly apposite to our own situation today"; and it concludes with the closing lines of the Gettysburg Address.

Copland quotes two songs of the period to give his music contemporary flavor: Stephen Foster's *Camptown Races,* and the ballad, *Springfield Mountain*. In neither case is the treatment a literal one. Otherwise, the melodic material is entirely Copland's.

André Kostelanetz directed the first performance of the *Portrait* with the Cincinnati Symphony Orchestra on May 14, 1942.

APPALACHIAN SPRING, ballet (1945).

Appalachian Spring was composed for Martha Graham on a commission from the Elizabeth Sprague Coolidge Foundation. Miss Graham
introduced it at the Library of Congress in Washington, D.C., on October
30, 1944. In the spring of 1945, Copland arranged some of the best passages
into an orchestral suite which has enjoyed numerous performances throughout the country. *Appalachian Spring* won the Pulitzer Prize and the award
of the New York Music Critics Circle, both for 1945.

The composer has provided us with a history of this, one of his most
successful works:

"The music of the ballet takes as its point of departure the personality
of Martha Graham. I have long been an admirer of Miss Graham's work.
She, in turn, must have felt a certain affinity for my music, because in 1931
she chose my *Piano Variations* as background for a dance composition entitled *Dithyramb*.... Ever since then, at long intervals, Miss Graham and I
planned to collaborate on a stage work. Nothing might have come of our
intention if it were not for the lucky chance that brought Mrs. Elizabeth
Sprague Coolidge to a Graham performance for the first time early in
1942. With typical energy, Mrs. Coolidge translated her enthusiasms into
action. She invited Martha Graham to create three new ballets for the 1943
annual fall festival of the Coolidge Foundation in Washington, and commissioned three composers—Paul Hindemith, Darius Milhaud, and myself—
to compose scores especially for the occasion.

"After considerable delay, Miss Graham sent me an untitled script.
I suggested certain changes, to which she made no serious objections. I began
work on the music of the ballet in Hollywood in June, 1943, but didn't
complete it until a year later, in June, 1944, in Cambridge, Mass.

"The title, *Appalachian Spring*, was chosen by Miss Graham. She
borrowed it from the heading of one of Hart Crane's poems, though the
ballet bears no relation to the text of the poem itself."

The première of the ballet took place in October, 1944. The setting
was designed by Isamu Noguchi, and Edith Guilford supplied the costumes.

The orchestral suite from the ballet score includes eight sections,
played without interruption:

I. Very Slowly—The Introduction of the Characters.

II. Sudden Burst of Unison Strings, marking the beginning of the
action. The sentiment here expressed combines elation with religious
feeling.

III. Moderate (Duo for the Bride and Her Intended), a tender and
passionate scene.

IV. Quite Fast (The Revivalist and His Flock). The feeling is folk-
like, with echoes of country fiddlers and suggestions of square dances.

V. Still Faster (Solo Dance of the Bride). The extremes of joy and
fear are here voiced.

VI. Very Slowly (as at first). This is a transition scene in which the music brings up recollections of the introduction.

VII. Calm and Flowing (Scenes of Daily Activity for the Bride and her Farmer-Husband). A Shaker theme is heard, followed by five variations. The theme (solo clarinet) is derived from an actual Shaker melody entitled *Simple Gifts*.

VIII. Moderate (Coda). The married couple are left alone in their new home. Music that is almost reverent is intoned by muted strings. The final measures recall the opening pages.

SYMPHONY NO. 3 (1946). I. Molto moderato, with simple expression. II. Allegro molto. III. Andantino quasi allegretto. IV. Molto deliberato (Fanfare); Allegro risoluto.

In the summer of 1944, during a stay in a small Mexican village, Copland began working on a new symphony that had been commissioned by the Koussevitzky Foundation. The first movement was completed the following April, the second in August of the same year. The third and fourth movements were written between January and September of 1946. On October 18, 1946, the symphony was introduced in Boston by the Boston Symphony Orchestra under Koussevitzky. The New York Music Critics Circle gave it its annual award for the best new work by an American composer.

Unlike so many other works by Copland written in this period, the symphony does not call upon ideas from folk-music sources, American or foreign. Except for the fact that it occasionally borrows brief subjects from earlier Copland works (in the opening movement a tonal device stems from *Appalachian Spring,* while the last movement quotes from *Fanfare for the Common Man*), the symphony contains only original material, all of it of compelling force and vitality. Serge Koussevitzky described it as "the greatest American symphony—it goes from the heart to the heart."

Copland has described the work in the following way:

"The opening movement, which is broad and expressive in character, opens and closes in the key of E major.... The themes—three in number— are plainly stated; the first in strings at the very start without introduction; the second, in related mood, in violas and oboes; the third, of a bolder nature, in trombones and horns.... The form [of the second movement] stays closer to normal symphonic procedure. It is the usual Scherzo, with the first part, trio, and return.... The third movement is the freest of all in formal structure. Although it is built sectionally, the various sections are intended to emerge one from the other in continuous flow, somewhat in the manner of a closely knit series of variations.... The final movement follows without pause. It is the longest movement of the symphony, and closest in structure to the customary sonata-allegro form."

CONCERTO FOR CLARINET AND STRING ORCHESTRA
(1948). I. Slowly and Expressively; Cadenza. II. Rather Fast.

Since this work was commissioned by Benny Goodman, "The King
of Swing," it was to be expected that popular elements would be introduced into its musical texture. And the popular ideas employed by the
composer stem not only from American but also from South American
sources: the secondary material, for example, is based on a popular Brazilian
melody. The first movement, in simple song form, is ingratiatingly melodic
throughout. A cadenza for the solo instrument is the transition to the
second and final movement which comes without interruption, and is in
the form of a free rondo.

The Concerto was adapted into a ballet, *The Pied Piper,* and introduced by the New York City Ballet.

HENRY COWELL   1897—

The phrase "tone clusters" inevitably leaps to mind when the name
Henry Cowell is spoken. Almost from the time he began playing the piano,
Cowell experimented with new tonal effects, originating new kinds of chords
through the use of simultaneous seconds, produced on the piano keyboard
by utilizing the fists, forearms, or the palms of the hands. On March 12,
1912—one day after his fifteenth birthday!—he gave a recital of his own
music, all of it exploiting this revolutionary method, which has since
then acquired the name of "tone clusters." Tone clusters were not entirely
his invention, however. They had been utilized before him by Rebikoff and
Charles Ives. But Cowell had arrived at this technique independently of the
composers who had preceded him, and without knowing of their efforts
in this direction.

In his more recent works, Cowell has for the most part turned to
a more conventional style of composition, frequently searching in American
folk music, hymnology, and backgrounds for his ideas and materials. He
has been writing music of considerable charm and aural appeal, and his
more recent works, extensively performed, have greatly broadened the base
of his public appeal.

Cowell was born in Menlo Park California, on March 11, 1897. Study
of the violin was begun at the age of five, and two years after that he

appeared in a sonata recital. Compelled by serious illness to abandon the violin, he turned to composition, writing an opera when he was eleven. By the time he reached his fourteenth birthday, he could afford to buy a secondhand piano, on which he began experimenting with new harmonies.

In his seventeenth year, with more than a hundred compositions to his credit, Cowell was sent by his friends to the University of California for formal study with Charles Seeger. For three and a half years he attended music classes. Then, following an interruption of more than a year, during which time he was a bandmaster in the Army, he spent two additional years of study at the Institute of Applied Music in New York.

Between 1923 and 1933 Cowell toured America and Europe extensively in performances of his own piano music. His concerts frequently provoked riots, frequently inspired satiric comments from the critics. After 1933, by virtue of a Guggenheim Fellowship, Cowell devoted himself to musicological studies for two years.

Cowell has consistently been the champion of new music. He has founded organizations which published and performed new works; he has edited magazines which propagandized for them. He also has written numerous articles, has lectured, and has taught extensively. Between 1941 and 1943 he directed the Editorial Project for Latin American Music for the Pan-American Union, and was in charge of the Music Distribution Project, which loaned musical scores and recordings of American works to twenty Latin American countries. During World War II, he served in the Office of War Information, in charge of short-wave broadcasts of music. In 1948, he received a grant from the American Academy of Arts and Letters.

The following works by Cowell are discussed below: *Hymn and Fuguing Tune No. 2; Short Symphony (No. 4); Tales of Our Countryside.*

TALES OF OUR COUNTRYSIDE, suite for piano and orchestra (1940). I. Deep Tides. II. Exultation. III. The Harp of Life. IV. Country Reel.

In its original form, the *Tales* consists of a series of piano pieces composed between 1922 and 1930. In 1940, they were expanded by the composer, integrated as a four-movement suite, and scored for piano and orchestra. Each of the four movements was written in a different state in this country: the first in California; the second in the hills of the Hudson River Valley; the third in Iowa; and the fourth in Kansas.

The origin of the *Tales* as a work for solo piano has influenced its style. Tone clusters are utilized (though discreetly) in the solo piano part, and inject dramatic color into the entire composition. However, though the spice of dissonance is present, the suite is romantic and for the most part conservative. American country tunes exerted a strong, if possibly unconscious, influence on the thematic material, which is folkloristic in character, even though entirely original with the composer.

The first performance took place in Atlantic City, New Jersey in May, 1941. The composer was at the piano, and the All-American Orchestra was conducted by Leopold Stokowski.

HYMN AND FUGUING TUNE NO. 2, for string orchestra (1944).

In or about 1941, Cowell came across William Walker's collection of hymns by the old singing-school masters, *Southern Harmony,* which suddenly brought back memories of the music he had heard as a boy sung by the Primitive Baptists in Kansas and Oklahoma. "Cowell began to wonder," his wife has written, "what the result would have been if our musical culture had not cut itself off from its living roots as it did during the last century, overawed by the achievements of Europe. Suppose the musical elements which formed the style of the shaped-note hymns had been allowed to develop and to penetrate our art music, what might they have become in the modern symphonic fabric?

"The result of this query has been a series of pieces for various instrumental combinations, all under the title of *Hymn and Fuguing Tune.* Among these are two for strings, one for full orchestra, one for symphonic band, several for piano, one for voice or instruments in three parts, and another in five parts for viola and piano, another for string quartet....

"The famous New England tanner, William Billings, is credited with the invention of what he called 'fuguing tunes.' Their polyphony consists of an innocent kind of approximate imitation, but the separate entries of the voices lend interest, so the idea was widely adopted, and 'fuguing tunes' are still sung with enthusiasm at least as far west as the Ozarks."

The second *Hymn and Fuguing Tune* is one of the most successful works that Cowell has produced in this form. It was introduced in March, 1944, by the NBC Symphony Orchestra, Henri Nosco conducting. The first public performance took place in Boston on March 8, 1946, with Koussevitzky conducting the Boston Symphony Orchestra.

It is music that is intense in its expression and occasionally exalted in mood, written with almost severe simplicity and classic purity. Its effect is derived from its sustained contrapuntal eloquence.

SHORT SYMPHONY (NO. 4) (1946). I. Hymn. II. Ballad. III. Dance. IV. Fuguing Tune.

Like Cowell's *Hymn and Fuguing Tunes,* this symphony is inspired by old hymns. These hymns are not imitated or reproduced, but are developed—as the composer's wife has explained—"with increased variety of rhythm and tempo, modal modulation, contrast of tonal color, and more extended polyphony."

Mrs. Cowell has also analyzed the symphony:

"The first movement (Allegro) presents without any introduction the melodic material on which the entire composition is based. The movement consists of three contrasting hymn-like tunes. The first is in chorale or psalm-tune style, with variations; next comes a flowing Andante melody, and last an energetic modal melody more strictly in the shaped-note hymn tradition than the first two. Each of these is repeated with extended melodic development.

"In accordance with symphonic convention, the next two (Andante and Vivace) are in song form and in dance form, based on secular American rhythmic and melodic elements. The second movement is built on a melody of the unaccompanied, narrative-ballad character, set in a tonal atmosphere suggestive of a backwoods landscape rather than a literal instrumental accompaniment. The dance movement, an elaborately developed jig melody, has a strong Irish flavor and a strong family resemblance to the tunes played for square dancing and for the solo jig competitions among loggers from Maine to Washington across the northern United States....

"The last movement (Moderato con moto) consists of an introduction, a fuguing tune, and coda; the fullest development of the thematic material has been reserved for this moment. The fuguing tune is a development from the shaped-note style, with the addition of occasional dissonant notes in passing, retaining, however, the plainness of form and the polyphonic vigor of the style."

Richard Burgin and the Boston Symphony Orchestra introduced the *Short Symphony* in Boston on October 24, 1947.

PAUL CRESTON   1906—

A richness of melodic writing, which some critics have described as "Tchaikovskian," and an ingenious use of rhythmic schemes are two outstanding qualities of Creston's music. Others, as noted by Henry Cowell, are "a certain simplicity and delicacy of effect," "sustained lines," and "warmth and geniality."

Creston was born in New York City on October 10, 1906. Much of his music study took place autodidactically. Later, however, he studied formally with Pietro Yon, Randegger, and Gaston Dethier.

In 1932, Creston wrote his first work, a set of five dances for piano.

Two years later, he became organist at St. Malachy's Church in New York. Playing the organ and teaching composition have been the sources of his income ever since.

His *Threnody,* which received its world première in Pittsburgh in 1938, was the first of his works to attract national attention. In 1938 and again in 1939, Creston received the Guggenheim Fellowship; during this period he wrote numerous works, including the orchestral *Two Choric Dances.* His First Symphony, written in 1940, was outstandingly successful, and at once placed him among the leading American composers of our time.

On two occasions, in 1941 and again in 1943, he received the Citation of Merit from the National Association for American Composers and Conductors, and in 1956 became its President. In 1943, he was awarded a grant from the American Academy of Arts and Letters.

The following works by Creston are discussed below: Concerto for Piano and Orchestra; Symphony No. 1; Symphony No. 2; Symphony No. 3 ("Three Mysteries"); Symphony No. 4; *Threnody; Two Choric Dances.*

THRENODY, for orchestra, op. 16 (1938).

Though the composer suggests that this work is autobiographical he gives no clue about the specific event in his life that inspired this emotional music. The first performance took place in Pittsburgh on December 2, 1938, Fritz Reiner conducting the Pittsburgh Symphony.

Muted strings introduce the first theme, which is in the style of a plain song. Following the statement of the second subject by the violas, the emotional intensity increases until a climax is reached. From this point on, the work repeats preceding material, but in reverse: the second theme (slightly varied) appears before the first. The work ends elegiacally with a flute solo sounding a tender strain against a background of muted strings.

TWO CHORIC DANCES, for orchestra, op. 17 (1938). I. Slow. II. Majestic. III. Fast.

Creston originally wrote this work for chamber orchestra, in which form it was introduced at the Yaddo Music Festival, at Saratoga Springs, New York, under the direction of Arthur Shepherd. Creston soon rescored the work for full orchestra, and Arthur Shepherd once again conducted the première performance, this time in Cleveland with the Cleveland Orchestra.

The intention of the composer was to suggest through music the movements of a group of dancers rather than tell any specific story. While the composer suggests that the music might be adaptable for choreographic treatment, he insists that it is to be heard as pure music.

The first movement consists of an introduction and dance. "The unifying element in the dance," the composer writes, "is the undulating figure in the strings forming the accompaniment to the melody in the woodwinds. This figure is later transferred to the piano and tom-tom and becomes the basis of the climax with the whole orchestra taking part in it."

The second movement also begins with a brief introduction before a pronounced rhythmic figure is presented by the piano to introduce the dance. The second dance moves at a whirlwind pace (in contrast to the slow dance of the first movement), marked by frequent changes of rhythm, color, and mood.

SYMPHONY NO. 1, op. 20 (1940). I. With Majesty. II. With Humor. III. With Serenity. IV. With Gaiety.

Creston's First Symphony received its first performance in Brooklyn, on February 22, 1941, with Fritz Mahler conducting the N.Y.A. Symphony Orchestra. Two years later, on March 23, 1943, Eugene Ormandy and the Philadelphia Orchestra performed it, at which time it aroused considerable enthusiasm. The New York Music Critics Circle selected it as the most important new symphonic work by an American heard that season.

Creston has provided the following analysis:

"The opening movement is in free sonata-allegro form, the thematic material of which is presented in two distinct sections. Within the first six measures are announced three separate motives, rhythmic and vigorous in character, comprising the first group of themes; at measure sixteen is presented the contrasting lyric theme. During the development of this material the themes are intertwined, combined, fugally treated, and varied in many ways, and at times change their initial aspect so that the rhythmic themes become lyric and the lyric become dramatic.

"The second movement is a scherzo. Rhythm is the reigning element, with overlapping and subdivisional patterns abounding throughout. The middle section is cast in a lyric vein, but the rhythmic aspect of the movement is maintained in the alternating figure played by the cellos and the basses.

"In the third movement, the cellos present in its complete form the main theme which was suggested in the introduction by muted strings. The oboe takes up this theme and develops it differently. This leads to the second theme, which is passed from flute to clarinet to oboe to bassoon to trumpet, each time varied. After the climax, the movement returns to its original serenity with muted strings.

"The final movement is based on two themes, the first being again subdivided into two sections: one presented at the opening by the oboe and the other by the clarinet in the ninth measure. The second theme is presented by the brass choir in chordal structure. No new material is introduced at any time during the movement. Each time the first theme appears it does so in a different texture, is varied, and is treated in a different style. The conclusion presents a fragment of the second theme in augmentation with a fragment of the first against it."

SYMPHONY NO. 2, op. 35 (1944). I. Introduction and Song. II. Interlude and Dance.

Creston's Second Symphony was conceived as an apotheosis of what the composer believes are the two fundamentals of all music: song and dance. The juxtaposition of song and dance, or prelude and dance, has long intrigued the composer as a musical form. It is found in such works as the *Prelude and Dance,* op. 25, the *Pastorale and Tarantella,* op. 28, and the *Preludes and Dances,* op. 29. In the Second Symphony, the song-and-dance form receives its most ambitious treatment and its fullest realization.

The symphony was introduced in New York on February 15, 1945. Artur Rodzinski conducted the New York Philharmonic-Symphony Orchestra.

The following analysis is by the composer:

"In the opening of the Introduction are presented four themes as a cumulative ground bass, i.e., successively superimposed. Theme one, played by the cellos, and theme two, played by violas, are the main bases of the entire symphony. Whatever new thematic material emerges is either a ramification or a development of these two themes.

"The Song is largely built on a variation of theme one, tender and simple in character, presented first by the flute and then by the horn....

"The Interlude opens with a completely transformed theme one, quite aggressive and defiant, leading to a rather quiet section, but soon returning to the aggressive character. This last merges into the Dance without pause, which after a rhythmic introduction begins with another variant of theme one (muted trumpet). Each appearance of this variation of theme one alters further the rhythm and contour of the melody. As the excitement mounts, theme two soars above the ever-recurrent rhythmic pulses, developing to a climax and into the next section of the Dance. In the second section, based on a variation of theme one inverted, the rhythmic pattern has changed and there is a greater sense of driving forward. This theme variant goes through several metamorphoses as the section builds into a major climax and then subsides to an altered version of the original cumulative ground bass. Above the three concurrent rhythms which were presented earlier in the Dance, the flute theme of the Song (now played by the violins), becoming more and more intense, brings the composition to a close."

CONCERTO FOR PIANO AND ORCHESTRA, op. 43 (1949). I. Allegro maestoso. II. Andante tranquillo. III. Presto.

Creston completed his piano concerto in July, 1949, and dedicated it to the memory of Joseph D. Malkin, a Philadelphia music lover. It was introduced in the same year in France by Earl Wild and the Radio-Diffusion Française de Lille, Chauncey Kelley conducting.

Creston has prepared the following analysis of his concerto:

"The first movement opens with a vigorous presentation of the main theme by the full orchestra, soon taken up by the piano in a rather rhapsodic style and leading to the second theme (cellos and basses) with arabesque figurations in the solo. This second theme in augmentation forms the basis of a quietly lyric section which ensues. After a short orchestral interlude, a fuller development of the two themes and moods is presented, closing in brilliant style.

"The second movement is pastoral in mood and is also based on two principal themes, the first tranquil and lyric, and the second slightly agitated. The development of these themes is entrusted largely to the solo instrument.

"The third movement is quite rhythmic in character and has much the feeling of a Tarantella, although several un-Italian rhythms make their appearance here and there. The rhythmic drive is maintained throughout, even in the less impetuous section."

SYMPHONY NO. 3 ("Three Mysteries"), op. 48 (1950). I. The Nativity. II. The Crucifixion. III. The Resurrection.

Creston was commissioned to write his Third Symphony by the Worcester Music Festival to honor the memory of Aldus C. Higgins. It was completed in July, 1950, and was introduced in Worcester, Massachusetts, by the Philadelphia Orchestra under Eugene Ormandy on October 27, 1950.

The symphony, inspired by the "three mysteries," draws generously from the melodic storehouse of the Gregorian chant. It is not, the composer insists, a narrative or a painting, but rather "a musical parallel of the inherent emotional reactions" aroused by these religious events.

The first movement (Lento; Allegro moderato) is based on two Gregorian themes: the first is heard in the horn in the middle of the slow introduction; the second appears in the flute in a subdued section which follows the main climax. The movement ends with a fugato on the first theme.

Another Gregorian melody, played on the solo cello against a brass accompaniment, opens the second movement (Adagio). This melody is transformed into a passacaglia-like theme for the cellos, and against it is set the fragments of a second Gregorian theme. The spiritual calm passes into a brief section of great agitation, but soon returns with a restatement of the two subjects.

In the third movement (Lento moderato; Allegro ma calmo) a Gregorian melody is present in its entirety (cellos and basses). This leads to the second theme, a Gregorian theme heard in the horns. The introduction ended, the Allegro section emerges with animation. This section, says the composer, is "based primarily on the sequence for Easter, *Victimae paschali laudes,* perhaps the best known of all the themes utilized in this work. The original rhythmic structure of the Gregorian melodies is more closely retained in the second and third movements than in the first, although the actual melodic contour is evident in all of them."

SYMPHONY NO. 4, op. 52 (1951). I. Maestoso. II. Andante pastorale. III. Allegretto giocoso. IV. Vivace saltellante.

This symphony was commissioned by Viola Malkin as a memorial to her husband, Joseph D. Malkin. It was introduced by the National Symphony Orchestra under Howard Mitchell on January 30, 1952 in Washington, D.C.

The first movement opens with an introduction which leads to the Allegro, in which the first principal theme is announced by the clarinet, and the second by the violins. Fragments of the thematic material are tossed from choir to choir, resolving into a full orchestral presentation of the first theme. The lyrical and gay elements are alternately presented in an increasing measure of excitement until the final triumphant outburst of the second principal theme in the brasses against the first principal theme in the rest of the orchestra.

The second movement is in three-part form, the first consisting of a pastoral melody, the second of a slightly restrained shepherd's dance, and the third a recapitulation of the pastoral song. The third movement is also in three sections, the outside parts featuring a jesting theme in various solo instruments and a muted pizzicato section for strings, with the middle portion devoted to a legato and lyric passage for strings. The fourth and concluding movement has the character of a tarantella. The pitch of excitement is almost constantly high, with intricate rhythms abounding throughout. The concluding section is a rapid resumé of all themes previously presented.

LUIGI DALLAPICCOLA   1904—

Dallapiccola is both the first and the most important of the Italian composers to write in the twelve-tone technique. He assimilated this style comparatively late in his career: in 1939, with *Night Flight* and *Greek Lyrics*. Before then he had produced numerous works of distinction—many of them introduced at the various festivals of the International Society for Contemporary Music—in which his writing passed from romanticism to impressionism to neo-classicism.

Even in his works after 1939, elements of the other styles are not absent. His significance rests in the success with which he has combined atonality with lyricism, astringency with genuine emotional feeling.

Dallapiccola was born in Pisino, Istria, on February 3, 1904. A protracted stay in Austria, where he became acquainted with the music of Mozart and Wagner, convinced him that he wanted to become a composer. His musical studies took place at the Cherubini Conservatory in Florence. In 1931, he became instructor of piano at the Conservatory, and after World War II, teacher of composition. In 1932, his *Three Studies for Soprano and Chamber Orchestra* was successfully introduced at the International Society for Contemporary Music Festival in Venice. After that, works of his were repeatedly performed at the festivals of the Society, performances which placed him in the very front rank of the younger Italian composers. In the summer of 1951, he visited the United States for the first time. Since 1956 he has been professor at Queens College, New York.

The following works by Dallapiccola are discussed below: *Marsia; Il Prigioniero.*

MARSIA, ballet (1943).

This ballet is one of Dallapiccola's most successful works in the twelve-tone technique. But like most of his major works in this style, it also contains, at times, impressionistic and neo-classical writing. The music, for the most part, is full of tension and power; but poetic moods provide welcome contrasts.

A symphonic suite from this score has been frequently performed. In 1950, it was heard in this country in performances by the NBC Symphony, under Guido Cantelli, and the New Orleans Symphony, under Massimo Freccia.

The story of the ballet is as follows:

Marsia discovers sound by blowing into a flute. Excited by the music he is making, he goes into a feverish dance, at the climax of which he comes upon Apollo. Challenged by Marsia to a contest in producing beauty of sound, Apollo calls on the Muses to act as judges. Marsia plays and dances, and with such fire that the forest nymphs come to join him in his dance. But when Apollo goes into his music and dance there can be no question that he is the superior. The Muses condemn Marsia to death by being skinned alive, and they raise Apollo high on their shoulders. Marsia dies in the arms of the forest nymphs, who grieve at his passing until their bodies become tears and mingle with Marsia's blood to form the Marsia River.

IL PRIGIONIERO, opera (1947).

Dallapiccola regards this one-act opera as his most important work up to the time it was composed. He derived his own libretto from a short story by Villiers de l'Isle Adam, *La Torture par l'Esperance,* and from a scene in Charles de Coster's *Ulenspiegel.* The theme concerns the incarceration and torture of a Flemish Protestant political prisoner during the reign of Philip II, his unsuccessful attempt to escape, and the loss of his mind as he is being led to the stake. This theme assumed particular significance to the composer, who had seen many political prisoners tortured during and before World War II. He developed it (much as Beethoven did in *Fidelio*) into a paean to freedom.

Il Prigioniero was heard for the first time over the Turin Radio in 1949. The first stage performance took place on May 20, 1950 at the Florentine May Music Festival. On March 15, 1951, it was introduced in this country by the Juilliard School of Music in New York. Describing the opera, in his review for the *New York Times,* Howard Taubman wrote: "It is a work that, in its music and its bare, symbolic action, projects the horror of a fear-ridden world.... His music... seems to be an amalgam of the newest and oldest trends in music.... Dallapiccola reserves his most eloquent writing for the orchestra. He is a master of vivid and moving tonal combinations. And when he combines his orchestra with chorus toward the end, he achieves a shattering effect.... In sum, this is a composer and a work of individuality." This opera is written in the twelve-tone technique.

CLAUDE DEBUSSY   1862—1918

When Debussy was a young man the artistic cults most frequently discussed in the cafés of Paris were those of the Impressionists in painting (Manet, Pissarro, Renoir) and the Symbolists in poetry (Verlaine, Mallarmé). Their artistic theories and ideas of technique struck a responsive chord with Debussy, who truth to tell, had also been drifting (somewhat instinctively) in their direction anyway.

The Impressionists, turning away from photographic realism, were more concerned with color and light than with form and substance. To them, the subject matter was of less importance than the *impression* the subject aroused—the impression as interpreted by the painter through unorthodox use of patterns and through exploitation of shadows and color patches. The symbolists in poetry were an analogous school. Not only the idea of the poem was important but also the sensuous sounds of the words.

The symbolists were interested in the music of versification; words were not only to be the carriers of ideas but were also to be used for evoking moods and sensations in much the same way that music does.

The seeds of these ideas fell on fertile soil as Debussy listened to them, absorbed them, and made them a part of his own *Weltanschauung*.

His own musical ideas had been undergoing several changes up to this time. After a visit to Bayreuth, he had become a passionate disciple of Wagner; a second visit to Bayreuth dissipated his enthusiasm and converted him into a skeptic. Painstakingly he now tried to free himself from the influence that the Wagnerian music-drama had been exerting on him. In Erik Satie he found a kindred spirit who was even more articulate in expressing resentment against Wagnerian principles. More than ever, the German romantic school repelled Debussy, with its indulgence in excessive sentiment, its love for expounding metaphysical ideas and Faustian struggles in music, its preferences for inflated structures.

Debussy sensed the need of reducing music to smaller proportions. He wanted to exchange exaggerated feeling for reason; he yearned for precision, economy, understatement. His goal was an essentially French art which would be a negation of Germanic ideals. And his conversations with Satie clarified his thinking.

From his contact with the Impressionists and Symbolists, Debussy arrived—at last—at those artistic principles which were to shape and form his composition. He, too, no longer concerned himself with the *thing* he was writing about, but rather the impressions and sensations the *thing* aroused in him. He, too, became concerned with color, atmosphere, mood, and not with form and the traditional development of thematic material. In his search for new effects of the most subtle kind, he evolved an harmonic language of his own which exploited unresolved discords and permitted chords to move with independence from a tonal center. He arrived at new exotic melodies through the use of unorthodox scales: the Oriental pentatonic scale; the whole-tone scale; the seven-note scale of the Church modes. He achieved vagueness and mystery through avoidance of cadences and through deft alternations of rhythmic patterns. Such technical elements were absorbed into his art, opening up vistas of sensitive, delicate, exquisite, dreamlike impressions that music had rarely known up to his time.

The father of musical impressionism was born on the outskirts of Paris, in Saint-Germain-en-Laye, on August 22, 1862. He passed the entrance examinations for the Paris Conservatory in his eleventh year. For another eleven years he studied at the Conservatory with Durand and Lavignac (harmony), Marmontel (piano), and Guiraud (composition). Despite occasional excursions from the tenets of the harmony textbook in search of new chord combinations, Debussy was an excellent student, winning prizes in solfège and sight-reading. When the wealthy Russian lady, Mme. Nadejda von Meck—the same who was Tchaikovsky's patroness and "beloved friend"—applied to the Conservatory for a talented young student to serve as pianist, Debussy was recommended. For a few months, Debussy traveled with the von Mecks in Italy, Austria, Russia—the young musician's first glimpse of the world outside Paris—officiating as a pianist and, incidentally, making love to one of the daughters. Mme. von Meck thought highly of him as a composer, as a pianist, and as a typical son of the Paris boulevards. For two succeeding summers (1881 and 1882), she invited him to her Russian home as a household pianist.

As a Conservatory student, Debussy became increasingly restive with the accepted laws of harmony. He experimented with unrelated chords and with discords, to the horror of his masters. But he could play the game by their own rules, too. In 1884, he won the much-coveted Prix de Rome—the highest stamp of approval which the academic masters could place on him—with a cantata, *L'Enfant Prodigue.*

Settled in Rome, Debussy chafed under the restrictions imposed upon all winners of the Prix de Rome. He hated the city, its weather, its food. His fellow pupils bored him. He yearned to return to Paris (indeed, for a brief period in 1886, he did escape to his beloved city). As a respite from his unhappiness he plunged into the study of Wagnerian scores (*Tristan and Isolde* particularly). He also devoted himself to composition, fulfilling the official requirements of the Prix de Rome by writing "envois" at periodic intervals.

He had been composing since he was fourteen years old, mostly songs. Some of them have considerable originality and charm, and are still heard: the delightful serenade, *Mandoline* (Paul Verlaine), and *Paysage Sentimental* (Paul Bourget), written between 1880 and 1883. His sensitivity in translating the mood and the sentiment of French poetry into the appropriate musical equivalent is already evident. As Oscar Thompson remarked, Debussy, in these songs, is already a "landscape artist," but an artist who is more concerned with the "sentimental or emotional promptings of the scene" than with the scene itself. There is also a tendency in these songs to strive for greater harmonic freedom. "As there are no precedents," Debussy wrote self-confidently at this time, "I must create anew."

For his first envoi he composed an orchestral suite entitled *Printemps.* Here innovations are hinted at rather than realized. Yet so revolutionary did this music appear to the Conservatory officials that they denounced it firmly and refused to permit its performance. Debussy's second envoi was *La Demoiselle Élue* (*The Blessed Damozel*) a setting of parts of Dante Gabriel Rossetti's lyric poem, as translated into French by Gabriel Sarrazin, for women's voices and orchestra. Here color effects are given precedence to structural requirements; clarity makes way for vagueness and mystery; unusual modulations and unrelated chords replace the textbook formulas. Once again the officials were horrified, flinging at him for the first time the condemning designation of "impressionist." The first performance took place without their blessing, on April 8, 1893, five years after its completion. The orchestra of the Société Nationale was conducted by Gabriel Marie, and Julia Robert was the soloist. At this time several prominent musicians acclaimed the work, notably Vincent d'Indy and Julien Tiersot; and since that time it has been accepted as one of Debussy's early masterpieces.

The rejection of *La Demoiselle Élue* by the Conservatory officials convinced Debussy that he had had enough of the Prix de Rome. Henceforth he would have to go his own way without restriction. Without completing the prescribed three years, he abandoned Rome and settled in Paris. Now a habitué of the Montmartre cafés, he assimilated the new cultural ideas which were arising around him.

By 1893, Debussy had crystallized his thinking and arrived at his own manner of writing music. He now produced a series of masterpieces which forthwith placed him with the great creative men of his time and established him as one of the most provocative.

First came the Quartet in G Minor for Strings, op. 10, written in 1893 and introduced at a concert of the Société Nationale on December 29 of the same year. The audience was at turns puzzled and irritated by its daring style. The critics were outright denunciatory, one of them speaking derisively of its "orgy of modulations." Recognition was not to come for another decade; but in the early twentieth century it was recognized as one of the most important and original string quartets since Brahms. It set into motion musical impressionism as a compositional style; its influence on younger composers everywhere was incalculable.

Then came one of Debussy's most exquisite works, the orchestral prelude, *L'Après-Midi d'un Faune* (*The Afternoon of a Faun*), written between 1892 and 1894, and introduced on December 23, 1894, by the Société Nationale, Gustave Doret conducting. Inspired by the delicate poem of Stéphane Mallarmé (dean of the symbolists), it is a complete realization in music of the artistic concepts of both the symbolists and the impressionists.

With the three orchestral Nocturnes, written between 1897 and 1899, Debussy's tone-painting achieves the very quintessence of perfection. Debussy himself explained that this title of "Nocturne" was intended "to have a more general and, above all, a more decorative meaning," and that he was not concerned with the form of the nocturne, but with "everything that this word includes in the way of diversified impression and special lights." The first two Nocturnes, *"Nuages"* ("Clouds") and *"Fêtes"* ("Festivals"), were introduced by the Lamoureux Orchestra, Chevillard conducting, on December 8, 1900. The following year, on October 27, 1901, all three *Nocturnes*—the third of which was *"Sirènes"* ("Sirens"), scored for women's voices as well as orchestra—were performed at a Lamoureux concert.

The above-mentioned Debussy masterpieces were all written before 1900 and, consequently, are not discussed in detail in the pages that follow.

There was, however, no diminution of creative power in the music Debussy wrote after 1900. One after another the masterpieces left his pen as Debussy became the dominating figure in French music, one of the most inventive contributors of new techniques and methods that the music of his day produced.

With the outbreak of World War I, ill-health began to sap Debussy's energy to a point where composition required Herculean will power. Nevertheless, he kept on writing. His music was now uneven in quality, occasionally suggesting his one-time originality and inventiveness but occasionally relying for its effect on technique and the repetition of tried and true mannerisms.

The growth of a cancer (for this was Debussy's ailment) necessitated an operation in 1915. Thereafter he was only a shadow of himself, usually in terrible pain. After 1917 he never left his apartment. He died there on March 25, 1918, only eight days after he had applied for a recently vacated chair at the Académie des Beaux-Arts. The war had so completely absorbed the attention of France that few at the time noticed that her greatest musician had passed away.

The following works by Debussy are discussed below: *Children's Corner; En Blanc et Noir; Estampes;* Etudes; *Fêtes Galantes* (II); *L'Île Joyeuse; Images* (for orchestra); *Images* (for piano); *La Mer; Pelléas et Mélisande;* Preludes; Sonata No. 3, for Violin and Piano; *Suite Bergamasque; Trois Ballades de Villon.*

For *L'Après-Midi d'un Faune (The Afternoon of a Faun)*, see the biographical sketch above; for *"La Cathédrale Engloutie"* (The Engulfed Cathedral"), see Preludes; for *"Clair de Lune,"* see *Suite Bergamasque;* for *La Demoiselle Élue (The Blessed Damozel)*, see the biographical sketch; for *"Fêtes,"* nocturne for orchestra, see the biographical sketch; for *"La Fille aux Cheveux de Lin"* ("The Girl with the Flaxen Hair"), see Preludes; for "Golliwogg's Cakewalk," see *Children's Corner;* for *"Ibéria,"* see *Images* (for orchestra); for *"Jardins sous la Pluie,"* see *Estampes;* for *Mandoline,* see the biographical sketch; for Nocturnes, see the biographical sketch; for *"Nuages,"* nocturne for orchestra, see the biographical sketch; for *"Pagodes,"* see *Estampes;* for *Paysage Sentimental,* see the biographical sketch; for *"Poissons d'Or,"* see *Images* (for piano); for Quartet in G Minor, op. 10, see the biographical sketch; for *"Reflets dans l'Eau,"* see *Images* (for piano); for *"Soirée dans Grenade,"* see *Estampes.*

PELLÉAS ET MÉLISANDE, opera (1902).

With *Pelléas,* Debussy's career as a composer of opera both began and ended. It may be that *Pelléas* was so complete and perfect a realization of his art within the form of opera that Debussy may have felt that any other work in a similar vein could be only duplication. It may be, too, that Debussy had found in *Pelléas* a libretto so perfectly suited to his sensitive art that all other librettos approached thereafter appeared unsympathetic by comparison.

Debussy had specific ideas on the role of the librettist: He must be "one who only hints at things and will thus enable me to graft my thought on his; one who will create characters whose history and abode belong to no particular time or place; one who will not despotically impose set scenes on me, but will allow me now and then to outdo him in artistry and perfect his work."

He also had definite ideas on the part music should play within the operatic framework: "I shall not follow the usual plan of the lyric drama in which the music insolently predominates, whilst the poetry is relegated to the background and smothered by elaborate musical trappings. There is too much singing in musical dramas. The characters should sing only when it is worth while, and the pathetic note should be held in reserve. The intensity of the expression should vary in degree. At times it is necessary to paint in monochrome and limit oneself to gray tones. . . . Nothing should retard the progress of the dramatic action: all musical development that is not essential to the text is incorrect. Apart from the fact that any musical development which is at all protracted cannot possibly correspond to the mobile words . . . my dream is to find poems that will not condemn me to perpetrate long, ponderous acts; poems that will provide me with ever-changing scenes, varied as regards place and atmosphere, in which the characters will not argue, but live their lives and work out their destinies."

Debussy acquired a copy of Maurice Maeterlinck's play in 1892. It enchanted him from the very first. The theme was as old as literature itself. Golaud, King Arkel's son, discovers Mélisande at a fountain. Falling in love with her, he brings her back to his castle to become his wife. In the castle, however, Golaud's brother, Pelléas, meets Mélisande; almost at once they both fall deeply in love with each other. When Golaud discovers that he has been betrayed, he kills the lovers.

It was the simplicity with which the poet developed this age-old triangle, and enchantment which the story evoked, that delighted Debussy. He knew at once that this was the text for his opera, and forthwith he began to sketch out some ideas (one of which was ultimately utilized in the fourth act, fourth scene, and became one of the melodic embryos of the entire work).

But the opera did not come easily. He wrote and destroyed; wrote and revised. Again and again, he felt that he was succumbing to the pernicious influence of "the phantom of old Klingsor, alias R. Wagner," from which he had to free himself completely before he could arrive at his own personal idiom.

Finally, on April 30, 1902, *Pelléas* was introduced at the Opéra Comique. The première was preceded by a scandal that rocked artistic Paris. Maeterlinck had intended his mistress, Georgette Leblanc, as Mélisande. But Albert Carré, manager of the Opéra Comique, had other ideas: he wanted

Mary Garden for the role. Maeterlinck was furious. He threatened to cane Debussy, whom he suspected of having influenced Carré. He wrote a heated letter to *Le Figaro,* sixteen days before the première, denouncing the Opéra Comique management and maintaining that the work "is now strange and hostile to me. I can only wish its immediate and emphatic failure." There was even talk of a duel between Maeterlinck and Carré, though nothing came of that.

At the dress rehearsal a witty parody on the play was published and distributed at the entrance of the theater—said to be the work of Maeterlinck himself, though this has never been proved. Thus hilarity was injected into the already confused situation. The rehearsal went badly. Disturbances (possibly inspired by the poet) were introduced by members of the audience, with Mary Garden as their particular victim.

In any event, the première proceeded on schedule, and was awaited in Paris with no little electrified anticipation. As the unorthodox music progressed—rarefied, disembodied, seemingly amorphous—hisses and loud-voiced denunciations rose audibly in the theater. On the other hand, in the stalls and gallery pronounced enthusiasm gave answer to the skeptics. The critics, too, were divided in their opinion. "His music is vague, without color or nuance, without motion, without life. It is not even declamation, but a continual dolorous melopoeia without vitality or vigor, deliberately shunning all semblance of precision." Thus wrote Arthur Pougin in *Le Menéstrel.* The Paris correspondent of a London paper reported: "The composer's system is to ignore melody altogether, and his personages do not sing, but talk in a sort of lilting voice to a vague musical accompaniment of the text. The effect is quite bewildering, almost amusing in its absurdity." But other critics sensed that a new world had been opened for opera with this masterpiece; Gustave Bret, André Corneau, Henry Bauer spoke highly of Debussy's achievement.

Possibly because it was a *cause célèbre,* and possibly because its beauty began to cast a spell, *Pelléas* soon began to interest the Parisian public. By the seventh performance the house could not accommodate all those ready to buy a ticket. It was performed fourteen times in May and June of that year, and ten times the following season—surely a formidable achievement for a new, revolutionary opera.

Since its première, *Pelléas* has acquired a permanent place in the operatic repertory. Historically its influence has been decisive: modern opera has its roots in the innovations set forth in *Pelléas.* In the entire evolution of the operatic form, *Pelléas* remains one of the recognizable milestones. In its magic fusion of word and sound, it has evoked a world of enchantment whose spell is irresistible, unbroken from the first bar to the last.

ESTAMPES, for piano (1903). I. Pagodes. II. Soirée dans Grenade. III. Jardins sous la Pluie.

This set of three portraits for piano was introduced by Ricardo Viñes at a concert of the Société Nationale, on January 9, 1904, and was well received: so great was the enthusiasm at the end of the work that the third piece had to be repeated. Since then it has become one of Debussy's best known works for the piano, one of his most successful efforts in projecting impressionistic effects through descriptive music.

In *"Pagodes"* Debussy employs the Oriental pentatonic scale (which he heard at the Paris Exposition in 1889, performed by Javanese and other Far Eastern musicians) with considerable skill; an exotic picture emerges. Bell-like effects are sounded throughout the piece.

The "Evening in Granada" (the most famous of this trio of pieces) describes the Spanish city with its Moorish backgrounds as dusk descends. In the distance is heard the strum of a mandolin as a Spaniard raises his voice in a serenade. The rhythm of a habanera is here employed so felicitously that Manuel de Falla has called this piece "characteristically Spanish in every detail." It conjures, wrote Falla, "the effect of images mirrored by the moonlight upon the limpid waters of the large cisterns adjoining the Alhambra."

Two French folk songs appear in the "Gardens In the Rain" (*Nous n'irons plus au Bois,* and *Do, Do, l'Enfant, Do*), which describes a garden drenched by the rain and combed by the fingers of the wind.

FÊTES GALANTES, second series, for voice and piano (1904). I. Les Ingénus. II. Le Faune. III. Colloque Sentimental.

In 1892, Debussy had composed the first series of *Fêtes Galantes* to poems by Paul Verlaine. This series included *"En Sourdine," "Clair de Lune"* (not to be confused with the more celebrated piece for the piano), and *"Fantoches."* The second set came twelve years later.

In the first of the three songs, Debussy's good humor is evident as he carries over in his music Verlaine's delightful description of the mischievous play of youthful lovers. The second song imitates the timbre of the flute (voice) and the tambourine (piano) in this description of the faun who guards the enchanted woods where lovers meet. In the final number, the feeling of disillusionment is beautifully caught as two former lovers meet again in a lonely park and recall their now-dead rapture.

L'ÎLE JOYEUSE, for piano (1904).

Though originally planned for the *Suite Bergamasque,* this celebrated piece was published independently. It interprets Watteau's *Embarquement pour Cythère* in as sensual a piece of music as Debussy has written. Its ingenious deployment of rhythm and its use of orchestral timbres are particularly interesting. It was introduced by Ricardo Viñes on February 18, 1905.

SUITE BERGAMASQUE, for piano (1905). I. Prelude. II. Minuet. III. Clair de Lune. IV. Passepied.

Though begun as far back as 1889, the *Suite Bergamasque* was not completed until 1905. In it Debussy attempted, for the first time, to create music with the grace and charm of the seventeenth-century French clavecinists, without sacrificing his own harmonic experiments. This combination of the old and the new gives the music its greatest fascination.

The most famous movement of the four is the *Clair de Lune,* a sensuous picture of a moonlit night. Guido Gatti said about this exquisite piece of music: "What an airy flowering of arpeggios ascends the keyboard, to leap up again like a fountain jet which scatters its water on the air, then relapses into calm again in solid tonic and dominant undulations, on which the theme spreads out, ample, sonorous, expressive."

LA MER, three symphonic sketches for orchestra (1905). I. De l'aube à Midi sur la Mer. II. Jeux de Vagues. III. Dialogue du Vent et de la Mer.

Debussy's love of the sea is revealed in these effective tone pictures which present three facets of its personality. "I was intended for the fine career of a sailor," he wrote to a friend in 1903. And in 1905, following the crossing of the Channel, he wrote to his publisher: "The sea has been very good to me. She has shown me all her moods."

Debussy worked on *La Mer* from 1903 to 1905. On October 15, 1905, its first performance took place in Paris, with Camille Chevillard conducting the Concerts Lamoureux. M. D. Calvocressi, writing in the *Guide Musicale,* felt that the work marked a new phase in Debussy's development, with a "more robust inspiration, stronger colors, and more definite lines than his preceding works." But there were antagonistic reviews as well. "I neither hear, nor see, nor feel the sea," wrote Pierre Lalo with finality in *Le Temps*.

It is not easy to append a definite program to this nebulous music. And while it is possible to say with Lalo that one cannot specifically hear, see, or feel the sea in the music, it is impossible to deny that the personality of the sea is magically suggested. It is the poet's conception of the sea that is invoked in this music—the reveries, moods, and nostalgic longings which it inspires in a sensitive lover of Nature.

The mystery of the sea is suggested in the first sketch as a muted trumpet and English horn present the principal subject. In the second part we have a description of the play of the waves, caressed by the gentle winds. The music becomes more dramatic in the closing section as the sea grows more restive, participating in a dialogue—"of cosmic things," Oscar Thompson believes—with the wind.

IMAGES, for piano (1905; 1907).

Debussy wrote two sets of *Images* for the piano. He regarded these pieces highly. In dispatching the first set to his publisher he wrote: "I think

I may say without undue pride that I believe these three pieces will live and will take their places in piano literature...either to the left of Schumann... or to the right of Chopin."

FIRST SERIES: *"Reflets dans l'Eau"* etches the shimmering reflections of figures and outlines in water with floating chords. Debussy has said that this, one of his most famous pieces for the piano, incorporates "the newest discoveries in harmonic chemistry." *"Hommage à Rameau"* pays tonal tribute not only to Rameau (whom Debussy admired greatly) but also to the music of Rameau's period. *"Mouvement"* creates a "perpetual motion" in a succession of gay triplets, relieved midway by a slow subject.

SECOND SERIES: *"Cloches à travers les Feuilles"* delicately echoes the murmur of forest leaves as they vibrate to the sounds of ringing bells. *"Et la Lune Descend sur le Temple qui fut"* received its title from Louis Laloy after the music was written. An exotic atmosphere is created, somewhat archaic and remote. *"Poissons d'Or"* was inspired by a piece of oriental lacquer on which was painted goldfish swimming in a stream.

CHILDREN'S CORNER, suite for piano (1908). I. Doctor Gradus ad Parnassum. II. Jimbo's Lullaby. III. Serenade for the Doll. IV. Snow Is Dancing. V. The Little Shepherd. VI. Golliwogg's Cakewalk.

Debussy wrote this suite for his little daughter Chouchou (then only four years old). In the entire literature of music for children there are few works which re-create a child's world so simply and charmingly.

The composer himself provided the work with English titles, thereby suggesting that each section was a game played by a little French girl and her English governess.

In the first movement the struggles of a child with the Clementi piano exercises are amusingly reproduced. There follows a lullaby to a stuffed elephant named Jimbo, one of the most cherished possessions of Chou-Chou, with whom she shared her bed. Chou-Chou tells bedtime stories to Jimbo and sings her elephant to sleep. After the lullaby comes a child's piquant serenade to her doll. In the fourth movement, the child watches the falling snow from her window and waits for the return of the sun. A pastoral piece in Debussy's most refined manner is the fifth number, and the sixth is an American cakewalk, revealing Debussy's interest in American popular music; the interpolation of a phrase from Wagner's prelude to *Tristan* injects a satiric note.

TROIS BALLADES DE VILLON, for voice and orchestra (1910). I. Ballade de Villon à s'Amye. II. Ballade que Feit Villon à la Requeste de Sa Mère pour Prier Nostre-Dame. III. Ballade des Femmes de Paris.

Debussy's fascination for musical medievalism—expressed in his use of Gregorian modes and in his love of old liturgical music—found satisfaction in his setting of three Villon poems. Modal writing is here utilized extensively; and to Léon Vallas the "restrained art attains its highest perfection" in this music.

On February 5, 1911, the three *Ballades* were introduced (with piano accompaniment) by Poule de Lestang. The orchestral version was heard for the first time on March 5 of the same year, with Charles W. Clark as soloist and the composer conducting.

The first song is declamatory, conveying the bitterness of the poet in discovering that his loved one is a hypocrite. The second creates a medieval atmosphere through modal writing, and is contrapuntal. The third (one of Debussy's most spirited songs) describes the chattering of Parisian women in gay and infectious music.

PRÉLUDES, for piano (1910; 1913).

There are many authorities—Ernest Newman is among them—who consider Debussy's twenty-four Preludes as the quintessence of his art. All the technical and artistic devices with which he had been experimenting up to this time are completely realized, as new resources of color and resonance are explored for the piano.

Each of these pieces is a miniature—a brief improvisatory sketch—in which, to paraphrase Newman, infinitely delicate auditory and visual sensations are suggested in music. The form is free. Inspired by the fragment of a theme, or a rhythmic device, or an original chord combination, the composer develops the most refined mood portraits.

The Preludes are in two volumes, the first of which was completed in 1910, and the second three years later. It is interesting to note that the title of each piece was placed by the composer not at the head of each, but at the end—possibly because the titles did not occur to him until after he had completed the music.

BOOK I: I. *"Danseuses de Delphes."* A Greek sculpture, representing three women in a slow dance, was the composer's inspiration for this tranquil, mysterious music.

II. *"Voiles."* Sailboats are anchored in port as the wind gently flutters the sails. This piece is one of the most successful in utilizing the whole-tone scale.

III. *"Le Vent dans la Plaine."* A picture is here evoked, as Alfred Cortot has described it, of wind "gliding over the grass, fastening on the bushes, tumbling the hedges and sometimes in the young ardor of the morning, with a more brusque breath, bowing the springing corn with a long trembling wave."

IV. *"Les Sons et les Parfums Tournent dans l'Air du Soir."* (The title is drawn from a poem by Baudelaire.) This is one of the most voluptuous pieces of music that Debussy wrote. Sound and fragrance draw intoxication from the evening air.

V. *"Les Collines d'Anacapri."* The piece has a folklore character, with a tarantella-like rhythm and a Neapolitan-style melody.

VI. *"Des Pas sur la Neige."* Debussy himself indicated that the rhythm should "have the sonorous value of a melancholy snow-bound landscape." The entire piece has a subtle melancholy character.

VII. *"Ce qu'a vu le Vent d' Ouest."* A vivid description of a hurricane suggested in whirling arpeggios and in discords.

VIII. *"La Fille aux Cheveux de Lin."* This exquisite melody is deservedly one of the most famous written by Debussy, a portrait of a maiden in diaphanous lines. The inspiration for this piece came from Leconte de Lisle's *Chanson Ecossaise.*

IX. *"La Sérénade Interrompue."* A Spanish atmosphere is evoked through suggestion of strumming guitar and Andalusian rhythms.

X. *"La Cathédrale Engloutie."* A mystic representation of an old Breton legend which told that on clear mornings, when the sea is transparent, the Cathedral of Ys rises to view; clearly audible are its tolling bells and chanting priests. Slowly the vision is dissipated. The cathedral returns to its sleep in the depths of the sea.

XI. *"La Danse de Puck."* A roguish sketch, with ironic shadows, of the Shakespearean character in *A Midsummer Night's Dream.*

XII. *"Minstrels."* A music hall is depicted, in which suggestions of an old-time shuffling roadway song gives basis to the belief that Debussy had black-faced minstrels in mind.

BOOK II: I. *"Brouillards."* Vague tonalities—said to be the precursor of polytonality—create an amorphous picture.

II. *"Feuilles Mortes."* A series of melancholy ninth chords describe the descent of dead leaves to the ground.

III. *"La Puerta del Vino."* The famous gate of the Alhambra in Granada—which Debussy saw on a picture post card—is described in dance rhythms and Andalusian ornamented melodies.

IV. *"Les Fées sont d'Exquises Danseuses."* With quicksilver movement, the grace of fairy dancing is re-created.

V. *"Bruyères."* An unforgettable picture of natural beauty, of sunlight streaking through leaves in a woodland.

VI. "General Lavine—Eccentric." A wooden puppet, famous at the Folies Bergère for his ungainly steps, is immortalized in this ironic piece, which has the character of an American cakewalk.

VII. *"La Terrasse des Audiences du Clair de Lune."* A phrase from a letter by René Puaux, published in *Le Temps,* provided Debussy with this title. Echoes of the famous French song *Au clair de la lune* are heard in sevenths in this tonal picture of a "moon-drenched scene."

VIII. *"Ondine."* A water nymph is the heroine of this vaporous piece of music.

IX. *"Hommage à S. Pickwick, Esq., P.P.M.P.C."* The celebrated Dickens character is here caricatured as amusing quotations are made from *God Save the King*.

X. *"Canope."* A brief, melancholy threnody which, as Oscar Thompson put it, "is that of an impersonal sort of reverie."

XI. *"Les Tierces Alternées."* Debussy's predilection for the music of the old clavecin composers is here reflected.

XII. *"Feux d'Artifice."* This is a musical picture of a display of pyrotechnics, possibly one for Bastille Day, since strains of the *Marseillaise* are heard.

IMAGES, for orchestra (1912). I. Gigues. II. Ibéria. III. Rondes de Printemps.

It is the contention of Léon Vallas that the three Images which Debussy created for orchestra were each based on the folksongs of different countries. He finds that *"Gigues"* was derived from the English, with emphasis on the English jig; *"Ibéria,"* from the Spanish; and *"Rondes des Printemps,"* from the French.

"Gigues" (originally called *"Gigues Tristes"*—"Sad Gigues") was completed on January 4, 1909 in a piano version. André Caplet completed the orchestration in 1912, and on January 26, 1913, introduced it at a Colonne concert. Caplet saw in this music "the portrait of a soul in pain, uttering its slow lingering lamentation on the reed of an oboe d'amore." The gigue—the theme of which is believed to have been borrowed from a song by Charles Bordes—is heard in an unaccompanied solo by the oboe d'amore after twenty measures of introduction. A second principal theme is Scottish in character, and is heard in the bassoons.

"Ibéria" is the most famous section of this suite, and the one most frequently performed separately. Few portraits in music have caught so authentically the color and exotic charm of Spain. It is quite true that Debussy (as he himself insisted) did not try to write Spanish music, though suggestions of the Spanish idiom are recognizable. What he wanted to do, what he accomplished with telling effect, was to express in music the impressions that Spain made on him. It might be added, for further clarification, that the sum total of Debussy's experiences in Spain was a one-hour excursion to Saint-Sebastian. But, as Manuel de Falla remarked, "he preserved a lasting remembrance of the impression made on him by that peculiar light of a Plaza de Toros: the striking contrast between the part flooded by sunlight and that covered by shadow. 'The Morning of a Fête-Day' in *'Ibéria'* might perhaps be accepted as an evocation of that afternoon spent on the threshold of Spain."

"Ibéria" has three sections:

I. "In the Streets and Byways" (Assez animé). The garish sunlight that floods the streets of Spain is suggested in the luminous orchestral colors that open this section. In the background is heard the persistent throb of castanet rhythm. The music grows in intensity, ebbs, develops into powerful climaxes and subsides as numerous thematic ideas are skillfully intertwined. The principal subjects are a jaunty theme for two clarinets, accompanied by oboes and bassoons and a pulsing tambourine, and a beautiful melody for viola and oboe.

II. "The Odors of the Night" (Lent et rêveur). An evocative picture, dreamlike and diaphanous, emerges in the glissandi of violins and chromatic runs of the woodwinds; it is nighttime in Spain. A note of melancholy is interpolated by the oboe. After the music becomes agitated, a solo horn restores an atmosphere of mystery and enchantment. Bells peal in the distance.

III. "The Morning of the Festival Day" (Dans un rhythme de marche lointaine, alerte et joyeuse) proceeds from the second movement without interruption. Thematic material from the preceding movement is recalled as the orchestra collects its strength and joyously injects power and brilliance to describe a characteristic festival day; people dance in the streets.

Though begun in 1906 (as a piece for two pianos), "Ibéria" was not completed until two years later as a work for orchestra. On February 20, 1910, Gabriel Pierné conducted the première at a concert by the Colonne Orchestra.

The French folk tune Nous n'irons plus au bois is the basic subject of the third of the Images—"Rondes de Printemps." This single idea, Laloy tells us, "now glides, now runs through light fronds of melody, till it joins in a breathless dance, whirls wildly for a moment, then grows calm and vanishes in clear air."

Debussy began the "Rondes de Printemps" in 1909. The première performance took place on March 2, 1910, with the composer conducting one of the Concerts Durand. The published score quotes the following line from the Maggiolata: "Vive le mai! Bienvenu soit le mai avec son gonfalon sauvage!" ("Long live the month of May! Welcome to May with its savage banner!")

EN BLANC ET NOIR, for two pianos (1915). I. Avec emportement. II. Lent, sombre: sourdement tumultueux. III. Scherzando.

Each of these three pieces (intended to suggest a picture in black-and-white) carries a motto which provides a clue to its meaning. The first piece, dedicated to Serge Koussevitzky, quotes a line from the Gounod opera, Roméo et Juliette: "He who keeps his place and does not join in the ring silently confesses to some disgrace." A waltz melody is here developed with fervor.

The second number carries a motto from a Francois Villon ballad, and is dedicated to a French lieutenant killed in World War I. It begins solemnly, then develops into an agitated mood when, suddenly the strains of Luther's hymn, *Ein feste Burg* are injected. The music finally, as Debussy put it, "cleanses the atmosphere of the poisonous fumes of the chorale, or rather of what it represents."

The third piece (dedicated to Stravinsky) quotes Charles, the Duke of Orleans: "Winter, you are nothing but a villian!" This is a fanciful Scherzo written in rather slow tempo. It is believed to describe an old chateau standing bleakly in solitary splendor as a storm rages; this is the scene for a legend recounted by an old castellan. The storm subsides, and the setting becomes peaceful.

ÉTUDES, for piano (1915).

More than any composer since Chopin, Debussy opened up new resources for the piano. In these Études (dedicated, appropriately enough, to Chopin), Debussy explored, as he has written, "a thousand ways of treating pianists according to their deserts."

Each Étude faces a technical problem and attempts its solution. The first book opens with a five-finger exercise (a somewhat satiric commentary on Czerny) and continues with exercises in thirds, fourths, sixths, and octaves, ending with an eight-finger exercise. The second book treats problems of chromatic intervals, grace notes, reiterated notes, contrasted sonorities, arpeggios, and chords.

But these two books are more than a *Gradus ad Parnassum* for pianists. They actually embody all of Debussy's experiments in harmony, counterpoint, tonality, and rhythm, and highlight his melodic idiosyncrasies.

SONATA NO. 3, FOR VIOLIN AND PIANO (1917). I. Allegro vivo. II. Intermède. III. Finale.

In 1915, Debussy planned the writing of a series of six sonatas for various instruments, in which a conscious effort would be made to return to the traditional classical forms of the seventeenth- and eighteenth-century French instrumental masters. Only three of these six sonatas were completed. The first, for cello and piano, was written in 1915. The second sonata, for flute, viola, and piano, followed several months later. The third, though begun in 1915, was not completed until two years later. This last work was written under great duress. The composer was seriously ill, and had to undergo a serious operation for cancer which sapped his energy and strength. Besides his illness, there was the harrowing fear that at any day the advancing German armies might enter Paris. Only by dint of Herculean effort was he able to complete his violin sonata. On May 5, 1917, it was introduced in Paris by Gaston Poulet; the now-emaciated composer was at the piano.

Though some of the material sounds labored, the entire work is exemplary for mastery of workmanship. The first movement has particular rhythmic interest. It is followed by a scherzo-like movement of faun-like grace. The finale is the most effective of the three movements, binding the whole work into an integrated unity by quoting at the very opening the main theme of the first movement.

FREDERICK DELIUS   1862—1934

Refinement of speech, delicacy of touch, restrained emotions, tranquillity, and repose are some of the qualities of Delius's music. It is impressionistic tone-painting of the most subtle kind. An unnamed critic of the *London Times* described it further as follows: "It is the richly decadent beauty of autumn colors; its feeling is not so much sad as pensive; there is an absence of rhythmic vitality which marks it off sharply from the new music of his younger contemporaries.... His is music of sensibility."

Delius was born on January 29, 1862, in Bradford, England. Though he showed marked musical talent, his father intended him for the wool business, in which he worked for two years. In 1884, Delius escaped from the drudgery of the business world by emigrating to Solano, Florida, to take care of an orange plantation his father had bought for him. In Florida, he studied the violin by himself and began composing. At last, he received the belated permission of his father to study music seriously. He now went to Europe and studied under Sitt, Jadassohn, and Reinecke at the Leipzig Conservatory. After Leipzig, Delius went to Paris to assimilate its cultural life and to devote himself there more actively to creative work. In 1892, his first published work appeared, a *Légende* for violin and orchestra. This was followed by *Over the Hills and Far Away* and a Concerto for Piano and Orchestra.

After marrying Jelka Rosen, Delius settled in Grez-sur-Loing, which was to remain his home for the remainder of his life. For the next decade and a half following 1899 he produced a series of masterpieces which placed him with the foremost composers of his time, the most important of which were a series of sensitively beautiful tone-poems for orchestra.

Success and recognition came slowly. The elusive beauty of his music required intimacy before it could be appreciated, and performances of Delius's works were sporadic. It was in Germany that Delius's music first found a receptive public, following several important performances there of major works. However, there were a few disciples in England who fought Delius's battle patiently, the most notable of whom was Sir Thomas Beecham. It was through their indefatigable efforts that Delius ultimately achieved acceptance. When, in 1929, a festival of six concerts devoted entirely to Delius was launched in London, there were few to deny that he was one of England's great creative figures.

Meanwhile, soon after World War I, Delius began to disclose alarming symptoms of physical disintegration. At first, he suffered only from intense fatigue and attacks of inertia; but by 1922, he was a hopeless paralytic. Paralysis was followed, in 1925, by total blindness. Delius accepted his crushing fate with a calm and serenity that amazed those near him. Nor did he abandon composition. With the aid of Eric Fenby, who came to live with him and served as his amanuensis, Delius wrote several works, patiently dictating them note by note.

Delius died at his home in Grez-sur-Loing on June 10, 1934. One year later, his body was transported to its final resting place, in a churchyard in Limpsfield, in southern England.

The following works by Delius are discussed below: *Brigg Fair; In a Summer Garden; A Mass of Life; On Hearing the First Cuckoo in Spring; Sea-Drift; A Song of the High Hills; Song of Summer; Summer Night on the River; A Village Romeo and Juliet.*

A VILLAGE ROMEO AND JULIET, opera (1901).

Though Delius is not known as a composer of operas, he wrote six works in that form, the fourth of which is his most important. Delius himself referred to this opera—*A Village Romeo and Juliet*—as a "lyric drama in six pictures." He aimed for a work in which the stage action served merely to elucidate the music—to suggest through words and gesture what the music had realized completely. One commentator has referred to the opera as a kind of symphonic poem in which the play serves as the program.

Delius himself prepared the libretto (assisted by his wife), adapting a tale of Gottfried Keller, *Die Leute von Seldwyla.* The daughter of one family falls in love with the son of another—even though a bitter feud exists between the households. The lovers decide to escape. On the road they meet a vagabond fiddler who tries to induce them to follow him to a life of abandoned delights. The lovers are not interested; they prefer going their own way. That way eventually leads to suicide on a river barge.

The opera is written with subdued strokes: there are no climaxes, no emotional peaks, no dramatic thrusts. It is an amazingly quiet work, which, however, "burns with such white heat at the center (wrote Bernard van Dieren) that it seems little else than a bewildering number of lost opportunities."

One of the orchestral interludes has become familiar through performances at symphony concerts: "The Walk to the Paradise Gardens."

This entr'acte occurs between the fifth and sixth "pictures," and is said by Phillip Heseltine to be an epitome of the whole opera.

The opera was introduced in Berlin at the Komische Opera under the direction of Fritz Cassirer on February 21, 1907. Its first performance in England did not take place until 1910.

SEA-DRIFT for baritone, chorus and orchestra (1903).

The first poem in Walt Whitman's *Sea-Drift* ("Out of the Cradle Endlessly Rocking") provided Delius with his text. The shape of the music, as the composer told Eric Fenby, "was taken out of my hands, so to speak, as I worked, and was bred easily and effortlessly of the nature and sequence of my particular musical ideas, and the nature and sequence of the particular poetical ideas of Whitman that appealed to me."

Except in some of his shorter orchestral works Delius rarely achieved such a consistently high level of inspiration as he did in this music. He absorbed the wind-swept rhythms of Whitman's poetry, and the pathos and solemnity of its emotions; music and poem seem magically one, almost as if they had been created together, and by the same man.

Arthur Hutchings has pointed out that the work is not essentially a "seascape," even though the presence of the sea is felt; that the principal concern of the composer was to reproduce in music the emotions of such lines as:

> Soothe! Soothe! Soothe!
> Close on its waves soothes the wave behind,
> And again another behind embracing and lapping,
>   every one close,
> But my love soothes not me, not me.

Sea-Drift was introduced in 1906, three years after its composition, by the Allgemeiner Deutscher Musikverein in Essen.

A MASS OF LIFE, for double chorus, quartet, and orchestra (1905).

A Mass of Life was developed out of *Night Song of Zarathustra,* which Delius had composed in 1898. The *Night Song* is suggested in the early part of the *Mass,* and appears in the last movement as the principal theme.

The *Mass* was introduced in London on June 7, 1909 under Beecham's direction. Delius thought highly of this work, an expression of his almost religious fervor for the philosophy of Nietzsche.

The music, which gives the impression of improvisatory writing, is ideally suited to the mystical writings of Nietzsche. The music is, as Hugh Ross remarked, a series of mood pictures, in which a mood of revery alternates with dramatic passages.

BRIGG FAIR, rhapsody for orchestra (1907).

Brigg Fair is a famous English folksong, rediscovered and arranged by Percy Grainger. It is the basic material which Delius enlarged and developed in this rhapsody. *Brigg Fair* was written one year after Grainger had published the setting of the song, and was introduced by the Liverpool Philharmonic under Sir Granville Bantock on January 18, 1908.

The folksong is first heard in the oboe, before being subjected to development. The pastoral mood of the song dominates the atmosphere of the entire rhapsody, which, from beginning to end, has calm beauty.

IN A SUMMER GARDEN, fantasy for orchestra (1908).

Two mottoes appear in the printed program, providing clues to both the emotional and programmatic implications of the music.

The first of these is by Dante Gabriel Rossetti:

> All are my blooms; and all sweet bloom of love
> To thee I give while Spring and Summer sing.

The other, of unknown authorship, appears in a German text and might serve as the program: "Roses, lilies, and a thousand scented flowers. Bright butterflies flitting from petal to petal, and gold-brown bees humming in the warm, quivering summer air. Beneath the shade of ancient trees, a quiet river with water-lilies. In a boat, almost hidden, two people. A thrush is singing in the distance."

In a Summer Garden was introduced on December 11, 1908 by the London Philharmonic, the composer conducting.

A SONG OF THE HIGH HILLS, for chorus and orchestra (1911).

In a prefatory note within the published score of this composition, the composer wrote: "I have tried to express the joy and rapture felt in the High Mountains and to depict the lonely melancholy of the highest altitudes and of the wide expanses. The vocal parts typify Man in Nature."

Although written for chorus and orchestra, the work is essentially an orchestral composition, the choral parts being used as color background. It received its première in London nine years after its composition, on February 26, 1920, under Albert Coates's direction.

When *A Song of the High Hills* was introduced in this country, under Percy Grainger, the conductor provided the following description of the music, published in the program:

"The entire work, from start to finish, is singularly solemn and uplifted in mood, and full of that rare quality of freshness and purity that is so striking a characteristic of things born of the hills—their flowers, their poets, their painters, etc.... Nothing is consciously descriptive on the composer's part, yet the analogy between much of the music and certain nature impressions is easily recognized.... Noteworthy is the scale in which the musical form of the work is cast—vast dimensions that recall little else in music except certain creations of Bach."

ON HEARING THE FIRST CUCKOO IN SPRING, tone-poem for orchestra (1912).

Delius's summer vacations were invariably spent in Norway, in the hills of Jotenheim; he was happiest surrounded by the natural beauties of that country.

In *On Hearing the First Cuckoo in Spring,* he not only transfers to music the feelings of a composer at the awakening of springtime (a feeling magically suggested with the very opening luminous chord) but also his own nostalgic yearnings for Norway. Thus, the second theme is a Norwegian folksong, "In Ola Valley." The first theme, however, is English in character and is Delius's own; it consists of a sequence of echoing phrases suggesting the exchange of cuckoo calls.

This work is one of Delius's masterpieces, an unforgettable picture of the vernal season, and one of the happiest examples of Delius's sensitive style. It was introduced together with *Summer Night on the River* in Leipzig on October 2, 1913.

SUMMER NIGHT ON THE RIVER, tone-poem for orchestra (1912).

This exquisite tone-poem is a companion piece to *On Hearing the First Cuckoo in Spring.* It was introduced together with that work in Leipzig on October 2, 1913.

It was not intended as an impressionist picture in the way that the *Cuckoo* work was. The pictorial description is here direct rather than suggestive. The vague harmonies bring up a picture of mists settling over the river; the rhythms suggest the rocking of small boats. A cello solo is the principal melodic idea—a beautiful song creating an atmosphere of peace and mystery that embraces the river on a summer night.

SONG OF SUMMER, tone-poem for orchestra (1930).

During the last years of his life, Delius (now totally blind) dictated his music to his amanuensis, Eric Fenby. In this way the *Song of Summer* was written, based on sketches which Delius had written out many years earlier for a projected piece to be called *Poem of Love and Life.*

To Fenby, Delius provided the following description of this music: "I want you to imagine that we are sitting on the cliffs in the heather and looking out over the sea. The sustained chords in the high strings suggest the clear sky and stillness and calm of the scene.... You remember that figure that comes in the violins when the music becomes more animated.

I'm introducing it there to suggest the gentle rise and fall of the waves....
The flutes suggest a seagull gliding by."

NORMAN DELLO JOIO   1913—

By his own admission, Dello Joio has been most strongly influenced by his teacher, Paul Hindemith. The younger man belongs with the neo-classicists, whose aim is the revival of old classical forms and styles and their adaptation to twentieth-century use. He may write a ricercare, passa-caglia, or chaconne—forms which belong to the seventeenth century; but his writing is the percussive, dissonant, and richly colored music of a modernist.

He is always a splendid technician; but beyond this, when he is at his best, he creates music that is clear, forcefully motivated, poetic, and highly personal.

Dello Joio was born in New York City on January 24, 1913, and his studies took place at the Musical Institute, the Julliard Graduate School, the Berkshire Music Center (with Paul Hindemith), and privately with the organist Pietro Yon. He first attracted attention with a Piano Trio, written while he was still a student at the Musical Institute, which won the Elizabeth Sprague Coolidge Award. His *Magnificat,* which won the Town Hall Composers Prize in 1943, further increased his reputation. There followed performances of major orchestral works throughout the country, and the receipt of numerous honors (including a Guggenheim fellowship twice, and a grant by the American Academy of Arts and Letters). In 1957 he won the Pulitzer Prize in music for *Meditation on Ecclesiastes* (see Supplement). Dello Joio taught composition at Sarah Lawrence College, in Bronxville, New York, between 1944 and 1950.

The following works by Dello Joio are discussed below: Concerto for Harp and Orchestra; *New York Profiles; Ricercari; Variations, Chaconne, and Finale.*

CONCERTO FOR HARP AND ORCHESTRA (1944). I. Introduction and Passacaglia. II. Scherzo—March.

This concerto was introduced in New York on November 3, 1947, by the Little Orchestra Society, Thomas Scherman conducting; Carlos Salzedo was the soloist.

The following information about this work is by the composer:

"The first movement is a passacaglia whose entrance is prepared by an extended introduction. This introduction has in it the melodic elements that emerge into the full passacaglia theme set forth by the cellos and basses. The movement closes with direct references to the introduction.

"The second movement is an amiable Scherzo. The rhythmic character of this movement affords the harp the opportunity for a varied virtuoso display. Most of the characteristics of the instrument are exploited to their maximum degree of sonority. The two contrasting themes that serve as the frame for the movement are in a constant state of kaleidoscopic treatment between the harp and the orchestra."

RICERCARI, for piano and orchestra (1946). I. Allegretto giocoso. II. Adagio. III. Allegro vivo.

A ricercare is a sixteenth- and seventeenth-century musical form in which the vocal motet is adapted to instrumental music. Generally speaking, the form presents a germinal idea (originally, the ricercare employed several ideas) which it develops fugally.

Dello Joio restores the old form to contemporary usage, retaining the classical structure but endowing it with modern writing. The three movements represent three different ways of developing the germinal idea: the first, harmonically; the second, melodically; the third, rhythmically.

This work was introduced on December 19, 1946, by the New York Philharmonic-Symphony Orchestra. George Szell conducted, and the composer was at the piano.

VARIATIONS, CHACONNE, AND FINALE, for orchestra (1947).

When this work was introduced by the Pittsburgh Symphony Orchestra under Fritz Reiner, on January 30, 1948, it was called *Three Symphonic Dances*. The composer soon felt that to describe a work so serious in character as "dances" was something of an incongruity. He affixed a new title, by which the composition is now known. It has been extensively performed both in Europe and America; in 1949 it won the New York Music Critics Circle Award.

The basis of the entire work is a theme of liturgical character (first heard in the oboe) which the composer derived from the Kyrie of the *Missa de Angelis*. In the first movement, following a brief prologue, the theme experiences six variations: Semplice grazioso; Andante religioso; Vivacissimo; Allegro pesante; Amabile; Funebre. The chaconne that follows is built around the framework of the first four notes of the theme (in chromatic form). A veritable orgiastic outburst of energy marks the finale, in which the theme repeatedly asserts itself. This is joyous music—the religious music of the first two movements here becomes secular!—in which an almost carnival spirit of merrymaking prevails. With a thunderous enunciation of the first four notes of the theme, fortissimo, the music comes to a triumphant close.

NEW YORK PROFILES, suite for orchestra (1949). I. The Cloisters. II. The Park. III. The Tomb. IV. Little Italy.

This work was commissioned by Augustus L. Searle, honorary Vice-President of the Musical Arts Society of La Jolla, California. The première performance took place in La Jolla, on August 21, 1949, under the direction of Nikolai Sokoloff.

Dello Joio provides, in this charming suite, four vignettes of New York City. In the first piece, the composer draws from the Gregorian chant to describe the magnificence of The Cloisters as it overlooks the Hudson. The second movement captures the spirit of fun and play among children in Central Park. A chorale fantasy next evokes Grant's Tomb, culminating in a brief quotation from *The Battle Hymn of the Republic*. The suite ends with a spirited Italian dance such as might be witnessed in the streets of New York's Italian neighborhoods. The composition ends with a reference to the Gregorian chant first heard in the initial movement.

DAVID DIAMOND   1915—

In his earlier works—the *Psalm,* for orchestra, the Concerto for String Quartet, and the *Elegy,* for orchestra—Diamond was the unashamed romanticist who spoke his heart freely with emotional outbursts, rich harmonic textures, and vivid orchestral colors. Subsequently, he has tended to simplify his writing, and to make it more transparent; but the romantic vein is still an outstanding trait. He is perhaps best in his slower pages, which he endows with eloquent language and intense feelings. But he has passionate drive, too, the vigor of a strong and magnetic personality.

Diamond was born in Rochester, New York, on July 9, 1915, and received the first part of his musical training at the Cleveland Institute of Music and the Eastman School of Music in Rochester. A scholarship for the Dalcroze School of Music brought him to New York in 1934; and another for study with Nadia Boulanger later sent him to Paris. In Paris, he wrote several works, the best of which was his *Psalm,* which received the Juilliard Publication Award and was introduced by the San Francisco Symphony Orchestra. In 1938, a Guggenheim Fellowship enabled him to complete his music study in Europe, study which finally brought him to full maturity as a composer, as was made evident by his First Symphony, written in 1940 and introduced by the New York Philharmonic under Dimitri Mitropoulos one year later. From then on, Diamond wrote prolifically in virtually all the major forms of music, except the opera. Significant performances of his works by leading American orchestras, chamber-music groups, and artists, established him as one of the most important of our younger composers. Diamond received the Paderewski Award in 1943, and a grant by the American Academy of Arts and Letters one year later.

The following works by Diamond are discussed below: *Romeo and Juliet; Rounds;* Symphony No. 3; Symphony No. 4.

ROUNDS, for string orchestra (1944). I. Allegro molto vivace. II. Adagio. III. Allegro vigoroso.

The round—of which the twelfth-century *Sumer Is Icumen In* is both a classic example and a prototype—is more generally associated with vocal than with instrumental music. But in this work for chamber orchestra, Diamond demonstrates how its artistic possibilities can be extended. Diamond wrote it on a commission from Dimitri Mitropoulos, then conductor of the Minneapolis Symphony Orchestra, who introduced it in Minneapolis on November 24, 1944.

In the first movement, the different choirs of strings enter canonically as a kind of prelude to the main melody, which is played by the violas. The Adagio is a page of sustained lyricism, "a resting point between the two movements," in the words of the composer. The finale is a kind of fugal movement in the rondo form, in which the rhythmic device of the first movement is repeated, "so helping," wrote the composer, "to 'round' out the entire work and unify the formal structure."

SYMPHONY NO. 3 (1945). I. Allegro deciso. II. Andante. III. Allegro vivo. IV. Adagio assai. V. Allegro con impeto.

Diamond's Third Symphony, dedicated to his parents, was given its first performance in Boston by the Boston Symphony Orchestra under Charles Munch, on November 3, 1950.

The composer explains that the symphony consolidates the cyclic form "by amalgamating all thematic, harmonic, and rhythmic material throughout the five movements." The composer adds further: "Apart from the principal thematic materials and their development in all movements, two 'motival' themes link together the entire symphony cyclically, appearing in their disguised forms . . . completely or in fragments."

SYMPHONY NO. 4 (1945). I. Allegretto. II. Andante. III. Allegro.

Diamond's Fourth Symphony was the result of a commission from the Koussevitzky Foundation. On January 23, 1948, it was heard for the first time in a performance by the Boston Symphony Orchestra under Leonard Bernstein. Its première took place before that of the Third Symphony.

The work is of comparatively small dimensions. The first movement (in sonata form) opens with a tender theme which is projected in two sections, the first stated by muted strings and clarinets, and the second in the strings with a bassoon accompaniment. The second theme is gay and carefree (oboe solo). After a rather extended development in which the two themes are skillfully transfigured, there comes a powerful climax in which both of them are joined. The movement ends with a return of the first theme and a brief coda.

The introduction of the second movement is a chorale-like melody heard first in the brass and then repeated in the strings. The main idea of the movement is then unfolded, a long and sustained melody for viola. The third movement—full of dynamic power—opens with a vigorous subject for the brass. A rhythmic figure which follows in the tenor drum recurs throughout the movement and acquires increasing significance. This third movement has been described by its composer as combining the features of the scherzo and the rondo.

ROMEO AND JULIET, symphonic suite (1947). I. Overture. II. Balcony Scene. III. Romeo and Friar Laurence. IV. Juliet and Her Nurse. V. Death of Romeo and Juliet.

This suite was commissioned by Thomas Scherman, conductor of the Little Orchestra Society, and was heard for the first time on October 20, 1947, in New York City, at a concert in which the Little Orchestra Society made its debut.

In writing this suite, the composer has informed us, he wished to "convey as fully and yet as economically as possible the innate beauty and pathos of Shakespeare's great drama without resorting to a large orchestral canvas and a definite musical form."

Describing his suite further, Diamond adds: "The Overture holds all the characteristics of the play in a very concentrated formal structure. The second movement needs no explanation. The third movement depicts those scenes of the drama in which the characters of Romeo and Friar Laurence appear, and in the music thematic material of two distinct styles is used to describe them. The fourth movement is similarly descriptive. The last movement is the death of Romeo and Juliet."

ERNST VON DOHNÁNYI   1877—

The admiration—adulation might be the apter word—which young Dohnányi had for Johannes Brahms had a marked influence on his musical writing. There were those facetious critics who referred to Dohnányi's op. 1, the Piano Quintet in C Minor, as "Brahms' Second Piano Quintet." Indeed, there is no mistaking the Brahmsian romanticism, spaciousness, and emotional climaxes in this first Dohnányi composition. But even in subsequent Dohnányi music, the Brahmsian fingerprints are still in evidence. Yet, for all its debt to the master, these Dohnányi compositions have a charm of their own, due largely to Dohnányi's sound technique, inventive and often spontaneous lyricism, and (in the orchestral music) particularly interesting instrumentation.

Dohnányi never did succeed in achieving a personal identity in his music. He never allowed himself to be influenced by the new ideas and techniques and idioms springing up all around him. Even on those less frequent occasions when he derived his materials from Hungarian folk music—following the lead of his celebrated compatriots, Bartók and Kodály—his music never assumed a distinguished personality. He simply never outgrew his love for German postromanticism; and by the same token he never quite developed from an interesting and a charming composer into a great one.

Dohnányi was born in Pressburg, Hungary, on July 27, 1877. After some piano study with Carl Förstner, he entered the Royal Academy in Budapest in 1894. He made rapid strides both as pianist and composer. His youthful Symphony in F Major won first prize at the Academy in 1897 and was performed soon thereafter. In the same year, he also began his career as a concert pianist, a career in which he was soon to gather notable successes. His concert career, however, did not stem the tide of his creative output. When only eighteen years old, he wrote an admirable *Piano Quintet* (op. 1), which inspired the praise of Brahms, who was responsible for getting it performed. Other works followed, all noticeably influenced by Brahms.

From 1905 to 1911, Dohnányi was professor of the piano at the Berlin Hochschule. After 1916, he was professor of the piano at the Landesakademie in Budapest, of which he became full director in 1934. He was also active with the baton, serving for many years as musical director of the Budapest

Philharmonic Orchestra, and in 1925 appearing as a guest conductor with American orchestras.

After World War II, Dohnányi returned to the concert platform as pianist. In November 1948 he returned to the United States, settling in Tallahassee, Florida, where he was appointed instructor at the Florida State College.

The following works by Dohnányi are discussed below: *Ruralia Hungarica;* Suite in F-sharp Minor; *Variations on a Nursery Theme.*

SUITE IN F-SHARP MINOR, for orchestra, op. 19 (1909). I. Andante with variations. II. Scherzo. III. Romanza. IV. Rondo.

This suite is in Dohnányi's best romantic vein. The influence of Brahms is obvious—as, for example, in the unmistakably Brahmsian song in the first movement, the subject of six variations. These variations run the gamut from gentle tranquillity to gay animation, from quiet introspection to passionate romanticism. Their often subtle and elusive relationship to their theme is once again reminiscent of Brahms' use of the variation form.

Dohnányi's bent for wit is found in the Scherzo, a piquant little movement that moves with quicksilver grace. Plucked strings introduce the Romanza, in which the principal subject is spoken by the solo cello (once again the image of Brahms is reflected). An energetic rondo brings gaiety to the closing pages of the score.

VARIATIONS ON A NURSERY THEME, for piano and orchestra, op. 25 (1913).

The nursery theme exploited here in a series of witty variations is a familiar one. It is the old French song, *Ah, Vous Dirai-Je, Maman,* which Mozart also used for variations, and which in this country is sung with the alphabet.

Dohnányi's *Variations* opens with the utmost sobriety which seems to set the stage for the entrance of an impressive and dignified melody; then the gay little tune is introduced by the piano. The nine variations that follow are full of lighthearted, satiric, and gay ideas. It becomes understandable why the composer dedicated this work "to the enjoyment of lovers of humor, and to the annoyance of others." In the finale, a robust fugue develops into a climax, after which the nursery theme returns in a slightly altered form.

RURALIA HUNGARICA, for piano, op. 32a (1924). I. Andante poco moto, rubato. II. Presto ma non tanto. III. Allegro grazioso. IV. Adagio non troppo. IV. Molto vivace.

Only infrequently did Dohnányi stray from the Brahmsian fields to sport in those Hungarian pastures cultivated by Bartók and Kodály. And when he did, his efforts were usually not rewarded with success. *Ruralia*

Hungarica, for the piano (Dohnányi also orchestrated it), is an exception. Elements of Hungarian song and dance are utilized charmingly. The most effective movement, from the melodic point of view, is the fourth, which is touched with a gentle melancholy; rhythmically, the last movement is of considerable interest—a kind of tarantelle.

PAUL DUKAS   1865—1935

No more than a handful of works have survived Paul Dukas, the most famous of which is the delightful and witty scherzo, *The Sorcerer's Apprentice,* written before 1900. His best works are characterized by such mastery of technique, such fastidious workmanship, and such elegance of style that the right of their composer to belong with the best French composers of the twentieth century cannot be denied. Despite his excursions into modern writing, Dukas succeeded in bringing to his music a classic repose and serenity, so much so that (as G. Jean-Aubry wrote when Dukas was still alive) many of Dukas' pages already have "the assuaging quality of the past."

Dukas was born in Paris on October 1, 1865. After pursuing classical studies at the Lycée Charlemagne, at Turgot, he entered the Paris Conservatory in 1882. As a pupil of George Mathias (piano), Theodore Dubois (harmony), and Ernest Guiraud (composition), he won first prize in counterpoint and fugue, and the second Prix de Rome.

After a period of military service he returned to Paris to devote himself to composition. In 1892, he attracted attention with the overture *Polyeucte,* performed by the Lamoureux Orchestra. One critic went so far as to say that this piece was "one of the most remarkable works of recent years." His reputation grew further with the Symphony in C major (1896). And it virtually encircled the globe with the triumphs of his *The Sorcerer's Apprentice.* Dukas wrote this masterpiece—today acknowledged not only as his best work but also as one of the finest symphonic pieces by a contemporary composer—in 1897, inspired by the Goethe ballad, *Der Zauberlehrling,* which in turn was a poetic adaptation of an old folk tale. In few works of our day has programmatic writing been achieved with such vivid and telling strokes—so much so that it is almost possible to follow the progress of the merry tale without recourse to a printed program.

The Sorcerer's Apprentice was introduced in the year of its composition at a concert of the Société Nationale and was immediately a great success.

In 1909, Dukas became professor at the Paris Conservatory, a post he retained until the end of his life. Thereafter, as though disdainful of public acclaim, he refused to send his new works to publishers, and did little to encourage performances of his music. Toward the end of his life he even destroyed most of his later manuscripts.

Dukas died in Paris on May 17, 1935. A few months before his death he was invited to occupy the chair of the Academy of Fine Arts vacated by Alfred Bruneau.

The following works by Dukas are discussed below: *Ariane et Barbe-bleu; La Peri.*

For *The Sorcerer's Apprentice* (*L'Apprenti Sorcier*), see the biographical sketch above.

ARIANE ET BARBE-BLEU, opera (1907).

It is the opinion of many French authorities that Dukas' opera (though rarely heard) is one of the two great achievements of the French lyric theater of the twentieth century, the other being Debussy's *Pelléas et Mélisande.* Comparison between these two masterpieces is inescapable. Both are derived from plays by Maeterlinck. Both have a unanimity of style and mood. Both are negations of the Wagnerian principles so much in vogue in the early twentieth century. Both are impressionistic in their utilization of symbolism, indulgence in atmospheric writing, and preference for subtle suggestion rather than outright statement.

The play of Maurice Maeterlinck revolves around the sixth wife of Bluebeard—Ariane—who refuses to believe that Bluebeard has killed his other wives and that a similar fate awaits her. She is given seven keys by her husband: six are silver, giving access to vaults containing precious jewels—and these she may use at will. The seventh, of gold, opens a strange door; the use of that key is strictly denied her.

In that room are Bluebeard's wives, huddled in rags. Ariane arranges for their escape, brings them to her castle, and decks them out in fine clothes and lavish jewels. Meanwhile, Bluebeard engages in a fight with the villagers, is beaten, tied, and brought back to his home as captive. There, freed of the bonds that tie his wrists, he is astonished to find his beautiful wives. Ariane decides to leave Bluebeard forever; but her entreaties to the other wives to imitate her fall on deaf ears.

Ariane was introduced at the Paris Opéra Comique on May 10, 1907. "The Maeterlinck drama might perhaps dispense with a musical commentary," wrote Gabriel Fauré in *Figaro* following the première, "but this music of Paul Dukas, so clearly delineated, so sharp and eloquent, does it not throw more light on the personages of the drama, who walk in a somewhat imprecise atmosphere and express themselves in a similarly imprecise manner?"

Several months after the composer's death, *Ariane* was introduced into the repertory of the Paris Opéra.

LA PÉRI, dance-poem for orchestra (1910).

La Péri was written for the dancer Mlle. Trouhanowa, to whom it was dedicated. It was introduced at the Chatelet Theatre in Paris in 1912, with the composer conducting.

The original program contained the following story-outline of the music:

"It happened that at the end of his youthful days... Iskender went about Iran seeking the flower of immortality.

"The sun sojourned thrice in its dozen dwellings without Iskender finding the flower. At last he arrived at the end of the earth.... There, on the steps that lead to the hall of Ormuzd, a Peri was reclining, asleep in her jewelled robe. A star sparkled above her head; her lute rested on her breast; in her hand shone the flower.

"Iskender noiselessly leaned over the sleeper and without awakening her snatched the flower, which suddenly became between his fingers like the noonday sun over the forests of Ghilan. The Peri, opening her eyes, clapped the palms of her hands together and uttered a loud cry, for she could not now ascend toward the light of Ormuzd.

"Iskender, regarding her, wondered at her face, which surpassed in deliciousness even the face of Gurda-ferrid. In his heart he coveted her. The Peri knew the thought of the King, for in the right hand of Iskender the lotus grew purple and became as the face of longing.

"Thus the servant of the Pure knew that this flower of life was not for him. To recover it, she darted forward like a bee. The invincible lord bore away from her the lotus.

"But the Peri danced the dance of the Peris; always approaching him until her face touched his face; and at the end he gave back the flower without regret. Then the lotus was like unto snow and gold, as the summit of Elbourz at sunset. The form of the Peri seemed to melt in the light coming from the calix and soon nothing more was to be seen than a hand raising the flower of flame, which faded into the realm above. Iskender saw her disappear. Knowing from this that his end drew near, he felt the darkness encompassing him."

EDWARD ELGAR 1857—1934

Elgar's severest critics have often said that he lacks originality, profundity, a personal style; that too much of what he has written is derivative from other composers (Schumann and Wagner particularly). Yet it should not be denied that his language, at its best, has beauty. The charm of his lyricism, the distinction of his form, the robustness of his orchestration, together with the poetry and mysticism that touch his best pages, do not fail to enchant the ear and senses. It is music with attributes like those of the man who wrote them: suave, genial, witty, sentimental, polished, cultured. Unfortunately, it is also the kind of music that ages quickly; much of it has already worn a bit thin. But while its day is brief, this music, nevertheless, spreads the warmth of sunshine to those who come into contact with it for the first time.

Sir Edward Elgar was born at Broadheath, near Worcester, England, on June 2, 1857. Though he showed pronounced musical talent, he was at first trained for law. His love for music eventually drove him away from his legal studies. After immersing himself in varied musical activities, he went to London and studied the violin with Adolf Pollitzer. These lessons soon were terminated. Returning to his home, Elgar became bandmaster at the county lunatic asylum at Worcester, and began composition.

In 1885, Elgar was appointed organist of the St. George Cathedral, in Worcester, and four years after that he married Caroline Alice Roberts. Now convinced that what he wanted to do more than anything else was to compose, he gave up his organ post, transferred himself to London, and began writing in larger and more ambitious forms than heretofore. The most important productions at this time were a concert overture, *Froissart,* op. 19, and an oratorio, *The Light of Life,* op. 29.

The next half-dozen years saw the first performances of several major choral works. Early in 1899, Elgar completed his first important work for orchestra, the *Variations on an Original Theme,* better known today as the *Enigma Variations,* op. 36. Elgar referred to these variations as an "enigma" because of a "concealed theme" which is never actually heard but which is suggested in each of the variations, sometimes as a "silent accompaniment." Another enigmatic feature was the imposition of a set of initials before each variation, these initials identifying some Elgar friend of whom the variation was intended as a tonal characterization.

Hans Richter, the conductor, was delighted with this work and introduced it in London in June, 1899. Its success not only in London, but also in Germany and Austria, brought Elgar recognition for the first time. To this day, it remains one of Elgar's best and most popular works.

His fame made further secure with the triumph of his oratorio, *The Dream of Gerontius,* Elgar now proceeded to identify himself as an *English* composer by writing a set of six nationalistic marches entitled *Pomp and Circumstance,* and an Ode for the coronation of Edward VII. In 1904, Elgar was honored with knighthood and a three-day festival of his music at Covent Garden. In 1924, he was appointed Master of the King's Musick, and seven years later received the highest honor that the Crown could offer a composer—a baronetcy.

During World War I, Elgar served first in the Hampstead Division as special constable, then in the Hampstead Volunteer Reserve. The war over, he returned to serious writing. His vein now became more personal. He turned to chamber music, producing several intimate works which are rarely performed.

The death of his wife in 1920 was a major blow. He swore he would never again write a bar of music. In 1929, however, his patriotism brought him back to his music. King George V was stricken by a serious illness. As a hymn of prayer for his recovery, Elgar wrote a Christmas carol— his first piece of music in nine years. Thus reawakened, his creative urge led him to plan a new symphony—his third.

He was never destined to complete that symphony. In 1934, a serious illness from which he never recovered, sent him to bed. He died at his home in Marl Bank on February 23, 1934. His last request was that no one should meddle with the sketches of his Third Symphony, that it remain permanently unfinished and unpublished.

The following works by Elgar are discussed below: *Cockaigne;* Concerto in B Minor for Violin and Orchestra; *The Dream of Gerontius; Introduction and Allegro; Pomp and Circumstance;* Symphony No. 1 in A-flat Major; Symphony No. 2 in E-flat Major.

For *Enigma Variations,* see the biographical sketch above.

COCKAIGNE, concert overture for orchestra, op. 40 (1900).

This overture, subtitled by the composer *In London Town,* is a realistic and sometimes witty picture of London: its scurrying crowds and busy streets, its sounds and sights. Two lovers are taking a stroll. Their aural and visual impression of the goings-on in the city streets are spiritedly and colorfully reproduced in the music.

THE DREAM OF GERONTIUS, oratorio for soloists, chorus, and orchestra, op. 38 (1900).

If the *Enigma Variations* first brought Elgar into the limelight, it was this oratorio that kept him there. Based on the famous poem of Cardinal Newman, the oratorio consists of a series of lyric and dramatic episodes portraying the doctrine of Purgatory as taught by the Catholic Church.

The Dream of Gerontius was introduced at the Birmingham Festival under Richter on October 3, 1900. It was, at first, something of a failure. A few discerning musicians (among whom was Bernard Shaw) recognized it as a masterpiece, and were strongly moved by the mysticism and poetry of the music, the beauty of the sounds, the effective choral writing, the vivid musical imagery, the high-minded sincerity. But the public had come expecting a traditional oratorio with arias, choruses, and ensemble numbers in the style of Handel. Elgar's unconventional form proved puzzling. For Elgar had molded his music to his text in the Wagnerian manner, creating a continuous musical flow which received its shape and form from the demands of the poem.

On December 19, 1901, *The Dream of Gerontius* was heard at the Lower Rhine Festival. It was immediately and immensely successful. This was possibly the first time that the work of an English composer inspired such enthusiasm in Germany. Richard Strauss did not hesitate to describe it as a "masterpiece." The German acclaim inevitably encouraged repeat performances in England. Eventually, the beauty and the poetry of the music impressed themselves on the English music public. *The Dream* now became one of the most frequently heard and one of the best-loved oratorios on the English concert stage, exceeded in popularity only by Handel's *Messiah* and Mendelssohn's *Elijah*.

POMP AND CIRCUMSTANCE, five marches for orchestra, op. 39 (1901).

In 1901, Elgar planned a set of six stately marches to prove that march music need not necessarily be banal. He had in mind the same serious approach to the march that other composers had brought to other popular forms, such as the waltz or the polonaise. Of the six marches, he succeeded in writing only five, entitling the set *Pomp and Circumstance*.

He was as proud of these marches as of his major works. While they are not all of equal merit, they are rousing without being pompous, filled with vigorous melodic ideas and rhythmic strength.

Of the five marches, it is the first, in the key of D major, that is the most famous, and the one that is usually referred to when the name *Pomp and Circumstance* is mentioned. Probably no other single piece of music—except, perhaps, the anthem *God Save the King*—is so inextricably associated with the British Empire. In strict march form, the piece opens with a robust melody, strongly rhythmic, which serves to introduce the stately melody which has become for the English people something of a second national anthem. Today, this middle section is frequently heard separately, sung to the words of Laurence Housman's *Land of Hope and*

Glory. This melody also appears in the Ode which Elgar wrote in 1902 to honor the Coronation of King Edward VII.

The first and second marches from this set received their world première in Liverpool on October 19, 1901. The keys of the five marches are: I. D major (*Land of Hope and Glory*); II. A minor; III. C minor; IV. G major (*Song of Liberty*); V. C major.

INTRODUCTION AND ALLEGRO, for strings, op. 47 (1905).

One day while on a visit to Wales the composer heard the distant music of singing. The cadence of a falling third caught his ear and suggested to him the idea for a theme, characteristically Welsh. Subsequently he heard in the valley of the Wye a true Welsh song, which, in his own words, "reinforced my Welsh impressions and led me to the completion of the work." It was first given in London on March 8, 1905.

The work—*Introduction and Allegro*—is scored for solo string quartet and string orchestra, and is in the style of the old concerto grosso, which utilized the solo quartet as a "concertante" with the rest of the orchestra as "tutti."

The solo quartet and strings pronounce the opening subject, and a second theme of contrasting character is posed by the quartet itself. After the development comes the Welsh melody that inspired the entire work, heard in the solo viola. The Introduction ends, and the second of the two opening themes returns, transformed from minor to major, in the Allegro section that follows, and is allowed to develop. After the solo quartet presents a new subject, an ingenious development grows into a powerful climax. Still another new idea becomes the germ of a fugato movement. The work ends in a recollection of the opening theme of the Allegro, in a resounding restatement of the Welsh melody by quartet and orchestra, and in a final recapitulation of the opening theme of the Allegro movement.

SYMPHONY NO. 1 IN A-FLAT MAJOR, op. 55 (1908). I. Andante nobilmente e semplice. II. Allegro molto. III. Adagio. IV. Lento; Allegro.

Elgar's First Symphony was several years in the planning. He had originally intended it as a tribute to General Gordon, whom he admired profoundly. But the subject restricted his musical thinking and he dropped the idea. When the symphony was finally completed in 1908, the composer provided the following clue to its emotional and spiritual content: "It is written out of a full life-experience and is meant to include the innumerable phases of joy and sorrow, struggle and conquest, and especially between the ideal and actual life." But the symphony, as Basil Maine suggests, is neither a tribute to any one man or even an autobiographical document, but—in its majestic strides, epical structure, and melodic grandeur—is actually the glorification of an entire era.

Power is generated throughout the entire work; but introspection and deep thinking are also present. After the first movement, with its heroic breadth and grandeur which tempted one critic to speak of it as "the British Empire in tones," a somber mood pervades the music, most strongly assertive in the slow movement, which reaches stirring emotional depths. Structurally, the symphony is well integrated, with the principal thematic ideas of the entire work posed in the introduction of the first movement, and returning as a summation in the closing movement.

It was introduced in Manchester by Hans Richter on December 3, 1908, and was received so successfully that within the next twelve months it was repeated many times.

CONCERTO IN B MINOR FOR VIOLIN AND ORCHESTRA, op. 61 (1910). I. Allegro. II. Andante. III. Finale: allegro molto.

Elgar completed the writing of his violin concerto with the technical advice and assistance of his violinist-friend, William H. Reed. It was heard for the first time at an informal social gathering at Gloucester, with Reed playing the solo part and the composer accompanying him on the piano. On November 10, 1910, Fritz Kreisler introduced the work officially with the London Philharmonic Orchestra, conducted by the composer.

On the flyleaf of the published score appears the following brief motto: "Here is enshrined the soul of...." Without question, the concerto is a personal work into which the composer poured his most intimate feelings, thoughts, reveries, emotions. In few other works is his romanticism more ardent than it is in the spacious opening movement, built around four themes developed into passionate, intense, and sensitive moods. In few other works is his feeling spoken with such warmth and tenderness as in the slow movement, a veritable poem recited alternately by orchestra and the solo instrument. Rarely does his flair for light-paced wit achieve such grace as in the Finale.

The concerto occasionally exploits interesting devices. One of these is the *accompanied* cadenza in the third movement; another (in the same section) is the novel effect achieved by the violinists in the orchestra drumming their fingers on the strings. In the very opening movement an ingenious method is realized when the solo violin plays the concluding bars of the orchestral introduction. But, for all such novel turns, the concerto is traditional in its form, faithful to the romantic concepts of the late nineteenth century, of which it is both a characteristic and a successful product.

SYMPHONY NO. 2 IN E-FLAT MAJOR, op. 63 (1911). I. Allegro vivace e nobilmente. II. Larghetto. III. Rondo: presto. IV. Moderato e maestoso.

The Second Symphony which followed the first by almost three years, is on a different emotional level. Where the earlier work is both grandiose and somber, the second (though beginning on a note of despair) achieves increasing good spirits as the symphony progresses. It erupts with veritable joyousness in the Rondo, and ends on a triumphant note of undisguised optimism. In comparing the two symphonies, Robert H. Hull finds that the second "is more immediate in its attractions," while the first is "more urgent in its ultimate meaning." To Hull, the general impression of the Second Symphony is one "of spontaneous gaiety. This atmosphere is common to each of the four movements, notwithstanding the sense of tranquil reflection discernible in the Adagio."

Elgar dedicated this symphony to "the memory of His Late Majesty King Edward VII." Its première took place in London on May 24, 1911.

GEORGES ENESCO   1881—1955

Enesco's most famous works are those in which the personality of his native land is reflected through the exploitation of folk-music elements. With considerable vitality, Enesco transferred to many of his works the vivid harmonic schemes, oriental atmosphere, irresistible dance rhythms, and melodic contours found in Rumanian folk music. But not all of Enesco's works are Rumanian. Some of his major compositions are not national in idiom, but are the creations of a modern composer who brilliantly utilizes contemporary techniques without sacrificing sensitivity of expression and emotional outpourings.

Enesco was born in Liveni, Rumania, on August 19, 1881. As a pupil at the Vienna Conservatory he studied with Joseph Hellmesberger. One of his most important contacts in Vienna was with Brahms, whom he admired greatly and later imitated.

After winning prizes in Vienna, Enesco completed his studies at the Paris Conservatory. His teachers, who included Fauré, Massenet, and Gédalge, spoke well of him both as violinist and composer. And it was not long before the young musician justified their opinion. In concert appearances as violinist, he received almost instant recognition as a virtuoso of first importance. He also made his mark as a composer. A concert of his chamber music and songs, which took place in Paris in 1898, was well received. One year later, the première of his *Poème Roumain* by the Colonne Orchestra gave evidence of his creative growth.

Just before the outbreak of World War I, Enesco returned to his native land, settling in Bucharest, and at once becoming one of his country's major music forces. He became conductor of the Bucharest Philharmonic; he organized concerts of contemporary music; he did everything he could to promote the interests of young Rumanian composers.

The war over, Enesco transferred his home to Paris, where he lived for the next decade and a half, filling a triple role in the world of music as composer, conductor, and violinist. Once each year, however, he returned to his native land for a visit—as if to maintain contact with his people.

During the years of World War II, Enesco lived on a farm near Bucharest, tending to his stock and occasionally composing. After the war, Enesco resumed his activity as conductor and violinist throughout the music world until July 1954 when he suffered a stroke in Paris. He died a year later in Paris on May 4, 1955.

The following works by Enesco are discussed below: *Rumanian Rhapsodies Nos. 1 and 2;* Suite No. 2 in C Major; Symphony No. 1 in E-flat Major.

SYMPHONY NO. 1, IN E-FLAT MAJOR, op. 13 (1905). I. Assez vif et rhythmé. II. Lent. III. Vif et vigoureux.

The composer once had this to say about the influences shaping his early creative life: "The god of my own youthful adoration was Brahms, and I wrote my early work quite flagrantly in the manner of the immortal Johannes." Enesco actually proved what he said in his First Symphony. It is obviously the work of a composer who adored Brahms, for many of Brahms' recognizable traits as a composer—the warmth of his romanticism, the spacious melodies, the luxurious harmonic and contrapuntal language, the adherence to classic form—are found here. But though the speech emulates that of Brahms it still has personal accents of its own; and in this symphony classic form is combined with freedom of expression without sacrificing the feeling of spontaneity. Consequently, though this is the earliest of Enesco's symphonies, it is the one most frequently heard.

The symphony received its première in Paris on January 21, 1906, in a performance by the Colonne Orchestra. Its success, the composer has written, "awakened an interest among my colleagues in my abilities as a composer, as heretofore they had regarded me only as a fiddler....Ysaÿe wanted it immediately for Brussels, but I had already promised it to another conductor in London. That performance was so poor that...it took many years after this initial failure to achieve success in London. Since those early days, the symphony has been printed and performed throughout the world."

RUMANIAN RHAPSODIES NOS. 1 and 2, op. 11 (1907).

Though Enesco has written profounder and more original music than these two scintillating rhapsodies, none has equaled them in popular appeal. It is easy to understand why these rhapsodies are so famous. In their ever-changing moods, abundance of spirited and wistful folk melodies, and breath-taking utilization of folk-dance rhythms (principally those of the *hora* and *sirba*) these two works cast an almost irresistible spell. There is nothing subtle or elusive about their charm. They wear their effects on the surface for all to see at first glance.

The first *Rhapsody* (A major)—by far the more popular of the two—treats a varied assortment of folk melodies in variation form: the melodies are now boisterous and gay, now sensuous, now languorous, now nostalgic. The second *Rhapsody* (D major) is more melancholy. It is built around two principal melodies: the first opens the work and is heard in the strings; the second, tender and expressive, is played by the English horn.

Both rhapsodies were introduced in Paris on February 7, 1908, with the composer conducting the Pablo Casals Orchestra.

SUITE NO. 2 IN C MAJOR, for orchestra, op. 20 (1915). I. Overture. II. Saraband. III. Gigue. IV. Minuet. V. Air. VI. Bourrée.

The neo-classical bug which bit and infected so many contemporary composers did not pass by Enesco. He composed this Second Suite in an attempt to re-create in modern terms the classical dance suite of Bach; it is possible that Bach's third orchestral suite was Enesco's immediate model. Since this suite originated in 1915 it must be regarded as one of the earliest examples of neo-classicism.

The orchestral writing is modern throughout, but the rigid rhythmic pattern of the respective dances is respected. In spite of the frequent employment of present-day harmonic techniques, a classic spirit prevails and provides the work with much of its charm.

The suite opens with a robust Overture for full orchestra and piano. The stately dance of the Saraband follows (solo violin, flutes, horns). The strings then present the lively Gigue. The Minuet is first suggested by bassoons, celli, and bass, then finally presented by full orchestra. After the beautiful song of the fifth movement (first played by oboe, then taken up by flute and clarinet) the work ends with a vivacious Bourrée, the longest and most complex of the six movements, and the only one to suggest even faintly a folk character.

MANUEL DE FALLA   1876—1946

Falla wrote only a handful of compositions, for he was hypercritical of his efforts and was not easily satisfied. But each one is a masterpiece, fastidious in its workmanship, rich in poetic beauty, evocative of the colorful personality of Spain.

Like Albéniz before him, Falla was directed toward the expression of Spanish backgrounds and subjects through the utilization of techniques, methods, and styles of Spanish folk music by Felipe Pedrell, the *grand homme* of Spanish music. Already, Falla's first important work, *La Vida Breve,* derived its spirit and inspiration from Spanish folk music; and virtually everything he wrote thereafter was intimately concerned with the backgrounds, people, and folklore of his native land.

What Falla once said about national Spanish music in general provides an illuminating insight into Falla's own music in particular. "Our music must be based on the natural music of our people, on the dances and songs that do not always show close kinship. In some cases the rhythm alone is marked by clapping and drumsticks, without any melody; in others, the melody stands out by itself; so that no one should employ vocal melody alone as a manifestation of folk music, but everything that accompanies it or exists without it, never losing sight of the milieu wherein all this has its being.... It has occasionally been asserted that we have no traditions. We have, it is true, no written traditions; but in our dance and our rhythm we possess the strongest traditions that none can obliterate. We have the ancient modes which, by virtue of their extraordinary inherent freedom, we can use as inspiration dictates."

W. R. Anderson wisely pointed up in Falla's music the combination of "typically regional qualities of fancy and form" with the mysticism that evokes "the soul as well as the scenery of his land." Ancient Spanish ecclesiastical chants and modes and flamencan song may have been vital influences on Falla, but they were not reproduced by the composer but absorbed by him until their spirit was carried over in music that is essentially his own.

Falla was born in Cadiz, Spain, on November 23, 1876. After preliminary music study with his mother and local teachers, he went to the Madrid Conservatory, where he came under the influence of Felipe Pedrell. After completing his studies at the Conservatory (where he won highest honors in piano playing), he earned his living by composing light musical scores for the theaters (*zarzuelas*) and teaching the piano. But he also devoted time to serious composition. His first important work was *La Vida Breve,* which in 1905 won first prize in a competition among Spanish composers sponsored by the Academy of Fine Arts of Madrid.

In 1907, Falla went to Paris for a seven-week visit; but he remained seven years. He moved in a musical circle that included some of the great names in French music (Debussy, Dukas, Ravel, Fauré, Satie, Schmitt, Roussel). During this long stay in Paris he wrote little; he was too busy gathering impressions, absorbing musical experiences, and studying the forms and techniques of French music.

Just before he returned to his country, Falla witnessed successful performances of *La Vida Breve* in Nice and Paris. After that, it was introduced in Madrid, where its success was so instantaneous that the composer's reputation was at once established. For the next few years, Falla traveled throughout Spain, during which time he wrote two important works with which contemporary Spanish music can be said to have come of age: the ballet-pantomime, *El Amor Brujo,* in 1915, and the *Nights in the Gardens of Spain,* one year later.

In 1922, Falla settled in Granada, in the shadow of the Alhambra, where he lived in a retirement only infrequently interrupted by visits to European capitals to attend performances of his works. He detested publicity, avoided attention, refused to woo fame. His was the life of a recluse. He took solitary walks, attended church services, and always worked hard at composition.

Intensely religious, he was at first drawn sympathetically to Franco during the Spanish Civil War, feeling that in Franco's victory the antireligious tendencies of the then new democracy would be aborted. But disenchantment with the Franco regime set in after the war. Now ill, Falla expatriated himself. He lived the last five years of his life at Alta Garcia, in the province of Cordoba, Argentina. There he died on November 14, 1946.

The following works by Falla are discussed below: *El Amor Brujo;* Concerto for Harpsichord, Flute, Oboe, Clarinet, Violin, and Cello; *Nights in the Gardens of Spain; The Three-Cornered Hat; La Vida Breve.*

For *"Ritual Fire Dance,"* see *El Amor Brujo;* for "Spanish Dances Nos. 1 and 2," see *La Vida Breve.*

LA VIDA BREVE, opera (1905).

Falla's first important essay in the Spanish idiom, his opera *La Vida Breve,* has not survived in the repertory. But the two Spanish dances from this opera are among the composer's most popular compositions. Justifiably so! The very heart of Spanish song and dance is found in these two pieces: the poignancy and passion, the subtle and complex rhythms, the warm blood of oriental melody. The first Spanish dance is not only familiar in its original orchestral version, but also in the transcription for violin and piano by Fritz Kreisler. It has also been transcribed for two pianos.

La Vida Breve, written to the text of Carlos Fernandez Shaw, was at first refused a performance even though it had received first prize in a national competition sponsored by the Academy of Fine Arts of Madrid for an authentic Spanish work by a native composer. However, in 1913, the opera was introduced successfully at the Municipal Casino in Nice, and repeated a few months later at the Paris Opéra Comique. The warmth with which it was received by French audiences of both the north and the south encouraged a Spanish performance in Madrid in 1914, a performance that was so successful that overnight its composer became famous.

NIGHTS IN THE GARDENS OF SPAIN (NOCHES EN LOS JARDINES DE ESPAÑA), symphonic impressions for piano and orchestra (1915). I. In the Gardens of the Generalife. II. A Dance Is Heard in the Distance. III. In the Gardens of the Sierra de Cordoba.

"If these 'symphonic impressions' have achieved their object," said Falla of this work, "the mere enumeration of their titles should be a sufficient guide to the hearer. Although in this work—as in all which have a legitimate claim to be considered as music—the composer has followed a definite design regarding tonal, rhythmical, and thematic material... the end for which it was written is no other than to evoke places, sensations, and sentiments. The themes employed are based... on the rhythms, modes, cadences, and ornamental figures which distinguish the popular music of Andalucía, though they are rarely used in their original forms; and the orchestration frequently employs, and employs in a conventional manner, certain effects peculiar to the popular instruments used in those parts of Spain. The music has no pretensions to being descriptive; it is merely expressive. But something more than the sounds of festivals and dances has inspired these 'evocations in sound,' for melancholy and mystery have their part also."

These picturesque tone-portraits of Spanish gardens at night are not only among the most poetic works produced by Falla but, as Turina pointed out, among his saddest. "In the peculiar flavor of the orchestral sonority, one can in fact discern a feeling of bitterness, as if the composer had striven to express a drama of an intimate and passionate nature."

Since the composer has provided no specific program for his three nocturnal pictures, W. R. Anderson has admirably filled the gap with the following description: "We hear the first nocturne, 'In the Generalife'—the hill garden at Granada with its fountains and ancient cypresses contemplating the city below.... In the influence of the night, the fountains, dreamy patios, melancholy thickets and flowering pomegranates in the summer palace of the Moorish sultan, we can feel a sense of mystery and the ghosts of the past.... The hazy sound of the orchestral horn ceases, and we move in imagination to another garden, for the second nocturne, the 'Dance in the Distance.' About us again are the orange trees, the myrtles and the palms, the splashing waters. Mandolines and guitars play scraps of oriental-sounding tunes, coming nearer in the gentle wafts of tone now upborne, now falling, on the light breeze. In the last piece, we are 'In the Gardens of the Sierra de Cordoba,' on the mountainside, at a party where surely the gypsies are playing, singing, and dancing. Here is music wilder, rougher than before, still more deeply rooted in the East, in impassioned feeling and primitive power."

Nights in the Gardens of Spain was composed between 1909 and 1915, and was introduced in April, 1916, by the Orquesta Sinfónica of Madrid with Fernandez Arbós conducting and M. Cubiles as piano soloist.

EL AMOR BRUJO (LOVE, THE MAGICIAN), ballet-pantomime (1915).

El Amor Brujo (which the composer subtitled *Gitanería,* or *Gypsy Life*) is based on a play by Gregorio Martinez Sierra, which, in turn, was derived from an old Andalusian gypsy folk-tale.

Candela, a sensuous gypsy, falls in love with Carmelo after the death of her husband. The love affair is troubled by the husband's ghost, which comes to haunt the pair. In despair, Candela decides on a happy solution. Knowing that her husband, while alive, was unable to resist the wiles of a beautiful gypsy, she calls on her friend Lucía to flirt with the ghost. Candela's husband succumbs to Lucía's beauty, leaving the lovers free, at last, to devote themselves to each other.

It was the Spanish dancer, Pastora Impervio, who suggested to Falla that he compose music for a ballet-pantomime in which Impervio could sing as well as dance; and it was Impervio's mother who related the old Andalusian tale to Sierra. When the ballet was first introduced at Teatro de Lara in Madrid on April 15, 1915, the following note was published in explanation: "The composer, whose feeling for and command of his country's folk music are well known, saw that it would be impossible to write true gypsy music by restricting himself to instrumental dances alone, and without resorting to the gypsies' most characteristic feature: their songs. But he has by no means used actual melodies. Every song is of his own invention, and it is his particular glory that he has succeeded in making it almost impossible to believe that the songs are not actual popular material."

The first performance was only moderately successful. One year later, Fernández Arbós directed the première of a suite (for contralto and orchestra) which included the major sections of the ballet score. The suite was acclaimed; and it has since become one of the most popular works in the contemporary symphonic repertoire.

This suite comprises twelve numbers: I. Introduction and Scene. II. The Gypsies—Evening. III. Scene of Sorrowing Love (with voice). IV. The Homecomer. V. Dance of Terror. VI. The Magic Circle. VII. Ritual Fire

Dance. VIII. Scene. IX. Song of the Will-o'-the-Wisp (with voice). X. Pantomime. XI. Dance of the Game of Love (with voice). XII. Morning Chimes. The voice is sung backstage; it is an occasional practice of some conductors to dispense with the voice and to substitute a wind instrument, preferably the horn.

The "Ritual Fire Dance" is the most famous single number of the suite. It is also one of the most celebrated pieces by Falla, and one of the most representative works of the contemporary Spanish school. It is familiar not only in its original orchestral version, but also in transcriptions for the piano and for two pianos.

THE THREE-CORNERED HAT (EL SOMBRERO DE TRES PICOS), ballet (1919).

On a visit to Falla in Granada, Serge Diaghilev listened to parts of a score which Falla had written for a "pantomime." Its text, by Martinez Sierra, was based on a novel by Antonio de Alarcón entitled *The Three-Cornered Hat*. Diaghilev's talent for sensing a potential masterpiece did not betray him now. He recognized the potentialities for a Spanish ballet which would synthesize all Spanish folk arts and which would provide a novel and significant addition to his repertory; and he commissioned Falla to develop and enlarge his score for that purpose.

The first performance of Falla's ballet, which took place in London on July 22, 1919, was extraordinarily successful. Besides Falla's music, which evoked a new world of mystery and magic for London's ballet enthusiasts, there were Pablo Picasso's imaginative scenery and costumes (some of them based on paintings of Goya), Leonide Massine's choreography, and the dancing of Massine and Karsavina to create an artistic conception of striking originality, beauty, passion, exotic charm, and even wry humor.

At that première performance, the following synopsis of the scenario was published: "Over the whole brisk action is the spirit of a frivolous comedy of a kind by no means common only to Spain of the eighteenth century. A young miller and his wife are the protagonists, and if their existence be idyllic in theory, it is extraordinarily strenuous in practice—choreographically.... The miller and his wife between them, however, would hardly suffice even for a slender ballet plot. So we have as well an amorous Corregidor, or Governor (he wears a three-cornered hat as badge of office), who orders the miller's arrest so that the way may be cleared for a pleasant little flirtation—if nothing more serious—with the captivating wife. Behold the latter fooling him with a seductive dance, and then evading her admirer with such agility that, in his pursuit of her, he tumbles over a bridge into the mill-stream. But, as this is comedy and no melodrama, the would-be-lover experiences nothing worse than a wetting, and the laugh, which is turned against him, is renewed when, having taken off some of his clothes to dry them, and gone to rest on the miller's bed, his presence is discovered by the miller himself, who, in revenge, goes off in the intruder's garments after scratching a message on the wall to the effect that 'Your wife is no less beautiful than mine!' Thereafter, a 'gallimaufry of gambols' and—curtain!"

This amusing text had also been utilized by Hugo Wolf, for his opera *Der Corregidor,* composed in 1895.

An orchestral suite from this ballet score, comprising three major dances, is frequently heard at symphony concerts. The three dances are: I. The Neighbors. II. The Miller's Dance. III. Final Dance. The second dance is perhaps the best of the three, successfully combining Andalusian rhythms with an ornamental Moorish melody. The final dance is a jota.

CONCERTO FOR HARPSICHORD, FLUTE, OBOE, CLARI-NET, VIOLIN, AND CELLO. I. Allegro. II. Lento. III. Finale: vivace (1926).

During a visit to Falla in Granada, the celebrated harpsichordist Wanda Landowska discussed with the composer the artistic possibilities of her instrument. Actually, Falla had been sufficiently interested in the harpsichord to incorporate it into the orchestration of his *Retablo,* on which he was then at work. But Landowska now intensified his enthusiasm to a point where he decided he would write a major work for it. He spoke of a concerto, and he promised Landowska that she would give the première performance.

As always with Falla, composition went slowly: the concerto took him three years. When it was completed, it did not prove to be a virtuoso work glorifying any one instrument, but a chamber-music work in which six instruments had equal importance.

Wanda Landowska introduced the concerto in Barcelona in November, 1926, with Pablo Casals conducting the Casals Orchestra.

Gilbert Chase, the eminent authority on Spanish music in general and Falla's music in particular, considers this concerto Falla's masterpiece, the one in which the "eternal essence" of Spain has been most completely embodied. The Spanish characteristics of this work are readily recognizable. In the first movement, the harpsichord suggests the subtle guitar perform-ances of Spanish gypsies, weaving an intoxicating rhythmic background to melodies richly evocative of folk music. The second movement describes a religious processional, with plain songs providing some of the melodic material. "In this movement," wrote Ralph Kirkpatrick, "are all of Spain, the harsh bitter fervor, the restraint of ceremony, the intellectual esctasy that are the inseparable constituents of the Spanish character." Spanish dance rhythms give the final movement of the concerto an engaging vitality.

GABRIEL FAURÉ   1845—1924

The delicacy and refinement of Fauré's style, his classic restraint and tendency toward understatement, his purity of expression, his fastidious attention to detail, and his exquisite workmanship—all these qualities betray the nationality of the composer. Indeed, so French is Fauré's art that it is sometimes said that only a Frenchman can properly appreciate it. His is an intimate art which does not wear its heart on its sleeve. In his music, modern technique is beautifully blended with the classic spirit of ancient Greece (twenty years before Debussy, he wrote impressionistically, while the harmonic language of his later works is an independent one). As Julien Tiersot once said of Fauré, "It is the spirit of Hellenism, as well as its forms, which is reborn in him."

Fauré was born in Pamiers, Ariège, on May 13, 1845. His music study took place at the École Niedermeyer in Paris. He began his professional career in music as an organist for various churches, including the St. Sulpice and the Madeleine in Paris. Then he turned to teaching, first becoming professor of composition at the École Niedermeyer, after that holding a similar post at the Paris Conservatory, and finally, in 1905, succeeding Dubois as the director of the Conservatory. An entire generation of French musicians studied under him and were influenced by him, including Maurice Ravel, Florent Schmitt, Roger-Ducasse, and Nadia Boulanger.

He first emerged as a composer with a group of songs published in 1865, in which there could already be discerned the qualities that were soon to make him one of the greatest exponents of the French art song. The best of these included *Après un Rêve, Sylvie, En Prière, Les Roses d'Ispahan, Au Cimetière, Soir,* and *Prison.*

Fauré's first major work in a large form was his monumental Requiem —up to this day one of his unquestioned masterpieces. He composed it in 1887 and introduced it at the Madeleine one year later. It is one of the noblest and most moving works in all French music—gentle, tender, contemplative. Other notable works include the beautiful Sonata in A Major, for violin and piano, op. 13 (1876), in which the style of César Franck is foreshadowed and the Quartet in C Minor, for piano and strings, op. 15 (1879). Fauré also produced several significant works for orchestra, the most successful of which were the *Ballade,* for piano and orchestra, op. 19 (1881), and the incidental music for *Pelléas et Mélisande,* op. 80 (1898).

In 1909, Fauré was elected to the Académie des Beaux-Arts, and thirteen years later, the object of national tributes, he was promoted to the highest class in the order of the Legion of Honor. During the closing years of his life, Fauré suffered from deafness, which compelled him to resign his directorship of the Conservatory in 1920. He died in Paris on November 4, 1924.

The following works by Fauré are discussed below: *La Chanson d'Ève; L'Horizon Chimerique;* Nocturnes (Nos. 9-13); Préludes; Quartet in E Minor; Quintet No. 2.

For Requiem, see the biographical sketch above.

NOCTURNES (Nos. 9-13), for piano, opp. 97, 99, 104, 107, 119.

In his earliest piano works (he composed his first three nocturnes, op. 33, in 1883), Fauré was strongly influenced by the style and stylistic mannerisms of Chopin and Schumann. Perhaps this was inevitable. But it was not long before he evolved his own style. The Nocturnes nos. 9 through 13 are among his finest creations for the piano. These are not gentle pieces of the night—as the nocturne frequently was with John Field and Chopin—but lugubrious music filled with despair and gloom. The ninth Nocturne (B minor) is restless and febrile; this atmosphere is created by the unusual modulations. The eleventh Nocturne (F-sharp minor) is a funeral elegy inspired by the death of Pierre Lalo's young wife. The thirteenth Nocturne (B minor)—Fauré's farewell to the piano—is one of the most eloquently tragic pieces of music he ever put to paper.

LA CHANSON D'ÈVE, song cycle for voice and piano, op. 95 (1910). I. Paradise. II. Prima Verba. III. Roses Ardentes. IV. Comme Dieu Rayonne. V. L'Aube Blanche. VI. Eau Vivante. VII. Veilles-tu Ma Senteur de Soleil? VIII. Dans un Parfum de Roses Blanches. IX. Crépuscule. X. O Mort, Poussière d'Étoiles.

It is indeed appropriate that the first published work of one destined to become France's greatest living master of the art song should have been a set of songs. Few composers of our time—few composers of any time, for that matter—have equaled Fauré's fresh and tender melodic vein, refinement of style, sensitivity to the poetic text, and gift for translating the subtlest atmospheres or feelings into tones. His more than one hundred songs are among his greatest achievements, and are among the most treasured items in the repertoire of French music.

In the songs written in the closing two decades of his life, Fauré had a simpler and more individual approach to both melody and harmony. His means are more economical; his harmonic language subtler and more suggestive. There is not a wasted phrase or a misspent note.

The best of his later songs are found in song cycles. *La Chanson d'Ève* is a setting of ten pantheistic poems by Charles van Lerberghe. In these

poems, young Eve looks around the newly created world and interprets what
she sees. The poems are vivid in their imagery and touched with mysticism;
and to these poems Fauré always brought the musical *mot juste*. The cycle
is prefaced by a five-bar motto phrase in the piano which resembles a plain
chant, and which, so to speak, sets the stage for the cycle and creates the
mood. The songs are delicate in feeling and fragile in construction.

PRÉLUDES, for piano, op. 103 (1911).

One French critic (who is anonymous) spoke of these preludes as the
"purest and strongest music" written by Fauré. The preludes have a single-
ness of mood and a unity of form; the melodic ideas do not come fully
developed, but are allowed to grow out of germinal ideas.

The finest of these nine preludes are the first (D-flat major), which
has a wonderful serenity; the second (C-sharp minor), with its exotic atmosphere produced by the whole-tone scale; the fifth (D minor), which is in a
stormy mood; and the exquisite sixth (E-flat minor), considered by Aaron
Copland to be comparable to any one of the preludes in Bach's *Well-
Tempered Clavier*.

QUINTET NO. 2, for piano and strings, op. 115 (1921). I. Allegro
moderato. II. Allegro vivo. III. Andante moderato. IV. Finale: allegro molto.

Fauré composed his first piano quintet, in the key of C minor, in 1906.
Koechlin described it as "the first classic work of our times." Even more
successful, and a much more integrated masterpiece, is the second quintet
which came fifteen years later.

The first movement opens with a single bar for the piano, after which
the viola enters with a fragment of the first principal theme. One by one the
strings enter, until the theme is completely and fully realized. Sharp and
agitated chords make up the second principal idea of the movement. The
Scherzo, which follows, is in one of Fauré's vivacious moods: the touch is
light; the movement, mercurial. Music of great emotional stress is found in
the slow movement. A four-bar theme, speaking of unfathomable grief, is
brought up by the strings. A dialogue of exquisite tenderness then takes
place between violin and piano, after which a second melody—no less
melancholy than the first—is heard in the piano. The sadness is completely
dissipated in the agitation and rhythmic force of the last movement.

L'HORIZON CHIMÉRIQUE, song cycle for voice and piano, op.
113 (1922). I. La Mer est Infinie. II. Je Me Suis Embarqué. III. Diane, Séléné.
IV. Vaisseaux, Nous Vous Aurons Aimés.

Fauré's last work for voice and piano was based on four poems written
by Jean de la Ville de Mirmont (a young poet killed in World War I). These
poems use the sea as a symbol of the undiscovered. To the seventy-seven-year-

old composer in the shadow of death, the sea becomes a symbol of the great Beyond. The songs are filled with a quiet and dignified pathos.

QUARTET IN E MINOR, for strings, op. 121 (1923). I. Allegro moderato. II. Andante. III. Allegro.

Fauré's last composition for a chamber-music ensemble, his only string quartet, is often compared to the last quartets of Beethoven. Fauré's work, like that of Beethoven's last period, is rich in spiritual content. As in Beethoven, the expressiveness of the melodic ideas transcends the music itself and seems to speak of mystic and philosophic concepts. One other point of resemblance is important. Both composers were completely deaf when they wrote these works, and, in their isolation from the world of actual musical sound, were led to employ unusual progressions, modulations, and thematic sequences.

However, in Fauré—as is not often the case in the later Beethoven— the concentration of writing is so great that the music is stripped down to essentials. There is no diffuseness; no superfluity. Every line, every phrase, has its calculated mission; each is indispensable to the design of the whole.

The greatest of the three movements (and here, once again, we are reminded of Beethoven) is the slow one. This is music of quiet and gentle melancholy, music of autumnal moods—the introspection of a mature man who knows he has not much longer to live. Fauré's poetic speech here rises to a plane of eloquence rarely realized even by him. What Julien Tiersot said of Fauré in general applies most strongly to music such as this: "He ... thrusts himself beyond the spheres in order to bring back pure beauty."

ARTHUR FOOTE   1853—1937

The New England school of composers, which included George Chadwick, Frederick Converse, Henry Gilbert, Horatio Parker, and Arthur Foote, was a conservative group which never outgrew the traditions of its teachers. These composers believed in using the sound forms of classical and romantic music and filling them with robust melodies, attractive harmonies, and the accepted contrapuntal techniques of the textbook.

Although Foote lived into the fourth decade of the twentieth century and saw composers everywhere shattering long-accepted rules and evolving new styles, he kept on producing the kind of music he had written in the closing years of the nineteenth century. For Foote, major innovations in musical style ended with Wagner and Brahms. Maturity and experience, of course, brought to his music enrichment of speech and refinement of writing, but did not alter its essential character, which remained romantic and direct in its appeal, academic and skilled in its technique, and always filled with ingratiating ideas stated simply and pleasingly.

Foote was born in Salem, Massachusetts, on March 5, 1853. He took music courses at Harvard University, but serious music study did not begin for him until after he had graduated from that institution in 1874. His teachers now included B. J. Lang and John Knowles Paine. He received his Master of Arts degree in 1875 and his doctorate in music in 1919.

For thirty-two years, beginning in 1878, Foote was organist of the First Unitarian Church in Boston. During this period he achieved full recognition as a composer. In 1886, the Boston Symphony Orchestra successfully introduced his Suite in E Major, the first of many important orchestral works of his which the Boston Symphony was to introduce over the years. To celebrate Foote's eightieth birthday in 1933, the Boston Symphony performed *A Night Piece*. Foote died in Boston on April 8, 1937.

The following works by Foote are discussed below: *A Night Piece;* Suite in E Major.

SUITE IN E MAJOR, for string orchestra, op. 63 (1907). I. Prelude. II. Pizzicato. III. Fugue.

This is one of Foote's best-known works. It was introduced by the Boston Symphony Orchestra under Max Fiedler on April 16, 1909.

The short Prelude which opens the suite is built on a phrase of eight notes heard at the outset. The plucking of the strings in the Pizzicato is only briefly interrupted by a melody for muted strings (Adagietto) played with the bow. The suite ends with a conventional fugue, the first four notes of whose theme are often heard by themselves before the projection of the fugue.

A NIGHT PIECE, for flute and string quartet (1918).

Foote wrote few works so pure in their musical expression, so completely deriving their effect from beauty of sound, as this nocturne. Marked *Andante liquido,* this piece is music diaphanous in harmonic texture, tender in melody, touched with the most delicate tone colors. Philip Hale wrote that the listener "is not conscious of anything but charming sounds skillfully and logically succeeding each other, so that there is a thing of beauty."

This composition originated as a chamber-music work in 1918, in which form it was introduced by the San Francisco Chamber Society on January 28, 1919. Pierre Monteux asked the composer to adapt the music for flute and string orchestra. In the new version, the work was introduced by the Boston Symphony Orchestra under Monteux on April 13, 1923.

LUKAS FOSS   1922—

As a young student in Paris, Lukas Foss—then only in his early teens —wrote music in the style of Hindemith. Less than a half-dozen years later he became Hindemith's pupil—only to find his musical thinking turning sharply from Hindemith's neo-classicism to a more romantic and emotional expression. Hindemith himself had nothing whatsoever to do with this change (to this day Foss admires that composer profoundly); what took place was just the natural evolution of a young composer who always wrote as he felt.

In his more recent works there may occasionally be found certain procedures which owe their origin to the contrapuntal techniques of the seventeenth century (particularly in the two Biblical cantatas, *The Song of Anguish* and *The Song of Songs*). But in spite of this, neo-classicism belongs with Foss's past performances. Today his style is melodic and harmonic rather than contrapuntal. "Dramatic power," wrote his friend Robert Strassburg, "is matched by lyric warmth and spaciousness of concept." There can be found humanity in his music, and deeply personal sentiments, in forms that are precise and clear and usually in richly colored orchestral dress.

Foss was born in Berlin on August 15, 1922, and began the study of music early. In his eleventh year, he went to Paris for further study, and, in 1937, came to this country to establish his home permanently. He completed his music study here at the Curtis Institute of Music (with Scalero, Reiner, and Vengerova) and with Paul Hindemith. In 1942, his incidental music to Shakespeare's *Tempest* won him the Pulitzer Traveling Scholarship (he was the youngest musician ever to win this honor). Three years after that, he received a Guggenheim Fellowship; once again he was the youngest musician ever to get this award. Meanwhile, several of his works received major performances in New York and Philadelphia, climaxed by the success of his cantata *The Prairie*.

Besides composing, Foss has been active as pianist, having appeared as soloist with many major American orchestras. For several years he was staff pianist of the Boston Symphony Orchestra, resigning in 1950. Since 1953 he has been professor of composition at the University of California in Los Angeles.

The following works by Foss are discussed below: *The Prairie; The Song of Anguish; The Song of Songs.*

THE PRAIRIE, cantata for solo voices, chorus, and orchestra (1943).

In the summer of 1941—four years after coming to this country—Foss conducted a performance of Copland's Suite from *Billy the Kid.* Copland's use of cowboy melodies, and the apt way in which the music interpreted America, intrigued Foss. The young man now felt the impulse to write a work of his own dedicated to and inspired by the land of his adoption. The reading of Carl Sandburg's poem *The Prairie* provided the necessary stimulus. The reflection of the soil and spirit of America in Sandburg's poem— with the prairie, as Foss puts it, as a "symbol for the all-embracing principle of *growth* itself"—called for music. Foss set to work on a large cantata in 1943. On October 15 of that year, an orchestral suite from the score was introduced by the Boston Symphony under Koussevitzky. On May 15, 1944, the entire cantata was heard for the first time in New York City, performed by the Collegiate Chorale under Robert Shaw. It was selected by the New York Music Critics Circle as the best new American work of the season.

Spacious in its design, with broad, wind-swept melodies and sweeping sonorities suggestive of "vast open landscapes and lots of fresh air," *The Prairie* is American music without once quoting or even simulating American folk music.

Foss's description of the work follows:

"The opening movement, which has the nature of a prologue, speaks of the prairie, as we are accustomed to visualize it. The author, in a pastoral tenor solo, sings of open valleys and far horizons, and the music breathes fresh air. After this pastoral introduction, a fugue is heard in the orchestra, above which the chorus takes up a new theme in the manner of a chorale. This is the voice of the prairie. . . . As a complete contrast, a folk-like movement follows, but the melodies remain original throughout the work. . . . With the re-entry of the chorus, the prairie becomes 'mother of men, waiting.' Then the author reaches far back into the past and we see the cities rising on the prairie, out of the prairie, while the chorus chants of the years when the red and white men met. . . . In rugged . . . rhythms follows what may be styled the industrial section, ending with a fugue for male voices. . . . A lyrical intermezzo brings us back to the prairie. This consists of a short a cappella chorus, a soprano song, and a scherzando duet . . . held together by a dreamy little shepherd's lay, a nostalgic woodwind refrain of the prairie. The tenor's voice introduces the seventh and last section, and everyone joins in the final hymn to the future, expressing the healthy and sunny optimism unique to this country."

THE SONG OF ANGUISH, cantata for baritone and orchestra (1945).

Foss wrote two biblical cantatas, the first being *The Song of Anguish,* on a text from Isaiah. This cantata was completed in 1945 on a commission from the Kulas Foundation in Cleveland. But the first performance took place, not in Cleveland, but in Boston, with Foss himself conducting the Boston Symphony Orchestra on March 10, 1950. Marko Rothmüller was the assisting artist.

A long orchestral prelude (Andante sostenuto; Allegro) sets the mood of the music, which fluctuates from the poetic to the dramatic, from the elegiac to the passionate, following the demands of the text.

The passages from Isaiah open with the following lines:

Woe unto them that call evil good and good evil,
That put darkness for light and light for darkness,
Woe unto them that are wise in their own eyes
That are prudent in their own sight.
Woe—Woe—Woe.

THE SONG OF SONGS, cantata for soprano and ochestra (1946). I. Awake, O North Wind. II. Come, My Beloved, Let Us Go Forth Into the Field. III. By Night on My Bed. IV. Set Me as a Seal upon Thine Heart.

Foss's second biblical cantata, drawing its text from the Song of Solomon, was commissioned by the League of Composers for the Negro sopano Ellabelle Davis. Completed in the summer of 1946, it was introduced by Ellabelle Davis and the Boston Symphony Orchestra, Serge Koussevitzky conducting, on March 7, 1947. Koussevitzky's enthusiasm for this new work was so great that he broke all precedent by performing it eight times in nine days: twice in Boston, twice in New York City, and once each in Philadelphia, Brooklyn, New Haven, and Northhampton, Massachusetts.

The music—sensual in style and containing many pages of great emotional intensity—has caught the essence of the text. It is at turns joyous and tragic, ecstatic and religious, delicately sweet and acrid. The opening section, intended as an introduction to the whole work, opens with a free fugue before the entrance of the voice. The second part is a broad and elastic melody—a *da capo* aria. The third part, in contrast, is a recitative, intermittently interrupted by orchestral interludes. The concluding movement, which follows the third section without a pause, is in the nature of a prayer.

JEAN FRANÇAIX   1912—

In his music, Françaix is as Gallic as his name. Lightness of touch, effervescence of spirit, irony that sometimes approaches malice, briskness of movement—the vein so many French composers adopt with such skill—are found in all of Françaix's major works. He has been greatly influenced by the neo-classic manner of Stravinsky, to a point where slender form, conciseness, brevity, simplicity, and clarity of writing become almost a fetish. But there is enough acidity in the harmony and robustness in the rhythm to give his music contemporary spice. Profundity of thinking and deeply felt emotions are not to be found in his works—and for these reasons, perhaps, Françaix has never quite lived up to the brilliant promises that his remarkable technique and freshness of style gave in the 1930's. But if his music is rather slight in its esthetic intentions, it nevertheless has a bright-faced sparkle and elegant manner that are captivating.

Françaix was born in Le Mans on May 23, 1912, the son of the director of the Le Mans Conservatory. He began composing early—a piano suite written when he was nine was published by Maison Senart. He was first a pupil in his father's class at Le Mans, then a private student of Nadia Boulanger, and after that was enrolled at the Paris Conservatory. He won numerous prizes. *Eight Bagatelles,* for string quartet and piano, played at the International Society for Contemporary Music Festival in Vienna on June 21, 1932, gave strong evidence of his rapidly developing creative talent. On November 6 of the same year, the Orchestre Symphonique de Paris under Pierre Monteux introduced his Symphony. Thereafter, Françaix was frequently represented on major concert programs, and was often referred to as the "white hope" of French music. He visited the United States in 1938.

The following works by Françaix are discussed below: *L'Apostrophe;* Concertino for Piano and Orchestra; Concerto for Piano and Orchestra.

CONCERTINO FOR PIANO AND ORCHESTRA (1934). I. Presto leggiero. II. Lent. III. Allegretto. IV. Rondo: allegretto vivo.

The neo-classicist's ideal—music reduced to its very essentials—is realized successfully in this early and ingratiating work. The simplicity and directness of this music almost approaches the ingenuous. The solo piano presents a brief headstrong theme in the first movement, which is immediately taken up by the orchestra. This theme is the spine of the entire movement, which is light and capricious throughout. The second movement is only thirty bars long. Against a hauntingly tender background of strings, the piano presents a nostalgic melody. The trumpet injects a rakish and jazzy melody in the Allegretto that follows—to be answered soberly by the piano; but the mood throughout is carefree and abandoned. The last movement is the gayest of the four, effervescent in its good spirits.

The Concertino was introduced on December 15, 1934, by the Lamoureux Orchestra under Jean Morel, with the composer at the piano.

CONCERTO FOR PIANO AND ORCHESTRA (1936). I. Allegro. II. Andante. III. Scherzo. IV. Allegro.

The usual spacious dimensions and bigness of style found in concerto music are not to be encountered in this work. The texture is thin; the design fragile. There is no development of thematic material to speak of.

There are four little themes in the first movement, which is rhythmic and sprightly. A pensive note is injected in the Andante, the piano presenting a tender melody out of which the entire section is built. The mercurial Scherzo has three basic ideas, each introduced by the piano before being taken over by the orchestra. The vertiginous finale exploits four ideas with brilliant effect, as the healthy animal spirits of the composer are allowed full freedom of movement and expression.

This concerto (with which, incidentally, Françaix made his American debut in 1938) was first heard in Berlin on November 8, 1936, the composer as soloist.

L'APOSTROPHE, comic opera (1950).

The gaiety and mockery of Françaix's style lends itself naturally to the requirements of comic opera. The text of L'Apostrophe was derived from one of Balzac's Droll Tales, and concerns the futile love of the hunchback Darandas for the lovely and coquettish Tascherette, a love that brings him doom at the hands of Tascherette's husband.

The opera was introduced at the Holland Music Festival in Amsterdam on July 1, 1951. Reviewing the work, a correspondent for the New York Times described the score as follows: "The music is the essence of theatricalism ... with an utter lack of inhibition in rhythm, melody, and orchestration. ... The score is more ingenious than important, but since Françaix is attempting no more than a broad satire, the result is completely effective—so much so that even the non-French speaking section of the audience often was lured into laughter solely by the caprices of the score."

GEORGE GERSHWIN 1898—1937

It is mainly since Gershwin's death that complete awareness of his musical importance has become almost universal. The little defects in his major works—those occasional awkward modulations, the strained transitions, the obscure instrumentation—no longer appear quite so important as they did several decades ago. What many did not realize then—and what they now know—is that the intrinsically vital qualities of Gershwin's works reduce these technical flaws to insignificance. The music is so alive, so freshly conceived, and put down on paper with such spontaneity and enthusiasm that its youthful spirit refuses to age. The capacity of this music to enchant and magnetize audiences remains as great today, even with familiarity, as it was yesterday, when it came upon us with the freshness of novelty.

Gershwin lacked the technical adroitness and the *savoir-faire* that come with a conservatory education. What he did have—and what no conservatory can teach—was an infallible musical instinct.

That he had a wonderful reservoir of melodies was, of course, self-evident when Gershwin was alive. What was not quite so obvious then was that he had impressed his identity on those melodies—his way of shaping a lyric line, his use of certain rhythmic phrases, the piquant effect of some of his accompaniments—so that they would always remain recognizably his. His best songs sound as fresh today as they did when first written. Their piquancy, wistfulness, charm, and tenderness have not been dissipated by time. And those lyric outbursts in his larger works—the fabulous middle section of the *Rhapsody in Blue,* the slow movement of the Concerto in F, the best songs of *Porgy and Bess*—are the creations of a born melodist.

Beyond the fact that he produced several works that are among the treasured contributions to present-day music in America, Gershwin's significance lies in his influence on contemporary musical writing. When Gershwin came upon the musical scene, our popular music was a rather disreputable idiom, even though several major composers like Debussy, Satie, Stravinsky, and Milhaud had experimented with it. It was Gershwin, however, more than any other single composer who brought artistic respectability to it. He set the example which encouraged composers throughout the world to emulate him. Krenek, Weill, Lambert, Walton, Copland, Gould—to mention just a few—owe a considerable debt to Gershwin which they readily conceded.

Gershwin was born in Brooklyn on September 25, 1898. He was by no means a prodigy, and his musical education was spasmodic. He took lessons at the piano (his first important teacher being Charles Hambitzer), and later studied harmony briefly with Rubin Goldmark. In his teens, he acquired a job as song plugger at Remick's, one of Tin Pan Alley's largest publishing houses. Before long he was writing songs of his own; and, in 1919, he was the proud parent of a "hit" that swept the country, *Swanee*. In 1920, he began writing the music for George White's *Scandals;* thereafter his rise as one of the most successful composers for the Broadway stage was rapid. In 1924, he composed his first serious work in the jazz idiom, the historic *Rhapsody in Blue,* the success of which made Gershwin famous throughout the world of music. After that, he divided his activities between writing popular music for the Broadway stage (and later for the Hollywood cinema) and serious works for concert-hall consumption. In both fields, he was extraordinarily successful and popular. He died in Hollywood on July 11, 1937, after an unsuccessful operation on the brain. In 1945, the story of his life was told in the motion picture, *Rhapsody in Blue*.

The following works by Gershwin are discussed below: *An American in Paris;* Concerto in F for Piano and Orchestra; *Porgy and Bess;* Three Preludes for Piano; *Rhapsody in Blue*.

RHAPSODY IN BLUE, for piano and orchestra (1924).

Paul Whiteman asked Gershwin to write a large work in the jazz idiom for a concert of popular music he was planning to give at Aeolian Hall in New York on February 12, 1924. The work Gershwin finally wrote (and which Ferde Grofé orchestrated for him) was the *Rhapsody in Blue,* which not only proved to be the tour de force of Whiteman's concert—the work that gave point and significance to Whiteman's experiment—but was also the turning point in Gershwin's career. It made him world-famous and rich. Royalties from the sale of sheet music and records, and from public performances on stage and screen, were astronomical. It was heard in every possible arrangement, even adapted into a ballet, and prepared for a tap dance. Its principal theme became Paul Whiteman's identifying signature on the radio. Its name provided the title for Gershwin's later screen biography. Perhaps no other work in musical history enjoyed such a fabulous success in so short a period.

But the *Rhapsody* accomplished even more than making Gershwin rich and famous. By "making a lady out of jazz," it set into motion an entire new trend in modern music. Composers in many different parts of the world were encouraged by it to write serious works in the jazz idiom, often with great artistic success.

The *Rhapsody in Blue,* besides being very good music, has the additional strength of being very good *American* music. Few works written by Americans before 1924 have such an unmistakable national identity as this one. It is American to its very core, just as rodeos, baseball, and tabloids are American. The nervousness, energy, youth, optimism, strength, and infectious charm of this country are caught in its infectious rhythms. The color and background of America are reflected in its harmonies. The *Rhapsody* is music about an age of steel and speed; it is the voice of the great modern metropolis. Surely future historians will come to know what we were during the fabulous era of the 1920's by listening to the *Rhapsody,* just as today we know what Vienna was a century ago by hearing the waltzes of Lanner and Johann Strauss, and what France of the Second Empire was by listening to the *opéra comique* of Offenbach.

CONCERTO IN F, FOR PIANO AND ORCHESTRA (1925).
I. Allegro. II. Andante con moto. III. Allegro con brio.

The tremendous success of the *Rhapsody in Blue* in 1924 brought Gershwin a major commission: to write a concerto for piano and orchestra for Walter Damrosch and the New York Symphony Society. Gershwin knew so little about the concerto form that before beginning work he had to buy a textbook to guide him. He planned to write a work more ambitious in form and scope than his *Rhapsody;* besides he intended to orchestrate it himself, instead of relying on Ferde Grofé, as had been the case with the *Rhapsody.*

The première of the concerto took place in New York on December 3, 1925, with the composer playing the piano part and Damrosch conducting the orchestra. The work met a mixed reaction. Samuel Chotzinoff used the word "genius" without reservation; but other critics felt that too much of the concerto was derivative (from Debussy, for the most part), and too much of it was marred by technical flaws.

Since that first performance, the concerto has grown in popularity, and today it is one of Gershwin's best-loved works. Several years after it had been introduced, Albert Coates—the eminent English conductor—included it as the only American composition in a list of fifty of the most important musical works of our generation.

A Charleston motive appears in the introduction of the first movement, after which the bassoon presents the first major theme. This is developed. A second theme, more lyrical than the first, is introduced by the solo piano. The major part of the movement is devoted to discussing these two ideas. A brief coda, in which the rhythmic fragment of the introduction returns, brings the movement to a close. The second movement is poetic music, bringing up a moody subject for muted trumpet, followed by a sprightlier secondary theme for piano. After a development, a new melody comes forth, first in the strings and woodwinds, then in the piano, finally in the full orchestra. After an impressive climax, the first theme returns, and the movement ends in an atmosphere of questioning and mystery. In the final movement Gershwin unleashes his rhythms and sprightliest jazz themes, then throws a reminiscent glance toward his first movement by repeating its second theme. A new idea for muted trumpet and strings is imposed. After some development, a fugato passage—based on the second theme of the finale—comes as a kind of summation. After the return of the main theme the movement ends with a brief but effective coda.

THREE PRELUDES FOR PIANO (1926).

Gershwin's only work for solo piano, the Three Preludes—represents three moods in jazz. The first (B-flat major) is an excursion in uninhibited adandon, and the third (E-flat major) is a fleeting expression of pure joy; in both of these preludes the rhythmic element predominates strongly. Between these two preludes is found one of the loveliest pages of music Gershwin ever wrote, and one of the most poignant (in C-sharp minor). Against a provocative harmonic background rises a three-part blues song of extraordinary tenderness and beauty, growing in expressiveness as the harmony grows richer and more piquant. This prelude has achieved considerable popularity not only in its original piano version, but also in transcriptions for orchestra, and in an arrangement for violin and piano effectively performed by Jascha Heifetz.

AN AMERICAN IN PARIS, tone-poem for orchestra (1928).

In the spring of 1928 Gershwin escaped from his many business and social commitments in this country for a European vacation. He hoped to devote himself to serious music study. He never did get around to studying, but he did succeed in writing a major work for orchestra. The exhilaration and intoxication of being in Paris inspired him to re-create these moods in his music, together with the inevitable feeling of homesickness which every American inevitably experiences. Gershwin completed his sketches in Paris, began his orchestration in Vienna, then completed the entire work on a return visit to Paris. On December 13, 1928, it was introduced in New York by the New York Philharmonic-Symphony Orchestra, Walter Damrosch conducting.

A brisk and energetic theme for strings at the opening of the composition suggests the light-footed pace of the American walking through the Parisian streets. The noise of taxicab horns (the score calls for four actual taxi horns) assails his ears. A brief theme in the trombone suggests a music hall which the American passes. A second walking theme is then heard in the clarinet. After some development of both walking themes, a solo violin introduces a brief melody—it is a young lady who is approaching our American. But for all his exhilaration, our American cannot suppress a measure of homesickness. A plangent blues song—the principal melodic idea of the entire work—unfolds. The walking themes and the blues return, and then a vigorous finale proclaims the fact that while it will be good to be home again, it is even better to be in Paris.

PORGY AND BESS, opera (1935).

Having successfully tackled the forms of the rhapsody, concerto, and overture, Gershwin began thinking of writing an opera. But the problem of suitable libretto had to be solved. He remembered a Theatre Guild production he had seen some years earlier, a play called *Porgy* by DuBose Heyward. The American flavor of this play, and the poignant story of the love of Bess for the crippled Porgy, impressed themselves strongly on Gershwin's consciousness. The more he thought of it, the more he felt that this was the ideal subject for an opera, a *native* American opera, possibly a folk opera.

The libretto was prepared by DuBose Heyward in collaboration with Ira Gershwin. Then George Gershwin set to work on his music. To get the proper feel of the locale of his story, he went for several weeks to Charleston, South Carolina, living in a shack on the waterfront. There he absorbed the music of the Gullah Negroes. Thus saturated with the music and ritual of the Charleston Negro, Gershwin began collating his melodic ideas. Within the texture of his writing he incorporated something of the piquant melodies of Charleston street-cries, something of the savage rhythms of Negroes at work or in prayer, something of the plangent melody of a sad race. His writing did not go easily by any means. It took him eleven months to put his opera down on paper; and an additional nine months were consumed in the orchestration.

The première of the opera took place in Boston on September 30, 1935. On October 10, it began its run in New York City. It cannot be said that the opera was successful at first. The critics felt that though there were lovely songs in it, the work was neither opera nor musical comedy, but a sort of hybrid product. Olin Downes said that it did not "utilize all the resources of the operatic composer or pierce very often to the depths of the simple and pathetic drama."

But like all genuinely important works, *Porgy and Bess* did not have to wait indefinitely for full recognition. In 1937, it received the David Bispham Medal as an important contribution to native American opera. In 1938, it was produced in Los Angeles and San Francisco with outstanding success. Four years after that it was revived in New York, this time to become one of the great theatrical successes of the season and to enjoy the longest run ever known by a revival. The Music Critics Circle now embraced the work, selecting it as the most important musical revival of the year. Some of the leading critics, re-evaluating it, found it good. Between 1952 and 1956, an American-Negro company toured with *Porgy and Bess* throughout Europe, the Middle East, the Soviet Union, and Latin America, scoring triumphs everywhere equalled by few contemporary operas, if any; it became the first opera by an American-born composer performed at the historic La Scala in Milan. In 1959, Samuel Goldwyn produced a motion-picture adaptation of the opera.

That *Porgy and Bess* should have wonderful melodies is to be expected from a born song writer; these melodies are not only among the best that Gershwin has written but among the best to be found in contemporary American music: *Summertime, I Got Plenty of Nuttin', Bess, You Is My Woman Now, My Man's Gone Now*. But the opera is much more than just a collection of choice songs. It has piquant wit, genuine poignancy, and—as in the closing scene—telling dramatic effect. Sometimes it rambles, and sometimes it lacks cohesion. But these flaws are minor considerations in comparison to the power and vitality of Gershwin's inspiration at its best.

HENRY F. GILBERT   1868—1928

A hearing of Charpentier's opera *Louise* in 1901 was a crucial hour in the life of Henry F. Gilbert. That performance motivated him to return to composition, which he had abandoned for a few years. Equally important, it convinced him of the necessity of deriving his materials and inspiration from American folk and popular styles, in much the same way that *Louise* was influenced by Parisian street cries. From then on, Gilbert went to American sources—popular and serious—for ideas and techniques. His first major symphonic work, *Americanesque* (1903), developed three minstrel-show tunes. Subsequently, Negro, Creole, ragtime, cakewalk music—as well as other minstrel melodies—played vital roles in his compositions.

His historic importance cannot be disputed: at a time when most American composers were feeble imitators of French impressionism or Germanic postromanticism, he pointed the way to a robust Americanism that was sincere and artistically valid. His music is vigorous, sometimes unconventional, made vital by rhythmic energy, and given humanity by an engaging sense of humor. Its American identity is unmistakable; and therein, perhaps, lies its greatest strength.

Born in Somerville, Massachusetts, on September 26, 1868, Gilbert received his musical education first at the New England Conservatory and then with Edward MacDowell. The necessity of making a living made it difficult for him to devote himself to composition. During the years when he worked as a printer, arranger, and engraver, he became a student of American cultural backgrounds. This brought him into contact with American folk and popular music, which he came to admire. He was fired with the ambition of encouraging the emergence of an American nationalist school of music. With Arthur Farwell he founded the Wa-Wan Press, devoted to the publication of native American music. Then, after hearing *Louise,* he turned to composition and became one of the first serious American composers to utilize American popular idioms successfully.

During most of his life, Gilbert suffered not only from intense poverty but also from miserable health. He had been born with an abnormally large right ventricle which sent forth a great amount of blood through the skin capillaries. With this deformity, the doctors insisted, Gilbert could not be expected to live beyond his thirtieth year. He lived twice that number of years, but they were years of great physical suffering.

Despite his poor health, he continued composing and produced several works of distinction. In 1927, he was one of two American composers (the other was Aaron Copland) represented at the International Society for Contemporary Music Festival, held in Frankfurt-am-Main, Germany. Though now an invalid, he went to Europe to attend the performance of his *The Dance in the Place Congo.* He died one year later at his home near Cambridge, Massachusetts, on May 19, 1928.

The following works by Gilbert are discussed below: *Comedy Overture on Negro Themes; Dance in the Place Congo.*

DANCE IN THE PLACE CONGO, tone-poem for orchestra (1906).

The music of the Creoles of Louisiana provided Gilbert with thematic subjects for this successful work. Five Creole songs are utilized "much after the manner of Grieg or Tchaikovsky," as the composer frankly pointed out. An atmosphere of eerie unreality is created for the frenetic slave dances, which pass from nimbleness to outright savagery. A bell tolls funereal sounds to call the slaves back to their tasks. The composition ends on a note of despair.

Gilbert composed his orchestral work in 1906. A decade later he decided to transform it into a ballet, and wrote his own scenario. The ballet was introduced at the Metropolitan Opera House on March 23, 1918 (on the same evening that Cadman's opera, *Shanewis,* was first performed). It was excellently received.

It was the symphonic poem, not the ballet, that represented American music at the International Society for Contemporary Music Festival in 1927. The Germans, who referred to Gilbert as the *"Uramerikaner"* ("primary American"), received the work with outstanding enthusiasm.

COMEDY OVERTURE ON NEGRO THEMES, for orchestra (1910).

For many years, Gilbert worked on an opera based on the Uncle Remus tales of Joel Chandler Harris. He had completed a great part of the score before he discovered that the operatic rights had been assigned to another composer. Gilbert's opera was therefore never published or produced.

From the music of this score he was able to create two independent works. One of these was his *American Dances,* for piano. The other was this overture. Renamed *Comedy Overture on Negro Themes* (and rescored for large orchestra), it has become one of Gilbert's most famous compositions.

The overture develops several authentic Negro melodies. One of them is of Bahaman origin. Another is a roustabout tune frequently heard and danced to along the Mississippi River (*I'se Gwine to Alabamy, Oh!*). The third, a spiritual named *Old Ship of Zion,* was utilized by the composer as the theme for a sprightly fugue.

The first performance of the overture took place at an open-air concert in Central Park, New York City, on August 17, 1910. It was not particularly successful; nor did it create a much deeper impression when it was repeated by the Boston Symphony Orchestra the following April. The serious treatment of native American tunes was still too novel for audiences (and even the critics) to allow recognition of the wit and skill with which the composer developed this material. Since then, however, native American idioms and themes have often been exploited in serious musical forms. Gilbert's overture is no longer new or original; but it remains to this day music of considerable charm.

ALEXANDER GLAZUNOV   1865—1936

Glazunov was one of the last of the Russian masters to carry on the traditions of the school of the "Five," and to bring those traditions forcefully to the attention of the Western world. When Prokofiev's *Scythian Suite* was introduced in St. Petersburg in 1916, Glazunov is said to have rushed out of the hall in horror, holding his hands over his ears to deafen them to Prokofiev's dissonances. This gesture was symbolic of Glazunov's career as a composer. He lived through the years in Russia which saw the changing of traditions and the making of epochs. Throughout his own life he saw and heard composers around him—beginning with Mussorgsky and continuing with Prokofiev and Stravinsky—adventurously striking out in new directions. Yet to all these new styles and sounds he closed his ears and went his own way, unaffected by the powerful oceanic surges of musical movements that swept so many composers along in their tide. Glazunov was certainly no revolutionist, no experimenter. He often confessed that he was most strongly influenced by Brahms. By this he meant that, like Brahms, he had a healthy respect for (and extraordinary skill in) architectonic construction. But with his remarkable technique he combined feeling for beauty; and for this reason some of his works continue to be heard and admired.

Some of Glazunov's most important works were written before 1900—notably the tone-poem *Stenka Razin,* op. 13, the *Five Novelettes* for string quartet, op. 15 (1888), the Fourth, Fifth, and Sixth Symphonies, opp. 48, 55, and 58 (1893, 1895, and 1896), and the *Scènes de Ballet,* for orchestra, op. 52 (1895). These works do not come within the scope of the present volume. But Glazunov continued to produce music with fertility after the turn of the twentieth century, and wrote a few works which keep his name alive in our concert halls.

Glazunov was born on August 10, 1865, in St. Petersburg. He began studying the piano in his ninth year, and was only thirteen when he started composing. Balakirev, impressed by his talent, urged him to study with Rimsky-Korsakov, under whose vigilant eye young Glazunov composed his First Symphony, op. 5 (1881). Introduced by Balakirev at a Free School concert in St. Petersburg, this symphony was outstandingly successful; Cui described it as an "amazing work, frightening in its precocious maturity." The symphony was no flash in the pan, as young Glazunov proceeded to prove by writing the excellent String Quartet in F Major, op. 10 (1884), the brilliant *Overture on Greek Folk Themes* (his second such overture), op. 6 (1885), and the tone-poem *Stenka Razin.* Though he was only twenty, he was already considered by some to be one of Russia's foremost composers.

But his reputation was not confined to the boundaries of his own country. In 1884, his First Symphony was successfully introduced by Franz Liszt in Weimar. *Stenka Razin* scored decisively at the Paris Universal Exhibition of 1889. So famous had Glazunov become throughout the world of music that, in 1893, he even received a commission from across the ocean: to write a Triumphal March for the Chicago Exhibition.

In 1899, he was appointed professor of instrumentation at the St. Petersburg Conservatory, beginning a long and eventful career as teacher which was to influence an entire generation of Russian composers. In 1909, he became director of the Conservatory, holding the office with great distinction until 1922.

Well before the outbreak of World War I, Glazunov went into an artistic decline—a fact which he himself obviously recognized, since his last-known large work, the incidental music to *The King of the Jews,* was written in 1914. He lived on for two more decades, but remained creatively sterile, satisfied to allow his fame to rest on the works of his youth and early manhood.

Though he was not altogether in sympathy with the Revolution, he remained in Russia until 1928, even holding official positions. In 1928, he transferred his home to Paris. Now a sad and tired musician, a man who long since had abandoned composition, but now had even abandoned the land of his birth, he lived for the remainder of his life in the Parisian capital. Occasionally he visited other countries to conduct his music, appearing for the first time in the United States on November 21, 1929, as a guest conductor of the Detroit Symphony Orchestra.

Glazunov died in Paris on March 21, 1936. The announcement of his death came as a shock to many, who, so long associating him with the music of the past rather than the present, thought that he had been dead for many years.

The following works by Glazunov are discussed below: Concerto in A Minor for Violin and Orchestra; *The Seasons*.

THE SEASONS, ballet, op. 67 (1900).

The book and choreography of *The Seasons* were conceived by Marius Petipa. It was introduced at the Hermitage Theatre in St. Petersburg on February 23, 1900.

The ballet gives picturesque interpretation to the four seasons of the year; appropriately, it is in four scenes (and an apotheosis). Winter opens the ballet, surrounded by his friends, Frost, Ice, Hail, and Snow. They are frolicking amid the snowflakes when two gnomes arrive and set fire to a bundle of faggots. The warmth causes Winter to disappear. Spring now arrives with Zephyr, Birds, and Flowers, all of whom join in a dance. With the golden beams of the sun, Spring and his companions leave. It is now Summer. The Spirit of the Corn arrives. The flowers go through a dance, then stretch out exhausted on the earth. Naiads arrive, carrying azure veils for which the flowers reach eagerly. Satyrs and fauns, playing on their pipes, come to capture the Spirit of the Corn. But the flowers protect him and Zephyr sends them scurrying away. In the final autumnal scene, the Bacchantes dance in the company of the Seasons under the falling leaves. In the Apotheosis, stars are seen glistening in the sky.

Glazunov extracted the most important sections from the ballet score and developed them into a suite whose popularity on concert programs has exceeded that of the ballet itself. The suite contains the following divisions: I. Winter: Introduction; The Frost; The Ice; The Hail; The Snow. II. Spring. III. Summer: Waltz of the Cornflowers and Poppies; Barcarolle; Variation; Coda. IV. Autumn: Bacchanale—Petit Adagio. Finale—The Bacchantes and Apotheosis.

CONCERTO IN A MINOR FOR VIOLIN AND ORCHESTRA, op. 82 (1905). I. Moderato. II. Andante. III. Allegro.

This concerto is good Glazunov, and has established itself permanently in the violin repertoire. It is pleasing melodically; it is soundly constructed; it is effectively written for the violin. It was written for Leopold Auer. One day, the story goes, Glazunov visited Auer's class and heard one of the prodigies performing. The composer was so impressed by what he heard that he begged Auer to allow the pupil to introduce his concerto. Graciously, Auer consented. On October 17, 1905, the young prodigy—his name was Mischa Elman—gave the first performance of the concerto in London.

Though in three traditional movements, the concerto is played without pause. The principal subject of the first movement (moderato) is heard in the opening, announced by the solo violin; it is a melancholy melody, and sentimental. The Andante consists of two main themes, once again both introduced by the solo violin. The entire movement is pleasingly lyrical. A protracted cadenza leads directly into the finale, the main theme of which appears in a dialogue between the solo violin and orchestra. After a second melody, the music moves joyously to a spirited closing.

REINHOLD GLIÈRE   1875—1956

Glière's style was subjected to three distinct influences. In the early years of his creative life, he carried on the traditions and style of the Russian nationalist school. Later on, his music became more romantic and impressionistic, as French and German influences replaced Russian ones. Subsequently, Glière returned to Russian subjects and idioms in an effort to glorify Soviet ideals. He was never a particularly original composer; but he was a consummate craftsman, had a particular flair for orchestral effect, and filled his works with warm melodic themes and striking dramatic effects.

Of Belgian descent, Glière was born in Kiev on January 11, 1875. Music study began in Kiev, and was continued at the Moscow Conservatory where he was a pupil of Taneiev and Ippolitov-Ivanov. His First Symphony, op. 8 (1899-1900) was received so apathetically, when introduced in Moscow in 1902, that Glière was convinced of the need of additional study. He went to Berlin and worked hard at theory. His *Second Symphony,* op. 25 (1907) reveals the influence of this stay in Germany in its increased maturity and heightened romanticism.

In 1913, Glière became professor of composition at the Kiev Conservatory, rising to the post of director one year later. In 1921, he went to Moscow to become professor of composition at the Conservatory, beginning a successful career there as teacher. He turned to writing proletarian music, achieving a formidable success with his ballet *The Red Poppy,* the first successful Soviet ballet on a revolutionary subject. He won the Stalin Prize in 1948 for his Quartet No. 4, and in 1950 for his ballet, *The Bronze Horseman.* He died in Moscow on June 23, 1956.

The following works by Glière are discussed below: *The Red Poppy;* Symphony No. 3 in B Minor ("Ilia Mourometz").

SYMPHONY NO. 3 in B MINOR (ILIA MOUROMETZ), op. 42, (1911). I. Wandering Pilgrims: Ilia Mourometz and Sviatogor. II. Solovei the Brigand. III. The Palace of Prince Vladimir. IV. The Feats of Valor and the Petrification of Ilia Mourometz.

Glière's most important work to date is his Third Symphony, introduced by the Russian Musical Society in Moscow under Emil Cooper in 1912. It received the Glinka Prize.

Inspired by ancient Russian folk legends and tales, Glière has here glorified the hero Ilia Mourometz, who is believed to have lived in the twelfth century, and whose exploits in war and peace were fabulous. Ultimately, Ilia was converted to Christianity.

Glière's symphony calls for a detailed program, which the composer supplied in his published score:

First movement: Ilia Mourometz, son of a peasant, is selected by two gods, disguised as wandering pilgrims, to become a bogatyr. He joins the all-powerful bogatyr Sviatogor to wander over the Holy Mountains. When Sviatogor dies, his heroic force passes on to Ilia, who now goes on to Kiev.

Second movement: In a dense forest lives Solovei the mighty Brigand. Ilia comes to the forest, wounds Solovei with his giant arrow, and drags him tied to the palace of Vladimir, the Sun.

Third movement: There is a royal feast at the palace of Vladimir, at which the mighty have gathered. When Ilia arrives, he commands Solovei to raise his ferocious cry, which causes the palace to shake and overcomes all the great men within. Ilia now slices off Solovei's head. Vladimir invites Ilia to the feasting table where he is royally welcomed.

Fourth movement: Batyagha the Wicked and his pagan army arise in Orda, the land of gold. Ilia, at the head of twelve bogatyrs, comes to do them battle. For twelve days the mighty battle continues, until the enemy is finally destroyed. Ilia, with seven bogatyrs, now goes forth to the limpid land. Two warriors come to challenge them. When they are destroyed, four rise in their place; when the four are overcome, there appear eight. The bogatyrs flee to the mountains, one after another of them being turned to stone, even the great Ilia. And since that day bogatyrs have disappeared from Holy Russia.

Several themes recur throughout the symphony, almost like leitmotifs. There is a chorale-like subject, written in free meter, which opens the symphony and suggests the Christian faith that drives Ilia Mourometz to his heroic deeds. This subject appears in several alterations, and is heard climactically at the end of the symphony, symbolic of the victory of Christianity over the bogatyrs. Two other major themes describe the hero, Ilia Mourometz, and appear throughout the work: the first is heard in the strings (low register) and bassoons; the second, more grandiose in character, is played by the trombones.

THE RED POPPY, ballet (1927).

What is generally accepted as the first successful Soviet ballet employing a revolutionary subject was introduced, to outstanding acclaim, at the Bolshoi Theatre in Moscow on June 14, 1927. Since that time, it has been performed frequently in the Soviet Union, where it is regarded in high favor for its spirited music, so vibrant with melody and color, its vital dances, and the dramatic thrust of M. T. Kurilko's book.

The first act takes place in a Chinese port. Soviet propaganda appears in the depiction of the exploited Chinese coolies, an exploitation which is relieved by the sailors of a Soviet ship in the harbor. This act reaches a whirlwind climax with a series of dances for sailors of different nationalities. It is here that there appears the celebrated "Russian Sailors' Dance" (*"Ekh Yablochko"*), which has become so popular in this country. For the rest of the ballet, the port commander, enraged by the action of the Soviet sailors, tries to kill their captain. A maneuver to kidnap him fails. Meanwhile, beautiful Tai-Hao has fallen in love with the Soviet captain and is fired with the ideal of fighting for the freedom of the masses. Realizing that a plot is afoot to poison her beloved, she thwarts it. The port commander eventually shoots and kills Tai-Hao, who is now aboard the Soviet vessel. With her dying words she urges the children around her to fight for liberty, giving them a flower that is symbolic of that liberty—a red poppy. An epilogue, which hails the ultimate victory of the Chinese proletariat, utilizes for its principal melodic material a fragment of the *Internationale*.

MORTON GOULD   1913—

Among the composers who have utilized popular styles of American music in serious forms, Gould has been one of the most important and successful. He has been a singularly prolific writer but, despite his abundance, haste is rarely evident in his music. He has a fine compositorial technique which occasionally succeeds in bringing to some of his works greater interest than their comparatively second-rate material would warrant. A natural gift for orchestration gives additional luster to his writing. Frequently his works are purely functional, adequately serving the purposes for which they were intended. All this does not mean that Gould is a minor creative personality. His music at times achieves genuine distinction; several of his major works are original in concept and effectively written.

Gould was born in Richmond Hill, New York, on December 10, 1913. His unusual musical gift became apparent early: when he was only six he wrote a waltz that was published; and not much later he made appearances as a prodigy virtuoso of the piano. His musical studies took place at the Institute of Musical Art and at New York University. Following this, he held several musical jobs, the most important of which was that of staff pianist for the Radio City Music Hall. When he was eighteen, he made a significant bow as a composer, when the Philadelphia Orchestra under Stokowski introduced his *Chorale and Fugue in Jazz*.

He became associated with the radio for the first time when he was twenty-one—as conductor of an orchestra. For the next few years he conducted radio orchestras, becoming famous for his dynamic performances and brilliant orchestral transcriptions. He also wrote a number of serious works which were widely performed.

The following works by Gould are discussed below: *Fall River Legend; Interplay; Philharmonic Waltzes; Spirituals;* Symphony No. 3.

For *American Concertette,* see *Interplay.*

SPIRITUALS, for string choir and orchestra (1942). 1. Proclamation. II. Sermon. III. A Little Bit of Sin. IV. Protest. V. Jubilee.

The idiom which Gould utilized in this highly successful work does not stem from Tin Pan Alley but from the treasury of American folklore: specifically spirituals, black and white. Actual spirituals are not reproduced; what Gould tried to do was to create melodies of his own which have the mood and the structure of authentic spiritual music. Since spirituals are varied in their emotional content, the melodies of Gould's work traverse a wide gamut, from lighthearted gaiety to tragedy, from wistfulness to deep feeling.

Structurally, the work is interesting for its utilization of a string choir as if it were a vocal chorus. Thus string choir and orchestra are often used antiphonally.

The five movements are sharply contrasted in atmosphere and mood. The first, described by the composer as "slowly rhapsodic and intense," is declamatory in character. A lighter mood is created through syncopated rhythms in the second section, which is "in a simple story style." The accouterments of the dance orchestra are enlisted to project a gay and devilish mood in the third part, while the fourth is a powerful utterance which increases in intensity as the section comes to a close. The last part, "Jubilee," is in three sections, the first a hoe-down heard in the strings alone, the second with a kind of boogie-woogie bass against a sustained melody for violins and violas, and the third for the entire orchestra, with which the work comes to an exciting culmination.

INTERPLAY (AMERICAN CONCERTETTE), for piano and orchestra (1943). I. With drive and vigor. II. Gavotte. III. Blues. IV. Very fast.

Interplay was written for a radio concert conducted by Gould, which presented the pianist, José Iturbi, as soloist. Its original title was *American Concertette*. The composer, in his description of the music, informs us that "the first movement is ... very rhythmic and brash in the accepted classical form of two contrasting themes and a short development. The second movement ... is a gay, short dance with a sly glance back to the classical mode. The third movement is a Blues and what the title implies—a very simple and, in spots, 'dirty' type of slow, nostalgic mood. The fourth and last movement brings the work to a rousing close."

Soon after the première of the work, Jerome Robbins, the choreographer, utilized the music for a ballet called *Interplay,* which was first seen in Billy Rose's *Concert Varieties* in the summer of 1945. On October 17 of the same year it was presented at the Metropolitan Opera House by the Ballet Theatre. The ballet, divided in four parts (I. Free Play. II. Horseplay. III. Byplay. IV. Team Play), contrasts the classic ballet with present-day dances with such freshness that it has become one of the outstanding successes in the Ballet Theatre repertoire, and was played on the Theatre's tour through the United States, Europe, and South America.

FALL RIVER LEGEND, ballet (1947).

In August 1892, in Fall River, Massachusetts, Lizzie Borden was accused of murdering her father and his second wife with an ax. Her trial made the front pages, as did her ultimate acquittal. This celebrated case has been the subject of stories, plays, and books. It was also utilized for a ballet, with scenario and choreography by Agnes De Mille with music by Gould, introduced by the Ballet Theatre in April, 1948.

"The ballet," we are informed by the composer, "deals with the psychological motivations that led Lizzie Borden to commit murder, and its structure alternates between dramatic sequences and set-pieces, so that, in a sense, it combines the qualities of both pure and pantomimic dance."

An orchestral suite, consisting of six movements, was prepared from the ballet score by the composer and has been heard at orchestral concerts. "The suite," the composer explains further, "consists of the music for the more strictly balletic portions of the work; the composer feels that the freely dramatic sequences would lose some of their effect without the accompanying stage action, and, therefore, has limited the suite to the less literal parts of the score. The music makes many idiomatic references to New England hymns and dances of the '90s. The composer does not quote any such tune literally, but has fashioned his own thematic material in their guise in order to achieve an appropriate stylization."

PHILHARMONIC WALTZES, for orchestra (1947).

This light and infectious piece of music is Gould's apotheosis of the three-quarter time of the waltz. Though played as an integrated unit, it is in three sections. In the first, the composer recalls, and amplifies, the old-fashioned, sentimental waltz of the Gay Nineties. In Gould's own words: "The character is very bawdy and gay, and the orchestra echoes the colors of a player-piano and the old-time picnic and street music." There follows a straight-forward romantic waltz, which, in turn, gives way to a continental-type waltz, with its "swirling patterns and broad lyrical lines."

Gould wrote these waltzes at the request of the Philharmonic League of New York, to be performed at the annual ball and Pension Fund concert of the New York Philharmonic. The première performance was conducted by Dimitri Mitropoulos on November 16, 1948.

SYMPHONY NO. 3, for orchestra (1947). I. Rhapsodic and intense. II. Moderately slow and relaxed. III. Moderately fast. IV. Slowly moving—fast.

One of Gould's most important works, the Third Symphony, was given its world première in Dallas, Texas, with the composer conducting the Dallas Symphony, on February 16, 1947. Some time after this première Gould subjected the symphony to revision, writing an entirely new last movement for it. The revised version was introduced by the New York Philharmonic-Symphony Orchestra, with Dimitri Mitropoulos conducting, on October 28, 1948.

As in so many other works of Gould, the symphony reaches to American popular idioms—jazz and blues—for its materials, developing them with breadth and considerable dexterity.

Gould's own analysis of the symphony follows:

"The first movement is rhapsodic and dramatic. Rather than self-contained themes, the melodic line is sort of long and unwinding and there are two contrasting sections which are developed. The movement ends on a grim and driving sort of funereal processional.

"The second movement is simple and lyrical and almost 'sweetness and light' as compared to the first. There are singing melodies throughout, and the harmonic and melodic scheme stays pretty close to the Blues tonality.

"The third movement corresponds to the Scherzo. It opens on a jazz fugue which grows wilder and wilder. The trio is blatant and humorous. There is a short return to the first theme and then a driving coda.

"The last movement is a Passacaglia and Fugue. The opening Passacaglia theme is austere and reserved. The whole passacaglia section is dynamically very soft, the variations changing in texture rather than impact. There are allusions to the thematic material of previous movements. The fugue opens with a sudden attack. Thematically the fugue is derived from the passacaglia, and the movement ends with the passacaglia theme announced double forte."

ALEXANDER GRETCHANINOFF   1864—1956

The field of music which Gretchaninoff tilled with greatest fertility—indeed, he made that field his own—was that of church music for the various services of the Russian Orthodox Church. It is here that he is most authentically Russian in his inspiration, most original in his thinking. His natural gift for writing for voices, his skill at counterpoint, his ability to create powerful choral effects, and his deep religious feeling are the qualities which place his various liturgies on a high artistic plane.

Apart from his church music, Gretchaninoff was most famous for his songs, of which he has written more than 250. As Sabaneyev said of him, he knows "ideally and to perfection the properties of the human voice," knows how to realize the fullest potentialities of the voice for artistic expression. More important still, he has an abundant melodic gift (made piquant with vivid Russian colors) and a vein of tenderness. The most famous of his songs—and they are among the best written by a contemporary

Russian—were composed before 1900. They include *Triste est le Steppe,* op. 5, no. 1, and *Cradle Song,* op. 1, no. 5.

Gretchaninoff was born in Moscow on October 25, 1864. His musical training came comparatively late. After a casual study of the piano, he entered the Moscow Conservatory when he was seventeen. A pupil of Safonov, Arensky, and Laroche, he proved to be a mediocre student, so much so that Arensky advised him to give up all thoughts of becoming a musician. After leaving the Conservatory, Gretchaninoff went to St. Petersburg, entering its Conservatory as a pupil of Rimsky-Korsakov. He wrote a string quartet that won a prize and a symphony that was successfully performed.

In 1901, Gretchaninoff completed his opera, *Dobrinya Nikitich,* which was introduced at the Bolshoi Theatre in Moscow in 1903 with Chaliapin. The opera was a triumph, soon entering into the repertory of virtually every Russian opera house. A second opera, *Sister Beatrice* (based on a text of Maurice Maeterlinck) was written in 1912. Meanwhile, Gretchaninoff made his mark as a composer of church music and songs.

In 1925, he abandoned his native land to settle in Paris, from which city he frequently embarked on extensive concert tours (including several to this country). He arrived in the United States in 1939. His ninetieth birthday was celebrated in New York on October 25, 1954 with a concert of his works. He died in New York a few months later, on January 3, 1956.

The following works by Gretchaninoff are discussed below: *Missa Oecumenica;* Symphony No. 5.

MISSA OECUMENICA (ECUMENICAL MASS), for soloists, chorus, orchestra, and organ, op. 142 (1936). I. Kyrie. II. Gloria. III. Credo. IV. Sanctus. V. Benedictus. VI. Agnus Dei.

In writing this mass, the composer did not intend a religious service for any one church, but a service embodying the universal meaning of all churches. In his own words, he intended a mass "in which there could be combined the musical character of the Eastern and Western churches.... The text—in Latin—is the one used in Catholic Churches."

Though in his liturgical music Gretchaninoff is most identifiably a Russian composer, this work reaches for its style not to the school of the "Russian Five," but to Franz Liszt. It is built along massive lines, is more rhapsodic and dramatic than lyrical, and is Germanic in its romanticism. Powerful and massive climaxes predominate (e.g., in the *"Gloria"* and *"Sanctus"*), and even in the *"Benedictus"* and *"Agnus Dei"* the effect is more dramatic than poignant.

There are no separate solo numbers. The chorus is utilized throughout the entire work (often with stunning effect), with the music for solo voices sometimes alternating with the chorus and sometimes integrated with it.

The Mass was written between 1938 and 1943, begun in Paris and completed in this country. On February 25, 1944, it was introduced by the Boston Symphony Orchestra under Koussevitzky.

SYMPHONY NO. 5, op. 153 (1939). I. Allegro. II. Andante. III. Intermezzo. IV. Allegro moderato.

Gretchaninoff has written five symphonies, which are melodious, harmonically pleasing, and structurally sound. While agreeable to listen to, they are not of outstanding artistic importance. Stylistically, they depend more upon German postromanticism than upon the idioms of the Russian school; emotionally, they are reminiscent of Tchaikovsky. The best of his five symphonies is the last, introduced by the Philadelphia Orchestra under Stokowski on April 5, 1939. The symphony abounds with graceful themes of romantic character, intriguing shifting rhythms, and telling climactic effects. The best movements are the second, which is rhapsodic, with a beautiful lyric middle section, and the propulsive last movement, built out of a number of subjects, including a delightful rondo episode and a lilting melody for strings.

CHARLES T. GRIFFES   1884—1920

There can be little doubt that the early death of Griffes, at the premature age of thirty-six, robbed American music of a major creative figure. With each succeeding work, Griffes demonstrated increasing creative powers, growing imagination, stronger individuality, and an increasing gift for projecting beauty in music with sensitivity and poetry. His two masterpieces, *The Pleasure Dome of Kubla Khan* and the *Poem,* for flute and orchestra— written in the last years of his life—represent him at the height of his achievements, and can only suggest how much higher he could have risen had he lived to write more works.

Griffes was born in Elmira, New York, on September 17, 1884. He began the study of the piano early, and showed such talent that he was encouraged to prepare for a concert career. He went to Berlin in his nineteenth year to complete his piano studies. There he came under the influence of Humperdinck, who steered him away from a virtuoso career and toward composing. In Berlin, Griffes wrote his first works (some songs and a few piano pieces), in which the influence of German postromanticism is marked.

Returning to the United States in 1907, he became a teacher of music at the Hackley School in Tarrytown, New York, a position he held until the end of his life. His salary was so meager that he had to supplement this job with hack work. But he did not neglect serious composition. A slow worker, he labored painstakingly on each composition, producing only a few scores. But these scores are all sensitive in their construction and of a fragile, exotic beauty in which French impressionism is blended with a kind of Russian orientalism.

A few friends recognized his talent and worked for his recognition. Through them, there came about several performances of his works— between 1918 and 1920. The Flonzaley Quartet introduced his *Two Sketches on Indian Themes*, for string quartet; the Philadelphia Orchestra, with Marcia von Dressen as soloist, performed his *Three Songs*, for soprano and orchestra; George Barrère and the New York Symphony Society presented the *Poem*; and the Philadelphia Orchestra gave *The White Peacock*. While there were some critics who spoke well of the works, these performances did not succeed in bringing the composer out of his poverty and obscurity.

Griffes realized his first triumph just before his death. On November 8, 1919, the Boston Symphony Orchestra under Monteux introduced *The Pleasure Dome of Kubla Khan*. So successful was this performance that Griffes became famous overnight. Unfortunately, this recognition came too late. Always delicate in health, he had strained his sensitive constitution to the breaking point by working night after night copying out the parts of his score for the Boston performance. Pneumonia set in, and he never recovered. He died on April 8, 1920, in New York.

The following works by Griffes are discussed below: *The Pleasure Dome of Kubla Khan; The White Peacock*.

THE WHITE PEACOCK, for piano, also for orchestra (1915).

Peacocks—white peacocks especially—held a strange fascination for Griffes. When he was in Berlin, where he visited the Zoological Gardens, he wrote: "Among the peacocks was a pure white one—very curious." It is said that whenever he came upon pictures of white peacocks he clipped and saved them. It is, therefore, not surprising that the poem of William Sharpe should have impressed him profoundly.

He wrote the piece originally for piano. It was published as the first of a set of four piano pieces entitled *Roman Sketches*, op. 7. In 1918, the composer introduced these *Sketches* at the MacDowell Club in New York.

Griffes orchestrated *The White Peacock* for a performance scheduled in—of all places!—a motion-picture theatre in New York. It was to serve as background music for a stage ballet at the Rivoli Theatre and (to add to the incongruity) the ballet was interpolated between a Mack Sennett comedy and a picture about the Civil War. The orchestral version of *The*

White Peacock received its concert première in Philadelphia, with Leopold Stokowski conducting the Philadelphia Orchestra, on December 19, 1919.

The tone-poem creates a most delicate mood, sustained uninterruptedly throughout the composition. The following lines, from the poem of William Sharpe that inspired the piece, probably provide the best clue to the emotional and pictorial intentions of the music:

> Here as the breath, as the soul of this beauty
> Moveth in silence, and dreamlike, and slowly,
> White as a snowdrift in mountain valleys
> When softly upon it the gold light lingers:
> Moves the white peacock, as tho' through the noontide
> A dream of the moonlight were real for a moment.
> Dim on the beautiful fan that he spreadeth....
> Dim on the cream-white are blue adumbrations....
> Pale, pale as the breath of blue smoke in far woodlands,
> Here, as the breath, as the soul of this beauty,
> Moves the white peacock.

Harlan Cozad McIntosh wrote a novel called *This Finer Shadow* in which this Griffes work plays a vital part in the plot development.

THE PLEASURE DOME OF KUBLA KHAN, symphonic poem for orchestra (1918).

The following lines from the celebrated poem by Coleridge are quoted in the published score of Griffes' symphonic poem:

> In Xanadu did Kubla Khan
>   A stately pleasure-dome decree;
> Where Alph, the sacred river, ran
> Through caverns measureless to man
>   Down to a sunless sea.
> So twice five miles of fertile ground
> With walls and towers were girdled round:
> And here were gardens bright with sinuous rills...
> Enfolding sunny spots of greenery.
>
> The shadow of the dome of pleasure
>   Floated midway on the waves;
> Where was heard the mingled measure
>   From the fountains and the caves.
> It was a miracle of rare device,
> A sunny pleasure-dome with caves of ice.

In translating the poem to music, Griffes has explained, "I have given my imagination free rein.... The vague, foggy beginning suggests the sacred river, running 'through caverns measureless to man down to a sunless sea.' The gardens with fountains and 'sunny spots of greenery' are next suggested. From inside come sounds of dancing revelry which increases to a wild climax and then suddenly breaks off.... There is a return to the original mood suggesting the sacred river and the 'caves of ice.' "

The Boston critics acclaimed this new work of Griffes when the Boston Symphony under Monteux introduced it on November 28, 1919. The critic of the *Boston Globe* put Griffes in the same class as Ravel, Rachmaninoff, and Stravinsky. Philip Hale, the most important of these critics, praised Griffes' "gift of expression ... as he has found new harmonic and orchestral colors.... The music, from the strange, unearthly opening, which at once arrests the attention, to the exquisitely fanciful close, is fascinating throughout."

FERDE GROFÉ   1892—

Grofé has been a contributor to the movement which developed American jazz as a serious idiom. He is not one of our great composers. The area of his creative activity is a highly restricted one. But it is pleasantly landscaped and adds to the variety of our musical scene. On the credit side are his inventiveness in orchestral colors, his ability to exploit unusual timbres, his broad, likable melodies, his pleasing verve; on the debit side, a sometimes naive literalness in translating his program into tones, and superficiality in his musical thinking. He established his reputation with two entertaining musical works, *Mississippi Suite* and the *Grand Canyon Suite,* the popularity of which he has never quite equaled in his subsequent compositions (*Tabloid, Hollywood Suite, Metropolis,* etc.).

Grofé was born in New York City on March 27, 1892. He studied the piano, violin, and harmony with his mother, and the viola with his grandfather. For ten years he played the viola in the Los Angeles Symphony; during the later years of this period he also played in jazz bands and wrote novel instrumentations of popular songs. Paul Whiteman heard one of his arrangements in 1919 and engaged Grofé to work for him as pianist and arranger. Thereafter, Grofé's name was intimately linked with that of Whiteman in the development of jazz music. All of Whiteman's orchestral arrangements were written by Grofé. It was Grofé, too, who wrote the orchestration for Gershwin's *Rhapsody in Blue.*

From orchestration Grofé soon passed on to original composition, writing his first work in a larger form, *Broadway at Night,* in 1924. With the *Grand Canyon Suite,* in 1931, Grofé had arrived as a composer. He has frequently conducted his own music in concert halls and over the radio, and since 1940 has worked in Hollywood writing music for the screen.

The following works by Grofé are discussed below: *Grand Canyon Suite; Mississippi Suite.*

MISSISSIPPI SUITE, for orchestra (1924). I. Father of Waters. II. Huckleberry Finn. III. Old Creole Days. IV. Mardi Gras.

Mississippi Suite was Grofé's first serious work to achieve popularity. He wrote it for Paul Whiteman, who introduced it with his orchestra at Carnegie Hall in 1925.

A stately melody, with traces of Indian character, unfolds in the first movement to portray the mighty river. Jazz intrudes in the second section to provide a saucy and impudent flavor to this tonal characterization of Huckleberry Finn. The theme is first suggested by the tuba and is later taken up by the strings. A nostalgic picture is brought up in the third movement as a melody, suggestive of a Negro song, is carried from muted trumpet to strings, and from woodwinds again to the strings. The last movement—the most famous of all—is a gay carnival. The excitement and fever of the Mardi Gras is re-created in the opening through a brisk and rhythmic subject which soon makes way for a beautiful song for strings—for the Mardi Gras is not only the time for frenetic merrymaking but for romance as well. The opening jaunty subject returns briefly, but the movement ends with the recapitulation of the song by the full orchestra.

GRAND CANYON SUITE, for orchestra (1930). I. Sunrise. II. The Painted Desert. III. On the trail. IV. Sunset. V. Cloudburst.

Grofé's utilization of the jazz idiom is much more discreet in this work than it is in his other compositions, and is found in such subtle rhythmic and melodic suggestions that its presence might not be detected by the casual listener. It is only the spice giving piquancy to the dish Grofé is preparing; and the dish is an American recipe compounded, for the most part, of sound classical ingredients.

Grofé has here achieved vivid pictorial writing; the *Suite* is an unforgettable travelogue in tones. Five pictures are evoked with a brush of many colors—four different facets of the awe-inspiring beauty of the Grand Canyon and the emotions they stir in the composer.

The first picture is that of the sunrise. A roll of the kettle-drums suggests the rising sun as dawn breaks. Against a background of chords, the principal theme is given by the muted trumpet. The music then grows and develops, gaining luster and brilliance much as the sun does when dawn grows into daytime.

An atmosphere of mystery and grandeur is next etched. Ominous chords suggest an eerie picture. A beautifully lyric middle section brings relief, but the movement ends as it began, in mystery.

The third picture is the most famous of the entire set. A halting rhythm describes the gait of a burro as he carries the visitor down the rim of the Canyon. Against the first subject a cowboy tune is introduced contrapuntally. The trip is interrupted when the visitors stop off for refreshment, then continues.

After a series of distant animal calls, a beautiful melody emerges in the fourth section. It is sunset, and the peace and melancholy of dusk descend on the Canyon. Suddenly the clouds darken and gather, lightning flashes streak across the sky, and Nature erupts with thunder and showers. A summer storm is presented with vivid realism. Then all is peace again, and the Canyon is once again touched with indescribable grandeur.

The *Grand Canyon Suite* received its première performance in Chicago on November 22, 1931, with Paul Whiteman conducting his orchestra.

LOUIS GRUENBERG   1884—

In the early 1920's, Gruenberg's style was influenced by jazz techniques. In a series of excellent compositions—including *Daniel Jazz* (for tenor and eight instruments), *Jazz Suite* (for orchestra), and *Jazzettes* (for violin and piano), he employed a popular style with dignity and artistic validity. Two of Gruenberg's later works employed, in varying degrees, American idioms other than jazz: the opera *Emperor Jones,* in which a Negro spiritual is heard, and the Concerto for Violin and Orchestra, inspired by spirituals and hillbilly music.

Whatever his style—be it the impressionism of his apprentice days, the jazz of early manhood, the utilization of advanced rhythmic and harmonic devices and tonalities of contemporary style—Gruenberg is a master of his technique, and an artist who is extraordinarily articulate. He has brought vitality, the force of a dynamic personality, into present-day American music.

Born in Brest-Litovsk, Russia, on August 3, 1884, Gruenberg came to this country when he was two years old. He began the study of the piano early, with Adele Margulies. Later on, in 1903, he attended the Vienna Conservatory, and was a private pupil of Busoni. In 1912, his professional career began in two fields: he entered the concert world as pianist; and he won a prize of one thousand dollars for a symphonic poem, *The Hill of Dreams*. He returned to the United States in 1919. From this time on he devoted himself intensively and exclusively to composition. During the past decade or so, Gruenberg has been writing many original works for Hollywood, some of which have won Academy Awards.

The following works by Gruenberg are discussed below: Concerto for Violin and Orchestra; *The Emperor Jones*.

THE EMPEROR JONES, opera (1932).

Though in the climax of the opera, Gruenberg calls upon the famous Negro spiritual, *Standin' In the Need of Prayer,* not the style of Negro music but that of an ultramodern composer prevails in this work. To translate into music the high tensions, savagery, and terror of Eugene O'Neill's famous play, Gruenberg had recourse to modern techniques. His melodic line, rather than imitating the *melos* of the Negro, is midway between song and speech; in its unorthodox line it sometimes even simulates the *Sprechstimme* of Alban Berg. A complicated and subtle use of rhythm, and harmonic effects of the most intense kind, generate a driving power that sweeps through the entire opera, and—as in the final orgy—carries the listener through a profound emotional experience. The piercing interludal cries of the chorus are of an almost brutal strength. To these vital elements of modern writing, Gruenberg brought what one critic described as a "dramatic instinct and intuition for the theater" which was "unfailing," and a musical technique characterized by "a very complete modern knowledge and a reckless mastery of his means."

The libretto, prepared from the O'Neill play by Kathleen de Jaffa, follows the original quite closely. The pullman porter, Brutus Jones, having murdered a friend in a crap game, escapes to a distant Caribbean island where he becomes an "emperor." Overthrown, he escapes into the nearby forest, equipped with a pistol that has six bullets, one of them (a silver one) reserved for his own suicide if all else fails. Distant voodoo drums are heard in the forest as Jones sees fantastic phantoms of people he has killed. He fires at five of them. Terror-stricken, he suddenly remembers an old spiritual, *Standin' In the Need of Prayer,* which he sings to God in his appeal for forgiveness. The following morning, the natives catch up with him. Jones presses the pistol to his body and releases the silver bullet. As he stretches out, dead, the natives dance around his body, and then pass out of the forest.

The opera, which was fourteen months in the writing, was introduced at the Metropolitan Opera House on January 7, 1933, with outstanding success. Lawrence Tibbett sang the part of Emperor Jones. The critics the following morning echoed the report of the *New York Times* that the opera was "swift, tense, emotional, with fantastical music and spectacular finale"; they considered it one of the major American operas of our time.

CONCERTO FOR VIOLIN AND ORCHESTRA, op. 47 (1944). I. Rhapsodic. II. With Simplicity and Warmth. III. Lively and with Good Humor.

Jascha Heifetz, seeking a major American composition to add to his repertoire, asked Gruenberg to write one for him. Gruenberg completed his concerto on August 7, 1944. A few months later, on December 1, Heifetz introduced it in Philadelphia; Eugene Ormandy conducted the Philadelphia Orchestra.

To endow his music with American flavors, Gruenberg incorporated into the second movement fragments of two spirituals, while in the third movement he introduced thematic ideas suggesting hillbilly music and the prayer music of revival meetings.

The first movement is, as marked, rhapsodic in character—a free fantasy, along elaborate lines, on several original themes. After a pyrotechnical cadenza for the solo instrument, the movement comes to a placid close. In the second movement, the violin is heard in two Negro spirituals, *Oh, Holy Lord* and *Master Jesus*. In the final movement, the scene passes from the world of the Negro to that of rural America. Strains of *The Arkansas Traveler* mingle with those of a fox trot to bring up the picture of a barn dance. Suddenly, a shift is made to a revival meeting, with whose passionate, frenetic music the concerto ends.

CAMARGO GUARNIERI   1907—

Brazil—the country of which Heitor Villa-Lobos is the musical dean— has produced several other creative figures; and of these one of the most original and forceful is Camargo Guarnieri. Donald Fuller wrote in *Modern Music* that Guarnieri "lacks the sudden, new-sounding flashes of a Villa-Lobos, but then it is not primarily for his coloristic nationalist traits that we appreciate him. He moves in a more universal sphere, though he is completely of his country." Skillfully combining the techniques and idioms of modern music with native folk elements, Guarnieri is usually more interesting for his rhythmic and harmonic originality than for his folklore strains.

To a consummate technique he adds a wide emotional span; to forcefulness
and vigor he also brings sensibility and poetry.

Guarnieri was born in Tieté, Brazil, on February 1, 1907. He studied
with local teachers, then at the São Paulo Conservatory, where he was
an honor student. After graduating, he was appointed professor. In 1938,
he won a government award that enabled him to go to Paris for further
study with Ruhlmann and Koechlin. The outbreak of World War II
interrupted this period of study. Back in his native land, he won first
prize in a competition sponsored by Samuel S. Fels of Philadelphia for a
violin concerto; a few years later, his Symphony won the important
Alberto Penteado de Rezonde Prize. In 1946, Guarnieri paid a six-month
visit to this country, returning for a second trip three months after leaving
here. He has conducted many of our major orchestras in his own works.

The following works by Guarnieri are discussed below: *Albertura
Concertante;* Symphony.

ALBERTURA CONCERTANTE, for orchestra (1942).

This short orchestral work—introduced by the São Paulo Orchestra
on June 2, 1942—was designated by its composer as a "concertante" because
it features an alternation of wind and strings in the exposition section, much
in the way the concerto grosso of old alternated solo instruments with
orchestra. The vigorous principal theme appears in the flute in the fifteenth
measure. After a dialogue between strings and wind, the tympani introduces a transitional passage which precedes the second part of the work.
This consists of an extended development of old material. A new transition
restores the first part, after which recapitulation and coda follow. At the
close of the work, the tympani project the rhythm of the principal theme.

SYMPHONY NO. 1 (1944). I. Rude. II. Profondo. III. Radioso.

This symphony is generally recognized to be one of Guarnieri's most
important works. He completed it in 1944, in which year it was introduced
in São Paulo and received first prize in a contest for authentic Brazilian
music. Dedicated to Koussevitzky, the symphony was heard in the United
States on November 29, 1946, with the composer directing the Boston Symphony Orchestra.

All the themes of the symphony are of folk origin, and are often
written in the ancient modes characteristic of many Brazilian folksongs. The
rhythmic patterns are also Brazilian in their complex variety and dynamic
surge. The construction of the symphony is traditional, the first and third
movements being in sonata form, and the second in the A-B-A song form
(with coda).

HOWARD HANSON 1896—

As a conductor, and as the director of the American music festivals in Rochester, New York, Hanson has always been both receptive and encouraging to advanced musical thinking. But as a composer he has preferred to hew to the traditional line. As he put it: "Though I have a profound interest in theoretical problems, my own music comes from the heart and is a direct expression of my own emotional reactions." He has the traditionalist's respect for classical form and his satisfaction with the accepted harmonic and tonal structures of the past. Hanson is at his best writing in a romantic vein, giving freedom of movement to his supple and expressive lyricism; but even then—possibly because of his Nordic blood—his feelings are held in check, and are subdued.

It is the comparative restraint with which Hanson speaks his heart—his restraint in the use of color, dynamics, and tender melodies—that has tempted some commentators to describe him as "the American Sibelius." This characterization will serve. He is American to the core—no question about that. As for being another Sibelius, the somber moods and melancholy strains so often found in his music, the bleak effects he achieves through use of modal harmonies, the dramatic thrusts of his climaxes, the objective beauty of his melodies, all have a kinship with the symphonies of the Finnish master.

Hanson was born in Wahoo, Nebraska, on October 28, 1896. After studying at the School of Music of Luther College, he came to New York and became a pupil at the Institute of Musical Art. His academic and musical studies were completed at Northwestern University. In 1915, he became professor of theory and composition at College of the Pacific in San José, California, becoming the dean of its Conservatory of Fine Arts three years later. In 1921, he won the Prix de Rome of the American Academy. During his three-year residence in Rome, he composed his first major work, the *Nordic Symphony,* which he himself introduced in Rome, with the Augusteo Orchestra, in 1922.

In 1924, he returned to this country to receive an appointment as director of the Eastman School of Music, a post he has held since that time. He has been a cogent force in American music—as an educator, propagandist for new music, and composer. The number of musical organizations with which he is associated—and whose mission it is to develop musical education and culture in this country—is legion. As the artistic director of the music festival in Rochester he has, in a period spanning two decades, been responsible for the performance of one thousand works by six hundred composers—most of these compositions being heard for the first time.

The following works by Hanson are discussed below: *The Lament for Beowulf; Merry Mount;* Symphony No. 1 ("Nordic"); Symphony No. 2 ("Romantic"); Symphony No. 3; Symphony No. 4.

SYMPHONY NO. 1 ("Nordic"), op. 21 (1922). I. Andante solenne; Allegro con fuoco. II. Andante teneramente con semplicita. III. Allegro con fuoco; Finale.

Though a youthful work (it was written in Hanson's twenty-fifth year), this symphony is a work of impressive beauty and sound structural logic. It has been widely performed. The first performance took place in Rome in 1923, with the composer conducting the Augusteo Orchestra. Though the Italian audiences were not usually partial to new American works, they acclaimed this symphony.

The material for the entire symphony is found in the first movement— "strongly Nordic in character," as the composer described it, singing of the "solemnity, austerity, and grandeur of the North, of its restlessness and surging and strife, of its sombreness and melancholy." The second movement, inscribed to the composer's mother, is gentle in character, touched with sadness. The third movement (for his father) is more virile: it utilizes several thematic subjects suggestive of Swedish folksongs. The finale proceeds without pause.

THE LAMENT FOR BEOWULF, for mixed chorus and orchestra, op. 25 (1925).

The sagas of the North always appealed strongly to Hanson. While on a visit to England he came upon a copy of *Beowulf,* translated by William Morris and A. J. Wyatt. He decided to set some of it to music, choosing the scene of Beowulf's death. Except for the brief orchestral introduction, which sets the somber mood of the entire work, the music is entirely choral. "My intention," Hanson has said, "has been to realize in the music the austerity and stoicism and the heroic atmosphere of the poem. This is true Anglo-Saxon poetry and may well serve as a basis for music composed by an American."

The music follows the text closely. A summary of the text has been provided by the composer: "There is a brief picture of the great burial mound by the sea on which the funeral pyre of the hero is built. A great beacon mound is constructed and on it are placed the trophies of the hero, mementos of his famous battles and victories. The women lament as the mound is built by the warriors. Then follows an episode in which the wife of the hero and her handmaidens voice their grief. The young warriors in a group surround the bier of their dead king and tell of his prowess. The work ends with the eulogy of the great hero."

Hanson began writing his work in Scotland "in an environment rugged, swept with mist, and wholly appropriate to the scene of my story." He continued it in Rome, and completed it on his return to this country. It was heard for the first time at the Ann Arbor Festival in 1926.

SYMPHONY NO. 2 ("Romantic"), op. 30 (1930). I. Adagio; Allegro moderato. II. Andante con tenerezza. III. Allegro con brio.

Hanson's Second Symphony followed his First by eight years. It was commissioned by Serge Koussevitzky for the fiftieth anniversary of the Boston Symphony Orchestra, which introduced it on November 28, 1930.

The composer's analysis of this symphony follows: "The first movement begins with an atmospheric introduction in the woodwinds, joined first by the horns, then the strings, and finally the brass choir, and then subsiding. The principal theme is announced by four horns with an accompaniment of strings and woodwinds, and is imitated in turn by the trumpets, woodwinds, and strings. An episodic theme appears quietly in the oboe and then in the solo horn. A transition leads into a subordinate theme, with the theme itself in the strings and a countersubject in the solo horn. The development section now follows.... The climax of the development section leads directly to the return of the principal theme in the original key by the trumpets.... The movement concludes quietly in a short coda.

"The second movement begins with its principal theme announced by the woodwinds with a sustained string accompaniment. An interlude in the brass, taken from the introduction of the first movement and interrupted by florid passages in the woodwinds, develops into a subordinate theme, which is taken from the horn solo of the first movement.

"The third movement begins with a vigorous accompaniment figure in strings and woodwinds, the principal theme of the movement—reminiscent of the first movement—entering in the four horns and later in the basses. The subordinate theme (Molto meno mosso) is announced first by the cellos and then taken up by the English horn; its development leads into the middle section. A brief coda...leads to a final fanfare and the end of the symphony."

MERRY MOUNT, opera (1933).

In 1932, Richard Stokes published a poem based on Nathaniel Hawthorne's *The Maypole of Merry Mount*. This poetic description of Puritan life in New England made such a deep impression on Hanson that he forthwith planned to use it as the basis of an opera. The libretto was prepared by the poet himself. On May 20, 1933, it was heard for the first time, presented in concert form, at the Ann Arbor Festival, the composer conducting. One year later, on February 10, 1934, it was introduced at the Metropolitan Opera

House, with Lawrence Tibbett in the principal role. It was well received (there were fifty curtain calls at the première performance) and was given twelve performances that season. Despite the fact that the critics spoke highly of it and the audience found the opera appealing, it was withdrawn from the Metropolitan repertoire.

The plot revolves around the sensual dreams of Pastor Bradford in old New England. Though he is engaged to a Puritan girl, his restless fancies send his amorous thoughts in another direction. When the Cavaliers arrive, bringing with them beautiful Lady Marigold Sandys, Bradford is overwhelmed by his desire for her. On Merry Mount, Lady Marigold is to be married to Gower Lackland. But the Puritans, provoked by Bradford, arrive to disrupt the proceedings. When Indians come upon the scene there ensues such confusion that Bradford is able to abduct Lady Marigold to a nearby forest where he confesses to her his passion. Gower finds them; in the struggle that follows he is killed by Bradford. Sleep finally overtakes the murderer, who dreams that he is in Hell, that Gower is Lucifer, and that he kills Gower in order to take Lady Marigold for himself. Awakened by his own betrothed, Bradford is told that the Indians have ravaged their village. The villagers are aroused against Lady Marigold because they feel she is the cause of all their misfortunes. Sensing that a terrible doom awaits Lady Marigold, Bradford seizes her and drags her with him through the leaping flames of the burning church.

"*Merry Mount,*" the composer has written, "is essentially a lyrical work, and makes use of broad melodic lines as often as possible. There is less perlando than one might expect to find in a contemporary opera, and a greater tendency toward the old arioso style. The form of each small scene within the larger scene is considered as an entity in itself, a series of small forms within a large form, almost as if in symphonic structure. Both harmonically and rhythmically, the listener will hear certain Americanisms. In orchestration, too, use has been made of certain orchestral colors and devices which were born on this side of the Atlantic....A word might be said concerning the rather frequent use of modal writing, especially in the music of the Puritans. It seemed to me that the characteristics of such melodic modes as the Aeolian, Dorian, Phrygian, and, in exalted moments, the Mixolydian, are very much in keeping with the Puritan character."

Hanson has prepared an orchestral suite from the opera score, which was heard for the first time in Rochester, New York, on December 17, 1936, with the composer conducting the Rochester Philharmonic. It contains four sections:

I. Overture (Lento). The Puritan character of the score is briefly forecast.

II. Children's Dance (Allegro molto). The children, left by their elders who go to church, are taught games by Prence, a Cavalier mountebank—games which bring trouble both to the children and to Prence.

III. Love Duet (Largamente molto espressivo). The passionate outburst of Bradford for Lady Marigold in Act III is here reproduced.

IV. Prelude to Act II and Maypole Dances (Allegro grazioso). The christening of Merry Mount and the erection of a maypole take place (Act II), a ceremony that includes Puritan dances.

SYMPHONY NO. 3, op. 33 (1936). I. Andante lamentando; Agitato. II. Andante tranquillo. III. Tempo scherzando. IV. Largamente e pesante.

The Third Symphony (in A minor) bears a closer affinity with the First than with the Second. It was commissioned by the Columbia Broadcasting System, and three movements were introduced under the composer's direction on September 19, 1937. The entire symphony was given its first performance by the Boston Symphony Orchestra, the composer conducting, on November 3, 1938.

The symphony, as the composer explains, "pays tribute to the epic qualities of pioneers" who founded the first Swedish settlement on the Delaware in 1638 and who in a later period forged westward to open up new territory. Hanson's own descriptive analysis follows: "The first movement is both rugged and turbulent in character, alternating with a religious mysticism. The second movement is, as its name implies, for the most part peaceful and brooding. The third movement is in the tempo of a fast scherzo, and is vigorous and rhythmic. The fourth movement begins with the brooding character of the first movement, developing into an extended chorale in antiphonal style, rising to a climax in the full orchestra out of which appears the principal theme of the second movement, the symphony ending in a note of exultation and rejoicing."

SYMPHONY NO. 4, op. 34 (1943). I. Kyrie. II. Requiescat. III. Dies Irae. IV. Lux Aeterna.

The Fourth Symphony was inspired by the death of the composer's father, to whose memory it is dedicated. It is an elegiac work, and one of the most personal and emotional of Hanson's symphonies. The four movements draw their subtitles from the Requiem Mass. On December 3, 1943, it was publicly introduced in Boston by the Boston Symphony Orchestra, the composer conducting.

The composer asked his former pupil, William Bergsma, to prepare an analysis of this symphony. The analysis, which has been widely quoted and can be considered definitive, is repeated here in part:

"The work...is concise and highly elided, taking barely twenty minutes to perform. The four movements can be characterized briefly; the first (Andante inquieto) is a turbulent and varied movement, a Kyrie theme alternating with dance and song-like sections, and a chorale statement preceding a stormy coda. The second (Largo) is a simple and tender treatment of a scale-like theme in eighth notes, given a first statement in the solo bassoon. The third (Presto) is a furious and bitter scherzo. The last (Largo pastorale), a pastorale with stormy interpolations, has a simple 2/4 ending, dying off on the second inversion of a major triad."

In 1944, the symphony was awarded the Pulitzer Prize in music, the first such work ever to win this honor.

ROY HARRIS   1898—

Few American composers of our time have achieved so personal a style as Roy Harris. His music is easily identified by many stylistic traits to which he has clung through his creative development. The long themes which span many bars before pausing to catch a breath, the long and involved developments in which the resources of variation and transformation are utilized exhaustively, the powerfully projected contrapuntal lines, the modal harmonies, and the asymmetrical rhythms are a few of the qualities found in most Harris works.

Though Harris has frequently employed the forms of the past (toccata, passacaglia, fugue, etc.), has shown a predilection for ancient modes, and on occasion has drawn thematic inspiration from Celtic folksongs and Protestant hymns, he is modern in spirit. His music has a contemporary pulse, the cogent drive and force of present-day living; there is certainly nothing archaic about it. More important still, it is essentially American music, even in those works in which he does not draw his ideas from our folk or popular music. The broad sweep of his melodies suggests the vast plains of Kansas, the open spaces of the West. The momentum of his rhythmic drive is American in its nervousness and vitality. But in subtler qualities, too, Harris's music is the music of America. "The moods," Harris once wrote, "which seem particularly American to me are the noisy ribaldry, the sadness, a groping earnestness which amounts to suppliance toward those deepest spiritual yearnings within ourselves; there is little grace or mellowness in our midst." Such moods—noisy ribaldry, sadness, groping earnestness—are caught in Harris's music; and to these moods are added other American qualities: youthful vigor, health, optimism, and enthusiasm.

Harris was born in Lincoln County, Oklahoma, on February 12, 1898. He was the son of pioneers who had set out in an ox-cart for Oklahoma, and there staked a claim. While still a child, he learned to play the clarinet and the piano. But not until after World War I did he consider music as a career. He enrolled as a harmony student in the Southern Branch of the University of California, and after that became a private pupil of Arthur Farwell. In 1926, he went to Paris to study with Nadia Boulanger. In Paris he wrote his first major works: of these, the Concerto for Piano, Clarinet and String Quartet (1927) was the most successful. After returning to the United States, he wrote several important works in which his personal style was being realized, notably the *String Sextet* (1932), the *Symphony: 1933,* and the Second Quartet (1936). Since then, Harris's position as one of the foremost composers in this country has never been seriously threatened.

Harris has filled several major positions. From 1934 through 1938 he headed the composition class of the Westminster Choir School in Princeton, New Jersey. Subsequently he was Composer-in-Residence at Cornell University, Colorado College, the State Agricultural College, Peabody Teachers College in Nashville and the Pennsylvania Women's College in Pittsburgh. During World War II, he served as chief of the Music Section for the Office of War Information.

The following works by Harris are discussed below: Quartet No. 3; Quintet for Piano and Strings; Symphony No. 3; Symphony No. 4 ("Folk Song"); Symphony No. 5; Symphony No. 6.

QUARTET NO. 3, for strings (1937).

In his Third Quartet, Harris's predilection for modal writing is revealed most strongly and, in certain ways, achieves its highest degree of artistic expressiveness. The quartet (it is actually a suite) comprises four preludes and fugues, in which is utilized what Slonimsky calls "the spectrum of modes," ranging from infradark to ultrabright. The preludes all have a medieval character, their remoteness and exoticism being their most ingratiating qualities. The fugues are the last word in contrapuntal dexterity, but they make their impression on the listener not for their technical ingenuity but for the driving power of their momentum.

In 1939, the Roth Quartet—which had introduced the quartet and made it a permanent part of their repertory—chose it as the only contemporary composition by an American to be heard at the International Congress of Musicologists, held in New York.

QUINTET FOR PIANO AND STRINGS (1937). I. Passacaglia. II. Cadenza. III. Fugue.

This, one of Harris's acknowledged masterpieces, was—like the Third String Quartet—written in 1937. Like its companion piece, it represents a successful attempt to modernize old forms and stylistic elements. Modal writing here, too, brings a distinctive flavor to the music. A beautiful and highly personal modal subject is the kernel of the Passacaglia, which, as the form demands, undergoes a series of effective transformations. With a virtuoso passage for the violin, the Cadenza is launched. Its highlight is a kind of recitative for string quartet, which is among the most tranquil pages of music ever written by Harris. The closing fugue has dramatic impact, containing some of the most vigorous pages in the entire work.

SYMPHONY NO. 3 (1938).

Though this is one of Harris's earlier symphonies, it is one of the most powerful works he has written in this form, and one of the most successful. It was introduced by the Boston Symphony Orchestra under Serge Koussevitzky on February 24, 1939. At that time, Dr. Koussevitzky told an interviewer that he considered it one of the greatest American works he knew. This verdict was soon echoed by many leading critics throughout the country, as the symphony was performed by practically every major American orchestra. The critic of *Modern Music* wrote: "For significance of material, breadth of treatment, and depth of meaning; for tragic implication, dramatic intensity, concentration; for moving beauty, glowing sound, it can find no peer in the musical art of America."

The symphony, in a single uninterrupted movement, contains five sections. The following convenient outline, prepared by the composer himself, is a valuable guide for the work:

"I. Tragic (bow-string sonorities).

"II. Lyric (strings, horns, woodwinds).

"III. Pastoral (emphasizing woodwind color).

"IV. Fugue—dramatic. (Brass, percussion predominating; canonic development of Section II material constituting background for further development of fugue; brass climax, rhythmic motif derived from the fugue subject).

"V. Dramatic—tragic. (Restatement of violin theme of Section I. Tutti in strings in canon with tutti woodwinds. Brass and percussion develop rhythmic motif from climax of Section IV.)"

SYMPHONY NO. 4 ("Folk Song"), for chorus and orchestra (1939).
I. Welcome Party. II. Western Cowboy. III. Interlude. IV. Mountain Love Song. V. Interlude. VI. Negro Fantasy. VII. Finale.

This functional work, whose explicit purpose was to provide practical music for symphony orchestras desiring to collaborate with their local high school or college choruses, is so effective in its utilization of American folk-song materials and so genuinely American in its atmosphere and spirit that it ranks among the composer's major efforts. The chorus, the writing for which is simple and direct, is heard in five of the seven movements.

Numerous familiar folk and popular songs are skillfully woven into this elaborate fabric. *When Johnny Comes Marching Home* is heard in the finale (not to be confused with the overture of the same name, also by Harris). Delightful cowboy songs are interpolated into the second movement, notably *Oh Bury Me Not on the Lone Prairie.* Western fiddle tunes are introduced into the third movement, while in the fifth, such popular folk ditties as *Jump Up My Lady* and *The Blackbird and the Crow* are skillfully exploited.

The Symphony was introduced (in parts) by the Eastman-Rochester Symphony Orchestra under Howard Hanson on April 25, 1940. On December 26 of the same year, the entire symphony was heard in Cleveland, Rudolf Ringwall directing the Cleveland Orchestra. Following this performance, the work received a prize of five hundred dollars from the National Federation of Music Clubs as the best symphonic work of the year. Subsequently, Harris reshuffled the order of his movements. In this now definitive version it was presented by the New York Philharmonic-Symphony under Mitropoulos on December 31, 1942.

SYMPHONY NO. 5 (1942). I. Prelude. II. Chorale. III. Fugue.

This symphony is closely identified with the political temper of the year in which it was written. At the time, the Soviet army was savagely resisting the invading Nazi armies, which, for the first time since the outbreak of the war, introduced hope and optimism for the cause of the Allied countries. Excited by this turn of events, Harris dedicated his Fifth Symphony to "the heroic and freedom-loving people of our great ally, the Union of Soviet Socialist Republics." It was introduced by the Boston Symphony Orchestra under Koussevitzky on February 26, 1943, a performance which, incidentally, was transmitted by short-wave to the Soviet Union. The work was also heard by short-wave eleven times by our armed forces around the world.

A martial note is injected into the first movement with a theme played by the horns that resembles an army bugle call, a theme out of which the entire movement is developed. It is powerful and highly rhythmic music. By way of contrast comes the lyrical second movement, something of a rhapsody, melancholy in character; of particular poignancy is a melodic middle passage for violin (Maestoso). A complicated and brilliantly contrived double fugue ends the work with irresistible force.

SYMPHONY NO. 6 (1944). I. Awakening. II. Conflict. III. Dedication. IV. Affirmation.

Harris was born on Lincoln's birthday, and in a log cabin. "The shadow of Abe Lincoln has hovered over my life since childhood." The Sixth Symphony reflects the composer's great admiration for and spiritual affinity with the Great Emancipator. It was written on a commission by the Blue Network, was dedicated "to the Armed Forces of Our Nation," and was introduced on April 14, 1944, by the Boston Symphony Orchestra under Koussevitzky.

The symphony draws its program from the Gettysburg Address. "In Lincoln's *Gettysburg Address,*" wrote the composer, "I find a classic expression of that great cycle which always attends any progress in the intellectual or spiritual growth of the people: (1) awakening, (2) conflict of the old against the new, (3) terrible suffering resulting from the conflict, and (4) the triumph of the new over the old, which is the affirmation of the eternal youth of the human spirit."

The first movement of the symphony expresses the opening of the speech. The second reflects on the passage, "Now we are engaged in a great civil war, testing whether that nation, or any nation so conceived and so dedicated can long endure." The third part, a chorale to the dead, begins with "We are met on the great battlefield of that war," and ends with "The world will little note nor long remember what we say here, but it can never forget what they did here." The concluding section, which is in fugal form, is devoted to the final lines of the Address, beginning with: "It is for us, the living, rather, to be dedicated here to the unfinished work which they who have fought here have thus far so nobly advanced."

PAUL HINDEMITH   1895—

Those writers who enjoy finding a spiritual kinship between one famous composer and another have described Hindemith as "a twentieth-century Bach." The relationship between these two composers is not difficult to trace. Hindemith's *Ludus Tonalis* has a strong similarity in purpose and method to the *Well-Tempered Clavier;* and the works grouped under the title of *Kammermusik,* or *Chamber Music,* can be described as contemporary Brandenburg Concertos. The bond that ties Hindemith to Bach is—counterpoint. With both composers, polyphony is the basis of their thinking; with both, polyphony serves as the material out of which mighty architectural structures are built. Yet one might say for Hindemith what Deems Taylor once said so well of Bach: "The best way to listen to Bach's music is to forget the word *counterpoint* and to listen just for the music."

With Hindemith, counterpoint is not the end, but the starting point. He is no neo-classicist living in the past, but a very modern composer belonging to our times. Though counterpoint is his method, there is independence in his thinking. His music is linear, by which we mean that the voices move with complete freedom of harmonic relationships. It has intensity, concentration, energy—qualities that we associate with contemporary expression rather than with Bach. It is sometimes dissonant, sometimes atonal.

Hindemith's music is highly complex, even though his later works have shown a tendency towards clarification of structure and a greater simplicity of style. This is music not easy to understand at first hearing. But as one gets to know a Hindemith work intimately, the resourcefulness and skill that Hindemith brings to polyphony become of secondary importance; we are more fascinated by the vigor of his language, his subtle intellectual processes, his high-minded ideals; we are fascinated by the inexorable logic of his writing.

In his treatise, *The Craft of Musical Composition*—which some writers consider to be the most important theoretical work on music since Rameau's —Hindemith has given us a clue to his technique by analyzing the techniques of contemporary composers. All tone combinations are possible as an altogether new conception of "key" is realized; melody is freed from its dependence on harmony.

Strange to say of a composer whose method is so complex and whose language is so remote, Hindemith has not kept himself altogether aloof from his public. He has, as a matter of fact, felt strongly the responsibility of the composer to society. Consequently, he has produced a great number of works for mechanical organ, radio, pianola, theater, etc. This music has been described as *Gebrauchsmusik*—functional music—a term invented for Hindemith.

Hindemith was born in Hanau, Germany, on November 16, 1895, and studied at the Frankfort Conservatory. In Frankfort, Hindemith distinguished himself as a violinist (he was concertmaster of the Frankfort Opera House Orchestra), conductor, founder and violist of the Amar String Quartet (which specialized in contemporary chamber music), and, finally, as a composer. His early works, introduced at the Donaueschingen Festivals in Baden-Baden between 1921 and 1923, attracted attention. In the half-dozen years that followed, Hindemith became one of the major creative figures in Germany, particularly after the successful premières of his operas *Cardillac* (1926) and *Neues vom Tage* (1929).

In 1927, he was appointed professor of composition at the Berlin Hochschule, a post he held up to the time of Hitler. Soon after the Nazis took over Germany, Hindemith became the center of a celebrated political and musical controversy. The Nazis did not look with favor on Hindemith, despite his international fame. He was married to a non-Aryan; his music (they said) was a negation of the artistic principles of the *Kulturkammer*. When Wilhelm Furtwaengler planned to direct the première of Hindemith's opera *Mathis der Maler*, the Nazis prohibited the performance. In vain did Furtwaengler try to influence the *Kulturkammer* to revoke its decision. For his stouthearted support of Hindemith, the conductor was removed from the German musical scene for a year. And Hindemith's music was banned on all German concert programs.

Leaving Germany, Hindemith went to Turkey, on the invitation of that government, to help reorganize its musical life. After that, Hindemith came to this country, became a citizen, and taught at Yale. In 1953 he settled in Zurich, Switzerland, and in 1954 he won the Sibelius Prize.

The following works by Hindemith are discussed below: *Chamber Music (Kammermusik)*; Concerto for Piano and Orchestra; Concerto for Violin and Orchestra; *Mathis der Maler; Nobilissima Visione;* Quartet No. 3; Quartet No. 4; Quartet No. 5 in E-flat Major; *Der Schwanendreher; Symphonia Serena; Symphonic Metamorphoses on a Theme by Carl Maria von Weber;* Symphony in E-flat Major; *Theme With Variations according to the Four Temperaments.* For *Saint-Francis,* see *Nobilissima Visione.* For *Die Harmonie der Welt,* see Supplement.

QUARTET NO. 3, for strings, op. 22 (1922). I. Fugato. II. Quickly and Energetically. III. Calm and Flowing. IV. Lively. V. Rondo.

In the Third Quartet, introduced at the Donaueschingen Festival in Baden-Baden on November 4, 1922, Hindemith crystallized his linear writing. The first movement is an atonal fugato in which the various voices achieve complete freedom of movement. The scherzo bursts in without a break; this is sharply accentuated and powerfully propelled music, often in irregular rhythms. The longest of the movements, the third, brings to polytonality singular expressiveness. After a fantasialike section, virtuoso in character, the final movement, a rondo, enters without interruption.

QUARTET NO. 4, for strings, op. 32 (1924).

The Fourth Quartet followed the Third by two years and represents some of the most brilliant and complex contrapuntal writing Hindemith has done in the quartet form. A fugue and a double fugue appear in the first movement, while in the second the contrapuntal writing is developed with remarkable inventiveness and variety of mood. A brisk march brings a measure of relief from these polyphonic elaborations, but the relief is only temporary. The closing passacaglia, which consists of twenty-seven variations of a theme, is an elaborate web that ends in a climactic fugato.

CHAMBER MUSIC (KAMMERMUSIK), nos. 1-7.

Hindemith composed seven important works for chamber orchestra, or for solo instrument and chamber orchestra, in which his rebellion against Wagnerian postromanticism and Debussian impressionism was complete. Here his own linear style was finally realized. In these works contrapuntal writing is combined with modern techniques to achieve fluidity of movement, together with high tensions and concentrated power. German critics, mindful of Hindemith's modern approach to counterpoint, used to describe these works as "Brandenburg Concertos—upside down."

It was with these works that Hindemith first attracted notice to himself. The first was introduced at the Donaueschingen Festival, at Baden-Baden, in 1922; the second was first heard at the International Society of Contemporary Music Festival in Venice, in 1925. Both performances were successful, and as a result Hindemith became one of the important representatives of the younger school of German composers.

The seven works in this group are:

No. 1, for chamber orchestra, op. 24, no. 1 (1922).
No. 2, for piano and twelve instruments, op. 36, no. 2 (1924).
No. 3, for cello and ten instruments, op. 36, no. 1 (1925).
No. 4, for violin and chamber orchestra, op. 36, no. 2 (1924).
No. 5, for viola and chamber orchestra, op. 36, no. 3 (1927).
No. 6, for viola d'amore and chamber orchestra, op. 36, no. 4 (1930).
No. 7, for organ and chamber orchestra, op. 46, no. 2 (1930).

MATHIS DER MALER, Symphony (1934). I. The Concert of the Angels. II. The Entombment. III. Temptation of Saint Anthony.

What is perhaps Hindemith's most famous and successful work has known two lives. It originated as an opera. Writing his own libretto, the composer developed the few known facts about Matthias Grünewald, the early sixteenth-century painter, into a romantic story set against the turbulent background of the Peasants' War of 1524. Matthias (Mathis), employed by Cardinal Albrecht, abandons his lifework (painting religious pictures) to join the cause of Hans Schwalb, leader of the uprising peasants against the Church. Once plunged into the revolutionary struggle, Matthias is assailed by doubts. He sees on his side as much injustice, murder, pillage, as he had formerly witnessed on the other. He escapes with his beloved, the beautiful Regina, daughter of Schwalb, to seek peace of mind in the Oden-wald. Ugly apparitions come to haunt him. They disappear. Then beautiful visions—panels from the Isenheim Altar—appear to bring him back to his art. Matthias is back in his studio working. His beloved Regina is no longer with him. With quiet and peaceful resignation he gives up the outside world.

Hindemith completed his opera in 1934. Its première was scheduled for that year at the Berlin State Opera, Wilhelm Furtwaengler directing. But the theme of the opera—the defeat of German liberalism—was too delicate for the times; and the details of the plot had overtones too sensitive for the ears of the Nazis. They denounced the work vigorously, banned the première, then attacked all of Hindemith's music as objectionable to the State. It was several years before the opera was introduced. This took place, not in Germany, but in Zurich, under the direction of Robert Denzler, on May 28, 1938. At that time the opera received an ovation. "It is ironical," wrote H. H. Stuckenschmidt, "that Mathis, which can be named beside Beethoven's Fidelio and Pfitzner's Palestrina in German essence and ethical earnestness, should start its course outside of Germany; but there is no doubt that this course will lead all over the world."

Meanwhile, Hindemith selected three orchestral excerpts from the operatic score and developed them into a "symphony"—though it actually is more like a suite than a symphony. Despite Nazi disapproval, Wilhelm Furtwaengler conducted the première of the symphony with the Berlin Philharmonic on March 12, 1934.

Here the composer endeavored to re-create the emotions aroused in a sensitive spectator by the three celebrated Grünewald paintings of the Isenheim Altar, at the Museum at Colmar. Utilizing a flexible style that ranges from medieval modes to suggestions of the twelve-tone system, Hindemith has created tonal symbols that are extraordinarily expressive without being pictorial. The pervading mysticism and religious intensity of the paintings has been caught in the music. As Heinrich Strobel remarked, polyphonic writing acquired here "a symbolic force which is something entirely new for Hindemith.... Effects are obtained here which could not have been realized by dramatic expressiveness."

The first movement, "The Concert of the Angels," is the overture of the opera. The principal theme is a melody utilized throughout the entire opera—"*Es sungen drei Engel.*" The second movement is derived from the sixth scene; the final one comes from the intermezzo of the opera's final scene, describing the painter's mellow resignation and dismissal of the world outside his workshop. "The development of the three movements is singularly clear," write Strobel. "The dynamic curve descends from the festive and happy *Concert of the Angels* of the beginning to the quiet elegy of *The Entombment,* and then proceeds, after the music of the Saint's ordeal, to the concluding hallelujah hymn of the final visionary exaltation."

DER SCHWANENDREHER, concerto on old folk melodies for viola and orchestra (1935). I. Langsam—Mässig bewegt mit Kraft. II. Sehr ruhig; Fugato. III. Finale: variations on *Seid ihr nicht der Schwanendreher*—Mässig schnell.

The name of this concerto is derived from the melody which appears, and then is varied, in the last movement, *Seid ihr nicht der Schwanendreher.* The translations of the word *Schwanendreher* are varied, the most familiar being *hurdy-gurdy player.*

On November 14, 1935, this concerto was introduced by the composer and the Amsterdam-Concertgebouw Orchestra, Mengelberg conducting.

The following explanatory note appears in the published score: "A minstrel, joining a merry company, displays what he has brought back from foreign lands: songs serious and gay, and finally a dance piece. Like a true musician, he expands and embellishes the melodies, preluding and improvising according to his fancy and ability. This medieval scene was the inspiration of the composition."

Folk melodies are the kernel of Hindemith's thinking in this work. In the first movement is heard *Zwischen Berg und tiefem Tal,* a folk tune of the fifteenth century; the two melodies of the second movement are both folk melodies, *Nun laube, Lindlein, laube* and *Der Gutzgauch auf dem Zaune sass,* both from the fifteenth or sixteenth centuries. In the last movement, the early seventeenth-century melody *Seid ihr nicht der Schwanendreher* is subjected to seven variations.

NOBILISSIMA VISIONE, suite for orchestra (1938). I. Introduction; Rondo. II. March. III. Passacaglia.

In 1937, Hindemith was commissioned by Serge Diaghilev to collaborate with the choreographer Leonide Massine in the writing of a ballet for the Ballet Russe. The subject of Saint Francis was finally chosen. The ballet, or "choreographic legend," as it was designated by its authors, attempted (as Massine explained) to "translate the moving simplicities and mentality of the strange world of Saint Francis into the highly formalized language of the ballet." *Saint Francis* was introduced by the Ballet Russe in London on July 21, 1938.

One year after the première of the ballet, Hindemith extracted several sections from the ballet score—those that in his words were "self-sufficient and comprehensible in concert music, and which do not depend upon supplementary stage action"—and developed them into an orchestral suite which he called *Nobilissima Visione.* The suite was heard for the first time in Venice in September, 1938. On March 23, 1939, its American première took place in Los Angeles, with the composer conducting the Los Angeles Philharmonic.

Hindemith's own description of this orchestral suite follows: "The Introduction consists of that part of the original music during which the hero of the action is sunk in deep meditation. The Rondo corresponds to the music in the stage score for the mystic union of the Saint to Mistress Poverty, the scene having been inspired by an old Tuscan legend. The music reflects the blessed peace and unworldly cheer with which the guests at the wedding participate in the wedding feast—dry bread and water only. The second movement pictures the march of a troop of medieval soldiers. First heard but distantly, their gradual approach is observed. The middle portion of this movement suggests the brutality with which these mercenaries set upon a traveling burgher and rob him. The third and closing movement corresponds to the portion of the ballet score representing the Hymn to the Sun. Here all the symbolic personifications of heavenly and earthly existence mingle in the course of the different variations through which the six-measure long theme of the Passacaglia is transformed."

CONCERTO FOR VIOLIN AND ORCHESTRA (1939). I. Moderato. II. Andante. III. Vivace.

This work is not to be confused with the *Chamber Music,* no. 4 (op. 36), which is sometimes programmed as a Concerto for Violin and Chamber Orchestra.

Early in 1940, the Violin Concerto was introduced in Amsterdam. On March 14, 1940, Ruth Posselt performed it in this country with the Boston Symphony, Richard Burgin conducting.

Though Hindemith does not abandon his contrapuntal style in this piece, he recognizes the lyrical nature of the solo instrument by indulging in long and expansive melodic ideas. One of these is heard in the very opening of the first movement; another, the principal theme of the second movement, has an even greater span. The slow movement has perhaps the most expressive and intense of these melodic ideas, heard in the solo instrument after a few introductory measures by the woodwind. The pace changes in the last movement, as soloist and orchestra indulge in music of sprightly character. An elaborate cadenza employing earlier material is heard toward the end of the work.

THEME WITH VARIATIONS ACCORDING TO THE FOUR TEMPERAMENTS, for strings with piano (1940).

In this music, originally intended as a score for a ballet that never materialized, Hindemith tried to give musical expression to the different moods of melancholic, sanguine, phlegmatic, and choleric people. The "four temperaments" consequently are variations on the theme of human nature. The work is described as a theme with variations, but actually consists of three themes projected in three different sections; each variation, in turn, appears in the same order as the themes, and is divided into three sections of its own.

Themes: The first subject is heard in the strings (Moderato); the second is played by the piano (Allegro assai); the third appears in the entire orchestra (Moderato).

Variation I. Melancholic. Against a piano background, a muted violin is heard in a supple melody. A presto passage for orchestra follows, after which the variation ends with a slow march for piano.

Variation II. Sanguine. A delightful waltz melody is played by the piano and strings.

Variation III. Phlegmatic. A subject for strings alone (Moderato) is followed by a sprightly idea for piano (Allegretto). Strings and piano bring the variation to its end (Allegretto scherzando).

Variation IV. Choleric. A succession of vigorous chords in the piano are answered just as vigorously by the orchestra. After a Vivace section for the orchestra, a passionate and emotional passage is heard. The work ends Maestoso.

This work was heard for the first time in Boston on September 3, 1943, with Richard Burgin conducting members of the Boston Symphony Orchestra, and Lukas Foss playing the piano obbligato.

SYMPHONY IN E-FLAT MAJOR, for orchestra (1940). I. Sehr lebhaft. II. Sehr langsam. III. Lebhaft. IV. Massig schnell halle.

Though the symphony has a specific tonality—E-flat major—it is written with Hindemith's customary tonal freedom; there is no key signature in the music itself, beyond that on the title page. It was introduced by the Minneapolis Symphony Orchestra under Dimitri Mitropoulos on November 21, 1941.

Two principal themes dominate the first movement. The first is a vigorous and rhythmic subject heard in the horns; the second, which is much more lyrical, is set against the pizzicati of the strings and introduced after the development of the first. The second movement opens with the principal idea stated by the English horn, clarinet, and trumpet against the quarter-note background of the tympani. The subsidiary subject is played by the oboe accompanied by violin chords, later to be taken up by the entire orchestra. The third movement has the nature of a scherzo, which develops into the finale without pause. The principal subject of this last movement similar in some respects to the principal theme of the first movement, is announced by the first violins; following its development, a subject of decided strength and energy is heard in the brass. Following a climactic development there comes a lull in the form of an intermezzo; but the earlier unrest returns and slowly grows in strength and proportion into a dynamic close.

QUARTET NO. 5 IN E-FLAT MAJOR, for strings (1943). I. Very quiet and expressive. II. Lively and very energetic. III. Quiet; Variations. IV. Broad and energetic; Allegretto grazioso.

Hindemith here designated a key, a not altogther frequent procedure with him. But the tonality, though stated, is not too restricting. Through the work it is free, marked by abrupt modulations and even by occasional polytonality. Counterpoint does not play quite the important role here that it did in earlier quartets. The emphasis is rather on thematic material and its development. This increased bent for lyricism, together with a simplification of writing and refinement of texture, makes this quartet more pleasurable on first contact than any of his preceding works in the form.

SYMPHONIC METAMORPHOSES ON A THEME BY CARL MARIA VON WEBER, for orchestra (1943).

Hindemith borrowed four Weber themes from the master's more obscure works in this elaborate "symphonic metamorphosis"; and in their order the four movements suggest a symphony. The first, third, and last of the movements are derived from themes taken from the eight pieces for four-hand piano entitled *All' Ongarese,* op. 60; the second movement

(Scherzo) utilizes a subject from Weber's overture to incidental music to Schiller's *Turandot*. Hindemith took pains to explain that none of these Weber excerpts represents the composer at his best and that they are, consequently, altered and elaborated by him whenever necessary.

On January 20, 1944, this work was introduced by the New York Philharmonic-Symphony Orchestra, Artur Rodzinski conducting.

CONCERTO FOR PIANO AND ORCHESTRA (1945). I. Moderately fast. II. Slow. III. Medley on the Medieval Dance, *Tre Fontane*.

Hindemith composed this concerto on a commission from the pianist Jesús María Sanromá, who introduced it with the Cleveland Orchestra, George Szell conducting, on February 27, 1947.

There are three principal subjects developed in the first movement: a theme played in the very opening of the section by the clarinet, and then taken up by the solo piano; a lyrical idea brought up by two clarinets and bass clarinet; and a subject for muted trumpet. The second movement, in simple three-part form, is interesting for its orchestral color and appealing for its pure melodic writing. For his finale, Hindemith created a medley on the fourteenth-century dance theme, *Tre Fontane,* which he found in Volume I of the *Archiv der Musikwissenschaft*. This section opens with a canzone (solo piano) and develops into a march and a slow waltz. The melody of *Tre Fontane* returns in the piano and orchestra to conclude the work.

SYMPHONIA SERENA, for orchestra (1946). I. Moderately fast. II. Geschwindmarsch by Beethoven, Paraphrase. III. Colloquy. IV. Gay.

Antal Dorati, then music director of the Dallas Symphony Orchestra, commissioned Hindemith to write a new orchestral work for his organization. On February 2, 1947, Dorati introduced it with the Dallas Symphony Orchestra in Dallas.

For this première, Dorati provided an analysis of the work which is complete and authoritative: "The first movement is in sonata form.... It is very alive and vivid music, with contrasting and strong themes...developed in the usual symphonic fashion.... The second movement takes the place of the scherzo. Under a fluent and steady current of woodwind passages, which provide a continuous thematic background, the Beethoven theme (a military march composed by Beethoven between 1809 and 1810) is stated in little bits at a time first, and gradually becomes stronger, more and more coherent, and develops into a very fast march, with which the scherzo closes brilliantly. The third movement is written for string orchestra divided into two groups. The first puts forth a serious and tender slow theme. The second group plays a faster scherzando passage, pizzicato. These two sections are connected by a recitative-like passage for two solo violins, one of them playing backstage.... The finale is the most complex and challenging of the four movements. It introduces a wealth of new thematic material, and...is of tremendous impact, and at the same time, full of enormous contrapuntic detail. Its form is quite new and individual, yet the roots are clearly entrenched in the classical symphony finale form, which is a mixture of the old sonata and rondo forms."

GUSTAV HOLST   1874—1934

Literary influences played an important part in Holst's earliest works. Always an avid reader of poetry, his passion for Walt Whitman and his admiration for William Morris are discernible in the *Whitman Overture* (1899), *The Mystic Trumpeter* (1901), and the second movement of the *Cotswold Symphony* (1900), which was dedicated to the memory of William Morris.

In or about 1905 religious philosophy—as found in Sanskrit literature— began influencing Holst's musical thinking. *Sita* (1906), an opera based on an episode from the *Ramayana;* four choral hymns composed to the *Rig-Veda* (1912); and an opera di camera, *Savitri,* based upon an episode from *Mahabharata,* (1908) are products of this period. Not the methods of Indian music (though the exotic scales and irregular rhythms of Eastern music are occasionally heard), but the mysticism, poetry, and spiritual over-tones of Eastern philosophy interested Holst.

By 1915, Holst had more or less abandoned the oriental trend to arrive at his own identity. He now produced a work which was instantly successful, and which to this day remains the most frequently performed of his works—*The Planets.* The Wagnerian tendencies so long prevalent in his music were once and for all overcome. With skill in harmonic and rhythmic writing, a wealth of orchestral color, and a genuinely effective melody derived from English folk music, Holst arrived at full maturity.

After World War I, Holst's style became more austere. A profound interest in English folk music (to which he had been drawn as a result of his friendship with and admiration for Ralph Vaughan Williams) made him seek a simpler style, a purification of idiom, a greater flexibility of melodic line. He never did attempt to imitate the English folksong; and only on very rare occasions did he actually incorporate folk materials in his works. It is the artistic impulses behind the English song—its economy and austerity—that impressed him. At the same time, he became drawn more and more to nonharmonic counterpoint, and to the utmost freedom in the use of tonality. The strength and passionate speech and brilliance of color which were found in *The Planets* now gave way to the lean and cold music of the *Twelve Songs,* to lyrics of Humbert Wolfe (1929), and the Concerto for Two Violins and Orchestra (1929). The music of this last period of Holst's creative life, however, has never gained either the circulation or the popularity of his earlier efforts.

Holst was born in Cheltenham on September 21, 1874. His mother, a concert pianist, taught him the elements of music. In 1893, Holst entered the Royal College of Music, where he won a scholarship in composition. After completing his studies, Holst played the trombone in several orchestras. In 1903 he assumed his first post as teacher of music. One year later he became director of the Passmore Edwards Settlement. For the next two decades, Holst was particularly active as a teacher, holding important posts at the St. Paul's Girls' School, Morley College, and the Royal College of Music.

During World War I, he was active in organizing the musical activities of the British troops in the Near East. In February, 1923, he suffered a concussion as the result of a fall. His physical deterioration was so rapid that he was soon compelled to give up all musical activities except composing. For the next decade he lived in seclusion, from which he emerged briefly in 1932 to visit this country and conduct the Boston Symphony Orchestra. He died in London on May 25, 1934.

The following works by Holst are discussed below: *The Planets; St. Paul's Suite.*

ST. PAUL'S SUITE, for orchestra, op. 29, no. 2 (1913). I. Jig. II. Ostinato. III. Intermezzo. IV. Finale.

This delightful music was written for the school orchestra of St. Paul's Girls' School in Hammersmith, of which Holst was musical director. It came as an expression of gratitude for the new music wing, with a special sound-proof studio, which the school had that year built for the composer.

English folksong influence is felt strongly in this music. Occasionally actual folk themes are quoted; most often, however, the music derives only its rhythmic impetus and its clarity and simplicity from folk tunes. The opening jig has an exotic flavor, due to its modal writing. The second movement has the character of a perpetual motion. A beautiful cantabile melody dominates the third section, frequently interrupted by English dance rhythms. In the finale, two famous English songs are quoted: *Dargason* (which is repeated thirty times with various harmonic and rhythmic variations) and *Greensleeves,* which appears as a contrapuntal melody.

THE PLANETS, suite for orchestra, op. 32 (1916). I. Mars, the Bringer of War. II. Venus, the Bringer of Peace. III. Mercury, the Winged Messenger. IV. Jupiter, the Bringer of Jollity. V. Saturn, the Bringer of Old Age. VI. Uranus, the Magician. VII. Neptune, the Mystic.

What is unquestionably Holst's most popular work in this country, and one of his finest, was written between the years of 1914 and 1916. A private performance conducted by H. Balfour Gardiner in 1918 introduced it to a select audience. Five of the seven movements ("Venus" and "Neptune" were omitted) were publicly introduced on February 27, 1919, with Sir Adrian Boult directing the London Philharmonic. The complete suite was heard on November 15, 1920, under Albert Coates.

In an interview, Holst explained: "These pieces were suggested by the astrological significance of the planets; there is no program music in them, neither have they any connection with the deities of classical mythology bearing the same names. If any guide to the music is required, the subtitle to each piece will be found sufficient, especially if it be used in a broad sense. For instance, Jupiter brings jollity in the ordinary sense, and also the more ceremonial kind of rejoicing associated with religious or national festivities. Saturn brings not only physical decay, but also a vision of fulfillment. Mercury is the symbol of the mind."

Strong rhythms and counterrhythms, and a vigorous melodic subject stated by trumpets and horns, bring up the martial character of the first section. A gentler mood is evoked with "Venus"—a soft horn call, answered by the delicate music of flutes, immediately brings up an atmosphere which to Richard Capell suggests "cool, clear air." Swift-winged movement is evoked in the third part, a fleet scherzo. Good spirits abound in "Jupiter," which has been called "an overture for an English country festival"; the core of this part is a fully articulated folksong which spans some forty bars. According to Capell, "a profound peacefulness" pervades the fifth movement. Bright-faced humor returns in "Uranus," who, Capell explains, "might have been called the god of laughter if after a point the prodigiousness of his pranks did not pass a joke." *The Planets* ends in an atmosphere of quiet mystery. "Neptune" is a movement that is played entirely pianissimo, "its hushed interrogation," says Capell, "coming as a beautiful relief, slackening the strain set up by the dynamic assertiveness that we have heard in the hour." In the final pages, a hidden choir of women's voices is heard on a sustained note, with the flute and clarinet as a background.

ARTHUR HONEGGER   1892—1955

Honegger first became known (at the close of World War I) as a member of a school of young composers known as the "French Six." This group included, besides Honegger, Darius Milhaud, Georges Auric, Louis Durey, Francis Poulenc, and Germaine Tailleferre. Actually, the "French Six" was not a school in the accepted sense of the term—that is, a number of composers united by the same ideals and artistic purpose. And its creation was due not to the composers themselves, but to a French critic. Reviewing an album of piano pieces by these six young composers Henri Collet—in an article published in *Comoedia* on January 16, 1920—likened these composers to the more famous Russian nationalist school, "The Five." The name of "French Six" stuck to these six composers, even though they had little in common and tried their best to disassociate themselves from the label.

Honegger is a case in point. He might mingle socially with the other members of the "Six"; he might even allow his works to be performed with theirs. But he never subscribed wholeheartedly to their artistic ideals. For one thing, their interest in jazz and music-hall idioms never intrigued him (though even he succumbed briefly in his Concertino for Piano and Orchestra). Nor could he adopt their fetish for neo-classic simplicity. Strong-willed and artistically independent, Honegger listened to the esthetic discussions of his friends (who were influenced and inspired by Erik Satie) and to their music; then in his composing he went his own way, in those directions where his artistic conscience led him.

Characteristic of his independent thinking was the fact that he achieved his first striking success with a work that clung to the traditions and styles of the past: the oratorio *King David*. With this work the conservatives in Paris embraced him. But the conservatives were soon to disown him completely, as the linear austerity and harmonic ruggedness of such works as the highly provocative *Pacific 231* (1923) suggested his growing emancipation from the idioms of the past.

His stylistic mannerisms were now becoming set. The language is muscular, passionate, spiced with dissonance. The rhythmic sense is strong. The tonality is free. The contrapuntal writing is linear. And yet lyricism is not sacrificed.

Lyrical abundance with strength of idiom—together with an occasional indulgence in mysticism and religious feeling—are found in his later works, many of which have been performed with outstanding success in the leading musical capitals of the world.

Honegger was born in Le Havre on March 10, 1892. He received his early musical training from his mother and local teachers. For two years he attended the Zurich Conservatory, and after that attended the Paris Conservatory, where he was a pupil of Gédalge, Widor, and Vincent d'Indy. While still at the Paris Conservatory, he composed several works in which his writing was markedly influenced by Debussy and Ravel. His first important work was the incidental music to the play, *Le Dit des Jeux du Monde,* performed in Paris in 1918. The oratorio, *King David (Le Roi David),* came in 1921. Its première in Paris brought Honegger fame. Thereafter he became a provocative figure in French music as his writing grew increasingly individual.

All through World War II, Honegger remained in Paris, active in the Resistance movement. In 1947, he visited this country for the second time (the first visit having taken place in 1929) to teach at the Berkshire Music Center in Tanglewood. He died in Paris, November 27, 1955.

The following works by Honegger are discussed below: Concertino for Piano and Orchestra; *Joan of Arc at the Stake; King David (Le Roi David); Pacific 231; Pastorale d'Été;* Symphony No. 2; Symphony No. 3 (*"Liturgique"*); Symphony No. 5.

For *Mouvement Symphonique No. 3,* see *Pacific 231;* for *Rugby,* see *Pacific 231.*

PASTORALE D'ÉTÉ, for small orchestra (1921).

There are several conductors (Toscanini has been one of them) who have programed this quiet and bucolic music together with *Pacific 231,* as a kind of study in contrasts. *Pastorale d'Été* preceded *Pacific 231* by two years. It is a gentle etching of Nature. Two themes comprise its musical materials: one for horn, heard immediately after a three-bar introduction, and a second, more vivacious, for clarinet.

Pastorale d'Été was first heard in Paris on February 17, 1921.

KING DAVID (LE ROI DAVID), oratorio for narrator, soloists, chorus, and orchestra (1923).

Early in 1921, Honegger was commissioned to write music for *King David,* a "dramatic psalm" by René Morat, scheduled for performance at the Théâtre du Jorat in Mézières (near Lausanne), Switzerland. He adopted a conventional pattern and wrote a formal oratorio. Though on occasion brusque harmonies and atonality bring suggestions of the later Honegger, the form and approach are reminiscent of Handel. The première performance was outstandingly successful. For the time being, at any rate, Honegger was a favorite of the conservative group of French composers.

In 1923, Honegger reorchestrated the oratorio and adapted it for concert performance. Introduced that year in Winterthur, *King David* once again proved a great success. It was heard in Paris in 1924, in New York in 1925, and in Zurich and Rome in 1926. Then it virtually encircled the rest of the music world.

The oratorio is in three sections (which, in turn, are divided into twenty-eight parts). It tells the story of David, tracing his career from humble shepherd to king and prophet.

PACIFIC 231, for orchestra (1923).

As a child in Le Havre, Honegger used to watch trains for hours on end. Through manhood this passion for trains continued.

In writing *Pacific 231*, he did not attempt to imitate "the noises of the locomotive," he once told an interviewer, but to translate into music "the visual impressions made by the locomotive, and the physical sensation of it." Honegger explained further: *"Pacific 231* sets forth the objective contemplation; the quiet breathing machine in repose, its effort in starting, then gradual increase in speed, leading from the lyrical to the pathetic condition of a train of three hundred tons hurling itself through the night at a speed of 120 kilometers an hour."

Despite the composer's avowed intentions, the work is a realistic picture. What we get in this music is not so much the composer's emotional reactions to the locomotive as a picture of the locomotive itself—its puffings, snortings, and increased momentum.

Pacific 231 was introduced in Paris by Serge Koussevitzky and his orchestra on May 8, 1924. It received considerable attention, favorable and otherwise. Together with *King David,* it helped establish the composer's reputation.

In 1924, the dissonances of *Pacific 231* were provocative and disturbing. Today they no longer appear startling; and the reproduction of the sounds and movement of a train now seems almost naïve in its realism.

Honegger subsequently wrote two additional short works for orchestra which, together with *Pacific 231,* he intended as a three-movement symphonic work: *Rugby* (1928) and *Mouvement Symphonique No. 3* (1933).

CONCERTINO FOR PIANO AND ORCHESTRA (1924). I. Allegro molto moderato. II. Larghetto sostenuto. III. Allegro.

This disarmingly pleasing little concerto is one of Honegger's few works to simulate a popular music-hall idiom. It is the kind of jaunty, insouciant music the French wrote so well in the 1920's—occasionally impudent and malicious, but always ingratiating for its simple approach, fresh lyricism, and rhythmic vitality.

On May 23, 1925, the concertino was introduced in Paris. Andrée

Vaurabourg (Honegger's fiancée) was soloist, and the orchestra was conducted by Serge Koussevitzky.

The first movement begins with a sustained dialogue between piano and orchestra. A syncopated theme for piano appears after a run. Following a brief fugal development, the opening material is repeated. The principal material of the second movement is a piquant little melody for the piano, with various embellishments by the orchestra. The interest here is exclusively lyrical, just as the interest in the finale is primarily rhythmic. In the closing movement both piano and orchestra participate in highly syncopated passages as the music gathers force and grows into a telling climax, which, however, is dissipated.

JOAN OF ARC AT THE STAKE (JEANNE D'ARC AU BÛCHER), dramatic oratorio for two narrators, soloists, chorus, and orchestra (1938).

Honegger wrote this oratorio for Ida Rubinstein, who appeared in the title role when the work was introduced, in Basel, Switzerland, on May 10, 1938. In 1939, it was heard in Orléans and Paris; in 1940, in Brussels. After successful performances in most of the principal cities of Europe, it was introduced in the United States on January 1, 1948, by the New York Philharmonic-Symphony Orchestra, directed by Charles Munch. Vera Zorina appeared as Joan of Arc.

The composer has designated the oratorio as a *mimodrame,* by which he meant that he intended it as a stage production, with scenery and costumes. However, the work has been heard more frequently as a concert-oratorio.

Paul Claudel wrote the text, which, in the opinion of Olin Downes, is "mystical and symbolic . . . a bravura feat by a scholar and literary virtuoso." Honegger's music caught many of the symbolic and mystic nuances of this text; a great measure of the artistic success of the oratorio was due to the felicitous union of poem and music.

When *Joan of Arc* was introduced in Basel, Roger Secretain provided the following notes: "The work . . . is in an unusual dramatic form, on two separate stages. From the beginning to the end of the spectacle Joan is seen fastened to the stake. Her bonds permit her to make the Sign of the Cross only with difficulty—this sign, which, Claudel says, 'is the development of the four cardinal points of the human race . . . which is also the quartering of Joan between her earthly destiny and her divine vocation.' The cross is the struggle between earth and heaven. But Joan never flinches for a moment before the death which will clearly be conquered at last—at last convinced. She obeys the injunction of the Virgin who, from the top of the pillar, conjures her to let herself be embraced by her 'Brother Fire' . . . to let herself be drawn into heaven.

"As well as Joan's stake—symbol of the final sacrifice, where she stands immovably throughout the oratorio—one can see the unfolding of various images of Joan's life, as through Joan's own eyes. The synthetic vision typifies the genius of Claudel. Through his function as a poet, he sets the action in the past as well as the present. She is a presence simultaneously in all corners of the earth, in possession of time and space, exposed to all earthly temptation. The hour has come for this sublime heroine, he says, 'to understand what she has done; to utter the supreme *Yes!'*"

The oratorio consists of a Prologue and eleven scenes. The scenes are entitled: I. The Voices of Heaven. II. The Book. III. The Voices of Earth. IV. Joan Delivered to the Beasts. V. Joan at the Stake. VI. The Kings, or the Invention of the Card Game. VII. Catherine and Marguerite. VIII. The King Who Goes to Rheims. IX. Joan's Sword. X. "Trimazo"— Rehearsal of the Merry Month of May. XI. Joan of Arc in Flames.

SYMPHONY NO. 2, for string orchestra (1941). I. Molto moderato; Allegro. II. Adagio mesto. III. Vivace non troppo.

Honegger's Second Symphony was written in the gray year of 1941, when the Nazi troops were in Paris. Willi Reich believes that the music has caught "much of the mood of occupied Paris." Few other Honegger works are so deeply felt, or reach for such emotional heights.

An ostinato figure for violas, heard early in the first movement and repeated throughout, provides an atmosphere of gloom, which is intermittently interrupted by dissonances and vigorous sweep of defiant rhythms. Despair is also evident in the second movement, a passacaglia consisting of eight variations on a ground bass. This part opens gently enough in the violins, but midway grows in intense suffering until uncontrolled grief erupts. The finale, however, has overtones of good spirits, as one theme after another is nimbly projected before the presto-like coda is realized. Optimism is sounded loud and clear in the chorale of the closing page.

The Second Symphony was dedicated to the Swiss conductor Paul Sacher, who introduced it in Basel on May 23, 1942.

SYMPHONY NO. 3 ("Liturgique") (1946). I. Allegro marcato. II. Adagio. III. Andante con moto.

Honegger dedicated his Third Symphony to Charles Munch, who introduced it in Zurich on August 17, 1946. Munch believes that this work "poses the problem of humanity vis-à-vis God," expressing as it does the revolt of man against a Higher Will, then his voluntary subjugation to and acceptance of that Will.

The composer has provided explanatory Latin subtitles to the three movements. The first is a *"Dies Irae"* which, to Arthur Hoerée, "is irresistible in its fulguration, in its abruptness, its panic and trepidation, its ever-present lyricism." To Hoerée the second movement, a *"De Profundis,"* is a "long cry of distress"; and the closing movement, *"Dona Nobis Pacem,"* aspires to "new peace through a long phrase in the violins whose inspiration borders upon the sublime."

SYMPHONY NO. 5 (1950). I. Grave. II. Allegretto. III. Allegro marcato.

Honegger's Fifth Symphony came four years after the Fourth, and was heard for the first time in Boston on March 9, 1951, with Charles Munch conducting the Boston Symphony Orchestra.

A mighty chorale for full orchestra opens the symphony, succeeded by a gentler idea, stated first by the clarinets, then by the English horn. The original chorale returns in a gentler vein, after which the movement ends softly. A staccato theme, appearing as a duet for clarinet and first violins, opens the second movement. Following a climax, an Adagio section appears. This Adagio section brings the movement to a close after the original subject has been stated. The third movement is in the nature of a perpetual motion, opening with a staccato phrase for trumpets soon to be taken up by the strings. Despite the rhythmic agility of this movement there is a pronounced suggestion of tragedy.

An interesting integrating feature of this symphony is the recurrence of a drum tap in D, pianissimo, as the last note of each movement.

JACQUES IBERT   1890—

Ibert has utilized impressionistic devices in the way Maurice Ravel did; but, actually, he is no impressionist. He goes in for vivid orchestrations, subtle effects, chords moving in parallel motion. His writing has clarity and deftness; there is self-assurance in his technique; and occasionally there is wit as well. As André George said of him: "An air of good fellowship and delicate amiability reveals him to be an artist of breeding."

Ibert was born in Paris on August 15, 1890. Since his father objected to his receiving musical training, he had to learn harmony and the piano secretly. Eventually he overcame his father's resistance: in 1911, he entered the Paris Conservatory, where his teachers included Gédalge and Fauré. World War I interrupted these studies. During this period Ibert served first in the Navy, then as an officer in the French Naval Reserve. The war over, he returned to music study and won the Prix de Rome with his cantata, *Le Poète et la Fée*. In Rome, in 1921, he wrote his first important composition, *The Ballad of Reading Gaol*, for orchestra, inspired by Oscar Wilde's moving ballad of abuses suffered in an English prison. This composition was successfully introduced at a Colonne Concert in Paris, Gabriel Pierné conducting, on October 22, 1922. This was followed by an even more successful work, *Escales*, for orchestra. Ibert's importance in French music was now established.

In 1937, he was appointed director of the Académie de France in Rome, the first musician ever to hold this post. After World War II, he became assistant director of the Paris Opéra. During the summer of 1950, Ibert visited the United States for the first time, to serve on the faculty of the Berkshire Music Center at Tanglewood. Between 1955 and 1957 he was director of the combined management of the Paris Opéra and the Opéra-Comique.

The following works by Ibert are discussed below: *Concertino da Camera for Alto Saxophone and Orchestra; Divertissement; Escales.*

For *The Ballad of Reading Gaol*, see the biographical sketch above.

ESCALES, suite for orchestra (1922). I. Rome—Palermo. II. Tunis—Nefta. III. Valencia.

During his duties in the Navy in World War I, Ibert visited many Mediterranean ports. They attracted him for their local color and their native popular tunes. In 1922, he wrote a musical travelogue of three such ports. The atmosphere and individuality of each is re-created musically. A free-flowing Italian melody (flute) brings up the picture of an Italian port. A chromatic theme (oboe) set against oriental rhythms transports us to Africa. In the last section, a languid and sensual Hispano-Moorish subject in the strings, developed in an improvisatory manner, evokes Spain.

Escales was heard for the first time on January 6, 1924, at a Lamoureux Concert in Paris. Since its première, it has been one of Ibert's most frequently heard works.

DIVERTISSEMENT, for orchestra (1930). I. Introduction. II. Cortège. III. Nocturne. IV. Valse. V. Parade. VI. Finale.

Like the *Concertino da Camera* described below, the *Divertissement* finds Ibert in one of his lighter and happier moods. The music was drawn from the score of a musical comedy, *Le Chapeau de Paille d'Italie*, produced in 1929. The Suite was introduced in Paris on November 30, 1930.

Following a lively Introduction built out of a single theme, there comes a march made up of two ideas: one is fast, played by the strings; the second is a vigorous subject for the trumpet. A powerful climax develops, after which, suddenly, there is heard an amusing quotation from the "Wedding March" of Mendelssohn's *A Midsummer Night's Dream*. The Nocturne is a short and simple melody. Infectious moods are posed by the Valse (in which there is an amusing passing reference to Johann Strauss's *The Blue Danube Waltz*) and the Parade, after which there comes the Finale, in which an effective climax is achieved with a characteristic Offenbach "can-can." The piano adds to the gaiety of the proceedings by interpolating strident and dissonant notes into the harmonization.

CONCERTINO DA CAMERA FOR ALTO SAXOPHONE AND ORCHESTRA (1935). I. Allegro con moto. II. Larghetto—animato molto.

This charming chamber concerto is not an excursion into jazz, as the solo instrument might suggest. Tart modern harmonies and cross-rhythms appear within the old chamber-concerto structure with delightful effect. The music is brisk and witty. Its artistic intent may be slight; but what it sets out to do—namely, to produce a workmanlike and aurally pleasing vehicle for an unorthodox solo instrument—it does successfully. There is skillful virtuoso writing for the saxophone. There is buoyant, lyrical material that is fresh and singable: the principal themes of both the first and the Larghetto movements, each one introduced by the soloist. In the Larghetto, Ibert's melodic writing grows mellow and thoughtful. But besides being lyrical the concertino is witty, as in the fugato of the first movement, in which the various voices take part in a kind of rowdy abandon; or as in the leapfrog pranks of the rhythms in the closing page.

VINCENT D'INDY   1851—1931

D'Indy was a pupil of César Franck; subsequently he became the master's disciple and partisan. The Franck influence on d'Indy's music is found in the use of the cyclic form, in the high-minded thinking, and in the spiritual radiance of the speech. To these qualities derived from Franck, Vincent d'Indy added some of his own; an objectivity and detachment that never permitted his music to indulge in dramatics or emotional extravagances. D'Indy does not overwhelm his listeners with powerfully projected climaxes; he does not excite them with splendors of color and overpowering sonorities. His appeal is more to the intellect than to the emotions. The processes of his thinking provide esthetic pleasure; those who follow these processes will come upon subtle moods that prevent the composer from yielding to austerity or cerebralism.

Vincent d'Indy was born in Paris on March 27, 1851. He began the study of music early—harmony with Lavignac and piano with Diémer and Marmontel. In 1872, he entered the Paris Conservatory, but the routines of conservatory life and study irritated him. He then became a private pupil of César Franck, whose influence on the younger man has already been discussed. From 1875 to 1879, d'Indy was chorusmaster of the Colonne Orchestra (after having played the kettledrum there). Meanwhile, in 1876, there came the first performance of one of his earliest ambitious works—the symphony *Jean Hunyade,* which was introduced by the Concerts Populaires, with Pasdeloup conducting.

With Franck, Vincent d'Indy founded the Société Nationale de Musique in Paris, whose mission was the encouragement and performance of contemporary music. The Société was responsible for bringing about first performances of works by most of the important younger French composers. When Franck died in 1890, d'Indy succeeded him as president.

In 1893, d'Indy was invited by the French government to be a member of a committee formed to reform the Paris Conservatory. The plan he helped to evolve proved too revolutionary, and it was shelved. Meanwhile, in 1894, d'Indy founded the Schola Cantorum, a school for the study of church music which, six years later, extended its curriculum to include every branch of music. The Schola Cantorum became one of France's great musical institutions; and d'Indy, who taught there for many years and then became professor at the Paris Conservatory, was one of France's greatest teachers of composition.

Two of d'Indy's most frequently heard works were written before 1900. The first was the famous *Symphony on a French Mountain Air,* op. 25, written in 1886, and heard for the first time one year later at a Concert Lamoureux in Paris. The principal thematic idea of the symphony, recurring throughout the work, is a mountain air the composer heard during a trip in the French Alps. A decade after the symphony came the *Istar Variations,* op. 42, which was inspired by the Babylonian poem, *The Epic of Izdubar.* There is here an unorthodox treatment of the variation form. The theme is not heard at the beginning, as is customary, but is allowed to grow and develop from embryo until, after the last variation, it is allowed to appear in its entirety. The first performance of the *Istar Variations* at an Ysaÿe concert in Brussels on January 10, 1897, was outstandingly successful.

Besides being a great teacher and composer, Vincent d'Indy also distinguished himself as a theorist, conductor, editor, and writer. He died in Paris on December 2, 1931, the same year in which he received one of the most impressive ovations of his career after conducting a performance of his *Symphony on a French Mountain Air.*

The following works by d'Indy are discussed below: *Summer Day on the Mountain;* Symphony No. 2 in B-flat Major.

For *Istar Variations* and *Symphony on a French Mountain Air,* see the biographical sketch above.

SYMPHONY NO. 2 IN B-FLAT MAJOR, op. 57 (1904). I. Extréme-ment lent—Très vif. II. Modérément lent. III. Modéré—Très animé.

Eighteen years separated d'Indy's two symphonies. The Second Symphony was introduced in Paris by the Lamoureux Orchestra on February 26, 1904.

Here d'Indy makes consummate use of the cyclical form evolved by his teacher César Franck, a form in which ideas stated in one movement are repeated in subsequent sections to give the work greater integration. The thematic material of the Second Symphony is found in the first four measures of the introduction to the first movement: the first theme, rather somber, is heard in the cellos and double basses; the second, a phrase for the flute, features an ascending flight of the interval of the seventh. These two ideas are varied and elaborated; they constitute the kernel of all the melodic materials of the symphony.

A slow introduction opens the work. A dramatic quasi-lyrical section follows. The second movement is a song for orchestra, the second section of which has the character of a funeral march. A folk-like melody opens the final movement and passes without interruption into the finale, which con-sists of an introduction, fugue, and finale.

D'Indy's style in this symphony consists mainly of chromatic har-monies and occasional excursions into whole-tone writing. There is little in the symphony to shock or arouse the listener—even in the year in which it was written. It is reserved and objective, rather than iconoclastic. Yet when the symphony was heard in America for the first time—on January 7, 1905, with the composer conducting the Boston Symphony Orchestra—Louis Elson wrote as follows in the *Boston Advertiser:* "D'Indy's symphony (????) is so unutterably shocking to us that we hesitate to express our frank opinion. It is evident that harmony books are now mere waste paper, that there are no more rules, that there is to be an eleventh commandment for the com-poser—'Thou shalt avoid all beauty.'" Philip Hale, however, was much more discerning. "We believe," wrote Hale, "that this symphony is one of the most important works of modern times....It contains deep and impres-sive thoughts, pages of beauty that is almost unearthly."

SUMMER DAY ON THE MOUNTAIN, rhapsody for piano and orchestra, op. 61 (1905). I. Dawn. II. Day. III. Night.

This effective triptych of nature portraits (which Daniel Gregory Mason once described as d'Indy's "masterpiece in the realm of program-matic music") is a veritable *Symphonie Pastorale.* We find painted in the first movement the break of dawn, as Nature gently awakens from her slumber. In the second section, a picture of Nature—as evoked by a sensitive artist reclining under the shade of a pine tree—is vividly reproduced. Night comes. As the country becomes enveloped in serenity and darkness, the music takes on a pastoral character.

The work is pictorial and impressionistic. It was introduced by the Colonne Orchestra in Paris on February 18, 1906.

CHARLES IVES   1874—1954

In one of Ives' earliest works, *Song for the Harvest Season* (1894), we find startling polytonal combinations: the song is set for voice, cornet, trombone, and organ, and each voice is written in a different key. A string quartet and a symphony (his first) followed in 1896; in these works the traditional concepts of harmony and rhythm, acceptable to other composers of this period, were abandoned. And as Ives kept writing, his daring grew.

That all of Ives' music was written before 1920, and much of it in the first few years of the twentieth century, presents an interesting phenomenon. Before Stravinsky, Ives worked with polyrhythm; before Bartók, he utilized agonizing dissonances; before Milhaud, he employed polytonality; before Alois Hába, he experimented with quarter-tones; before Henry Cowell, he exploited tone-clusters.

Strange as it is to contemplate, the complex scores that were collecting dust on his shelf for so many years contained (and often fully realized) innovations in tonality, rhythm, harmony, and melody which other, and more famous, composers arrived at years later, and frequently only after long and laborious experiments.

And if he was an ultramodern composer long before the ultramodern composers received notice, he was also an authentically American composer at a time when the American composer was only a faded carbon copy of the Europeans. With a sublime disregard for European examples and traditions—to which virtually all other American composers of the time felt bound—Ives wrote music which drew its breath and spirit from American backgrounds and experiences. Almost everything American served to inspire him: American culture as found in the New England writers of a century ago; American customs, as found in revival meetings, camp meetings, barn dances, town meetings; American scenes, such as one sees in picturesque New England; American history, holidays, politics, and even songs.

With his ungovernable spirit, he was driven by these American experiences to write music which in its brusqueness, independence, severity, and wind-swept movement could have come from nowhere but this country. It is the intrinsic Americanism of Ives' music that gives it its significance and assures its permanence in our cultural heritage. When he fully realized his identity in his music, Ives did much more than create new techniques. He created a vibrant art, an American art.

Charles Edward Ives was born in Danbury, Connecticut, on October 20, 1874. His iconoclasm was a heritage from a remarkable father. George E. Ives, a bandmaster during the Civil War, also tried to find new horizons for music. He was always experimenting: now with acoustics, now even with a system of quarter-tones. He made his son sing *Swanee River* in one key while he himself played the accompaniment in an opposing tonality, in order to train the boy to new sound relations. He was Charles Ives' first teacher. After that the young Ives studied with Dudley Buck, Rowe Shelley, and Horatio Parker. For a while, he worked as an organist. Then he entered the insurance business, in which he was to achieve considerable success and in which he was to remain until 1930. He combined business with the writing of music for the greater part of his life; he had no wish to make money out of his music. The first of his masterpieces came between the years of 1901 and 1904—the Third Symphony; but not until over forty years later was it performed, at which time it received a special citation from the New York Music Critics Circle and a few months after that the Pulitzer Prize. He continued working in obscurity and neglect. When success finally did come—and it came in his old age—he took little notice of it, avoiding interviewers and photographers and continuing to live the life of the recluse. He died in New York on May 19, 1954.

The following works by Ives are discussed below: Sonata No. 2 for Piano ("Concord"); Symphony No. 3; *Three Places in New England*.

SYMPHONY NO. 3, for orchestra (1904). I. Andante maestoso. II. Allegro. III. Largo.

Of the four symphonies composed by Ives, the Third was destined to be his most successful; it is, as a matter of fact, the work that was to bring him his belated recognition. Though written between the years of 1901 and 1904, it was not heard until forty-two years later, when Lou Harrison conducted it in New York City with the New York Little Symphony Orchestra (April, 1946). On May 12 of the same year it was repeated on an all-Ives program in New York, at which time the work was acclaimed by the critics. It received a special citation from the New York Music Critics Circle and after that the Pulitzer Prize in music.

The symphony was inspired by the camp meetings once rampart in the town of Danbury, Connecticut. Its melodic ideas are drawn from actual old hymn tunes: *O for a Thousand Tongues,* which is treated fugally in the first movement; and *Just Am I,* introduced in the last movement. The middle section of the symphony has been described by the composer as a game played by children at a camp meeting while their elders listen to the Holy Word.

As one might expect in a work by Ives, the symphony is unorthodox. It is filled with unusual progressions and cross-rhythms. But it does not give the appearance of being exclusively an experimental work, filled as it is with a speech that is strong and personal, authentically American in every accent. What Lawrence Gilman wrote about another Ives symphony applies even more strongly to this one: "This music is as indubitably American in impulse and spiritual texture as the prose of Jonathan Edwards."

THREE PLACES IN NEW ENGLAND for orchestra (1914). I. Colonel Shaw and His Black Regiment. II. Putnam Park, Connecticut. III. The Housatonic at Stockbridge.

Ives began writing his *Three Places in New England* in the year he completed the Third Symphony; but he did not finish this orchestral trilogy until 1914. Whereas New England hymns had been the inspiration for the symphony, New England geography provided the stimulation for *Three Places.* Of technical interest is the amazing use of polyrhythm in the section describing the approach of two different bands into town, each band playing a different melody in a different tempo. Of esthetic interest is the exquisite and subtle impressionistic tone-painting of the Housatonic at Stockbridge with which the work ends.

The composer provided the following information regarding the programmatic background for this music. The first movement was inspired by *The St. Gaudens in Boston Common* of which the following are the opening lines:

> Moving—Marching—Faces of Souls!
> Marked with generations of pain.
> Part-freers of a Destiny,
> Slowly, restlessly—swaying us on with you
> Towards other Freedom!

The setting of the second movement is a small park near Redding Center, Connecticut, which served as the winter quarters of General Putnam's soldiers in 1778-79. Slonimsky describes this section as a "musicorama of the American Revolution." Snatches of Revolutionary War songs and marches are interpolated.

For the third movement, Ives quoted Robert Underwood Johnson's poem, *The Housatonic at Stockbridge:*

Contented river! in thy dreamy realm—
The cloudy willow and plumy elm ...

Thou hast grown human laboring with men
At wheel and spindle; sorrow thou dost ken. ...

Thou beautiful! From every dreamy hill
What eye but wanders with thee at thy will,
Imagining thy silver course unseen
Conveyed by two attendant streams of green. ...

This work was first heard on January 10, 1931, in New York City, with
Nicolas Slonimsky directing members of the Boston Symphony Orchestra.

SONATA NO. 2 FOR PIANO ("Concord, Mass.: 1840-60") (1915).
I. Emerson. II. Hawthorne. III. The Alcotts. IV. Thoreau.

The intellectual heritage of the Concord writers has here provided
Ives with the inspiration for his most important work for the piano. From
transcendental philosophy Ives drew the essence of his musical thinking,
particularly in the first movement, which is music of mystery and revelation.
Hawthorne's "fantastical adventures into the half-childlike, half-fairylike
phantasmal realms" (in the words of Ives) are interpreted in the wild music
of the second movement. A more idyllic and gentle vein is tapped in the
music for the Alcotts and Thoreau.

The most advanced and experimental devices of rhythm, tonality, and
harmony are explored in this fabulous score. But, as is so characteristic of
Ives, this music is not only completely free in self-expression; it is also uninhibited in its use of unorthodox techniques and interpolations. In the Hawthorne section, a ruler or strip of wood is utilized by the pianist to play an
expansive two-octave cluster. In the Alcott music, the first four notes of
Beethoven's Fifth Symphony are quoted (the Alcott children used to prac-
tise Beethoven indefatigably). In the Thoreau section, Ives suggests that "a
flute may play throughout the page," because Thoreau "much prefers to
hear the flute over Walden."

The sonata was written between 1909 and 1915 and was published
privately in 1920. Its first complete public performance was given by John
Kirkpatrick in New York City on January 20, 1938.

To explain this complex and formidable work, Ives published a slim
pamphlet entitled *Essays Before a Sonata*. With his customary wit, Ives
dedicated these *Essays* to "those who can't stand his music—and the music
for those who can't stand his essays; to those who can't stand either, the
whole is respectfully dedicated."

LEOS JANÁČEK 1854—1928

"The Moravian Mussorgsky" is the way Janáček has been described by some critics; and this description puts a finger precisely on his stylistic manner. His indebtedness to Moravian peasant music was profound (he even used old Slavonic scales), just as Mussorgsky's debt to Russian folk music was great. But the similarity of musical ideal of these two composers is what makes then artistic brothers under the skin. Like Mussorgsky, Janáček tried to evolve his melodies out of speech patterns—"melodies of the language," he called them. The inflections, cadences, rhythms peculiar to the Czech language provide the contours for his melodic line. Janáček felt that, under different circumstances—among different kinds of people, and under different stresses and impacts—speech patterns change; and so must the melody. There is, consequently, a personal element in the harsh and stark lyricism found in Janáček's music. And the personal manner is also evident in his strong, robust harmonizations, in his ever-present feeling for dramatic effect, and in his avoidance of thematic development. He was not a skillful or sophisticated workman (once again there is a striking resemblance to the Russian!); but there are times when he seems to gain in force and passion because of the comparative crudity of his methods.

Janáček was born in Hukvaldy, Moravia, on June 3, 1854. Music study began in Brünn, continued at the Organ School in Prague, and was completed at the Leipzig and Vienna Conservatories. In 1881, Janáček settled in Brünn to become conductor of the Philharmonic Society and to organize the Organ School. He later became a teacher at the Prague Conservatory. As a composer, he first became known for his operas, achieving international fame with *Jenufa*. On the occasion of his seventieth birthday, the opera houses of Prague and Brünn gave cycles of Janáček's operas. He died in Ostrau, Moravia, on August 12, 1928. The tenth anniversary of his death was commemorated throughout Czechoslovakia with performances of his major works.

The following works by Janáček are discussed below: *Jenufa; Sinfonietta; Taras Bulba.*

JENUFA, opera (1902).
Janáček composed eleven operas, many of them on Russian subjects. But his chef d'oeuvre is based on Moravian peasant life. His lifelong researches into the folk music of Moravia now provided him with the neces-

sary musical materials with which to build a folk opera. A peasant play by Gabriela Preissová—a realistic drama of lust and murder—provided Janáček with the strong musical language he had been evolving; he himself adapted the play into a suitable libretto.

Jenufa, a peasant girl of Moravia, has been loved by two stepbrothers, one of whom, Stewa, is the father of her child. But Stewa no longer loves Jenufa; he has found pleasurable company elsewhere. The other stepbrother, Laca, is ready to accept Jenufa as his bride. Jenufa's mother notices the instinctive horror of Laca towards accepting a son who is not his own. She gives Jenufa a sleeping potion, and while the girl is asleep, drowns the baby in the river. When Jenufa awakens, she is told by her mother that the baby has died naturally. Jenufa marries Laca. The wedding ceremony is interrupted by the discovery of the dead body in the river. For a while, Jenufa is accused of murder, until the mother confesses her crime and is led away. Jenufa is ready to call off the marriage, but Laca remains true to her.

Much of the dramatic power of the opera—and its dramatic power is its outstanding quality—lies in the force of Janáček's melodies. But, as Rosa Newmarch has pointed out, not all of these melodies follow strictly the patterns of speech. "Sustained passion and tenderness forge their own melodies.... Jenufa's opening song, the Ave Maria, and the final duet are all 'singable' music."

Jenufa was introduced at the Brünn Opera two years after its composition. It did not create much of an impression, and was allowed to lie neglected for the next twelve years. It was revived by the Prague Opera in 1916, and was introduced in Vienna in 1918, achieving a great success on both occasions. It was then heard in most of the leading opera houses of Europe, and came at last to the Metropolitan Opera House on December 6, 1924.

TARAS BULBA, rhapsody for orchestra (1918). I. Death of Andrey. II. Death of Ostap. III. Prophecy and Death of Taras Bulba.

Russian literature provided Janáček with considerable artistic stimulation. He wrote operas based on a novel by Dostoyevsky, a drama of Ostrovsky, a poem of Lermontov. His String Quartet in E minor was inspired by Tolstoy's *Kreutzer Sonata*.

The epic novel of Nikolai Gogol about the fifteenth-century Cossack, Taras Bulba, and his two sons, Ostap and Andrey, was the spark to set Janáček's musical imagination aglow in this rhapsody. In the conflicts between the Ukrainian Cossacks and the Poles, Bulba's son, Andrey, turns traitor because of his love for a Polish girl. Captured, Andrey is brought before his father who, without hesitation, shoots him as a traitor. Bulba's second son, Ostap, is captured, tortured, and executed in the presence of his father, who has come within the enemy lines to rescue him. Seeking revenge, Taras Bulba descends with his troops on Polish towns, wreaking havoc. He is captured and burned alive; with his last gasps, Bulba prophecies that a Czar will arise to bring complete victory to the Russian Orthodox faith.

From this novel, Janáček drew the three major tragic episodes to set to music the respective deaths of Andrey, Ostap, and Taras Bulba. The music is dramatic throughout, highly expressive, vivid with colors and dynamics. Turbulent, vehement, sometimes full of terror, the music nevertheless acquires effective contrast by lapsing into exquisite elegiac moods (as in the theme for English horn, speaking of Andrey's love for the Polish girl, and the beautiful song for violins in the second movement, describing Ostap's death). The work acquires radiance in the closing section for full orchestra— the prophecy of Taras Bulba.

Janáček wrote *Taras Bulba* in 1918. A decade later it was introduced by the Leipzig Gewandhaus Orchestra, directed by Bruno Walter.

SINFONIETTA, for orchestra (1926). I. Allegretto. II. Andante. III. Moderato. IV. Allegretto. V. Allegro.

This sinfonietta originated as a series of fanfares for brass instruments, intended for open-air performance at an athletic meet in Prague. Hearing his fanfares, Janáček felt they deserved more extended musical treatment. He revamped them into a five-movement Sinfonietta. The origin of this work is revealed in the use of fanfare music for brass at the opening and close of the first movement, and in the fanfares of the last two.

Each movement is composed of several sections (some of them only a few bars), which proceed from one to another without much development, and often with the most tenuous transitions. The melodic and rhythmic ideas are all derived from Moravian folksongs and dances—and much of the work radiates peasant health and vigor.

In its final form, the Sinfonietta was introduced by the Czech Philharmonic Orchestra in Prague in May, 1926.

DMITRI KABALEVSKY   1904—

Like so many other Soviet composers, Kabalevsky has utilized music to glorify the political and social ideologies of his country, as well as to pay tribute to the historic and cultural past of the Russian people. Even when his music does not have a stated program, its intention is usually to portray some phase of Soviet life and aspirations. He is satisfied to write in traditional forms, uses stout harmonies and broad melodies, and fills his music with subjective feelings. A vein of pleasing wit often courses through his music and provides it with an infectious charm. Uncomplicated, direct, forceful, always aurally agreeable, his music makes an immediate appeal to listeners.

Kabalevsky was born in St. Petersburg on December 30, 1904. Though he early revealed his talent for music, he did not begin intensive study until his fourteenth year, when he entered the Scriabin Music School in Moscow. He completed his studies at the Moscow Conservatory with Miaskovsky (composition) and Goldenweiser (piano); upon his graduation in 1930, his name was inscribed on the honor plaque in the hall of the Conservatory.

Meanwhile, in 1925, he was appointed by the government to a teaching post in a children's school, where he composed several delightful works expressly for children's use. Subsequently, he taught at the Scriabin Music School, and was finally appointed professor of composition at the Moscow Conservatory. In 1939, he was elected President of the Organizing Committee of the Union of Soviet Composers. In 1940, he received the Order of Merit, and in 1946 the Stalin Prize.

The following works by Kabalevsky are discussed below: *Colas Breugnon; The Comedians;* Concerto No. 2 in G Minor for Piano and Orchestra; Concerto for Violin and Orchestra; Sonata No. 3 for Piano; Symphony No. 2.

SYMPHONY NO. 2, op. 19 (1934). I. Allegro quasi presto. II. Andante non troppo. III. Prestissimo; Scherzando; Molto agitato; Allegro.

Kabalevsky's Second Symphony is actually his third: his first two major works for orchestra, entitled *Poem of Struggle* (1932) and *Requiem for Lenin* (1933), are sometimes designated as symphonies. He completed the "Second" in 1934, and it was introduced in Moscow on December 25 of that year, Albert Coates conducting the Moscow Philharmonic.

In his First Symphony, Kabalevsky spoke of man's adjustment to life after numerous inner conflicts. In the Second Symphony, op. 19, he is more positive in his ideological approach. Man takes an active part in the reconstruction of his society, and thereby achieves his salvation.

The cogent first movement might be interpreted as man's triumph over the obstacles placed in his way in the building of a new society. The movement opens with a loud chord, much like the thrust of a clenched fist against possible opposition. A virile theme in the clarinet and a more lyrical second subject undergo dramatic development. Serenity comes in the second movement, which is beautifully melodic—as if man has found peace within himself. But this inner peace develops into an exultant feeling of triumph in the last movement, which glows with brilliant orchestral colors and is swept by powerful rhythmic forces.

CONCERTO NO. 2 IN G MINOR FOR PIANO AND ORCHES-
TRA, op. 23 (1935). I. Allegro. II. Andante. III. Allegro molto; Alla breve.

Kabalevsky's Second Piano Concerto is one of his finest and most
successful works. It was written soon after the Second Symphony and was
introduced in this country over the radio on May 9, 1943. Leo Schmit was
the soloist, and the NBC Symphony was directed by Frank Black.

The concerto is classical in form, and filled with bright, vigorous
melodies. The principal theme of the first movement is aggressive, contrasting with a second theme of singing character; both themes are ingeniously
synthesized at the end of the movement. The entire second movement is
melancholy; there are two main themes, one tender, the other passionate. A
toccata-like third movement moves precipitously to impressive climaxes. The
principal idea of this section is an adaptation of the first theme of the first
movement.

COLAS BREUGNON, opera (1937).

A novel by Romain Rolland, adapted by V. Bragin into a libretto,
was the source for Kabalevsky's famous opera. The character of Colas
Breugnon—the witty, cunning Burgundian craftsman of the sixteenth century, who had such a laughing, lusty view of life—dominates the Rolland
novel. And it dominates the opera, but with a difference. The Rolland tale
consists more of the reflections of the hero, of his attitudes to situations,
incidents, and characters with which he is brought into contact; it has no
particular social or political philosophy. But in Bragin's libretto, the story
becomes a social criticism of the sixteenth century, with many interpolations
of proletarian concepts. When the opera was introduced at the Leningrad
State Opera early in 1938, some Soviet critics—strange to report!—took the
composer to task for the liberties he took with the Rolland story. But Rolland
himself seemed highly pleased with the result and wrote to the composer:
"You possess the gift of dramatic development which is absent in so many
good composers. You also have your own harmonic language."

In preparing to write the opera, Kabalevsky made an intensive study
of French folksongs—Burgundian folksongs in particular. "My aim was to
convey the local color and nature of the epoch." Though only two brief
themes are borrowed directly from Burgundian folk music, much of the
score has retained the distinct flavor and personality of the French folksongs,
even where the melodies are Kabalevsky's own. For this procedure Rolland
particularly commended the composer. "The folk songs are highly successful.
You have grasped their essence perfectly and have given them form in your
music."

The overture to this opera has often been performed by American
symphony orchestras, and is probably the best-known single work by Kabalevsky. It is, in miniature, a characterization of the principal character. Its

sparkling and laughing measures are an admirable portrait of a man who loved the good things of life.

The overture is only one part of an orchestral suite containing parts of the operatic score. The other portions are three entr'actes entitled "People's Rebellion," "People's Calamity," and "People's Festival."

THE COMEDIANS, suite for orchestra, op. 26 (1938). I. Prologue. II. Galop. III. March. IV. Waltz. V. Pantomime. VI. Intermezzo. VII. Little Lyrical Scene. VIII. Gavotte. IX. Scherzo. X. Epilogue.

In 1938, Kabalevsky wrote incidental music for a children's play, *The Inventor and Comedians,* produced in Moscow. The play centered around a band of itinerant comedians and their often amusing escapades as they travel from town to town, appearing in public squares, at fairs, and so on. In writing the music for this play, Kabalevsky assumed a simple and direct style, now witty, now pictorial, now nostalgic, now ingenuous. From this score, Kabalevsky prepared an orchestral suite comprising ten numbers, which was introduced in Moscow in 1940. Since then, the suite has been heard with equal success at children's concerts and on symphony programs for adults.

SONATA NO. 3 FOR PIANO, op. 46 (1946). I. Allegro con moto. II. Andante cantabile. III. Allegro giocoso.

Kabalevsky's Third Piano Sonata was heard for the first time in Moscow, at the Moscow Conservatory, in a performance by Yakov Zak.

A pleasant little tune opens the sonata. The sonority grows and the harmonic texture becomes detailed before the appearance of the second theme —another delightful melody. Both of these themes are quiet and restrained, but an incidental theme, march-like in character, has rhythmic strength and dissonant harmonies. The original material then returns, though sometimes in accelerated tempo and sharply accentuated rhythms.

A song of haunting beauty unfolds in the second movement; it has the simplicity and poignancy of a folk melody. But, almost as if the composer felt that such peace is ephemeral, the music suddenly becomes stormy and febrile as great power is generated. Then the original vein comes back: beauty triumphs over ugliness.

A martial mood is created in the last movement—music of galvanic power and great rhythmic surges which makes one suspect that the recent war was still in the composer's mind. This suspicion is further strengthened by the outcries of jubilation that follow, the uninhibited joy of total victory.

CONCERTO FOR VIOLIN AND ORCHESTRA, op. 48 (1948). I. Allegro molto e con brio. II. Andantino cantabile. III. Vivace giocoso.

Louis Kaufman, the violinist who introduced this work in America (over the NBC Pacific network on May 14, 1950) prepared the following terse analysis:

"The first movement, in the fresh, unconstrained and sincere language of Kabalevsky, is an Allegro con brio which is candidly traditional in form and lively and ingratiatingly warm in content. The Andantino cantabile opens with a beautiful melody worthy of the great Russian romantic tradition, which is immediately contrasted with a rhythmically developed motive of capricious character that leads back to the first subject intoned by the orchestra. This is gracefully accompanied by the solo violin in muted scale and trill passages and ends with the soloist singing the basic theme simply, without the slightest deviation. The concluding third movement is ...full of vitality and good-natured zest. This infectiously gay section includes a witty homage to Mendelssohn in the cadenza, after which the headlong pace is resumed to terminate in a brief and triumphant coda."

ARAM KHATCHATURIAN   1903—

Up to the time of his twentieth year, when he began music study, the only music Khatchaturian knew was the folksongs and dances of his native Armenia. The first piece he wrote and published, the *Dance* for violin and piano (1926), drew its stylistic traits from the folk art of the trans-Caucasian peoples. And though for a brief period he was attracted to and influenced by the modern style and techniques of the contemporary French school, he soon rejected them and developed his personal idiom through the absorption of the folk elements found in the music of his people.

The intonations, the rhythmic patterns, the oriental colorings, and the dramatic emotional contrasts found in Armenian folksongs and dances are the predominant traits of Khatchaturian's music. The improvisational character of the songs of the *ashugs*—Armenian bards—is caught in his rambling melodies. Highly lyrical, rich in colors and dynamics, endowed with a powerful rhythmic momentum, his music has a forceful impact even on first acquaintance.

Khatchaturian was born in Tiflis, Armenia, on June 6, 1903, and began the study of music twenty years later at the Gniesen School of Music in Moscow. Six years after that, he entered the Moscow Conservatory, where his teachers included Miaskovsky and Vasilenko. His First Symphony, written in 1934 and introduced in the same year, brought him his first success. Subsequently, he won the Stalin Prize (twice) and the Order of Lenin; and his name has been inscribed on an honor plaque in the hall of Moscow Conservatory. Along with nine other important composers, Khatchaturian was condemned by the Central Committee of the Communist Party for his indulgence in "antipopular trends" and "bourgeois formalism" on February 10, 1948 (*see* Shostakovich).

The following works by Khatchaturian are discussed below: Concerto for Piano and Orchestra; Concerto for Violin and Orchestra; Concerto for Violoncello and Orchestra; *Gayne; Masquerade;* Symphony No. 1; Symphony No. 2.

For "Saber Dance" see *Gayne.*

SYMPHONY NO. 1 (1931). I. Andante maestoso; Allegro mon troppo. II. Adagio sostenuto. III. Allegro risoluto.

The first of Khatchaturian's major works was written to honor the Soviet Armenia on its fifteenth anniversary. It was introduced the same year by Eugene Szenkar and the Moscow State Philharmonic Orchestra, scoring a decided success, and bringing the composer to the limelight for the first time.

Though it does not utilize actual folksongs, the symphony is rich with the colors, rhythms, and personality of Armenian folk music. The improvisational character of the introduction (which contains the basic thematic ideas of the entire symphony) is derived from the bardic songs of the *ashugs.* This first movement is of epical structure. Khubov, who described it as "monumental," considers it a "perfectly independent symphonic poem." The first theme, Khubov continues, develops "immediately and organically" out of the prologue, while the second, an Armenian melody in a different tempo, "emerges against a background provided by the dying away of a metamorphosis of the principal theme." These same ideas are found in the next two movements, worked out with deep feeling in the slow section and with powerful dramatic impulses in the closing movement.

CONCERTO FOR PIANO AND ORCHESTRA (1935). I. Allegro ma non troppo e maesto. II. Andante con anima. III. Allegro brillante.

With his Piano Concerto, which Khatchaturian wrote one year after his First Symphony, he solidified his success as a composer. The concerto enjoyed extraordinary popularity in the Soviet Union. After its American première on March 14, 1942, when it was performed by Maro Ajemian and the Juilliard Orchestra under Albert Stoessel, it became one of Khatchaturian's most frequently heard and widely admired works in this country.

Its popularity is understandable. Its folk character endows it with rhythmic and harmonic vitality and an exotic oriental personality. It is brilliant in its virtuoso writing. The fast movements have an electrifying momentum, and are suggestive of Borodin and Liszt in their breadth and scope. The middle section catches its breath from the athletic movement which precedes it, to give way to introspective and poetic brooding; a fascinating contrast to the drive of the outside movements is thereby provided.

The vigorous and joyous theme with which the first movement opens (a theme characteristically Armenian in its cadential structure) dominates the entire section, returning in the finale with a renewed burst of energy. "The exotic romanza-like effect of the Andante," wrote the Soviet critic Khubov, "is achieved through a combination of fresh harmonies, folk mood, and laconic expression, the whole giving an impression of severe simplicity."

CONCERTO FOR VIOLIN AND ORCHESTRA (1938). I. Allegro confermezza. II. Andante sostenuto. III. Allegro vivace.

Three years after he wrote his Piano Concerto, Khatchaturian wrote a Concerto for Violin which is no less attractive in its use of engaging folk materials and no less brilliant in its exploitation of the virtuoso possibilities of the solo instrument. Like its predecessor for the piano, this concerto opens with a powerfully rhythmic first movement. The first theme sweeps with a heroic stride; the second subject, equally virile, is also intensely passionate. The second movement resembles a lament; it is one of the most poignant pieces of music written by this composer. The singing and romantic quality of the violin is utilized with great effect. A vertiginous finale has gypsy abandon.

MASQUERADE, suite for orchestra (1939). I. Waltz. II. Nocturne. III. Romance. IV. Mazurka. V. Galop.

In 1939, Khatchaturian composed incidental music for a play by Mikhail Lermontov, *Masquerade,* dealing with the licentious life of the Russian upper classes in the 1830's. From this score, the composer prepared a concert suite of five numbers which the Moscow Radio Orchestra introduced in 1944. The music is lilting, infectious, throughout—of the summer "pop" variety—full of engaging melodies and whirling rhythms.

GAYNE, ballet (1941).

Gayne (or *Gayaneh,* as it is known abroad) is a patriotic folk ballet with libretto by K. N. Derzhavin. On December 9, 1942, it was introduced by the Kirov Theatre for Opera and Ballet (which is connected with the Leningrad State Academy) in the city of Molotov. N. A. Anisimova was the producer and principal ballerina. In 1943, it received the Stalin Prize, first degree.

The action takes place in a collective farm, with its everyday work and play activity providing much of the background material. Giko, a traitor to the Soviet Union, joins up with a group of smugglers. He sets fire to his own collective farm and attempts to murder his wife, Gayaneh, and their daughter. They are saved by Kazakov, who is in love with Gayaneh, and who marries her when Giko meets the fate that is his due.

Khatchaturian's score is a veritable cornucopia of Armenian folk dances, thirteen of which he later gathered into two orchestral suites that have achieved considerable popularity on orchestral programs. The thirteen dances have a wide variety of pace and mood, ranging from the tender and the nostalgic (as in the famous "Lullaby") to the corybantic (as in the even more celebrated "Saber Dance"). Shepherd dances, peasant dances, a Ukrainian *hopak,* and a Georgian lezghinka are also represented.

Three of these dances ("Lullaby," "Saber Dance," and "Dance of the Rose Maidens") were first heard in this country in 1945, in a performance by the Kansas Philharmonic Orchestra under Efrem Kurtz. When these dances were performed for the first time in New York at the Lewisohn Stadium, the "Saber Dance" had to be repeated. This dance has been heard so frequently over the radio—even in arrangments for the piano or for popular orchestra—that for a time it enjoyed the status of a hit song.

SYMPHONY NO. 2 (1943). I. Andante maestoso. II. Allegro risoluto. III. Andante sostenuto. IV. Andante mosso; Allegro sostenuto.

Khatchaturian's Second Symphony was a child of World War II. He began writing it soon after the Nazis invaded the Soviet Union. The "superhuman sufferings caused to the Soviet people by the Nazi monsters," said Khatchaturian, "are portrayed in the third movement." In the fourth, the heroism and unconquerable spirit of the Soviet people are powerfully delineated.

Khubov, who subtitled the work *Symphony with a Bell,* has written the definitive analysis of this work:

"The first movement has an introduction consisting of two elements—a bell motive, which shudders loudly through the entire orchestra, and a following theme for strings. The principal subject of the movement appears first in the lower strings, and with its statement there ensues a rather headlong development, embodying some harking back to previous material, plus hints of things to come. A brooding song now comes through the musical web, and it is intertwined with earlier themes. On the heels of this we enter into a march episode, introduced, however, by a repetition of the 'bell' idea. The march persists almost to the end of the section.

"The second movement presents an insistent rhythmic figure which grows to the dimensions of an irresistible danse macabre. The sinister quality of the music suddenly changes to a more genial section in a tune which comes floating into the scene. It lives its rather brief life, soon to be supplanted by the preceding business....

"The third movement is of tragic import. Basically it is a funeral march featuring a doleful theme of Azerbaijan folk origin. Shouted quite frenetically over the march is the *Dies Irae*. The music increases in power, and it ends in a great climax with the 'bell' motive.

"In the fourth movement, exultation is the feeling. Piercing fanfares open the section. The brass hurls out what is perhaps aptly described as a 'Brass Chorus of Glory.' Some softer fragments follow with the echoings of previous themes. Then a grand climax is attained as the 'bell' theme and the 'Brass Chorus' thunder out an idea symbolic of triumph."

The symphony was heard for the first time on December 30, 1943, with Boris Khaikin conducting the Moscow Conservatory Orchestra. The symphony, as it was heard in this country for the first time, on April 13, 1945, with Leonard Bernstein directing an improvised orchestra, was somewhat different from that introduced in Moscow. There were various revisions by the composer in the score, the most important being the shifting of the Andante sostenuto from the second movement to the third, and putting the Scherzo in its place.

CONCERTO FOR VIOLONCELLO AND ORCHESTRA (1946). I. Allegro moderato. II. Andante sostenuto. III. Allegro.

This vigorous work—like the concertos for the piano and for the violin—is indebted to Armenian folk music for its personality and stylistic traits. An impressive orchestral prologue inaugurates the first movement. The soloist then presents the principal theme, which is allowed to develop in a virtuoso manner throughout the movement (the longest and most fully developed of the three). A prolonged orchestral introduction, in which a flute solo is prominent, also opens the second movement. The cello then appears with a languorous oriental melody, which passes on to the orchestra. A climax follows. After the return of the principal melody, the third movement enters without any interruption. This part is highly rhythmic, containing flashing passages for the cello.

This concerto was introduced in Moscow on October 30, 1946.

ZOLTÁN KODÁLY   1882—

Like his friend and compatriot, Béla Bartók, Zoltán Kodály went on extensive expeditions throughout Hungary in search of authentic folk music. In a few years' time, Kodály had collected between three and four thousand of these melodies, many of which he published jointly with Bartók. These melodies were far different from the puling, sentimental gypsy songs that the world up to then had accepted as Hungarian folk music. The Hungarian folksongs and dances which Kodály and Bartók uncovered in different parts of the country lack (as Paul Rosenfeld wrote) "the meretriciousness of gypsy music, and is not sinuous, sliding, or suggestive as that is. It is much severer, earthier, and homelier ... and has some of the strength and savorsomeness of Mussorgsky's folk-born Slavic music."

Intimacy with this folk music was a profound influence on Kodály's development as a composer. Formerly he had written works that betrayed stylistic traits of Brahms and Debussy. Now (after 1905) his melodic line acquired the rhythm and inflection of the Hungarian language; the brusqueness of accent, the modal quality of the tonality, the persistent repetition of a melodic or rhythmic pattern, the narrative recitative-like character of his writing became the identifying qualities of his own music, just as they were qualities that distinguished Hungary's musical folk art.

Though he was stimulated by the same source as Bartók, Kodály's music is of a completely different character than that of his friend. Bartók is often explosive and brutal, while Kodály is generally gentle and melancholy; where Bartók uses primarily discords and complicated rhythms, Kodály favors a tender lyricism.

Kodály was born in Keczkemét on December 16, 1882. He entered the Budapest Conservatory when he was eighteen years old, and at the same time was enrolled as a student at the University of Budapest. In 1905, he began his intensive research into the folk music of his country, inspired to do so by Bartók, with whom he took frequent expeditions throughout the length and breadth of Hungary, writing down the native melodies and dances of different localities. Kodály's first major work was the *Psalmus Hungaricus,* which he wrote in 1923 to celebrate the fiftieth anniversary of the union of Buda and Pesth. With the opera *Háry János,* written in 1925, Kodály became one of the most important composers of his country. After 1906, he taught composition at the Budapest Conservatory. Thereafter he became one of the leading musical spirits of Hungary, influential as a teacher, composer, and writer. During World War II, in Nazi-occupied Hungary, he was influential in helping numerous Jewish refugees escape from the hands of the Nazis, and though his activities were discovered by the Gestapo, his fame and popularity saved him from the concentration camp. In the winter of 1946, Kodály visited the United States for the first time as an official delegate to the Congress of International Confederation of Authors Societies, meeting in Washington, D.C.

The following works by Kodály are discussed below: *Dances of Galanta; Dances of Marosszék; Háry János; Psalmus Hungaricus; Te Deum.*

PSALMUS HUNGARICUS, for tenor solo, chorus, and orchestra, op. 13 (1923).

In 1923, Kodály was commissioned by the Hungarian government to write a work for performance in conjunction with the festivities commemorating the fiftieth anniversary of the union of Buda and Pesth. Kodály selected an old Hungarian text dating from the sixteenth century, in which the poet, Michael Veg, had adapted the Fifty-fifth Psalm but had filled it with so many personal and national associations that it had become a Hungarian psalm. In setting this text to music, Kodály drew copiously from old Hungarian styles and folk idioms and produced a work of singular power and beauty. It is not only one of his finest works, but is also one of the outstanding choral works of our time. Its first performance took place in Budapest on November 19, 1923. After that it was translated into numerous languages and was given hundreds of performances throughout the world.

The work opens with sixteen measures for orchestra, following which the altos and bassos enter with an unaccompanied unison passage beginning: "Sad Was King David, Dismal and Downcast." When this choral passage ends, there enters a tenor psalm of supplication, "Lord in Thy Mercy, Hear," which is periodically interrupted by the return of the unison chorus chanting "Sad Was King David, Dismal and Downcast." An Adagio orchestral intermezzo of compelling beauty precedes a final solo for tenor: "Now Does Fresh Courage Enter My Sad Soul."

HÁRY JÁNOS, opera (1925).

Kodály's most famous work is an opera centered around the character of Háry János, a figure familiar in Hungarian folklore. Háry János is a picaresque character, boastful, somewhat pompous, and addicted to fabulous lies, which he himself soon believes to be the truth. In Kodály's opera, János moves against the background of the Vienna of more than a century ago. To a group of incredulous listeners, he spins a yarn that Marie Louise, daughter of Emperor Francis and the wife of Napoleon, is arriving in Vienna. Indeed, she *does* arrive, and during her visit falls in love with Háry and wants to take him back with her to Paris. Háry is willing, but only on condition that his sweetheart, Orze, joins them. Thus Háry is the center of a situation he enjoys no end: Two women compete for his affections, while Napoleon is enraged with jealousy. Napoleon's anger leads him to declare war on Austria, a war in which Háry—who is on the side of the Austrians, of course—is a hero; single-handed he destroys the enemy. Napoleon is put in the humiliating position of begging for mercy. Marie Louise, repelled by Napoleon's cowardice, is more than ever convinced of her love for Háry and is eager to marry him. Háry, meanwhile, is welcomed back to Vienna in triumph. But in Vienna, he suddenly realizes that it is Orze he loves. With a magnificent gesture, he rejects Marie Louise, returns her to Napoleon, and accepts Orze as his wife, taking her back with him to his native village.

There (in the final scene of the opera) we find old Háry János telling his tall tales to the villagers as Orze arrives to take him home for his dinner.

Háry János was produced with outstanding success in Budapest on October 10, 1926. Americans know it through the delightful orchestral suite that Kodály arranged from the opera score.

The suite opens with an orchestral glissando, representing a sneeze; for it is a superstition in Hungary that a statement is true if the speaker sneezes as he talks. In the first part, "Prelude: The Fairy Tale Begins," Háry tells his wondrous story; as his imagination grows, so do the orchestral sonorities and dynamics. Háry comes to Vienna. In "Viennese Musical Clock" he stands in front of the Imperial Palace and listens to the chimes of the musical clock, at the same time watching the rotating mechanical figures. In "Song" he nostalgically recalls the gentle evening that would descend on his little village and touch it with peace. The fourth section, "The Battle and Defeat of Napoleon," is war let loose in the orchestra: a march rhythm sets the armies into motion; they clash; a funereal melody ends the section, speaking of the dead enemy. In the fifth part, "Intermezzo," a Hungarian dance is heard—vital, electrifying, full of gypsy blood. The concluding movement, "Entrance of the Emperor and his Court," finds Háry at the height of his triumph, contemplating the grandeur of Viennese royalty.

DANCES OF MAROSSZÉK, for piano (1929).

Marosszék is a town in the province of Szekely, Hungary, which Kodály visited during his intensive researches into Hungarian folk music. Here he found a valuable store of autochthonous songs and dances. Six of these native melodies were woven by the composer into an integrated work, for the piano, which resembles a rondo in form. In this music, as the pianist Edward Kilenyi remarked, "one visualizes...these Szekelys in their quaint costumes, singing and dancing at their holiday celebrations."

The *Dances of Marosszék* are also familiar in a version for small orchestra, prepared by the composer at the special request of Arturo Toscanini. The première, however, was directed by Fritz Busch, in Dresden, on November 28, 1930, two weeks before Toscanini's New York performance.

DANCES OF GALANTA, for orchestra (1934).

In the published score, Kodály appended the following information:

"Galanta is a small Hungarian market town known to travelers between Vienna and Budapest. The composer passed there seven years of his childhood. There existed at that time a gypsy band which has since disappeared. Their music was the first 'orchestral sonority' which came to the ears of the child. The forebears of these gypsies were known more than a hundred years ago. About 1800, some books of Hungarian dances were published in Vienna, one of which contained music 'after several gypsies from Galanta.' They have preserved the old Hungarian traditions. In order to continue it, the composer took his principal subjects from these ancient editions."

There are here five gypsy dances, played without interruption. A breath-taking momentum is achieved in these *Dances*. The composition opens sedately, but as it progresses the tempo is accelerated until the music erupts into an orgiastic outburst. Though each dance is independent, thematic ideas are repeated throughout to give the work integration.

TE DEUM, for soloists, chorus, and orchestra (1936).

This profoundly religious work—one of Kodály's masterpieces—combines power with spirituality. Power is generated through the frequent employment of dissonance and harsh rhythms; spirituality is achieved through the utilization of old church modes. Two basic motives are prominent throughout the work: a trumpet call that opens the work, and the expressive melody accompanying the words *"Pleni sunt"* ("The Heavens and Earth Are Filled with the Majesty of Thy Glory"). Despite the religious character of the music, elements of Hungarian folksongs and dances are introduced into the musical texture. The two principal lyric passages—both of luminous beauty, and both for soprano—have an unmistakable Hungarian identity.

The *Te Deum* was written to commemorate the 250th anniversary of the delivery of Budapest from the Turks. It was heard for the first time on September 11, 1936, in the Budapest Cathedral.

ERNST KRENEK   1900—

Krenek's music has not always been so cerebral and so difficult to assimilate as it is today. He came to his present atonal style by a long and devious route. First he wrote in the postromantic style of Franz Schreker. Then, for a brief period, jazz interested him. After that he tried to arrive at the simple romanticism of Franz Schubert. Finally, the need for "an ever freer and more incisive articulation of musical thought," as he himself put it —the artistic necessity of arriving at emotional restraint, compressed thinking, economy of materials—led him to embrace the Schoenberg twelve-tone system, which he has employed in most of his works since 1933 with particular brilliance and technical astuteness.

Krenek was born in Vienna, of Czechoslovakian origin, on August 23, 1900, and was a pupil of Franz Schreker. The warmth and emotional appeal of his chamber music attracted some attention before World War I. In the early 1920's he turned to opera, becoming a conductor and stage director (his most important post was as conductor of the Prussian State Theatre). His first opera was produced in Frankfurt in 1924—*Der Sprung über den Schatten.* Two years later, the success of *Jonny Spielt Auf* made him an international figure. In 1928 he settled in Vienna, where he came closely into contact with Arnold Schoenberg and his group. Though an Aryan, he was found unacceptable to the Nazis, and had to leave Austria. He established his permanent home in this country, holding teaching or directorial positions at Vassar College, Hamline University, and the Chicago Musical College.

The following works by Krenek are discussed below: Concerto No. 3 for Piano and Orchestra; *Jonny Spielt Auf;* Symphony No. 4; Symphony No. 5.

JONNY SPIELT AUF, op. 45, opera (1926).

In the 1920's, the popularity of American jazz spread like a contagious disease throughout Germany and Austria. Many of the serious composers of those countries were so fascinated by jazz colors, rhythms, instrumentation, and blues melodies that they borrowed these stylistic details for their own major works.

One of the first of these composers to use jazz within the framework of the opera was Krenek. He wrote the libretto and the score of *Jonny Spielt Auf* "to interpret," as he said, the rhythms and atmosphere of modern life in this age of technical science."

A Negro jazz-band leader, Jonny, is the principal protagonist. He steals Daniello's violin, goes in for jazz fiddling, and wins over with his intoxicating music all those who come into contact with him. Eventually, he bestrides the world; as he plays his seductive music the people of the world dance helplessly to the energetic strains.

This was a novel operatic subject for 1926. The music Krenek wrote for it—mostly music-hall melodies, blues melodies, kinesthetic jazz rhythms slightly diluted—was equally novel. Several opera houses turned it down before the Leipzig Opera decided to take a chance with it. It was introduced on February 11, 1927—and it was a sensation. Jazz-mad Germany took it to its heart. People spoke rapturously of Jonny, whistled its many tunes. Before many months passed *Jonny* began a triumphant march through the world of music. In a few years' time, it was seen in the opera houses of more than one hundred European cities; it was translated into eighteen languages. In 1929, it was performed at the Metropolitan Opera in New York.

CONCERTO NO. 3 FOR PIANO AND ORCHESTRA (1946).

Krenek wrote his first two piano concertos in 1923 and 1937. The

Third came in 1946. On November 22, 1946, the work was introduced by the Minneapolis Symphony Orchestra, with Dimitri Mitropoulos filling the dual role of pianist and conductor.

Unlike other Krenek works of recent years, the concerto does not employ the twelve-tone technique. But it is nevertheless bald and austere music. It is in five movements, played without interruption. A unique instrumental characteristic is the use of a different section of the orchestra as background for the solo instrument in each of the five movements. In the first (Allegro con passione), it is the brass and tympani; in the second (Andante sostenuto), a fugue, the strings; in the third (Allegretto scherzando), the woodwinds; in the fourth (Adagio), for the most part a cadenza for solo piano, harp and percussion; and in the fifth (Vivace), a rondo, full orchestra. In the concluding movement, the thematic ideas of the earlier movements are repeated.

SYMPHONY NO. 4 (1947). I. Andante tranquillo; Allegro appassionata; Allegro vivace. II. Adagio. III. Allegro pesante; Allegro agitato; Allegro deciso.

Krenek's Fourth Symphony was introduced in New York by the New York Philharmonic-Symphony Orchestra, Mitropoulos conducting, on November 27, 1947. This is complex and cerebral music, austerely objective. The writing is in the twelve-tone technique.

The composer has provided the following analysis:

"First movement. Technically, the movement consists of a quiet, fairly slow introduction, an agitated transition and a sonata-allegro with two themes, a brief development section and an abridged recapitulation....

"Second movement. This movement consists of alternating variations on two themes. The general mood is one of resignation, in an essay of getting along without fighting for the 'ideal.' ...

"Third movement. A long, elaborate introduction and a dramatic Allegro with some characteristics of a rondo appear in this movement, which is the longest of the three and contains the dramatic climax of the whole work."

SYMPHONY NO. 5 (1949).

While Krenek's Fifth Symphony is not in the twelve-tone technique, it is atonal music. It is classical in its concept of form; the material is developed concisely and economically. Played without interruption, the symphony is in five sections: I. Introduction. II. Sonata. III. Rondo. IV. Theme and Variations. V. Fugue. The concluding fugue is used as a kind of summation.

Material is repeated throughout the five movements: the theme of the fourth section (which undergoes eight variations) is derived from the coda of the third; and the thematic subjects which become the basis of the concluding double fugue are likewise derived from earlier ideas.

This symphony was introduced by the Albuquerque Symphony under Kurt Frederick on March 16, 1950.

ANATOL LIADOV   1855—1914

"Art," Liadov once wrote, "is the realm of the non-existing. Art is a figment, a fairy tale, a phantom. Give me a fairy tale, a dragon, a water sprite, a forest-demon—give me something unreal and I am happy."

In his music Liadov lived continually in that make-believe world of enchantment peopled by unearthly spirits. It was his escape from the reality around him which he found to be "tedious, trying, purposeless, terrible." Thus he succumbed to the spell of folklore; his music is most original and virile when it draws its ideas from that source.

A national composer, Liadov belongs to that group of Russian composers, beginning with Glinka and continuing with the "Russian Five," who built an art out of folksong materials. Liadov's sphere is essentially a more limited one than that of his celebrated compatriots. He worked exclusively in the less ambitious forms—tone-poems and adaptations of folksongs. In the best of his work he revealed elegance of style and fine taste.

He was incorrigibly lazy. Rimsky-Korsakov has told us that Liadov was suspended from the St. Petersburg Conservatory because he not only refused to do any studying but, in time, even avoided classes. The same inertia and lethargy remained with him throughout his life. In certain seasons—when it was warm and fair—he could do no work at all. In others, he preferred doing tomorrow what he had planned for today. Ambitious projects, like an opera, never reached beyond the planning stage. He drove himself to complete other ventures, slighter in scope than operas. He avoided assignments like the plague; when he did accept them he was never quite certain when he would complete them, or *if* he would.

It is a fascinating footnote to the musical history of our times that it was due to Liadov's indolence that the most dynamic and influential composer of our time was able to realize his first success. For it was to Liadov that Diaghilev came for a score to *The Fire-Bird;* and it was only because Liadov was dilatory that the assignment was finally turned over to Igor Stravinsky.

Anatol Liadov was born in St. Petersburg on May 11, 1855. He was a student at the St. Petersburg Conservatory. After unfavorable beginnings (at one time he was even suspended) he eventually emerged as an outstanding student. Just before his graduation, he wrote his first orchestral work, *The Bride of Messina,* which so impressed the Conservatory authorities that they appointed him professor of harmony and theory. Besides his activity as a teacher, Liadov also distinguished himself as the conductor of the Musical Society, which was significant in bringing performances to prominent works of younger Russian composers. As a member of the Ethnographic Society, Liadov made intensive researches in the field of Russian folk music; he made several excellent adaptations of folksongs and dances. He died in St. Petersburg on August 28, 1914.

The following works by Liadov are discussed below: *Baba Yaga, Eight Russian Folk Songs; The Enchanted Lake; Kikimora.*

BABA-YAGA, fairy tale for orchestra, op. 6 (1904).

Liadov wrote three fairy tales for orchestra, the first of which was *Baba-Yaga.* (The other two fairy tales were *The Enchanted Lake* and *Kikimora,* discussed below.) Baba-Yaga is a witch whose home is protected by a fence constructed out of the bones of human beings. Her swift flight through space, as she sweeps her path with a broom, is picturesquely described in this music, which is a literal portrayal in tones of air-locomotion.

EIGHT RUSSIAN FOLK SONGS, for orchestra, op. 58 (1906).

This is a companion piece to *Kikimora,* both of them originally being intense researches into Russian folk music. For Liadov this was a labor of love; all his life he had passionately admired folklore and folk music. Out of the treasurehouse of this art he selected eight poignant songs, integrated them into a single composition, and clothed them in a rich harmonic and orchestral garb.

The first song is a religious chant sung by children in a procession. The second is a Christmas carol, and the third a plaintive village melody. In the fourth, a humorous song is accompanied by an amusing dance of young peasants with a mosquito. The fifth is a song of the birds, in which their chirpings and pipings are imitated. A cradle song is heard in the sixth, a round dance in the seventh, and a village dance song in the last.

THE ENCHANTED LAKE, fairy tale for orchestra, op. 62 (1909).

This is a companion piece to *Kikimora,* both the them originally being sketches for an opera that never passed the outline stages. Unlike *Kikimora, The Enchanted Lake* has no specific program. But it is descriptive music, easily lending itself to programmatic interpretation. The opening rippling theme for muted strings (the principal melodic idea of the entire work) tells of the magic lake in which the grim encircling forests are reflected. Sprightly rhythmic subjects bring up suggestions of the water nymphs who inhabit the lake. *The Enchanted Lake* was published in 1909.

KIKIMORA, fairy tale for orchestra, op. 63 (1909).

A folk tale by Sakharoff is the source of this imaginative work, published in 1910.

The published score provides the following program:

"Kikimora (the phantom) is brought up by a sorceress in the mountains. In her youth she is beguiled from early morn to late at night by the tales of foreign lands told by the sorceress's Magic Cat. From night to dawn, Kikimora is rocked in a crystal cradle. In seven years the phantom grows up. Tiny and black, her head is small as a thimble, and her body as thin as straw. Kikimora makes all manner of noises from morning to night, and then whistles and hisses from early evening to midnight. Then the phantom spins until daylight—spins and stores up evil in her mind against all mankind."

CHARLES MARTIN LOEFFLER   1861—1935

Though Loeffler lived the last fifty-four years of his life in this country, became an American citizen, and wrote all of his works here, he never attempted to endow his music with an American identity. His background was international. He was Alsatian by birth; he spent his boyhood in Russia; he received his musical training in Germany and France; and he served his professional apprenticeship in France. His music was equally international. His first work, *Les Veillées de l'Ukraine* (1891), was of Russian character. Later compositions revealed stylistic traits of Scriabin or Debussy. All of his works were influenced by Germanic respect for form and architectonic construction. He was at his best, however, when his poetic temperament expressed itself impressionistically, at which time his writing had singular beauty and aristocracy.

Loeffler was born in Mulhouse, Alsace, on January 30, 1861. As a boy, he lived in the Russian city of Kiev, where his father, a scientist, had come to work for the Russian government, and where he assimilated many vivid impressions of Russian folk music. In his fifteenth year he was sent to Berlin to study the violin with Rappoldi and harmony with Kiel. Further study took place in Paris with Massart and Guiraud. After playing the violin in the Pasdeloups Orchestra, he came to the United States in 1881, joined the Boston Symphony Orchestra in 1882. From 1885 to 1903 he shared the concertmaster's desk in Boston with Franz Kneisel. The need to express himself creatively led him to resign from the Boston Symphony in 1903 to devote himself exclusively to composition. In 1907 he realized his first substantial success as a composer with *A Pagan Poem*. The last thirty years of his life were lived in retirement and seclusion on a farm in Medfield, Massachusetts, where he died on May 19, 1935.

The following works by Loeffler are discussed below: *Evocation; Memories of My Childhood; Music for Four Stringed Instruments; A Pagan Poem.*

A PAGAN POEM, for orchestra, with piano, English horn, and three trumpets, op. 14 (1906).

Among Loeffler's impressionist compositions, the most successful is *A Pagan Poem*. Rarely in his music does he achieve such refinement of writing as here; rarely is his feeling for beauty so sensitively realized. There is serene music, aglow—as Philip Hale once put it so well—with a "cool fire," and a cool fire that "is more deadly than fierce, panting flame."

The literary source of this music was Virgil's eighth eclogue, in which a Thessalian maiden calls upon her necromantic gifts to restore to her a deserted lover. The music does not attempt to follow this program literally, but strives to suggest through impressionistic means the emotions and moods evoked by the poem.

Originally, *A Pagan Poem* was scored for a small chamber orchestra, comprising a piano, two flutes, oboe, clarinet, English horn, two horns, three trumpets, viola, and double bass. Two years after it appeared in this form in 1903, Loeffler scored it again, this time in an even more unorthodox manner: two pianos and three trumpets. Still dissatisfied, Loeffler finally rewrote it for full orchestra and the obbligato of piano, English horn, and three trumpets. On November 23, 1907, this definitive version was introduced by the Boston Symphony Orchestra under Karl Muck.

MUSIC FOR FOUR STRINGED INSTRUMENTS (1917). I. Poco adagio; Allegro comodo. II. Easter Sunday: adagio ma non troppo; Allegro. III. Moderato; Andante quasi allegretto; Allegro vivo; Tempo di marcia; Allegro; Adagio.

Religious mysticism fills the pages of this work and gives it its identifying character. Loeffler wrote this quartet to honor the memory of an American aviator, Victor Chapman, who died in World War I. The melodic ideas are derived from the Gregorian chant, and provide the work with a remote and spiritual quality. The slow sections (the opening introduction and the second movement) are among the most poignant pages of the entire composition, reflecting a funereal strain often in evidence in Loeffler's music.

MEMORIES OF MY CHILDHOOD, tone-poem for orchestra (1924).

In this orchestral work, the composer remembers nostalgically his Kiev childhood and his association with Russian folk music. It won the first prize of one thousand dollars in a competition sponsored by the Chicago North Shore Festival, and received its first performance in Evanston on May 29, 1924.

The composer provided the following information:

"Many years ago, the composer spent more than three years of his boyhood in a Russian small town.... He now seeks to express by this music what still lives in his heart and memory of those happy days. He recalls, in the various strains of his music, Russian peasant song, the Yourod Litany prayer, 'the happiest of days,' fairy tales and dance songs. The closing movement of the tone poem commemorates the death of Vasinka, an elderly Bayan, or story-teller, singer, maker of willow pipes upon which he played tunes of weird intervals, and the companion and friend of the boy who now, later in life, notes down what he hopes these pages will tell."

EVOCATION, for speaking voice, women's chorus, and orchestra (1930).

On February 5, 1931, Severance Hall, the new home of the Cleveland Orchestra, was dedicated with a special concert. For that concert, Loeffler composed his *Evocation,* the text of which was taken from T. W. Mackail's *Epigrams of the Greek Anthology.*

The following paragraph, printed in the preface of the published score, can serve as a program for the music: "The imagined form of this music is to tell the building of a beautiful temple of the Muses; of the god Pan's rhapsodic lay and the nymphs' love for him; of their vain endeavors to fetter him to their beloved sunny fields whence Echo is listening for the pure fun of answering; of Syrinx, Pan's most beloved naiad, whom Artemis metamorphosed into a reed to save her from Pan's amorous pursuit; of the strange account given by the Singing Stone of itself; awed by solemn wonder at it we now seek the little stream running down the hills to meet us, the reeds bowing to us in the breeze. The nymphs are still calling, 'Pan, abide here on these sunny greens.'"

The work opens with a slow and stately fugue, symbolic of the temple of music (Severance Hall). This fugue is shortly interrupted by a motif of the Singing Stone. There then comes a lyrical passage describing the nymphs enjoying their Arcadian happiness and meeting the great god Pan. This interlude over, the principal theme (which grew out of the opening fugue) returns to lead to the encounter with the Singing Stone.

The final scene takes place in the favorite stream of the nymphs and naiads where Artemis metamorphosed Syrinx. Pan's rustic lay is heard from the distance.

The narrator who speaks the lines of the Singing Stone is heard in a hushed voice offstage.

NIKOLAI LOPATNIKOFF   1903—

Like the two contemporary composers he admires most, Stravinsky and Hindemith, Lopatnikoff is a neo-classicist who merges contemporary thinking and techniques with the forms of the past. It is revealing to compare Lopatnikoff with both Stravinsky and Hindemith. Like Stravinsky, Lopatnikoff is economical and lean in his writing, and employs forms of modest proportions. But in spirit he is even closer to Hindemith.

Lopatnikoff, however, is not a stencil of any other composer. His thinking and feeling are essentially his own, even where his techniques may have been influenced by others.

Lopatnikoff was born in Revel (Tallinn) Estonia, on March 16, 1903, and attended the St. Petersburg Conservatory, where he studied piano with Sacharoff and theory with Zhitomirsky. Further music study with Toch and Rehberg took place in Helsingfors and Heidelberg. His First Piano Concerto, introduced in Cologne in 1925, and his First String Quartet, heard one year earlier in Karlsruhe, drew attention to his creative talent. For the next decade and a half he wandered over Europe, living at different times in Berlin, Helsingfors, and London. In 1939, he made this country his permanent home, becoming a citizen in 1944. In this country, he has been active not only as a composer but also as a teacher, holding positions in Hartford and White Plains, and at the Carnegie Institute of Technology and the Berkshire Music Center.

The following works by Lopatnikoff are discussed below: Concerto for Violin and Orchestra; Sinfonietta.

CONCERTO FOR VIOLIN AND ORCHESTRA, op. 26 (1941).
I. Allegro moderato. II. Andante. III. Allegro con brio ma non troppo.

Lopatnikoff's Violin Concerto was introduced by Richard Burgin and the Boston Symphony Orchestra, Serge Koussevitsky conducting, on April

17, 1942. Three ideas comprise the first movement, which is soundly constructed and marked by a powerful rhythmic force. The lyrical second movement has a Russian personality. Vigor returns to the third movement, which is occasionally infectiously gay, to be contrasted midway with a contemplative melody for two clarinets.

SINFONIETTA, for orchestra, op. 27 (1942). I. Allegro. II. Andantino. III. Allegro molto.

This intimate work, which has the texture of chamber music, is in Lopatnikoff's most successful neo-classic vein. Within the structure of a classic concerto grosso, the composer has injected modern linear writing in which the instrumental effects and sonorities bring irony and wit. Against the background of the orchestra, seven wind instruments (trumpet, horn, oboe, clarinet, flute, bassoon, and piccolo) provide the melodic materials. A lively theme opens the first movement; this, and a countertheme heard in the clarinet, are the main threads out of which the composer weaves his polyphonic fabric. In the second movement, an ensemble of wind instruments is effectively set against the orchestra in the style of the concerto grosso. The finale, a rondo, gives vigorous play to the full orchestra, with emphasis on the family of percussions; this movement has been described as a true Russian dance.

GUSTAV MAHLER   1860—1911

Mahler once wrote: "All music since Beethoven is program music." He was probably influenced by the kind of music he himself was writing. Most of his works are programmatic, not as realistically as are the tone-poems of Richard Strauss, but suggestively, in the vein of Beethoven, who in his last works tried to make music speak abstract ideas.

Mahler was a complex individual. His entire life was obsessed by inner turmoil and conflicts, spiritual doubts, *Weltschmerz*. Restlessly he searched for a meaning to life. And in his music he continually posed metaphysical questions. He sought to prove the meaning of life and death, to seek out the mysteries of Nature. Above all else, he wanted to resolve the cosmic questions that continually troubled him. In a way, his music is a spiritual autobiography.

Those who dislike Mahler (and they are as passionate as those who

worship him) find him bombastic and garrulous. It is not difficult to uncover his weaknesses. He was given to profusion. His works are often
mammoth in size and orchestral equipment. They indulge in emotional
extravagances. His melodies, often stemming from Austrian folk sources,
are sometimes naïve and sentimental.

But at his best Mahler could rise far above his defects and arrive at
an eloquence found in few other musical works. His music, when it is
good, is shattering in emotional impact. It is full of human qualities, yet
profound in its extramusical implications. Like the man who wrote it, it is
uncompromising in its artistic ideals, passionate in sincerity, high-minded
and noble in thinking. It is the last word in technical mastery, displaying
a knowledge of the orchestra that few other composers have been able to
match.

Though Mahler has written remarkable music in the form of the
song and the song cycle, the essence of his art is to be found in his
symphonies, of which only the first two were written before 1900. Like
Beethoven, Schubert, and Bruckner, Mahler wrote nine symphonies (a
tenth was left uncompleted); like Beethoven, Schubert, and Bruckner, he
belongs with the great symphonists of all time. These nine Mahler symphonies fall into three distinct groups. The first, including the first four
symphonies, was subjective; here, as Paul Stefan wrote, there took place "a
great and intensely personal struggle with the world and the universe." In
the second group, embracing the fifth through the eighth symphonies, the
musician-philosopher became a tone-poet. "As though moving in lofty
spheres," wrote Stefan, "he has now mastered his own musical language,
penetrating into it more intensely, spiritualizing it, so that he now no longer
needs human language." The final group includes the Ninth Symphony
and that song cycle which Mahler liked to designate as a symphony, *Das
Lied von der Erde*. The composer no longer drew his inspiration from the
emotions and struggles of his life. As Bruno Walter remarked, he had now
disassociated himself spiritually "from the sphere of life—a loosening of all
former connections had changed the entire aspect of his feelings." He was
now bidding the world farewell, sometimes with sorrow (as in *Das Lied
von der Erde*), sometimes with peace and resignation (as in the closing
movement of the Ninth Symphony).

Gustav Mahler was born in the Bohemian town of Kalischt on July
7, 1860. At the age of fifteen he entered the Vienna Conservatory, where
he remained for three years, receiving prizes for piano playing and composition. He began conducting immediately after his graduation from the
Conservatory, and achieved his first major success with a performance of
Mendelssohn's *St. Paul* in Leipzig in 1885. Subsequently he conducted in
opera houses in Prague, Pesth, and Hamburg, before coming to the Vienna
Royal Opera, where his regime proved to be one of the most lustrous

chapters in the history of that opera house. His importance as a conductor was an accepted fact; his incandescent performances of both operatic and symphonic music set a standard which few have equaled. From 1908 until 1911, Mahler conducted in this country at the Metropolitan Opera House and with the New York Philharmonic-Symphony Orchestra.

Despite his activity with the baton, Mahler found time and energy for composition. He wrote his First Symphony in 1888, and on November 20, 1889, it was introduced in Budapest. Mahler, who subtitled the symphony "The Titan," regarded it as an adventure of the soul. It was a highly subjective work into which Mahler poured his turbulent feelings regarding life, youth, nature, death. The audience that heard this symphony for the first time did not respond sympathetically; it regarded Mahler's overwhelming outpourings as pretentious, and was vocally hostile.

The audience reacted somewhat more favorably to Mahler's Second Symphony, "Resurrection," which he completed in 1894 and the première of which was conducted by Richard Strauss in Berlin on March 4, 1895. But the critics were still hostile. Mahler's probing into the "whys" of human existence and the purpose of human suffering, along with his reaffirmation of life, seemed pompous stuff; one of the critics described Mahler as "cynical" and "brutal."

Hostility followed Mahler's creative work almost to the end of his life. Notwithstanding these attacks, he continued to write ambitious symphonies, song cycles, and songs, in which his *Weltanschauung,* his philosophical questionings, his search for truth, found expression. Even in that field in which his greatness was generally accepted—conducting—he met bitter enemies. His high-minded principles, his intransigence, his driving will, his refusal to curry favor with anyone, made him a victim of numerous cabals and intrigues. His physical collapse in New York on February 21, 1911, was as much a result of the attacks of his enemies as it was of hard work. He was taken to Paris for serum treatments, then returned to Vienna where he died on May 18, 1911.

The following works by Mahler are discussed below: *Kindertotenlieder; Das Lied von der Erde;* Symphony No. 4 in G Major; Symphony No. 5 in C-sharp Minor; Symphony No. 9.

For Symphony No. 1 ("Titan") and Symphony No. 2 ("Resurrection"), see the biographical sketch above.

SYMPHONY NO. 4 IN G MAJOR (1900). I. Gay, deliberate, unhurriedly. II. With leisurely motion. III. Peacefully. IV. Very easily.

The darkness and the despair we find expressed in so many Mahler symphonies are not found in this music. This symphony is sunshine and warmth. The shortest of the Mahler symphonies, and the lightest in orchestral texture, it is also the most good-humored and bright-faced. Its première performance took place in Munich on November 25, 1901, with Felix

Weingartner conducting. The symphony was—as was the case with most Mahler symphonies—poorly received. One critic described it as a "musical monstrosity."

An illuminating commentary by Bruno Walter in his biography of Mahler serves as an admirable guide: "After the works of pathos, a yearning for gaiety or, rather, for serenity had sprung up in Mahler's heart, and so he created the idyll of the Fourth, in which a devout piety dreams its dream of heaven. Dreamlike and unreal indeed is the atmosphere of the work—a mysterious smile and a strange humor cover the solemnity which so clearly had been manifested in the Third. In the fairy tale of the Fourth everything is floating and unburdened.... The blissful feeling of exaltation and freedom from the world communicates itself to the character of the music. The three orchestral movements take their course without a condensation of the peculiar moods out of which they grew into a definite idea.... The first movement and the *Heavenly Life* are dominated by a droll humor which is in strange contrast to the beatific mood forming the keynote of the work. The scherzo is a sort of uncanny fairy-like episode. Its demoniac violin solo and the graceful trio form an interesting counterpart to the other sections of the symphony without abandoning the character of lightness and mystery. Referring to the profound quiet and clear beauty of the Andante [the third movement], Mahler said to me that they were caused by his vision of one of the church sepulchers, showing the recumbent stone image of the deceased with the arms crossed in eternal sleep. The poem whose setting to music forms the last movement depicts in words the atmosphere out of which the music of the Fourth grew. The childlike joys which it portrays are symbolic of heavenly bliss, and only when, at the very end, music is proclaimed the sublimest of joys, is the humorous character gently changed into one of exalted solemnity."

In the fourth movement, Mahler interpolates verses from an old Bavarian folksong, *Der Himmel hängt voll Geigen,* and from his own song cycle, *Des Knaben Wunderhorn;* these are sung by a soprano.

KINDERTOTENLIEDER, song cycle for voice and orchestra (1902). I. "Once More the Sun Would Gild the Morn." II. "Ah, Now I Know Why Oft I Caught You Gazing." III. "When My Mother Dear." IV. "I Think Oft They've Only Gone Aboard." V. "In Such a Tempest."

Those who have been moved by the immense grief of this music, and who are familiar with the fact that Mahler lost his daughter in 1906, are likely to infer that this work was stimulated by the composer's personal tragedy. Actually, Mahler wrote the *Kindertotenlieder* several years before the death of his child. He was inspired by the moving elegies that the poet Friedrich Rückert wrote on the loss of his children. Of these he selected five and set them to music of profound sadness. Incidentally, following the death of his own child, Mahler was continually haunted by the superstition that death had come to his daughter because he had written this elegiac music!

Paul Stefan has provided the following admirable guide to this cycle of songs in his biography of Mahler: "The first...seeks in vain for consolation in the Universe. Again and again a double stroke of the glockenspiel sounds like a doleful reminder...and dies away gently with the greeting to the sun....In the second, the eyes of the dead children brighten again— *only* eyes before, *only* stars now. In the third, the voice with its empty fourths, deep, muted, as though speaking alone, joins the sorrowful cor anglais melody. The glance seeks the vanished child on the threshold beside the entering mother. A violent outbreak of grief, and all becomes silent again; only a low G of the harp is struck. Then violins and horns begin a hurrying melody....A furious storm; the children would never have been allowed in this weather. Anxiety is vain today. The glockenspiel is heard again, and over the celesta and violins sounds in major 'like a cradle song' the message of hope and lasting peace."

SYMPHONY NO. 5 IN C-SHARP MINOR (1902). Part One— I. Funeral march; II. Stormily agitated, with great vehemence. Part Two— III. Scherzo: vigorously, not too fast. Part Three—IV. Adagietto: very slowly; V. Rondo—Finale: allegro.

This symphony is so gargantuan in size (though not the largest of the Mahler symphonies) and so overladen in its instrumentation that it has been called "The Giant." Mahler was dissatisfied with his original scoring and revised it repeatedly up to the year of his death, when he reorchestrated it completely. In its original version, it was introduced in Cologne on October 18, 1904, with Mahler conducting. It was unsuccessful.

Numerous programs have been superimposed upon this highly descriptive and dramatic music. But Bruno Walter informs us that Mahler had insisted to him that "not a single note points to the influence of extramusical thoughts or emotions upon the composition of the Fifth." Walter goes on to describe the music of the symphony as "passionate, wild, pathetic, buoyant, solemn, tender, full of the sentiments of which the human heart is capable—but still 'only' music, and no metaphysical questioning, not even from very far off, interferes with its purely musical course."

The symphony opens with a funeral march, music of such grandeur that it might well serve to describe the passing of a hero. A second movement is rebellious in mood and stormy, and brings the first part of the symphony to a close. The second part consists of a rather whimsical scherzo, the spine of which is a solo for horn. The third part opens with what is perhaps the most famous section of the entire work, a charming, delicate Adagietto. There follows the climax of the symphony, a rondo-finale movement, the crowning section of which is a grandiose triple fugue.

DAS LIED VON DER ERDE, song cycle for tenor, contralto, and orchestra (1908). I. Drinking Song of the Misery of the Earth. II. The Lonely One in Autumn. III. Of Youth. IV. Of Beauty. V. The Toper in Spring. VI. The Farewell.

Das Lied von der Erde and the Ninth Symphony represent Mahler's farewell to the world. Though there appears to be a tranquil resignation in the symphony, there is only the profoundest pessimism in the song cycle. In what is perhaps one of his most personal works, Mahler expresses his maladjustment to the world around him, and his bitter renunciation of it. "Dark is life, dark is death," is only one line in the cycle; but it might serve as the motif for the entire work.

Das Lied is a cycle of six songs, alternately sung by tenor and contralto. It is based on Chinese poems by Li-Tai-Po, Tchang-Tsi, Mong-Kao-Yen, and Wang-Wei, which Hans Bethge adapted in his *Die Chinesische Flöte*. The somber mood of the poems, and the rich Chinese imagery, inspired Mahler to write music that is persistently dark and brooding in feeling and yet occasionally touched with vivid oriental colors.

Mahler referred to *Das Lied* as a "symphony"—though its relation to the classical symphonic form is, at best, remote. Keeping Mahler's designation in mind, Eric Blom finds the first song serving as the opening movement of the symphony; the second (poignantly elegiac music) is, then, the slow movement; the third (the only section that is not pessimistic) might be the scherzo; the fourth is in the nature of a minuet and trio; the fifth assumes the form of a rondo; and the last might approximate a slow-movement finale such as is found in Mahler's Ninth Symphony. In the last song, the despair of the preceding movements achieves a heart-rending and climactic intensity.

SYMPHONY NO. 9 (1909). I. Andante comodo. II. Im Tempo eines Gemächlichen Ländlers. III. Rondo burleske. IV. Adagio.

Mahler wrote his last complete symphony realizing that his life was drawing to a close and with the feeling that this would be his final work in the symphonic form. (He actually began a tenth symphony, but it was never completed.) The music of the Ninth Symphony is filled with sadness and world-weariness, the conflicts of a man searching restlessly for the peace and tranquillity life has thus far denied him. There is a great deal of soul-searching in the music, and the drama of inner turmoil; but there is also a note of resignation, particularly in the radiant music of the closing Adagio.

The first movement, described by Alban Berg as the most beautiful ever written by Mahler, opens in an atmosphere of foreboding and mystery. It continues in a somber vein to project the most intense sadness and yearnings of the composer. There are two principal melodic ideas: one has the calmness of resignation, while the other (twenty measures later) is passionate and intense, its expression of agony stressed by piercing chords for the trumpets. In the second movement one might reasonably expect an escape from this mental anguish, for here Mahler writes a Viennese Ländler, a peasant dance which in the hands of Schubert had lightness and gaiety. But Mahler writes his dance music with a suggestion of mockery, as if to comment with scorn on wordly pleasures. Irony, too, is injected into the third movement, which, Paul Bekker says, "is also a backward glance upon life with its indomitable activity, in which the song of creation is but an undercurrent to the always renewing changes of surging power. The artist mocks himself in a mockery which gives voice to the feelings of all those whose home is not in this world and its errors, who yearn for other shores. A movement of burning scorn."

But the mockery and the irony die on the lips, and in the final movement—one of the most incandescent pages ever written by Mahler—comes resignation. This is music of ethereal serenity and of other-worldly beauty. Mahler, having gone through his herculean struggles with himself, has at last found peace of soul.

The first performance of the Ninth Symphony took place in Vienna on June 26, 1912—a little more than a year after Mahler's death—with Bruno Walter conducting the Vienna Philharmonic.

GIAN FRANCESCO MALIPIERO 1882—

Malipiero's painstaking and monumental researches into the music of Italy's past—which have resulted in definitive editions of Monteverdi, Vivaldi, Cavalieri, Galuppi, etc.—have had an inescapable influence on his own musical thinking. Without sacrificing modern techniques, he reaches into Italy's past for subtle stylistic qualities and suggestions; these set his music apart from those of other contemporary Italians by endowing it with a kind of medieval quality. Like that of Monteverdi, his melodic line frequently resembles a recitative, carrying powerful dramatic impact. Like those of Vivaldi and Tartini, his slow passages often have serenity, even spirituality. And like so many of the old Italians, Malipiero emphasizes counterpoint; his style is frequently evolved from the old Gregorian chant.

Not only old Italian music, but old Italian culture as well, has left the imprint of its personality on his music. Sometimes Malipiero models his themes after the cadences and strophes of old Italian poetry; sometimes his very structures are imitative of poetic forms. And there are occasions when he re-creates in his music the spirit and atmosphere, the social and cultural backgrounds, of the Italian Renaissance.

Malipiero was born in Venice on March 18, 1882, a descendant of an old Venetian family that numbered several famous musicians. For a year, he studied at the Vienna Conservatory; but most of his training was received from Enrico Bossi. A protracted stay in Paris, where he came into intimate contact with progressive cultural ideas and the latest trends in music, influenced his technique, just as old Italian music (with which he first associated himself in 1902) molded his style.

As a composer he attracted attention in Europe immediately after World War I with two distinguished orchestral works. The first was the *Pause del Silenzio,* written in 1917, which reflected the shattering effect that the gruesome experiences of World War I had had upon him. *Pause del Silenzio* was introduced in Rome on January 17, 1918, under the direction of Bernardino Molinari. The next work was *Impressioni dal Vero,* three impressions which scenes of nature inspired in the composer. Written in 1918, *Impressioni dal Vero* was first heard in London on August 22, 1918.

In 1920, Malipiero won the one-thousand-dollar Elizabeth Sprague Coolidge Prize for the string quartet *Rispetti e Strambotti,* thereby becoming known in this country.

He has lived the greater part of his life in the seclusion of the little town of Asolo, not far from Venice. There he has worked hard at his studies, at teaching, and at composing. For many years he conducted a class in composition at the Liceo Benedetto Marcello in Venice, of which he became director in 1939.

The following works by Malipiero are discussed below: *La Passione; Rispetti e Strambotti; Sonata a Tre;* Symphony No. 2 ("Elegiaca"); Symphony No. 4 ("In Memoriam").

For *Impressioni dal Vero* and *Pause del Silenzio,* see the biographical sketch above.

RISPETTI E STRAMBOTTI, for string quartet (1920).

Rispetti and *strambotti* are two ancient Italian forms of poetry. The former is an address of love from a gentleman to a lady; the other is a kind of roundelay.

In adapting these two forms of poetry to music, Malipiero attempted to sketch a varied picture of society against the background of the Renaissance, from the peasant to the clergy. In one movement, this quartet contains twenty loosely connected episodes in which two themes are prominent: one, based on the plain chant, suggests the clergy; the other, consisting of acrid chords, speaks for the peasantry.

This quartet received the Elizabeth Sprague Coolidge prize of one thousand dollars. The world première took place at Pittsfield, Massachusetts, on September 25, 1920, in a performance by the Letz Quartet.

SONATA A TRE, for violin, cello, and piano (1927). I. Allegro impetuoso. II. Ritenuto. III. Allegro impetuoso.

In 1927, Malipiero was commissioned by Elizabeth Sprague Coolidge to write a chamber-music work. In conceiving a trio for violin, cello, and piano, Malipiero arrived at an original scheme. He wrote the first movement for cello and piano and the second for violin and piano; only in the concluding movement is the trio heard. The writing is impressionistic, with alternations of turbulent and placid moods. There is a richness of melodic ideas throughout. Themes used in the first two movements are repeated in the last.

The first public performance—by the Elshuco Trio—took place on September 20, 1928, in Pittsfield, Massachusetts.

LA PASSIONE, oratorio, for soloists, chorus, and orchestra (1935).

Malipiero has composed two oratorios which set to music the sixteenth-century mystery play by Pierozzo Castellani, *Rappresentazione della Cena e Passione,* the first being *La Cena,* composed in 1927. *La Passione* was introduced successfully at the Augusteo in Rome early in 1936.

The text is a primitive one; for it, Malipiero produced music that has an archaic quality, derived from medieval Italian folksongs and Gregorian chants. It is simple to a point of being, at times, stark and bare. The melodic writing is fluid, with little difference between actual lyricism and recitative.

"In the main," wrote Raymond Hall, reporting the première performance in Rome, "the music adheres closely to the text...since the composer is dominated by the pictorial conception of the fresco.... Thus the outward dramatic events of the opening, such as Judas' betrayal, the arrest and trial, are not given much relief, and the characters themselves—the angel, Judas, the captain, the high priest, Pontius Pilate, Herod—are scantily differentiated in the score, but are rather reduced to a synthetic common denominator, Mary excepted. The orchestra...in its accompaniments and brief interludes creates the atmosphere of each situation in a few masterly strokes.... The compenetration of subject and medium reaches a high degree of expertness."

SYMPHONY NO. 2 ("Elegiaca") (1936). I. Allegro non troppo. II. Lento non troppo. III. Messo. IV. Lento; Allegro; Lento quasi andante.

The year of 1936 was a tragic one for Malipiero. Though he tried to keep music outside the periphery of his own emotional crises, he could not help endowing the symphony he was writing with an elegiac character. "The first movement," wrote the composer, "is the least elegiacal, for the principal theme is full of vigor. The last movement, almost more than the second movement, justifies the character of an elegy. The third movement has a groundwork of ill-conceived melancholy."

The entire symphony has many pages of gentleness, and it is the opinion of Malipiero's wife that it has absorbed the quiet and serene character of the Italian countryside at Asolo, where it was written.

The symphony was introduced in this country on January 25, 1937, in a performance by the Seattle Symphony Orchestra under Basil Cameron.

SYMPHONY NO. 4 ("In Memoriam") (1947). I. Allegro moderato. II. Lento funebre. III. Allegro. IV. Lento.

World War I inspired Malipiero to write the bitter music of *Pause del Silenzio*. Out of World War II (and its aftermath) came the Fourth Symphony, a veritable elegy. "This terrible postwar period," Malipiero wrote, "is a huge cemetery in which is brought together all that is no more, so that one's soul has been disposed to draw into itself and make its own the grief of a friend."

The great tragedy through which Malipiero and his fellow Italians went during the years of World War II sets the mood for the entire symphony. The composer has explained that in the first and third movements he attempted to speak of hope; in the second and fourth movements, the mood is that of resignation. The fourth movement, which brings up the image of a funeral procession, utilizes the pealing of church bells as the principal theme; this is subjected to six variations. This theme occurred to the composer thirty-six years before he put it into this symphony, and remained in his mind "until the day when I found its rightful place in the fourth movement of the symphony."

Commissioned by the Koussevitzky Foundation, the symphony was introduced in Boston on February 27, 1948, with Koussevitzky conducting the Boston Symphony Orchestra.

FRANK MARTIN   1890—

Though Frank Martin has long been regarded as one of Switzerland's outstanding composers, recognition in this country has been slow in coming. In Europe he has enjoyed a long record of successful performances since 1918. But not until 1939 did a major work of his receive performance in the United States: the *Ballade* (for saxophone, piano, percussion, and strings), heard on an all-Swiss program. And not until a decade after that did he realize substantial success in the United States. And the work that now placed his name on the programs of most of our major symphony orchestras was the *Petite Symphonie Concertante.*

Through the years of his long and rich creative activity, Martin has allowed his style to undergo several transformations. At first he wrote academically, remaining faithful to accepted traditions. But, as one nameless Swiss critic remarked, though "the art of music has stood still with Martin in that no new realms of sound have been explored, it has been immeasurably enriched with a group of unpretentious works whose only claim to importance is that they bring the listener new worlds of beauty." Between 1922 and 1928, his works explored rhythmic problems, culminating with *Rhythmes,* for orchestra (1928). For brief periods after that, Martin turned to folk idioms (*Niques à Satan*), then to experiments with the twelve-tone technique (Symphony; *Musique de Ballet*). Finally Martin arrived at a style which is identifiably his, and in which he has produced his most important works to date. This style was characterized by Jacques de Menasce as "broad melodic lines of a chromatic nature, subtle harmonic and rhythmic patterns, and a sustained contrapuntal texture."

Frank Martin was born in Geneva, Switzerland, on September 15, 1890. He studied music there with Joseph Lauber. For a long period he lived in Paris, assimilating its musical influences and associations. Returning to his native city, he became one of the leaders of its musical life. He has served as head of the Dalcroze Institute of the Conservatory of Geneva, and was the founder of the Technicum Moderne de Musique. From 1952 to 1958 he taught at the Cologne Conservatory, after which he returned to Switzerland.

PETITE SYMPHONIE CONCERTANTE, for harp, harpsichord, piano, and two string orchestras (1945). I. Adagio; Allegro molto. II. Adagio; Allegretto alla marcia.

This work, completed in 1945, reveals the influence of the twelve-tone technique; but traditional procedures are not altogether abandoned. The blending of the old and the new is achieved gracefully.

This little symphony is in two movements, each with a slow and fast section. The opening Adagio contains the thematic material utilized throughout the work. Structurally, as Jacques de Menasce noted, the symphony reveals "the impulse of what might be called a symphonic cycle without a scherzo, leading from the introduction to the finale through the agitations of an initial Allegro and the more contemplative moods of a slow middle section."

The symphony is dedicated to Paul Sacher, conductor of the Basel Chamber Orchestra. That orchestra, under Sacher, introduced the work in Zurich on May 27, 1946. Two years later it was heard in this country for the first time, with Ernest Ansermet conducting the NBC Symphony over the NBC network.

CONCERTO FOR SEVEN WINDS AND ORCHESTRA (1949). I. Allegro. II. Adagietto. III. Allegro vivace.

This work was introduced by the Musical Society of Bern (to whom it is dedicated), Luc Balmer conducting, on October 25, 1949. It scored such a success that performances followed immediately in the leading cities of Switzerland, as well as in Amsterdam, Berlin, Cologne, and New York.

The three movements begin with the same syncopated theme which serves as a kind of motto. In the first movement, this motto theme introduces each of the seven wind instruments, which appear in the following order: oboe, clarinet, horn, trumpet, trombone, bassoon, and flute. A principal lyrical idea appears in the clarinet and is developed by the flute; a second major subject is later heard in the trombone. This second subject, transferred to the violins, introduces the recapitulation section. A reentry of the respective solo instruments in their original order concludes the movement. The second movement consists of a variation and development of an atmospheric melody in the violins. The finale, in free rondo form, begins with a vivacious scherzo theme, with a secondary important subject later found in the trumpet. Both themes are worked out in great detail and then repeated. The movement ends with a variation of the scherzo theme.

BOHUSLAV MARTINU   1890—

The music of Martinu has been subjected to two important influences. One is found in his use of form, in his exceptional partiality to the classical concerto grosso. The other is discernible in his style, dependent on Czech folk elements.

Though he draws copiously from Czech folk music (not so much from actual melodies as from the stylistic traits of these melodies), Martinu is by no means a present-day Smetana. The Czech influence is subtle, sometimes even elusive; it is not possible to regard Martinu's music as a glorification or extension of Czech folk art. For the French manner has also contributed much to his writing: clarity, economy, precision, refinement.

The Swiss conductor Ernest Ansermet has remarked that a pithy characterization of Martinu's music is not easy. His forms are, for the most part, classic. His harmonic language (though sometimes complex) is usually orthodox. His melodies, even when they have assimilated Czech elements, are not unique. But Ansermet goes on to put a finger on the essential quality that distinguishes Martinu's music—its expressiveness, attained "through media of his very own." There are few composers of our times who have achieved such true sentiment as is found in many Martinu works without resorting to the conventional idioms of romanticism.

Martinu was born in Polička, Bohemia, on December 8, 1890. His musical talent revealed itself early, encouraging some of his townspeople to create a fund for the purpose of sending him to the Prague Conservatory. After his graduation, he played the violin in the Czech Philharmonic Orchestra; during this period he wrote a ballet, *Istar* (produced at the National Theatre in 1921) and two symphonic poems. In 1923, he went to Paris for a prolonged stay of seventeen years. *Half-Time* (a musical description of a football match), performed at the International Society for Contemporary Music Festival in Prague in 1925, and *La Bagarre* (a musical interpretation of a crowd), heard in Paris in 1926, drew attention to him. His stature grew rapidly with successive works. By 1932, when he won the Elizabeth Sprague Coolidge Prize for his Sextet, he was recognized as an important figure in contemporary music.

When the Nazis took Paris, Martinu escaped to Southern France. After many trying experiences, he came to this country in 1941, and has remained here ever since. Though always a prolific composer, he has never before written so many works of ambitious scope and impressive quality as he has done here.

The following works by Martinu are discussed below: Concerto for Violin and Orchestra; Concerto Grosso; Double Concerto; Symphony No. 1; Symphony No. 2.

For *Concerto da Camera in F Minor,* see Concerto for Violin and Orchestra.

CONCERTO GROSSO, for chamber orchestra (1937). I. Allegro non troppo. II. Lento. III. Allegretto.

The composer has written: "The traditional form of concerto grosso has not been followed here, but rather the characteristic alternation of 'soli' and 'tutti,' which I have given to the pianos, woodwinds, and strings. The violins are divided into three sections in order to diffuse the full sonority of the strings and to provide more polyphonic activity.... In the first movement I work with a little rhythmic germ of a half-measure which binds the different developments of the other motives and which appears in the most diversified forms up to the end, where there remains nothing but this little germ within the fullness of the orchestra. The andante of the second movement is an extended song by the cellos and other strings, which continues forceful and expressive. But a few measures before the end, the song subsides into tranquillity. In the third movement, of lively character, the two pianos take the foremost place as soloists, setting forth the themes (somewhat rhythmic) of a rondo. At first they are enveloped always by the polyphony of the orchestra; then the orchestra takes them up, relegating the contrapuntal ornamentation to the pianos."

This work has had a strange and involved history. It was scheduled for publication in Vienna, but the project was abandoned with the *Anschluss* in 1938. A Paris première was canceled because the music could not be procured from Vienna at this time. A performance then scheduled for Prague had to be canceled because of the Munich crisis. Now earmarked for a Paris première, the work once again had to be abandoned, this time because the Nazis had entered the city. In all the ensuing confusion, the manuscript appeared to be lost, only to be discovered in this country in the possession of the conductor George Szell, who had brought it from Prague. At long last, the first performance did take place—in Boston, on November 14, 1941, with Serge Koussevitzky conducting the Boston Symphony Orchestra.

DOUBLE CONCERTO, for two string orchestras, piano, and tympani (1938). I. Poco allegro. II. Largo. III. Allegro.

Martinu was working on this concerto in 1938 when the tragedy of Munich descended cataclysmically on the Czech people. Into his music the composer transferred the tremendous impact that this historic event had on him; the concerto is actually the musical expression not only of Martinu but of all the Czech people during this period of crisis. "Its notes," says the composer, "sang out the feelings and sufferings of all those of our people who, far away from their home, were gazing into the distance and seeing the approaching catastrophe....It is a composition written under terrible circumstances, but the emotions it voices are not those of despair but rather of revolt, courage, and unshakable faith in the future. These are expressed by sharp, dramatic shocks, by a current of tones that never ceases for an instant, and by a melody that passionately claims the right to freedom."

This is one of Martinu's most emotional works, and one of his best. The power and feeling of this music were immediately recognized at the first performance, which took place in Basel, Switzerland, on February 9, 1940, with Paul Sacher conducting the Basel Chamber Orchestra. R. Aloys Mooser, the Swiss critic, wrote: "We find in the Double Concerto miraculous fantasy, irresistible dynamism, and an exceptional sense of construction. But we also find here a tragic sentiment and fascinating expression in which this talent attains its ripeness, today in full blossom."

Though the première performance went well, the rehearsals that preceded it were not without incident. It seems that the orchestral musicians rebelled against the complexity of the music. "Gentlemen," the conductor said firmly, "you do not realize that this is a masterpiece." The musicians agreed to work further on the music (actually, the composition had to be rehearsed over a period of six months!), and were eventually won over by the concerto.

SYMPHONY NO. 1 (1942). I. Allegro. II. Scherzo. III. Largo. IV. Allegro.

Martinu did not undertake the writing of his First Symphony until after his fiftieth birthday. The symphony was, as a matter of fact, his first composition for a large orchestra in fourteen years. But if the composer approached his most ambitious artistic task up to that time with any degree of uncertainty, technical or otherwise, it is not apparent in the music. The symphony was Martinu's most significant production up to that time, a work of fine integration, forceful expression, sound workmanship. It was written on a commission from the Koussevitzky Foundation and was introduced in Boston on November 13, 1942, by the Boston Symphony Orchestra, directed by Koussevitzky.

"My symphony," wrote the composer, "follows the classical division into four parts.... In preserving this plan, I have also followed an aesthetic plan which my conviction dictates, and this conviction is that a work of art must not transcend the limits of its possibility in expression.... I have avoided elements which seem to me alien to the expressive purpose of the work. The basis of the orchestra is a quintet of strings, which does not prevent solo passages for woodwinds, while the brass and percussion fulfill their due part. I have tried to find new sound combinations and to elicit from the orchestra a unified sonority in spite of the polyphonic working which the score contains. It is not the sonority of impressionism, nor is there the search for color, which is integral in the writing and the formal structure. The character of the work is calm and lyric."

CONCERTO FOR VIOLIN AND ORCHESTRA (1943). I. Andante; Allegro. II. Poco moderato. III. Poco allegro.

In 1941, Martinu had written a chamber-concerto for violin and orchestra—the *Concerto da Camera in F minor*—with an unmistakable Czech identity. A more ambitious work for violin and orchestra followed two years later. In 1943, Mischa Elman, the violin virtuoso, attended a concert of the Boston Symphony Orchestra in which a new symphony by Martinu was performed. This music made such an impression on him that he contacted the composer after the concert and asked him to write a violin concerto for his use. Subsequently, Elman gave an informal recital for Martinu; it is said that in writing his concerto, Martinu kept in mind the individual style of the violinist. Mischa Elman introduced the concerto in Boston on December 31, 1943, with the Boston Symphony Orchestra under Koussevitzky.

This concerto is essentially lyrical, just as its predecessor had been dramatic. The composer explained his artistic intentions as follows:

"The idea for the concerto presented itself to me with the following order—Andante, a broad lyric song of great intensity which leads to an Allegro, exploiting the technique and the virtuosity of the instrument, and has the aspect of a single-movement composition. The definitive form complies with concerto structure. I have preserved its grave character, lyric in the first part; and even in the middle Allegro, the Andante theme returns to end the movement. The second part is a sort of point of rest, a bridge progressing towards the Allegro finale. It is almost bucolic, accompanied by only a part of the orchestra and progressing *attacca* into the finale, which is Allegro.... The concerto ends with a sort of stretto, Allegro vivace."

SYMPHONY NO. 2 (1943). I. Allegro moderato. II. Andante moderato. III. Poco allegro. IV. Allegro.

The Second Symphony is more pastoral than the First, having been conceived as intimate music with the proportions of a chamber-music work. It approaches the simplicity of a classic symphony. The principal theme of the first movement, reflective and tender, sets the mood for the entire work. This tranquillity is extended in the second movement, which assumes the personality of a Moravian folksong and is a pastoral poem. Only in the third movement is the intimacy temporarily abandoned with a rousing march for full orchestra. A transition leads to the finale (a rondo) in which the texture and sensitive expression of the earlier movement returns. A broad and simply constructed melody, also like a Moravian folksong, is the basis of the final movement.

The symphony was introduced by the Cleveland Orchestra under Erich Leinsdorf on October 28, 1943. Dedicated "to my fellow countrymen in Cleveland," this work was performed to commemorate the twenty-fifth anniversary of the founding of the Czechoslovak Republic.

DANIEL GREGORY MASON   1873—1953

Mason was essentially a conformist who had a healthy respect for classical forms and was not afraid to use them to express his romantic temperament. Though there are occasional modern suggestions in his harmonic writing and tonality, these are rather hasty excursions for particular effects; they do not shatter the intimate link that binds his music with the past. He acknowledged his conservative tendencies and justified them. As he wrote: "To conserve the great influences of the past seems to me the way to put oneself in touch with what is most seminal and enduring in art. No music-loving individual, whether composer, performer, or listener, can hope fully to realize his own powers except as, escaping from the narrow walls of his egotism, he breathes the great air of musical tradition."

He is so articulate in his music, so much the master of his technique, so strong a personality, that, despite his debt to the past, he has not been imitative, and has succeeded in arriving at a pronounced individuality.

Mason was born in Brookline, Massachusetts, on November 20, 1873, a member of one of America's most famous musical families: his grandfather was the well-known music educator, Lowell Mason; his uncle was William Mason, the concert pianist and teacher; his father was Henry Mason, founder of the piano-manufacturing firm of Mason & Hamlin.

Daniel Gregory Mason was graduated from Harvard University in 1895, following which he engaged in intensive music study with Nevin, Chadwick, and Whiting. In the summer of 1913, he became a pupil of Vincent d'Indy in France. Meanwhile, eight years before this, he had joined the music faculty of Columbia University. He remained there until 1942, eventually becoming head of the music department. Besides his teaching activities, he engaged actively in writing about music, publishing numerous books which were permanent additions to the music library.

As a composer, Mason came to prominence before World War I, when the Kneisel Quartet and Ossip Gabrilowitsch introduced his Quartet for Piano and Strings, and the Philadelphia Orchestra gave the première of his First Symphony. He died in Greenwich, Conn., on December 4, 1953.

The following works by Mason are discussed below: *Chanticleer;* Symphony No. 2; Symphony No. 3 ("Lincoln").

CHANTICLEER, concert overture for orchestra (1926).

The following motto from Thoreau's *Walden* appears in the publisher's score: "I do not propose to write an ode to dejection, but to brag as lustily as a chanticleer in the morning, standing on his roost, if only to wake my neighbors up."

The crow of the chanticleer (trumpet) is the first theme. This is immediately followed by two other subjects: one is for woodwind, the other for four horns, and both (as the composer explained) "suggestive of the exuberant joy of many responding to the joy of Nature." After a repetition of the chanticleer theme by three trumpets and full orchestra, a tranquil section follows; this is high-lighted by a theme for solo bassoon and a second subject for muted strings and solo horn. Human exuberance (full orchestra) is restored in the closing page.

Chanticleer was heard for the first time in Cincinnati on November 23, 1928, Fritz Reiner conducting the Cincinnati Symphony.

SYMPHONY NO. 2 (1929). I. Allegro maestoso. II. Andante soste-nuto. III. Vivace scherzando. IV. Finale: lento; Allegro maestoso.

Mason's Second Symphony came fifteen years after his first. It was written between 1928 and 1929, and was introduced in Cincinnati on November 7, 1930, Fritz Reiner conducting the Cincinnati Symphony. Following the première performance, it was repeated by numerous American orchestras with great success.

In structure, the symphony digresses from classical models by dispensing with the development and recapitulation sections in the first movement. Like all of Mason's symphonies, the themes are treated cyclically. The music is romantic, powerful, and sometimes stark in the fast movements. It is poetic in the slow movement, built around an expansive melody.

SYMPHONY NO. 3 ("Lincoln") (1936). I. The Candidate from Springfield. II. Massa Linkum. III. Old Abe's Yarns. IV. 1865.

American composers have been partial to the subject of Abraham Lincoln. Mason has been no exception. His *Lincoln Symphony* was introduced in New York by the New York Philharmonic-Symphony Orchestra under John Barbirolli on November 17, 1937.

In the first movement, descriptive of Lincoln's early manhood, a popular song of the 1860's, *Quaboag,* is used prominently. The second movement is patterned after a spiritual (English horn) to portray the Negro's tenderness for Lincoln. A scherzo of peasant wit depicts Lincoln's flair for broad humor. The symphony ends with a poignant threnody to the assassinated President.

HARL McDONALD   1899—1955

Though Harl McDonald's music embraced a wide gamut of styles, he brought to each work such musicianship and original thinking that it never fails to carry conviction. He wrote realistically, in a tender postromantic vein, and impressionistically. His interest in folk music had led him to produce compositions equally varied in style and technique, embodying American, Negro, Hebrew, Spanish, and French-Canadian themes. What he attempted to do, however, he did skillfully, and though he never achieved an identity that bears the unmistakable fingerprints of its author, he, at any rate, produced music that makes for pleasurable listening.

McDonald was born in Boulder, Colorado, on July 27, 1899. At four, he began studying the piano, and at seventeen he wrote his first work, a set of dances for the piano, utilizing Hispanic rhythms. His music study began with private teachers, continued at the University of Southern California and Redlands University, and was completed at the Leipzig Conservatory. He became lecturer, then professor, and finally director of the Music Department at the University of Pennsylvania. He conducted its various choral groups, as well as the Philadelphia Mendelssohn Club; after 1939, he became manager of the Philadelphia Orchestra. He died in Princeton, N.J., on March 30, 1955.

The following works by McDonald are discussed below: *"Rhumba"; Saga of the Mississippi; Three Hebrew Poems.*

For Symphony No. 2, see *Rhumba.*

RHUMBA, for orchestra (1935).

One of Harl McDonald's most famous and most frequently heard compositions is a rhumba which, though actually the third movement of his second symphony, has acquired fame independent of the symphony itself.

The entire symphony was a product of the era in which it was written —the early 1930's. The music aimed to speak of an age of breadlines, labor strife, experimental legislation in Washington, and the almost feverish attempt on the part of most people to escape from reality.

The gaiety of the rhumba movement interpreted "the spirit of restlessness of the period," in the words of the composer, "its passionate search after good times and diversions, its pursuit of intoxicated pleasures."

The composer also had this to say about the interpolation of a rhumba movement in a symphony. "Several years ago, quite by accident, I heard a Cuban band doing wonderful things in rhumba rhythm, and my first thought was that when I had sufficiently saturated myself with the style of Cuban music, I should write a rhumba for symphony orchestra. Shortly after this the dance became popular in the United States, and while many of our dance bands failed to preserve the exotic and violent style of the native dance, it became for me one of the most interesting and exciting things in jazz music. My *Rhumba Symphony* was not planned as a setting for the dance; but rather, as I considered the plan of the symphony, I felt that the rhumba instead of the conventional scherzo was almost essential."

The entire symphony was introduced in Philadelphia in October, 1935, by the Philadelphia Orchestra, Leopold Stokowski conducting.

THREE HEBREW POEMS, for orchestra (1936).

A collection of Aramaic and Hebrew folk music came to McDonald's

attention in 1936. Seven themes (four Aramaic and three Hebraic), all similar in style and spirit, are woven into the texture of this music, which was
written in 1936 and was introduced in the same year by the Philadelphia
Orchestra under Ormandy. "While I have felt free to reshape the original
material even to the point of inverting lines, I have tried at all times to maintain the important rhythmic and phrase peculiarities of the originals. In the
matter of harmonic language and, to a certain extent, the orchestral style,
I have attempted to preserve the character of the traditional material rather
than to allow myself too many excursions in a too personal vein."

The first poem is gay, the opening being described by the composer
as a "nature poem." An Aramaic chant follows, punctuated with a fragment
of the famous Jewish melody, *Eili, Eili.* An Aramaic and a Hebraic tune
are blended into a song of lamentation for the second poem. The third comprises three themes, two of which are dance tunes.

SAGA OF THE MISSISSIPPI, for orchestra (1947). I. Prehistoric
Mississippi. II. Father of the Waters.

In this descriptive work (which McDonald began in 1945 but revised
and completed in 1947), the saga of the Mississippi River is told in two parts.
The first represents "the rise of the great stream from its primeval geologic
sources"; the second narrates "the human history of the river." The first
movement, which hints at antiquity through suggestions of modal writing,
comprises two conventional themes and an epilogue. The second is a graphic
description of an Indian ceremony.

The following outline of the music is provided by the composer:

"I. Born of the Highlands and the Lakes; the Glaciers, the Mountains
and the Prairies. The picture of your birth is clouded in the ice and mists
of ancient ages, but your spirit remains our life stream.

"II. The Red Man knew your bountiful gifts and gave thanks to the
great Spirit on your banks. The Spanish and French Fathers brought the
glory of Christianity to America on the Mississippi. But all men, white and
dark—Indian, Spaniard and Negro, Bourbon and Yankee—combined to
make Mississippi the heart of America."

The world première took place in Philadelphia on April 9, 1948, with
Eugene Ormandy conducting the Philadelphia Orchestra.

NICOLAS MEDTNER   1880—1951

Though Medtner wrote several fine songs and three sonatas for violin and piano, he is most important in his works for the piano. He has been called the "Russian Brahms"—the implication being that, like Brahms, his music is classical in structure, and that it has some of Brahms' austerity and power.

Though Medtner was himself an outstanding virtuoso of the piano and consequently knew the instrument as perhaps only a performer can—his writing is not always pianistically grateful. His music tends to get involved in its harmonic and contrapuntal textures, in its rhythmic play, to a point where it becomes somewhat cumbersome, even for virtuoso hands. But though his music may not come easily to the performer—and sometimes, due to its intellectual concentration, it does not come easily to the listener either—it is music which deserves the effort it must get. For at its best it has grandeur and passionate sweep.

Medtner was particularly successful in the smaller forms: *Arabesques, Novellen, Fairy Tales, Improvisations, Marches, Musical Pictures, Etudes, Caprices, Moments Musicals, Romantic Sketches,* etc. These pieces are filled with fine melodies, deeply felt emotion, and a gift for conveying varied tone colors and atmospheres. Technically, these pieces are derived from the piano music of Schumann, and Schumannesque in their imaginativeness and subtle suggestions, and in their delicate poetry.

Medtner was born in Moscow on January 5, 1880. He entered the Moscow Conservatory when he was only twelve years old, studying composition with Arensky and Taneiev and piano with Safonov. Before his graduation, which took place in 1900, he published some songs and piano pieces which revealed his creative talent. In 1902, Medtner began the first of his many concert tours, which, in the years that followed, were to bring him around the world and establish his reputation as a virtuoso of first importance. He left Russia in 1921, stayed for a while in Germany, and then in 1936 settled permanently in England, where he lived in seclusion. In 1948, the Maharajah of Mysore provided the funds to record the entire creative output of Medtner, most of it in his own performances—the first time that the entire lifework of a composer was put on records. Medtner died in London on November 13, 1951.

The following works by Medtner are discussed below: Concerto No. 1 in C Minor for Piano and Orchestra; *Fairy Tales.*

CONCERTO NO. 1 IN C MINOR FOR PIANO AND ORCHESTRA (1918).

Medtner wrote this one-movement concerto in 1918, and in the same year he introduced it in Moscow as a soloist with the Koussevitzky Orchestra. In structure it is an elaboration of the classic sonata form, consisting—as the composer explained—"of an exposition, a series of variations on two chief themes constituting the development, and a recapitulation."

The principal theme is heard in the violins after three strong measures of introduction by the piano. The cellos give the second theme against an ascending passage of chords and octaves in the piano. After a rhapsodic passage for piano, which is soon taken up by a solo horn, a brief development takes place. A short cadenza for the piano follows, following which come the nine variations. A coda, in which the two principal themes are combined, comes after a recapitulation, and the concerto ends brilliantly.

FAIRY TALES, for piano.

Of all the forms utilized by Medtner, he was perhaps best in the one which he himself invented—the fairy tale. Thirty of them appear in opp. 8, 9, 14, 20, 26, 34, 35, 42, and 51. In these fairy tales, his music unfolds like a narrative. While they have no definite program, they are so rich in dramatic and emotional content that it is not difficult to find some extramusical interpretation in them, though what that interpretation is each listener must decide for himself.

Leonid Sabaneyev points out that a Medtner fairy tale does not recreate the world of elves and witchery, or the romanticism of enchantment. It is, rather, "the poetry of ancient heroic legends, and most of all an echo of the underworld Nibelungs, gnomes, and mountain kings.... It has no brightness or radiance, but dusk and darkness. Occasionally, it has an ominousness, and a certain closeness. In his *Fairy Tales* Medtner is neither heavenly nor ethereal, nor in the clouds, but earthly, even earthy—subterranean."

GIAN-CARLO MENOTTI 1911—

Through the years the lament has been sounded periodically that opera is a dying—or a dead—art form. And through the years there has always emerged some new composer to give opera a new lease on life, to prove that it is still a vibrant form. Sometimes a composer has done this by the application of new techniques and approaches, as was the case of Debussy and Alban Berg. Less frequently, opera has been revitalized only because the composer has brought to it the freshness and vigor of a talented personality. The latter is the case of Menotti.

The opera as a form has been changed little by Menotti. When he writes in a comic vein, he carries on the traditions of Italian opera buffa, established through the centuries from Pergolesi to Wolf-Ferrari. In his more serious manner, he takes the torch from the hands of Puccini. And yet in his hands the opera has acquired pulse and heartbeat; it is living theatre.

Menotti's feeling for the stage is an instinct which he has revealed from the very first, both in his librettos (which he has always written himself, *Amelia Goes to the Ball* in Italian, and the rest in English), and in his scores. The music meets the most fastidious and subtle demands of his text. It has brisk pace, contrasts, moods of varying shades and hues, dramatic thrust. Menotti has a born gift for characterization; and in painting an atmosphere he is virtually unique. He can be melodramatic and sardonic, realistic and fanciful, sordid and poetic—sometimes all within the same opera. But always he is capable of finding the musical *mot juste* with which to point up an emotion, a conflict, a climax.

Menotti was born in Cadigliano, Italy, on July 7, 1911. A prodigy, he began composing at the age of six, wrote his first opera when he was eleven, and soon after that was a favorite in the salons of Milan as a concert pianist. In 1928, he came to this country, and has remained here ever since. He attended the Curtis Institute on a scholarship; later he succeeded his teacher, Rosario Scalero, as head of the composition department. He was only twenty-three when he wrote *Amelia Goes to the Ball,* which forthwith established him as an important operatic composer. Subsequent operas—performed extensively throughout the world—justified the high promises of this maiden effort.

In 1945, Menotti received a one-thousand-dollar grant from the American Academy of Arts; in 1954 he was awarded the Pulitzer Prize for *The Saint of Bleecker Street* (see Supplement).

The following works by Menotti are discussed below: *Amahl and the Night Visitors; Amelia Goes to the Ball; The Consul; The Medium; The Old Maid and the Thief; The Telephone.*

AMELIA GOES TO THE BALL, comic opera (1934).

As a boy pianist, Menotti was the darling of Milanese society. From the intrigues and the banter of the salon, he drew his inspiration for this gay and impudent comedy—his first major effort in the operatic form, and his first important success. He wrote it when he was only twenty-three years old. It was introduced by members of the Curtis Institute of Music, under Fritz Reiner's direction, on April 1, 1937, in Philadelphia. The same group brought the opera to New York a few days later. Its success was immediate. It was not long before it entered the repertory of many major opera companies, including that of the Metropolitan Opera Association on March 3, 1938.

Menotti wrote his own libretto, in rhymed Italian meter: In Milan, Amelia is dressed for a ball. Her husband discovers a love letter addressed to her. On learning that the culprit is his downstairs neighbor, he storms out with threats of murder. While he is gone, the lover enters through the window, pouring out his love for Amelia, whom he begs to run away with him. When the husband returns, the two rivals discuss the triangle. This discussion irritates Amelia, for it is making her late for the ball. In despair, she throws a vase at her husband, and calls to the police to arrest her lover for attacking his rival. The husband goes to the hospital; the lover to jail. And Amelia (in the company of the police officer) goes to the ball.

It is a witty, tongue-in-cheek little play. For it, Menotti wrote an infectious score, engaging for its lightness and gaiety. It oozes with blood-rich melodies; and it is made piquant with a discreet use of dissonance. Within the formal pattern of the opera-buffa, aria, romanza, duet, trio, recitative, etc., Menotti produced a work that is abundantly fresh and spirited; and a work that is highly personal.

THE OLD MAID AND THE THIEF, opera (1939).

The Old Maid and the Thief is one of Menotti's most frequently heard operas. It is in the vein of *Amelia Goes to the Ball,* of which it was the immediate successor. Written on a commission from the National Broadcasting Company, it was introduced in a concert version over the NBC network on April 22, 1939. The first stage performance was given by the Philadelphia Opera Company on February 11, 1941.

Like its predecessor, the score is in the traditions of the opera buffa: witty, brisk, satiric, infectious. And, like its predecessor, it boasts a broad farce as a libretto. Miss Todd and her servant—starved for a man—eagerly welcome a tramp in their house, and prevail on him to remain indefinitely. He is treated royally. Miss Todd even goes to the length of stealing, to satisfy the ever-increasing demands of her lodger; on one occasion she raids a liquor establishment to get him a drink. The neighbors, ascribing the recent thefts to the tramp, demand that the police raid the house and arrest the culprit. Miss Todd begs him to escape. When the tramp learns that she has been stealing for him, he insists that she go to jail for her crimes. Upset by his lack of gratitude, Miss Todd goes to the police. During her absence, the tramp and Miss Todd's servant elope, stealing from the house whatever they can carry away. Thus is demonstrated—so says the author in his subtitle—"how a virtuous woman made a thief of an honest man."

THE MEDIUM, opera (1945).

That the gifted composer of the irrepressible *Amelia Goes to the Ball* was equally gifted in a more somber and dramatic vein was proved with *The Medium,* a two-act opera composed on a commission from the Ditson Fund. It was introduced on May 8, 1946, at the Festival of Contemporary Music at Columbia University in New York City.

The strange theme for this opera came to Menotti when he was visiting Austria in 1937. He was invited by a baroness to accompany her to her private chapel, where she spent an hour in communion with her dead daughter. "Though skeptical myself," Menotti has confessed, "I was impressed by her faith. Skepticism is a barren thing compared to faith. I try to show this in the opera."

In writing his macabre play, Menotti planned to describe the "tragedy of a person caught between two worlds, the world of reality which she cannot wholly comprehend, and the supernatural world in which she cannot believe." Madame Flora, a medium, defrauds her clients with fake séances— with the aid of a mute, Toby, and her daughter, with whom the mute is in love. During one of these séances, a cold, clammy, supernatural hand reaches for Madam Flora's throat.Terrified, she confesses to her clients that she is a fake—only to find that they do not believe her. Believing that the hand was that of Toby, she beats him and drives him out of the house. Then, as an escape, she takes to drink. In a stupor, she hears Toby returning to her home to claim her daughter. Lifting a revolver, she shoots Toby dead.

Though the play is rather contrived, it achieves dramatic strength through the originality and power of the music. With an infallible theatrical instinct, Menotti skillfully contrasts his somber colors with bright ones. His score, while essentially tragic, has sardonic overtones; it introduces notes of gaiety and levity which come as a blessed relief from the gruesome proceedings. Structurally and stylistically, the opera may stem from Puccini; but in its alternation of light and shade, the somber and the fanciful, it is a characteristic product of Menotti's theatrical talent.

In 1951, *The Medium,* filmed in Italy, was converted into a motion picture, the screen adaptation having been made by the composer.

THE TELEPHONE, opera (1946).

This amusing one-act opera has been described as a "skit with music." Subtitled by the composer, *"L'Amour à Trois,"* this play is slight indeed. But it is treated so deftly, and so admirably does it provide a stimulus for Menotti's satirical and always appropriately descriptive music that it serves well the composer's operatic purposes. Music and text, song and stage action, are wonderfully integrated, so that a "trite gag," as one New York music critic referred to it, becomes a fresh and well-paced composition.

A young lover tries to propose to his girl, only to be repeatedly frustrated by the ringing of the telephone. In despair, the lover rushes to the corner drugstore to propose to his girl—by telephone.

Introduced in New York City in a small uptown theatre on February 18, 1947, *The Telephone* was so well received that it was transferred to the Broadway stage on May 1, to settle down for an extended and successful run, paired with *The Medium.*

THE CONSUL, musical drama (1949).

Out of the tragedy of our times has come a poignant musical drama— the most ambitious operatic work Menotti has produced up to this time. The reading of a newspaper account which told of a European woman committing suicide because she could not get a visa to this country provided Menotti with the theme for his play. In a police state, a woman is seeking a visa for another country (both countries remain unidentified) in order to join her husband. She haunts the offices of the consul as frequently and as relentlessly as the secret police haunt her own home. The consul himself never appears on the scene; as a kind of disembodied spirit, never seen—but whose presence is always felt—he becomes the very personification of Fate itself, against whom the victim is helpless. The visa is never granted. The husband returns from his freedom to join his wife, who commits suicide.

In the creation of the grim parts of this opera, such as the overpowering closing suicide scene, Menotti again demonstrates the powerful gift for drama and atmosphere that made *The Medium* so effective. *The Consul* is macabre—but much more than that. Throughout the entire play there courses a profound feeling of pity which brings a humanity and emotional depth found in no other opera by Menotti. The composer feels intensely the tragedy of his characters, and the helpless situation in which they find themselves; and he projects that tragedy with crushing effect.

The resources of grand opera, together with the techniques of contemporary music, serve Menotti in his search for the appropriate musical counterpart for his moving text. Now he utilizes the crisp and cogent lines of song-speech, much as an atonalist might; and then, as in the magnificent aria sung by Magda to close the second act, or the exquisite lullaby the grandmother sings to the dying child (also in that act), he allows his melodic fancy to soar without inhibition. In the same way, he passes without warning from formal harmony and counterpoint to polytonality, dissonance, free rhythms, etc., as the text develops from pathos to bitterness, from the diaphanous world of dream fantasies into sordid reality. And the same extraordinary technique that blends text and music into an indissoluble whole coalesces the varied styles and techniques into an inextricable unity.

The Broadway run of *The Consul* (after tryouts in Philadelphia) began at the Ethel Barrymore Theatre in New York City on March 15, 1950. There were cheers after the première performance; and the cheers were echoed by the critics. Virgil Thomson described the work as "a music drama of great power." Olin Downes wrote ecstatically: "He has produced an opera of eloquence, momentousness, and intensity of expression unequalled by any native composer ... written from the heart, with a blazing sincerity and a passion of human understanding." *The Consul* received the Pulitzer Prize and the Drama Critics Award. Such success proved several things: that a vibrantly contemporary subject can be the basis of an effective opera; and that a serious opera need make no artistic concession to public taste to be box-office magic on Broadway.

AMAHL AND THE NIGHT VISITORS, opera (1951).

This is the first opera written expressly for television; and since the broadcast was sponsored, it is also the first opera whose world première was financed by a commercial organization. That première took place on Christmas eve, 1951, over the television network of the National Broadcasting Company, which had commissioned the work. The opera was repeated over television the following Easter, and was also successfully presented as a stage production by several opera organizations, including the New York City Opera Company.

The inspiration for the opera came to Menotti from the Flemish painting of Hieronymous Bosch, *The Adoration of the Magi.* Settings and costumes of the opera were directly influenced by it, as were the planned simplicity and naivete of Menotti's text. The story centers around the crippled boy, Amahl, who is miraculously healed when he gives his crutches to the Three Wise Men, on their way to the Manger in Bethlehem, as a gift to the Holy Child.

In reviewing the opera for the *New York Times,* Olin Downes remarked that "television, operatically speaking, has come of age." His analysis of Menotti's score follows: "The music is written often in recitative but with intensifying beauty at climactic moments, as when the child walks and the king chants of the power and majesty of the Savior. ... The choruses of the approaching and departing shepherds and other ensemble pieces are always poetical and atmospheric, never obvious or banal. Mr. Menotti has used no folk-airs or Christmas chants in this score, but he has written delightfully and characteristically in his music for the peasant dances. His tune of the beggar boy's pipe which begins and ends the play...is one of his happiest ideas."

OLIVIER MESSIAEN   1908—

On June 3, 1936, there took place in Paris, at the Salle Gaveau, a concert of music by young (and then comparatively unknown) French composers. This concert marked the emergence of a new school of contemporary musicians, self-styled *"La Jeune France."* In its manifesto, published in the program of that concert, the school dedicated itself to "the dissemination of works youthful, free, as far removed from revolutionary formulas as from academic formulas." The manifesto said further: "The tendencies of this group will be diverse; there only unqualified agreement is in the common desire to be satisfied with nothing less than sincerity, generosity, and artistic good faith. Their aim is to create and promote a living music."

This school of young French composers included Daniel-Lesur, Yves Baudrier, André Jolivet, and—most important of all—Olivier Messiaen.

Though a member of a school, Messiaen has always gone his own way in his music, frequently venturing into foreign worlds of musical expression far removed from those in which his fellow composers moved. He is a complex and original thinker. His music abounds with complicated polymodal and polyrhythmic writing and with intricate ideas. He is not afraid to be expansive: He has written a ten-movement symphony—and a piano work of 175 pages, requiring two hours for performance. He is partial toward the exotic: he calls upon rhythms derived from Hindu practice, archaic modes and scales, melodic ideas imitative of the plain song. Rhythm has particularly occupied his attention. He has used it with the variety and flexibility of a virtuoso. His ten-movement symphony, *Turangalîla* (commissioned by the Koussevitzky Foundation and introduced by the Boston Symphony under Leonard Bernstein on December 2, 1949) is, indeed, a veritable apotheosis of rhythm. Not only is it from beginning to end a most complex and elaborate exercise in the use of rhythm, but it also exploits an amazing variety of percussion instruments, including temple blocks, wood blocks, the Chinese cymbal, the tam-tam, tubular bells, etc.

There have been several influences in Messiaen's artistic development, as he himself has confessed. One has been of particular significance: the

Catholic Church. Profoundly religious, Messiaen has frequently turned to the liturgy and scriptures of the Catholic Church for the materials of his musical works; and he has suffused his writing with deep religious feeling and mysticism.

Messiaen was born in Avignon, France, on December 10, 1908, and attended the Paris Conservatory, where he won several prizes as a pupil of Dukas and Dupré. In 1931, he became organist at the Trinité Church in Paris; in the same year, his first major work—*Les Offrandes Oubliées*—was performed publicly. After a decade of teaching composition at the Schola Cantorum and the École Normale de Musique, he was appointed professor of harmony at the Paris Conservatory. During World War II, he served in the French Army, and for a period was interned by the enemy as a prisoner. In the summer of 1949, he visited the United States for the first time. Since 1952 he has been the organist at the Trinité church in Paris.

The following works by Messiaen are discussed below: *L'Ascension; Les Offrandes Oubliées; Les Visions de l'Amen.*

For *Turangalîla,* see the biographical sketch above.

LES OFFRANDES OUBLIÉES, for orchestra (1930).

In the published score there appears the following paragraph, intended by the composer as a clue to the emotional content of this music:

"With arms extended, sad unto death, on the tree of the Cross, sheddest Thou Thy blood. Thou lovest us, Gentle Jesus, but we had forgotten. Urged onward by madness and the sting of the serpent, in a frenzied, panting race that gives no release, fell we into sin as into a tomb. Behold the table pure, the spring of charity, the banquet of the poor; behold adorable compassion, offering the bread of life and love. Thou lovest us, Gentle Jesus, but we had forgotten."

Les Offrandes Oubliées was Messiaen's first major work to be performed. It was first heard on February 19, 1931, in Paris. It was also the first of his works to give an indication of the extent of his talent.

L'ASCENSION, four symphonic meditations for orchestra (1934).

The Ascension draws its text from Catholic liturgy and scripture, comprising Christ's prayers to the Father and the emotional responses of his followers to his words. The composer provided each movement not only with a title but also with an explanatory caption, that latter serving as the program for the music:

I. (*Très lent et majestueux.*) Majesty of Christ Beseeching His Glory of His Father. "Father, the hour is come; glorify Thy Son, that Thy Son may glorify Thee."

II. (*Pas trop modéré et clair.*) Serene Hallelujahs of a Soul That

Longs for Heaven. "We beseech Thee, O Lord...that we may dwell in Heaven in the spirit."

III. (*Vif et joyeux.*) Hallelujah on the Trumpet, Hallelujah on the Cymbal. "God is gone up...with the sound of a trumpet....O clap your hands, all ye people; shout unto God with the voice of triumph."

IV. (*Extrêmement lent, ému et solennel.*) Prayer of Christ Ascending to His Father. "Father...I have manifested Thy name unto men... and now I am no more in the world, but these are in the world, and I come to thee."

The first movement, scored for brass and woodwinds, is hymn-like. An archaic mannerism enters in the second part, in which a serene and spiritual atmosphere is evoked. The expression of joy becomes unconfined in the third section, for full orchestra. Only the strings are used in the concluding part, which is a devout prayer.

The Ascension was completed in 1934 as a suite for either solo piano or organ. It was later orchestrated by the composer. The first American performance took place in San Francisco on February 27, 1947, with Pierre Monteux conducting the San Francisco Symphony.

LES VISIONS DE L'AMEN, for two pianos (1943). I. Amen of the Creation. II. Amen of the Stars, of the Planet Saturn. III. Amen of the Agony of Jesus. IV. Amen of Desire. V. Amen of the Angels, of the Saints, of the Song of the Birds. VI. Amen of Judgment. VII. Amen of Consummation.

This is one of Messiaen's major works, and one of the most important works for two pianos written in our time. Davidson Taylor, who heard a private performance in Paris, described the music as follows in *Modern Music:*

"*Les Visions* is full of the music of bells, mellow bells and cracked harsh bells like those of Rennes, near bells and distant bells, deep bells and high delicate bells, and there is no trace of monotony in the music....

"The first section of this grand and dramatic sevenfold Amen bears the quotation, 'Let there be light, and there was light.' The Amen of the stars quotes Baruch, 'God calls them and they say, Amen, we are here!' It is a savage dance. The final movement is headed *'De clarté en clarté.'* The two sections which remain most acute...are the one about the angels and the birds, with a long, serene melody decorated by the most intricate fretwork, and the one about the judgment, in which futile supplications are broken by great frozen chords like pronouncements from the throne of God."

NIKOLAI MIASKOVSKY   1881—1950

Miaskovsky was the most prolific of today's composers of symphonies. He wrote in all twenty-seven works in that form. In his earliest symphonies (of which the Sixth is the best example), he was the subjective composer who imparted personal thoughts and feelings into his music. A more objective approach becomes evident with the Seventh Symphony. Influenced and inspired by the revolution in his native land, Miaskovsky turned to Soviet life and activity for his inspiration. Thus his Twelfth Symphony is known as the *Collective Farm Symphony*. In the next six symphonies—from the Thirteenth to the Eighteenth—an attempt is made to reconcile subjective and objective expressions. This was not satisfactory, as Miaskovsky himself realized. With the Nineteenth Symphony, still another approach is perceptible. From now on, the composer aims for simplified writing, consciously attempting the kind of music that is easily assimilable and can have immediate and direct appeal to large masses. His Twenty-First Symphony, generally credited as his best work, is the most successful realization of this point of view.

Though Miaskovsky was prolific in writing symphonies, he has also produced music in other forms as well, and with no diminution of quantity. His works include symphonic poems, concertos, sinfoniettas, quartets, piano music, songs, one work for band (the Nineteenth Symphony), and various other works for other media.

His earlier works are, for the most part, melancholy. In the description of Igor Glebov, this is music of "utter darkness—a gray, awesome, autumnal darkness, transformed into a moonless night, a tenebrous darkness." But his later works radiate optimism. To continue Glebov's metaphor, the sun is allowed to pierce the darkness and bring warmth and light.

Nikolai Miaskovsky was born in Novogeorgievsk, Russia, on April 20, 1881. The study of music came comparatively late, as he prepared himself for a career as an army engineer. However, once he assumed a post as engineer, the need for musical self-expression led him to abandon his profession for intensive music study. He entered the St. Petersburg Conservatory, where he was a pupil of Glière and Liadov. Soon after graduating from the Conservatory, Miaskovsky began composing, revealing exceptional talent from the very first. During World War I, he was wounded and shell-shocked in the Russian army. After the October Revolution, he settled in Moscow, becoming professor of composition at the Conservatory and holding that post with distinction. However, when the Central Committee of the Communist Party sternly denounced the leading composers of the Soviet Union for "formalism" in February, 1948 (see Prokofiev), Miaskovsky was not exempt: he was brought to task not only for the "formalism" of his compositions but also for his insistence on introducing "inharmonious music" into the educational system. He died on August 9, 1950.

The following works by Miaskovsky are discussed below: Sinfonietta (op. 32, no. 2); Symphony No. 6 in E-flat Minor; Symphony No. 21 in F-sharp Minor.

SYMPHONY NO. 6 IN E-FLAT MINOR, op. 23 (1922). I. Poco largamente; Allegro feroce. II. Presto tenebroso. III. Andante appassionato. IV. Finale.

The Sixth Symphony was written in 1922 and received its first performance in Moscow on May 4, 1924, Golovanov conducting. Like all the early symphonies of Miaskovsky, this is highly personal music. The composer himself has provided the following information regarding its origin:

"The first impulse was given to me by the singing of the French revolutionary songs, *Ça ira* and *Carmagnole,* by a French artist, who sang them exactly as they do in the workers' districts of Paris. I made notes of his version, which was different from the printed versions, and I was particularly impressed by the rhythmic energy of *Carmagnole.* When, in 1922, I started my Sixth Symphony, these themes naturally found their place in the music. The confused state of my world outlook at that time had inevitably resulted in a conception of the Sixth Symphony which sounds strange to me nowadays, with the motives of a 'victim,' 'the parting of the soul and body,' and a short apotheosis symbolizing 'beatific life' at the end; but the creative ardor I then felt makes this work dear to me even now."

Further information regarding the emotional impulses that led to the writing of this music is found in the published score:

"At the time of its writing, Miaskovsky was deeply impressed by the passing of two persons particularly dear to his heart.... Some portions of the symphony are also influenced by *Les Aubes* of Emile Verhaeren, the Belgian poet."

Generally speaking, the symphony is somber in character, brooding in the slow movement and passionate and virile in the fast pages. Even in the last movement, aflame with Miaskovsky's revolutionary ardor, there is a strange feeling of portentous doom as a quotation of the *Dies Irae* appears. In this movement, a chorus, singing a wordless chant, adds to the despair, and the symphony closes as it began, with quiet melancholy.

SINFONIETTA, for string orchestra, op. 32, no. 2 (1929). I. Allegro pesante e serioso. II. Andante. III. Presto.

Of Miaskovsky's two sinfoniettas for string orchestra, this one is more frequently heard. It was written eighteen years after the first. Character-istic of later Miaskovsky music, this work is pleasingly melodious. The first movement is robust, the principal melody being heard in unison strings. A gentle touch of melancholy enters the second movement with a melody for solo violin; this melody undergoes four variations. Spirit and vigor return in the last movement, which proceeds at a brisk pace from beginning to end, and in which the richness of the tonal texture is enhanced by the use of divided strings.

SYMPHONY NO. 21 IN F-SHARP MINOR, op. 51 (1940).

This is both the best and the most successful of Miaskovsky's sym-phonies. It was completed in 1940, and introduced on November 16 of the same year by the Moscow Philharmonic under Alexander Gauck. It was successful from the first. Gregory Schneerson reported: "There were shouts of *bis,* demands for repetition, a rare case in the symphonic annals." The sym-phony was selected to inaugurate a ten-day festival of Soviet music; one year later, it received the Stalin Prize, first degree.

This comparatively short work (requiring only fifteen minutes for per-formance) is in a single movement, pleasurable music from the opening bar to the last. A meditative introduction contains the material of the entire work, the principal idea, out of which the other thematic subjects are evolved, is stated by the clarinet. With varied moods (repeated alternation between fast and slow sections) the symphony gains in power and brilliance until, after a fugal development, it arrives at a "festive and triumphant culmina-tion," as Schneerson described it. In concluding the symphony, the composer returns to the material and mood of the introduction. "It is as though," Schneerson commented, "the composer returns to the initial mood of lyric reflection, which has now acquired a deeply transfigured character."

FRANCISCO MIGNONE   1897—

From the rhythms, melodies, instrumental colors, and personality of Brazilian folk music (which, in turn, has assimilated Indian, African, and Portuguese traits), Mignone has acquired both the inspiration and the ma-terials for his composition. Interest in the folk music of his native land came to him early, even before his official emergence as a composer; and it has remained a vital influence throughout his creative career. However, other

influences have also been discerned more recently in his music: notably religious and social ones. But it is principally those works with a pronounced
national identity that have been most widely performed, and that have placed
him with the foremost composers of South America. Mignone's best music,
like the best music of Brazil, is harmonically colorful, strongly rhythmic,
sometimes exotic in character, and always imaginatively conceived.

Mignone was born in São Paulo on September 3, 1897. For a while he
combined the study of music at the São Paulo Conservatory with the playing
of the piano in a local theater. In 1918, his official debut as a composer took
place when he himself introduced a few piano pieces and his father conducted
the première of *Caramarú,* for orchestra. For nine years, beginning with 1920,
Mignone lived in Europe as the recipient of a government grant. There he
studied, composed, and assimilated musical influences. Back in his native
country, he became professor of harmony and piano at the São Paulo Conservatory. In 1941, he played a major part in the reorganization of the musical
life of his country. One year later, he visited the United States for the first
time as a guest of our State Department.

The following works by Mignone are discussed below: *"Congada";*
Four Churches.

For *Contratador de Diamantes,* see *"Congada."*

CONGADA, dansa Afrobrasileira, for orchestra (1920).

In 1920, Mignone went to Italy on a government grant to study with
Ferroni. Coming in contact with Italian opera in its native setting had its
effect on the young composer, who proceeded to write an opera in the traditional Italian manner: *Contratador de Diamantes.* The setting was eighteenth-century Brazil; the theme, the exploitation taking place in the Brazilian diamond mines. But it is not the voice of a Brazilian deeply concerned
with folk idioms that is heard in this score; rather, it is an apprentice composer imitating a foreign style.

However, there are intermittent passages in which Mignone's nationalism asserts itself; and these are the best pages of the opera. One such section
is the Afrobrazilian dance, *"Congada,"* found in the second act. This is
vertiginous music, adopting the ingenious rhythms, brilliant colors, and
exotic character of Brazilian Negro music.

This piece is one of Mignone's most famous works. It was introduced
in São Paulo on September 20, 1922, under the composer's direction, and
since that time has been extensively performed.

FOUR CHURCHES, symphonic poem for orchestra (1940).

In this symphonic poem, the composer attempted the evocation in
music of the feelings and ideas inspired by the festivities of the Catholic
Church in Brazil. Though the music is inspired by the Brazilian Church, it

is not religious music. The composer took pains to explain that these Brazilian religious fiestas combine the sacred with the profane, blending the religious chant of the church with the superstitious song of the Negro.

The first section brings up the hubbub of a fiesta day, as street noises mingle with the pealing of organ music from within the Church of Saint Francis of Bahia. The plain chant is heard; also the music of choir, organ, and church bells. The fiesta comes to an end. Colonial Brazil is now described; the Negro slaves are building a church. Here Negro song mixes with the religious chant. There follows a portrait of the Gloria Church in Rio de Janeiro, in music that is serene and gentle. Then the church bells ring and the organ sounds its majestic voice to honor Our Lady of Brazil. All the people are united by their common devotion to the Church, and to Nossa Senhora Aparecida do Brasil, whose image looks down on them from her corner in the wall.

Four Churches was introduced in this country on April 21, 1942, with Mignone himself conducting the NBC Symphony over the NBC network.

DARIUS MILHAUD   1892—

Like the old Kapellmeisters of the sixteenth and seventeenth centuries, Darius Milhaud writes music as naturally as he breathes. He is not one of those composers who pours his very lifeblood into every work he produces, to whom the creative process is a life-and-death struggle. Nor is he a composer to work so painstakingly on every bar and note that a year's effort usually results in a single major work. Milhaud writes music all the time, writes it with such extraordinary facility and ease that nothing seems able to stem the tide of his production. He has suffered serious illness; he has lived through the trials of two world wars, the second of which uprooted him from his native land and sent him to find a new home in a new country; he has traveled frequently and extensively. And yet, despite circumstances which have often stultified the efforts of others, he has kept on writing abundantly.

He has written so many works that to catalogue them would be a futile task, one which—even if accomplished—would forthwith become out of date, in view of the many new compositions that would have been written in the interim. He has written in every possible form of music and he has utilized many different styles. The remarkable part of it all is that he is not a superficial composer. His music rarely betrays carelessness, haste, or glib thinking. What he has written invariably has revealed consummate mastery of technical equipment—that and the enviable capacity to arrive at the most felicitous musical expression with economy. Even when he adopts a popular vein—which he has done on many occasions—he brings to his writing such a personal charm and such a wealth of musical inventiveness and ingenuity that this music rises above popular appeal to achieve artistic dignity.

He was one of the six composers whom Henri Collet gathered into the school now known as the "French Six" (see Honegger). But Milhaud has never marched under any banner other than that of complete artistic independence. He has always gone his own way. With amazing flexibility, he has employed now one style, now another, bringing to each assignment a completely fresh approach. He has written works in the idioms of South American folk music and American jazz; he has produced Hebrew music; he has written music that is ultramodern in technique (he may be called the first successful polytonalist). But through whatever vein he chooses for a given work he sends the rich flow of lyricism. This melodic invention, together with the inexorable logic of his thinking and an engaging feeling of spontaneity, are the traits that give his music the great appeal it enjoys both with connoisseurs and amateurs.

Darius Milhaud was born in Aix-en-Provence, France, on September 4, 1892. In his eighteenth year he entered the Paris Conservatory, where his teachers included Gédalge, Widor, and Vincent d'Indy. The outbreak of World War I interrupted his studies, and during this period he joined the French Legation in Rio de Janeiro. It was at this time that he came into contact with the South American folk and popular music which he was to utilize in his own works; and it was during this period, too, that the French writer Paul Claudel was to create for him the texts of several important operas.

When the war ended, Milhaud returned to Paris and became associated with a group of other young French composers in a school known as the "French Six." In 1922, he visited the United States for the first time, appearing as pianist, conductor, and lecturer. During the period between the two world wars, his reputation as composer grew until there were few to deny him the position of France's foremost living composer upon Ravel's death. With the coming of World War II, Milhaud settled in this country, teaching at Mills College in Oakland, California, and making intermittent appearances as conductor of his own works with leading American orchestras. He also taught for one summer at the Berkshire Music Center in Tanglewood, Massachusetts. After the war, Milhaud returned to France, but he has since that time visited this country regularly.

The following works by Milhaud are discussed below: *Le Boeuf sur le Toit* (*The Nothing-Doing Bar*); Concerto No. 2 for Cello and Orchestra;

Concerto No. 2 for Piano and Orchestra; *La Création du Monde;* Quartet No. 6; Quartet No. 14; Quartet No. 15; *Saudades do Brasil; Suite Française; Suite Provençale;* Symphony No. 1; Symphony No. 2; Symphony No. 3 ("Te Deum"); Symphony No. 4.

For Octet, see Quartets Nos. 14 and 15.

LE BOEUF SUR LE TOIT (THE NOTHING-DOING BAR),
pantomime, or farce, with music (1919).

There is a famous bar in Paris called Le Boeuf sur le Toit. It is some-times believed that Milhaud's pantomime was named after this bar; actually, the reverse is true.

It is also interesting to point out that the text (or synopsis) was writ-ten *after* Milhaud had composed his music. Jean Cocteau heard a two-piano version of the score. He was so taken with its stage possibilities that he offered to adapt a fantastic pantomime to it. The pantomime was introduced in Paris on February 21, 1920, with the clown Fratellini in the principal role and Vladimir Golschmann conducting.

Though the setting for Milhaud's ballet is an American speakeasy, and the characters (all of whom are required to wear masks three times the normal size) are all drawn from American life, the music is derived not from jazz but from Brazilian folk music.

The Nothing-Doing Bar, noisy and crowded, is filled with a strange assortment of people: a huge Negro boxer who puffs at an enormous cigar; a Negro dwarf; a flashy bookie; a woman with paper hair; and another with a dashing red evening gown. During a crap game, the fashionable lady slings the dwarf over her shoulder and takes him to the nearby billiard room. The boxer makes a play for the other woman, but is knocked out by the bookie. After the bookie goes through a tango, the sound of a police whistle is heard. Since this is the era of prohibition, everyone in the bar is upset. But the bartender calmly removes the liquor from view and hangs a sign reading: "Only Milk Served Here." The policeman enters, sniffs around, tastes the milk, and proceeds to do a dance. As he is dancing, a huge re-volving fan falls on his head and decapitates him. If the patrons are upset by these events, they do not betray it. The dwarf sings a romance; the bartender presents the head of the policeman to the fashionable lady, who dances around it. The principal characters then make their exit, including the Negro boxer, who has since been restored to consciousness. When the dwarf refuses to pay his bill, the bartender replaces the head on the body of the policeman. Revived, the policeman is given the dwarf's bill—two feet long.

SAUDADES DO BRASIL, suite for orchestra (1921). I. Sorocabo.
II. Botofogo. III. Leme. IV. Copacabana. V. Ipanema. VI. Gavea. VII. Cor-covado. VIII. Tijuca. IX. Sumaré. X. Paineras. XI. Laranjeiras. XII. Paysandú.

A "saudade" can be translated as a "nostalgic recollection." In these twelve saudades the composer brings to mind memories of Brazil, where he lived for two years during World War I. The rhythms of Brazilian dances—principally that of the tango—are evoked. Actual Brazilian dances, however, are not reproduced, but merely suggested: Milhaud regarded these saudades as a kind of composite and idealized portrait of Brazilian dances. The twelve movements derive their names from different districts of Rio de Janeiro.

The *Saudades* were first introduced in Paris in 1921, Vladimir Golschmann conducting. At this performance, the dancer Lois Fuller interpreted the music.

LA CRÉATION DU MONDE, ballet (1922).

During his visit to the United States in 1922, Milhaud visited the Harlem section of New York City and spent many hours listening with fascination to the jazz music of Negro bands. When he was later asked to write the music for a Negro ballet, *La Création du Monde*—scenario by Blaise Cendrars—he decided to utilize the jazz idiom. He scored the music for eighteen solo instruments (including the saxophone). His style was that of jazz: the opening theme was a plangent blues melody set against an intriguing accompaniment that combined major and minor keys; there was a fugue based on a jazz motive; there was syncopation and ragtime. So admirably did Milhaud re-create the jazz style that Paul Rosenfeld called this work "the most perfect of all pieces of symphonic jazz," while Aaron Copland remarked that symphonic jazz had here succeeded in producing "at least one authentic small masterpiece." Equally important is it to remember that *La Création du Monde* was one of the first large works in this genre, antedating Gershwin's *Rhapsody in Blue* by a year.

The story of the ballet concerns the creation of the world—but as seen through the eyes of an aborigine. The action takes place in semidarkness. Some of the dancers, portraying herons, appear on stilts; others, representing animals, clamber about on all fours.

La Création du Monde was introduced by the Swedish Ballet at the Théâtre des Champs Élysées on October 25, 1923. An orchestral suite from the ballet score is better known than the ballet itself, having been performed frquently in this country and abroad. The suite comprises the following sections:

Overture.

I. The chaos before Creation. Giant deities of Creation hold council.

II. The confused mass begins to move. Suddenly a tree appears, and then various animals.

III. The animals join in a dance during which two bodies emerge limb by limb from the central mass.

IV. While the pair perform the dance of desire, the remaining mass dissolves into human beings, who join in a frenetic round to the point of vertigo.

V. The crowd disappears in little groups, leaving the Negro Adam and Eve embraced in a lasting kiss. It is springtime.

QUARTET NO. 6, for strings (1922). I. Souple et animé. II. Très lent. III. Très vif et rythmé.

Milhaud's Sixth Quartet, dedicated to Francis Poulenc, is one of his tersest and most compact works in this form. The first movement opens with a theme for viola (against a cello accompaniment) which progresses to the second theme, introduced by the cello. The development treats both themes succinctly. The recapitulation that follows is virtually a duplication of the opening exposition. The second movement grows out of a long-flowing melody, gentle in mood. A pastoral theme (violin and viola) opens the closing movement. This theme is followed by an extended quiet section. The music becomes more animated and complex in the development of these ideas. After a brief return to the opening theme, the quartet ends in a burst of sonority.

SUITE PROVENÇALE, for orchestra (1936). I. Animé. II. Très modéré; Vif. III. Modéré. IV. Vif. V. Modéré. VI. Vif. VII. Lent. VIII. Vif.

In this infectious and simply written suite of eight dances, Milhaud has gathered a few of the eighteenth-century folk tunes of his native Provence (mostly by Campra) and dressed them with a pleasing orchestral raiment, adding an occasional piquant color of polytonal writing. The suite was presented for the first time as background music for a ballet at the Opéra Comique in Paris. It was performed at a symphonic concert for the first time in Venice on September 12, 1937, with the composer conducting.

SYMPHONY NO. 1 (1939). I. Modérément. II. Très vif. III. Très modéré. IV. Animé.

Milhaud completed his First Symphony during the first weeks of World War II, while he was still in France. It was completed in Aix-en-Provence and introduced by the Chicago Symphony on October 17, 1940.

If the cataclysmic events of the times had any effect on the composer, they reveal no traces in this music, which is, for the most part, serene and poetic. The composer has described the first movement as "very melodic, and quiet, with a great feeling for nature." The first principal theme is stated by the flutes and first violins; the second, by the woodwinds. The second movement, comprising three subjects, is "rather dramatic and robust, with a fugue in the middle." Tranquillity returns in the third part, which "begins with a theme like a chorale, the character of the movement being deeply tender; the chorale theme alternates with a melody very expressive and clear." The symphony ends as it began, in a placid mood, though touched now with slightly more joyous feelings. It is built out of three principal themes (the first for woodwinds, harp, and plucked strings; the second for strings and woodwinds; the third for woodwinds, horns, and trumpets).

CONCERTO NO. 2 FOR PIANO AND ORCHESTRA (1941).
I. Animé. II. Romance. III. Bien modérément animé.

The Second Piano Concerto came five years after the first. It was heard for the first time in Chicago, on December 18, 1941, with Milhaud as soloist and Hans Lange conducting the Chicago Symphony.

The concerto opens with a nervous, rhythmic theme that is used extensively throughout the movement. An extended section for orchestra follows in which a new idea is unfolded against a background utilizing the rhythmic pattern of the first subject. Another rhythmic passage is introduced and given considerable importance before the original material is repeated.

Twelve measures of piano solo introduce the second movement, following which the orchestra enters with the same theme, but stated canonically. Variations of the theme are at the same time heard in the piano. The orchestra then enters with the second theme, after which the piano injects a new idea. The two main themes are used in conjunction just before the coda.

Three ideas are utilized in the closing movement: a dialogue between piano and orchestra; a second theme set against a rhumba rhythm; and a third subject which comes in the orchestra in canonic form. The three ideas are heard independently, then mingled one with another. The concerto ends brilliantly.

SUITE FRANÇAISE, for band or for orchestra (1944). I. Normandie. II. Bretagne. III. Isle de France. IV. Alsace-Lorraine. V. Provence.

The folk music of France provided Milhaud with the melodic materials for this suite—materials which he utilized with the utmost creative freedom. The composer has written in explanation: "The five parts of this suite are named after the French Provinces, the very ones in which the Americans and Allied armies fought together with the French underground for the liberation of my country." The composer adds further that his purpose in writing this work was to have young Americans "hear the popular melodies of those parts of France where their fathers and brothers fought to defend the country from the German invaders."

This suite was written both for band and for symphony orchestra. In the former version it was introduced by the Goldman Band under Edwin Franko Goldman in New York on June 13, 1945. As a work for orchestra, it was heard for the first time on July 29, 1945, at a concert at the Lewisohn Stadium in New York; Maurice Abravanel conducted the New York Philharmonic-Symphony Orchestra.

SYMPHONY NO. 2 (1944). I. Paisible. II. Mystérieux. III. Doul-oureux. IV. Avec sérénité. V. Alléluia.

Milhaud wrote his Second Symphony in this country on a commission from the Koussevitzky Foundation. He himself conducted the première per-formance in Boston with the Boston Symphony Orchestra on December 20, 1946.

Throughout the five movements, the composer maintains an atmos-phere of serenity which at times develops into mystery and melancholy. Only occasionally does an eruption of dynamic power take place, and only to give greater emphasis to the expressive sadness and tranquillity of the music that precedes and follows it. The symphony ends with a fugue built out of a hymn-like subject pronounced by full orchestra and growing into a tri-umphant and exalted expression.

CONCERTO NO. 2 FOR CELLO AND ORCHESTRA (1945). I. Gai. II. Tendre. III. Alerte.

The Second Cello Concerto followed its predecessor by eleven years. It was commissioned by the cello virtuoso Edmund Kurtz, who introduced it with the New York Philharmonic-Symphony Orchestra under Artur Rod-zinski on November 28, 1946.

In the first movement, a music-hall theme plays a prominent part. It is heard in the nine-bar introduction, and is repeated by the solo cello in its first entrance. Immediately after the first theme has been unfolded, a second theme enters, as gay as the first. In the development, the playful atmosphere created by the two delightful themes is maintained. The second movement is very lyrical and very expressive: the main melody is introduced by the cello. The second theme of the movement is first heard in the orchestra and then repeated by the cello. The two themes are integrated into one in the closing page of this movement. The sprightly closing movement opens with a six-bar statement by the solo cello, after which the vigorous first theme is heard. The music then develops into fleeting passages, with effective virtuoso writing for the solo instrument, before coming to a decisive climax.

SYMPHONY NO. 3 ("Hymnus Ambrosianus"), for chorus and orchestra (1946). I. Fièrement. II. Très recueilli. III. Pastorale. IV. Te Deum.

Soon after the liberation of France, the French government commis-sioned Milhaud to write a *Te Deum* to commemorate the event. The com-poser decided to extend the idea to symphonic proportions. He arrived at the following procedure: the first and third movements were for orchestra alone; the second, for orchestra and chorus, but without any text; the fourth, for chorus and orchestra, setting the complete text of the *Te Deum*.

The music, owing as it does its origin to the liberation of France from the Nazi invaders, is a work of great emotional force. The varied feel-ings of the composer, inspired by this momentous event, are reflected throughout the work. The first movement is stately, as if to suggest the indomitable spirit of France, unbowed after several years of oppression and degradation. A more introspective mood is caught in the second movement, music of quiet reflection. The third movement was intended by the composer as a "return to the earth, to grass roots." Exultantly, the symphony erupts in music of religious ardor and consecration in the closing movement.

The symphony was heard for the first time during a Milhaud festival in Paris on October 30, 1947.

SYMPHONY NO. 4 (1947). I. Insurrection. II. To the Dead of the Republic. III. The Peaceful Joys of Liberty Regained. IV. Commemoration, 1948.

Milhaud wrote his Fourth Symphony on a commission from the French government as part of the centenary celebration of the 1848 revolution against Louis Philippe, "the citizen king," which set up the Second Republic. The symphony was written during a forty-day ocean trip from San Francisco to Le Havre aboard a freighter during the summer of 1947. On May 20, 1948, the composer conducted the première performance over the French Radio.

Henri Mahlerbe, the eminent French critic, provided the following definitive analysis of the symphony for the French première performance:

"In the first movement (Animé), composed of fragments of song of popular aspect, interlaced, entangled, embroiled and penetrated with seditious cries, the composer portrays for us the joyful exaltation of the armed mob, at first scattered, then gradually united to struggle and triumph in an explosion of joy. The second movement (Lent) is simply a long lamentation, of a sad and intimate intensity, constantly sustained. Its pathetic effect is the more profound in that the composer marshals his potent forces with moderation and tellingly employs but a very few instruments. The third movement (Modérément animé) shows us, between bucolic episodes, the noble and tender emotion that prevailed in every heart at the triumph of liberty. Finally, in the last movement (Animé), the popular and heroic themes of the beginning are resolutely recapitulated and, with impressive mastery, varied, transformed, enriched, expanded, and, as it were, projected towards the future."

QUARTET NO. 14, for strings (1948). I. Animé. II. Modéré. III. Vif.
QUARTET NO. 15, for strings (1949). I. Animé. II. Modéré. III. Vif.

Milhaud devised the original scheme of writing two quartets, each of which has an independent identity and is self-sufficient as an artistic product, which can also be played simultaneously as an octet for strings. The two quartets were played separately and together at the same concert by the Paganini Quartet at Mills College in Oakland, California, on August 10, 1949.

The two quartets were planned to contrast each other. The opening movement of the Fourteenth is lively and highly accented, while that of the

Fifteenth has sustained lyricism; the middle movement of the Fourteenth seems like an accompaniment to that of the Fifteenth, which is a delicate melody of sensitive beauty; against the bright syncopation of the closing movement of the Fifteenth is the robust and animated vigor of the Fourteenth.

ITALO MONTEMEZZI 1875—1952

In the half-dozen or so operas that Montemezzi contributed to the modern Italian lyric theater, he demonstrated that he completely absorbed, and was satisfied with, the accepted traditions of Italian opera. Like the great Italians who preceded him, his principal concern was for lyricism, an abundant stream of which courses through his best operas. His secondary interests were emotion, dramatic action, atmosphere. He was, on the other hand, unsympathetic to realism, or to the opening up of new vistas for the operatic form.

A certain enrichment to Italian operatic writing comes in Montemezzi's works through his interpolation of Debussy's sensitive atmospheric etchings, and through the Wagnerian enlargement of symphonic scope found in his orchestrations. But, for the most part, Montemezzi was quite content to walk in the footsteps of the mighty Verdi; and it is greatly to his credit that he was able to do this gracefully.

Montemezzi was born in Vigasio, Verona, on August 4, 1875. He was originally intended for an engineering career. But in Milan, where he went to complete his technical studies, he entered the Conservatory and developed rapidly under Saladino and Ferroni. In 1905, the first of his operas to be performed was seen in Turin—*Giovanni Gallurese.* Some critics hailed Montemezzi then and there as an important composer. His second opera, *Hellera,* passed unnoticed. But with his third opera, *L'Amore dei Tre Re,* he achieved international fame.

In 1939 Montemezzi settled in California. He returned to his native land shortly before his death, which took place in Verona on May 15, 1952.

L'AMORE DEI TRE RE, opera (1913).

L'Amore dei Tre Re is the acknowledged masterpiece among Montemezzi's operas. It has deservedly been called the finest product of the Italian

lyric theatre of our time. Some critics go even further and call it the finest
Italian opera since Verdi.

The text by Sem Benelli—excellent theatre throughout, and sometimes
filled with poetry of flaming beauty—is a powerful stimulant for a composer.
Montemezzi confessed that he was "gripped by the beauty of this Benellian
tragedy," and that he knew at once that he had "embarked on a work of
great importance." He added further: "The tragedy responded absolutely to
my conception which was to construct an art work, different from anything
done before—a real Italian music drama, with dynamism, drama, poetry—all
of it bathed in an atmosphere of musical rapture."

When Montemezzi first contacted Sem Benelli it was to acquire the
operatic rights for *The Jest*. But Benelli had just sold those rights for a paltry
hundred dollars; in place of *The Jest,* the dramatist offered to write a new
tragedy expressly for the composer. He outlined his idea to Montemezzi, who
was so taken with it that then and there he took Benelli to his publisher,
Ricordi, who signed both dramatist and composer to a contract.

It took Montemezzi more than two years to write his score. On April
10, 1913, the opera was heard for the first time, at La Scala in Milan, Tullio
Serafin conducting. It was outstandingly successful. Nine months after that,
it was performed at the Metropolitan Opera House under Arturo Toscanini.
After that, it entered the repertory of virtually every major opera house.

Montemezzi brought to his score not only his fully developed and
original lyricism (at times, as in the last act, achieving incandescent beauty),
but also a sense for dramatic effect (which in the climactic scenes of both the
second and third acts has shattering force) and a keen sense for characterization. The portrait of the blind King Archibaldo is touched with pity and
grandeur, compassion and terror—surely one of the great characterizations in
all operatic literature.

Archibaldo's son, Manfredo, is married to the princess Fiora, who, in
turn, is in love with Avito. When Fiora confesses that she loves someone
else and not Manfredo, Archibaldo strangles her. Then, in an attempt to pun-
ish her guilty lover, he puts poison on her dead lips. Avito comes upon the
dead Fiora, kisses her lips passionately, and dies. But Manfredo also sees the
dead body of his wife. He, too, kisses her—and dies. Archibaldo momentarily
succumbs to a feeling of triumph when, coming on the scene, he feels he has
trapped the dead man. But when he recognizes his son Manfredo and sees
him dead, his grief becomes overpowering.

DOUGLAS MOORE   1893—

It is not easy to classify Douglas Moore. He has often used modern techniques; but he cannot be considered an ultramodern composer. He has frequently turned to the American scene and backgrounds for his material; yet he is not essentially a nationalist composer. On occasion he is not reluctant to give his emotions freedom of expression; yet it would be difficult to consider him a romanticist.

The truth is that Moore has approached each of his subjects with a freshness of viewpoint, bringing to it that style which is best suited for his artistic purpose. Generally speaking, his works are characterized by a freshness in melody and by striking dramatic contrasts. He writes particularly well for the voice, for which he has shown partiality. This lyrical gift has made him particularly successful in the writing of song and opera.

Moore was born in Cutchogue, Long Island, on August 10, 1893. His education took place at the Hotchkiss School and at Yale University. After World War I, he continued his music study in Paris with Vincent d'Indy and Nadia Boulanger, and with Ernest Bloch in Cleveland. In 1928, he joined the music faculty of Columbia University, becoming head of the department in 1940. In 1946 he was made president of the National Institute of Arts and Letters and in 1952 director of the American Academy of Arts and Letters. He received the Pulitzer Prize in music in 1951.

The following works by Douglas Moore are discussed below: *The Devil and Daniel Webster; The Pageant of P. T. Barnum;* Quartet; Symphony No. 2 in A Major.

THE PAGEANT OF P. T. BARNUM, suite for orchestra (1924). I. Boyhood at Bethel. II. Joice Heth. III. General and Mrs. Tom Thumb. IV. Jenny Lind. V. Circus Parade.

With this delightful orchestral suite, which the Cleveland Orchestra introduced in the year of its composition, Moore achieved his first substantial success as a composer. It is witty music, spontaneous, fresh, and rich with American flavor. In relating episodes in the fabulous career of a great showman, Moore first describes Barnum's boyhood, introducing the village music of country fiddles and bands, which Barnum no doubt heard in Bethel. Joice Heth was the 160-year-old Negress who was the first of Barnum's attractions; legend had it that she was the first person to put clothes on George Washington. In this section, there is a skillful interpolation of a Negro spiritual—a version of *Nobody Knows de Trouble I've Seen*. The General and Mrs. Tom Thumb, midgets, were another of Barnum's attractions; the music has a mock military air about it. Jenny Lind was, of course, one of the greatest triumphs of Barnum's career; a melody for the flute suggests the incomparable coloratura voice of the Swedish nightingale, as she must have sung at her first American appearance in Castle Garden. In the concluding section, the circus of Barnum is described—with spirited, even raucous circus-parade music suggesting animals, clowns, acrobats, and calliope.

QUARTET, for strings (1933). I. Allegro comodo. II. Allegro giusto. III. Andante cantabile. IV. Allegro.

This chamber-music work—successfully introduced by the Roth Quartet in 1936—is one of Moore's finest compositions. Graceful in its construction, melodically fresh, endowed with a spontaneous feeling, this quartet is a distinguished contribution to contemporary American chamber music.

Otto Luening succinctly described this quartet in *Modern Music:* "The first movement is polymodal, remarkably lucid, with a great feeling for transparent part-writing. Carefully spaced dissonances augment the natural resonance of the quartet in a unique manner. The lyric mood is personal and poetic. In the second movement a march-like, American, folkish tune is clearly developed. Both movements reveal a growing mastery of form. The third is less definite in outline, but the melodic lines are in themselves expressive. The finale is dance-like in character, carefully developed and in sharp rhythmic contrast to the others."

THE DEVIL AND DANIEL WEBSTER, folk opera (1938).

Moore's folk opera is based on a story by Stephen Vincent Benét (which, incidentally, was also used for a motion picture). It was introduced in New York on May 18, 1939, by the American Lyric Theatre.

The protagonist of Benét's story is a New Hampshire farmer, who, Faust-like, sells his soul to the devil—but for the coin of material prosperity which will enable him to get married. The wedding festivities are interrupted by the devil, who arrives (in the person of a Boston attorney) to claim the soul. Daniel Webster pleads the case for the farmer—before a jury composed of resurrected traitors and blackguards of the distant past; and he pleads it so eloquently that the farmer is released from his bargain.

Moore's approach to the opera form is a traditional one, and *The Devil and Daniel Webster* is pleasingly set in arias, ensemble numbers, etc. In his melodies, Moore frequently resorts to popular and folk idioms, with fine effect. The harmonic writing and orchestration are simply realized. The major appeal of the opera lies in its ingratiating lyricism, excellent writing for the voice, and dramatic strength.

SYMPHONY NO. 2 IN A MAJOR (1945). I. Andante con moto; Allegro giusto. II. Andante quieto a semplice. III. Allegretto. IV. Allegro con spirito.

The composer has provided the following analysis:

"First Movement: There is a lyric introduction in which features of the principal Allegro are gradually evolved. The Allegro giusto begins with the principal theme in the first violins. This theme consists of several ideas which are developed and varied in the music that follows. There is a transition in C-sharp Minor, where a woodwind dialogue leads to a subsidiary theme in E Major. These themes serve as the principal material of the movement, which follows the classical pattern of design. There is a short coda at an accelerated close.

"Second Movement: The mood ... was suggested by a short poem of James Joyce which deals with music heard at the coming of twilight. This is a lyric movement in one long section. The principal elements are the introduction, a broad melody against a guitar-like accompaniment, and a third motive, which appears briefly at the end of each phrase of the principal melody and is heard in its entirety just before the conclusion.

"Third Movement: This is a polyphonic piece, somewhat resembling a minuet but more rapid, and if there is any elegance about it, it is of the rural rather than the court variety.

"Fourth Movement: The finale is an attempt to write an entertainment piece of the classic type rather than an apotheosis of the entire symphony. There is a four-bar introduction preceding the principal theme, which is heard in the first violins. This theme has a shifting rhythm of two and three which dominates the movement. There is a lyric theme for contrast, which, as it unfolds, contains a new rhythm that plays an important part in the development and coda."

The symphony is dedicated to the celebrated American poet, Stephen Vincent Benét, friend and, at times, collaborator of the composer. It was introduced in Paris—by the Paris Broadcasting Orchestra under Robert Lawrence—on May 5, 1946. After its American première in Los Angeles on January 16, 1947, it received honorable mention from the Music Critics Circle of New York.

GABRIEL PIERNÉ   1863—1937

One can say of Gabriel Pierné what has been said of other conservative French composers of our time. He had technical adroitness; his style was always elegant; sensitivity and refinement characterized his speech; poetic beauty filled its content. What he lacked in originality he compensated for in charm; while discovering no new worlds in music he revealed the old ones with freshness of viewpoint.

Pierné was born in Metz on August 16, 1863. At the Paris Convervatory he was a classmate of Debussy; his teachers included Marmontel, César Franck, and Massenet. Pierné won the highest honors, including the Prix de Rome, which was awarded for the cantata *Edith,* in 1882. In 1890, he succeeded César Franck as organist of Sainte-Clotilde. After eight years in this post, he became the conductor of the Colonne Orchestra, in which he won international distinction over a period of almost a quarter of a century. He was a prolific composer in virtually every musical form. He died in Ploujean, France, on July 17, 1937.

The following works by Pierné are discussed below: *The Children's Crusade; Cydalise and the Satyr.*

THE CHILDREN'S CRUSADE, cantata for chorus and orchestra (1902).

With his Flemish legend, *The Children's Crusade*—text by Marcel Schwob—Pierné achieved international recognition as a composer; and to this day it remains one of his most distinguished works. In 1905 it won the City of Paris prize of ten thousand francs, and on January 18 of the same year it was introduced with outstanding success by the Colonne Orchestra, directed by Edouard Colonne. Soon after its première, it was heard throughout the world of music.

Pierné has told the legend of the thirteenth-century crusade of children to the Holy Land with poetic sensitivity. In the published score the following introductory explanation is found: "About that time, many children, without leader and without guidance, did fly in a religious ecstasy from our towns and from our cities, making for the lands beyond the seas. And to those who asked of them whither they were bound, they did make the answer: 'To Jerusalem, in search of the Holy Land.' ... They carried staves and satchels, and crosses were embroided on their garments.... They traveled to Genoa, and did embark upon the seven great vessels to cross the sea. And a storm arose and two vessels perished in the waters....And to those who asked of such of the children who were saved, the reason for their journey, these replied: 'We do not know.' "

The cantata is divided into four sections, or scenes: I. The Departure of the Children. II. Their Journey to Genoa. III. The Scene by the Sea. IV. The Savior in the Storm.

In the first scene, the heavenly hosts summon the children to their crusade, a summons they answer enthusiastically in spite of the pleading of their parents to ignore it. In the second scene, the children are on their way, marching through meadows and countrysides during the warm mornings of spring. The delight of the children at seeing the sea is described in the third scene, while in the fourth, the storm, shipwreck, the children's prayer for help, and the celestial vision of the Savior are reproduced.

CYDALISE AND THE SATYR, ballet (1913).

Pierné's most famous ballet, *Cydalise and the Satyr,* was written in 1913. Though accepted immediately by the Paris Opéra, its première was delayed for several years by the outbreak of war. It was finally performed at the Opéra on January 15, 1923, achieving a great success. Emile Vuillermoz wrote as follows: "Gabriel Pierné has written...a score of extraordinary youthfulness and allurement; he has brought into play all the subtleties of modern instrumentation, as also a great knowledge and routine without the aggressive audacities of our modern experimenters....This score abounds in coquetries of excellent quality, and is of vivacity and freshness which will enchant the public."

The text, based on Rémy de Goncourt's *Lettres d'un Satyr,* combines classic mythology with eighteenth-century French court life. An old satyr conducts a class in dancing and in the playing of Pandean pipes. Styrax, one of the pupils, is mischievous, and is expelled. He wanders into the woods, where he is met by a coach bearing a group of dancers, one of whom is Cydalise. Falling in love with Cydalise, Styrax hides in the coach and is brought into a French royal court. There he reveals himself to his beloved, makes love to her, and is about to win her over when, from the distance, come the voices of satyrs calling him back to the forests. Torn between his love for Cydalise and his desire to rejoin his companions, Styrax finally succumbs to the latter.

From the ballet score, Pierné prepared two orchestral suites. The first includes the following sections: I. The School of the Fauns (or, The Entrance of the Little Fauns). II. The Lesson on the Pandean Pipes. III. March of the Nymphs. IV. The Dancing Lesson. The second suite has seven sections: I. Ballet of the Sultan of the Indies. II. Entrance. III. Pantomime. IV. Dance of the Apothecaries. V. Dance of the Slaves. VI. Variation of Cydalise. VII. Finale.

The opening movement of the first suite—The Entrance of the Little Fauns, or, as it is sometimes called, The School of the Fauns—is outstandingly popular. It is a sprightly little piece, in which a piquant tune (muted trumpets) is heard against the background of piccolos. An infectious rhythm is provided by snare drum, tambourine, and violinists tapping lightly on the strings with the wood of their bows.

WILLEM PIJPER   1894—1947

Teacher, critic, editor, composer—Willem Pijper was one of the dominating figures (if not *the* dominating figure) in the contemporary music of Holland. As a composer he was in the vanguard of the Dutch ultramodern school, writing in a forceful and concentrated style that incorporated many of the techniques of twentieth-century music, notably polytonality and atonality. But these techniques, for Pijper, were always a means to an artistic end, never an end in themselves. He was in his best vein when he generated power; but on occasion he could also produce music expressive of strongly felt emotion.

Pijper was born at Zeist, Utrecht, on September 8, 1894. Music study took place with Johan Wagenaar and Mme. von Lunteren. Some chamber-music works, a rhapsody for piano and orchestra, and a First Symphony spoke for his creative talent. These works were romantic, after the manner of Mahler and the early Richard Strauss. But a reaction of style set in after 1920, and more and more Pijper began experimenting with new devices until he evolved an idiom of his own, fully realized in such works as the Third Symphony (1926), the opera *Halewijn* (1920), and the last two string quartets.

Besides composing, Pijper was active as critic and teacher. Early in his career, he was a music critic of the *Utrechts Dagblad,* and subsequently became coeditor (with Paul F. Sanders) of the influential journal, *De Muziek*. From 1918 to 1921, he was a music teacher at the Amsterdam Music School, then professor of composition at the Amsterdam Conservatory, and after that director of the Rotterdam Conservatory. Always frail of health, Pijper died prematurely at the age of fifty-two at Leidschendam, near The Hague, on March 19, 1947.

SYMPHONY NO. 3 (1926).

Pijper's last symphony is the one work by which he is best known in this country; it has enjoyed numerous performances by many of our major symphonic organizations. It is also one of Pijper's most important compositions. On October 28, 1926, it was introduced by the Concertgebouw Orchestra of Amsterdam under Pierre Monteux. A quotation from the *Aeneid*, which appears on the flyleaf of the published score, gives a clue to the composer's emotional intentions: "If I cannot influence the Gods, I will move the powers of Hell."

Though in three distinct sections, the symphony is played without interruption. The main theme comes at the very outset and consists of phrases that ascend and descend in intervals of the fourth. (This theme is repeated at the close of the symphony, too.) A countersubject is a piquant melody for violins and flutes. A fermata leads into the slow movement, music of great emotional depth, reflecting the composer's state of mind during this period of personal tragedy. The quiet and expressive sorrow is punctuated with orchestral outbursts, but at the conclusion of this section tranquillity returns. A solo violin introduces the return of the opening theme, now heard in the basses, after which the final movement brings music of herculean strength and defiance. The symphony ends in a sudden and frenetic climax, fortissimo.

WALTER PISTON   1894—

Some critics (mindful perhaps of his long career as professor of music, or aware that he has shown a marked partiality for such traditional forms as the symphony, the concerto, the suite, etc.) have described Piston as an academic or a classical composer. He is neither. There is so suggestion of the schoolroom or the textbook in his music. And though he likes classical forms, he is very often vibrantly contemporary in his idiom. But when he writes atonally, or when he uses dissonant counterpoint, he absorbs such modern techniques completely into writing which, for the most part, is derived from older styles.

It is not easy to classify a composer who at times is complex and at other times simple, at times coldly logical and at other times emotional. Piston writes as he pleases, adapting his style to the esthetic requirements of the music he is writing. He is usually strongly melodic, with a fine sense of design and construction. He writes with economy, directness, force, and charm. And what he writes is invariably well worth hearing.

Piston was born in Rockland, Maine, on January 20, 1894, was graduated from the Massachusetts Normal Art School in 1916, and studied music with Harris Shaw, Fiumara, Theodorowicz, and Winternitz. After World War I, in which he served in the Navy, he entered Harvard University, specializing in music and graduating *summa cum laude* in 1924. For two years he was a pupil of Nadia Boulanger in Paris. Then, returning to this country, he joined the faculty of Harvard University, where he has remained ever since as professor of music. In 1928, he first attracted attention to his music when the Boston Symphony Orchestra under Koussevitzky performed his *Symphonic Piece*. Subsequent performances of his major orchestral works, principally by the Boston Symphony, added to his reputation. In 1935, he was the recipient of a Guggenheim Fellowship, and in 1940 he was appointed a member of the American Academy of Arts and Sciences.

The following works by Piston are discussed below: *The Incredible Flutist;* Quartet No. 3; Symphony No. 2; Symphony No. 3.

THE INCREDIBLE FLUTIST, ballet (1938).

Piston has always preferred writing abstract music, feeling freest when he can allow his musical ideas to grow, develop, and change because of the musical logic involved rather than because of the demands of some text or program. Thus he has avoided programmatic music, with one notable exception—the ballet *The Incredible Flutist*. He has brought to the score of his ballet so rich a fund of wit, so much vivid imagery, and such an uncanny ability to translate subtle innuendos of the text to their musical equivalents that it becomes obvious that he has avoided program music not because he is less gifted in that vein, but out of preference.

The Incredible Flutist was written in collaboration with the dancer Hans Wiener, who—with his dancers—introduced it at one of the concerts of the Boston Pops Orchestra on May 30, 1938. The action takes place in a village market place, which early in the morning awakens and becomes alive with activity. A circus enters: at its head, a juggler, a clown, and a flutist. The miraculous piping of the flutist is able to charm snakes—and women. It charms one of the merchants' daughters. Suddenly the clock strikes eight. Romance is in the air, and it infects all those in the market place. Couples are seen whispering tender sentiments. A rich widow kisses a merchant and, discovered by her lover, passes away into a swoon. The flutist strikes up one of his pretty tunes, and the widow recovers. A march is suddenly struck up. The circus leaves town.

An orchestral suite from the ballet score, introduced on November 22, 1940, by the Pittsburgh Symphony under Fritz Reiner, has become one of Piston's most successful and best-known symphonic works. It includes the following sections: I. Introduction. II. Siesta Hour in the Marketplace and Entrance of the Vendors. III. Dance of the Vendors. IV. Entrance of the Customers. V. Tango of Four Daughters. VI. Arrival of Circus and Circus March. VII. Solo of the Flutist. VIII. Minuet—Dance of the Widow and Merchant. IX. Spanish Waltz. X. Eight O'Clock Strikes. XI. Siciliano—Dance of the Flutist and Merchant's Daughter. XII. Polka. XIII. Finale.

SYMPHONY NO. 2 (1943). I. Moderato. II. Adagio. III. Allegro.

The Alice M. Ditson Fund of Columbia University commissioned Piston to write a symphony. On March 5, 1944, Hans Kindler conducted its première with the National Symphony of Washington, D. C. Following its performance in New York City by the New York Philharmonic-Symphony Orchestra, the work received the Music Critics Circle Award.

A broad legato subject in the violas and cellos opens the symphony; this is the major theme of the first movement. It is subjected to elaborate development, and at the end of the movement appears in canonic form (pianissimo). A second idea—rhythmic rather than melodic—is heard in the oboe, clarinet, and bassoons. In the Adagio, a delicate melody appears in the bassoon and sinuously winds its ways throughout the movement, which is continuous and fluid rather than sectional. Three themes are heard in the concluding section of the symphony: one is robust and rhythmic (cellos and horns); a second is a march (clarinets and bassoons), and a third is melodic (English horn and clarinet).

QUARTET NO. 3, for strings (1947). I. Allegro. II. Lento. III. Allegro.

Piston's Third String Quartet was written on a commission from Harvard University for its Symposium of Music Criticism. The work was introduced by the Walden Quartet in Cambridge, Massachusetts, on May 1, 1947. The first movement is vigorously rhythmic with occasional passages of lyric interest; the second theme calls for a rubato style. The slow movement is based on a single melodic phrase played by the viola. This melody undergoes several variations, is developed to a dramatic climax, and then is allowed to end quietly. A rondo, based on three themes, constitutes the closing movement. Light and spirited throughout, this is ingratiating music from beginning to end; the first of the three themes undergoes considerable fugal treatment.

SYMPHONY NO. 3 (1947). I. Andantino. II. Allegro. III. Adagio. IV. Allegro.

The Third Symphony, which followed the Second by four years, was commissioned by the Koussevitzky Foundation. It is one of Piston's most important and successful works to date. Music of exceptional communicative power, it has a wider emotional range than most of Piston's work, passing from an almost delicate wit to a pastorale-like serenity, from introspective calm to dramatic intensity.

The first movement is based on three thematic ideas (the first in the oboe; the second in the horn, clarinet, and English horn; the third, in the brass) which are developed singly and in combination. The second movement is a three-part scherzo, with the principal theme played by the violas and bassoons. The Adagio comprises four large and closely connected sections of musical development: in the first the theme is stated; in the second it is presented in varied form; in the third it rises to a climax; and in the fourth it returns in its original form. A three-part finale consists of two major themes, one treated fugally, the other march-like in character.

Serge Koussevitzky conducted the first performance of the Third Symphony with the Boston Symphony Orchestra on January 9, 1948. It was outstandingly successful from the first. Late the same year, the symphony received the Hornblit Award and the Pulitzer Prize.

ILDEBRANDO PIZZETTI   1880—

That Pizzetti's music is not more frequently heard in this country is an irreparable deprivation. Few composers in our time have achieved such a sensitive fusion between the intellect and emotion, between the old and the new, as Pizzetti. Always music of high-minded principles, his works have a character all their own in the dramatic expressiveness of his melodic line; in his unique harmonic atmosphere, achieved at times through the use of Gregorian modes; in the force and originality of his musical thinking. In whatever medium he chooses to write, he reveals the hand of a master and the aristocratic intellect of a scholar. His position as one of Italy's foremost living composers is unassailable.

Three influences have fed his inspiration. The first has been the Greek drama, which was responsible for several works, the most important of which was the opera *Fedra* (1909-12), after Gabriele d'Annunzio. Then Pizzetti turned to the Bible for the themes of such major works as the opera *Debora e Jaele* (1915-21) and the incidental music to *La Sacra Rappresentazione di Abram e d'Isaac* (1917). Finally, he found stimulation in old Italian history, as a result of which he wrote the operas *Fra Gherardo* (1926), *Orseolo* (1931-35) and *Vanna Lupa* (1947), and the incidental music to *La Rappresentazione di Santa Uliva* (1933).

Pizzetti was born in Parma on September 20, 1880. He received his musical education at the Parma Conservatory, and proved his talent by writing two operas. After his graduation in 1901, he held various minor posts as conductor and teacher. In 1909, he became professor of theory and composition at the Music Institute in Florence, becoming its director nine years later. From 1924 to 1936 he was director of the Verdi Conservatory in Milan, then went to Rome to succeed Respighi as professor of composition at the St. Cecilia Academy. His first major success as composer came in 1915 with the opera *Fedra,* performed at La Scala on March 20. In 1930, Pizzetti visited the United States.

The following works by Pizzetti are discussed below: *Concerto del-l'Estate; Fra Gherardo; Rondo Veneziano;* Sonata in A Major for Violin and Piano.

SONATA IN A MAJOR FOR VIOLIN AND PIANO (1919).

I. Tempestoso. II. Preghiera per gli innocenti. III. Vivo e fresco.

The reaction of the composer to World War I is revealed in the poignantly tragic music found in this sonata. One of the composer's most personal utterances, the sonata is among his more emotional creations, and among his unquestioned masterpieces. Grief unrelieved—grief in all its unrestrained intensity and piercing sting—is heard in the tempestuous first movement. The first theme, heard in the piano, is intense and passionate; the second theme, following immediately in the violin, is elegiac. The second movement is a "prayer for the innocents." Appended to the opening measures is the following line: "O Our Lord, have pity upon all the innocents who do not know why they must suffer." Against modern chords, and with altered rhythms, comes a melody of sustained beauty—"a gospel of charity," Castelnuovo-Tedesco called it. An element of joy comes at last in the concluding movement, a rondo, almost as if, after the grief and suffering, a reaffirmation of life comes. The principal theme resembles a folksong.

FRA GHERARDO, opera (1926).

In his operas, Pizzetti sought to realize a more intimate association between the musical theater and life itself. He put it this way: "Dramatic music should express life in action—conflicts of matter and mind, of instincts and aspirations, of egotism and moral duty; and lyrical music should express the transcendence, the overcoming of these conflicts." In Pizzetti's operas, as in life itself, action is combined with repose, dramatic conflict with introspection.

Pizzetti diverged sharply from those traditions of Italian opera that had hardened in stereotyped patterns. The singer in his operas is only one of many elements and never given exaggerated importance. Nor is the music ever allowed to become dominant: it must be inextricably wedded to the text so that to separate one from the other is to lose something vital. There are no formal arias in Pizzetti's operas. His melodic line usually consists of strong and expressive declamations (molded to the inflections of the Italian language); and when he allows greater freedom and flight to his lyricism, it must always grow naturally out of the texture of the play. The choruses, too, are never allowed to assume excessive importance, but are integrated into the texture of the whole design, and must always serve a dramatic purpose. The fluidity and continuity of the opera as a whole is more important to Pizzetti than the effect of any one scene; his operas, consequently, may occasionally appear static, but they have a unity of conception and purpose which is one of their strongest attributes.

The best-known of Pizzetti's operas in this country is *Fra Gherardo,* heard at the Metropolitan Opera House in 1929. Its première took place at La Scala, in Milan, on May 16, 1928.

The text, by the composer himself, is based on the thirteenth-century Chronicles of Salimbene de Parma. Gherardo is a weaver who rescues the lovely Mariola from attack, falls in love with her, and takes her to live with him. He repents this indiscretion and is driven to join the Flagellant Order. Nine years later, he is known as Fra Gherardo of the White Friars, a saintly man worshipped by the masses. He becomes the spearhead of the attack of the citizens of Parma against their nobility. Meanwhile, Mariola comes to him to confide that, some years back, she has given birth to their child, who has died. Fra Gherardo would like to make amends by devoting himself to Mariola. But she remind him that his first duty is to the people of Parma in their uprising. The uprising is aborted when Fra Gherardo is arrested for heresy. For her part in the insurrection, Mariola is condemned to burn at the stake. Only one thing can save Mariola: Gherardo's expression of allegiance to the state. This he cannot give. Mariola rushes to him to be with him when they die. Gherardo is burned, and Mariola becomes the victim of an insane woman.

CONCERTO DELL'ESTATE, for orchestra (1928). I. Mattutino. II. Notturno. III. Gagliarda e finale.

Though Pizzetti confesses modeling this work after the concerto grosso of Vivaldi, there is little in the writing (which is modern in spirit and impressionistic in character) or even in the architectonic construction to remind us of the eighteenth-century classical form, beyond the rather superficial fact that two vigorous movements are separated by a lyrical one. The first part of this concerto is built around five themes, three appearing at once and almost simultaneously; the fourth is an oboe solo; the fifth, a largamente for full orchestra. Unaccompanied violins voice the lyric and poetic melody which comprises the entire middle section. For his closing part, Pizzetti re-creates an ancient dance, with brusque and dynamic rhythms.

On February 28, 1929, Arturo Toscanini gave the première performance of the Concerto in New York City with the New York Philharmonic-Symphony Orchestra.

RONDO VENEZIANO, for orchestra (1929).

In the published score of this work, the composer himself provides an admirable analysis: "This composition consists of three 'strophes,' preceded and followed by a less extensive musical period in the guise of a 'ritornello' (refrain); whence the title *Rondo*. But just as there are, in Italian poetry, songs and odes in rondo form whose strophes differ in content as well as in expression, so the three 'strophes' of this rondo differ not only in thematic material, but in movement and character.

"If the musical period that serves as a ritornello (opening and closing the composition) be regarded as an expression of the fundamental and immutable traits of the Adriatic city, the first strophe might be considered an expression of aristocratic Venice, luxurious and pompous (but without particular reference to any specific period of the past) and the third strophe as an expression of plebeian Venice. The middle strophe is a sort of intermezzo, both idyllic and impassioned."

Rondo Veneziano was given its world première in New York City on February 27, 1930, with Arturo Toscanini conducting the New York Philharmonic-Symphony Orchestra.

QUINCY PORTER   1897—

Quincy Porter has thus far produced his best music within the frame of the string quartet. His is the kind of music that suggests intimate confidences, the kind of music that demands small forces: now delicately playful, now amiable and charming, now tender and gentle, now moody and thoughtful. Though his music is always masterfully realized, with the fullest technical resources, there is an almost effortless quality about it—in the presentation of the melodic ideas, in their development, and in the transparent texture of his harmonic and contrapuntal writing—which gives it an engaging feeling of spontaneity. Herbert Elwell put it well when he said that Porter had acquired the skill of the professional without losing the enthusiasm of the amateur. In what Elwell has described as its "fine blend of simplicity and sophistication" lies perhaps the greatest appeal of Porter's music.

Quincy Porter was born in New Haven, Connecticut, on February 7, 1897. After extensive preliminary study of music, he entered the Yale School of Music, where his teachers included Horatio Parker and David Stanley Smith. There he won the Osborne and the Steinert prizes in composition. Following his graduation from the School of Music, he went to Europe for additional study with Capet and Vincent d'Indy; then he returned to this country to study with Ernest Bloch.

In 1923, Porter was appointed to the faculty of the Cleveland Institute of Music, where he soon became head of the theory department. This was the beginning of a long and fruitful career as teacher. For six years he was professor of music at Vassar College; for several years he was associated with the New England Conservatory of Music, first as dean of the faculty, then as director; in 1946, he joined Yale University as professor of music.

In 1928, Porter received a Guggenheim Fellowship, in 1943 the Coolidge medal in chamber music, and in 1954 the Pulitzer Prize for the Concerto for Two Pianos (see Supplement).

The following works by Porter are discussed below: Concerto for Viola and Orchestra; Quartet No. 4; Quartet No. 7.

QUARTET NO. 4, for strings (1931). I. Allegro moderato. II. Lento. III. Allegro molto.

This quartet was introduced by the Cleveland Institute Quartet in Cleveland on November 15, 1931. It is predominantly lyrical, with long spans of melody in the first movement, decorated by small rhythmic cells which jump from one instrument to another. The slow movement is built on one single theme. The form is contributed more by the motion of the rhythm, which increases to a climactic point before returning to the theme in its original form. The last movement has irregular rhythms, with a long theme for the cello.

QUARTET NO. 7, for strings (1943). I. Allegro moderato. II. Adagio molto. III. Allegro moderato; Allegro molto.

Porter's Seventh Quartet was commissioned by and dedicated to Elizabeth Sprague Coolidge. It was first performed at the Founder's Day Concert at the Library of Congress by the Coolidge Quartet on October 30, 1943.

The chief interest of the first movement is in the variety of rhythmic feeling that is worked into a consistent meter of 3/8 time, which does not change till the coda, which is in 2/8 time. A number of themes are woven together, but not treated in strict sonata form. The slow movement is somber and built on long dynamic lines, with frequent use of crossing instrument timbres. At the climax, the chief theme of the first movement is heard. The last movement begins with an energetic introduction, but soon settles into a fast triplet movement. It includes some references to themes from the first movement.

CONCERTO FOR VIOLA AND ORCHESTRA (1948).

Though Porter is at his best in smaller forms for more intimate combinations, he has produced effective music in the symphonic and concerto forms. The viola concerto is possibly his best work in the larger forms. On May 16, 1948, it was introduced in New York by Paul Doktor and the CBS Symphony Orchestra, Dean Dixon conducting, during the American Music Festival held at Columbia University.

The three movements are played without pause. The first movement (Adagio) contains much of the melodic material used later on, especially the main theme announced by the horn at the beginning. The viola plays in quasi obbligato, but introduces a number of melodic elements which are also made much of throughout the concerto. The second movement (Allegro) in in fast 6/8 rhythm, but with considerable lyric melody for the viola, interspersed with virtuoso passages. The slow movement (Largo) is meditative, and contains an important cadenza for the solo instrument. The last movement (Allegro giusto) is gay and contains some dance rhythms, a climactic return to the material of the opening of the first movement, and a fast, brilliant coda.

FRANCIS POULENC   1899—

Though Poulenc has invested many of his songs with tender sentiments and intense feelings, and though on occasion he has written such strong and forceful works as the cantata *Figure Humaine,* he is most often associated with the kind of music modern Frenchmen, from Erik Satie to Jean Françaix, write so well. That music is witty, satiric, whimsical, occasionally impudent; it is written with lightness, grace, in slight designs and with fragile textures. In such a vein, Poulenc is, indeed, a master. His touch never loses its delicacy; his wit and malice are razor-edged; his technical assurance never wavers. He writes with a simplicity that is deceptive, for it conceals the extraordinary skill that goes into the fashioning of the music. He is brief and clear. And he is always infectiously charming.

Poulenc was born in Paris on January 7, 1899. Study of the piano with Ricardo Viñes was interrupted by World War I, at which time Poulenc served in the French Army. Mustered out in 1918, Poulenc returned to study

—principally with Charles Koechlin—and to composing. He published his first work, the *Negro Rhapsody,* in 1917, and followed this with several gifted sonatas. At about this time, he came into contact with Erik Satie, who influenced him greatly. Like several other young French composers who had been influenced by Satie, Poulenc was regarded as a member of the new school of young French composers known as the "French Six" (see Honegger). But like the other members of the "French Six," he went his own way in his music, uninfluenced by what others around him were writing. Major performances brought him to the front rank of contemporary French composers. The most notable of these were that of his ballet, *Les Biches,* by the Diaghilev Ballet Russe in 1924, and of his Concerto for Two Pianos and Orchestra at the International Society for Contemporary Music Festival in Venice in 1932.

During World War II, Poulenc was active in the Resistance movement in France. The war over, he added a certain measure of notoriety to his fame when his opera-burlesque, *Les Mamelles de Tirésias,* created a scandal in Paris on June 10, 1947. In 1948, Poulenc visited the United States for the first time, appearing as piano soloist with major orchestras, and in joint recitals with Pierre Bernac.

The following works by Poulenc are discussed below: *Le Bestiare* (*The Zoo*); *Concert Champêtre;* Concerto in D Minor for Two Pianos and Orchestra; Sinfonietta; Sonata in D Major for Violin and Piano.

LE BESTIARE (THE BESTIARY), cycle for mezzo-soprano, string quartet, flute, clarinet, and bassoon (1918). I. Le Dromadaire. II. La Chèvre du Thibet. III. La Sauterelle. IV. Le Dauphin. V. L'Écrevisse. VI. La Carpe.

Though Poulenc is best known for his larger works, he is one of the foremost and one of the most sensitive song composers of our time. His natural and ever-apparent lyric gift has a seemingly inexhaustible palette of colors, variety of mood, and shades of emotional expression. As in so many of his larger works, he can be gay and sophisticated in his songs; but he can also write songs in a deeper and profounder vein, songs that reveal a completely different facet of his artistic personality from that found in his orchestral music.

Le Bestiare belongs with Poulenc's early works, having been written while the composer was still greatly under the influence of Satie. Here Poulenc reveals the same apt gift for animal characterization—and with equally economical strokes—that Saint-Saëns had shown in his *Carnival of Animals,* or, for that matter, that Poulenc himself was later to exploit in his ballet adaptation of La Fontaine's *Fables, Les Animales Modèles.* To words of Guillaume Apollinaire, Poulenc describes, with his customary charm and wit, six specimens of animal and marine life: the dromedary, goat, grasshopper, dolphin, crawfish, and carp.

CONCERT CHAMPÊTRE, for harpsichord (or piano) and orchestra (1928). I. Adagio; Allegro molto. II. Andante (Mouvement de sicilienne). III. Finale: presto (très gai).

In writing this delightful work for the harpsichordist Wanda Landowska, Poulenc had a double mission. For one thing, he tried to show that the harpsichord was by no means an archaic instrument. Besides this, he tried to re-create in modern terms the style of seventeenth-century French keyboard music, in the way Ravel did in the *Tombeau de Couperin*. "I decided to use the full orchestra against the harpsichord," the composer has said. "If they carry on a dialogue, the one does not harm the other. As soon as they play together I extract from the mass isolated instruments, and in turn each group strengthens, without crushing, the sonority of the harpsichord."

Except for the peroration, which is dignified and expressive, the entire work is replete with delightful tunes, sometimes set against tart harmonies, and—particularly in the last movement—is filled with the laughter and lightheartedness which we invariably associate with Poulenc. The spirit of the seventeenth century is preserved in the freshness and delicacy of the music, but there is never much doubt that this is the work of a contemporary composer.

The work was introduced by Wanda Landowska and the Paris Philharmonic Orchestra under Pierre Monteux on May 3, 1929.

CONCERTO IN D MINOR FOR TWO PIANOS AND ORCHESTRA (1932). I. Allegro ma non troppo. II. Larghetto. III. Finale.

This slight but highly ingratiating work has become one of Poulenc's most frequently heard compositions. It is in his finest witty vein, and is full of simple and engaging little tunes and droll rhythmic effects, many of which belong in the music hall rather than the concert auditorium. It was first heard at the festival of the International Society for Contemporary Music, held in Venice, on September 5, 1932. The composer and Jacques Fevrier were the soloists, and the La Scala Orchestra was directed by Desiré Defauw.

Two powerful chords introduce the composition, after which the first piano enters with a brilliant passage which is soon taken up by the second piano. There then comes a sprightly first theme—a staccato four-note phrase. The second theme is of the music-hall variety, and is introduced by the woodwinds and solo horn. The music then becomes sentimental, and after a brief cadenza for the two pianos the thematic material is revived. The movement ends quietly. In the Larghetto, the principal theme is a melody of great charm and wistfulness, announced first by the first piano. The second piano repeats the melody against an ingenious accompaniment provided by its partner. The tempo quickens, a climax is reached, and then the first theme returns to restore the original mood. The concerto closes with music-hall tunes, one of them resembling a march, another lyrical. The music passes from the lyrical to the virtuoso, and the movement ends with an outburst of exuberance.

SONATA IN D MAJOR FOR VIOLIN AND PIANO (1943).
I. Allegro con fuoco. II. Intermezzo: très lent et calme. III. Presto tragico.

This sonata was dedicated to the memory of Federico García Lorca, the celebrated Spanish poet who was killed by the Franco fascists in 1936. It is one of the most intensely and deeply felt of Poulenc's works, and one of his most lyrical effusions. The first movement goes from outright vehemence to sentimentality and back to vehemence. To the second movement, the composer appended the following Lorca quotation: "The guitar makes dreams weep"—a reminder that Lorca was also famous as a guitarist who accompanied himself in the singing of Spanish folksongs. Plucked violin strings give a faint suggestion of the guitar, but the body of the movement consists of a broad languorous melody, gentle rather than intense in its sadness; this is as tender and expressive a lyric page as can be found in Poulenc's works. The spell is broken: the turbulent, passionate third movement is the expression of grief at the contemplation of tragedy.

SINFONIETTA, for orchestra (1947). I. Allegro con fuoco. II. Molto vivace. III. Andante cantabile. IV. Finale: très vite et très gai.

This unpretentious, witty little orchestral work, which is in the vein of the Concerto for Two Pianos and Orchestra, was heard for the first time over the B.B.C. in London, Roger Désormière conducting, on October 24, 1948.

It is a delightful excursion into levity, aptly described by G. H. L. Smith as "amiable without being banal, popular without concession, haunted with nimble dances and songs that each hearer will think he remembers, but which are new, nevertheless." The first movement is made up of several episodic ideas presented in a spirit of gaiety. The scherzo that follows carries on this carefree attitude. A lyrical third movement makes no pretense at profound emotion, but is pleasantly tuneful. The closing movement opens with a piquant little theme which injects insouciance; a second theme is more lyrical.

SERGE PROKOFIEV

Not many contemporary composers write music which has such an unmistakable identity as that of Prokofiev. What is particularly interesting is that Prokofiev's music, stylistically, changed little over the decades; the same qualities and mannerisms by which his later works are recognized can be found in many of his earlier productions. A saucy, infectious impudence is the attitude usually associated with his music. The mocking reeds, the mischievous leaps in the melody, the tart and often disjointed harmonies, the sudden fluctuation from the naïve and the simple to the unexpected and the complex—these are a few of the fingerprints that can be found in most of Prokofiev's works. Certain little idiosyncracies appear and reappear: for example, beginning a theme in a rather hackneyed pattern and then having it suddenly and inexplicably leap to an unexpected interval; or consciously setting a trite tune against a piquant and original harmony; or utilizing simple schoolbook chords in unorthodox relations. Somehow, whenever these and other similar devices emerge— though they are expected —they manage to bring surprise and delight.

In his attempt to free music from literary, metaphysical, or mystical associations and to have it appear as music and nothing else, Prokofiev's ironic and satiric vein has, of course, become famous. But it would be a mistake to assume that his is a one-string lyre—that he is witty and sardonic, and nothing more. As a matter of fact (and particularly in his more recent works), Prokofiev is also capable of music of great dramatic power, of sensitively projected emotions, of meditative moods, and of noble concepts.

Prokofiev was born in Sontsovka, Russia, on April 23, 1891. Extraordinarily precocious, he began studying music early with his mother and with Glière and Taneiev. At five he wrote his first piano pieces, and at eight a complete opera. In 1903, he entered the St. Petersburg Conservatory, where he was a pupil of Liadov, Rimsky-Korsakov, and Nicolas Tcherepnine, graduating with the highest of honors seven years later. His *Scythian Suite,* whose dissonances at once established him as a kind of *enfant terrible* of Russian music, was written in 1914. And in the next few years he was performed and he was published; his original music made its influence felt in Russian musical circles.

In the spring of 1918, Prokofiev left the Soviet Union to circle the world. It is said that when he applied for his visa, the People's Commissar of

Education said to him: "You are a revolutionary in music just as we are revolutionary in life, and we ought to work together. But if you want to go, we will not stand in your way." By way of Siberia, Japan, and Honolulu, Prokofiev came to the United States, arriving in August, 1918. He appeared here as a pianist and as a composer, and was regarded as very much of a musical curiosity because of his modern thinking. While in this country, he received a commission from the Chicago Opera Company to write an opera—*The Love for Three Oranges.*

In October, 1923, Prokofiev began a ten-year residence in Paris. During this period he established his world reputation as one of the most powerful, original, and provocative composers of our time. His native land did not forget him. Reports on Prokofiev's works appeared continually in the Soviet press; his music was published by the State Publishing House; and the Soviet critics did not hesitate in acclaiming him one of Russia's greatest composers. When, in 1927, Prokofiev returned to the Soviet Union for a three-month visit, he was given a hero's welcome.

At last, in 1932, Prokofiev decided to return to his native land for good. In explaining his long absence, he said: "I had not grasped the significance of what was happening in the U.S.S.R. I did not realize that the events there demanded the collaboration of all citizens—not only men of politics, but men of art as well." Before long, he assumed a position of first importance in Soviet musical life, a position he maintained for the next sixteen years. And, as Nicolas Slonimsky remarked, his music became "probably the greatest single influence in Soviet music."

And then suddenly and without warning—as such things happen in a totalitarian state—he was in disgrace.

On February 10, 1948, the Central Committee of the Communist Party of the U.S.S.R. issued a public resolution denouncing the leading composers of the Soviet Union for "decadent formalism," or "cerebralism." The Committee felt that Russian composers had allowed themselves to be infected by Western musical thinking, with the result that the complex, dissonant, iconoclastic music they wrote was far removed from the masses. The principal targets for this attack were Prokofiev, Khatchaturian, Shostakovich, Miaskovsky, Shebalin, Muradeli, and Popov.

The resolution was specific in its denunciation. Characteristics in these composers which it found lamentable were "the negation of the basic principles of classical music; a sermon for atonality, dissonance, and disharmony, as if this were an expression of 'progress' and 'innovation' in the growth of musical composition as melody; a passion for confused, neuropathic combinations which transform into cacophony, into a chaotic piling up of sounds. ... Many Soviet composers, in pursuit of falsely conceived innovation, have lost contact with the demands and the artistic taste of the Soviet people, have shut themselves off in a narrow circle of specialists and musical gourmands, have lowered the high social role of music and narrowed its meaning, limiting it to a satisfaction of the distorted tastes of esthetic individualists."

The Soviet composers thus rebuked did not lose time in trying to regain official favor. All of them rushed to admit that they had been at fault, that they now saw the truth and would mend their ways. Here is the way Prokofiev put it in a letter to Khrennikov: "As far as I am concerned, elements of formalism were peculiar to my music as long as fifteen and twenty years ago. Apparently the infection was caught from contact with some Western ideas. When formalistic errors in Shostakovich's opera *Lady Macbeth* were exposed by *Pravda,* I gave a great deal of thought to creative devices in my own music, and came to the conclusion that such a method of composition is faulty. As a result, I began a search for a clearer and more meaningful language.... The existence of formalism in some of my works is probably explained by a certain self-complacency, an insufficient realization of the fact that it is completely unwanted by the people. The Resolution has shaken to the core the social consciousness of our composers, and it has become clear what type of music is needed by our people, and the ways of the eradication of the formalist disease have also become clear.... This is the direction which I intend to take in my new opera on a contemporary Soviet subject, *A Tale of a Real Man* by Polevoy. I am highly gratified that the Resolution has pointed out the desirability of polyphony, particularly in choral and ensemble singing.... In my above-mentioned opera, I intend to introduce trios, duets, and contrapuntally developed choruses, for which I will make use of some interesting northern Russian folksongs. Lucid melody, and as far as possible a simple harmonic language, are elements which I intend to use in my opera."

But Prokofiev was too honest a creative artist and too independent a musical thinker to be able suddenly to write his music to measure. *A Tale of a Real Man,* introduced in concert form in Leningrad in 1948, did not quite turn out the way he had planned; in fact, the style remains unmistakably that of Prokofiev. Consequently, on December 29, 1948—at the conclusion of a nine-day discussion of Soviet music by the Union of Soviet Composers—Prokofiev came in for another stinging attack in a resolution drawn up by Khrennikov. "The plenum concedes that the creative reorientation of these composers proceeds very slowly, as revealed by the presence of some unliquidated formalistic elements in their music. Defeated ideologically, formalism still lives in the music of Soviet composers. This is demonstrated by the new opera of Prokofiev, *A Tale of a Real Man."*

Eventually, however, he was able to rehabilitate his position in the Soviet Union. He wrote an oratorio, *On Guard for Peace,* which bitterly condemned the Western "warmongers" while extolling the Soviet "international peace movement." He also wrote a vocal-symphonic suite, *Winter Bonfire,* which (like the oratorio) adopted the realistic and pleasing style demanded by the new Soviet esthetics. These works brought Prokofiev the Stalin Prize early in 1951. To emphasize still further his return to the good

graces of the ruling clique, there took place on April 23, 1951, a special
Prokofiev concert celebrating the composer's sixtieth birthday. Prokofiev died
in Moscow on March 5, 1953.

The following works by Prokofiev are discussed below: *The Age of
Steel* (*Le Pas d'Acier*); *Alexander Nevsky; Classical Symphony;* Concerto
No. 3 in C Major for Piano and Orchestra; Concerto No. 5 in G Major for
Piano and Orchestra; Concerto No. 1 in D Major for Violin and Orchestra;
Concerto No. 2 in G Minor for Violin and Orchestra; *Lieutenant Kije; The
Love for Three Oranges; Peter and the Wolf;* Quartet No. 1; Quartet No. 2
in F Major; *Romeo and Juliet; Scythian Suite* (*"Ala and Lolli"*); Sonata
No. 7 for Piano; Sonata in D Major for Violin and Piano; Symphony No. 5;
Symphony No. 6 in E-flat Minor; *War and Peace.*

For Symphony No. 1, see *Classical Symphony.*

CONCERTO NO. 1 IN D MAJOR FOR VIOLIN AND ORCHES-
TRA, op. 19 (1913). I. Andantino. II. Scherzo. III. Moderato.

Prokofiev's First Violin Concerto is not a concerto in the traditional
meaning of the term. The virtuoso character of the solo instrument is never
exploited (there are no cadenzas or passages of bravura writing), just as the
orchestra is never allowed to assume the subsidiary role of an accompanying
body. Solo instrument and orchestra are treated as a symphonic unit, both
used inextricably in the development and embellishment of the musical ideas.

The concerto (which is sometimes played without interruption) opens
in a contemplative mood set by the plaintive and lyrical opening subject in
the solo violin. The movement gains in force as the solo instrument becomes
more energetic; but the general feeling of repose is not altogether abandoned.
The flashing Scherzo that follows has those characteristic leaps in the melody
and nervous accentuations that make for Prokofievian whimsy. Broad lyricism returns in the concluding movement, and the concerto ends as it began,
with the plaintive opening subject soaring in the upper registers.

The concerto, while written in 1913, was not heard until October 18,
1923. Marcel Darrieux was the soloist in Paris, and the orchestra was led by
Serge Koussevitzky.

SCYTHIAN SUITE ("ALA AND LOLLI"), for orchestra, op. 20
(1916). I. Invocation to Veles and Ala. II. The Evil God and the Dance
of the Pagan Monsters. III. Night. IV. The Glorious Departure of Lolli, and
the Cortege of the Sun.

Soon after being graduated from the St. Petersburg Conservatory,
Prokofiev planned a ballet about a legendary race known as the Scythians,
and their gods. The Scythians were said to have inhabited a region southeast
of Europe near the Black Sea, and to have become extinct in or about 100 B.C.
Prokofiev outlined his ideas to Diaghilev, who was not impressed. Conse-

quently, the composer revised his plans and decided to write an orchestral suite instead.

The first movement (Allegro feroce), in music of brilliant colors and vehement passion, describes an invocation to the Sun, leading deity of the Scythians. A sacrifice to Ala, daughter of Veles, follows. In the second section (Allegro sostenuto), a frenetic dance by the Evil God takes place. He is surrounded by the seven pagan monsters he has evoked. Night descends. The Evil God comes to Ala in the third section (Andantino) and brings her great harm. The Moon Maidens descend to console her. The suite ends (Tempestuoso) with the Scythian hero, Lolli, setting forth to save Ala. He is no match for the Evil God and would be overcome but for the help given him by the Sun God. Sunrise comes like a benediction; and the suite comes to an end.

The suite was heard for the first time on January 29, 1916, in St. Petersburg, with the composer conducting. Its advanced harmonic and rhythmic writing and its dissonances disturbed many who heard this music. It was treated harshly by the critics. One such criticism was written by Leonid Sabaneyev, and thereby hangs a tale. The original date set for the première had been postponed at the last moment—too late for Sabaneyev to retract the devastating criticism which he had sent in for publication. To make matters worse for the critic, he had not only written the review without having heard the music, but also without any possibility of having had access to the manuscript score. This incident created considerable disturbance against Sabaneyev and drew some sympathetic interest to the composer.

CLASSICAL SYMPHONY, op. 25 (1917). I. Allegro. II. Larghetto. III. Gavotte: non troppo allegro. IV. Finale: molto vivace.

This delightful symphony is a twentieth-century adaptation of the classical symphony of Mozart and Haydn. The form and instrumentation are of classical proportions; classical, too, are the economy and transparency of the orchestral writing and the brevity of the developments. But the harmonic progressions, the angular melodic lines with their capricious octave leaps, and the Prokofievian whimsy belong to our times. The strange blend of the past and the present, however, offers no contradiction. With all his customary mastery, Prokofiev has admirably synchronized old styles and new to create a living artistic product. This music is so simple and direct in its approach, so precise in the presentation of its thematic materials, and so terse and logical in its development that it can readily be assimilated at first hearing; and for these reasons it has been one of the most popular of Prokofiev's works.

The two principal subjects of the first movement are heard in the first violins: the first, headstrong and impetuous, opens the movement; the second, gay and brisk with capricious octave leaps, follows after a brief transition in the flute. In the second movement, a piquant melody—characteristically Prokofievian—rises in the violins against a murmuring background. A running passage for pizzicato strings is the middle section, after which the violins return with their haunting song. In the Gavotte, the fusion of an old form with new writing is perhaps most brilliantly realized; the middle part is a musette. The closing movement opens with a loud chord, after which the music erupts with élan and exuberance and progresses with uninterrupted momentum until the end of the work.

The *Classical* is the first of Prokofiev's symphonies. It was written in 1916-17, dark years in Russia, torn as that country was by war and the threats of impending revolution. (Strange, is it not, that music as bright-faced and gay as the *Classical Symphony* should be born in such a critical period of suffering?) On March 21, 1918, the composer conducted the première performance in St. Petersburg.

THE LOVE FOR THREE ORANGES, opera, op. 33 (1919).

Prokofiev was commissioned by Cleofante Campanini, general director of the Chicago Opera Company, to write *The Love for Three Oranges*. Campanini found the work too difficult for performance and shelved it. When the opera company came under Mary Garden's direction she decided to go ahead with the project. The opera, now somewhat revised, was heard for the first time on December 30, 1921. It was repeated once in Chicago and once in New York. It was not successful. While a good spectacle to the eye, its complicated and ironic libretto and the modern harmonies and lyricism of the daring score proved too puzzling. The opera passed into oblivion until the New York City Opera Company revived it in November, 1949.

For his libretto Prokofiev took an eighteenth-century fantastic tale by Carlo Gozzi and converted it into a knife-edged satire on grand opera. On the stage he placed an opera audience of twenty-four, comprising Glooms, Joys, Cynics, Empty-Heads—each group with its own pet esthetic theories—who, from time to time, interrupt the play with comments and suggestions. The stage within the stage unfolds the fantastic story of a Crown Prince, long ill, who can be cured only through laughter. A sorceress comes to prevent his recovery. Attacked by the palace guards, her struggles prove so comical that the prince bursts into laughter. Though now recovered, his woes are not over: the sorceress has stricken him with a curse of having to fall in love with three oranges. The prince now goes in quest of his love. He finds two oranges and opens them up, only to find the beautiful princesses within them dead from thirst. In the third orange, the princess lies dying. The Cynics from the stage audience rush with a pail of water and revive her. The prince gets his love—while the stage audience takes the sorceress as prisoner.

For this strange, and often nonsensical play, Prokofiev created music that passes from wit to whimsy, from drollery to burlesque, with particularly brilliant writing for the orchestra. There is a great deal of impudence in his frequent quotations from Russian and French operas. The sum total is not only a broad burlesque of opera plots, so often both confused and confusing, but also something of a parody of romantic operatic composition. One critic put it this way in 1921: "He strips grand opera of its glamour and makes it no longer grand."

The "March," the "Scherzo," and the *"Scène Infernale"* have become famous at orchestral concerts. The whimsical "March" (used as the signature for the radio program *The F.B.I. in Peace and War*) is one of Prokofiev's best-known orchestral pieces.

CONCERTO NO. 3 IN C MAJOR FOR PIANO AND ORCHES-TRA, op. 26 (1921). I. Andante; Allegro. II. Theme and Variations: andantino. III. Allegro ma non troppo.

For many years, Prokofiev had been accumulating the themes he was to develop in this concerto: the principal theme of the second movement came to him in 1913, while an episode in the first movement dates from 1911. He began to work with concentration on the concerto in the summer of 1921, completing it on September 28. The world première took place in Chicago on December 17, 1921, with the composer as soloist and Frederick Stock conducting the Chicago Symphony Orchestra. The work was well received; and ever since its première it has been one of Prokofiev's most successful and frequently heard compositions.

The composer's own analysis, as published in the score, follows: "The first movement opens quietly with a short introduction. The theme is announced by an unaccompanied clarinet, and is continued by the violins for a few bars. Soon the tempo changes...which leads to the statement of the principal subject by the piano.... A passage in chords for the piano alone leads to the more expressive second subject, heard in the oboe with a pizzicato accompaniment. This is taken up by the piano and developed at length.... At the climax of this section, the tempo reverts to Andante, and the orchestra gives out the first theme, *ff*. The piano joins in, and the theme is subjected to an impressively broad treatment. On resuming the Allegro, the chief theme and the second subject are developed with increased brilliance, and the movement ends with an exciting crescendo.

"The second movement consists of a theme with five variations. The theme is announced by the orchestra alone. In the first variation the piano treats the opening of the theme in quasi-sentimental fashion.... The tempo changes to Allegro for the second and third variations.... In variation four, the tempo is once again Andante, and the piano and orchestra discourse on the theme in a quiet and meditative fashion. Variation five is energetic (Allegro giusto). It leads without pause into a restatement of the theme by the orchestra, with delicate embroidery in the piano.

"The finale begins with a staccato theme for bassoons and pizzicato strings, which is interrupted by the blustering entry of the piano.... Eventually, the piano takes up the first theme and develops it into a climax. With a reduction of tone and slackening of tempo, an alternative theme is introduced in the woodwinds. The piano replies with a theme that is more in keeping with the caustic humor of the work. This material is developed and there is a brilliant coda."

THE AGE OF STEEL (LE PAS D'ACIER), ballet, op. 41 (1925).

In 1925, Serge Diaghilev outlined to Prokofiev an idea for a ballet about Soviet life. Diaghilev had a specific plan for such a ballet: the first part was to describe the crumbling of the old order, while the second part would be devoted to the building of a new Soviet world. He had engaged Georgi Yakulov to write the book, and he wanted Prokofiev to prepare the score.

The ballet was in essence a glorification of the growth and development of industrialization in the Soviet Union. It called for strident and realistic music in which factory noises and the rhythms of machines and engines in motion were to play a prominent part. Prokofiev's score fulfilled the assignment completely. It was highly dissonant, and with an almost stark naturalism. The occasional flavoring of Russian melodies, in which Prokofiev simulated the folksongs of his land, did not conceal the acrid bitterness of the music as a whole. This music was as tense as steel, an "apotheosis of machinery," as one unnamed critic described it.

At its première performance, which took place in Paris on June 8, 1927, the ballet was received with comparative apathy. Diaghilev expected a scandal, but he received neither riots nor enthusiasm. However, when the ballet was introduced in London, the following July 4, it scored a decided success, and was played eight times. The *Musical Times* called it the most powerful Diaghilev ballet since *Les Noces,* and the *Empire News* felt that it expressed the spirit of modern Russia better than all the efforts of orators and writers.

A symphonic suite prepared from the ballet score (op. 41a) comprises eleven sections, of which the following six are most often heard: Train of Men Carrying Provision Bags; Sailor with Bracelet and Working Women; Reconstruction of Scenery; The Factory; The Hammer; Final Scene.

QUARTET NO. 1, for strings, op. 50 (1930). I. Allegro. II. Scherzo. III. Andante.

The personal confidences that are usually spoken by the composer within the intimate form of the string quartet are to be found in this music. In few of his works has Prokofiev written music in which he plumbs his own feelings so deeply. In place of the customary wit and satire that we have come to expect in Prokofiev we find serene beauty (the second theme of the first movement) and the profoundest emotions (the opening of the scherzo). Perhaps in none of his other works has he maintained such a high level of spiritual and esthetic beauty as in the whole of the closing movement. The quartet is characterized by Israel Nestyev as "predominantly deep, calm, and contemplative."

Prokofiev wrote this work for the Library of Congress in Washington, D.C., where it was introduced on April 25, 1931.

CONCERTO NO. 5 IN G MAJOR FOR PIANO AND ORCHES-TRA, op. 55 (1932). I. Allegro con brio. II. Moderato ben accentuato. III. Allegro. IV. Larghetto. V. Vivo piu mosso; Coda.

The melodic ideas for this composition (as in the case of the Third Piano Concerto) had been in existence long before the composer sat down to write his work. Actually, there have been two Fifth Concertos. One was written in 1918, and, having been left in Russia when Prokofiev came to the United States, went astray. The other was developed in 1932 from the piano sketches of the original work, which the composer had preserved. The première of the concerto took place in Berlin on October 31, 1932. The composer was the soloist, and the Berlin Philharmonic was directed by Wilhelm Furtwaengler.

The composer's analysis follows:

"The first movement is an Allegro con brio with a Meno mosso as middle section. Though not in sonata form, it is the main movement of the concerto and fulfills the function and maintains the spirit of the traditional sonata form. The second movement has a march-like rhythm. I would not think of calling it a march because it has none of the vulgarity or common-ness which is so often associated with the idea of march, and which actually exists in most popular marches. The third movement is a toccata. This is a precipitate, displayful movement of much technical brilliance and requiring a great virtuosity; it is a toccata for orchestra as much as for piano. The fourth movement . . . is the lyrical movement of the concerto. It starts off with a soft, soothing theme; grows more and more intense in the middle portion, develops breadth and tension, then returns to the music of the beginning. The finale has a decided classic flavor. The Coda is based on a new theme, which is joined by the other themes of the finale. There is a reference to some of the material of the preceding movements in the finale.

LIEUTENANT KIJE, symphonic suite, op. 60 (1934). I. The Birth of Kije. II. Romance. III. Kije's Wedding. IV. Troika. V. Burial of Kije.

The first music written by Prokofiev after his permanent return to his native land in 1933 was for a film, Lieutenant Kije. The witty screen play concerns a mythical character, Lieutenant Kije, created by Tsar Nicholas I through the misreading of a military report. Rather than tell the Tsar that he has made a mistake, the courtiers are compelled to fabricate all sorts of military exploits for the invented character. Finally, pressed by the Tsar to bring the hero into the court, they bring about his noble death on the battlefield.

For this merry story, Prokofiev wrote a score in his best satirical vein. The character of Kije is virtually caricature; his exploits are told with tongue-in-cheek malice.

In 1934, the composer wrote a symphonic suite based on some of the best music of the motion-picture score. In the first part (Allegro), a fanfare of cornets and rolls of the drum evoke the character of the military hero, Lieutenant Kije. A march of somewhat hollow pomp is heard. In the succeeding part (Andante), our hero succumbs to love. This section calls for a baritone solo, but most of the time Kije's song of love is assumed by the tenor saxophone. With a great deal of ceremony—and with no less sentiment—Kije gets married in the third movement (Allegro fastoso). A Moderato section brings up the Russian winter with sleigh bells. Within a tavern a lusty song is heard. (Once again the tenor saxophone substitutes for the singing voice.) Poor Kije is put to rest with full military honors in the concluding pages (Andante assai), as high points of his career are reviewed. Prokofiev's music emphasizes the fact that for the courtiers this is not an occasion for grief, but for constrained rejoicing: Kije has become a trial to them, and his death is a blessed relief.

The suite was introduced in Paris under the composer's direction on February 20, 1937.

CONCERTO NO. 2 IN G MINOR FOR VIOLIN AND OR-CHESTRA, op. 63 (1935). I. Allegro moderato. II. Andante assai. III. Allegro ben marcato.

The Second Violin Concerto followed the First by twenty-two years. It was written for a French violinist, Robert Soetens, who introduced it in Madrid on December 1, 1935, with the Madrid Symphony Orchestra under Arbós. Prokofiev originally intended this work to be a sonata for violin and piano; but as his ideas grew more and more spacious, he realized that the concerto form was more suitable.

The Second Concerto is more melodic than the First and more romantic in its approach. The first movement (in sonata form) opens with a highly expressive melodic idea in the solo violin unaccompanied. This idea—the principal theme of the movement—is extended, after which a second melody, equally eloquent, is also proclaimed by the solo instrument against a background of soft strings. The working out of these two themes is elaborate, with the solo violin frequently indulging in pyrotechnical passages which decorate the melodies taken up by the orchestra. The second movement is classic in its emotional restraint and purity of writing. After two bars of prelude, the violin enters with the principal material—a moving and poetic melody out of which the entire movement develops. The concluding section of the concerto—a rondo in three sections—is more rhythmic than melodic, and gives play to Prokofiev's bent for satirical utterances.

ROMEO AND JULIET, three symphonic suites, op. 64 ter. (1935).

In 1935, Prokofiev wrote the music for a ballet based on Shakespeare's *Romeo and Juliet* for production by the Bolshoi Theater in Moscow. It was not successful. The Soviet critics did not like the inconsistencies in the libretto and its submission to what one of them described as "the worst traditions of the old form." There was also some resentment over the imposition of a happy ending (so much so that, after a trial performance, the original tragic ending of the drama was restored). Prokofiev's music was described as hard, cold, incongruous to the text. Prokofiev himself said: "I have taken special pains to achieve a simplicity which, I hope, will reach the hearts of listeners. If people find no melody and no emotion in this work I shall be very sorry. But I feel sooner or later they will."

Prokofiev was right in believing that audiences would learn to appreciate this music; but they did not do this until he had written three orchestral suites based on the ballet score. Of these, the second has proved the most successful, particularly for its effective tonal characterizations. This second suite was heard in the spring of 1937 in the Soviet Union and since then has been performed extensively everywhere.

The second suite has seven sections: I. Montagues and Capulets (Allegro pesante). II. Juliet, the Maiden (Vivace). III. Friar Laurence (Andante espressivo). IV. Dance (Vivo). V. The Parting of Romeo and Juliet (Lento poco piu animato). VI. Dance of the West-Indian Slave Girls (Andante con eleganza). VII. Romeo at Juliet's Grave (Adagio funebre).

The first suite, introduced in Moscow on November 24, 1936, also has seven sections: I. Dance of the People. II. Scene. III. Madrigal. IV. Minuet. V. Masques. VI. Romeo and Juliet. VII. Death of Tybalt.

The third suite is in six parts: I. Romeo at the Fountain. II. The Morning Dance. III. Juliet. IV. Nurse. V. Morning Serenade. VI. Juliet's Death.

PETER AND THE WOLF, symphonic fairy tale, for narrator and orchestra, op. 67 (1936).

That Prokofiev has a natural aptitude for writing music for children has been proved in his children's songs and in his delightful piano pieces, *Music for Children*. But his most successful achievement in this genre has been the symphonic fairy tale, *Peter and the Wolf*, written to teach children the sounds of the different instruments of the orchestra. As the narrator informs the listener in the opening monologue: "Each character in this tale is represented by an instrument in the orchestra: the bird, by a flute; the duck, by an oboe; the cat, by a clarinet in the low register; grandpapa, by the bassoon; the wolf, by three French horns; Peter, by the string quartet; and the hunter's rifle shots, by the kettledrums and bass drums."

The story then unfolds—in words and music. The narrator speaks the text, pausing to allow the music to give a tonal interpretation of what he has just described. During the recital, leitmotifs in the different instruments appear and reappear, and are woven into the orchestral fabric with extraordinary ingenuity. The themes for the various animals are highly descriptive; and the melodic subject describing Peter has all the insouciance and impudence of the reckless youth who goes unafraid to capture the wolf and who succeeds in dragging the animal back to the zoo.

Peter and the Wolf was introduced in Moscow on May 2, 1936.

ALEXANDER NEVSKY, cantata for mezzo-soprano, chorus, and orchestra, op. 78 (1938).

Prokofiev's ability to write music for a comparatively popular medium and yet to maintain the highest artistic integrity and standards was proved by *Alexander Nevsky*. Though originating as motion-picture music it is nevertheless one of the composer's finest creations, a work of great dignity and power.

The motion picture, directed by Sergei Eisenstein (in collaboration with Vasiliev), was built around the Russian defense of Novgorod in 1242 against the invading Knights of the Teutonic Order. The hero of this defense was Prince Alexander Yaroslavich Nevsky. Called to save his land, the Prince gathered around him a fighting force, met the enemy on the frozen waters of Lake Chud, and dealt them a disastrous defeat. (It must be recalled that when this motion picture was produced, in 1938—one year before the Soviet-Nazi pact—the sentiment against Germany was intense in the Soviet Union.)

The eloquent descriptive music that Prokofiev wrote for this motion picture impressed the composer, who realized that he had here the materials for a major musical composition. He extracted the most graphic pages of his score, amplified and extended them, and developed the whole into a cantata. In this form, *Alexander Nevsky* was introduced in Moscow (and with extraordinary success) on May 17, 1939, with the composer directing the Moscow Philharmonic Orchestra and Chrous.

The cantata is divided into seven sections, or "pictures."

I. "Russia Under the Mongolian Yoke." In somber music the composer evokes the feeling of desolation that seizes Russia following the Tartar invasion in the middle of the thirteenth century.

II. "Song of Nevsky." With ringing, soaring lines of music the chorus raises its voice in praise of the hero, Nevsky, who has helped bring about the defeat of the Swedes on the Neva River.

III. "Crusaders in Pskov." The Teutonic Knights, masquerading as religious crusaders, are depicted in music that pointedly combines Gregorian cadences (an ecclesiastical Latin text is set for chorus) with brutal, modern harmonies and sonorities.

IV. "Arise, Ye Russian People." The people of Russia are urged to rise against the invaders, the music now reflecting the intensity of this sentiment.

V. "The Battle on the Ice." A gruesome, realistic picture is drawn of the savage battle on Lake Chud.

VI. "Field of the Dead." Grief for the dead, expressed in a song by a Russian girl, mingles with the exaltation of patriotism.

VII. "Alexander's Entry into Pskov." A grandiose hymn of triumph is sounded by chorus and orchestra to celebrate the victory of Nevsky as he enters with glory into the city of Pskov.

WAR AND PEACE, opera (1942).

For many years Russian composers had been attracted to Tolstoy's epic novel as a subject for an opera, only to be discouraged by the seemingly impossible task of reducing the monumental proportions of the novel to libretto size. The year of 1941, which saw the invasion of the Soviet Union by the Nazis, gave new impact and significance to the Tolstoy novel. Prokofiev, who had long eyed the novel covetously for a possible opera, was driven by the momentous events of the times to creative action. His biographer, Israel Nesteyev, remarks that the speed with which Prokofiev wrote the opera, and the "dimensions and form of execution," may well be among the most amazing phenomena of the composer's career.

The libretto by Mira Mendelssohn, written in prose (much of which was directly expropriated from Tolstoy), concentrates exclusively on the Napoleonic invasion of Russia in 1812. In five acts (twelve scenes), the opera is intended for performance on two consecutive nights: the first part, Acts I and II, are called by the composer "scenes of peace," while the remaining three acts are the "scenes of war." "In the first six scenes," the composer has explained, "I wanted to depict the main characters' peaceful life, their smiles and tears, their thoughts and dreams. These scenes deal with the relationships between Natasha Rostova, Andrei Volkonsky, Anatoli Kuragin, and Pierre Bezhukov—what Tolstoy himself in one of his letters called 'the novel's core.' The libretto is written in such a way that the foreboding of war grows gradually stronger from the first to the seventh scene. Peaceful life is interrupted by Napoleonic invasion. Beginning with the seventh scene, interest is focused on the Russian people's struggle, their sufferings, wrath, courage, and victory over the invaders. In this part the people themselves constitute the hero of the opera in the person of the peasants of the popular militia, the regular Russian army, the Cossacks, and the guerillas. Field Marshal Kutuzov, the soldiers' and people's favorite, appears on the scene. The destinies of the main characters introduced in the first six scenes are closely linked with war events. I was particularly anxious to stress the profound changes which occurred in their mental and moral make-up as a result of the danger threatening the country...."

Sixty characters are employed in the opera, though most of them appear only once. There is the central love theme of Natasha and Andrei running through the entire work as a kind of coalescing agent, providing much of the lyrical interest in the opera (as, for example, the spring nocturne of Scene One). There are big mass scenes in which the historic events are projected on a vast scale (the chorus of the Smolensk refugees or the battle scene of Borodino). And there are subtle and highly picturesque orchestral tone-portraits (the picture of ruined Moscow that opens Scene Nine, and the vivid battle between the partisans and the French in Scene Eleven.

One of the outstanding qualities of Prokofiev's score is its gift for sharp character delineations. One Soviet critic elaborated on this point in the publication *Soviet Music:* "The principal characters of the opera have their own clearly defined idiom—one might almost say their own dialects, marking not only their aria passages but also their recitatives.... In this way Prokofiev may be said to give unity to separate groups of characters ... and, with all that, to distinguish between the social classes to which they belong.... In this way the composer attains an unusual expressiveness and psychological realism."

A few scenes of *War and Peace* were presented in concert form at the Moscow Conservatory in June, 1945, S. Samosud conducting. One year later, the first part of the opera was presented at the Maly Academic Theater in Leningrad. At that time, the Soviet critic A. Khokhlovkin exclaimed that it "is a work of tremendous significance." But that, of course, was before 1948—when Prokofiev and most of his major works came in for severe criticism (and proscription) by the Central Committee of the Communist Party.

QUARTET NO. 2 IN F MAJOR, for strings, op. 92 (1942). I. Allegro sostenuto. II. Adagio. III. Allegro.

Prokofiev himself has said that this quartet combines "one of the least-known varieties of folksong with the most classical form of the quartet." The variety of folksong alluded to is that heard and preserved in the region of Kabardino-Balkaria, in the East Caucasus, where Prokofiev was vacationing in the war year of 1942.

The melos of the Caucasian folksong dominates the entire quartet. It is found in the almost naïve first theme of the first movement, which sounds like a nursery tune; the second theme is more sophisticated, but the entire movement has a down-to-earth character. In the second movement, a Caucasian love song is heard in the cello against oriental embellishments in the other instruments. This song is plangent in character, but as the movement progresses some gaiety is injected, and the song returns devoid of sentimentality. The abrupt and varied rhythms of Caucasian folk dances bring vitality to the closing movement. A lyric strain enters in the second section, though the rhythmic energy is not controlled; but in the third section, rhythm gives way to a deeply felt melody. After a solo passage for the cello, a new section is introduced. But the earlier rhythmic and melodic material is soon repeated, and the movement ends with a return of the opening section.

SONATA NO. 7 FOR PIANO, op. 83 (1942). I. Allegro inquieto. II. Andantino. III. Precipitato.

This sonata has acquired the sobriquet of "The Stalingrad Sonata" because it was written during the heroic stand and victory of the Red Army. An event of such magnitude inevitably left its impress on the Russian people at the time, who sensed that the turning point of the war had come; and it left its influence on the sonata Prokofiev was writing.

There is no programmatic analysis appended to this music; but it is not hard to find in the music the tensions and the exaltations of the time. The powerful dynamism and the precipitous rhythmic sweeps of the first movement re-create the emotional disturbances that every Soviet citizen must have experienced at this historic hour. The shattering power and force of the closing movement are like the iron wall of flesh and steel set up by the Red Army against the besieging enemy. Felix Borowski put it this way: "Something of the inexorable rhythm of the finale ... gives a suggestion of the heroic inflexibility of a people who are not to know defeat." In between these two large and tempestuous movements there is a slender one: songlike music of rare delicacy which comes as a lull before the tempest that follows.

Svyatoslav Richter introduced the sonata in the Soviet Union in 1943, when it proved so successful that it was awarded the highly coveted Stalin Prize.

SONATA IN D MAJOR FOR VIOLIN AND PIANO, op. 94 (1943). I. Moderato. II. Scherzo. III. Andante. IV. Allegro con brio.

On one of the highly infrequent occasions that Bernard Shaw has returned to his early role of music critic, he described this sonata as a "humorous masterpiece of authentic violin music." Shaw was only partly right. Humorous this sonata occasionally is—particularly in the fleet and capricious scherzo, and in the playful and saucy impudence of the closing movement. But instead of humor, lyricism and tender feelings are the predominating traits of this work. It abounds in wonderful melodies. The sonata opens with one of these—a long, full, flowing song that dominates the entire first movement; and the graceful and delicate Andante is as gentle a piece of music as Prokofiev has written.

As for its being "authentic violin music": this sonata was *not* originally written for the violin but for the flute. In 1943, Prokofiev adapted his flute sonata for the violin, at whch time it was introduced in Moscow by David Oistrakh.

SYMPHONY NO. 5, op. 100 (1944). I. Andante. II. Allegro marcato. III. Adagio. IV. Allegro giocoso.

In writing his Fifth Symphony (which arrived fifteen years after his Fourth), Prokofiev voiced a hymn to the spirit of man—a spirit that could not be permanently subjugated by either oppression or war. This symphony was written in a single month during the summer of 1944 (though Prokofiev had been gathering sketches for it for several years), and reflects in many of its pages the impact of the war on the Russian people.

It opens with a majestic slow movement built around two themes; it grows in power and grandeur until the themes are evolved into a coda of epic stature. A scherzo-like section follows, nervous and abrupt in its sudden accentuations (some writers find this music expressive of the horrors of war). The third movement is a threnody of compelling emotional intensity— possibly what Prokofiev had here in mind was the terrible price that the Russians were paying for their heroic resistance to the Nazi invaders. The mood throughout is one of grief; at climactic moments, the tragedy becomes heart-rending. But Prokofiev does not succumb permanently to pessimism. In the last movement gaiety asserts itself through the ominous atmosphere and speaks for the future, in which the fruits of victory can be enjoyed.

The symphony was introduced in Moscow on January 13, 1945, with the composer conducting. When Serge Koussevitzky introduced this symphony in the United States, in November, 1945, he described it as one of the greatest works of our generation, and broke precedent by performing it twice in New York in the same season.

SYMPHONY NO. 6 IN E-FLAT MINOR, op. 111 (1946). I. Allegro moderato. II. Largo. III. Vivace.

The Sixth Symphony is slighter in texture than the Fifth, more economical in its means, more transparent in its writing, lighter in mood, and more melodious. Written simply and emotionally, it is one of the most grateful of Prokofiev's later works, and is the kind of music that can be appreciated at first hearing. It is therefore strange to remember that this symphony was also severely condemned as "formalist" (or "cerebral") by the Central Committee of the Communist Party when it hurled a blanket denunciation at most of the major Soviet composers in February, 1948. After its première performance (in Leningrad on October 10, 1947) it was put on the proscribed list and shelved.

Prokofiev's own description of this symphony is as terse and direct as the music itself. "The first movement, of agitated character, is lyrical at times, and austere at others. The second movement is brighter and full of song. The finale, rapid and major, is near in character to my Fifth Symphony, but for the austere reminiscences of the first movement."

GIACOMO PUCCINI   1858—1924

The last opera of the mighty Verdi, *Falstaff,* was produced in Milan in 1893. Less than a decade earlier the first opera of the twenty-five-year-old Puccini, *Le Villi,* was seen, also in Milan. Thus Italian opera did not have to wait long for Verdi's successor; the imperial line of Italian opera composers that began with Monteverdi remained unbroken.

Not that Puccini was another Verdi! He had little of Verdi's nobility and grandeur and sustained inspiration. The blemishes in Puccini's operas (which even his most enthusiastic admirers will not deny) could never have been perpetrated by Verdi: the excessive sentimentality; the often thin material with which he worked; the comparatively weak counterpoint; the excessive love for the voice which made him inflate an aria out of proportion to the requirements of the drama. Yet when these subtractions are made, there is enough value left in Puccini's operas to make them the most important and successful operatic creations after Verdi; enough to endear them permanently to an entire generation of music lovers as no other operas have succeeded in doing.

On a scale more limited than Verdi (or than Wagner, whom he admired so profoundly), Puccini was a master. He had a consummate understanding of the theater, its requirements, its strengths and weaknesses. He knew how to build a climax or big scene with a telling, often shattering effect. He knew how to transmute into his music, and often with the most economical means, every theatrical effect of the stage, however subtle or elusive—so much so that in his hands the music often became throbbing drama. He was a skillful hand at characterization—female characterization particularly. He could transform his style to simulate French music or Japanese music or Chinese music, when the text required it, without losing his identity. He was fastidious in his workmanship, and always elegant in his style. Beyond all this, he had a born gift for Italian melody—fluid, warm, passionate, of a rapturous beauty.

He always took from other composers whatever served his artistic purpose and so ingeniously integrated it into his own style that it became an inextricable part of his own idiom. Thus he always kept amplifying his technical resources, always kept extending the gamut of his artistic expression—and always kept growing as a creative artist.

He was first attracted to the new naturalism—or *verismo,* as it is known in Italian opera—that appeared in Mascagni's *Cavalleria Rusticana*

(1890) and Leoncavallo's *Pagliacci* (1892), and which had in turn been an outgrowth of operas like Bizet's *Carmen*. Into his own operas Puccini brought the freshness and vitality of realism, both in his selection of librettos and in his music for them. To *verismo* Puccini brought the Italian lyricism he had inherited from his predecessors; Wagner's enriched harmony; and— as the years passed—the subtle tints of Debussy's impressionism (even to the use of the whole-tone scale), a discreet use of dissonance and unorthodox progressions and tonalities learned from the moderns, and even (in his last opera) a suggestion of Schoenberg's bitonality.

Puccini was born in Lucca on December 22, 1858, descendant of a long line of musicians who had been famous in Lucca. He began to study music early, and completed his musical education at the Milan Conservatory, where his teachers included Bazzini and Ponchielli. His first opera, *Le Villi*— written soon after his graduation from the Conservatory, and submitted in a competition which was won by Mascagni's *Cavalleria Rusticana*—was heard in Milan on May 31, 1884, and was successful, winning for Puccini the support of the powerful publisher, Ricordi. His second opera, *Edgar* (1889)—commissioned by Ricordi—was a failure; but *Manon Lescaut,* which followed it four years later, was a veritable triumph and established Puccini's reputation. That reputation swelled to formidable proportions in the years that followed, as Puccini produced two of his masterpieces: *La Bohème* (adapted from Murger's *La Vie de Bohème*) was introduced in Turin on February 1, 1896, under the baton of Arturo Toscanini; *La Tosca* (from the drama of Sardou) was first witnessed in Rome on January 14, 1900. Both operas were extraordinarily successful, and made their composer both internationally famous and wealthy. Since both *La Bohème* and *La Tosca* were written before 1900, they are not discussed below.

Madama Butterfly, which followed *La Tosca* by four years, was at first a decided failure—but only for a while. After undergoing extensive revisions, it returned to conquer. Thereafter, Puccini's status as the leading Italian composer of his time was never again questioned. When he visited the United States in 1907 to attend the American première of *Madama Butterfly* at the Metropolitan Opera House, he was given a thunderous welcome. The result of this American visit was a commission from the Metropolitan Opera to write an American opera, *The Girl of the Golden West* (based on the play by David Belasco). Introduced at the Metropolitan on December 10, 1910, the opera was a triumph; but it has since become recognized as one of Puccini's lesser works. Lesser operas followed: *La Rondine* (1917), and the trilogy, *Il Tabarro, Suor Angelica,* and *Gianni Schicchi* (1918). None of these were of the stature of his earlier masterpieces, but they had enough charm and musical interest to enjoy a measure of success.

In 1924 a throat ailment developed into a cancer, necessitating an operation for Puccini. The operation itself was successful, but a heart ailment developed. On November 29, 1924, Puccini died of a heart attack in Brussels. Two years after his death, his last opera, *Turandot,* was performed in its unfinished state at La Scala under Toscanini. Subsequently, the opera was completed by Franco Alfano, and was performed throughout the world.

The following works by Puccini are discussed below: *Gianni Schicchi; Madama Butterfly; Turandot.*

For *La Bohème* and *La Tosca,* see the biographical sketch above.

MADAMA BUTTERFLY, opera (1904).

The fact that *Madama Butterfly* was one of the most decisive opera failures of our time at its première performance, and that it is today one of the best-loved operas in the repertory, is not entirely a paradox. For the *Madama Butterfly* we know and love today is not the same opera that was heard at La Scala in Milan on February 17, 1904.

When the news of the fiasco was told to Arturo Toscanini over the telephone, the conductor was not surprised. Toscanini had already pointed out to the composer some of the glaring faults of the opera, the most important being the second act, requiring an hour and a half for performance, which was much too long and much too static. There were other irritants in the opera: the annoying reminder of *La Bohème* in the music accompanying Butterfly when she appears in her wedding dress; and the unpleasant spectacle of the scene involving Butterfly's drunken uncle.

But Toscanini also knew that the opera, at its best, possessed a beautiful score and could, with revisions, become an opera of great tenderness and appeal. And to prove his faith, Toscanini offered to conduct the work in South America—despite its failure at La Scala—if Puccini made the necessary changes. Puccini—who loved his *Butterfly* more than any other of his operas and who was convinced of its ultimate success—went to work with a will. The two acts of the original score now became three; the unpleasant moments were deleted; the action was heightened; and the music was made more lyrical, with the inclusion of an entirely new aria, *"Addio, fiorito asil!"*

The new version was first heard in Brescia, Italy, on May 28, 1904, with Campanini (who had conducted the première performance) once again the conductor. The opera was now a triumph; Puccini was called to the stage ten times. The next month, Toscanini directed it in Buenos Aires, where the success of the opera was even greater. And thereafter *Madama Butterfly* conquered the world.

But when the opening night audience in Milan had revolted against the opera (the hissing became so great that it finally erupted into a violent uproar that shook the house), it had not only been alienated by the faults of the first version, but—ironically—by the virtues of the opera as a whole. For *Madama Butterfly* was Puccini's most original score up to that time, and it had proved too novel for ears accustomed to *La Bohème* and *La Tosca*. Harmonically, Puccini had taken a bold step forward, using Debussy's unusual suspensions, unresolved discords, and the exotic whole-tone scale to project the kind of atmosphere the Japanese play required; he even employed special instrumental and harmonic effects to simulate Japanese music, and he interpolated snatches of American melody to heighten the American context of the play.

In later performances, operagoers were to take this opera to their heart for its sentimentality, lyricism, and poignant drama. But the true strength of the opera lies in the original conception of the music as a whole, and the wonderful way in which music serves the drama. Arias like *"Un bel di"* and *"Addio, fiorito asil!"* may remain the tours de force of the opera whenever it is performed. But to the sensitive opera lover, there are greater and more original moments in the opera; the exquisite lullaby, *"Dormi amor mio,"* the picture of dawn painted by the orchestra, the shattering impact of the dissonant chords that end the opera.

The original source of *Madama Butterfly* was a short story by John Luther Long, which the author, in collaboration with David Belasco, adapted into a play. The libretto itself was the work of Giacosa and Illica (who had written the librettos of *La Bohème* and *La Tosca*). The story is a familiar one: Pinkerton, an American sailor, takes Cio-Cio-San as his "port wife" in Japan. After he leaves Japan, she gives birth to their child. When Pinkerton returns to Japan again he is accompanied by his American wife. Cio-Cio-San, heartbroken, gives her child over to the Pinkertons and commits suicide.

GIANNI SCHICCHI, opera (1918).

Puccini's trilogy of one-act operas, introduced at the Metropolitan Opera House in New York on December 14, 1918, is an interesting study in contrasts. The first, *Il Tabarro,* is a rather sordid drama of lust, jealousy, and murder; its music has force and bitterness. The second, *Suor Angelica* (exclusively for women's voices), is a tender work in which the ineffable peace of a convent is magically caught in music that is exquisitely delicate and sensitive. The last—and most famous—of the three operas is *Gianni Schicchi,* an excursion into wit, with the comic elements of the text carried over into music that chuckles warmly, occasionally erupts into burlesque humor, but moves from first bar to last with brisk gaiety. On occasion (as in the aria "O mio babino") Puccini even writes subtle satire—parodying his own sentimental vein in earlier operas!

The libretto, by Giovacchino Foranzo, is in the best traditions of opera buffa. The action is set in thirteenth-century Florence. The relatives of the recently deceased Buso Donati, wealthy Florentine, gather to mourn his death—and to learn the terms of his will. To their horror, they learn that Donati has bequeathed all his possessions to the Church. Heartbroken, they seek out the crafty lawyer, Gianni Schicchi, who devises an ingenious plan. Nobody but his relatives as yet knows of old Donati's death. They are sworn to strict secrecy, with the additional warning that, by Florentine law, they are all liable to severe punishment if their ruse is ever detected. Thereupon the body of the dead man is removed and Schicchi goes into Donati's bed. Simulating the dying man, he calls for two notaries and two witnesses and dictates a new will. The new will, however, is not what the relatives had expected—since crafty Schicchi gives them trifles and bequeaths the bulk of the dead man's fortune to himself! Afraid of the Florentine law which would hold them guilty as accomplices to a fraud, the relatives are helpless. After the will is drawn up, they attack the lawyer with fists and angry condemnations. But Schicchi disperses them with a club. Proud owner of Donati's fortune, he is able to realize the marriage of his daughter to her lover.

TURANDOT, opera (1924).

Puccini's last opera, left unfinished by his death, has the most original score he ever wrote—the most inventive in its orchestral effects, the most daring in its harmony and tonality, the most original in its melodic ideas. Dissonances, unusual timbres and colors, novel scales, even at times startling bitonalities are here integral parts of Puccini's style, and he uses them—together with his sentiment and lyricism—with overpowering effect. Chinese melodic ideas are interpolated to add local color—at times, as in the funeral music for the Persian Prince, with unusual effect; but the character of the music is not Chinese, but unmistakably Puccinian. Some critics go so far as to call *Turandot* Puccini's greatest opera, and Turandot herself Puccini's most eloquent characterization. This may be excessive praise; but there can be no doubt that in *Turandot,* more than in any other preceding opera, Puccini revealed the artistic potentialities which he might have realized had he lived.

The libretto was prepared by G. Adami and R. Simoni. In the Peking of legendary times, the beautiful, frigid Princess Turandot consents to marry anyone who can answer three questions, but who is also ready to forfeit his head if he fails. The Prince of Persia is the first victim. Just before the execution of the Prince, Calaf curses the cruelty of Turandot, but when he sees her he is so overwhelmed by her beauty that he is determined to try for her, too. He answers the three riddles, only to have Turandot renege on the bargain. No man, she pronounces icily, will ever possess her! Calaf chivalrously offers her a way out: if she can uncover his true identity by the following morning he is ready to die; if not, she must stick to her bargain. Liu, who is in love with Calaf, is brought before Turandot and is tortured so that she may reveal Calaf's identity. But love has sealed her lips, and when she feels that the torture is about to make her relent, she kills herself. Eventually, Turandot succumbs to Calaf's passion, and pronounces that his true name is—Love.

The first performance of *Turandot* took place at La Scala in Milan on April 25, 1926, with Arturo Toscanini conducting. At this performance, the opera was presented in its unfinished state. In the middle of Act III—just after the suicide of Liu—Toscanini put down his baton, turned to the audience and, with tears streaming down his face, announced: "Here—here— the master laid down his pen."

Subsequently, Franco Alfano completed the opera by adding a duet and finale which, though not of the high inspiration and subtlety of Puccini's music, represent nevertheless a creditable performance.

SERGEI RACHMANINOFF   1873—1943

In an artistic statement which Rachmaninoff once dictated to this author, he said: "I try to make my music speak simply and directly that which is in my heart at the time I am composing. If there is love there, or bitterness, or sadness, or religion, these moods become part of my music, and it becomes either beautiful, or bitter, or sad, or religious. For composing music is as much a part of my living as breathing and eating. I compose music because I must give expression to my feelings, just as I talk because I must give utterance to my thoughts."

Rachmaninoff inherited the artistic mantle of his distinguished predecessor Tchaikovsky, whom he admired so profoundly; he wore that mantle with such dignity and grace that it never appeared to be a borrowed garment. Like Tchaikovsky, Rachmaninoff was temperamentally opposed to composers who wrote music to dogmas or creeds or who tried to endow their works with mystic concepts; and so he had never much sympathy for the school of the "Russian Five" or the works of Scriabin, whose impress on Russian musical thinking was so far-reaching in the early years of Rachmaninoff's career. Like Tchaikovsky's, Rachmaninoff's roots were embedded in tradition. While he was intellectually stimulated by the innovations of Stravinsky and Prokofiev, he could never bring himself to think as they did. Like Tchaikovsky, Rachmaninoff was always a sad and lonely man, a man whose intense melancholy and perpetual feeling of desolation echo and re-echo in the music he wrote.

Rachmaninoff did not bring to music that which it did not have before him. He was satisfied that the materials he had acquired as a student served his artistic purposes fully. But how admirably he used those materials, with what mastery of formal structure and variety of lyrical expressiveness and harmonic beauty! With techniques and traditions acquired from others, Rachmaninoff nevertheless was able to bring to music a creative vein that was his own. He was never the innovator, never the original thinker. But what he felt so sensitively he was able to put down on paper—and in music of often overpowering sentiment and beauty.

Rachmaninoff was born in Onega, Novgorod, on April 1, 1873. At the St. Petersburg Conservatory he was more or less apathetic toward his music studies. Not until he was aroused by an imaginative teacher, Zverev, did he realize some of the potentialities of his native gifts. In 1885, he transferred to the Moscow Conservatory, where he was a brilliant pupil. He won prizes and he wrote an opera, *Aleko,* which was presented at the Moscow Opera. Soon after this, he achieved international fame as a composer with his Prelude in C-sharp Minor, for piano; and he made his mark as a pianist and a conductor.

But though success came early, it was not destined to remain with him permanently. The première performances of his First Piano Concerto and his First Symphony were outright failures, inducing in Rachmaninoff a morbidity which for several years frustrated all his attempts at composition. Not until 1901 was he able to emerge from this period of futility and despair; but when he did, he was to write a series of masterpieces which won the acclaim of the entire music world, the most important of which was the Second Piano Concerto.

Having found his stride as a composer, Rachmaninoff decided to escape from his many activities as pianist and conductor in order to devote himself unsparingly to creative work. He went to Dresden and lived there for several years, working intensively on such major works as the Second Symphony and *The Isle of the Dead*.

In 1909, Rachmaninoff began the first of many tours to the United States. In that first tour, he appeared in the triple role of conductor, pianist, and composer, receiving handsome appreciation in all three capacities. Subsequently, he relegated conducting to a minor role; but up to the end of his life, he maintained his industry as pianist and composer, achieving international prominence in both fields.

Unsympathetic to the Soviet regime, Rachmaninoff left his native land permanently in 1917, never to return. He established his home first in Switzerland and then in this country. An outspoken foe of the Soviets, Rachmaninoff was for a long time violently attacked in his own country: in 1931, for example, the Moscow *Evening Gazette* condemned his music for its "decadent ideas of a bourgeois." In the closing years of his life, Rachmaninoff not only found himself and his music accepted in the Soviet

Union, but even glorified. Since his death, the Soviets have considered him as a model for emulation.

In the winter of 1939, the Philadelphia Orchestra presented a three-concert cycle of Rachmaninoff's works, in which Rachmaninoff once again appeared in the triple role of composer, conductor, and pianist. His last major work, *Symphonic Dances,* was completed one year later. On March 28, 1943, Rachmaninoff died at his home in Beverly Hills, California.

The following works by Rachmaninoff are discussed below: Concerto No. 2 in C Minor for Piano and Orchestra; Concerto No. 3 in D Minor for Piano and Orchestra; Concerto No. 4 in G Minor for Piano and Orchestra; *The Isle of the Dead;* Preludes; *Rhapsody on a Theme of Paganini; Symphonic Dances;* Symphony No. 2 in E Minor; Symphony No. 3 in A Minor.

CONCERTO NO. 2 IN C MINOR FOR PIANO AND ORCHESTRA, op. 18 (1901). I. Moderato. II. Adagio sostenuto. III. Allegro scherzando.

Rachmaninoff wrote his first Piano Concerto, in F-sharp Minor, op. 1, in 1890-91, when he was still a music student. He himself introduced it in Moscow, with Safonov conducting, in 1891. It was a failure. A few years later, the equally emphatic failure of his First Symphony plunged the composer into a despondency which stultified all creative effort. Now convinced that he was without talent, Rachmaninoff could work no more. What was worse, his morbidity became so intense that a complete nervous breakdown seemed to be at hand. A prominent physician by the name of Dr. Dahl was enlisted to help the composer. Painstakingly, patiently, the physician worked on Rachmaninoff through the powers of autosuggestion. Eventually he succeeded in restoring the composer's shattered confidence. Reassurance returned, and with it the will to compose.

One of the works Rachmaninoff wrote in this period of revived self-confidence was the Second Concerto for Piano and Orchestra. Appropriately enough, it was dedicated to Dr. Dahl, who had made it possible. The concerto proved to be one of Rachmaninoff's greatest works, and one of his most successful. More than any other of his compositions—except perhaps for the fabulous C-sharp Minor Prelude—it helped to spread his reputation throughout the world of music. Its first performance, on October 27, 1901 (the composer was the soloist with the Moscow Philharmonic Society), was a triumph. Three years later it won the Glinka Prize. Since then it has been heard more often than any other of Rachmaninoff's large works. After Rachmaninoff's death, the popularity of the concerto continued to swell in this country. One of its principal melodies became a popular song and reached the "Hit Parade"; the concerto itself was used as the basis of three major motion pictures, including Noel Coward's *Brief Moment.*

Its popularity is not difficult to explain. It is a veritable treasure house of tender sentiments, expressive feelings, nostalgic moods. And what a wealth of fresh melodies there are here! The passionate sweep of the strings in the first movement, erupting immediately after the introductory chords of the piano, and offset by the second theme, so expressive of feminine yearnings and tenderness; the exquisite song for flute, against the arpeggios of the piano, evoking an atmosphere of indescribable peace in the second movement; the justly famous oriental and sensual melody for strings in the third movement—the emotional impact of such pages never seems to lose its force.

SYMPHONY NO. 2 IN E MINOR, op. 27 (1907). I. Largo; Allegro moderato. II. Allegro molto. III. Adagio. IV. Allegro vivace.

Rachmaninoff composed his First Symphony (in D Minor, op. 13) in 1895. The first performance, conducted by Glazunov, at a Belaiev concert in St. Petersburg, was a failure. The performance was a slipshod affair; besides, the music itself did not seem to have much of an appeal. The failure of this symphony, followed by that of the First Piano Concerto, brought the composer to the brink of a nervous breakdown. Out of this period of silence and morbidity, Rachmaninoff emerged creatively revitalized. He composed his first masterpiece, the Second Piano Concerto. Then, retiring to Dresden to devote himself to creative work entirely, he wrote his Second Symphony and *The Isle of the Dead*.

Completed in 1907, the Second Symphony was heard on January 26, 1908 in Moscow under the composer's direction. It was an unqualified success. It won the Glinka Prize (the second time the composer was thus honored).

The symphony—often music of intense melancholy—reflects Rachmaninoff's debt to Tchaikovsky. The long opening introduction (Largo) is the kind of plangent music that reminds us of the closing movement of the *Pathétique Symphony*. It is, perhaps, more introspective than Tchaikovsky; but the Russian pain is there. Powerful chords destroy the mood, and the violins begin the Allegro moderato section with a hint of the main theme, which, when fully realized, is somewhat excitable in nature. Strings and wind bring the second subject, quieter than the first. A shattering climax, in which the principal melody of the movement is quoted by the solo violin, is gradually evolved before the development begins. The return of the principal ideas follows, after which comes an elaborate coda.

The first movement is generally introspective and sad; the second, a scherzo, is vigorous, comprising two themes and a trio. The scherzo subject becomes the subject of an elaborate fugue.

The slow movement is rich with expressive ideas: one for the violins; another for the clarinet; a third for violins and oboe. This is the mood of the opening Largo—reflective music touched with an indefinable yearning and sadness.

A long, slow introduction starts the final movement. A march melody is played by the wind instruments; following this there comes a beautiful idea for violins, in octaves. An extended working-out of this material leads to the recapitulation and coda.

THE ISLE OF THE DEAD, tone-poem for orchestra, op. 29 (1908).

Between 1906 and 1908, Rachmaninoff lived in seclusion in Dresden, a refugee from his many activities in Russia as pianist and conductor. He had come to Germany to devote himself entirely to creative work.

In an art gallery in Leipzig one day, Rachmaninoff saw the Arnold Böcklin painting, *The Isle of the Dead*. The grim picture gripped the imagination of the composer. The tall, ghostly cypresses and menacing cliffs stood brooding over the waters, on which there approached a Stygian boatman conveying a flag-draped coffin and a lonely mourner. Rachmaninoff decided to set this picture to music. He completed his tone-poem in 1908. On May 1, 1909, he himself conducted its première performance in Moscow.

The gentle lapping of the waters is heard throughout the work in a musical figure in alternating rhythms, first played by the cellos, then by other instruments. The main theme, invoking an atmosphere of tranquillity, is given by the horns. But a plangent note is soon interpolated by a solo violin. Divided strings then bring up subdued expressions of mourning. The cellos suggest the Catholic Requiem, with a brief quotation of the *Dies Irae*. The despair deepens, the emotions become more tortured as woodwinds and brass bring the music to a climax. Then the intense feelings are relaxed. The thematic material of the opening returns to bring back dark serenity: the boat disappears into the blackness, and the lapping waters continue to murmur to the cypresses.

CONCERTO NO. 3 IN D MINOR FOR PIANO AND ORCHESTRA, op. 30 (1909). I. Allegro ma non troppo. II. Adagio. III. Alla breve.

The Third Concerto followed the Second by eight years. In 1909, Rachmaninoff came to this country for the first of his many tours here. Having just completed his Third Concerto, he decided to introduce it during his visit. On November 28, 1909, he performed it in New York City under Walter Damrosch's direction.

Two introductory measures for orchestra usher in the piano with the first major theme, which is Slavic in character. After this idea has been discussed, the second theme enters pianissimo in the strings, and is then elaborated in a passionate section. A rather detailed development follows, leading into a cadenza for piano which is one of the finest pages in the entire work; this cadenza, incidentally, is accompanied. Thematic material of the preceding pages returns, and the movement ends in a subdued mood.

The second movement is an intermezzo, the principal idea of which is a lovely Russian melody, first heard in the woodwinds, then repeated in turn by the strings and the piano. This melody is worked out extensively before a new theme (clarinet and bassoons) enters against the background of a waltz rhythm in the strings.

The final movement comes without pause, with an energetic passage for the piano. The orchestra replies with equal vigor. Music of considerable restlessness follows. There is a relaxation of this nervous energy as ideas from the first movement are recalled. But the agitation is soon resumed, and the concerto ends with a fiery and brilliantly sonorous coda.

PRELUDES, for piano, opp. 23, 32 (1903-1910).

If there is a single piece of music which is inextricably associated with the name of Sergei Rachmaninoff, that piece is surely the Prelude in C-sharp Minor, op. 3, No. 2, written in 1892. The composer could hardly have guessed that this little item—effective though it is—would blaze his name throughout the world of music; that, as a matter of fact, it would haunt him for the rest of his life. This prelude is the second of five pieces for the piano which Rachmaninoff wrote in 1892, almost a decade before he succumbed to his terrible desolation and artistic impotence. In performances and in publication, it traveled around the world. It was even responsible for Rachmaninoff's early successes as a pianist. Audiences everywhere came primarily to hear him play his own prelude whenever he gave a recital!

It is a vividly descriptive piece of music which, though without a program, invites extramusical interpretation. And it is characteristic of the best preludes that Rachmaninoff was to wr'·e later in his career. These preludes are more like miniature dramas than mood pictures or atmospheric vignettes. They are so vibrantly graphic that they encourage programmatic interpretation.

Rachmaninoff wrote twenty-five preludes: the C-sharp Minor, op. 3, no. 2, in 1892; the set of ten in op. 23, in 1903; and the set of thirteen in op. 32, in 1910.

Almost a rival in popularity to the Prelude in C-sharp Minor is the one in G Minor, op. 32, no. 5, music of stirring martial character that seems to suggest the marching of men to war; the contrasting lyric section seems to suggest the poignancy of homesickness. Other preludes suggest dramatic surges and conflicts—notably the E-flat Minor, op. 23, no. 9, and the F Minor, op. 32, no. 6. The yearning and anxiety of the F Major Prelude, op. 32, no. 7, is equally expressive. Occasionally, however, these preludes arrive at a simple, classical beauty, as those in E-flat Major, op. 23, no. 6, and G-flat Major, op. 23, no. 10.

CONCERTO NO. 4 IN G MINOR FOR PIANO AND ORCHES-TRA, op. 40 (1926). I. Allegro vivace; Alla breve. II. Largo. III. Allegro vivace.

Like the Third Concerto, the Fourth received its première in this country. On March 18, 1927, Rachmaninoff introduced it with the Philadelphia Orchestra, Leopold Stokowski conducting. Eleven years after the première, Rachmaninoff subjected the concerto to revision.

After six measures of introduction, the piano enters with a characteristic Rachmaninoff theme, a broad, majestic melody. Some subsidiary ideas are then contributed, after which the tempo changes to moderato and the piano enters with the second lyrical theme, less spacious than the first and more poignant. The slow movement opens with five introductory bars by the piano. The strings then voice the principal melody, full of Russian pathos, which is soon taken up by piano with some elaboration. After the strings, woodwinds, and horns continue with this theme, a brief agitated section is interpolated. A new idea is momentarily introduced (piano with accompaniment by clarinets), but the original melody soon returns. The third movement enters without interruption. A movement full of brilliant colors and dynamic rhythmic drive, it reintroduces thematic material heard in the preceding two movements.

RHAPSODY ON A THEME OF PAGANINI, for piano and orchestra, op. 43 (1934).

Though Rachmaninoff designated this work a "rhapsody" it is actually a set of twenty-four variations on a Paganini theme. The theme—taken from the Caprice No. 24 for solo violin—is the same one which served Brahms for his *Variations on a Theme of Paganini,* op. 35.

In Rachmaninoff's *Rhapsody,* the theme is first heard in its entirety (violins, later taken up by piano) only after the completion of the first variation. The brief orchestral prelude that opens the work gives a hint of it, however.

It is interesting to note that in this rhapsody (as in the earlier *Isle of the Dead*) Rachmaninoff interpolates a quotation of the liturgical melody *Dies Irae,* which appears in variations 7, 10, and 24. The climax of the entire work, as a matter of fact, comes with a brilliant and majestic statement of the *Dies Irae* in full orchestra. Rachmaninoff never explained the significance of this quotation.

Rachmaninoff completed this work in 1934 in Switzerland. On November 7 of the same year it received its first performance, in Philadelphia. The composer was the soloist, and the Philadelphia Orchestra was conducted by Leopold Stokowski.

SYMPHONY NO. 3 IN A MINOR, op. 33 (1936). I. Allegro moderato. II. Adagio non troppo. III. Allegro.

Thirty years elapsed between the Second and the Third Symphony. The latter was completed in Switzerland in 1936. On November 6 of the same year, Leopold Stokowski directed the première performance in Philadelphia with the Philadelphia Orchestra.

Lawrence Gilman characterized this symphony as a "profusion of those sweeping cantabile phrases, darkened by moods of melancholy and brooding and impassioned stress.... Somber, lyrical, defiant, it is a work wholly representative of the Slavic genius and Rachmaninoff in particular."

The symphony opens in a melancholy vein. A headlong movement of the strings and woodwinds invokes the first subject (oboes and bassoons). The second subject is a broad, mobile melody for the cellos.

A ten-measure theme for horn opens the second movement. Then there comes one of the most eloquent pages in the entire symphony—a melody for solo violin, set against chords in the woodwinds and brass. The melody grows in beauty and richness as it is taken up by all the violins in unison. A solo flute then enters with the second theme. The music now becomes more passionate and virile, but the movement ends as it began, moody and somber. The finale is impetuous music. The first theme is uncontrolled energy (violins and violas). The surge is kept in check for a while, as a somewhat more lyrical page of music is presented, but only for a while. The original momentum is re-created and reaches a climax. An elaborate fugue follows, the theme of which is derived from the first subject. There is a brief return of lyricism, and then the symphony ends in an orgiastic outburst of energy.

SYMPHONIC DANCES, for orchestra, op. 45 (1940). I. Non allegro. II. Andante con moto: tempo di valse. III. Lento assai; Allegro vivace.

Rachmaninoff's apotheosis of the dance was his last major work. He completed it in Huntington, Long Island, in 1940. The following January it was heard for the first time in Philadelphia, with Eugene Ormandy conducting the Philadelphia Orchestra.

The work was not intended by the composer as dance music, but rather as music inspired by the dance. It is essentially symphonic in its writing, devoid of any program. The composer originally intended appending the subtitles "Midday," "Twilight," and "Midnight" to the respective movements, but discarded this idea because he wanted the music to be disassociated from all extramusical suggestions. The hint of the dance is brought up, however, in the use of the waltz rhythm in the second movement, and in the exploitation of the rhythms of popular music in the closing movement. But the interest in the work lies exclusively in the music itself, in its rhythmic ingenuity and brilliant instrumental colors.

MAURICE RAVEL   1875—1937

When Ravel's *Histoires Naturelles* was introduced in Paris in 1907, a storm of controversy—long brewing—suddenly erupted. Some critics, headed by Pierre Lalo, accused Ravel outright of plagiarizing Debussy, of buying fame with the counterfeit coin of imitating a fashionable composer. It was not so much that the declamation of *Histoires Naturelles* made these critics recall the melodic line in *Pelléas et Mélisande,* nor that Ravel's harmonic language borrowed chords identified with Debussy. The simple truth was that they simply did not like *Histoires Naturelles*—Lalo called it a "café-concert with ninths"—and, provoked by this dislike, they launched an attack on Ravel's derivativeness. Other critics—of whom M. D. Calvocoressi and Georges Jean-Aubry were the most vocal—insisted that though Ravel had been influenced by Debussy, he had a pronounced artistic personality of his own.

From the perspective of time, it is not difficult to decide on which side the truth lay. Ravel's music is no more Debussy (even in those works which have such striking titular similarity to compositions by his celebrated contemporary) than it is later Stravinsky in creations that revert to the classical past. Whatever Ravel has written—and this goes even for his early Quartet in F Major—is characterized by his own individual approach to technique and style. Precise, direct, transparent, intellectual, almost classical in form, Ravel was actually the antithesis of Debussy—whose writing was vague, sensual, and loose in formal construction.

Debussy had been an influence, of course; it was hardly possible for a young composer to function in the Paris of the early twentieth century without reacting to the impact of Debussy's new music. But actually there were other influence's in Ravel's development which were more pronounced. There was the influence of Spanish music, to which Ravel had been susceptible from the very first, and which was responsible for works ranging from his early *Habanera* (1895) to such later masterpieces as *Rapsodie Espagnole, Bolero, L'Heure Espagnole, "Alborada del Gracioso,"* etc. There was the influence of Erik Satie, which resulted in the wry irony, subtle humor, and delicate wit of *Histoires Naturelles, L'Enfant et les Sortilèges, L'Heure Espagnole.* There was the influence of the Viennese waltz: *La Valse* and *Valses Nobles et Sentimentales.*

But in spite of all these influences—and in others—Ravel was no imitator of any existing style. It was, rather, the starting point for his own thinking; and the processes of that thinking—and the final thought—became distinctly Ravel's own. Hoerée put it well when he wrote that in subjecting himself to varied influences, Ravel was actually an innovator. "He works 'on a motif' like a painter. He installs himself before a Mozart sonata or a Saint-Saëns concerto as an artist does before a group of trees. When his work is finished, it is usually impossible to find any traces of the model." Or, to carry the idea still further, where the traces of the model are still in evidence, they have undergone such transformation that the model itself is completely forgotten. The personality of his melody (which often acquires a novel character through the use of Phrygian and Dorian modes), of his bold and adventurous harmony, of his exquisite workmanship, of his delicately projected moods, from wit and satire to outright enchantment, are the fingerprints by which his works are always readily identified.

Maurice Ravel was born in the town of Ciboure, in the Basque region of France, on March 7, 1875. Remarkably talented in music, he was taken to Paris when he was twelve years old to begin study seriously. In 1889 he entered the Paris Conservatory, where his teachers included Charles de Bériot, Pessard, Gédalge, and Fauré. Though he was an exceptional student and revealed an unmistakable creative gift, Ravel failed on four occasions to win the greatly desired Prix de Rome. The fourth attempt was in 1905—after he had written such remarkable works as the *Jeux d'Eau* and the tender elegy *Pavane pour une Infante Défunte,* both for piano, the *Schéhérazade,* for voice and orchestra, and the String Quartet in F Major. The injustice of denying the Prix de Rome to a composer of such gifts created a veritable scandal, which brought about the resignation of Théodore Dubois as head of the Conservatory, and his replacement by Fauré.

During World War I, Ravel enlisted in the French Army and served at the front in the motor corps. His health and spirit were shattered by the experiences of the war, and he was soon discharged. Soon after the war, Ravel bought a villa in Montfort l'Amaury, where he lived in comparative retirement for the remainder of his life. His life was devoted to his composition. A slow worker who was painstakingly fastidious about every detail, he did not produce many compositions; but what he did write was of the first order and placed him in the vanguard of contemporary composers, and among the foremost in France. In 1928, Ravel visited the United States, conducting orchestras and appearing as pianist in performances of his works.

An automobile accident in France brought about a lesion of the brain, necessitating an operation from which Ravel never recovered completely. He died in Paris on December 28, 1937.

The following works by Ravel are discussed below: *Bolero; Concerto for the Left Hand;* Concerto in G Major for Piano and Orchestra; *Daphnis et Chloé; L'Enfant et les Sortilèges (The Child and the Sorcerers); Gaspard de la Nuit; L'Heure Espagnole; Introduction and Allegro; Jeux d'Eau;*

Miroirs; Mother Goose (Ma Mère l'Oye); Quartet in F Major; *Rapsodie Espagnole;* Sonatina for Piano; *Le Tombeau de Couperin;* Trio in A Minor; *Tzigane;* La Valse; *Valses Nobles et Sentimentales.*

For *"Alborada del Gracioso,"* see *Miroirs;* for *Habanera,* see *Rapsodie Espagnole;* for *"Ondine,"* see *Gaspard de la Nuit;* for *Pavane pour une Infante Défunte,* see the biographical sketch above and *Jeux d'eau;* for Septet, see *Introduction and Allegro.*

JEUX D'EAU, for piano (1901).

A line from a poem by H. de Regnier—"a river god laughing at the waters as they caress him"—stirred Ravel's imagination and impelled him to write a descriptive piano piece. "This piece," explained the composer, "inspired by the sound of water and the music of fountains, cascades, and streams, is founded on two motifs, after the fashion of the first movement of a sonata, without, however, being subjected to the classical plan."

Jeux d'Eau is not only a gem of descriptive writing in which the water is made to laugh and play in scintillating cascades of tones: It is also the source of a new technique for the writing of piano music from which many of Ravel's contemporaries (even Debussy) were to profit. It brought to the piano sonorities and colors it had not known before; and its use of the highest register of the piano was revolutionary.

Ricardo Viñes introduced *Jeux d'Eau* at a concert of the Société Nationale in Paris on April 5, 1902. At this same concert he introduced still another Ravel gem for the piano: the delicate and tender *Pavane pour une Infante Défunte,* written in 1899.

Jeux d'Eau was well received; and in performances and in publication it soon traveled triumphantly throughout the world of music, making the name of its composer famous. Regrettably, Ravel himself thought so little of the commercial possibilities of this piece that he did not bother to copyright it; its phenomenal world-wide success, therefore, brought him few returns.

QUARTET IN F MAJOR, for strings (1903). I. Allegro moderato. II. Assai vif. III. Très lent. IV. Vif et agité.

Ravel's Quartet, the first of his masterpieces, was written when he was only twenty-eight. It is one of his most spontaneous works. Many years later, at the height of his mastery, Ravel regarded this youthful work with satisfaction; he said that though his later chamber music revealed greater technical adroitness, he preferred the Quartet for its freshness.

The Quartet, which Ravel dedicated to Fauré, was Ravel's first major success. Introduced by the Heyman Quartet on March 5, 1904, at a concert of the Société Nationale in Paris, it was a triumph. Some critics did not hesitate to call it a masterpiece. "In the name of the gods of music and of my own," Debussy wrote to the young composer, "do not change one thing in your Quartet!"

It is a melodious work, abundant in its lyric ideas. There is nothing remote or obscure about it; its charm is evident even with a casual acquaintance. The first movement, in sonata form, consists of two main themes, both suave and aurally pleasing, and built up with great effect. The scherzo that follows opens with a delightful pizzicato section; a broadly melodic middle section provides contrast. The slow movement is a poem of gracious moods and tender sentiments that makes us think of Debussy. The work ends effectively with music that alternates between storm and calm.

MIROIRS, for piano (1905). I. *"Noctuelles."* II. *"Oiseaux Tristes."* III. *"Une Barque sur l'Océan."* IV. *"Alborada del Gracioso."* V. *"La Vallée des Cloches."*

With *Miroirs,* Ravel entered a new phase of artistic development. The harmony becomes so daring that Ravel felt it would "put many musicians out of countenance who up to now have been most familiar with my style"; the modulations are freer; the rhythm patterns more varied; the developments more extended.

The five pieces of *Miroirs* are tone-pictures reflecting, rather than duplicating, their subjects, and completely divorced from the emotions of their creator.

Ravel considered *"Oiseaux Tristes"* the most typical of the group. "In it, I evoke birds lost in the torpor of a somber forest, during the most torrid hours of summertime."

"Une Barque sur l'Océan" is a shimmer of varying colors in its description of the changing sea. It is one of Ravel's most sensitive portraits. But to the French critics of 1905 it proved a baffling piece of music. Gaston Carraud thought that because the "spectacle changes every instant," it was a "bewildering kaleidoscope. One does not know what sort of weather is to be found on this ocean." (In 1908, Ravel orchestrated this piece.)

The most famous number of the entire suite is the *"Alborada del Gracioso."* *Alborada* is a morning serenade; and *gracioso* implies buffoonery. Utilizing a characteristic Spanish rhythm, Ravel brings about a delicate blend of irony and vivid tone-painting. This work is as famous in the orchestral transcription, which Ravel himself prepared in 1912, as in its original piano version.

Each of the five pieces is dedicated to a different member of a group calling itself the "Apaches"—young Parisian intellectuals (of whom Ravel was one) who met regularly to discuss art, music, and literature.

The first performance of *Miroirs* took place in Paris on January 6, 1906, at a concert of the Société Nationale. The pianist was Ricardo Viñes, to whom *"Oiseaux Tristes"* is dedicated.

SONATINA FOR PIANO (1905). I. Modéré. II. Mouvement de menuet. III. Animé.

This work is slight only in its architectonic dimensions; in artistic content it is a major work, one of Ravel's finest, stamped "with the double seal of youth and mastery," in the words of Roland-Manuel. On March 10, 1906, it was introduced in Lyons by Mme. de Lestang. Classical in its form, which is the very quintessence of perfection, it consists of a melancholy first movement, a minuet of rare grace, and a vitally dynamic concluding movement.

INTRODUCTION AND ALLEGRO, for harp with string quartet, flute, and clarinet (1906).

Ravel wrote the *Introduction and Allegro* for the Parisian harpist, Micheline Kahn. She introduced it in Paris on February 22, 1907, at a concert of the Cercle Musical.

The Introduction opens with a duet for flute and clarinet. The principal melodic idea of this section is an extended melody for the cello against the background of violin, flute, and clarinet. The intensity of the music grows, the tempo quickens, the sonority expands. The Allegro now enters without interruption, opening with a long and appealing harp solo. This melody is soon taken up by the flute, then by the other instruments. A rather involved development follows. Towards the end of the work a harp cadenza recalls some of the principal melodic ideas.

RAPSODIE ESPAGNOLE, suite for orchestra (1907). I. Prélude à la Nuit. II. Malagueña. III. Habanera. IV. Feria.

This rhapsody is one of several works in which Ravel's fascination for Spanish subjects is evident. And it is one of his major creations. On March 15, 1908, it was introduced at a Colonne concert, Eduard Colonne conducting; its success was so great that the second movement had to be repeated.

A four-note motif in muted strings brings up a tranquil scene. (This motif is used several times throughout the work.) One by one the sections of the orchestra pick up this theme. A cadenza for clarinets, and another for bassoon, leads into the second section, the main theme of which is heard in the double basses and after some evolution is repeated by bassoons, and then by muted trumpets. After a brief pause, the English horn enters with an improvisation. The Habanera movement (which is an adaptation of the *Habanera,* for two pianos, which Ravel wrote in 1895) is interesting for its rhythmic cogency. The Habanera rhythm (first projected in the clarinets) dominates the entire movement. In the concluding section, the music erupts with vital colors and spirited animation; the music is made rhythmically alive through an adroit use of the percussion. The gaiety subsides somewhat in the middle section (a song for English horn, followed by a repetition of the principal theme of the first movement). Then the excitement returns, and the music moves energetically to a grandiose climax.

GASPARD DE LA NUIT, for piano (1908). I. Ondine. II. Le Gibet. III. Scarbo.

Ravel was inspired by poems of Aloysius Bertrand to write a suite of three descriptive pieces for the piano under the collective title of *Gaspard de la Nuit*. It is one of his finest creations, in which he succeeded not only in producing piano music of "transcendental virtuosity" (in his own description) but also music full of the "fascination of dreams" and "the pervading enchantment of nocturnal visions" (Roland-Manuel).

"*Ondine*," the most famous of this trilogy, reproduces the sound of water with delicate broken chords. "*Le Gibet*," a musical portrait of the gallows, sounds the knell of doom in a persistent pedal point. "*Scarbo*" is an ironic scherzo describing a will-o'-the-wisp.

Gaspard de la Nuit was introduced by Ricardo Viñes at a concert of the Société Nationale on January 9, 1909.

L'HEURE ESPAGNOLE, comic opera (1908).

Ravel, who was always ineluctably drawn to Spanish subjects, Spanish rhythms, and Spanish melodies, came upon Franc-Nohain's mocking little comedy *L'Heure Espagnole*, and was intrigued by it. Having just completed the sardonic *Histoires Naturelles*, Ravel was in the mood to write another work in a similar vein; and *L'Heure Espagnole* seemed to provide a desirable subject.

It is a gay comedy of illicit love. Concepción is eager for her husband, the clockmaker Torquemada, to leave the shop, because she is expecting her lover. She reminds Torquemada that he must be off to regulate the town clock. No sooner is he gone when one of Concepción's lovers enters; then a second and a third. With Torquemada soon to return, Concepción insists that two of the lovers hide in the huge clocks. Torquemada finds them, but they have a ready explanation: they are customers and are only inspecting the insides of the clocks; indeed, they even buy the clocks to prove their integrity. A gay and impudent quintet ends the opera, in which the characters remind the audience that, after all, this takes place in Spain.

Ravel described *L'Heure Espagnole* as "a sort of musical conversation." It is an *opéra bouffe,* but with a difference. The touch is lighter, the mood is gayer and more ironic, the feeling more intimate than in traditional *opéras bouffes*. There is some exaggeration for humor, but it is in good taste and does not press its wit. The musical writing is crystal clear; the harmonic texture, refined; the instrumentation, always subtle.

Though written in 1908, *L'Heure Espagnole* was not performed until May 19, 1911, at which time it was presented by the Opéra Comique in Paris. The critics were only mildly appreciative. They admired Ravel's charm and technical astuteness; but many of them seemed appalled by the risqué theme of the text. However, one or two critics did sense the genuine merits of Ravel's score. Henri Ghéon, writing in the *Nouvelle Revue Française,* said: "It is miraculous to see how Franc-Nohain's buffoonery, whose comedy lies in gestures rather than words, becomes the jumping-off ground for those unexpected and unrestricted arabesques, based on the spoken word, but melodic all the same; to see how an art so concentrated and absorbed by the problems of expression can give the impression of being so natural. His grace and gaiety, in my opinion, are supremely vocal."

MOTHER GOOSE (MA MÈRE L'OYE), suite for orchestra (1908-1912). I. Pavane of the Sleeping Beauty. II. Hop o' My Thumb. III. Laideronnette, Empress of the Pagodas. IV. Conversations of Beauty and the Beast. V. The Fairy Garden.

In 1908, Ravel wrote a piano suite for four hands based on tales from Mother Goose for Mimi and Jean, two children of his friend, Godebski. "The idea of conjuring up the poetry of childhood in these pieces," wrote Ravel, "has naturally led me to simplify my style and clarify my writing." The four-hand version was introduced at a concert of the Musicale Indépendente in Paris on April 20, 1920; the performers were six-year-old Christine Verger and ten-year-old Germaine Duramy. In 1912, Ravel orchestrated the music for a ballet which was presented at the Théâtre des Arts in Paris on January 21 of that year.

The suite is in five sections. The first is a sad and stately dance of twenty measures. For the second, Ravel quoted the following passage from the Perrault tale to describe the music: "He believed that he would easily find his path by means of his bread crumbs, which he had scattered wherever he had passed; but he was very much surprised when he could not find a single crumb; the birds had come and eaten everything up."

In the third part, the story of Laideronnette is told. Laideronnette, daughter of a king, is cursed with ugliness by a wicked princess; her beauty is restored through the love of a prince.

The conversation between Beauty and the Beast consists of a little waltz melody, alternating with (then set against) a vulgar and brusque theme in the lower register. The suite ends with an enchanting theme for strings, out of which the entire concluding section is developed.

VALSES NOBLES ET SENTIMENTALES, for piano (1910).

La Valse was inspired by the waltz of Johann Strauss. *Valses Nobles et Sentimentales* had its roots in the infectious piano waltzes of Franz Schubert. It comprises seven waltzes and an epilogue played without interruption. The rhythms have the pulse and lilt of the Viennese waltz; but the harmonies are bold.

The waltzes were introduced by Louis Aubert at a concert of the Société Indépendante in Paris on May 9, 1911. That concert was unusual in that all compositions were presented anonymously. The intention was to confuse not only those academicians and reactionary critics in Paris who were continually attacking the new and the original, but also those gushing admirers who praised everything indiscriminately. Emile Vuillermoz revealed: "Ravel himself was seated in a loge in the midst of a group of society dilettantes who habitually swooned when they heard the sounds of Ravel's music. Heroically faithful to his oath as a conspirator, the composer of *Valses nobles et sentimentales* had not warned them that his work was included in the program. When they heard it, they began to jeer in the hope of pleasing Ravel by assailing this composition which they believed to be by someone else. Ravel accepted these manifestations in silence."

One year later, Ravel orchestrated the waltzes for a ballet called *Adelaide, or The Language of Flowers,* presented at the Théâtre de Chatelet on April 12, 1912, with Mlle. Trouhanova. The first concert version of the orchestrated waltzes took place in Paris on February 15, 1914, with Pierre Monteux conducting.

A motto by Henri de Regnier appears in the published score as a dedication "To the delicious pleasure of useless occupation."

DAPHNIS ET CHLOÉ, ballet (1911).

The impresario of the Ballet Russe, Serge Diaghilev, who was responsible for discovering the genius of Stravinsky, Manuel de Falla, and Prokofiev, also recognized Ravel's pronounced gifts early. In 1909, Diaghilev heard several Ravel works; immediately he sensed the promises they held. When, one year later, Fokine presented him with a scenario for a ballet about Daphnis and Chloë, Diaghilev went to Ravel for the music. Ravel took two years for the assignment. Strange to report of Diaghilev, whose musical instincts were so sound, he did not like Ravel's music. (A decade or so later, he was again to dislike a work that Ravel had written for him on commission—*La Valse!*) For a while, Ravel was tempted to abandon the entire project, but was prevailed upon not to do so by the music publisher Durand. After delays, caused mainly by internal dissensions in the ballet company, the Ballet Russe presented *Daphnis et Chloé* in Paris on June 8, 1912, with Pierre Monteux conducting. Nijinsky, Karsavina, and Bohm were the principal dancers. The choreography was by Fokine; the decor by Leon Bakst. The performance was not successful.

But there were some critics who recognized the distinction of Ravel's score. Jean Marnold wrote in the *Mercure de France:* "The score abounds in tableaux of the most exquisite plastic beauty.... *Daphnis et Chloé* really constitutes a 'musical drama' which offers the coherence and unity of a vast symphony. All of this music holds itself together and lives its own autonomous existence, to such an extent that the preliminary introduction of the leitmotifs would make even a blind man understand and follow the scenic action."

The source for the ballet scenario was a Greek pastoral, believed to have been written by Longus. But the original version was subjected to considerable change. In the ballet, the shepherd Daphnis dreams that Pan saves Chloë out of the memory of his love for the nymph Syrinx. Imitating Pan and Syrinx, Daphnis fashions a pipe out of reeds, and begins playing for Chloë, who dances until she falls into his arms. A general dance and a joyous tumult follow.

Even more famous than the ballet (which some now regard as one of the finest in the French repertory) are the two orchestral suites, or "series," which Ravel prepared from the score, and which have been extensively performed.

The first suite, or "series," includes the following sections: I. Nocturne. II. Interlude. III. Warlike Dance. It carries the following synposis: "A little flame suddenly burns on the head of one of the statues. The nymph comes to life and leaves her pedestal. Others descend, come together, and begin a slow and mysterious dance. They see Daphnis, bend over him, and dry his tears. Reanimating him and leading him to the rock, they invoke the God Pan. Little by little the form of the god assumes definite shape. Daphnis kneels in supplication. All is dark. Behind the scene, voices are heard, far off at first. And now there is a dim light. The pirates' camp is disclosed. There is a bold cast; the sea is in the background, with rocks to the right and left. A trireme is near the shore. Cypresses are here and there. The pirates, laden with booty, run to and fro. Torches are brought, which at last throw a strong light on the stage."

The second "series" is even more celebrated than the first. Its sections are: I. Daybreak. II. Pantomime. III. General Dance. The following synopsis appears in the score: "No sound but the murmur of rivulets fed by the dew that trickles from the rocks. Daphnis lies stretched before the grotto of the nymphs. Little by little the day dawns. The songs of birds are heard. Afar off a shepherd leads his flock. Another shepherd crosses the back of the stage. Herdsmen enter, seeking Daphnis and Chloë. They find Daphnis and awaken him. In anguish he looks about for Chloë. She at last appears encircled by shepherdesses. The two rush into each other's arms. Daphnis observes Chloë's crown. His dream was a prophetic vision; the intervention of Pan is manifest. The old shepherd Lammon explains that Pan saved Chloë in remembrance of the nymph Syrinx, whom the god loved.

"Daphnis and Chloë mime the story of Pan and Syrinx. Chloë impersonates the young nymph wandering over the meadow. Daphnis as Pan appears and declares his love for her. The nymph repulses him; the god becomes more insistent. She disappears among the reeds. In desperation he plucks some stalks, fashions a flute, and on it plays a melancholy tune. Chloë comes out and imitates the accents of the flute with her dance. The dance grows more and more animated. In mad whirlings, Chloë falls into the arms of Daphnis. Before the altar of the nymphs he swears on two sheep his fidelity. Young girls enter; they are dressed as bacchantes, and shake their tambourines. Daphnis and Chloë embrace tenderly. A group of young men come on the stage. Joyous tumult. A general dance. Daphnis and Chloë."

TRIO IN A MINOR, for piano, violin, and cello (1914). I. Modéré. II. Pantoum: assez vif. III. Passecaille; Très large. IV. Finale: animé.

Ravel once confessed that in this piano trio he was influenced by the early trios of Saint-Saëns; and what influenced Ravel particularly was Saint-Saëns' clarity and economy. Ravel's trio is a work reduced to essentials. It is a masterpiece of form and technique in its avoidance of all superfluous details.

Roland-Manuel wrote that the trio is a work "at once serious and impassioned, in which each instrument is clearly outlined in the enhancement of the melody." The best movements, according to Roland-Manuel, are the first (for the ingenuity of structure and the originality of metrical design) and the passacaglia (in which the problem of the opposing sonorities of piano and strings is solved "with consummate lightness and distinction"). The second movement, a scherzo, is called a "pantoum," after a Malayan poetic form calling for two independent thoughts moving in parallel lines.

LE TOMBEAU DE COUPERIN, suite for piano (1917). I. Prélude. II. Fugue. III. Forlane. IV. Rigaudon. V. Menuet. VI. Toccata.

During World War I, Ravel planned the writing of a musical composition honoring the memory of friends who had died in battle.

He had in 1914 begun work on a musical tribute to the great French composer of harpsichord music, François Couperin-le-Grand (1668-1733). It was a suite comprising seventeenth-century forms and dances and written with seventeenth-century economy and transparency. Work on this suite was interrupted when Ravel enlisted in the French Army. But in 1917, back in civilian life, Ravel resumed work on the suite, and at that time he decided to make this composition the gesture of homage to the war dead that he had been planning for some time. Though written for the war dead—and at a time when Ravel was further depressed by the death of his beloved mother— there is no undercurrent of either pity or sorrow beneath the serene classic surface of this music. It is music of tranquillity which has caught the spirit of an age long gone.

The suite was introduced in Paris in April, 1919. Some time later, Ravel transcribed the music for small orchestra (omitting the fugue and toccata movements). The orchestral version was heard for the first time on February 28, 1920, in a performance of the Pasdeloup Orchestra, Rhené-Baton conducting.

LA VALSE, for orchestra (1919).

Ravel loved the Viennese waltz, particularly the waltzes of Schubert and Johann Strauss. For many years he had planned writing a Viennese waltz of his own for use as a ballet. A commission by Diaghilev in 1919 set Ravel working on this idea. He conceived the ballet "as a kind of apotheosis of the Viennese waltz," as he later wrote, "linked, in my mind, with the impression of a fantastic whirl of destiny."

In the published score, the following descriptive paragraph is found: "Whirling clouds give glimpses, through rifts, of couples dancing. The clouds scatter, little by little. One sees an immense hall peopled with a twirling crowd. The scene is gradually illuminated. The light of the chandeliers bursts forth, fortissimo. An Imperial court, in or about 1855."

The waltz opens vaguely in the basses. Suddenly a waltz rhythm springs to life. It grows until a fully developed Viennese waltz is heard, in the best traditions of Johann Strauss. But suddenly the music becomes bitter as a few strident chords break the gay spell. The waltz returns, but it is now harsh and dissonant. The music grows more and more feverish. The mood is now that of despair. Discords bring the work to a close. In this transformation of the waltz from gaiety to tragedy, Ravel has portrayed Vienna itself, from its prewar abandon and light heart to its postwar futility and despair.

Diaghilev did not like La Valse, felt that it did not have choreographic possibilities, and refused to perform it. (Diaghilev's harsh opinion of the work brought about a permanent rupture between him and the composer.) But, perhaps as vindication for the work, it was extraordinarily successful when the Lamoureux Orchestra performed it on December 12, 1920, with Camille Chevillard conducting. Some years later, Ida Rubinstein included it in her repertory with equal success.

L'ENFANT ET LES SORTILÈGES (THE CHILD AND THE SORCERERS), fantasy (1924).

During World War I, the director of the Paris Opéra approached Colette, the novelist, to write a stage work—a *divertissement féerique* (a comedy of magic) that could be set to music. When this assignment was completed, both Colette and the director agreed that Ravel was the logical candidate to write the music. A copy of the text was dispatched to the composer. At that time, however, Ravel was at the front, in the motor corps, and the text never reached him. After the war, the comedy was brought to his attention. Though he reacted favorably to it (he always had a special weakness for fantasies of all kinds) he did not get around to the job of composition until 1924.

Colette's little play was, indeed, made to order for Ravel's temperament and talents. The fairy tale takes place in Normandy, where a mischievous boy, severely upbraided by his mother for his refusal to do his lessons, avenges himself by breaking up the furniture in the room and torturing domestic animals. The furniture suddenly comes to life and taunts the boy. Out of one of the books he has destroyed—his favorite—the Princess of a fairy tale comes into being to say she will have nothing more to do with him. Suddenly the child finds himself outside of the house. The trees, the squirrel, and the tree-frogs arrive to threaten him. But in the ensuing confusion, the squirrel is hurt. The boy tends to the animal. This kind act appeases the boy's attackers; the animals carry him back to his home, where his mother is waiting for him.

Ravel wrote his music, as he said, in the spirit of an "American operetta"—with an abundance of tongue-in-cheek humor. In one of his most provocative scenes he has a duet in cat language: the mewing of the cats grows out of the melodic line. In another scene—the dance of the cup and the teapot—he burlesques American fox-trot music. But Ravel's music is not exclusively satirical. At other places he evokes a world of enchantment— the child's magic world of imagination—in music of the greatest delicacy. He has given us few pages of music that are realized with such exquisite finesse as his musical description of the garden and its animal inhabitants in the opening of the second scene.

L'Enfant et les Sortilèges was introduced at the Monte Carlo Opera House on March 21, 1925, with Victor de Sabata conducting. It was so successful at this performance that the following season the Opéra Comique presented it in Paris under Albert Wolff's direction. This time the reaction was a mixed one. There were those who liked it greatly and spoke of it as a work of genius (Henri Malherbe, for example). Those who disliked it— André Messager was one of these—denounced the music for its ingenuous imitativeness as in the duet of the cats. *L'Enfant* received fifteen performances in two seasons, and could hardly be called a success.

TZIGANE, rhapsody for violin and orchestra (1924).

Ravel wrote *Tzigane* in 1924 for the violinist Yelly d'Aranyi. Conscious of her Hungarian nationality, Ravel wrote a stylization of Hungarian gypsy music. He did not intend to satirize or burlesque it. He meant to write a bravura piece of music that was Hungarian in personality and temperament. *Tzigane* exploits many of the well-known conventions of the Hungarian rhapsody form. It opens with a long slow cadenza for solo violin. After a second cadenza, this time for the harp, the main section begins with a fiery gypsy melody for the violin. Other gypsy tunes and dances follow, developed in a rhapsodic manner, and culminating in a whirlwind finish.

Tzigane was originally written for violin and "lutheal," a "lutheal" being an organlike attachment to the piano. In this version it was introduced in London on April 26, 1924, by Yelly d'Aranyi. Subsequently, Ravel orchestrated the accompaniment.

BOLERO, for orchestra (1928).

Bolero is a remarkable feat of compositional virtuosity; and, as a matter of fact, it was intended as such by the composer. For a long time Ravel had been intrigued by the idea of writing a piece of music consisting entirely of a single theme allowed to grow through harmonic and instrumental ingenuity.

In the summer of 1928, the dancer Ida Rubinstein asked Ravel to orchestrate for her Albéniz's *Iberia*. When Ravel discovered that the orchestration rights to *Iberia* belonged to Arbós, he offered to write a work of his own which would be Spanish in character. It was then that Ravel decided to experiment with his long-held idea. He took not one theme but two (a subject and its countersubject), both in the bolero rhythm. Without any development, change, or modulations, these themes were permitted to develop through change of instrumentation and sonority. The result was a musical tour de force. It was a success when Ida Rubinstein danced to it at the Paris Opéra on November 20, 1928. It was a sensation when Arturo Toscanini introduced it with the New York Philharmonic-Symphony Orchestra in New York City on November 14, 1929.

Since 1929, *Bolero* has become one of Ravel's most famous works. It has been heard in many different versions, including transcriptions for jazz band, harmonica, and two pianos; it has been incorporated into a Broadway revue; and it was the inspiration for a Hollywood movie.

Ravel himself described the work as follows: "It is a dance in a very modern movement, completely uniform in melody as well as harmony and rhythm, the latter marked without interruption by the drum. The only element of diversity is brought into play by an orchestral crescendo."

CONCERTO IN G MAJOR FOR PIANO AND ORCHESTRA

(1931). I. Allegramente; Andante a piacere. II. Adagio assai. III. Presto.

In this concerto—which took Ravel more than two years to write and sometimes kept him working ten hours a day—the composer felt he had expressed himself most completely and perfectly. Ravel explained that he conceived the work as a "concerto in the strict sense, written in the spirit of Mozart and Saint-Saëns." He completed it in 1931. On January 14, 1932, he conducted its première (as part of a Ravel festival) with the Lamoureux Orchestra; Marguerite Long was the soloist.

Henri Prunières, the eminent French critic, has provided the definitive analysis of this concerto:

"The first movement is constructed on a gay, light theme which recalls Ravel's early style. It appears first in the orchestra, while the piano supplies curious sonorous effects.... The development proceeds at a rapid pace with a surprising suppleness, vivacity, and grace. This leads to an Andante a piacere, where the piano again takes the exposition of the theme, while the bassoons, flutes, clarinets, and oboes surround it one after another with brilliant scales and runs. Then begins a grand cadenza. The orchestra enters again discreetly, at first marking the rhythm and then taking up the development, leading to a brilliant conclusion.

"The second movement consists of one of those long cantilenas which Ravel knows so well how to write.... Evolving over an implacable martellato bass, the melody is developed lengthily at the piano; then, little by little, the orchestra takes possession of it while the piano executes fine embroideries and subtle appoggiaturas.

"The Presto finale is a miracle of lightness and grace, and recalls certain scherzi and prestos of Mozart and Mendelssohn. The orchestra marks a syncopated rhythm while the piano leads the movement. The spirit of jazz animates this movement...but with great discretion."

CONCERTO FOR THE LEFT HAND, for piano left hand and orchestra (1931).

This concerto was written simultaneously with the Concerto in G Major; the two concerti represent Ravel's last major works. He wrote the left-hand concerto for the one-armed pianist Paul Wittgenstein, who introduced it in Vienna on November 27, 1931. A serious altercation between composer and performer, created by Wittgenstein's demand for certain changes in the music, drove Ravel to coach another pianist in this work: Jacques Février, who performed it in Paris on January 17, 1933.

In one movement (Lento; Allegro; Lento), this concerto utilizes jazz effects with exceptional skill. The composer explained the structure as follows: "After an introductory section, there comes an episode like an improvisation, which is succeeded by a jazz section. Only later is one aware that the jazz episode actually is built up from the themes of the first section."

MAX REGER   1873—1916

Though he liked using the contrapuntal style and forms of the sixteenth- and seventeenth-century composers, Max Reger was regarded by his own contemporaries as a revolutionary composer. For, in his attempt to enrich the articulateness of music, he utilized formidably complex harmonic and contrapuntal structures, generally too intricate for their own good; he developed monumental structures, often fussy with details; he was free in his use of modulation and abstruse in his notation.

Today we are more apt to consider Reger an academician than an iconoclast, an academician in whose music a fabulous technique and equally fabulous scholarship are more often ends in themselves rather than the means to an end. If Reger's music is not heard frequently, it is because it is too often ponderous and overelaborate. As one English critic put it: "He stifles his music with too many notes." Yet it has its role in twentieth-century music, and has had its influence. There is unquestionably great skill in this music; and at times there emerges out of the complexity a grandeur of writing.

He liked to use the old contrapuntal forms, which he did with outstanding skill, because he believed in abstract music and felt that counterpoint made possible the purest kind of music. He wrote toccatas, passacaglias, fugues, often breath-taking in their virtuosity. But he was perhaps at his best in writing variations on the themes of other composers (which would end in a fugue). Then he could give free play to all his technical adroitness and ingenuity by transforming a comparatively simple idea through all the resources of harmony, counterpoint, rhythm, and instrumentation into truly monumental structures.

Max Reger was born in Brand, Germany, on March 19, 1873. The son of a schoolteacher, he was at first intended for the teaching profession, even though he began studying music early and soon revealed exceptional talent. He passed the necessary teaching examinations. But before he assumed his first position, he met the eminent musicologist, Hugo Riemann, who, convinced of Reger's musical talent, urged him to devote himself completely to the art. In 1890, Reger enrolled at the Sonderhausen Conservatory as a student of Riemann; when Riemann went on to Wiesbaden, Reger followed him.

His studies over, Reger held minor posts as teacher of music before becoming musical director of the Leipzig University (in 1907) and professor of composition at the Leipzig Conservatory. Meanwhile, in 1906, he wrote his first major work, *Introduction, Passacaglia, and Fugue,* for two pianos. Work after work followed with amazing rapidity, increasingly complicated in style and ambitious in form, until Reger became one of the most provocative figures in German music before World War I.

When World War I came, Reger tried to volunteer in the German Army, but was found physically unacceptable. He settled in Jena to devote himself to composition, but—despite his poor health—broke his seclusion to undertake extensive concert tours. He died of a heart attack in Leipzig on May 11, 1916.

The following works by Reger are discussed below: *Four Tone-Poems after Böcklin; Variations and Fugue on a Theme by Mozart.*

FOUR TONE-POEMS AFTER BÖCKLIN, for orchestra, op. 128 (1913). I. Der geigende Eremit. II. Im Spiel der Wellen. III. Die Toteninsel. IV. Bacchanale.

Arnold Böcklin is the Swiss painter whose *Isle of the Dead* (*Die Toteninsel*) was the source of inspiration for Rachmaninoff's famous tone-poem of the same name. Reger, too, set that painting to music, in the third section of his *Four Tone-Poems;* the other three sections also owe their origin to famous Böcklin paintings.

The first, "The Hermit with a Violin," shows an old bearded friar playing on a violin for the Madonna; angels listen to him appreciatively. To give his music a medieval character, Reger used the Phrygian mode. The music of the friar is portrayed by a solo violin.

The second of Böcklin's paintings, "Sport among the Waves," describes Bacchic figures sporting in the waters. This music is a delicate but lively scherzo. A vigorous theme for horn describes the male figures; a gentle subject for strings speaks for the females.

"The Isle of the Dead," the third Böcklin painting, has been described in the section of Rachmaninoff which discusses the tone-poem of that name. Reger re-creates the mystery and desolation of the painting in a brief but highly atmospheric piece of music.

The concluding painting, "The Bacchanal," is laid outside a Roman tavern, where carousing and noisy merrymakers are involved in a brawl. The music is high-tensioned and nervous, full of contrasts, climaxes, abrupt changes of tempi, in reproducing a febrile atmosphere.

On October 12, 1913, Reger directed the première performance in Essen.

VARIATIONS AND FUGUE ON A THEME BY MOZART, for orchestra, op. 132 (1914).

The theme that Reger developed in this pretentious set of variations is the lovable subject which opens Mozart's Piano Sonata in A Major (K. 331), and which in the original setting is also subjected to variation treatment.

In Reger's work there are nine variations. In the first (L'istesso tempo), there are decorative passages in the strings around the theme, which is stated by the oboe. The rhythmic character of the theme is carried over in the second variation (Poco agitato), while in the third (Con moto) a fragment of the theme, played by clarinets and bassoons, is elaborated upon. Woodwinds and strings present the idea in the fifth variation (Quasi presto) before it is developed. The principal melody returns in the strings in the variation that follows (Sostenuto), but in a different meter. The original rhythm of the theme reappears in the seventh variation (Andante grazioso), with the theme itself stated in the horns. After the eighth variation (Molto sostenuto), there comes a culminating fugue (Allegretto grazioso) in which the theme is presented by first violins and answered by the second violins. The fugue is developed with great power, and a climax is reached with the principal melody promulgated by the trumpets.

On February 5, 1915, Reger directed the première performance in Berlin with the Orchestra of the Royal Opera.

OTTORINO RESPIGHI   1879—1936

Ottorino Respighi identified himself with the distant musical past not only through his many modern arrangements of old Italian classics, but also through many of his own works. We find him frequently indulging in the use of old modes, scales, and the plain chant: notably in such works as the *Gregorian Concerto* (for violin and orchestra), the "choreograph" *Belkis, Queen of Sheba,* and *Vetrate di Chiesa,* for orchestra.

But if Respighi's name survives in contemporary music it is not for his neo-modal music, nor even for his operas, one of which, *The Sunken Bell,* was presented at the Metropolitan Opera House in New York in 1928. Respighi's fame today rests securely on the trilogy of symphonic poems in which he recorded three different facets of Rome: its fountains, pines, and festivals. Here he is the modern composer who knows how to utilize contemporary idioms forcefully. Here he is the orchestrator of remarkable technique. Here he is the pictorial painter who can be so strikingly vivid.

It is through these poems for orchestra that Respighi earned the reputation of being one of Italy's foremost symphonic composers of our time. These successful works were responsible in encouraging other Italian composers to return to the cultivation of the symphonic field (a field which Italian composers had for so many years neglected for the sake of opera) and to bring about something of a symphonic renascence in Italy.

Respighi was born in Bolgona on July 9, 1879. His musical studies took place at the Liceo Musicale of Bologna with Sarti and Martucci; later with Rimsky-Korsakov in St. Petersburg and Max Bruch in Berlin. While still a student at the Bologna Liceo he wrote a set of symphonic variations. But it was as a concert violinist rather than as a composer that Respighi began his professional career. However, despite his successes with the violin, he felt himself drawn more and more to creative work. He wrote several major works, including a piano concerto, a quintet, and a fantasy for piano and orchestra.

In 1913, Respighi became a professor of composition at the Bologna Liceo Musicale. He remained there until 1924, when he was called to Rome to assume the post of director of the Santa Cecilia Liceo Musicale. In 1926, Respighi resigned his directorial post to devote himself completely to composition.

In the same year, Respighi visited the United States for the first time, touring the country extensively as composer and pianist. He returned to this country in 1928 to attend the Metropolitan Opera performance of his opera, *The Sunken Bell,* and again in 1932 to be present at a performance of his "mystery," *Mary of Egypt,* at Carnegie Hall, New York.

On December 17, 1932, together with nine other Italian composers (Pizzetti, Zandonai, Mule, Gasco, Toni, Pick-Mangiagalli, Guerrini, Napoli, and Zuffenato), Respighi signed a manifesto condemning those modern composers who write cerebral music. "We are against this art which cannot have and does not have any human content," ran the protest, "and desires to be merely a mechanical demonstration and a cerebral puzzle."

Respighi died in Rome on April 18, 1936, the victim of a heart attack.

The following works by Respighi are discussed below: Concerto for Piano and Orchestra; *Concerto Gregoriano for Violin and Orchestra; The Fountains of Rome; The Pines of Rome; Roman Festivals;* Toccata.

THE FOUNTAINS OF ROME, symphonic poem for orchestra (1916).

Though Respighi's *Fountains of Rome* is in four distinct sections, it is played without interruption; it is, consequently, to be regarded as an integrated symphonic poem in the manner of Liszt and Richard Strauss.

The four sections are given the following titles by the composer: I. The Fountain of Valle Giulia at Dawn. II. The Triton Fountain in the Morning. III. The Fountain of Trevi at Midday. IV. The Villa Medici Fountain at Sunset.

In the published score, the composer explained that his purpose in writing this work was "to give expression to the sentiments and visions suggested ... by four of Rome's fountains, contemplated at the hour in which their character is most in harmony with the surrounding landscape, or in which their beauty appears most impressive to the observer."

The composer also provides the program he was trying to interpret in his music: "The first part of the poem, inspired by the Fountain of Valle Giulia, depicts a pastoral landscape. Droves of cattle pass and disappear in the fresh, damp mists of a Roman dawn. A sudden loud and insistent blast above the trills of the whole orchestra introduces the second part. It is like a joyous call, summoning troops of naiads and tritons, who come running up pursuing each other and mingling in a frenzied dance between the jets of water.

"Next there appears a solemn theme, borne on the undulations of the orchestra. It is the Fountain of Trevi at midday. The solemn theme, passing from the wood to the brass instruments, assumes a triumphal character. Trumpets peal; across the radiant surface of the water there passes Neptune's chariot, drawn by sea-horses and followed by a train of sirens and tritons. The procession then vanishes, while faint trumpet blasts sound in the distance.

"The fourth part is announced by a sad theme which rises above a subdued warbling. It is the nostalgic hour of sunset. The air is full of the sound of tolling bells, birds twittering, leaves rustling. Then all dies peacefully into the silence of the night."

In *Music Since 1900* Nicolas Slonimsky notes that program annotators in this country have been perpetuating an error regarding the première performance. It took place on March 11, 1917, in Rome, with Antonio Guarnieri conducting the Augusteo Orchestra, and not (as has been generally believed) on February 10, 1918, under Toscanini.

CONCERTO GREGORIANO FOR VIOLIN AND ORCHESTRA (1922). I. Andante tranquillo; Allegro molto moderato. II. Andante espressivo e sostenuto. III. Allegro energico.

This violin concerto was introduced in Rome on February 5, 1922, with Mario Corti as soloist with the Augusteo Orchestra. When the concerto was heard in Paris a few years later, an anonymous program annotator provided the following information about the work: "The title ... was given to this work by the composer not only because the music was inspired by the Gregorian chant, but also because he sought to imbue his music with the purity and sobriety of form peculiar to the religious music of the Middle Ages. It will perhaps at first seem strange that the composer chose the form of the violin concerto as a medium wherewith to transport his listeners into the atmosphere of the church music of the Middle Ages—music so remote from all the complexities and the virtuosity of musical form in the last two centuries; a form predominantly instrumental. But, on closer examination of this score, one perceives that the work has few of the traits which usually characterize the instrumental concerto. The connection between the solo instrument and the orchestra has in this case quite a different significance: the solo violin plays, so to speak, the role of cantor in the old religious service, while the orchestra represents the choir of believers."

A few bars of ecclesiastical music ushers in the first theme, a tranquil melody for oboe which is soon taken up by the solo instrument. After the tempo changes to Allegro molto moderato, the solo violin introduces a new theme, more virile in character. A cadenza for the violin leads into the second movement, the principal theme of which (announced by solo violin against muted strings) is recognizably Gregorian. A second important idea, also of medieval character, is stated by the oboe. The music grows impassioned, but the emotions soon subside and the movement ends gently with a brief recollection of the opening subject.

The composer designated his concluding movement an "Allelujah." It is, indeed, joyous, exultant music, the emotional climate for which is set by the opening powerful theme for four horns in unison.

CONCERTO FOR PIANO AND ORCHESTRA (in the Mixolydian mode) (1924). I. Moderato. II. Lento. III. Allegro energico.

The Mixolydian is the seventh of the ecclesiastical modes. Respighi himself introduced his concerto at a concert of the New York Philharmonic-Symphony Orchestra on December 31, 1925. The theme of the first movement is derived from a Gregorian chant, *Omnes gentes plaudite manibus*. The second movement has the pervading atmosphere of medieval mysticism. The third movement—a passacaglia—follows without interruption.

THE PINES OF ROME, symphonic poem for orchestra (1924).

Like its celebrated predecessor, *The Fountains of Rome, The Pines* is in four sections, though the entire work is played without a break. The four parts are: I. The Pines of the Villa Borghese. II. The Pines near a Catacomb. III. The Pines of the Janiculum. IV. The Pines of the Appian Way.

In *The Fountains,* the composer sought to give a series of nature portraits. In the later symphonic poem, nature is used as the stimulus to arouse memories and reveries in the composer.

The published score contains the following programmatic information, provided by the composer:

"I. 'The Pines of the Villa Borghese.' Children are at play in the pine grove of the Villa Borghese, dancing the Italian equivalent of Ring-around-the-rosy, mimicking marching soldiers and battles, twittering and shrieking like swallows at evening, and they disappear. Suddenly the scene changes to—

"II. 'The Pines near a Catacomb.' We see the shadows of the pines which overhang the entrance of the catacomb. From the depths rises a chant which re-echoes solemnly, sonorously, like a hymn, and is then mysteriously silenced.

"III. 'The Pines of the Janiculum.' There is a thrill in the air. The full moon reveals the profile of the pines of Gianicolo's Hill. A nightingale sings (represented by a phonograph record of a nightingale's song, heard from the orchestra).

"IV. 'The Pines of the Appian Way.' Misty dawn on the Appian Way. The tragic country is guarded by solitary pines. Indistinctly, incessantly, the rhythm of innumerable steps. To the poet's fantasy appears a vision of past glories; trumpets blare, and the army of the consul advances brilliantly in the grandeur of the newly risen sun toward the sacred way, mounting in triumph the Capitoline Hill."

This work is probably the first to utilize a phonograph record as a part of the instrumentation. A recording of the song of an actual nightingale has been ingeniously interpolated into the closing part of the third movement, accompanied by trills of muted violins, chords of the harp, and a chord of the cellos and violas.

The first performance of *The Pines of Rome* took place on December 14, 1924, with Bernardino Molinari conducting the Augusteo Orchestra in Rome.

ROMAN FESTIVALS, symphonic poem (1928).

The third work in the symphonic trilogy about Rome is devoted to Roman festivals. On March 17, 1929, it was introduced in New York City with Arturo Toscanini conducting the New York Philharmonic-Symphony Orchestra.

The four sections are: I. The Circus Maximus. II. The Jubilee. III. The October Excursions. IV. The Eve of Epiphany in Piazza Navona.

As in the cases of the two earlier symphonic poems, the composer himself prepared the programmatic text for *Roman Festivals*.

"I. 'The Circus Maximus.' A threatening sky over the Circus Maximus, but the people are celebrating: Hail Nero! The iron gates open, and the air is filled with a religious chant and the roaring of savage beasts. The mob undulates and rages: serenely, the song of the martyrs spreads, dominates, and finally is drowned in the tumult.

"II. 'The Jubilee.' Weary, in pain, the pilgrims drag themselves through the long streets, praying. At last, from the summit of Mount Mario, is seen the holy city: Rome! Rome! And the hymn of jubilation is answered by the clangor of multitudinous church bells.

"III. 'The October Excursions.' Fetes of October, in the castles engarlanded with vine-leaves—echoes of the hunt—tinklings of horse-bells— songs of love. Then, in the balmy evening, the sound of a romantic serenade.

"IV. 'The Eve of Epiphany in Piazza Navona.' A characteristic rhythm of bugles dominates the frantic clamor: on the tide of noise float now and again rustic songs, the lilt of saltarellos, the sounds of the mechanical organ in some booth, the call of the showman, hoarse and drunken cries, and the stornello in which the spirit of the populace finds expression: 'Let us pass, we are Romans.' "

TOCCATA, for piano and orchestra (1928).

In this neo-classic work, Respighi adopted the toccata form of Frescobaldi, filling it (as he himself put it) "with the modern spirit, and modernized through the character of the harmonies." It is in three sections, played without pause: I. Prelude (in the form of a fantasia). II. Adagio. III. Allegro vivo.

The composer provided the following analysis:

"The prelude is based on a principal theme which is followed by a number of small episodic ideas of rhythmic character, and in the form of a cadenza-recitative. The Adagio consists of a melodic idea which is developed at great length in a sustained dialogue between piano and orchestra. The final movement begins with a brilliant theme which is developed through manifold rhythmic transformations, interrupted by a brief episode of scherzo character."

SILVESTRE REVUELTAS   1899—1940

The Mexican music of Silvestre Revueltas was intensely nationalistic; but Revueltas' approach to musical nationalism was different from that of his famous colleague, Carlos Chávez. Revueltas did not go exploring into distant regions of Mexico in search of old songs and dances. ("Why should I put on boots and climb mountains for Mexican folklore, if I have the spirit of Mexico deep within me?") He did not try to bring to his music the old dances, rhythms, and instruments of his native land—though by subtle suggestion and imitation he did simulate the melodies, rhythms, and sonorities of folk music. Nor did he attempt through his music to re-create the ancient culture of Mexico. It is Mexico itself—the Mexico that fascinates the visitor—that we find in Revueltas: its exotic streets, byways, alleys; its market places; its customs and games; its delightful resort towns and dives; its people and their native dress. His musical works evoke vivid sketches and mood pictures of the land, its lore, its people.

His style is primitive, given to brusque rhythms, angular melodies, garish colors. His orchestration is often derived from popular dance-band performances. Formal harmonic procedures and a concern for form and symphonic development are not to be found in his works. But his style is imaginative and powerful. It is a Mexican art to its very core, even though it is a Mexican art different in character and spirit from that realized by Chávez.

Revueltas was born in Durango, Mexico, on December 31, 1899, and from 1913 to 1916 he studied composition at the National Conservatory in

Mexico City. Later study took place in Austin, Texas, at the Chicago Musical College, and with Sevčik.

He first considered becoming a concert violinist, but soon turned to conducting. After directing theatre orchestras in the United States, he became assistant to Carlos Chávez with the Orquesta Sinfónica in Mexico City. Chávez encouraged Revueltas to begin composing, and in 1931 Revueltas produced his first ambitious work, *Esquinas,* which was performed by the Orquesta Sinfónica under the composer in the same year.

For several years, Revueltas devoted himself to composition, conducting, and teaching. In 1937, during the Spanish Civil War, he went to Spain to join the Loyalists and work in their Music Section. Back in Mexico City he resumed his varied musical activities. There he died on October 5, 1940, a victim of pneumonia.

The following works by Revueltas are discussed below: *Caminos; Sensemaya.*

CAMINOS, tone-picture for orchestra (1934).

Caminos is a musical description of picturesque Mexican streets, those "rather tortuous byways," wrote the composer, "probably unpassed, over which limousines won't venture; short enough so that one doesn't feel their roughness, and gay enough so that one forgets it." It is a gay piece of music, full of verve and excitement. The principal theme (first heard in the oboe) is imitative of a Mexican folk tune.

On July 17, 1934, Carlos Chávez introduced *Caminos* with the Orquesta Sinfónica of Mexico City.

SENSEMAYA, tone-poem for orchestra (1937).

Sensemaya ("Chant to Kill a Snake") is a poem by Nicolas Guillen, an Afro-Cuban poet. The opening lines are as follows:

> Mayombe—bombe—Mayombe!
> Mayombe—bombe—Mayombe! ...
> The snake has glossy eyes
> The snake comes and coils itself around a tree
> With its glossy eyes around a tree
> With its glossy eyes around a tree.

"Sensemaya," wrote Revueltas' sister, "is simply a fanciful, whimsical name; it has no interpretation and no sense. The poet used it solely as an idiomatic rhythm in his poem ... and this poem inspired Revueltas to compose his tone-poem of the same name."

In its original form, as written in 1937, *Sensemaya* was scored for voice and small orchestra. One year later, Revueltas rescored it for large orchestra without voice. It carries over the rhythmic pulse of the poem in strong and vigorous accents, and in its primitiveness it is suggestive of a pagan rite.

JEAN RIVIER 1896—

Jean Rivier belongs with a school of French composers called the Triton, which also includes Henri Barraud. These composers are not so much *for* anything concrete. Rather they are *against* many things in modern French music: the involved mysticism of Olivier Messiaen; the equally involved atonalism of René Leibowitz; the lean neo-classicism of Jean Françaix. If this Triton school believes in anything, it is moderation—moderation in venturing with new idioms and in absorbing old ones.

Rivier's music is the music of moderation. He punctuates his writing with dissonance and with modern rhythms; and he uses classical forms. But a neat balance is achieved between the old and the new in music that is generally emotional and tender, sometimes witty, always graceful and pleasing to the ear. It has clarity of design and writing and is created with economy of means.

Rivier was born at Villemonble, Seine, France, on July 21, 1896. Before World War I, he completed his academic studies. When war broke out, he volunteered for the French Army, and in 1918 was gassed. For several years he was ill. In 1922, he was well enough again to resume his music study where it had for so long a time been interrupted. He entered the Paris Conservatory, where he was a pupil of Causade and where he won prizes in counterpoint and fugue. Performances of several orchestral works by the major French orchestras brought him recognition in the middle 1920's. His Piano Concerto won first prize in a contest sponsored by the principal symphonic organizations of Paris.

SYMPHONY NO. 3 IN G MINOR, for string orchestra (1938). I. Allegretto quasi pastorella. II. Vivo e leggiero. III. Lento e nostalgico. IV. Allegro molto e fugato.

Rivier wrote his Third Symphony in 1938 on a commission from the French government. It was introduced in Paris on November 25, 1940, with Jane Evard conducting her own orchestra.

This work achieves thematic unity through the use of a melodic device:

several of the major themes utilize the same motive, descending down the interval of a fifth.

The first movement begins in a pastoral vein, but vigor is soon injected. The music becomes animated, but the second theme restores calm. The movement ends eloquently as divided violins and violas repeat the opening pastoral subject. A scherzo of delicate texture and light heart follows. It is in two contrasting sections, the first rhythmic, the second lyrical. The brief slow movement that succeeds the scherzo is poignant. The main melody, given to the first violins, is wistfully tender. Some agitation develops in the middle section, breaking the spell, which returns, however, with the restatement of the main melody in the cellos just before the coda. The last movement opens on a note of jollity. A sprightly idea is announced by the cellos and carried over to the other strings in a fugal manner. The development pays great attention to this theme. After this a new subject— march-like—is imposed. An impressive climax comes after the return of the opening measure in a series of augmentations.

MANUEL ROSENTHAL   1904—

During the years in which he emerged as an important composer, Manuel Rosenthal was a pupil of Maurice Ravel. Rosenthal did not fail to assimilate some of Ravel's compositional traits—the fastidious workmanship, the bent for wit and satire, the tender melodic line, the refinement of harmonic construction. But Rosenthal is no imitator of Ravel or anybody else; his music bears the unmistakable imprint of his own personality, which is forcefully projected in every page of music he has written. If in his music he frequently exploits programmatic ideas not usually subjected to musical treatment, he writes with such charm that both the material and its musical adaptation appear convincing rather than esoteric.

Rosenthal was born in Paris on June 18, 1904. Music study took place at the Paris Conservatory. In 1923, his first major work, a Sonatine for Two Violins and Piano, was performed in Paris. This work so impressed Ravel that he invited the young man to study with him. Study had to be postponed until Rosenthal completed his prescribed year of military service. But once begun, study with Ravel continued until Ravel's death in 1937, by which time Rosenthal's reputation was firmly established.

During World War II, Rosenthal enlisted in the French Army. As an infantry corporal, he won the Croix de Guerre for heroism. After being wounded, he was captured by the Germans, who incarcerated him until March, 1941. Back in France, Rosenthal was active in the Resistance movement, and was unsuccessfully hunted by the Nazis.

After the war, Rosenthal became the head of the Orchestre Symphonique of the French Radio, which he had conducted in 1939. In 1946, he visited the United States as a guest conductor of leading orchestras, appearing in performances of his own works and those of his compatriots. In 1949, he was appointed principal conductor of the Seattle Symphony Orchestra and composer-in-residence at the College of Puget Sound, in Tacoma, Washington. Rosenthal's contract in Seattle was suddenly terminated in the fall of 1951 after he had been denied readmittance to this country on charges of "moral turpitude."

The following works by Rosenthal are discussed below: *La Fête du Vin; Musique de Table.*

LA FÊTE DU VIN, for orchestra (1937).

Rosenthal wrote this musical tribute to wine for the French Exposition, where it was introduced. "There is no real program," the composer has explained, "but a kind of connecting thread, which is, in sum, the dream of a man who loves the juice of the vine; that is to say, all good Frenchmen. In the course of the dream there are evoked successively the various activities concerning the care of the vine and of the vintages, as also the libations which follow. The principal episode has utilized in this piece a Bacchic song of French folk origin, as well as some popular Canadian airs, whose frank and joyous allure seems to belong in the program."

MUSIQUE DE TABLE, suite for orchestra (1942). I. Maestoso (Guests Enter the Dining Room); Tempo allegro giocoso (Salade Russe). II. Moderato (Eels in Red Wine). III. Moderato (Quenelles Lyonnaise). IV. Allegro moderato, tempo di marcia (Beef Tenderloin). V. Allegro non troppo (Mixed Fresh Vegetables). VI. Allegro giocoso (Loin of Venison). VII. Moderato (Salade de Saison); Allegro non troppo (Fromage de Montagne). VIII. Finale: allegro ritmico.

During the bleak and bitter year of 1942—when half of France was invaded by the Nazis, and the other half in the hands of Nazi collaborators— Manuel Rosenthal was a member of the French underground, working actively and dangerously for the liberation of his beloved country. Food was scarce in those days, particularly for members of the Resistance, who had to work and live clandestinely; and hunger was something of an occupational disease. Rosenthal took to imagining sumptuous feasts at which he could gorge himself. At one time, in 1942, he was intrigued with the idea of setting one of these lavish meals to music. With wit and vivid realism,

Rosenthal produced tonal cameos descriptive of delicacies ranging from the
salade russe to cheese (probably goat cheese). The concluding finale, in
which each section of the orchestra is heard in turn, was intended as a
rousing hymn to gastronomy.

ALBERT ROUSSEL   1869—1937

As a young man, Roussel was inevitably attracted to the style of his
provocative contemporary, Debussy; and as a former pupil of Vincent
d'Indy, he tried to reconcile impressionism with classical forms. Roussel's
earliest works (the most important of which was the sensitive portrait of
Nature, *Poème de la Forêt,* written in 1905) reveal the unmistakable influence of both Debussy and d'Indy on his thinking. But this influence was,
to be sure, a passing one. There came his voyages as a sailor, which brought
him into contact with the orient and its songs and dances. Highly impres-
sionable, Roussel now turned to exotic orientalism, producing such nostalgic
works as *Evocations* (1910–11) and the opera with which he earned his first
major success, *Padmavati* (1918). Then he abandoned exotic subjects. With
the Second Symphony, op. 22 (1921), Roussel began to explore the artistic
possibilities of modern techniques; and with the Suite in F Major, op. 33,
he came upon neo-classicism.

Thus Roussel has gone through several phases before arriving at his
own identity; in arriving at his own identity he has assimilated the best
elements of the many phases through which he has passed. His tendency
toward a long, undulating melodic line and his interest in complex rhythms
are derived from his oriental period. From his teacher Vincent d'Indy he
acquired his healthy respect for classical structure, an occasional use of the
cyclic form, and a preference for the process of lyrical germination rather
than for symphonic development. He uses modern writing—polytonality or
polymodality—when it serves his artistic purpose; and he uses it without
abandoning that poetic vein which he inherited from Debussy and d'Indy.

Albert Roussel was born in Turcoing, France, on April 5, 1869. Planning a naval career, he was educated at the Stanislas College in Paris and the
Naval School, and served as an ensign on a vessel sailing the Chinese seas.
Recognizing the fact that he preferred music to the Navy, Roussel abandoned
his occupation to study first with Eugene Gigout and then with Vincent

d'Indy at the Schola Cantorum. In 1905, his Trio in E-flat Major was performed at the Société Nationale, and soon after this his symphony *Poème de la Forêt* was successfully heard at a concert of the Théâtre de La Monnaie Orchestra in Brussels. In 1909, he resumed his travels, visiting the orient, which inspired him to write several major works in an oriental style. The most important of these was the opera *Padamavati,* which took him many years to write, and which was performed with outstanding success at the Paris Opéra in 1923. Meanwhile, from 1902 through 1914, Roussel was professor of counterpoint at the Schola Cantorum.

In 1930, Roussel visited the United States to attend the première of his Third Symphony by the Boston Symphony Orchestra. He died in Royan on August 23, 1937.

The following works by Roussel are discussed below: *Bacchus et Ariane; Le Festin d'Araignée (The Spider's Banquet)*; Suite in F Major for Orchestra; Symphony No. 3 in G Minor; Symphony No. 4.

LE FESTIN D'ARAIGNÉE (THE SPIDER'S BANQUET), suite for orchestra, op. 17 (1912). I. Prelude. II. Entrance of the Ants. III. Dance of the Butterfly. IV. Hatching of the Ephemera; Dance of the Ephemera. V. Funeral March of the Ephemera.

Roussel was stimulated by Fabre's *Studies of Insect Life* to write a score for a ballet about the spider. Gilbert de Voisin wrote the scenario. On April 3, 1913, the work was introduced at the Théâtre des Arts in Paris, and soon afterward became a permanent fixture in the repertory of the Opéra Comique.

Though the ballet is little known in this country, much of its music is famous by virtue of a symphonic suite which Roussel prepared from the score and which has since become one of his most celebrated works. The suite was heard for the first time in New York City on October 23, 1914, with Walter Damrosch conducting the New York Symphony Society.

The Prelude describes a garden on a summer afternoon. In the second section, the ants, in the words of the composer, "industriously explore the garden until they find a rose petal, which they carry off with great difficulty." The Dance of the Butterfly follows. "The gay creature dances into the spider's web, where she dies after a brief struggle." After the hatching, the dance, and the death of the ephemera, "all the insects join with great pomp in the funeral procession.... Night falls on the solitary garden."

SUITE IN F MAJOR FOR ORCHESTRA, op. 33 (1926). I. Prelude. II. Sarabande. III. Gigue.

With this suite, written for the Boston Symphony Orchestra, Roussel abandoned impressionism, orientalism, modernism—styles which he had been cultivating—in order to enter the neo-classical world, grown so inviting to composers in France at that time. The first performance of the Suite took place on January 21, 1927, in Boston, Serge Koussevitzky conducted the Boston Symphony Orchestra.

The composer's own analysis follows:

"The Prelude is conceived after the manner of the instrumental toccata of ancient days. The first theme is based upon a continued rhythm of rapid eighth notes, announced by the strings and with rhythmic punctuation by the woodwinds and the horns. Then by successive expositions this principal motive gives birth to various countersubjects. . . .

"The violins in octaves sing the principal phrase of the Sarabande, which is later doubled by solo flute. A second melodic phrase appears in the clarinet, and the violoncellos and double basses provide a rhythmic background based on the first subject. . . .

"The final movement is based on the rondo form. The violins present a bright and lively motive, the basis of the couplet, while the answering motive of the recurring refrain is obviously related to the first. These two ultimately combine to develop a conclusion at once brilliant and vigorously rhythmical."

BACCHUS ET ARIANE, ballet, op. 43 (1930).

Roussel wrote the score to a classical ballet, *Bacchus et Ariane,* the scenario of which was written by Abel Hermant. Theseus, slayer of the mighty Minotaur, is feted with Ariadne on the island of Naxos. This feast is interrupted by Bacchus, who disperses the revelers and seizes Ariadne. With Bacchus, Ariadne forgets Theseus entirely, giving herself up to the joys of her new surroundings.

With choreography by Serge Lifar, and decor by Giorgio de Chirico, *Bacchus et Ariane* was successfully introduced at the Paris Opéra in May, 1931. "The infinitely varied rhythms may best be described as exhibiting the resilience of elastic strings," wrote the French critic, Henri Prunières, about Roussel's score. "Everything progresses with an irresistible movement and native force."

Roussel prepared two orchestral suites from the ballet score, the second of which has become popular at symphonic concerts. Its première took place in Paris on November 26, 1936, with Charles Munch conducting the Orchestre Philharmonique. The published score of the second suite has outlined the action described by the music: "Introduction—Awakening of Ariadne—She looks around her, surprised—She rises, runs about looking for Theseus and his companions—She realizes that she has been abandoned —She climbs with difficulty to the top of a rock—She is about to throw herself into the stream—She falls in the arms of Bacchus, who has appeared from behind a boulder—Bacchus resumes with the awakened Ariadne the dance of her dreaming—Bacchus dances alone—The Dionysiac spell—A group marches past—A faun and a Bacchante present to Ariadne the golden cup, into which a cluster of grapes has been pressed—Dance of Ariadne—Dance of Ariadne and Bacchus—Bacchanale."

SYMPHONY NO. 3 IN G MINOR, op. 42 (1930). I. Allegro vivo. II. Adagio. III. Vivace. IV. Allegro con spirito.

Roussel's Third Symphony was written on a commission from the Boston Symphony Orchestra to honor its fiftieth anniversary. Completed in 1930, it was introduced by the Boston Symphony under Koussevitzky on October 24 of that year. The composer—on his first visit to this country—attended the first performance.

The symphony is integrated through the repetition of a five-note motive in three of the four movements. The first movement is in sonata form. Three measures of introduction are followed by a highly rhythmic first theme (violins and woodwinds); introduction and first theme are written in the Phrygian mode. Brief ideas follow each other, each highly lyrical until the second main theme is heard in the flute. Development proceeds in the accepted manner, rising to a climax in which the five-note motive emerges resplendently.

The second movement opens with the motif theme. The tempo develops from Adagio to Andante to Più mosso, when a huge fugue, based on the motto theme, is launched by the flutes.

The third movement was described by the composer as a kind of valse-scherzo. It is diaphanous and light-footed. The finale opens with a vigorous theme for flute and continues with an expressive idea for strings. The music becomes very lyrical. At the end the motto theme returns twice.

SYMPHONY NO. 4, op. 53 (1935). I. Lento; Allegro con brio. II. Lento molto. III. Allegro scherzando. IV. Allegro molto.

Five years separated Roussel's Third and Fourth Symphonies. The Fourth was introduced in Paris by the Pasdeloup Orchestra under Albert Wolff on October 19, 1935, and was so vigorously acclaimed that one of the movements (the third) had to be repeated.

After a slow introduction of seventeen measures, the Allegro con brio begins with a theme developed out of a phrase in the sixth measure. The subject undergoes development before the second theme is heard in the horn. The movement now quickens and a climax emerges. The original material then returns—the first theme now heard in the woodwinds and muted trumpets; the second, in the oboe.

The Lento molto is enveloped in mystery. It opens with a quiet melody for strings. The first oboe then enters with a recollection of an idea from the introduction of the first movement. The tempo quickens; the atmosphere becomes restless. But when the feverish agitation is dissipated, the clarinet brings back the opening melody against a contrapuntal background of a second melody in the bassoon. This material is extended. A climax is reached and dies down; the movement then ends gently.

Violins and cellos present a lively theme which is like a gigue to open the third movement. This is the integral material of this entire section, all other subsidiary ideas being derived from it.

A theme for oboe against a pizzicato background of strings brings in the finale, a vivacious rondo. After this theme has been adopted by the first violins, a new theme—moving in its eloquence—is presented by the first violins. The entire finale is spirited, but it is not without grace. It ends on a triumphant note with a proud and exultant restatement of the opening subject for full orchestra.

LAZARE SAMINSKY   1882—

As one of the founders of the Society of Hebrew Folk Song (organized in St. Petersburg in 1909), and as the musical director of the Temple Emanu-El Choir of New York for more than a quarter of a century, Saminsky has inevitably been linked with the field of Jewish music. He has made notable contributions to Jewish music, not only as a composer, but also as conductor, scholar, and writer. But it would be a mistake to regard him as an exclusively Jewish composer. Indeed, some of his most important works have no tangible relation with either the techniques or styles of Jewish music. They are Eurasian in artistic concept.

In his most important works, Saminsky combines craftsmanship with vibrancy of personality and sensitivity of feeling. His speech varies subtly from passion and power to tenderness and poetic delicacy. It is music romantic in its style, yet on occasion arriving at original tone-colors, harmonies, and rhythms.

Saminsky was born in Vale-Gotzulovo, a small town near Odessa, on November 8, 1882. He studied both at the University of St. Petersburg (where he specialized in philosophy and mathematics) and at the Conservatory. After leaving the Conservatory, he helped found the Society of Hebrew Folk Song, dedicated to research in the field of Hebrew music, and to encouraging Jewish composers to write music in a Hebrew idiom; this Society included Engel, Gniesin, and Rosowski. Saminsky was also commissioned to travel in the Caucasus and Georgia for research in the religious music of that region. Meanwhile, in 1913, his first work to receive a major performance, *Vigiliae,* was heard in Moscow, conducted by the composer.

In 1920, Saminsky settled in this country permanently. He has held the post of musical director of Temple Emanu-El in New York for more than a quarter of a century. In this position he has organized and directed the annual event known as the Three Choirs Festival. He has conducted extensively in this country and abroad and has also been active as lecturer and writer. In addition, he was one of the founders of the League of Composers in New York.

The following works by Saminsky are discussed below: *The Daughter of Jephtha;* Symphony No. 4.

SYMPHONY NO. 4, op. 35 (1926). I. Motto and Introduction. II. Quasi Sonata. III. Monologue and Postlude.

Saminsky's Fourth Symphony was heard for the first time in Berlin, on April 19, 1929, the composer conducting the Berlin Symphony Orchestra.

The opening movement ushers in without delay the main theme of the symphony, called the "Motto." Two subsidiary themes, of which the first appears initially as counterpoint to the main subject, provide dynamic material for the other sections. The middle part is in sonata form, with two developments and no recapitulation. It centers around the Motto theme, now drastically transformed. The altered Motto is prefaced by a faintly jazzy but sublimated prelude. Powerfully driven into the climax of the section, this Motto, again modified, is followed by a second development. A mighty coda-fugato presents once more the basic Motto theme in still another guise, now merged with a countertheme in double counterpoint.

The closing part begins with a Monologue. Its new theme, derived from the coda of the first part, flows into the Postlude, which turns out to be the missing recapitulation of the Quasi Sonata movement. The main theme now returns in a new harmonic light, breathing forth the spirit of vigor.

THE DAUGHTER OF JEPHTHA, opera-ballet (1928).

In writing his own libretto for this opera-ballet in three continuous scenes, Saminsky allowed himself a certain measure of freedom in adapting the Biblical story. He has Jephtha proclaim his vow to God (to sacrifice the first living thing he meets following his victory in battle) *after* the battle. The next scene is laid in his native village, where Jephtha's daughters and her maidens play ritual dance tunes and burn herbs in sacrificial urns. A slave rushes in to bring the news of Jephtha's victory. Amidst general rejoicing, trumpet calls are heard. Jephtha appears over the cliffs. When his daughter rushes eagerly to welcome him, he utters a wild cry. She is the first living thing he meets after his victory, and—true to his vow—he must sacrifice her to God. Her maidens sing a sacred dirge as sacrifice fires are lit.

Saminsky described this work both as an "opera-ballet" and as a "cantata-pantomime" to signify that it could be performed either in the theatre or on the concert stage. It is marked by a free play of music, drama, and dance, each element assuming equal importance in an integrated artistic whole. The music is perhaps best in its effective and unusual ensemble numbers for orchestra, and in its vivid dances with their polyrhythmic writing and brilliant instrumental colors. The entire work generates great power, which Lawrence Gilman once described as "puissant and barbaric."

Saminsky completed the work in the summer of 1928. The world première (in concert form) took place in Rome on April 5, 1929, the composer directing the Augusteo Orchestra and chorus. It was heard in this country two years later at a concert of the League of Composers in New York.

ERIK SATIE   1866—1925

It is not difficult to understand why his contemporaries were so puzzled by Erik Satie that they could not accurately measure his importance. Here was a composer who earned his living as a Montmartre cabaret pianist, who did not hesitate to write popular songs for music-hall entertainers or even to introduce popular elements in his serious works. Here, too, was a composer who in his music used such outlandish titles as *Desiccated Embryos, The Dreamy Fish, Flabby Preludes for a Dog, Disagreeable Sketches, Airs to Make You Run Away, Cold Pieces, Three Pieces in the Shape of a Pear*, and so on; who cluttered his music with whimsical instructions (at one point he instructed the pianist to put his hand in his pocket; at another, he asked the performer to play the music "dry as a cuckoo, light as an egg"; at still another, he described a phrase as being "like a nightingale with a toothache"). Was this man a charlatan—or a genius? His contemporaries did not know—and not knowing, they preferred to dismiss him as a poseur, a bad boy who refused to grow up.

And yet—for all his strange attitudes and excursions into whimsy—Satie was a very serious artist, a great innovator, a powerful force. He anticipated the harmonic writing of Debussy, as for example in *Sarabande* (1887); he suggested some of the experiments of the twentieth-century modernists with the barless notation of his *Avant Dernières Pensées* (1915) and in the daring thinking of *Le Fils des Étoiles* (1891). But even more important, he represented a complete break with nineteenth-century romanticism. By rebelling against composers who took themselves and their art too seriously, he made it more down-to-earth, more human. By revolting against excessive emotionalism, large forms, and pretentious writing, he brought to music a simplicity and freshness that were like a breath of pure air in a fetid atmosphere. By his queer titles and queerer instructions, he mocked the preciousness of Debussy and his followers, and helped to rid impressionism of some of its less desirable traits. He sent French music in a new and healthy direction, a direction taken up by the "French Six" (see Honegger), Ravel, and the Arcueilists.

Erik Siate was born in Honfleur, Calvados, on May 17, 1866. He entered the Paris Conservatory in 1883, but was not happy there. His rebellious thinking, already evident in his earliest piano pieces (written between 1887 and 1888), brought him into conflict with his masters. He was pronounced untalented. These pieces, however, include the first of his famous works, the *Sarabandes, Ogives,* and *Gymnopédies.*

A decoration on a Greek vase inspired Satie to write the famous set of three piano pieces known as *Gymnopédies.* Gymnopedia was a festival of naked youths held in ancient Sparta to honor Apollo, Pythaeus, and Leto. In these piano pieces, gymnopedia represents a stately dance performed by these naked youths before the statues of the gods. The music is serene, classical, at times even solemn—even though there are also new harmonic colors and unorthodox progressions which give strong indications of things soon to come in the world of music. Debussy orchestrated two of these three pieces.

Satie left the Conservatory and for a while earned his living playing the piano in a Montmartre cabaret. There he met Debussy, whom he influenced greatly with his esthetic ideas; it was on Satie's suggestion that Debussy wrote an opera on Maeterlinck's *Pelléas et Mélisande.*

By 1905, Satie was a provocative and notorious figure in French music, by virtue of his unorthodox style and whimsical ideas. Feeling that his technique was inadequate, he decided to return to formal study. He enrolled in the Schola Cantorum, and for the next few years was a pupil of Vincent d'Indy and Albert Roussel. This intensive period subsequently encouraged Satie to undertake more ambitious assignments, and he produced several major works in large forms, including the ballet *Parade* (1917) and the lyric drama *Socrate* (1918).

Having influenced Debussy and members of the "French Six"—and having set them off on the paths they were to travel—Satie was once again influential in creating a school of music. Founded in 1923, this school was called the "Arcueilists," after the district of Arcueil, in Paris, where the composers lived; it included, besides Satie, Henri Sauguet, Roger Désormière, Henri Cliquet-Pleyel, and Maxime Jacob. The school was dedicated to simplicity and economy.

Satie died in poverty and obscurity in Paris on July 2, 1925. Not until after his death was his influence on his generation understood and appreciated.

For *Gymnopédies,* see the biographical sketch above.

PARADE, ballet (1916).

Diaghilev commissioned Satie to write the music for this realistic ballet, the scenario for which had been written by Jean Cocteau. The first performance of this ballet—called *Parade*—took place at the Théâtre du Châtelet on May 18, 1917. Curtain, scenery, and costumes were designed by Pablo Picasso (his first venture into ballet decor). The choreography was prepared by Massine.

The first performance provoked a riot in the audience and savage hostility in the press. So vitriolic was one of the critics that Satie was impelled to send him an insulting letter. Sued by the infuriated critic, Satie was sentenced to eight days in jail for "public insults and defamation of character." (This sentence, however, was suspended.)

Parade is a realistic satire on the touring companies of entertainers who played in the city streets. To attract attention to their show, these companies always preceded their performance with a parade of the cast. The principal characters of the ballet include a Chinese juggler, two acrobats, a little American girl, and three managers. On a Sunday, outside a Paris music hall, there has taken place a parade of performers. The company managers are barking at passers-by, trying to get them to attend the performance. But the Parisians think that the parade is the actual performance and ignore the solicitations. Some of the performers then join the managers in attracting the passers-by to the show, but in vain. This is the entire action of the ballet, which Cocteau likened to a Punch-and-Judy show.

Satie explained his musical intentions as follows:

"I composed only a background to throw into relief the noises which the playwright considers indispensable to the surrounding of each character with its own atmosphere. These noises imitate waves, revolvers, typewriters, sirens, airplanes—music belonging to the same category as the bits of newspaper painted woodgrain, and other everyday objects that the cubist painters frequently employ in their pictures in order to localize objects and masses in nature."

Due to technical difficulties it was not possible to carry out Satie's intentions in using background noises for the characters. But even without the noises, the music was unorthodox in its use of broad burlesque and in its incorporation of popular elements (even American jazz).

Though violently denounced in 1917, *Parade* has since that time been regarded as one of Satie's most important scores. Darius Milhaud has written: "The performance of Satie's *Parade* will stand in the history of French music as a date equally important with that of the first performance of *Pelléas et Mélisande*."

FLORENT SCHMITT   1870—1958

In writing about Schmitt, music critics often speak of his allegiance to tradition and classical form. But though Schmitt's most famous works seem traditional enough today, they were highly original and adventurous in their time. It must be recalled that his three most famous works (*Psalm 47*, the Piano Quintet, and the *Tragedy of Salome*) were all written before 1908. For that time, these works were courageous in their use of compound meters, advanced harmonies, exotic orchestration. Time has robbed this music of much of its daring. But since the music did not depend on its originality for its interest, time has not robbed it of its power to delight audiences. As we listen to these works today, what impresses us profoundly is their eloquent expressiveness, their ardor and emotional force.

Florent Schmitt was born in Blamont, France, on September 28, 1870. He was nineteen when he entered the Paris Conservatory, where his teachers included Fauré, Massenet, and Dubois. In 1900, he won the Prix de Rome, and while at the Villa Medici wrote his first major work, *Psalm 47*. Its first performance, followed by the successes of his Piano Quintet and *Tragedy of Salome*, brought him to a major position in French music. For two years he was director of the Lyons Conservatory. After that he lived in comparative retirement. In 1932, he visited the United States, appearing as guest performer with leading orchestras. He was elected to the Institut de France in 1936. Schmitt died in Neuilly, near Paris, on August 17, 1958.

The following works by Schmitt are discussed below: *Psalm 47;* Quintet in B Minor for Piano and Strings; *The Tragedy of Salome*.

PSALM 47 (46 in the Vulgate), for chorus, soloists, organ, and orchestra, op. 38 (1900).

Though this setting of the Forty-seventh Psalm ("O Clap Your Hands, All Ye People") is one of Schmitt's earlier works, it is also one of his best; and there are many French authorities who consider it one of the Alpine peaks in contemporary French music. Schmitt wrote it in Rome, while holding down the Prix de Rome, in 1906. On December 27 of the same year it was introduced at a Prix de Rome concert in Paris. The critics were divided in their opinion. Some (like Arthur Pougin) spoke derisively of its "bizarre" orchestration, "ferocious" modulations, "infernal" dissonances. Others (notably M. D. Calvocoressi) described the music as of singular power and grandiloquence.

In *Le Temps,* Emile Vuillermoz provided a definitive analysis:

[The composition opens with a roll of the tympani. Trumpets join in, setting the stage for the chorus which enters with the majestic outcry: "Glory to God!"]

"The orchestra, which has supported this call with all its power, extends it in triumphal fanfares. The chorus sings with rhythmic insistence the words 'O Clap Your Hands, All Ye People.' The instruments respond with noisy chords...and follow it with a sort of barbaric ritual in five rhythms. But the dance seems to become a processional....The brasses take up the heavy rhythm of barbaric exaltation. A rapid crescendo, and the orchestra pauses abruptly, while organ and divided chorus proclaim a fortissimo of chords as massive as the colonnade of a temple. The trumpets resound anew and a repetition of 'Glory to God!' brings in a majestic vocal fugato, 'For the Lord is Very Mighty.' This whole evocation of the human race saluting its Creator is music of power and sovereign beauty....But the clamor subsides. ...Over a caressing equilibrium of divided violas, a violin solo sings a supple and expressive phrase....One by one the desks make their entrance to surround the simple voice which is exaltingly intoxicated and lost in its impassioned dream. We are in an oriental atmosphere....The chorus murmurs in ecstasy while sinuous arpeggios of the harp rise like incense. Trumpets and muted horns, muted strings, with a soft roll on the cymbal, add a drab halo of sound....The magic of the Far East evaporates....Now the music becomes once more alert. The orchestra resumes its mighty voice....Once more the portals of the celestial temples open, and the organ supports the enunciation, 'Because the Lord Is Very Formidable.' The crescendo mounts until all the forces of the orchestra and chorus proclaim, 'Glory to God!' The ending is a formidable tumult of transport in which the people fill the air with their savage and joyful cries."

QUINTET IN B MINOR FOR PIANO AND STRINGS, op. 51 (1905). I. Lent et grave. II. Lent. III. Animé.

Though Schmitt is at his best in the larger forms for orchestra or orchestra and chorus, he has produced at least one work of chamber-music dimensions which is an unqualified masterpiece. This is his Piano Quintet, op. 51—also one of his comparatively early works—begun in 1905 but not completed until 1908. Its first performance was outstandingly successful (M. D. Calvocoressi spoke of it as "one of the most moving...and revealing creations of the past few years") and did much to establish Schmitt's reputation.

A slow and expressive introduction opens the quintet, after which comes the Allegro movement, orthodox in form, but full of vigorous ideas and unusual harmonies. The slow movement is the best of the three, high-minded and poetic in speech and full of sensitive beauty. An athletic final movement of impressive structural dimensions is rhythmically interesting.

THE TRAGEDY OF SALOME, suite for orchestra, op. 50 (1907). I. Prelude; Dance of the Pearls. II. The Enchantment of the Sea; Dance of Lightning; Dance of Fear.

Schmitt's most famous orchestral work was inspired by a lurid poem of Robert d'Humieres for which the composer produced sensual music that is at times exotic and at other times barbaric. Originally intended as a "mute drama" (in which form it was introduced in Paris on November 9, 1907, under the direction of D. E. Inghelbrecht), *The Tragedy of Salome* was first scored for chamber orchestra. Subsequently, Schmitt rewrote it for large orchestra, in which version it was heard for the first time at a Colonne concert in Paris on January 8, 1911. On April 22, 1912, Natasha Trouhanova interpreted the music in dance, the first of several successful dance-mountings the work has received.

After a gloomy Prelude in which the tragedy of Salome is foreshadowed, there comes a frenetic dance describing Salome's joy at the jewels she has just received from her mother. Moody music introduces the second part, bringing back the lugubrious atmosphere of the Prelude. Out of this rises a melody (oboe) derived from a folksong of Aica. Salome then dances by the illumination of lightning. She disappears, then returns with the head of John the Baptist on a tray. At first she appears ecstatic, but terror soon seizes her. She hurls the head into the sea, the waters of which soon change to blood. Lightning tears through the sky. A bolt strikes the palace of Herod and shatters it.

ARNOLD SCHOENBERG

1874—1951

Not until after World War I did Schoenberg crystallize his thinking into that system of composition with which his name is inevitably associated: the twelve-tone technique (twelve-tone row).

In his earliest works he was the romanticist who was profoundly influenced by the Wagnerian music-drama. His first work, an unpublished string

quartet (1897), was full of soaring and expressive melodies and chromatic harmonies. The celebrated *Verklaerte Nacht* (1899) and the *Gurre-Lieder* (virtually completed in 1901), were also affected by the Wagnerian music-drama.
But Schoenberg soon abandoned his romantic vein. His writing grew bolder.
In his search for simplification and preciseness, he began to abandon tonality,
and in his experiments with new sounds he deserted consonance. The last
time he used a key signature for more than three decades was for the Quartet
in F-sharp Minor (1907). There followed the iconoclastic music of *Pierrot
Lunaire* (1912) and the *Five Pieces for Orchestra* (1912). He was making more and more of an effort to free music from what he considered
to be the tyranny of tonality: slavery to a key-center or tonic. He wanted
greater freedom of movement for his melodic ideas, and he sought to open
up new avenues of musical expression.

But atonality soon represented to him not freedom but anarchy. He
sensed the need for a set of new principles to replace the old ones of tonality
he had discarded—to discipline his thinking. In 1915, therefore, he wrote a
Scherzo in which the twelve tones of the octave (the black and white notes)
were used, even though not yet in any established pattern. In his *Piano Pieces,*
op. 23, written at about this time, he utilized a technique which he called
"composing with the tones of the basic motive." "In contrast to the ordinary
way of using a motive," he explained, "I used it already almost in the manner
of a basic set of twelve tones." Thus the idea of writing music around the
framework of twelve tones kept simmering within him, and sometimes over-
flowed into the music he was writing. At last, in his Suite for the Piano,
op. 25 (1925), the basic formula of the twelve-tone system was set for the first
time; and in the fourth movement of the *Serenade,* op. 24 (1924), it had been
also realized.

A few of the salient features of the twelve-tone technique can be succinctly summarized. The twelve tones are arranged in a definite order (or
row); each composition is built around its own row; the twelve tones can be
arranged in a melodic pattern in any order, provided that no tone is repeated
before the others are used; each tone is given equal importance and independence, without subservience to a tonic; the row may be inverted or reversed.

The first major twelve-tone works—the String Quartet No. 3, op. 30
(1927), and the *Variations for Orchestra,* op. 31 (1928)—utilize the technique
with extraordinary ingenuity. But unfortunately there is something hard and
cold about the logic of this music, something forbidding in its calculations,
something even repellent about the ugly sounds that are produced. Gone are
the passions and intensity and flaming beauty of *Verklaerte Nacht, Gurre-
Lieder,* and *Pierrot Lunaire.* This new music was the product of a highly
analytical brain that handled compositional problems as if they were mathematical equations and dispensed completely with human feelings. Schoenberg
might well say that a twelve-tone composer may—like any other composer—
be as "cold-hearted and unmoved as an engineer ... or may conceive in sweet

dreams, in inspiration. What can be constructed with these tones depends on one's inventive faculty." (Indeed, both he and Alban Berg were to prove that this was so.) But the music that Schoenberg put down on paper in the 1920's was desiccated, ugly. The layman heard only baffling, seemingly disorganized complexity. Even highly trained musicians could listen without affection, at the same time admiring the extraordinary skill that was involved and recognizing the latent potentialities of the style.

After 1933, Schoenberg was able to bring human as well as intellectual values to his music. Transplantation to this country proved healthy. Schoenberg was now taking his art out of its formerly cloistered isolation, making it not merely a brilliant application of his theories but also an expression of his inmost feelings toward the world around him. Thus he could now write musical works which drew their subjects, and their emotional impact, from the contemporary world. Thus he could write functional music for a school band. Thus he could produce a major abstract work and flood it with warmth and even *gemütlich* charm.

But besides bringing emotion and a human approach to the writing of music in twelve-tone rows, Schoenberg also managed to change his onetime ascetic approach to the technique. He no longer felt the compulsion to write exclusively in the style of his invention. In some of his last works, the twelve-tone technique is utilized in spasmodic pages; in others, it is not used at all. The gamut of expressiveness was, therefore, greatly extended. He even felt the urge to return to older romantic styles—and yielded to that urge.

He could now say: "If a composer does not write from the heart, he simply cannot produce good music.... I get a musical idea for a composition. I try to develop a certain logical and beautiful conception, and I try to clothe it in a type of music which exudes from me naturally and inevitably. I do not consciously create tonal, atonal, or polytonal music. I write what I feel in my heart—and what finally comes on paper is what first courses through every fiber of my body."

Arnold Schoenberg was born in Vienna on September 13, 1874. After some elementary study at the Realschule, he became a pupil of Alexander von Zemlinsky, who was a great influence in his early development. Under Zemlinsky's guidance, Schoenberg wrote his first works, which followed traditional romantic lines. But it was not long before Schoenberg became adventurous in his composition. From this time on, performances of his works in Vienna provoked scandals.

Soon after marrying Zemlinsky's sister, in 1901, Schoenberg went to Berlin, where he was a conductor at a cabaret. During this period, he continued with his composition, producing *Pelleas and Melisande* and the *Gurre-Lieder*. He was back in Vienna in 1903, devoting himself to composition and teaching. It was at this time that he began gathering around him pupils who were soon to become his devoted disciples: among them were Alban Berg,

Anton Webern, and Erwin Stein. The adulation of his students—and their complete faith in the direction he was traveling—was a measure of compensation for the violent hostility which greeted each new work of his in Vienna.

During World War I, Schoenberg served in the Austrian Army. The war over, Schoenberg returned to teaching and composition. He helped found the Society for Private Performances, which performed his own music, and that of his followers, under favorable auspices (all critics were excluded).

With the rise of Hitlerism in Germany, Schoenberg decided to abandon Europe. Settling in the Brentwood suburb of Los Angeles, he became professor at the University of Southern California and the University of California at Los Angeles, holding this latter position for several years. By now the hostility to his music had died down, and he was accorded that world admiration that he deserved. His seventieth birthday in 1944 and his seventy-fifth birthday in 1949 were celebrated throughout the country with extensive performances of his major works—and to appreciative audiences and critics. In 1947, he received the Special Award of Merit from the National Institute of Arts and Letters.

Schoenberg died at his home in Brentwood, California, on July 13, 1951.

The following works by Schoenberg are discussed below: Concerto for Piano and Orchestra; *Gurre-Lieder; Ode to Napoleon; Pierrot Lunaire;* Quartet No. 3; Quartet No. 4; *A Survivor from Warsaw; Theme and Variations; Verklaerte Nacht* (Transfigured Night).

GURRE-LIEDER, for narrator, solo voices, chorus, and orchestra (1901).

In the last of his major postromantic works, Schoenberg produced his most ardent and beautiful music. The *Gurre-Lieder* is, as Paul Rosenfeld said of it, "poetic, glamorous; that poetry is a fragile one, and an exquisite one, a sort of expression of the gleaming, evanescent moment of feeling." The style stems from the two mighty Richards—Wagner and Strauss—and is prodigal in its use of chromatic harmonies, swollen contrapuntal passages, sensuous surges of melody. It is music that perhaps only the hot blood of early manhood can produce. After letting himself go emotionally and romantically without inhibitions, it is perhaps little wonder that Schoenberg should wish to adopt a new creative style calling for discipline and austerity.

The *Gurre-Lieder* is a setting of a cycle of poems by Jens Peter Jacobsen which retells the story of the love of King Waldemar I of Denmark for Tove, in the castle of Gurre. It is in three sections. The first, comprising the songs of Waldemar and Tove, some of the most exquisite love music produced in our time, ends with the "Song of the Wood Dove," a lament over the death of Tove. In the second part, Waldemar rejects God. The third section is the most dramatic of the three, describing—in the words of Paul Stefan—"a spectral vision of a ride of Death," followed by "a melodramatic interlude...and finally a magnificent chorus greeting the sun."

The *Gurre-Lieder* belongs to Schoenberg's earlier creative period, having been conceived in 1900 and completed (except for its orchestration) by the end of 1901. For the next decade, however, the manuscript lay untouched. Not until 1911 did Schoenberg complete the instrumentation.

The first performance took place in Vienna on February 23, 1913, with Franz Schreker conducting. Despite its ardent romanticism, the work unloosed a veritable tempest of hostility. At the rehearsals, the first horn player attacked the composer with his instrument, and then left the hall in a violent fit of rage, saying that under no circumstances would he perform such music. (Actually, he was subsequently prevailed upon to play it, and he even grew to like it.) At the concert itself, shouts of denunciation drowned out some of the more vocal expressions of enthusiasm. Fist fights erupted; one woman fainted. Some years later, the reverberations of this concert were still felt. In a Berlin court, one of the men of that audience brought suit against another for assault. A prominent physician testified that the music had been so nerve-wracking as to arouse strange neuroses. Yet this supposedly "nerve-wracking" music was tame stuff compared to the writings of Debussy, Satie, Ravel, and the early Stravinsky, with which the audiences of 1913 were acquainted. It is difficult to understand why music as easily assimilable as the *Gurre-Lieder* should have inspired such a reaction—except for the fact that Schoenberg's music had already provoked scandals so often that antagonism to his music had become something of a reflex action in Vienna!

PIERROT LUNAIRE, for speaking voice, piano, flute (or piccolo), clarinet (or bass clarinet), violin (or viola), and cello, op. 21 (1912).

In his setting of the decadent symbolism of Albert Giraud's "three-seven melodramas" (or short poems), Schoenberg arrived at the threshold of expressionism. This is not yet twelve-tone music; but the essential traits of Schoenberg's later style are already being established. There is no identifying tonality; the dissonances are prominent; the melodic writing is tense and concentrated; the solo voice—*Sprechstimme*—is rigidly controlled in rhythm and pitch, and becomes a musical instrument, an integral part of the instrumental texture.

Because of its complexity and unorthodoxy, *Pierrot Lunaire* required forty rehearsals before it could be performed. The première performance took place in Berlin on October 16, 1912, and provoked a scandal. There were catcalls and hissing. The critics were poisonous. "If this is music," wrote Otto Taubman in the *Boersen Courier,* "then I pray my Creator not to let me hear it again!"

It is not necessary to know the text to respond to Schoenberg's taut, intense music, or to appreciate its ability to reflect many different moods and shades of feeling. As a matter of fact, the composer at times consciously made his music completely antithetical to the spoken words—as in the nineteenth song, in which the text speaks of the viola, but the music is written for the cello. This music is meant to be absolute, in the strictest sense of the term: self-sufficient music, deriving its force and interest exclusively from musical values, and arriving at altogether new avenues of musical expression.

The titles of the twenty-one songs are as follows: 1. "Moonstruck." 2. "Colombine." 3. "The Dandy." 4. "A Pale Washerwoman." 5. "Waltz of Chopin." 6. "Madonna." 7. "The Sick Moon." 8. "Night." 9. "Prayer to Pierrot." 10. "Theft." 11. "The Red Mass." 12. "The Song of the Gallows." 13. "Decapitation." 14. "The Crosses." 15. "Homesickness." 16. "Outrage." 17. "A Parody." 18. "Moonspot." 19. "Serenade." 20. "Journey Home." 21. "Oh, Olden Fragrance."

VERKLAERTE NACHT (TRANSFIGURED NIGHT), for chamber orchestra, op. 4 (1899–1917).

In 1917, Schoenberg transcribed for chamber orchestra a sextet he had composed in 1899—*Verklaerte Nacht;* it is in this version that this work is best known and most frequently heard. A few additional stylistic changes were made by the composer in 1943.

It is not the apostle of the twelve-tone technique who is heard here, but the ardent romanticist of the late nineteenth century—a romanticist passionately devoted to the Wagnerian music-drama. Chromatic in its writing, deeply emotional in feeling, sensuous in texture, *Verklaerte Nacht* is effective programmatic music which catches admirably the descriptive and emotional nuances of the poem that inspired it. That poem—*Weib und die Welt* by Richard Dehmel—tells of a walk through a moonlit grove by a man and a woman, the woman confessing that she has been unfaithful, the man ready to forgive and forget. Through this compassionate forgiveness the world becomes transfigured.

Verklaerte Nacht was adapted into a ballet by Anthony Tudor and retitled *The Pillar of Fire.* It was introduced in this form in New York City by the Ballet Theatre on April 8, 1942.

QUARTET NO. 3, for strings, op. 30 (1926). I. Moderato. II. Adagio. III. Intermezzo. IV. Rondo.

In Schoenberg's First String Quartet (1905), the writing was, for the most part, post-Wagnerian. The Second Quartet (1908) was his first departure from traditional tonality (here a female voice is used for the last two movements). The Third Quartet, produced in 1926, was his first quartet in the twelve-tone technique, the technique here being used with a certain amount of freedom, since repetition of notes is permitted in introductory and transitional passages. The quartet was introduced in Vienna by the Kolisch Quartet on September 19, 1927.

The first movement is identified by a rhythmic ostinato that courses throughout the entire section, frequently serving as the background for the terse themes. In the second movement, the theme-and-variation form is utilized. The last two movements have powerful rhythmic momentum, while the melodic material is austere.

QUARTET NO. 4, for strings, op. 37 (1937). I. Allegro molto; energico. II. Comodo. III. Largo. IV. Allegro.

In his Fourth Quartet, Schoenberg was able to realize what Lou Harrison described in *Modern Music* as a more delicate balance of forms, "which allows for greater differentiation of musical idea and intense dramatic contrast." This, as Harrison explains, made it possible for Schoenberg to "reintroduce the special expressive features of his early expressionist style without inferring either an esthetic regression or an upset in the solidity of his works."

Almost classic in form, this quartet has a simplicity and clarity which have distinguished some of Schoenberg's more recent works. Two themes comprise the first movement, the first energetic, the second highly syncopated. The second movement, a scherzo, opens with a swaying subject for viola which yields to melodic material strangely reminiscent of the old Viennese Ländler—heavy-stamping waltz music. The expressive third movement opens with the four strings playing in unison to create a highly effective mood; there then follows a melody of dark, rich character which bears some resemblance to the Hebraic *Kol Nidrei*. (Schoenberg had made a setting of the *Kol Nidrei* two years earlier.) A rhythmically forceful movement brings the quartet to a close.

CONCERTO FOR PIANO AND ORCHESTRA, op. 42 (1942).
Though this concerto is played without interruption, it is actually divided into four sections. The first is a waltz-like Andante consisting primarily of an extended lyrical passage for solo piano, following which the orchestra enters to participate in the development. This lyrical subject is the embryo out of which the entire concerto grows, and is subjected to numerous transformations and developments. A delightful scherzo-like section follows, in which the composer utilizes a wide gamut of colors and instrumental effects. An emotional Adagio ends in a cadenza, which serves as the transition to the concluding vigorous rondo.

The concerto is written entirely in the twelve-tone technique; but here Schoenberg's style is much less severe and forbidding than in earlier works. Indeed, pleasing sounds are achieved, along with romantic feelings and occasionally even an infectious charm.

On February 6, 1944, this concerto was introduced by Eduard Steuermann and the NBC Symphony under Stokowski.

ODE TO NAPOLEON, for speaking voice, piano, and string orchestra, op. 41b (1942).

The *Ode to Napoleon* is a setting of Byron's *Ode to Napoleon,* a bitter denunciation of the autocrat. It is Schoenberg's first musical work with political implications. Byron's poem was used by the composer as a protest of man against tyranny and dictatorship. Schoenberg's view of the German dictator, whose hordes were sweeping triumphantly across Europe in 1942, was no different from Byron's view of Napoleon. Byron's final lines of invocation to George Washington—who represented to the poet the very opposite of Napoleon—were to Schoenberg a veritable paean to democratic freedom.

Schoenberg's music is in the twelve-tone technique, but without the mathematical rigidity of his earlier works. The music for the speaking voice is the *Sprechstimme* of *Pierrot Lunaire,* but much more elastic, since no indication of pitch is given and many of the inflections are left to the performer. There is less austerity to Schoenberg's melodic writing in this score. Many of the melodic ideas are, indeed, rich with symbolic implications: that of Napoleon (ascending fourths, followed by descending minor seconds) gives a suggestion of the ruthlessness of the autocrat; that of Washington (fifths) represents, through harmonic inversion, the very antithesis of the dictator. Besides, there are pages in this music in which Schoenberg has brought genuine emotional warmth: the invocation to Washington is music of grandeur in breadth and feeling.

The *Ode to Napoleon* was introduced by the New York Philharmonic-Symphony Orchestra under Artur Rodzinski on November 23, 1944.

THEME AND VARIATIONS, for orchestra, op. 43b (1944).

In recent years, Schoenberg occasionally departed from his twelve-tone technique to write music utilizing more traditional styles. As he wrote in the *New York Times* on December 19, 1948: "A longing to return to the older styles was always vigorous in me; and from time to time I have to yield to that urge."

It may have been just such an urge—or it may have been the particular purpose for which the work was intended—that led Schoenberg to adopt both a definite key center (G Minor) and the resources of accepted harmonies for the *Theme and Variations.* For the work was intended for use by high-school bands, and Schoenberg never expected his twelve-tone technique to be the musical diet of youngsters. The band version was completed in 1943. Soon afterward, it was arranged by the composer for full orchestra, in which form it was introduced by the Boston Symphony Orchestra under Serge Koussevitzky on October 20, 1944.

The work consists of a theme (which is march-like in character, befitting a band) and seven variations. Of these variations the most impressive are No. 3 (Poco adagio), lyrical and expressive; No. 6 (Allegro, a charming simulation of the waltz; and No. 7 (Moderato), a chorale-prelude. The work ends in a finale which serves as a summation and as an emotional climax.

A SURVIVOR FROM WARSAW, cantata for narrator, men's chorus, and orchestra, op. 46 (1947).

Out of one of the ghastlier pages of the history of World War II—that concerning the Nazi concentration camps—Schoenberg has created one of his most stirring works. In the text, written by Schoenberg himself, the narrator begins with the following words: "I cannot remember everything. I must have been unconscious most of the time." He then describes grimly the clubbing of the old and the sick, and the lining up of the healthier ones for the gas chamber. The Nazis shout their orders in German. But above these cries there arises the traditional Hebrew prayer, "Hear O Israel"—first softly, but then growing in intensity until it becomes at once a shout of defiance and a promulgation of undying faith.

The realism of the text, which is one of its most striking features, is matched by the equally stark realism of Schoenberg's music, much of it written in his twelve-tone technique. Rarely before has he endowed his technique with such a wealth of human values. The atonality becomes expressive of mental anguish; the complex rhythms re-create the emotional turmoil; and the ascetic melodic line assumes cogent dramatic power.

Though commissioned by the Koussevitzky Foundation, *A Survivor from Warsaw* was not introduced by the Boston Symphony Orchestra under Koussevitzky, but by the Albuquerque Civic Symphony Orchestra, Kurt Frederick conducting. The performance took place on November 4, 1948.

WILLIAM SCHUMAN 1910—

In discussing Schuman's music, writers most often point to its invigorating and robust movement. Leonard Bernstein has noted its "energetic drive, vigor of propulsion"; Paul Rosenfeld has poetically praised it for its "force ... moving joyously ... with a gesture of embrace out towards life"; Alfred Frankenstein has singled out its "nerves, virtuosity, drive." And so on. While its motor activity is an engaging quality—bringing buoyant enthusiasm and overpowering strength to each of his major works—Schuman's music is by no means exclusively dynamic. Other qualities are no less appealing: his highly expressive counterpoint, complex in texture but nevertheless warm and intense; his long-breathed melodies, often of classical beauty; his ever-fresh instrumentation; and, in occasional works such as *Newsreel* or *Side Show,* even an infectious sense of humor.

Schuman was born in New York City on August 4, 1910, and was educated in the city public schools and at Columbia University. His early musical education was spasmodic until, late in adolescence, he decided to pursue the art seriously. After preliminary studies, he became a private pupil of Charles Haubiel and Roy Harris, then was enrolled at the Mozarteum in Salzburg. His First Symphony and First String Quartet were presented by the WPA Composers Forum in New York in 1936; neither work satisfied the composer, and he withdrew both. His Second Symphony, introduced by the Boston Symphony Orchestra under Serge Koussevitzky on February 17, 1939, first brought him to public attention; and the great success of his Third Symphony, also performed by the Boston Symphony under Koussevitzky, made him famous. Since then he has been performed extensively, and has been the recipient of numerous honors and awards, including the Pulitzer Prize, the New York Music Critics Circle Award, a Guggenheim Fellowship (twice), the Town Hall League of Composers Award, and numerous citations and honorary appointments.

For a decade, beginning in 1935, Schuman taught at Sarah Lawrence College. He resigned this post to become director of publications of G. Schirmer & Co. In a few months' time he left Schirmer to become president of the Juilliard School of Music.

The following works are discussed below: *American Festival Overture;* Concerto for Violin and Orchestra; *A Free Song;* Quartet No. 3; Symphony No. 3; Symphony No. 5; Symphony No. 6; *Undertow.*

AMERICAN FESTIVAL OVERTURE, for orchestra (1939).

An incisive three-note phrase opens this authentically American piece of music. This phrase was meant by the composer to simulate a familiar call —the syllables "Wee-awk-eem" which are used by boys in the New York City streets to convoke the gang for play. "This call," Schuman explained, "very naturally suggested itself for a piece of music being written for a special occasion—a festival of American music."

Schuman's own analysis of the piece follows: "The first section of the work is concerned with the material discussed above and the ideas growing out of it. This music leads to a transition section and the subsequent announcement by the violas of a fugue subject. The entire middle section is given over to this fugue. The orchestration is at first for strings alone, later for woodwinds alone, and finally, as the fugue is brought to fruition, by the strings and woodwinds in combination. The climax leads to the final section of the work, which consists of the opening materials paraphrased and the introduction of new subsidiary ideas."

The overture was introduced by the Boston Symphony Orchestra under Koussevitzky on October 6, 1939.

QUARTET NO. 3, for strings (1939). I. Introduction. II. Intermezzo.

Schuman's Third Quartet is one of his finest works for a chamber-music ensemble. It was written on a joint commission from the League of Composers and Town Hall in New York. The first performance took place in New York City on February 27, 1940, by the Coolidge Quartet.

The introduction is meditative music, poetic in concept, which culminates in an ingeniously contrived fugue. Material from the introduction returns in the second movement, after which comes a series of elaborately developed variations.

SYMPHONY NO. 3 (1941). I. Passacaglia; Fugue. II. Chorale; Toccata.

. Schuman wrote his First Symphony in 1935, and his Second four years after that. It was with his Third Symphony that he achieved his first major success as a symphonic composer. Its première—by the Boston Symphony Orchestra under Koussevitzky on October 17, 1941—was a triumph; the audience was enthusiastic, and the critics, virtually rhapsodic. The symphony received the New York Critics Circle Award in 1942, and after that was performed by virtually every major American symphony orchestra; it was also played with considerable success in London, Paris, Copenhagen, Berlin, etc.

Though seventeenth-century forms are utilized by Schuman, there is nothing archaic about the music, which is modern in idiom. There is polyphonic writing here of great complexity and dexterity but this polyphony frequently has vertical beauty and dynamic power, and is frequently warm and human in its expressiveness. The theme of the Passacaglia is heard in the violas, in the lowest register—a sturdy theme. It is then altered melodically and rhythmically in a series of inventive variations. The Fugue comes without pause; its theme (approximately four bars long) is heard in the horns. The Chorale that opens the second part is derived from the passacaglia theme and appears in the solo trumpet. It is treated in several different ways before the music flows naturally into the Toccata section. As its name implies, the Toccata is a display piece featuring brilliant virtuoso writing for the orchestra.

A FREE SONG, secular cantata no. 2, for chorus and orchestra (1942). I. Too Long America; Look Down, Fair Moon. II. Song of the Banner at Daybreak.

For the text to his second secular cantata, Schuman went to Walt Whitman, couching three Whitman poems (as Nicolas Slonimsky put it so well) "in a propulsive rhythmic style as a twentieth-century counterpart of old Handelian forms." The writing is elaborately contrapuntal (the second part opens with an involved fugue), but the counterpoint generates considerable power. The over-all effect is one of strength and brilliance.

On March 26, 1943, the cantata was introduced by the Boston Symphony Orchestra—in collaboration with the Harvard Glee Club and the Radcliffe Choral Society—under the direction of Serge Koussevitzky. Soon after this première performance, the cantata was awarded the Pulitzer Prize in music.

SYMPHONY NO. 5, for strings (1943). I. Molto agitato ed energico. II. Larghissimo. III. Presto leggiero.

Schuman's Fifth Symphony is among his most economical works in the symphonic form, comprising only basic materials made up of concentrated harmonic and contrapuntal writing. The first movement is highly rhythmic, and derives its effect from its motor energy; the second movement is meditative, growing into an impressive climax; the third, which utilizes pizzicato passages for the strings with fine effect, has brilliance of color.

The symphony was commissioned by the Koussevitzky Foundation, and was introduced by the Boston Symphony Orchestra under Koussevitzky on November 12, 1943.

UNDERTOW, ballet (1945).

When Schuman's ballet *Undertow* was introduced in New York by the Ballet Theatre on April 10, 1945, it was described as "a psychological murder story." Actually it was the case history of a psychopath. The book was by Anthony Tudor, based on a suggestion by John van Druten; settings and costumes were by Raymond Breinin.

The following summary was prepared by both Schuman and Tudor: "The ballet . . . concerns itself with the emotional development of a transgressor. The choreographic action depicts a series of related happenings, the psychological implications of which result in inevitable murder. The hero is seen at various stages, beginning with his babyhood when he is neglected by his mother. . . . Frustrations . . . are heightened during boyhood by his sordid experiences in the lower reaches of a large city. He encounters prostitutes, street urchins, an innocent young girl, a bridal couple, dipsomaniacs, and a visiting mission worker whose care and friendship he seeks. The emotions aroused in the abnormal youth by these episodes. . . result in climax after climax, reaching a peak in the murder of a lascivious woman. It is only when he is apprehended for this crime that his soul is purged."

For this grim scenario, Schuman produced a powerful score which derives much of its effect from continual reiteration, and in which the darker and more dramatic pages are offset by passages of gaiety and irony.

Schuman took the basic material of this ballet score, telescoped it, and prepared a symphonic version which he called *Undertow: Choreographic Episodes for Orchestra*. The orchestral piece maintains the continuity of the ballet score. It is in three sections: I. Prologue—Birth and Infancy. II. The City—Adolescence and Manhood. III. Epilogue—Guilt.

CONCERTO FOR VIOLIN AND ORCHESTRA (1947). I. Allegro risoluto; Molto tranquillo; Agitato—fervente. II. Interlude: andantino. III. Presto leggiero; Adagio; Alla marcia; Cantabile alternando con presto.

This concerto was introduced in Boston by Isaac Stern and the Boston Symphony Orchestra under Charles Munch on February 10, 1950. An expansive melody for the violin opens the concerto, undergoing some development and then being succeeded by a second melody, tranquil in mood, also played by the soloist. A rhapsodic passage for the violin is then heard. After a large cadenza, the movement ends dramatically. The second movement is intended as an interlude, consisting of a long, rhapsodic melody for the violin; it is intense in feeling, broad in design. A four-voice fugato introduces the final movement. After a climax for orchestra, the solo instrument enters. A short cadenza and a powerful climax then bring the concerto to an end.

SYMPHONY NO. 6 (1948).

In 1948, the Dallas Symphony Orchestra commissioned Schuman to write an orchestral work. On February 27, 1949, it was introduced by that organization under Antal Dorati in Dallas, Texas.

Though in one uninterrupted movement, the symphony consists of six parts, marked: Largo; Moderato con moto; Leggieramente; Adagio; Allegro risoluto—presto; Larghissimo. The framework of the symphony is the two outside slow movements, while the other four movements have a suggestion of the classical symphonic form. The major thematic material is presented in the opening section, with a contrasting theme appearing contrapuntally. After the material has been offered, there comes the march-like music of the second section, in which the themes appear in variation. A kind of cadenza for kettle-drum leads into the third part, which is vivacious. After a slow passage for strings, there comes the Adagio, built out of a chorale-like melody. A violin solo comes as a transition to a highly rhythmic development section. There then emerges the turbulence of the Allegro risoluto passage, whose concluding Presto is in the nature of a coda. After a climax, an intermediary passage leads to the concluding Larghissimo, eloquent music with suggestions of mysticism.

ALEXANDER SCRIABIN   1872—1915

Before he became a devotee of mysticism, Scriabin was a composer of exquisite miniatures which have been favorably compared with the best of Chopin. These miniatures are truly Chopinesque in poetic content, felicitousness of form, and reflection of magic moods; they belong with the very best writings in romantic piano music.

But then Scriabin succumbed to a grandiose religion-philosophy which he called the "Mystery," and tried to make his music at least a partial expression of such a philosophy. He evolved his own harmonic system, the spine of which was the "Mystic Chord"—built not out of thirds but fourths. His writing grew more and more nebulous, involved and remote, until it became virtually impossible for the listener to follow him in his strange, mystic dreams.

In or about 1900, Scriabin was drawn to the mysticism of Prince S. N. Trubetskoy, with whom he attended many meetings of the Philosophical Society, whose discussions made a deep impression on him. Two years after this, he was particularly attracted to Nietzsche's philosophy, identifying himself with the concept of the Superman. (He even planned at this time an opera about a Nietzschean hero who, through art, conquers the world.) From Nietzsche he went on to theosophy. Thus, as the years passed, he immersed himself deeper and deeper in the nebulous world of mysticism, until he arrived at a vision of his own.

His vision was not merely a new kind of music but a new kind of *Weltanschauung:* a unity of all social, religious, philosophic, and artistic thinking into a new system. "Art," he said, "must unite with philosophy and religion in an indivisible whole to form a new Gospel which will replace the old Gospel which we have outlived. I cherish the dream of creating such a 'Mystery.'" He wanted that "Mystery" to summarize the whole history of mankind from the beginning of time to the final cataclysm which he felt would some day be at hand to purge the world and make room for a new race of nobler men. He wanted to use every artistic means at his disposal: dancing, music, poetry, colors, even smells. He even thought of devising a new language for his "Mystery," made up of sighs and exclamations rather than words.

For the practice of that "Mystery" he envisioned a special globe-shaped temple in India, situated on a lake—for he knew that humanity was not ready for his concept. But the human race as we know it was doomed, and he felt that his "Mystery" would be the final expression of the dying race and the transition to the new race of man.

When World War I broke out, Scriabin was convinced that it would be the purification the world was waiting for, after which the new race could emerge. And he had no doubt that he himself was the Messiah pointing the way to the new world.

Scriabin never did get around to writing the "Mystery," which he planned over a great number of years. He merely finished the text and some musical sketches for a cantata called *L'Acte Préalable* (*Preliminary Act*), which was to have been the introduction to the entire philosophy. But the idea of the "Mystery" penetrated more and more into his writing after 1900, until it obsessed him entirely.

Scriabin was born in Moscow on January 6, 1872, the son of an excellent pianist. He was taught music early, first by his aunt, then by Conus and Zverev. In 1888, he entered the Moscow Conservatory, where his teachers included Safonov, Taneiev, and Arensky; in 1891 he won a gold medal for piano playing.

Meanwhile, he began writing little pieces for the piano which, while derivative from Chopin, revealed such talent that they attracted the attention of the publisher Belaiev. Belaiev decided to sponsor the young musician, gave him a handsome contract for his compositions, and subsidized a tour for him as piano virtuoso in programs of his works.

From 1898 to 1903, Scriabin taught piano at the Moscow Conservatory. But teaching proved a painful chore to him, and he abandoned it for composition and piano recitals. In 1906, he toured the United States with great success.

His writing had been undergoing a radical metamorphosis all this time, due to his increasing interest in mysticism and philosophy. However, though his music was growing more involved and abstruse, he did not lack recognition, due largely to the stouthearted efforts of the conductor Serge Koussevitzky in promoting his interests. Scriabin appeared frequently with the Koussevitzky Orchestra and in piano recitals which helped to propagandize his music to audiences everywhere. Scriabin's appearances came to a sudden end when he developed a tumor on his lip. This tumor was the cause of his death in Moscow on April 27, 1915.

The following works by Scriabin are discussed below: *The Divine Poem* (Symphony No. 3); *Études*; *Poem of Ecstasy* (Symphony No. 4); Preludes; *Prometheus: The Poem of Fire* (Symphony No. 5); Sonatas.

THE DIVINE POEM (SYMPHONY NO. 3), in C Major; op. 43 (1903).

The merging of music with philosophy was one of Scriabin's pet ideals. In this he was abetted by his common-law wife, Tatiana Schloezer, who wrote a programmatic text, rich with theosophic implications, which became the basis of *The Divine Poem*.

In this symphony (it is actually a tone-poem and not a symphony, Scriabin attempted to represent, as Tatiana's text explains, "the evolution of the human spirit which, torn from an entire past of beliefs and mysteries which it surmounts and overturns, passes through pantheism and attains to a joyous and intoxicated affirmation of its liberty and its unity with the universe (the divine 'Ego')."

Tatiana's text of the three movements follows:

"*Struggles.* The conflict between the man who is a slave of a personal god, supreme master of the world, and the free, powerful man—the man-God. The latter appears to triumph, but it is only the intellect which affirms the divine 'Ego,' while the individual will, still too weak, is tempted to sink into pantheism.

"*Delights.* The man allows himself to be captured by the delights of the sensual world. He is intoxicated and soothed by the voluptuous pleasures into which he plunges. His personality loses itself in nature. It is then that the sense of the sublime arises from the depths of his being and assists him to conquer the passive state of his human 'Ego.'

"*Divine Play.* The spirit finally freed from all the bonds which fastened it to its past of submission to a superior power, the spirit producing the universe by the sole power of its own creative will, conscious of being at one with this universe, abandons itself to the sublime joy of free activity—the 'Divine Play.' "

On May 29, 1905, *The Divine Poem* was introduced in Paris under the direction of Artur Nikisch.

POEM OF ECSTASY (Symphony No. 4), in C Major, op. 54 (1907).

In this work, Scriabin expatiated on the "Joy in Creative Activity," the ecstasy of unfettered action. The two themes heard in the prologue symbolize, respectively, the pursuit after an ideal and the Ego theme realizing itself. A sonata-form section follows the prologue, beginning with an ecstatic theme describing the soaring flight of the spirit. After a repetition of the two prologue themes, a Lento passage arrives speaking of human love. A trumpet subject calls to the Will to assert itself, and the creative force appears. All these melodic and rhythmic ideas are now developed with great variety, "at times spending dreamy moments of delicious charm and perfume," as A. Eaglefield Hull wrote in his definitive analysis of this work, "occasionally rising to a climax of almost hilarious pleasure; at other moments experiencing violent stormy emotions and tragic cataclysms."

Scriabin played parts of the *Poem* privately to a select group of Russian musicians which included Rachmaninoff, Glazunov, and Rimsky-Korsakov. This eminent jury denounced the work in no uncertain terms. Rimsky-Korsakov said bluntly: "He's half out of his mind."

However, the Belaiev organization accepted it for publication and even awarded it the second Glinka Prize. The first performance took place in New York on December 10, 1908, under Modest Altschuler's direction.

PROMETHEUS: THE POEM OF FIRE (Symphony No. 5), in F-sharp major, op. 60 (1910).

In *Prometheus*—Scriabin's last orchestral work—there are the roots of the "Mystery" which he was conceiving at this time. Man (represented by the piano) is set against the Cosmos (the orchestra). Adapting a later version of the Prometheus legend, Scriabin sets out to show how mankind, in primitive stages, lacked the Promethean spark; it was consequently without will or self-consciousness. Prometheus then gave mankind the divine spark, thereby bringing into being self-consciousness and the Creative Will. But the gift of fire is both a curse and a blessing: there are those who use it for good, and others who make it an instrument of evil.

A mystical atmosphere is created with a typical Scriabin chord at the opening of the work. The emergence of the Creative Will is heard in a trumpet call, after which the piano enters with a theme suggesting the Creative Will. The music grows in passion and sensuousness as self-consciousness is born, and with it human love. There are conflicts; but eventually Humanity merges with the Cosmos. The work ends ecstatically as a chorus of mixed voices joins the orchestra in a wordless chant.

One of the novel features of this composition is its marriage to actual colors; for Scriabin had intended having a keyboard instrument throw colors on a screen while the music was being played. However, when *Prometheus* was introduced (by the Koussevitzky Orchestra under Koussevitzky, with Scriabin at the piano on March 15, 1911, in Moscow) the colors were dispensed with, as they invariably are when the work is heard nowadays. A performance of *Prometheus* with colors, by the Russian Symphony Orchestra under Modest Altschuler, took place in New York City in 1915.

ÉTUDES, for piano.

The twenty-six Études for piano which Scriabin wrote are usually written in the grand manner, of which the dramatic op. 8, no. 2, is both a famous and a characteristic example. Albert Wier finds that the influence of Brahms can be found in two of the op. 8 Études (nos. 2 and 3), while that of Chopin is prevalent in the sixth of the set; that in op. 42, rhythmic problems are explored with considerable virtuosity, and that two of the Études of op. 65 are characterized by "excruciating effects in melody-writing," one being in ninths, the other in sevenths, and both filled with unusual harmonic progressions.

PRÉLUDES, for piano.

Scriabin wrote eighty-nine Preludes for the piano. Up to op. 31, the Preludes are Chopinesque in the delicacy of the melody and the refinement of style. The best of these Preludes—they are among the finest short works for the piano in contemporary music—traverse a flexible range of emotions. There is serenity in op. 11, no. 5, contemplation in op. 11, no. 2, lyric poetry in op. 22, no. 1, and gentle sadness in op. 11, no. 3; on the other hand, there is febrile restlessness in op. 11, no. 14, dramatic power in op. 11, no. 1, and intensity and turbulent feeling in op. 27, no. 1.

After op. 31, the harmonic writing becomes more involved and sometimes more acrid, and the atmospheric effect more subtle. With the last Preludes, opp. 67 and 74, the style reaches—as Sabaneyev said of all Scriabin's later piano music—"an extraordinary exquisiteness and refinement, the harmony a rare complexity, along with a saturation of psychologic content. . . .

We observe a dissolution of rhythm, a reduction of melody to the minimum, a severance of the musical web and line which turns into a series of spasmodic exclamations and destroys the impressions of unity and wholeness."

SONATAS, for piano.

Scriabin wrote ten sonatas for the piano. The first three (in two movements, with introduction and main section) reveal his indebtedness to Chopin and Liszt. With the Fourth Sonata, in F-sharp Major, op. 30, Scriabin adopted the one-movement form which he was henceforth to utilize. The Fourth Sonata is programmatic: the first movement is intended to be the motive of desire, and the second, the motive of anguish. Technically, this sonata is of interest because its harmonic construction—with its building up of the intervals of a fourth—suggests the later "Mystic Chord."

With each succeeding sonata, Scriabin penetrated ever deeper into mysticism. The Fifth Sonata, in D-sharp Minor, op. 53, bears the following quotation from the *Poem of Ecstasy*—intended as a program for the music:

> I call you to life, O mysterious forces,
> Submerged in depths, obscure!
> O thou creative spirit, timid of life,
> To you I bring courage!

The music is, for the most part, turbulent in the introduction, while in the prologue that follows it becomes at different times tender, mysterious, impetuous.

With the Sixth Sonata, op. 62, Scriabin dispensed with key signatures. The Seventh Sonata, op. 64 (completed before the Sixth) was the composer's favorite, possibly because of its rich vein of mysticism. The music is mostly harsh, ending with a frenetic dance. The Eighth Sonata, op. 66, is the longest. It begins with an expressive introduction, following which comes the complex main section built out of three principal ideas. The Ninth Sonata, op. 68, has been called "The Black Mask." It opens in an atmosphere of mystery and proceeds with the main section, in which four ideas are heard in succession, then developed. The peroration of this work, wrote Hull, "is masterful and striking, and the sonata ends in that dim and mysterious light in which the dream opened."

The last of the Scriabin sonatas, op. 70, is probably the most elusive in content, the most obscure in thought, and the most complex in technique.

ROGER SESSIONS   1896—

Roger Sessions is one of the most complex of living American composers. His music is high-tensioned and dissonant. Generally written around
more than a single tonal center, it emphasizes rhythm and harmony (both
extremely complicated in structure) rather than melody. The musical ideas
are involved and original, abounding with subtle processes of thought. Complexity of technique and involved thinking combine to make Sessions' music
difficult to assimilate at first hearing; but even then its vigor and independence are recognizable.

Sessions was born in Brooklyn, New York, on December 28, 1896.
His academic education was received at the Kent School in Connecticut and
at Harvard University, while his musical studies took place at the Yale
School of Music and privately with Ernest Bloch and other teachers. When
Bloch became director of the Cleveland Institute of Music in 1921, Sessions
was his assistant. For eight years after 1925, Sessions lived in Europe, compos-
ing several major works, including the Symphony in E Minor, which the
Boston Symphony Orchestra under Koussevitzky introduced in April, 1927.
Since his return to the United States, Sessions has held various important
teaching positions, notably at Columbia University, Princeton University,
and the University of California at Berkeley.
    The following works by Sessions are discussed below: Concerto in B
Minor for Violin and Orchestra; Symphony No. 2.

CONCERTO IN B MINOR FOR VIOLIN AND ORCHESTRA
(1935). I. Largo e tranquillo, con grande espressione. II. Scherzo. III.
Romanza. IV. Finale: molto vivace e sempre con fuoco.
    This violin concerto is a comparatively early work of Sessions; it was
begun in 1931 and completed four years later. Sessions considers the concerto
one of the first works in which his later characteristic style is evident. The
first performance of the concerto took place in 1935 at a concert at the New
School for Social Research in New York; Serge Kotlarsky was the soloist,
and the composer accompanied him at the piano. The first performance with
orchestra was given by the Illinois Symphony Orchestra, Izler Solomon conducting, with Robert Gross, violinist.
    The first movement is divided into three large sections, each of which
is introduced by a theme which opens the concerto (trombone, answered by

trumpet). The second movement is a vigorous Scherzo, the principal theme of which begins with two staccato chords and continues energetically in clarinet and flute; the second theme is even sprightlier. A middle trio section is tranquil in character. An involved melody, heard for the most part in the solo violin, dominates the Romanza section. An unaccompanied passage for violin heralds the approach of the final movement, which is the longest and most complex of the entire work. Sessions described the character of this movement as "that of ever-increasing intensity, relieved by a waltz-like episode which forms a large portion of the middle section."

SYMPHONY NO. 2 (1946). I. Molto agitato. II. Allegretto capriccioso. III. Adagio tranquillo ed espressivo. IV. Allegramente.

Though the ideas for this symphony date as far back as 1934, Sessions did not set to work on it until 1944, when it was commissioned by the Ditson Fund. He completed it two years later, and on January 9, 1947, it was introduced by the San Francisco Symphony Orchestra under Pierre Monteux. The symphony is dedicated to the memory of Franklin Delano Roosevelt, whose death occurred when the composer was writing the Adagio movement.

The composer has this to say about the work: "With reasonable accuracy it may be considered as in the key of D Minor—the movements being in D Minor, F Minor, B-flat Minor, and D Major respectively.... Those who would like a clue to what is sometimes called the 'emotional content' I would refer to the tempo indications of the various movements, which give a fair idea of the character of each—though the hearer may perhaps feel that the Adagio is predominately dark and somber, and find that the last movement is interrupted, at its climax, by a blare of trombones, introducing an episode which contrasts sharply with the rest of the movement, which returns to its original character only gradually."

The first movement is in five distinct sections, a Molto agitato part being heard at the opening, closing, and in the middle, and two tranquil sections providing contrast. The second movement is a brief intermezzo. Three sections comprise the third movement, the last of which corresponds in outline to the first. The concluding movement assumes the form of a rondo in seven sections.

The symphony was selected by the Music Critics Circle of New York as the best new work by an American performed during the 1949-50 season.

DMITRI SHOSTAKOVICH   1906—

No other composer of our time has commuted from acclaim to denunciation in quite the way that Shostakovich has—particularly in his own land. As the composer of the brilliant First Symphony—and the passionate advocate of music of Soviet ideology—Shostakovich soon became the darling of Soviet officialdom, the object of much praise, honor, and important performances. Then, with his position seemingly secure, he experienced the first of his setbacks. An opera based on a satirical play by Gogol, *The Nose,* was produced at Leningrad on January 13, 1930, only to be soundly denounced by the Association of Proletarian Composers as a product of "bourgeois decadence." It took Shostakovich a little time to rehabilitate his position in Soviet music—but rehabilitate it he did, particularly with the success of his Concerto for Piano. Then once again savage attack descended on him. His opera, *Lady Macbeth of Mzensk*—which had been running with considerable success for two years!—suddenly became the victim of a critical blitz. In an article in *Pravda* entitled "Confusion Instead of Music," the opera was described as vulgar, "the coarsest kind of naturalism.... The music quacks, grunts, growls, and suffocates itself in order to express the amatory scenes as naturalistically as possible." Hardly had the echoes of this attack died down when (one week later) another Shostakovich work came in for similarly rough treatment. The ballet *The Limpid Stream,* about a collective farm in Kuban, was described as "without character. . . . It jingles, it means nothing. The composer apparently has only contempt for our national songs."

Two such attacks within one week, and in an organ like *Pravda,* could mean only one thing: the pet of Soviet music had lost favor with the powers. Shostakovich was now avoided by other leading Soviet composers. He was henceforth not given much attention in the press in 1936 and 1937, and when he was it was always unfavorably. Those who had formerly been warmest in their praises—and these included intimate friends—were now contemptuous of him.

But with the most amazing resiliency, Shostakovich once again bounced back to success, abetted by the major triumph of his Fifth Symphony in 1937. When his Piano Quintet received the Stalin Prize of one hundred thousand rubles in 1940, there could no longer be a doubt that he was once again the leading composer of his land. With the outbreak of the war, he became even more than that: a national hero.

Now, surely, it appeared that his position was unassailable! But

Shostakovich was still to experience storm and stress. In 1946, his Ninth Symphony was denounced by *Culture and Life* for its "ideological weakness" and for its failure to "reflect the spirit of the Soviet people." In a totalitarian state, unfavorable criticism directed against a composer of Shostakovich's stature and prestige is usually the warning of greater attacks to come; and the denunciation of the Ninth Symphony was only the beginning. On February 10, 1948, Shostakovich was one of several major composers to be officially denounced by the Central Committee of the Communist Party for "decadent formalism" (see Prokofiev). The term "formalism" had been hurled at Shostakovich in 1936; it was now applied not only to him but to other major Soviet composers as well.

And yet once again Shostakovich was to return to grace! He beat his breast publicly and confessed his guilt: "I know that the Party is right; I know that the Party shows solicitude for Soviet art.... All the directives of the Central Committee ... and in particular those that concern me personally, I accept as a stern but paternal solicitude for us, Soviet artists.... I shall try again and again to create symphonic works close to the spirit of the people." And he turned to the writing of music fulfilling the new esthetic requirements of the Committee. In 1949, his oratorio *The Song of the Forests* received the Stalin Prize. This, and the fact that a few months earlier he had been sent by the Soviet government to the United States as a member of the Cultural and Scientific Conference for World Peace, was stout evidence that Shostakovich was once again favored.

In the Soviet Union, where musical criticism is so often dictated by political expediency and has very little to do with the quality of the music under discussion, these frequent changes of official attitude to Shostakovich's music are more interesting than significant. What is significant, however, is that Shostakovich has often been subjected to wide divergence of public reaction in the world outside the Soviet Union. He has been widely publicized, praised, and performed; and he has been severely criticized, too. His music has been described as vital, fresh, spontaneous, infectious, powerful; it has also been called vulgar, trite, commonplace. Frequently these disparate points of view have been expressed by one and the same critic; and frequently, too, they have been expressed about one and the same work.

The sad truth is that few major composers of our time have been so uneven in their production. In his best satirical vein, Shostakovich is inimitable; his scherzos are fleet-footed, rhythmically dynamic, aglow with wit and malice, full of spice and sting. Sometimes he achieves moments of genuine majesty. And in his more recent symphonies, he has written expressive melodies. But it often happens that after a grandiose page of music he suddenly becomes as naïve as a schoolboy, almost as if he cannot discriminate between the good and the bad. At his best, he is a powerful and original voice; at his worst, he is given to disturbing clichés and obvious writing. It is unfortunate, indeed, that he has produced so few works in which the good is not adulterated by the bad.

Shostakovich was born in St. Petersburg on September 25, 1906. From 1919 to 1925 he was a student at the Leningrad Conservatory, where his teachers included Sokolov and Steinberg. Hardly had he left the Conservatory when he achieved his first major success with his First Symphony.

He was only eleven when revolution changed the political and social structure of his country. He consequently knew no other society than that of the proletariat, to which, of course, he subscribed wholeheartedly. From the very first, he traveled under the banner of proletarian music, as articulated first by the Association of Proletarian Musicians (organized in 1924), and then by the Society for the Encouragement of Proletarian Composers (founded in 1925). "We are revolutionaries," Shostakovich said in an interview, "and as revolutionaries we have a different concept of music. Lenin himself said that 'music is a means of unifying broad masses of people.'" Music was to interpret the social and political ideals of the people; it was to reflect the pride of the people in their industrial and social achievements; it was to "reflect [as the platform of the Association of Proletarian Musicians noted] the rich, full-blooded psychology of the proletariat," and to penetrate "into the innermost masses of workmen and peasants, unite the thought and will of these masses and raise them for further struggle and construction."

The fluctuations of Shostakovich's fortunes as the people's composer have been described in detail in the preceding paragraphs. Notwithstanding these fluctuations, he has remained a dynamic figure in Soviet music. He visited the United States in 1949, and in 1956 he received the Order of Lenin on the occasion of his fiftieth birthday.

The following works by Shostakovich are discussed below: Concerto in C Minor for Piano and Orchestra; Preludes; Quartet No. 2; Quintet for Piano and Strings; Sonata for Cello and Piano; Sonata No. 2 for Piano; *Song of the Forests;* Symphony No. 1; Symphony No. 5; Symphony No. 6; Symphony No. 7; Symphony No. 8; Symphony No. 9.

SYMPHONY NO. 1, op. 10 (1926). I. Allegretto. II. Allegro. III. Lento. IV. Allegro molto.

When the First Symphony was rehearsed prior to its première performance, Glazunov voiced amazement at the composer's virtuosity in orchestration. Others were impressed by its freshness and kinetic drive; still others expressed amazement that so completely and maturely realized a work could be found in a "first symphony" by a young composer. When the symphony was introduced by the Leningrad Philharmonic under Nikolai Malko on May 12, 1926, there was an exceptional ovation for the composer. Not yet twenty years old, Shostakovich was realizing his first triumph.

There are those who consider this symphony the best Shostakovich has written. Certainly it never fails to magnetize the audience with its electric energy, and to delight with its wonderful spontaneity and youthful enthusiasm. Derivative though it may occasionally be (sometimes from Tchaikovsky; sometimes, Prokofiev), it still has a definite personality of its own. The ebullient second movement and the dramatic alterations of mood and tempo in the last movement are traces of Shostakovich's later, fully developed style.

A muted trumpet opens the first movement, the principal theme of which is a tripping melody for clarinet; the second theme is a sentimental idea in the vein of Tchaikovsky, heard in the flute against pizzicati of the strings. The themes stated, the atmosphere becomes feverish and a sudden climax erupts. The movement ends gently, however, with a restatement of the opening bars in clarinet and celli.

The music of the second movement is Shostakovich in a familiar pose of irresponsibility—spirited music, full of joyful impulsiveness. The Lento that follows is in an entirely different manner, romantic and touched with sadness, dominated by a tender song heard at the opening of the movement in an oboe solo against string tremolos. The finale has stirring emotions and sharp contrasts. It opens with a restrained theme (Lento), which is soon succeeded by a turbulent Allegro molto section; the movement then passes from slow to fast, from tranquillity to drama. The music ends brilliantly with a whirlwind presto.

CONCERTO IN C MINOR FOR PIANO AND ORCHESTRA, op. 33 (1933). I. Allegro moderato. II. Lento. III. Moderato. IV. Allegro.

One of the unusual features of this piano concerto is its instrumentation: it is scored for string orchestra and a single trumpet. The trumpet ushers in the first movement with a simple, almost ingenuous little melody. The piano then enters with the first theme; the piano also introduces the second theme, after the pace has quickened into an Allegro vivace. The development is frequently contrapuntal, growing all the while in sonority; it ends with a restatement of the first theme, set against low groans of the trumpet.

A waltz rhythm is prominent in the second movement, with the main melody—a long, sustained song—heard in the violins, then answered by the piano. The tempo quickens; the sonority grows to fortissimo. The melody is later taken up by the trumpet, and after that by the piano.

The third movement is a brief twenty-nine-bar intermezzo, in which two cadenzas for the piano are prominent, one of them accompanied. The final movement brims over with good spirits, with the trumpet assuming almost a harlequin's role. The tunes are gaily mocking, and there is even a witty parody of the kind of melodic material found in the classical sonatas, and a mischievous quotation of a Beethoven melody.

The concerto was introduced on October 15, 1933, by the Leningrad Philharmonic under Fritz Stiedry; the composer was soloist.

PRELUDES, for piano, op. 24 (1933).

Between December, 1932, and March, 1933, Shostakovich wrote twenty-four preludes for the piano, in which the traditions of Chopin, Scriabin, and Rachmaninoff (rather than those of Debussy) are carried on. For the Shostakovich prelude is a psychological rather than an impressionistic sketch.

There is a wealth of emotional feeling in these preludes, though it must be confessed that their quality is uneven, ranging from "the sublime to the downright banal," as Ivan Martynov points out. Martynov singles out the following preludes as outstanding: the sombre and tragic E Minor Prelude, which "calls to mind the lofty portals of a Gothic church"; the structurally interesting E-flat Minor Prelude, a fugato; the D Major ("Velocity Étude") Prelude, with its effective passage writing; and the jazzy D Minor Prelude, the last of the set.

Leopold Stokowski has made an orchestral transcription of the E-flat Minor Prelude.

SONATA FOR CELLO AND PIANO, op. 40 (1934). I. Moderato. II. Moderato con moto. III. Largo. IV. Allegretto.

This cello sonata, written in 1934, is one of Shostakovich's most lyrical works. The two themes of the first movement are rich in melodic interest, the first elegiac and the second (arriving in completed state after a series of modulations) brighter in character. The second movement is a lilting waltz with satirical suggestions. A depressive mood pervades the Largo, in which the cello chants a beautiful song of sorrow. This despair is completely abandoned in the closing Allegretto a rondo in form), which has irrepressible good spirits.

SYMPHONY NO. 5, op. 47 (1936). I. Moderato. II. Allegretto. III. Largo. IV. Allegro non troppo.

The great success of Shostakovich's Fifth Symphony—one of the greatest he has known—came at a critical moment in his career. For one thing, Shostakovich had up to now failed to write a symphony that could repeat the success and inspiration of the youthful First. The Second Symphony, op. 14 ("To October"), written in 1927, was a failure when it was introduced on November 6, 1927. If the Third Symphony ("May Day"), op. 20—which came two years later—did not duplicate the fiasco of the Second, it could hardly be considered a success either; it has rarely been heard. The Fourth Symphony was received so badly by the musicians when it was rehearsed that it never achieved public performance.

The première of the Fifth Symphony, therefore, did not promise much. But even more ominous to the possible success of the Fifth Symphony than the fact that its three predecessors had been outright failures was the fact that at this time, 1936, Shostakovich was out of public favor. The official blasts in *Pravda* against his opera *Lady Macbeth of Mzensk* and his ballet *The Limpid Stream* had discredited him. His works were now being rarely performed, while he himself was ignored. But in spite of such an unfavorable climate for the introduction of his new symphony, it was a success of the first magnitude when heard for the first time in Leningrad on November 21, 1937. The audience cheered; the critics—frigidly aloof to Shostakovich for the past year and a half—acclaimed it. Shostakovich's star had once again risen in Soviet music, to shine more luminously than ever.

The success of the Fifth Symphony has been duplicated wherever it has been heard, for, together with the First, it is the finest of Shostakovich's creations in the symphonic form. It is, for the most part, music of power and majesty, less spontaneous than the First, but more spacious in design and bigger in artistic scope.

The symphony opens powerfully with a big, wind-swept theme in the strings, which sets the stage for music of dramatic interest and striking contrasts. The second movement is slighter in texture, a scherzo that resembles a waltz and is in Shostakovich's satirical style. The slow movement is one of the most emotional and profound pieces of music that the composer has given us up to now. The melody is first heard in the strings and is allowed to grow and develop into a moving apostrophe. Music march-like in character is heard in the concluding movement, and is followed by a gentler section, with which the symphony ends.

SYMPHONY NO. 6, op. 54 (1938). I. Largo. II. Allegro. III. Presto.

The Sixth Symphony followed the fifth within a year. It was written in 1938 and was heard for the first time (but none too enthusiastically) on December 3, 1939, during a two-month festival of Soviet music in Moscow. Shostakovich had originally intended this symphony to be a tribute to Lenin, and conceived it along monumental lines for large chorus, orchestra, and soloists, with text provided by peasant poets. But somewhere during the writing of the music, Shostakovich abandoned the Lenin idea, as well as the ambitious scheme, and created a symphony for orchestra alone and without any program.

The symphony opens in an unorthodox manner: The usual sonata-allegro first movement is absent and we have in its place the second-movement Largo. This slow movement is long, involved, and emotional, opening with a lyric section for strings and woodwinds followed by an equally lyric theme, but more elegiac in character. The Scherzo that follows is light and frivolous, with occasional sardonic commentary interpolated by a xylophone. The symphony ends with a highly rhythmic Presto, in rondo form, with march and dance music taking turns in expressions of restrained mockery.

QUINTET FOR PIANO AND STRINGS, op. 57 (1940). I. Prelude and Fugue. II. Scherzo. III. Intermezzo.

The piano quintet is one of Shostakovich's foremost successes; and it is one of his finest works. On November 23, 1940, it was introduced and acclaimed at the Moscow Festival of Soviet Music. Soon after this, it won the Stalin Prize of one hundred thousand rubles.

Lyrical and human, the quintet (despite its unorthodox form) is easily appreciated at first hearing. It opens with a Prelude and Fugue. The form may be that of Bach; but the style is unmistakably Shostakovich. This introductory movement is in three parts (Lento, Poco piu mosso, Lento), with the thematic material presented in the first section; the Fugue derives its melodic idea from one of the melodies of the Prelude, and is charged with feeling. The Scherzo finds Shostakovich in a recognizable impish attitude. The rhythms are impulsive; the melody has infectious gaiety. The last movement has been described by Victor I. Seroff as "ballet music with a march rhythm"; one of the themes is a traditional melody of the Russian circus, announcing the approach of the clowns.

SYMPHONY NO. 7, op. 60. (1941). I. Allegretto. II. Moderato poco allegretto. III. Adagio. IV. Allegro non troppo.

Divorced from the stirring times in which it was created, the Seventh Symphony loses much of its emotional and dramatic interest. Recent rehearsings have confirmed the original suspicion that this is, for the most part, a vulgar work compounded of cheap and obvious effects. It can hardly hope to survive for its musical interest. But it is a piece of contemporary history, and as such may remain an interesting musical curiosity.

It was begun (it will be recalled) in July, 1941, a grim period for the Soviets. The Nazi hordes, which had invaded the land one month earlier, were sweeping relentlessly across the land, bringing defeat and devastation, searing the principal Russian cities with fire, and laying siege to Leningrad. Shostakovich, in Leningrad, planned his symphony as an expression of what he called "the majestic ideas of the patriotic war. Neither savage raids, German planes, nor the grim atmosphere of the beleaguered city could hinder the flow of ideas. I worked with an inhuman intensity I have never before reached."

When the government fled to Kuibyshev, Shostakovich followed. There he completed the symphony in December. The première performance took place in Kuibyshev on March 1, 1942, with the Bolshoi Theatre Orchestra conducted by Samuel Samosud. This concert was a gala political, as well as musical, occasion. High diplomatic and military officials attended, and responded enthusiastically to the new work.

The symphony was soon after this heard throughout the Soviet Union, acclaimed wherever it was performed. The score was microfilmed and flown by air to the United States. On July 19, 1942, Arturo Toscanini conducted the première American performance with the NBC Symphony over the radio.

Shostakovich has described his symphony in the following way:

"The first and longest movement bears a dramatic and, I would say, tragic character. Our peaceful life has been broken up by a threatening event, war, and everything has to be subordinated to its laws. The music also has another theme: a requiem expressing the people's sorrow over their dead heroes.

"The next two movements were intended as an intermezzo. They confirm life in opposition to war. I tried to express the thought that art, literature, and science must advance in spite of war. It is, if you like, a polemic against the statement that 'when the cannons roar the muse is silent.'

"The fourth movement is dedicated to our victory. It is an immediate continuation of the second and third movements; their logical outcome. It is the victory of light over darkness, wisdom over frenzy, lofty humanism over monstrous tyranny.

"On the whole, I feel that the Seventh Symphony is an optimistic conception. As a composition it is closer to my Fifth Symphony than to my Sixth; it is a continuation of the emotions and moods of the Fifth Symphony."

SYMPHONY NO. 8, op. 65 (1942). I. Adagio. II. Allegretto. III. Allegro non troppo. IV. Largo. V. Allegretto.

The Eighth Symphony came one year after the Seventh, and was heard for the first time at a festival of Soviet music in Moscow on November 4, 1943, with Eugene Mravinsky conducting the State Symphony Orchestra.

Shostakovich explained that this symphony was an attempt "to look into the future, into the postwar epoch." "Life is beautiful," Shostakovich wrote in explaining the mood of this work, "and all that is dark and ignominious will disappear. All that is beautiful will triumph." But though the composer intended it as an optimistic utterance, the symphony has a pervading feeling of deep tragedy, as though Shostakovich could not forget the war that was raging so bitterly all around him.

It opens with a long and very lyrical Adagio movement. The principal subject is a soaring melody for the first violins. This basic theme is preceded by a pleasing duet for high and low strings which opens and closes the movement. The second movement is a march. The next three movements proceed without interruption. The third carries on the rhythmic momentum of the second. The fourth is in a form suggesting a passacaglia, the bass of which recalls the opening theme of the symphony. The fifth is pastoral music in which a series of melodic ideas is presented by different solo instruments.

SONATA NO. 2 FOR PIANO, op. 64 (1943). I. Allegretto. II. Largo. III. Moderato.

Shostakovich's Second Piano Sonata was heard for the first time in Leningrad on November 11, 1943, with the composer performing. In reviewing the American première, Robert Bagar wrote in the *New York World-Telegram*: "The last movement is the great joy of the work, though there is joy unconfined in the beauties that unreel almost every second through it.... To contrast with the resolute and decisive feel of the first and third sections, there is the Largo, with its delicately exotic flavor. Some low chords are utilized in a kind of pallid and bleak rhythmic background against fragments of melody that fall gracefully and softly on the ear."

QUARTET NO. 2, for strings, op. 69 (1943). I. Overture. II. Recitative. III. Romance. IV. Waltz and Variations.

Shostakovich's Second String Quartet came seven years after the First (op. 49). It was introduced by the Beethoven Quartet in the Soviet Union on November 9, 1944. Ivan Martynov described the quartet as a "romantic poem" full of "light and space."

A propulsive theme, given an exotic character by use of plagal cadences, opens the quartet; a second important subject, tender and expressive, occurs in the high register of the violin against pizzicati of the other strings. In the next two movements, as Martynov notes, the listener is carried into "the sphere of lyrical contemplation." The Recitative reminds Martynov of the classical recitatives of Bach, while the Romance is a "calm song," interrupted briefly by passionate episodes. The waltz that follows is in the traditions of Glinka and Tchaikovsky (rather than the Viennese waltz); the melody is introduced by the cello.

SYMPHONY NO. 9, op. 70 (1945). I. Allegro. II. Moderato. III. Scherzo. IV. Largo.

The Ninth Symphony is the most joyous of Shostakovich's works in that form, "a merry little piece," as he himself described it. It is also the shortest and simplest. It was heard on November 3, 1945, in Leningrad, with Eugene Mravinsky conducting the Leningrad Philharmonic Orchestra.

There are some commentators who like to consider the Ninth Symphony as the third in a symphonic trilogy inspired by the war. The Seventh expressed the martial spirit of a people rising to defend its land; the Eighth echoed the tragic overtones of a grim war; the Ninth was the gay and uninhibited voice of victory.

Gregory Schneerson, the eminent Soviet critic, has prepared the following analysis:

"The opening bars of the first movement transported us at once to a bright and pleasant world. There was joyous abandon, the warm pulsation of life and the exuberance of youth in those whimsical dance themes and rhythms. There was something about the classical purity of form, the dynamic development of the themes, and the rich expressiveness emanating from a sheer pleasure in the interplay of sound images that reminded us of Haydn.... As the symphonic action developed, Haydn associations grew gradually fainter until at last we came to the kernel of the music, to Shostakovich himself. Shostakovich—ever original, ever fresh, ever the clever, witty narrator, eager and sincere.

"The second movement introduces a new mood, one of warm and gentle lyricism, faintly touched by wistful meditation. The Scherzo, built on the variational development of several dance melodies, is perhaps the culmination of the emotional content of the entire symphony. It is music of radiant joy, an almost childlike abandon to happiness. The swift movement of the Scherzo is interrupted by a brief but extremely significant episode—[the] Largo. Here, it seems to me, is a key to the understanding of the single idea uniting the three parts of this symphonic trilogy. The Largo is the link that joins the separate parts in spite of stylistic differences of musical idiom and emotional content.

"The finale scintillates with humor and inventiveness. Radiant in mood and simple in design, the theme passes through masterful elaboration until it reaches the whirlwind coda that completes the symphony. A brief upward scale ... and the symphony is ended."

Though the audience and critics liked this symphony, Soviet officialdom soon frowned upon it as "ideologically weak" and a poor reflection of the true spirit of the Soviet people. I. Nestiev denounced the cynicism and the cold irony of the music in *Culture and Life,* and found that these traits were the results of Stravinsky's influence. In reply to this denunciation, Serge Koussevitzky expressed the opinion in Boston that the Ninth Symphony was "one of the most beautiful of our contemporary works."

SONG OF THE FORESTS, oratorio for children's choir, mixed choir, soloists, and orchestra, op. 81 (1949). I. At the War's End. II. In Forests Let Us Clothe Our Land. III. Remembrances of the Past. IV. Children Plant the Forests. V. Arise to Great Deeds All Ye People. VI. Promenade in the Future. VII. Glory.

With this oratorio (Shostakovich's first large work for chorus), he reestablished himself as a leading composer in the Soviet Union after the destructive attacks leveled against him in 1948 by the Central Committee of the Communist Party. It was acclaimed in the Soviet press as a prototype of the kind of subject and the kind of music to which Soviet composers were expected to devote themselves, and the Stalin Prize was conferred on it. The text, by Eugene Dolmotovsky, glorifies the program of reforestation undertaken by the Soviet Union after World War II to reclaim desert areas.

Shostakovich's score makes extensive use of two principal melodic subjects. The first is a cyclical theme which is heard at the opening in the orchestral introduction. The second is a germ motive, appearing first in the bass solo to the words "With victory came the end of the war," which undergoes considerable transformation and development throughout the entire oratorio. Both subjects are heard simultaneously in chorus and orchestra in the concluding "Glory."

The oratorio is in seven sections. The first tells about the end of World War II and the project to reclaim the desert lands in central Russia. The second part echoes the joyous reaction of the people to this plan. A melancholy mood is evoked in the third movement as the wastelands, and the misery they create for the people, are described. A lighter part follows: The children join in the activity of planting the trees, singing as they work. The sixth part is a pastoral poem, evoking the beauty of Nature in the springtime. All the vocal and orchestral forces are combined with immense power and brilliance of color in the finale, a mighty fugal paean to the glory of reforestation.

JEAN SIBELIUS   1865—1957

Sibelius proved once again, if such proof is necessary, that no musical style or form is really dated or obsolete if the composer brings to it freshness, inventiveness, creative strength. Sibelius never completely broke with tradition. He invented no new idioms, fashioned no new forms. He used modern techniques comparatively sparingly. Yet his music is original—recognizably his own. There is no mistaking the authorship of those healthy, irresistible melodies of the fast movements, or of the bucolic tranquillity (so often touched with elegiac sadness) of the slow ones. There is no mistaking who is the creator of the architectural monuments of his symphonies, cathedrals of tone built idea by idea, theme by theme.

When Sibelius began composing, Brahms dominated the world of symphonic music; and Brahms influenced the young Sibelius profoundly. They met in Vienna in 1890, the young man coming to pay reverent tribute to the master. In his first works, an orchestral overture and an octet, Sibelius imitated the romanticism and the sensual surges of Brahms' music.

But it was not long before a new Sibelius emerged from the shell of the old, a Sibelius with a style and message of his own. Returning to his native land after travels in Germany and Austria, Sibelius was fired with patriotic ardor that influenced his musical writing. He now sought to express the soul of his land in music that derived its character from Finnish folk songs: *Kullervo* (1892), *En Saga* (1892), *Karelia* (1893), the *Lemminkäinen* (four legends), which includes the poignant "Swan of Tuonela," (1893-99) and the mighty "Finlandia" (1899-1900).

Just before writing "Finlandia," Sibelius composed his First Symphony (1898-99), and with it launched his career as the most famous symphonic composer of the twentieth century. The First Symphony and the Second which followed it in 1901 were true to Germanic traditions. But with the Third (1904-07), Sibelius began deviating slightly from symphonic form (here the Scherzo and the finale become a single movement); and with the Fourth (1911), he achieved more conciseness and greater intensity, economy, and directness. With the next three symphonies he reduced the orchestral forces, sacrificed long and spacious melodies for short, epigrammatic ideas, replaced expansive emotions with sober and restrained feelings, and simplified the orchestral fabric through diminution of contrapuntal writing and reduction of harmonic language.

The symphonies of Sibelius are, without question, the music of Finland; the country, its people, its backgrounds, its folklore, give character and personality to the musical content. For this reason, programs have been interpreted for these symphonies by many writers. But Sibelius has always insisted that his symphonies must be considered as absolute music. "My symphonies," he confided in an interview by Walter Legge of the *London Daily Telegraph,* "are music conceived and worked out in terms of music, and with no literary basis.... For me, music begins where words cease.... The germ and the fertilization of my symphonies has been solely musical."

Sibelius was born in Tavastehus, Finland, on December 8, 1865. Though he revealed talent for music when he was only five, he did not receive his first lessons until his ninth year, when he began studying the piano. After that he engaged a local musician to teach him the violin, and studied harmony by himself.

In 1885, he was sent to Helsingfors to study law. At the same time he was enrolled in the Musical Academy, where he was a pupil of Martin Wegelius. The intervention of an uncle, who recognized his great talent for music, enabled Sibelius to give up the law for music. Sibelius went to Berlin on a government grant to become a pupil of Albert Becker, and after that to Vienna, where one of his teachers was Robert Fuchs. In Vienna, Sibelius wrote a quartet and an octet, both strongly influenced by Germanic romanticism.

Back in his native land, Sibelius became aroused by national consciousness. He absorbed the national epic of Finland, the *Kalevala*. He acquainted himself with the history and traditions of his land. He was fired with the dream of freeing his country from the tyrannical rule of the Russians.

This national consciousness entered into his musical writing and motivated the production of the first works to make him famous. *En Saga,* op. 9, was the first major orchestral composition to reflect the spirit of

Finland, and with it Finnish national music achieved artistic significance for the first time. Sibelius wrote it in 1892 for the conductor Robert Kajanus, who introduced it in the same year with the Helsingfors Conservatory Orchestra. It was revised in 1901.

En Saga was followed by the exquisite tone-poem "The Swan of Tuonela," the third of four legends for orchestra collectively entitled *Lemminkäinen,* op. 22. This poignant picture of a swan gliding majestically to Tuonela, Kingdom of Death, was written in 1893 and heard for the first time in Helsingfors, Sibelius conducting, on April 13, 1896.

For several years, Sibelius taught at the Musical Academy. A government grant at last enabled him to give up teaching for composition. He retired to the small town of Järvenpää, twenty miles from Helsingfors, where he devoted himself exclusively to creative work. Visits to European capitals, where he attended performances of his works, interrupted his seclusion from time to time. In 1914, Sibelius visited the United States to conduct nine of his works at the Norfolk Music Festival.

After World War I, Sibelius became a national figure as well as a composer of international importance. Anniversaries of his birth—the sixtieth, seventieth, seventy-fifth, eightieth—became occasions for national celebration throughout Finland; they also inspired commemorative concerts in the rest of the world. He died in Järvenpää on September 20, 1957.

The following works by Sibelius are discussed below: Concerto in D Minor for Violin and Orchestra; *Finlandia;* Symphony No. 2 in D Major; Symphony No. 3 in C Major; Symphony No. 4 in A Minor; Symphony No. 5 in E-flat Major; Symphony No. 6; Symphony No. 7 in C Major; *Tapiola; Valse Triste.*

For *En Saga,* "The Swan of Tuonela," and Symphony No. 1, see the biographical sketch above.

FINLANDIA, tone-poem for orchestra, op. 26 (1900).

This tone-poem, as we know it today, was written in 1900; but it originated one year earlier as the fourth movement of a suite entitled *Finland Awakes.* Divorced from the suite, the music of the fourth movement was rewritten, retitled (at first it was called *Suomi*), and reintroduced (on July 2, 1900, in Helsingfors, by an orchestra conducted by Robert Kajanus). In this form it became world-famous.

Intended by the composer as the reflection of the emotions of an exile returning to his native land, the stirring music of this tone-poem has through the years become the very voice of Finland, the expression of its character, spirit, and aspirations. More than that, it has been an integral part of contemporary Finnish history. It owed its origin to the February Manifesto issued by the Russian government to abrogate the legislative Diet and to suppress free speech and press in Finland: to raise funds to fight this tyrannical move the Finnish people inaugurated a series of entertainments, for one of which Sibelius wrote *Finland Awakes*. Soon after this, when Sibelius had revamped the last movement of the suite into an independent tone-poem, it was introduced in Paris under the name of *La Patrie* and in Germany as *Vaterland,* pleading the cause of Finland to the outside world. When heard again in its native land, this tone-poem proved so provocative in arousing the patriotic ardor of the people that Russia suppressed further performances in Finland and allowed it to be played in the Empire only under the nondescript name of *Impromptu.*

After 1905, with Russia's hold on Finland becoming looser, the tone-poem was heard again in Finland. Now retitled *Finlandia,* it became what its name implied, the musical spokesman for its country, the voice of a people stubbornly dedicated to freedom. (Indeed, some writers have gone so far as to say that *Finlandia* did more to bring about Finnish independence than any speech, pamphlet, or published propaganda!)

It is a vibrantly national piece of music—so much so that there are some who persist in believing that many of its melodies spring from folk sources. The entire work, however, is of Sibelius' invention. The stirring opening bars suggest the unrest of a proud people in the face of dark tyranny. There follows the choir of reeds in a spacious national melody now grown more famous than the Finnish national anthem—sounding like a prayer to peace. The strings answer with an equally national theme, and the reeds and strings proceed to alternate in a paean to freedom, truth, self-respect. The work grows climactically into a grandiose proclamation of the triumph of the people over the forces of oppression.

SYMPHONY NO. 2 IN D MAJOR, op. 43 (1901). I. Allegretto. II. Tempo andante ma rubato. III. Vivacissimo. IV. Allegro moderato.

Sibelius' First Symphony in E Minor, op. 39, was completed in 1899, and introduced in Helsingfors on April 26 of the same year. The Second Symphony was not slow in following the first. It was begun in Rapallo, Italy, in 1901, completed in Finland at the close of the same year, and given its première in Helsingfors on March 8, 1902, under the composer's direction.

The second symphony—though long a favorite with audiences—has in recent years come in for severe criticism for its emotional plenitude and extravagances of color and sonority. Virgil Thomson, writing his first criticism in the *New York Herald Tribune* on October 9, 1940, called the symphony "vulgar, self-indulgent, and provincial beyond all description." Maybe so. The sobriety and reflectiveness of the later symphonies are surely more artistically satisfying than the uninhibited outpouring of sound and feelings of the Second. But if the Second has indiscretions, they are those of impetuous, emotional youth; it has also the virtues of youth—drive, buoyancy, gusto, excitement.

Eight introductory measures in the strings preface the entrance of the first theme by oboes and clarinets. The theme has a rustic quality that made

Georg Schneevoigt refer to the entire first movement as a picture of the pastoral life of the Finns. A second idea is briefly introduced by horns alone. After this material has been worked over, there comes a pizzicato passage for strings which serves as a prelude to the second theme—a passionate utterance for woodwinds which later grows in the strings into a song of intense longing.

A roll of the drums and a pizzicato passage for the strings usher in the first theme of the second movement, played by the bassoons. This is a somber theme. The tempo quickens, the sonority grows as a feeling of restlessness intrudes. Then another melody, no less plaintive than the first, is heard in divided strings. These two themes are developed in some detail, following which comes a sweeping climax, culminating in a pause. The beautiful, melancholy second melody returns, before a coda brings the movement to a close.

The exuberant and spirited third movement, which is actually a scherzo, is said by Schneevoigt to represent the awakening of the patriotic spirit of the Finns. Two themes are prominent, one for the violins, the other for flute and bassoon.

The symphony comes to an exultant close with majestic music. The principal theme is proclaimed by the trumpet, and receives prominent treatment throughout the movement. (Later on in the movement, in the recapitulation, it emerges with climactic force in the strings.) A second theme appears in the oboe and is developed by other woodwinds. To Schneevoigt this movement describes the hope for deliverance from tyranny that stirred in every Finn, and his confident belief that this deliverance was at hand.

CONCERTO IN D MINOR FOR VIOLIN AND ORCHESTRA, op. 47 (1903). I. Allegro moderato. II. Adagio di molto. III. Allegro ma non tanto.

Sibelius' only concerto was completed in 1903, revised in 1905, and introduced by Karl Halir on October 19, 1905, in Berlin with an orchestra conducted by Richard Strauss.

It is a work filled with romantic ardor, containing many rhapsodic passages for the violin. It opens with the solo instrument intoning a melody against an accompaniment of divided muted strings. When this idea—the principal one in the movement—has been fully realized, there is some passage work for the soloist. The entrance of the orchestra marks the transition to the second theme—subdued and lyrical—also presented by the violin.

The second movement is in a poetic vein. Five measures in the woodwinds preface a beautiful and poignant subject for the solo violin. The orchestra then enters with contrasting material, but the violin soon returns in the original mood.

The finale enters with an outburst of vitality, the rhythmic pattern being established at once by tympani and string basses. This movement is in the form of a rondo and contains two themes, the first played by the solo instrument and the second by the violins and cellos.

VALSE TRISTE, for orchestra, op. 44 (1903).

In 1903, Sibelius wrote incidental music for *Kuolema,* a play by his brother-in-law Arvid Järnefelt. Only one of these numbers was published, a sentimental piece called *Valse Triste.* This piece—one of Sibelius' least important works—achieved formidable success throughout all of Europe after Sibelius himself conducted its première performance in Helsingfors on April 25, 1904. It became a staple in the repertoire of café-houses.

The music literally describes the following program appearing in the published score:

"It is night. The son, who has been watching beside the bedside of a sick mother, has fallen asleep from sheer weariness. Gradually a ruddy light is diffused through the room: there is the sound of distant music ... strains of a waltz melody.... The sleeping mother awakens, rises from her bed, and begins to move silently. She waves her hands and beckons in time to the music. Strange visionary couples appear, turning and gliding to an unearthly waltz rhythm.... Then she seems to sink exhausted on her bed and the music breaks off. Presently she gathers all her strength and invokes the dance once more, with more energetic gestures than before. Back come the shadowy dancers, gyrating in a wild, mad rhythm. The weird gaiety reaches a climax; there is a knock at the door, which flies wide open; the mother utters a despairing cry; the spectral guests vanish. The music dies away. Death stands at the threshold."

SYMPHONY NO. 3 IN C MAJOR, op. 52 (1907). I. Allegro moderato. II. Andantino con moto quasi allegretto. III. Allegro.

The writing of the Third Symphony took Sibelius three years. On November 16, 1907, it was introduced at a Siloti concert in St. Petersburg, the composer conducting.

The first movement opens in a rugged spirit, then passes from pastoral moods, with idyllic passages in the woodwinds or strings, to stormy ones in grandiose climaxes for full orchestra. There are two main themes: that with which the symphony opens, vigorous and restless, is scored for the lower strings; the other, of greater repose, is suggested first by horns and woodwind, then emerges eloquently in the celli. The second movement is characteristic Sibelius music—poetic, slightly elegiac, restrained. There are three basic ideas: the first opens the movement and is voiced by two flutes; the second is introduced by the clarinet; the third comes in the celli. The concluding movement is a combination of scherzo and finale, with a heroic theme for horn serving as a kind of link between the two. The scherzo is vivacious and light-footed, with emphasis in the instrumentation on the woodwinds; the finale, grandiose and spacious, achieves eloquence with a majestic page for divided violas.

SYMPHONY NO. 4 IN A MINOR, op. 63 (1911). I. Tempo molto moderato quasi adagio. II. Allegro molto vivace. III. Il tempo largo. IV. Allegro.

With the Fourth Symphony—one of the finest of the seven—Sibelius passes from the emotion, expressiveness, and frequent overstatement of the first three symphonies to greater sobriety and impersonality. If the quiet restraint of the Fourth makes it less exciting listening than the dramatics of the Second, for example, it offers other and probably greater rewards: a gentle autumnal beauty that reminds one at times of Brahms in the master's most poetic writings; a simplicity of approach and in the presentation of materials that can come only from the most consummate mastery of technique. Besides all this, the Fourth Symphony represents the most progressive writing that Sibelius had done up to this time—so much so that when it was first heard, the symphony was regarded as highly rebellious music, even by discriminating listeners. After hearing the Fourth for the first time, W. J. Henderson wrote: "He is as frankly dissonant as the worst of them. He has swallowed the whole-tone scale, the disjointed sequences, the chord of the minor second, the flattened supertonic and all the Chinese horrors of the forbidden fifths." But, in all fairness to Henderson, he did pronounce the work "a noteworthy composition," filled with "elemental imagination, courage of utterance, and fearlessness of style."

The symphony opens in the Lydian mode, with the principal subject presented by the solo cello. Other ideas are interpolated—some of them nakedly brief—one succeeding the other as the music gains in austerity and strength. A scherzo movement follows, gently touched with laughter and gaiety. From this light mood we pass on to pastoral music evoking a world of serenity and beauty: the slow movement, built for the most part out of the whole-tone scale, is one of Sibelius' finest creations. The mood is broken with the crude, ungovernable strength of the concluding Allegro.

Sibelius conducted the première performance of the Fourth Symphony in Helsingfors, on April 3, 1911.

SYMPHONY NO. 5 IN E-FLAT MAJOR, op. 82 (1915). I. Tempo molto moderato; Allegro moderato ma poco a poco stretto. II. Andante mosso quasi allegretto. III. Allegro molto.

Written in the second year of World War I, the Fifth Symphony came in a period of great trial and suffering—financial as well as spiritual—for Sibelius. It was begun at a time when Sibelius was tempted into believing that the war would be of brief duration. It was completed during 1915, by which time Sibelius knew that the war would be long and bitter. Its completion proved, as Karl Ekman wrote, "an expression of its creator's great optimism, gained through suffering; an elevating testimony, in an evil period, to an unshakable faith in the ever-renewing power of life." On Sibelius' fiftieth birthday, December 8, 1915, the new symphony was introduced in Helsingfors, the orchestra conducted by Robert Kajanus. Subsequently, Sibelius revised the symphony extensively, not once but several times, so much so that after the final revision the composer considered the result practically a new work. The definitive version—the one with which we are familiar today—was heard for the first time in Helsingfors on November 24, 1919, the composer conducting.

The first movement is built out of germinal ideas which are introduced early, developed from embryo to full growth as the music progresses. The first of these ideas is an ascending theme for first horn with which the movement opens; another is a stark motive for the woodwind against quivering strings; a third is a bright, triumphant passage for three trumpets. A scherzo follows without pause, with a lilting tune for the woodwinds; the music gains in momentum until it erupts in a climax of shattering force. Two major themes provide the material for the concluding movement, the first, lyric, played by the violas, and the second, extraordinarily powerful, pronounced by the horns; this second theme is built into a climax of great dimensions toward the close of the movement.

SYMPHONY NO. 6, op. 104 (1923). I. Allegro molto moderato. II. Allegretto moderato. III. Poco vivace. IV. Allegro molto.

The Sixth Symphony came almost a decade after the Fifth. It was introduced on February 19, 1923, in Helsingfors with the composer conducting. Cecil Gray has remarked, in his biography of Sibelius, that the keynote of this symphony "consists in a sense of serenity and poise, avoiding every kind of extreme.... The coloring ... is neither opulent nor ascetic, neither bright nor somber, but in intermediate tones.... The tempi are neither conspicuously fast nor slow.... This suggestion of balance between extremes is further symbolically reflected in the tonality of the first movement, which is ostensibly that of D Minor, but with the B-natural giving the impression of hovering ambiguously between major and minor. This modal atmosphere ... can also be perceived in the other movements ... imparting an underlying spiritual unity to the whole four movements."

The symphony opens in a subdued rhapsodic vein which persists throughout the first movement. The Allegro moderato is more brusque and restless, essentially modern in its use of dissonance and unrelated tonalities. The slow movement (the shortest of the four) has the personality of folk music; it is simple, direct, sustained lyricism. Episodic ideas, rather than a sustained lyric line, dominate the closing movement, some of them also of folk character.

SYMPHONY NO. 7 IN C MAJOR, op. 105 (1924).

The Seventh Symphony is the only one Sibelius wrote in a single movement. It has changes of mood and tempi, but these changes are not formalized. The music is organically unified, subjected to a logic of its own, but this logic is as inexorable as that of the classical symphony.

It was introduced in Stockholm on March 24, 1924, with the orchestra directed by the composer.

The symphony is built episodically. It opens with a lugubrious subject for the strings, of which much use is to be made throughout the work. An idea for woodwinds against tremolo strings follows, but it soon makes way for a heroic theme for trombone, which is also subsequently elaborated. The music passes from passion to grandeur with occasional passages of brutal strength. After a climactic page, the tempo becomes vivace, and woodwind and strings join in music of lighthearted gaiety. But the levity passes. Once again the moods become in turn passionate, savage, grandiose, poetic. A monumental climax emerges. The turbulent emotions dissipate and a gentle passage for flute and bassoon is heard against tremolo strings. A crescendo is built up for the conclusion of the work.

TAPIOLA, symphonic poem for orchestra, op. 112 (1926).

Tapio is the ancient forest god of Finland, and *Tapiola* is just one more name for the country which is described in this tone-poem. The following four lines, appearing in the published score, give a clue to the music's meaning:

> Widespread they stand, the Northland's dusky forests,
> Ancient, mysterious, brooding, savage dreams.
> Within them dwells the Forest's mighty god
> And wood-sprites in the gloom weave magic secrets.

A theme descriptive of the forest is the principal idea of the work. It is heard at the opening in the strings, after a soft drum roll. From out of this basic subject, the entire work is evolved—the theme being allowed to grow, to change, chameleon-like, and to develop as the music becomes an eloquent and unforgettable portrait of Nature. Now melancholy, now idyllic, the music is finally driven by uncontrollable momentum to heights of dynamic power.

Tapiola was introduced by the New York Symphony Orchestra under Walter Damrosch on December 26, 1926.

ELIE SIEGMEISTER   1909—

Siegmeister's identification with American folk music has been complete. He has traveled extensively to different parts of the country gathering local folk tunes, putting them down on paper, and making arrangements for them. As a result of this intensive digging, he has uncovered a veritable mine of folk music, little known out of its own locale. He has performed much of this music with the American Ballad Singers, an organization he founded in 1939; he has also published much of it in his books. Most important of all, he has incorporated some of it in his serious musical works. But even in those works in which folksongs are not directly quoted, the influence of his researches is apparent: his melodies, rhythms, orchestrations, all derive distinguishable traits from either folk or popular sources. Siegmeister's music is always straightforward, lyrical, full of vitality, and rich with American flavors.

Siegmeister was born in New York City on January 15, 1909. He began to study the piano when he was nine, but not until he was graduated from Columbia University, in 1927, did he concern himself seriously with both music study and composition. From 1927 to 1931 he studied with Nadia Boulanger in Paris (having had preliminary study in composition with Wallingford Riegger); and from 1935 to 1938, he was a student of conducting at the Juilliard Graduate School. Hearing some Kentucky folksongs sung by Aunt Molly Jackson gave him the direction he needed; henceforth he dedicated himself completely to American folk music. With Olin Downes he edited *A Treasury of American Song*. He wrote the musical score for the Theatre Guild production, *Sing Out, Sweet Land!*

The following works by Siegmeister are discussed below: *Ozark Set;* Symphony No. 1; *Wilderness Road*.

OZARK SET, for orchestra (1943). I. Morning in the Hills. II. Camp Meeting. III. Lazy Afternoon. IV. Saturday Night.

In *Ozark Set,* four scenes in the life of the Ozark Mountain people of Missouri and Arkansas are described. The first movement paints the back country as it slowly awakens to a day of activity. The shouting, stamping, and frenetic religious singing of a camp meeting are re-created in the second part, while the third evokes a picture of open fields and prairies baked in the sun. The set ends with a square dance on a Saturday night.

Siegmeister wrote this suite when the Theatre Guild of New York asked him if he had any music that could be utilized for a play set in the Ozarks. Not having any such music, the composer sat down to write some. The play never materialized, but the music became the basis of one of Siegmeister's best orchestral works. The *Set* was introduced by the Minneapolis Symphony Orchestra under Dimitri Mitropoulos on November 7, 1944.

WILDERNESS ROAD, for orchestra (1944).

In *Wilderness Road,* Siegmeister creates a musical picture of the West, for which he has provided the following program: "Through the dark, ancient forest and over the silent hills stretched the Wilderness Road—gateway to the West. Over it came a great caravan: tall, cheerful men with their axes and rifles, their women and children, their wagons, dogs and horses; pioneers, seekers and builders of a new land. The wilderness echoed with their coming; they passed, leaving quietness, a hope and a dream."

Wilderness Road was written between August, 1944, and April, 1945. It was introduced by the Detroit Symphony Orchestra under Forstat in June, 1945.

SYMPHONY NO. 1, (1947). I. Andante. II. Vivace brioso; Allegretto grazioso. III. Moderato cantabile. IV. Maestoso; Allegro spiritoso.

On October 30, 1947, this symphony was given its world première in New York, with Leopold Stokowski conducting the New York Philharmonic-Symphony Orchestra.

The first movement has two principal themes: a slow, lyrical melody with which the symphony opens, and a ballad-like subject. The second movement is robust "in the general spirit of raising the roof," as the composer put it; a blues-like melody is heard midway. The third movement, slow and lyrical, adopts a popular style. The concluding movement opens gravely and becomes at turns dramatic, dance-like, and poetic, ending with a powerful climax.

RICHARD STRAUSS   1864—1949

Strauss's career as a composer ended as it had begun: with the writing of music classical in form, romantic in feeling, warm with pleasing melodies and gracious, conventional harmonies. After listening to both his earliest and latest works—the Brahmsian Piano Quartet (1884) and Violin Sonata (1887), and those compositions in which he nostalgically returned to the style of his youth, notably the concertos for horn and for oboe (1942, 1945)—it becomes difficult to remember that between these two periods Strauss produced music that shocked and outraged the world of music and made him one of its most provocative figures.

Hardly had the ink dried on his Violin Sonata when Strauss impatiently discarded his romantic style within classical forms to set off into the creation of what was for him a new kind of music—realistic, descriptive, utilizing the fullest modern resources of orchestration, adventurous in its use of form, harmony, and counterpoint. It was the music of his tone-poems. In this new direction he had been influenced by the philosopher-musician Alexander Ritter. In his many conversations with Ritter, Strauss had been convinced that it was his artistic duty to carry on the Wagnerian torch, even in the field of symphonic music: to exploit the dramatic expressiveness of music within the flexible form of the Liszt tone-poem. "His influence," Strauss confessed, "was in the nature of a stormwind. He urged me on to the development of the poetic, the expressive in music."

The first of the tone-poems, *Macbeth,* came in 1887. Then in rapid succession followed the series of orchestral masterpieces with which the name of Richard Strauss is inextricably associated:

Don Juan, op. 20, based on a poem of Nicolaus Lenau, was written in 1889, and introduced on November 11 of the same year by the Weimar Court Orchestra, Hans von Bülow conducting.

Death and Transfiguration (*Tod und Verklaerung*), op. 24, after a poem of Alexander Ritter, was written in 1889 and introduced in Eisenach on June 21, 1890, at a concert of the Allgemeiner Deutscher Musikverein, the composer conducting.

Till Eulenspiegel's Merry Pranks, op. 28, inspired by a famous German legend about a practical joker, was written in 1895 and first heard in Cologne on November 5, 1895, under the composer's direction.

Thus Spake Zarathustra, op. 30, freely after Nietzsche, was completed in 1896 and introduced at Frankfort-am-Main on November 27 of the same year, under the composer's direction.

Don Quixote, "fantastic variations on a theme of knightly character," op. 35, was written in 1897, and first performed at a Gürzenich concert in Cologne, Franz Wüllner conducting, on March 18, 1898.

A Hero's Life (*Ein Heldenleben*), op. 40, was completed in 1899 and first heard in Frankfort-am-Main on March 3, 1899, the composer conducting.

With these works, Strauss exploited the virtuosity of instrumentation boldly and adventurously, and gave form and harmony greater independence. The ability of music to describe extramusical ideas realistically was exploited to its fullest potential, even to the point of having new instruments of Strauss's own invention supplement the traditional ones to produce definite effects.

His tone-poems made him the storm center of the musical world in the closing decade of the nineteenth century. Their stark realism (far beyond that of any composer before him), their dissonances, their episodic forms, their attempt to extract the last ounce of expressiveness out of tones, their layer upon layer of orchestral color—all this inspired dissension, praise and vituperative criticism, satire and acclaim. Even so progressive a musician as Claude Debussy regarded one of Strauss's tone-poems as "an hour of music in an asylum." One of the German critics described *Till Eulenspiegel* as a "vast and coruscating jumble of instrumental cackles about things unfit to be mentioned."

But before many years passed, there arose other composers more rebellious in their use of form and technique than Strauss. In contrast to the atonal, polytonal, polyrhythmic writings of these new men, the tone-poems of Strauss appeared in their true light, not as essentially iconoclastic works, but as the last gasps of the dying Wagnerian epoch. Today, these tone-poems appear at times bombastic, at times oversensual, at times sentimental, at times even naïve. But other pages are filled with wonderful music: power, passion, grandiloquent speech, orchestral wizardry, poetic concepts. And since it is by their best pages rather than by the weak ones that these tone-poems are measured, their permanence in symphonic literature is assured.

At the same time that he was writing his tone-poems, Strauss was also producing songs in which the traditions of the German lied were brought to the threshold of the twentieth century. The more than one hundred songs he wrote are (like the tone-poems) uneven in quality. But at their best they deserve a place at the side of the greatest lieder of all time. The finest Strauss songs were all written before 1900, and include the following jewels: *"Zueignung,"* or "Dedication" (von Gilm), op. 10, no. 1; *"Allerseelen,"* or "All Soul's Day" (von Gilm), op. 10, no. 8; *"Cäcilie"* (Hart), op. 27, no. 2; *"Heimliche Aufforderung"* (Mackay), op. 27, no. 3; *"Morgen,"* or "Morning" (Mackay), op. 27, no. 4; *"Traum durch die Dämmerung,"* or "Dream in the Dusk," (Biernbaum), op. 29, no. 1; *"Wiegenlied,"* or "Cradle Song" (Dehmel), op. 41, no. 1, and *"Freundliche Vision,"* or "Friendly Vision" (Biernbaum), op. 48, no. 1.

Strauss may not always have been discriminating in the choice of his poetic texts, some of which are truly pedestrian; he may have indulged too frequently in excessive emotion; he may not always have achieved the happiest of balances between voice and piano accompaniment. But he was truly a lord of melody, a melody that expressed different shades of feeling and different atmospheres with great subtlety. His best songs, like the best pages of his tone-poems, are the products of a master.

Since his tone-poems and most famous songs were all produced before 1900, they are not discussed in detail in the pages that follow. In only one field—that of the opera—did Strauss produce acknowledged masterpieces after 1900. And even in that field he was to exhaust himself artistically before many years had passed, before 1914. Thereafter, and for the next thirty-five years of his life, he was to remain productive. But the flame of his genius was reduced to embers. The technical mastery remained, but little else. The master now took to imitating some of the styles, techniques, mannerisms, and effects that had once made him so famous.

Richard Strauss was born in Munich on June 11, 1864, the son of a well-known horn player who had played under Wagner. A precocious child, Richard was first given music lessons when he was four; and when he was six he started composing. His music study took place with August Tombo, Benno Walter, and F. W. Meyer. His progress was so rapid that well before his seventeenth birthday his Symphony in D Minor was directed by Hermann Levi (to receive the praises of none less than Brahms himself!), while several songs and a string quartet were also successfully performed. Academic study, however, was not neglected all this while: after completing studies at the Gymnasium, Strauss attended the University of Munich.

In 1883, he left the University without graduating. He went to Berlin, where he met Hans von Bülow, who encouraged Strauss by performing several of his works with his Meiningen Orchestra. Subsequently, von Bülow appointed Strauss as his assistant in Meiningen, and when he decided to retire as conductor he selected Strauss as his successor. Strauss's conductorial activity did not impede his creative efforts. During this period he wrote a new symphony (which received its world première in the United States in 1884, under Theodore Thomas) and a Piano Quartet, which won the Berlin Tonkünstlerverein prize.

Up to now, he had been influenced in his music by Brahms. But his friendship with the musician-philosopher, Alexander Ritter, opened up a new direction for him. Under Ritter's inspiration and guidance Strauss wrote the first of his tone-poems. These tone-poems made Strauss one of the most widely discussed and famous composers of his time. His fame—and notoriety—grew in the twentieth century with the writing of such operas as *Salome* and *Elektra*.

After serving for several years as conductor of the Berlin Royal Opera, Strauss was elevated to the post of director in 1898, a post which he held for a dozen years. In 1904, he toured the United States for the first time, conducting the German Wetzler Orchestra in programs of his own works. He returned to America a second time in 1921, this time as the guest of leading American orchestras.

Though there was a decline in his creative powers after World War I, there was no diminution in either his fame or significance. There were few to deny that he was the leading composer of Germany and one of the musical greats of our times. His importance as composer did not obscure his contributions with the baton. In his performances of opera and symphonic music in Berlin, Vienna, Munich, Salzburg, Bayreuth and elsewhere, Strauss proved himself to be an interpreter of major significance, particularly in his interpretations of the music-dramas of Wagner and the operas of Mozart.

When the Nazis came to power in 1933, Strauss openly allied himself with the new government, accepting the position of president of the Third Reich Music Chamber. It was not long before he came to grips with his Nazi superiors, particularly after his collaboration with a Jew, Stefan Zweig, in the writing of the opera *The Silent Woman*. Strauss resigned his official position, and retired to his villa in Garmisch-Partenkirchen, where he remained in virtual seclusion during the turbulent years preceding World War II. During a great part of the war, he lived in Switzerland, virtually destitute. The war over, he emerged from his prolonged retirement in 1947 to conduct a concert of his own works in London during a Strauss festival. His eighty-fifth birthday was celebrated in all the music centers of the world. Strauss died three months after, on September 8, 1949, at his home in Bavaria.

The following works by Strauss are discussed below: *Ariadne auf Naxos; Le Bourgeois Gentilhomme; Elektra; Metamorphosen; Der Rosenkavalier; Salome; Sinfonia Domestica.*

For *Death and Transfiguration* (*Tod und Verklaerung*), *Don Juan, Don Quixote, A Hero's Life* (*Ein Heldenleben*), Songs, *Thus Spake Zarathustra,* and *Till Eulenspiegel's Merry Pranks,* see the biographical sketch above.

SINFONIA DOMESTICA, op. 53 (1903).

The *Sinfonia Domestica* is the last of Strauss's exciting and provocative tone-poems, and the only one he wrote in the twentieth century. It was completed on the last day of 1903, and introduced in New York City on March 21, 1904, during Strauss's visit to this country with the Wetzler Orchestra.

When Strauss worked on this *Sinfonia,* he did not hesitate to explain that it was a piece of musical autobiography, illustrating "a day in my family... partly humorous—a triple fugue, the three subjects representing papa, mama, and baby." However, when the work was introduced, Strauss insisted that it must be listened to as pure music and refused to give any detailed programmatic explanations. Evidently he subsequently reconsidered the decision of passing this work off as absolute music. When it was played in Germany Strauss sanctioned the use of the following descriptive subtitles:

"I. Introduction and development of the three chief groups of themes. The husband's themes: (a) easygoing; (b) dreamy; (c) fiery.... The wife's themes: (a) lively and gay; (b) grazioso.... The child's theme: tranquil.

"II. Scherzo. Parents' happiness. Childish play.... Cradle song (the clock strikes seven in the evening).

"III. Adagio. Doing and thinking. Love scene.... Dreams and cares (the clock strikes seven in the morning).

"IV. Finale. Awakening and merry dispute (double fugue).... Joyous conclusion."

When the *Sinfonia* was introduced in London, Strauss allowed the following detailed analysis to be published in the program:

"The symphony continues without a break, but has four well-defined sections. . . . The Introduction is devoted to an exposition and treatment of the chief themes, or groups of themes, its most striking feature being the introduction of the child theme on the oboe d'amore. . . . The composer has spoken of this theme as being 'of almost Haydnesque simplicity.' On this follows a very characteristic passage, which has been interpreted as representing the child in its bath. The chief theme of the Scherzo is the child theme in a new rhythm. At its end the music suggestive of the bath recurs, and the clock strikes seven. We then come to the Lullaby, where we have another version of the child theme. . . . The elaborate Adagio introduces no new themes of any importance, and is really a symphonic slow movement of great polyphonic elaboration and superlatively rich orchestral color. The gradual awakening of the family is depicted by a change in the character of the music, which becomes more and more restless . . . and then there is another reference to the bath music, and the glockenspiel indicates that it is 7 A.M. In this way we reach the final fugue. . . . The subject of the dispute between father and mother is the future of the son. The fugue (the chief subject of which is another variant of the child theme) is carried on with unflagging spirit and humor and a great variety of orchestration, the introduction of four saxophones adding fresh colors to the score. . . . The father and mother, however, soon assert their former importance, and the whole ends with great spirit and in the highest good humor with an emphatic reassertion of the husband theme . . . suggesting that the father had the last word in the argument."

In 1925, Strauss took the first three bars of the child theme and elaborated it into a completely self-sufficient orchestral work which he entitled *Parergon to the Sinfonia Domestica*. It was scored for left-hand piano and orchestra, having been written for the one-armed pianist Paul Wittgenstein. Wittgenstein has this to say about this work: "Strauss told me that the first part describes the illness of the child and the second part his recovery. . . . What made him choose just the theme of the child, I do not know. Perhaps he felt that this theme had not been sufficiently developed in the *Sinfonia Domestica*. All the other themes are new and not contained in the *Sinfonia*."

SALOME, opera (1904).

A decade after he had written his first opera, *Guntram* (1894), Strauss demonstrated to the music world that he had not lost his capacity to shock and outrage. The choice of Oscar Wilde's play *Salome* as a text for an opera—with its emphasis on the insane passion of Salome for John the Baptist—was in itself highly provocative. But in matching the sensuality and neuroticism of Wilde's play with music no less erotic (vivid in its musical characterizations, passionate in harmonic colors and instrumental effects, lasciviously suggestive in its rhythms and sinuous melodies), Strauss was producing a work that could not help arousing moral indignation.

The planned première in Vienna was abandoned when the censors stepped in. For a brief period it seemed that no opera house would be courageous enough to present it, until Count Seebach, Intendant of the Royal Opera in Dresden, announced his intention of producing it. Despite an attempted strike by the principal singers because of the complexity of the music (Frau Wittig, the Salome, furiously asked how she could be expected to dance for ten minutes and follow it with the singing of exacting music for another quarter of an hour!), the first performance did eventually take place—on December 9, 1905, under Ernst Schuch. Instead of the angry protests and expressions of disgust which had been anticipated, there were thunderous ovations by the audience; Strauss took twenty-five curtain calls. The critics were equally enthusiastic. But this decisive victory for *Salome* did not mean the end of its trials. The Berlin performance was at first forbidden by the Kaiser himself—and when it was finally heard, in 1906, it was denounced for its "perverse depravity," and described as "repulsive." A scheduled London performance was called off, once again as a result of censor trouble. And the American première set off a storm which is surely one of the dramatic pages in the history of American opera.

That American performance took place on January 22, 1907, with the Metropolitan Opera under the direction of Heinrich Conried. The present author has written as follows about this episode in his book, *Music Comes to America:*

"Conried was not too farsighted when he arranged a special dress rehearsal for an invited audience to take place on Sunday morning. Many came straight from church services, and the shock of contrast was more than most of them could stomach. They left the opera house denouncing the 'lewd' spectacle. After the first performance, a righteous-minded citizenry descended on Conried with fury for permitting such a display of obscenity on his stage. The clergy rose up in battle. The critics, too, joined in this universal chorus of outraged feelings. Krehbiel wrote that 'the stench of Oscar Wilde's play had filled the nostrils of humanity,' while still another writer spoke of the opera as a 'decadent and pestiferous work.' One critic vented his spleen as follows: 'As to the mind and morals, they were diseased. Not to emphasize disgust, their state was one of decomposition far advanced. As to the music, it fits. It makes worse that to which nothing but music could give added degradation.' A few musicians (like Emil Paur) tried to defend the Strauss music, but their voices were drowned by the furor of the opposition. Before the second performance could be put on the stage, Conried received a curt note from the directors of the Metropolitan informing him that they considered 'the performance of *Salome* objectionable and detrimental to the best interests of the Metropolitan Opera House,' and protesting 'against any repetition of the opera.' There was nothing for Conried to do but withdraw *Salome* after one performance."

On November 25, 1910, the opera was revived in this country by the Chicago Opera Company with Mary Garden in the title role. In Chicago, too, the temperature rose high. The chief of police, who was required to attend the performance, described the opera and Mary Garden as "disgusting." After a second performance, the protests grew more shrill, and further presentations were canceled.

The shock is gone, and with it moral indignation. Recent revivals of *Salome* have drawn attention only to the remarkable qualities of the music, its extraordinary character delineations, its dazzling orchestration, the power and richness of its melodic and harmonic writing, and the incomparable way in which it blends with the play into a single, indivisible work of art. The conclusion, beginning with Salome's sensual dance of the veils and culminating with her passionate apostrophe, is surely one of the most stirring climaxes in all opera.

The story of *Salome,* coming to Oscar Wilde's play by way of the Scriptures, is well known. Salome, lascivious and perverted daughter of Herodias, has fallen in love with the prophet Jokanaan—a captive of her stepfather, Herod. She desires him and tries in vain to seduce him. Herod, who is in love with his stepdaughter, promises her anything she may desire if only she will dance for him. She dances—then demands the head of Jokanaan. The prophet is killed, and his head is brought on a tray to Salome. Passionately Salome caresses the head and delivers her final apostrophe. Realizing the extent of his stepdaughter's depravity, Herod orders her death.

ELEKTRA, opera (1908).

Elektra was Strauss's fourth opera, and the first in which he collaborated with the Austrian dramatist, Hugo von Hofmannsthal. Hofmannsthal's adaptation of the famous Greek drama of Sophocles is a highly individual one, filled with lusts and passions the original never knew. In the Hofmannsthal adaptation Elektra becomes a shrieking and hysterical personification of hate, and her mother, Klytemnestra, a loathsome picture of depravity. The whole drama becomes morbid and neurotic; yet it is filled with power and passion. And the music Strauss wrote for it is one of his most vividly realistic and sensual scores. Drama and music are so ideally mated to one another that the net result is a work of pathos and beauty. It is one of Strauss's unquestioned masterpieces for the theatre, one of the mighty productions of twentieth-century opera.

The theme of the Sophocles tragedy is famous. King Agamemnon is murdered by his wife Klytemnestra and her lover. Agamemnon's son, Orestes, is sent to exile; Orestes' sisters, Chrysothemis and Elektra, are objects of abuse. Elektra, stricken by her overwhelming grief at the death of her father, swears vengeance. She plans and is about to execute the murder of her mother and her mother's lover with the very weapon with which her father had been destroyed. Suddenly Orestes returns and completes the murder. Elektra, ecstatic that retribution has taken place, dances demoniacally until she falls dead.

The world première took place in Dresden on January 25, 1909, under the direction of Ernst Schuch. "It is a prodigious orchestral orgy," reported a correspondent of the *New York Times,* "and makes superhuman demands upon the mental and physical powers of the singers and players. The marvelous imitative effects of the orchestra are blood-curdling, drastic, and gruesome to the last degree. It is fortunate for the hearers that the piece is no longer, for else it would be too nerve-wracking!"

The German critics were appalled by what they saw and heard. "Lurid," "violent," "gruesome" were some of the adjectives used to describe the startling new Strauss opus. However, there were a scattered few who sensed the greatness of this provocative work. One of these was Alfred Kalisch, who described the overpowering climax of the opera, Elektra's dance, in the following way: "The mind has to travel far back to search for anything at all comparable to it in musical mastery and almost elemental emotional power.... Not only is there colossal skill in the way in which all the previous threads are woven into one, not only is there great art in the way the climax grows and the orchestral color gradually changes from darkness to the bright light of noonday; but the result is achieved without sacrifice of euphony or beauty, and the whole conception of the scene betrays a creative power which is certainly without rival in the present day."

DER ROSENKAVALIER, opera (1910).

Strauss expressed the desire to write a comic opera soon after finishing *Salome.* But not until after he had written *Elektra* did he set about realizing this ambition. He confided to his librettist, Hugo von Hofmannsthal, that he had in mind an opera combining the best qualities of Mozart and Johann Strauss; and Hofmannsthal proceeded to prepare a suitable text which, as he wrote to Strauss, "will to a certain extent correspond with your artistic individuality" in its "blending of the grotesque with the lyrical." He set his play in the eighteenth-century Vienna of Maria Theresa. Through his two principal characters—Baron Ochs and the Marschallin—he deftly mingled sentiment with broad comedy, tenderness with burlesque. The result was one of the finest librettos in all opera.

The story is spiced with the intrigues of the roué Baron Ochs, cousin of the Marschallin (Princess von Werdenberg). The Marschallin herself is carrying on a flirtation with the seventeen-year-old Octavian. Their little tête-à-tête is interrupted by the entrance of Ochs; Octavian quickly disguises himself as a maid. The Baron has come to ask his cousin to find someone who can bear a silver rose (symbol of a marriage proposal) to Sophia. Coming upon the disguised Octavian, Ochs flirts with "her" and invites "her" to a private supper. Meanwhile, the Marschallin gets rid of the Baron by promising to get him a suitable rose-bearer; and the one she has in mind for this assignment is Octavian.

Octavian brings the silver rose to Sophia; they fall in love with each other. To Baron Ochs Sophia is aloof, proof to the outraged roué that Octavian has stolen Sophia from him. He challenges his rival to a duel, in which he is slightly wounded. But the receipt of a letter from the Marschallin's "maid"—the disguised Octavian—soothes his pains and sends him dancing with joy; for the maid has written to remind him of their rendezvous. This takes place in a public tavern where the Baron makes impatient advances to the "maid." Things do not go well for the Baron. Strange faces appear in the windows of the tavern to haunt him. Suddenly there arrives a woman claiming him as her husband and the father of her children. A climax is reached when Octavian removes his female disguise and reveals himself. Baron Ochs leaves the tavern in fury. And the Marschallin, who in the meantime has made an appearance, magnanimously renounces Octavian to allow him to marry his beloved Sophia.

Some criticism has been levelled against the score Strauss wrote for this wonderful play—its length, verbosity, and occasional lapses into triteness. Such criticism, one must confess, is justified. But in spite of its defects, *Der Rosenkavalier* (music *and* words) is one of the glories of comic opera, the finest example of this genre since *Die Meistersinger*. If there are weak moments in *Der Rosenkavalier,* there are also many pages of grandeur, beauty, magic, and wit; and it is these pages that have assured the opera permanence in the repertory.

Though the waltzes that course throughout the opera are the best-known and most frequently heard portions, there are other passages which rank with the finest operatic writing of our time: the beautiful cantilena writing of the serenade and the nobility and pathos of the Marschallin's monologue, in which she laments her oncoming advanced age, both in Act I; and the trio, followed immediately by the love duet of Sophia and Octavian, with which the opera comes to a close. In such pages Strauss is truly the wizard who can not only bring up varying moods with great expressive power but who can also fill his music with heart.

The Dresden Opera accepted *Der Rosenkavalier* in 1910, but problems of staging slowed down the rehearsals until it seemed that the new opera would be doomed to failure. The celebrated director Max Reinhardt was called in, and saved the day. The first performance on January 26, 1911, under Ernest Schuch, went off magnificently; the new opera was an immediate success.

Soon after the première of the opera, Strauss collected the waltzes in an integrated and independent orchestral work which has gained considerable popularity throughout the world of symphonic music. (Strauss made a new orchestral adaptation of these waltzes in 1946.) He also wrote an orchestral suite combining some of the finest pages of the opera. The suite includes the introduction, the entrance of the rose-bearer, the duet of Sophia and Octavian, the waltz music, the trio, and the concluding love-duet.

ARIADNE AUF NAXOS, opera (1912).

This sparkling opera was originally written in 1912 as an interlude for the Max Reinhardt production of *Le Bourgeois Gentilhomme,* for which Strauss had written all the incidental music. Subsequently, Strauss revised this interlude extensively, revamped it into a one-act opera with a prologue, and in this form reintroduced it in Vienna in 1916. Like *Le Bourgeois Gentilhomme,* the opera does not call for large forces. It is written simply and with fine restraint; the form is intimate; the style is full of Mozartean sparkle and classic purity.

The libretto was prepared by Hugo von Hofmannsthal. It is a play within a play. The prologue takes place in the private theatre of a wealthy eighteenth-century European, who arranges the performance of *Ariadne* for his own and his guests' delight. Its young and idealistic composer is asked by his patron to vary the seriousness of his opera with comedy, and the patron insists that broad burlesque scenes be interpolated into the classic story. The young composer is upset, but he is advised by his music master to follow instructions. While contemplating his sad fate, the young composer is accosted by Zerbinetta, queen of the comedians, who is flirtatious. At first the young composer mistakes her coquetry for an interest in his artistic problems; but he is soon disenchanted. He takes his music master severely to task for forcing him to make concessions with his ideals and escapes from the theatre.

Then the opera, *Ariadne,* begins for the patron and his guests. Ariadne, feeling alone and forsaken, lies sleeping in a cave on the island of Naxos in ancient times. Her slumber is accompanied by the singing of Naiad, Dryad, and Echo. Awakening, Ariadne bemoans her sad fate. To dissipate her sorrow, Zerbinetta and four clowns come to her with song and dance; but Ariadne is too absorbed in her sorrow to notice them. The arrival of another visitor is announced by Naiad, Dryad, and Echo; he is young and handsome. Ariadne is ready to welcome him if he is Death—for she is weary of life and her sorrows. But he is Bacchus, who comes bringing with him the joy of life. Suddenly Ariadne's great sorrow passes. She joyfully falls into the arms of Bacchus.

LE BOURGEOIS GENTILHOMME, suite for orchestra, op. 66 (1912). I. Overture. II. Minuet. III. The Fencing Master. IV. Entrance and Dance of the Tailors. V. The Minuet of Lully. VI. Courante. VII. Entrance of Cleonte. VIII. Intermezzi: Dorante and Dorimene, Count and Marquise. IX. The Dinner.

On October 25, 1912, in Stuttgart, Max Reinhardt presented Hugo von

Hofmannsthal's adaptation of Molière's *Le Bourgeois Gentilhomme*. For this presentation, Strauss wrote the incidental music. The play was a failure. Neither the audiences nor the critics liked the way in which Hofmannsthal tampered with the Molière play. But there were no dissenting voices in the praise for the delightful music Strauss had written. Abandoning those gargantuan orchestras for which he had become famous, together with inflation of style, Strauss proved here that he could write directly, purely, and transparently. There is a great deal of charm and delicacy in this music; and delightful wit as well. Richard Specht has gone so far as to say that this is the most masterly music ever written for a dramatic play, incomparable for "its pseudo-archaic style ... its sparkling hilarity, and ... its fresh melodies."

One of the interludes of this music was later transformed into the one-act opera *Ariadne auf Naxos*. Most of the orchestral music was collected in a successful suite.

The theme of the Molière play revolves around the *nouveau riche* Jourdain, who, impelled to rise in station, summons tailors to fit him out in finery and teachers to instruct him in the social and artistic graces. He even entertains the thought of engaging in a little affair with an attractive Marquise, as befitting a man of his importance—a venture that is brusquely frustrated by his wife. For his daughter, he contemplates, of course, a worthy marriage. But his daughter is in love with Cleonte, who conceives the idea of dressing himself in Turkish garb and posing as the son of a Sultan. Jourdain—elevated by the "Sultan" to the rank of *mamaouchi*—blesses this marriage and gives over his daughter to Cleonte in disguise.

The play is a stinging satire; and Strauss's music is equally witty and satiric. The Overture is a malicious portrait of Jourdain. There follows a dainty Minuet, telling of Jourdain's grotesque efforts to learn fencing. The wit is extended into broad burlesque with the Entrance and Dance of the Tailors. Two classic dances ensue: the Minuet of Lully (an adaptation of a minuet Lully wrote for the original production of Molière's play) and a Courante. Cleonte enters with music that is now a bit solemn, now a bit gay (material is here also borrowed from Lully). In the Intermezzi that follow the rococo world of Louis XIV is evoked. The suite ends with a musical description of a lavish dinner: Strauss here amusingly interpolates a phrase from Wagner's *Das Rheingold* to suggest Rhine salmon, and a quotation from his own *Don Quixote,* the bleating of the sheep, to speak for the roast mutton.

The first revival of *Le Bourgeois Gentilhomme* since the première in 1912, with all of Strauss's music including the *Ariadne* interlude, took place at the Edinburgh Festival in 1950.

METAMORPHOSEN, study for twenty-three solo strings (1945). This unusual exercise in string sonority was introduced in Zurich by the Collegium Musicum under Paul Sacher on January 25, 1946.

The work, which assigns separate parts for ten violins, five violas, five celli, and three double basses, features solo instruments and groups of strings as well as the entire orchestra. Two theme groups of three subjects each are subjected to considerable development and transformation, with groups of strings used frequently in contrast to each other, and with lyric passages of solo character punctuating the elaborate texture. The music is touched with tragedy, opening as it does with somber chords (reminiscent of the Funeral March of Beethoven's *Eroica Symphony*) and concluding with this theme played contrapuntally with the actual one from the Beethoven symphony. It must not be forgotten that when Strauss wrote this music Germany was collapsing in the closing months of the war. Indeed, at the conclusion of his manuscript, Strauss wrote the two words, "In Memoriam" —in memory, no doubt, of the dying Germany, then being occupied by the Allied forces.

IGOR STRAVINSKY   1882—

Like a colossus, Stravinsky has straddled the world of contemporary music for almost half a century. One foot has been planted in the world of iconoclasm and revolt; the other, in the opposing world of neo-classicism, with its order and symmetry.

The rebel appeared in a series of masterpieces which many still consider among the greatest of Stravinsky's works: *The Fire-Bird, Petrushka,* and *The Rite of Spring*. Though he drew his strength and inspiration from Russian folklore and backgrounds, Stravinsky nevertheless struck a path of his own into new, formerly unexplored regions of musical sound. Orthodox harmony made way for dissonance, traditional tonality for polytonality. A severe, often crude, melodic line brought brutal strength. Rhythm was revitalized through the use of rapidly changing meters and polymeters. The orchestration exploited bizarre, sensational colors. This was a neo-primitive art, at one and the same time elemental and sophisticated.

This was the "music of the future." On the impressionistic and post-impressionistic world of 1912-14 it descended with shattering impact. It created fierce dissension between those who envisioned its composer as a prophetic voice in music and others who saw only sham and artifice in his tonal audacities. Few works were so violently attacked in their own time as these three scores; and few works have had such a decisive influence on the musical thinking of an entire generation. Consciously or otherwise, composers began imitating this fresh, vital speech. Younger men accepted Stravinsky as the spearhead of their attacks against formalism and tradition. In Italy, the futurist Marinetti paraded the streets with a banner proclaiming: "Down With Wagner! Long Live Stravinsky!"

Then just when these revolutionary works began slowly to gain general acceptance, and when the name of Stravinsky was conveniently identified with the *avant-garde* of contemporary music, a subtle evolution in style took place in his works. It was a breaking away from the complexity, the dissonance, and the hot blood of his Russian music. Stravinsky, seeking a more objective approach to his art, felt the need of greater clarity and lucidity in his writing, greater economy and simplicity. Indicative of this new attitude was the ballet *Pulcinella,* in which the creator of "the music of the future" was turning to the past by utilizing materials, and adapting the classical style, of Pergolesi! Brevity of forms, transparency of texture, avoidance of emotion in style, economy of instrumentation (with frequent excursions into novel combinations), a predilection for counterpoint—these were now the qualities of Stravinsky's works. From music that tended to be pictorial, Stravinsky turned to music that was abstract, pure, formal.

Once again acrid controversy raged around the personality of Igor Stravinsky, controversy between those who felt that the reservoir of his genius had now run dry and others who insisted that this new phase was a logical, even inevitable, development in the evolution of a great creative personality. To his many critics, Stravinsky insisted with calm self-assurance that just as they had refused to understand him when he wrote his Russian ballets, but later learned to accept him, so they would some day come around to his new way of thinking. "Their attitude certainly cannot make me deviate from my path," he wrote firmly in his autobiography. "I shall assuredly not sacrifice my predilection and my aspirations to the demands of those who, in their blindness, do not realize that they are simply asking me to go backwards. It should be obvious that what they wish for has become obsolete for me, and that I could not follow them without doing violence to myself."

And, it must be added, once again Stravinsky conquered. While not all of his neo-classical works have won full acceptance—some of them are singularly arid and unpalatable—the best of them (the *Symphony of Psalms,* say, or *Oedipus Rex*) have, in recent performances, made a profound impression. They are deeply moving in the intensity of expression and so inevitable in architectonic logic that many critics do not hesitate in referring to them as masterpieces.

In his most recent works, *Agon, Canticum Sacrum,* and an opera, *Threni,* introduced at the Venice Festival on September 23, 1958, a twelve-tone idiom known as "serial technique," and influenced by Anton von Webern, has replaced neo-classicism. His style may change; but there will be few to deny that Stravinsky is still one of the most dynamic personalities in the world of contemporary music.

Stravinsky was born on June 17, 1882, in Oranienbaum, a suburb of St. Petersburg, the son of a well-known singer of the Maryinsky Theatre. Law had been selected for him by his father. Though Igor Stravinsky detested it, and was by his own admission a poor student in academic courses, he managed to survive both the preparatory schools and the University. Meanwhile he found himself drawn more and more to the making of music. In the study of the piano, which he began when he was nine, he made excellent progress; later on, he combined his legal studies at the University with immersion in harmony and counterpoint textbooks.

During a visit to Germany, made when he was twenty, Stravinsky discovered that Rimsky-Korsakov was vacationing in Heidelberg. Since Rimsky-Korsakov's son was Igor's fellow-student at the University, the establishment of personal contact with the master was not difficult. Patiently, Rimsky-Korsakov went over some piano pieces Stravinsky had recently written and found a few things to praise, but much more to blame. His verdict: considerably more study was called for, but the profession of law was not to be abandoned.

The following year, Stravinsky wrote his first large work, a sonata for piano. Once again he went to Rimsky-Korsakov for criticism. The critical scalpel of an eminent theorist went to work, dissecting the composition for its strength and weakness. This time the praise outweighed the blame—so much so that Rimsky-Korsakov no longer had any hesitation in advising the young man to abandon law for music.

By the end of 1905, his course of study at the University ended, Stravinsky was definitely through with the legal profession. For the next two years he studied intensively with Rimsky-Korsakov, under whose guidance he wrote a symphony (in E-flat major), and *Faune et Bergère,* a suite for voice and orchestra after three poems by Pushkin. Both works were strongly influenced by Rimsky-Korsakov. They were performed privately by a court orchestra in 1907, while *Faune et Bergère* was introduced by Belaiev and the Russian Symphony Orchestra at one of its subscription concerts—Stravinsky's public debut as a composer.

Other works for orchestra—*Scherzo Fantastique* (inspired by Maeterlinck's *Life of the Bee*), and *Fireworks,* written for the marriage of Rimsky-Korsakov's daughter to Maximilian Steinberg—showed increasing technical assurance. It was these two works that attracted the attention of the impresario, Diaghilev, who recognized in them elements of genius. Diaghilev decided to join that genius to his recently organized Ballet Russe.

The first assignment was hardly calculated to give wings to the young man's talent: the orchestration of two Chopin pieces for a ballet, *Chopiniana*. But in 1909 Stravinsky's first major assignment came, the writing of an original score for a projected ballet, *The Fire-Bird*. It was Stravinsky's rendezvous with destiny. With *Petrushka* and *The Rite of Spring,* also written for Diaghilev, Stravinsky became the apostle of modern music.

After the outbreak of World War II, Stravinsky transferred his permanent home from Paris, where he had lived since World War I, to the United States. For a while he occupied a lecturer's chair at Harvard University. Subsequently he established his home in California. Since coming to this country, Stravinsky has devoted himself intensively to his creative work, interrupting it at intervals to conduct the great American orchestras.

The following works by Stravinsky are discussed below: *Apollo, Leader of the Muses (Apollon Musagète)*; *Capriccio; Card Game (Jeu de Cartes);* Concerto in D Major for Strings; Concerto in E-flat Major ("Dumbarton Oaks"); Concerto for Piano and Wind Orchestra; Concerto in D Major for Violin and Orchestra; *The Fire-Bird (L'Oiseau de Feu);* Mass; *Mavra; Ode; Oedipus Rex; Orpheus; Persephone; Petrushka; Pulcinella; The Rake's Progress; The Rite of Spring (Le Sacre du Printemps)*; *The Soldier's Tale (L'Histoire du Soldat)*; *The Song of the Nightingale (Le Chant du Rossignol)*; Symphony in C Major; *Symphony in Three Movements; Symphony of Psalms; The Wedding (Les Noces)*.

For "Dumbarton Oaks" Concerto, see Concerto in E-flat Major; for *Suite Italienne,* see *Pulcinella;* for Suite for Violin and Piano, see *Pulcinella.*

THE FIRE-BIRD (L'OISEAU DE FEU), ballet (1910).

The Russian legend of the Fire-Bird was planned as a ballet for Diaghilev by Fokine even before the commission for writing the score went to young Stravinsky. Another Russian composer had been assigned the job— Liadov. But Liadov procrastinated so long in completing this commission that the impatient Diaghilev decided to entrust it to Stravinsky. It was a bold gamble on the part of the impresario—for, up to then, Stravinsky had written little to suggest that he was able to fulfill so ambitious a project.

Stravinsky devoted the winter of 1909 and the early months of 1910 to the writing of this music. He was guided by the indefatigable Fokine, who had prepared the scenario, and who was ever at the composer's side with advice, criticism, and valuable suggestions.

On June 25, 1910, the Ballet Russe introduced *The Fire-Bird* at the Paris Opéra, with Fokine, Mme. Fokine, and Karsavina as the principal dancers. The settings were designed by Bakst and Golovina. Gabriel Pierné conducted.

That première was a resounding success. It made Stravinsky famous overnight. It also brought to the repertoire of the Ballet Russe one of its most strikingly original and famous works.

The Fokine scenario developed the traditional Russian legend without much variation. Ivan Tsarevitch, roaming aimlessly one night, stumbles across the Fire-Bird and captures it as it is in the act of plucking golden fruit from a silver tree. As a reward for its release, the Fire-Bird presents Ivan with one of its glowing feathers, which he accepts. Suddenly the thick darkness of the night dissipates. A castle comes into view, from whose doors thirteen maidens of surpassing beauty emerge. Little realizing that they are being observed, they play with the silver tree and its fruit. Emerging from his hiding place, Ivan receives from one of the maidens a golden fruit as a gift, and they dance out of sight. The night passes into dawn. Suddenly, Ivan realizes that the castle is the home of the dreaded Kastchei, who captures wayfaring strangers and subjects them to his will. Determined to conquer this ogre, Ivan enters the castle, which is guarded by terrifying monsters. Kastchei attempts to bewitch Ivan; but his power is impotent before the magic feather Ivan holds in his hand. Then the Fire-Bird comes into view, reveals to Ivan a casket, and informs him that Kastchei's fate is concealed in it. Ivan opens the casket and withdraws an egg, which he smashes to the ground. Death emerges from the smashed egg shell and obsesses the body of Kastchei. As Kastchei perishes, the castle suddenly disappears and the maidens are freed from their bondage. As a reward, Ivan receives in marriage the hand of the most beautiful of the captive maidens.

For this picturesque theme, Stravinsky produced a score of sheer magic. It was not without derivative echoes, but its boldness of imagination and its originality were unmistakable. With a stunning harmonic language, brilliant orchestral palette, distinctive melodic line, and irresistible rhythmic cogency Stravinsky evoked the most subtle tonal images. His was a style that could embrace barbarism (Dance of the Kastchei) and delicate tenderness (Berceuse).

It is quite true that many were outraged by Stravinsky's audacious harmonic and rhythmic language. Pavlova, who was supposed to dance in the première, refused to be associated with such "horrible music." Others considered the music noisy, brutal, vulgar. But there were also many who recognized its importance, who knew that a new master had just appeared. After the rehearsals, Diaghilev confided to a friend: "Mark that man, Stravinsky. He is on the eve of celebrity." And, following the première performance, Debussy rushed to young Stravinsky to embrace him, as if to hail a worthy successor.

Stravinsky prepared three different orchestral suites from the ballet score. It is the second which is heard most often at symphonic concerts. This one consists of six sections: I. Introduction—Kastchei's Enchanted Garden and the Dance of the Fire-Bird. II. Supplication of the Fire-Bird. III. The Princesses Play with the Golden Apples. IV. Dance of the Princess, and Berceuse. V. Infernal Dance of All the Subjects of Kastchei. VI. Finale.

This second suite differs from its predecessor in its simpler orchestration and in the deletion of two minor sections.

More recently, Stravinsky has prepared a third version, retaining the more economical orchestration of the second suite and restoring the Adagio and Scherzo movements from the first. He also interpolated transitional sections between the respective parts, in order to create integration and unity.

PETRUSHKA, ballet (1911).

Early in 1911, or some months after the successful première of *The Fire-Bird,* Diaghilev visited Stravinsky at Clarens, Switzerland, to listen to sections of a new ballet score upon which the composer was at work at that time. Diaghilev expected to hear the music for the ballet later known as *The Rite of Spring.* What he found Stravinsky immersed in was quite a different score: music of irony and capricious moods which, because the composer could not find a better name for it, he called a *Konzertstück.* What Stravinsky was trying to portray in this work was a pathetic sawdust puppet so frequently seen at Russian fairs: Petrushka. Diaghilev was not only enthused with the portions he heard Stravinsky play, but immediately recognized the value of Petrushka as a theme for a ballet. Together with the composer he now worked out the general lines of a scenario, setting the action in a Russian fair.

With this as a working basis, Stravinsky elaborated and developed his *Konzertstück* into a ballet score, now named *Petrushka.* He wrote not only the music but the scenario as well; the scenario was later put into final form by Alexandre Benois.

Petrushka was introduced by the Ballet Russe in Paris on June 13, 1911. Karsavina and Nijinsky were the principal dancers. Benois designed the scenery; Fokine prepared the choreography; Monteux conducted.

Philip Hale quotes the following admirable description of the action without crediting his source:

"This ballet depicts the life of the lower classes in Russia with all its dissoluteness, barbarity, tragedy, and misery. Petrushka is a sort of Polichinelle, a poor hero always suffering from the cruelty of the police and every kind of wrong and unjust persecution. This represents symbolically the whole tragedy in the existence of the Russian people, suffering under despotism and injustice. The scene is laid in the midst of the Russian carnival, and the streets are lined with booths, in one of which Petrushka plays a kind of humorous role. He is killed, but he appears again as a ghost on the roof of the booth to frighten his enemy, his old employer, an allusion to the despotic rule of Russia."

Into the musical atmosphere of 1911 the music of *Petrushka* came like a clap of thunder; and there were few who could ignore it. The rhythmic drive and variety, the unique instrumental effects, the incisive melodic line, the coruscating tone colors, were all projected with mastery and self-assurance. For the first time Stravinsky utilized polytonality; and the resultant effect was brilliant.

The score of *Petrushka* was an advance over *The Fire-Bird.* There was greater technical skill, and greater independence, in the later music. Stravinsky's bent for ironic and sardonic suggestions gave his new ballet score an intriguing and piquant flavor the earlier work did not possess. The tonal characterizations of *Petrushka* were subtler and more imaginative; the evocation of ever-changing moods was more skillful.

The following sections from the ballet were adapted by Stravinsky into an orchestral suite often heard at symphony concerts: Carnival; The Magician; Russian Dance; Petrushka; The Arab; Dance of the Ballerina; Nurses' Dance; The Bear and the Peasant Playing a Hand-Organ; The Merchant and the Gypsies; The Dance of the Coachman and the Grooms; The Masqueraders; The Quarrel of the Arab and Petrushka; The Death of Petrushka.

THE RITE OF SPRING (LE SACRE DU PRINTEMPS), ballet (1913).

Soon after completing *The Fire-Bird,* Stravinsky had a "vision," as he himself described it. He saw a girl dancing herself to death in a sacrificial pagan rite. He reported this transport to the painter Nicolas Roerich, who, impressed, agreed that this could be elaborated into a new ballet. Roerich helped Stravinsky work out a general outline in which images of pagan Russia were evoked.

The writing of this new ballet was delayed while another one, of quite a different character, engaged Stravinsky—*Petrushka.* Not until *Petrushka* was out of the way did Stravinsky return to *The Rite* and complete it.

The Rite of Spring has no detailed specific program. In abstract terms it portrays a ritual of pagan Russia. Symbolic or anecdotal details are not permitted to intrude. An exquisite orchestral introduction of seventy-five bars sets the mood of springtime: the earth is reborn; life is regenerated. There then takes place the Ballet of the Adolescents, who accompany their uneven stamping on the ground with an incantation. A second ceremonial consists of a kind of community contest, during which the Sage of the tribe appears to consecrate the soil. A pagan night, touched with mystery and sadness, descends. The Mysterious Circle of Adolescents begin a frenetic dance. A victim for the sacrifice is now chosen; and she dances herself to death.

The première performance, at the Théâtre de Champs Elysées in Paris on May 29, 1913, created a scandal which has been frequently described. Nijinsky's exotic choreography and Roerich's bizarre settings and costumes were partially responsible. But it was Stravinsky's revolutionary score which, more than any single factor, stirred that first-night audience to dynamic reactions. The performance had not progressed very far when catcalls, shouts, and stamping of feet began to drown out the music. On the one hand, musicians like Maurice Ravel and Debussy arose to exclaim that this was a work of genius; on the other, people like the critic André Capu, the Austrian Ambassador, and the Princess de Pourtalès pronounced it a fake. Blows were exchanged. One woman spat in the face of a demonstrator. Pandemonium followed. Very little of the music could now be heard.

Such was the birth of a musical work which has justifiably been described as one of the epochal landmarks in the music of our generation. More than any other single composition, it has influenced composers throughout the world, setting forth a new trend in musical composition, helping to evolve a new idiom. The dynamism of Stravinsky's rhythmic writing—the rapidly changing meters, the counterpoint of different rhythms—had a devastating kinesthetic appeal; the tension of the music, built up through dissonance and polytonality, had a terrifying effect; the brazen colors produced by unorthodox instrumentation were dazzling; the primitive appeal to the elementary senses of masses of sound and disjointed melodies had overwhelming impact. All this destroyed the complacency not only of a first-night audience but also of an entire musical era.

When *The Rite of Spring* was introduced in London at the Drury Lane Theatre on July 11, 1913, the audience was better mannered than the one which had witnessed the première performance in Paris. But the critics were just as savage. "It has no relation to music at all as most of us understand the word," one of them wrote. Another remarked: "A crowd of savages ... might have produced such noises."

Appreciation for this powerful and original music did not come suddenly. When the orchestral suite was introduced in this country by Pierre Monteux and the Boston Symphony in 1924, there was still profound antagonism to this music. One wit contributed the following verse to the pages of the *Boston Herald:*

> Who wrote this fiendish *Rite of Spring?*
>   What right had he to write this thing?
> Against our helpless ears to fling
>   Its crash, clash, cling, clang, bing, bang, bing!

If acceptance came slowly, it came inevitably as well. The score is now heard often—more often in the symphony hall than in the theatre—and much of the original surprise is gone. Instead, we now appreciate the incomparable vitality, the richness of speech, the audaciousness of thinking in this music. Indicative that this work is no longer for esoteric ears alone is the fact that it was incorporated in a Walt Disney motion picture, *Fantasia,* which was seen by millions.

The Rite of Spring, as heard in the concert auditorium, is divided into two parts:

I. The Adoration of the Earth. Introduction—Harbingers of Spring—Dance of the Adolescents—Spring Rounds; Games of the Round Cities—the Procession of Wise Men—The Adoration of the Earth—Dance of the Earth.

II. The Sacrifice. Introduction——Mysterious Circle of the Adolescents

—Glorification of the Chosen One—Evocation of the Ancestors—The Sacrificial Dance of the Chosen One.

THE SONG OF THE NIGHTINGALE (LE CHANT DU ROSSIGNOL), symphonic poem for orchestra (1914). I. The Palace of the Chinese Emperor. II. The Two Nightingales. III. Illness and Recovery of the Emperor of China.

The Song of the Nightingale has emerged in three different musical forms. It originated as an opera. After that, it was transformed into a ballet for the Diaghilev repertory. Subsequently it was revamped into symphonic form, the form in which it is best known.

The delightful fairy tale of Hans Christian Andersen appealed to Stravinsky as early as 1909, when he planned a "lyric tale in three acts" to a libretto by his friend Mitusov, and actually completed the entire first act. Not until 1914, however, was he able to complete the opera. It was then introduced at the Paris Opéra on May 26, Pierre Monteux conducting. One month later, it received four performances in London. Then—as an opera, at any rate—it passed into oblivion.

Diaghilev suggested to Stravinsky the conversion of the opera into a ballet. For this purpose, the composer adapted the last two acts into an integrated orchestral piece which could be utilized as the musical background for a ballet sequence. It was as an orchestral piece—or symphonic poem—that this new version was first heard: in Paris, on December 16, 1917, with Ernest Ansermet conducting. As a ballet (scenery by Matisse and choreography by Massine), it was introduced by the Ballet Russe in Paris on February 2, 1920, once again with Ansermet conducting.

The three sections of the symphonic poem are played without interruption. They describe the following program:

I. The Palace of the Chinese Emperor. The festivities attending the arrival of the Emperor into court are described. Following this—and with considerable pomp and ceremony—the nightingale, whose exquisite singing is world famous, is brought into the presence of the Emperor.

II. The Two Nightingales. The nightingale raises his voice in a song of such beauty that tears come into the eyes of the Emperor. A mechanical nightingale is then introduced into the court. It, too, sings beautifully, much to the chagrin of the live bird, who disappears. Angry, the Emperor orders the banishment of the live bird and gives the place of honor beside his bed to the mechanical nightingale.

III. Illness and Recovery of the Emperor of China. The Emperor is dying. Together with the pains of his illness come pangs of conscience for evils committed. Frantically he calls to his mechanical bird to sing, to drive out his thoughts and pains with beautiful music. But the mechanical bird is silent; the mechanism has broken. Suddenly the sweetest music is heard. It is that of the real nightingale, who has returned. The music so calms the

Emperor that he falls into a deep sleep, from which he awakens fully recovered. A funeral march announces the arrival of the courtiers, who expect
to find their Emperor dead. But they find instead a vigorous and healthy
ruler.

The songs of the nightingale, played in turn by a solo flute, an E-flat
clarinet, and a solo violin, are among the most eloquent pages in the score—
a welcome relief from the recurrent dissonances and acrid sounds that pre-
cede and follow them. Subtle suggestions of irony give the work considerable
spice: for example, the mock-heroic entrance of the Emperor in the first
section (written, appropriately, in the pentatonic scale of oriental music);
or, once again, the satiric funeral march in the last part for an Emperor who
proves to be vulgarly healthy.

THE SOLDIER'S TALE (L'HISTOIRE DU SOLDAT), ballet (1918).

Only three characters, a narrator, and seven instruments are required
for the performance of this intimate ballet. This economy was dictated not
by artistic necessity but by simple expediency. Many theatres and ballet companies had to suspend operations during World War I. Ambitious ballets,
requiring large forces, had almost no chance of being produced. Such being
the situation Stravinsky, planning a ballet in 1918, decided to write one that
made only limited demands on the production facilities of any theatre.

The Swiss poet C. F. Ramuz prepared the text, based on a Russian folk
tale. A soldier, returning from the wars, meets a devil disguised as an amiable
gentleman. The devil offers the soldier a magic book, capable of answering
any question, in return for his violin. Eagerly, the soldier accepts the bargain,
only to discover that knowing the answers to all the questions induces in him
an insatiable wanderlust. He loves a Princess and loses her. Finally, when
homesickness brings him home, he is seized on the border by the devil.

The première took place in Lausanne, Switzerland, on September 28,
1918, under Ernest Ansermet's direction.

One of the interesting musical features of this work is its occasional
use of the jazz style. One year earlier, Ansermet had brought back with him
from America examples of New Orleans jazz which he showed to Stravinsky. Evidently this music made a deep impression on the composer, for ragtime rhythm and dance—and even jazz improvisation—are ingeniously incorporated into this score. Stravinsky's use of the percussion instruments also
reveals the influence of the drums in the New Orleans jazz bands.

An orchestral suite, drawn from the ballet score, includes the follow-
ing numbers: I. Soldier's March. II. The Soldier's Violin—Music at the
Brook. III. Pastorale. IV. Royal March. V. Little Concerto. VI. Three
Dances—Tango, Waltz, Ragtime. VII. The Devil's Dance. VIII. Grand
Chorale. IX. Triumphal March of the Devil.

PULCINELLA, ballet (1919).

The music of Giovanni Battista Pergolesi (1710-1736)—discovered in manuscript form in Naples—provided the musical material for this Stravinsky ballet. Stravinsky wrote *Pulcinella* for Diaghilev. It was produced by the Ballet Russe in Paris, at the Opéra, on May 15, 1920. Pablo Picasso designed the scenery and costumes; Massine prepared the choreography; the principal dancers included Massine and Karsavina; Ernest Ansermet conducted.

Pulcinella is a traditional character of the early Neapolitan theater. In Stravinsky's ballet, he is the source of envy of all his neighbors because the girls are in love with him. They plot to kill him. Pulcinella simulates death. Believing they have achieved their aim, the Neapolitans assume Pulcinella's costume and proceed to make love to their respective girls. Meanwhile, Pulcinella puts on a sorcerer's robe and brings to life his double. However, vengeance is not in Pulcinella's heart. He attends the love-making of his neighbors and benevolently arranges for their respective marriages—while he himself weds Pimpenella.

An anonymous Swiss annotator remarked that, in adapting Pergolesi's music, Stravinsky "did more than transcribe.... In the case of some numbers, which he took as a point of departure, he elaborated a work which it is necessary to regard as to some extent original.... Feeling certain sympathetic affinities with the music of Pergolesi, Stravinsky reverted in his imagination to the environment of the Neapolitan music-makers of the early eighteenth century and provided what is, in effect, a 'portrait' of Pergolesi and his times.... He borrowed from Pergolesi not only the melodies and their characteristic harmonies, but also the strains of style and the form of these pieces."

Stravinsky adapted a concert suite for orchestra from the ballet score. The suite was introduced in Boston by the Boston Symphony Orchestra under Pierre Monteux on December 22, 1922. The suite includes the following movements: I. Sinfonia (Overture). II. Serenata—Larghetto. III. Scherzino, Allegro, Andantino. IV. Tarantella. V. Toccata. VI. Gavotte with Two Variations. VII. Duetto. VIII. Minuetto-Finale.

The music from *Pulcinella* also provided Stravinsky with the material for two different suites for violin and piano. One of these he entitled simply *Suite,* completed in 1925. This work contains the following movements: I. Introduction. II. Serenata. III. Tarantella. IV. Gavotte with Two Variations. V. Minuetto-Finale. A second suite was called *Suite Italienne,* written in 1933. Its movements are as follows: I. Sinfonia. II. Canzona. III. Danza. IV. Gavotta with Two Variations. V. Scherzino. VI. Moderato—Allegro vivace.

MAVRA, comic opera (1922).

Stravinsky conceived this opera because, as he put it, he had "a natural sympathy...for the melodic language, the vocal style and conventions of the old Russo-Italian opera. This sympathy inevitably led me back to a tradition ... which represented no tradition from the historical point of view and answered no musical necessity.... The music of *Mavra* is in the direct tradition of Glinka and Dargomijsky. I wanted merely to try my hand at this living form of opera buffa."

Boris Kochno adapted Pushkin's amusing story, *The Little House in Kolomna,* into a one-act libretto for Stravinsky. Parasha and Basil are in love. When Parasha's mother laments the loss of her cook, Parasha brings Basil, in woman's disguise and under the assumed name of Mavra, as a replacement. The ruse is discovered when Parasha and her mother return suddenly and discover their cook—shaving. The mother faints. When she recovers, Basil jumps out of the window and escapes as Parasha calls after him.

The plot is characteristic of the opera buffa tradition. For it Stravinsky produced one of his most engaging scores, rich with wit and lyricism, and occasionally marked by novel treatment in the instrumentation. Recitative is dispensed with altogether. The score consists of a continuous stream of melodies for solo voice and of ensemble numbers, both varied in character. As Paul Collaer pointed out, four sources yielded the styles of Stravinsky's lyricism: Russian occidental melody as found in Glinka and Dargomijsky; classical Italian melody; gypsy melody; and chromatic melody.

On June 3, 1922, the opera was introduced by the Ballet Russe at the Paris Opéra.

THE WEDDING (LES NOCES), cantata (1923). I. The Tresses. II. At the Bridegroom's Home. III. The Bride's Departure. IV. The Wedding Feast.

Stravinsky adopted an unconventional form for his "Russian choreographic scenes," which he designated as a cantata. *The Wedding* is a setting in four tableaux of scenes describing a Russian wedding ritual. It is scored for solo voices, chorus, and instrumentalists with the instrumental ensemble consisting of the unusual combination of four pianos and a battery of percussion. Unusual, too, is the placement of the singers—not on the stage, but in the orchestra pit.

Several popular Russian poems, collected by Kirievski, an authority on Russian folklore, provided the subject for this cantata. While there is no integrated plot as such, the action can be readily described:

I. "The Tresses." The bride is being dressed and prepared by her friends for the wedding ceremony.

II. "At the Bridegroom's Home." A similar ritual takes place at the home of the groom. Friends of both families shower the parents of the bride and groom with congratulations. The marriage ceremony then takes place.

III. "The Bride's Departure." After being blessed by his parents, the groom joins his bride as voices of congratulation are heard. The married couple leave, followed by the guests.

IV. "The Wedding Feast." The parents of both the bride and the groom lament the loss of their children. The wedding feast begins. Revelry takes place as the bride is formally presented to the guests before being passed over to her husband. A couple are chosen to prepare the bridal room and (as was then customary) to warm the bed. The bridal pair are conducted to the room, while the parents dally outside. The voice of the bridegroom is heard through the closed door, in praise of love.

All this is a picture of rather primitive people with primitive customs. For it, Stravinsky conceived an equally neo-primitive score. Brief snatches of melodic ideas replace sustained lyricism. Harsh and complicated rhythms, monotonous tone colors, piercing sonorities bring elemental power. The awkward lines and abrupt phrases suggest the illiteracy of the characters. This is not music that makes for pleasurable listening. But it cannot be denied that this is powerful music, or that it achieves its effect with sledgehammer blows.

No other work by Stravinsky took so long to crystallize. The first sketches were begun in 1914, and the first draft was completed in 1918. But not until 1923 was the orchestration completed. On June 17, 1923, *The Wedding* was introduced by the Russian Ballet at the Théâtre de la Gaieté in Paris, choreography by Bronislava Nijinsky. It was only moderately successful.

When it was introduced in London three years later (this performance was notable for the fact that the four pianos were played by composers—Poulenc, Auric, Dukelsky, and Rieti), it created a minor scandal. The audience booed and jeered. The critics were poisonous. The music, however, found a stouthearted protagonist in none other than H. G. Wells, who wrote an open letter declaring: "I do not know of any other ballet so interesting, so amusing, so fresh, or nearly as exciting as *The Wedding*....I protest against this conspiracy of willful stupidity that may succeed in driving it out of the program....The ballet is a rendering in sound and vision of the peasant soul, in its gravity, in its deliberate and simple-minded intricacy, in its subtly varied rhythms, in its deep undercurrent of excitement."

CONCERTO FOR PIANO AND WIND ORCHESTRA (1924).
I. Allegro. II. Larghissimo. III. Allegro.

The scoring of this piano concerto is unorthodox, calling for a wind orchestra supplemented by double basses and tympani. This instrumentation is characteristic of Stravinsky's continual experiments with unusual combinations of instruments following World War I. In line with Stravinsky's neo-classical thinking, the concerto re-creates the concerto grosso style of the seventeenth century—but with modern techniques.

Stravinsky introduced this concerto in Paris on May 22, 1924, at a Koussevitzky concert. The first movement is the most ambitious of the three. It is a toccata conceived along spacious lines; the main subject is a three-part

invention in the vein of Bach. The slow movement is introduced by the
piano with an expressive idea which is then carried by the orchestra before
receiving elaboration. In the final Allegro, the first subject consists of the final
cadence of the preceding movement, but in fast time: the theme is treated
fugally, and then is allowed to assume various shapes and forms. This section carries reminiscences of musical ideas heard in the opening and slow
movements.

OEDIPUS REX, opera-oratorio (1927).

In planning a major dramatic work based on the majestic tragedy of
Sophocles, Stravinsky called upon Jean Cocteau to prepare a new text.
Stravinsky felt that the language of the new text should be a dead one
(Latin), in order to give the subject a kind of remoteness, or, as he put
it, "a statuesque plasticity and a stately bearing entirely in keeping with the
majesty of the ancient legend." When Cocteau completed his play in French,
it was turned over to Jean Danielou for translation into Latin.

In order to make the play more comprehensible to the audience, Stravinsky adopted the device of having a narrator (in evening dress) appear on
the stage at intermittent periods to sum up the action that is to follow.

It was as an oratorio that *Oedipus* was first performed. Stravinsky
planned it as a surprise for Diaghilev, commemorating the twentieth anniversary of the impresario's activities. Since a dramatic presentation demanded
Diaghilev's collaboration—and since funds for such a presentation were
lacking anyway—Stravinsky decided to introduce it in concert form. Stravinsky himself conducted the première performance on May 30, 1927, in Paris.
That evening also included stage presentations of several ballets made famous
by Diaghilev. *Oedipus* was not well received. Heard between two colorful
ballets, it appeared dull and pretentious.

Subsequent performances—both in oratorio and operatic versions—
have since proved that this music, for all its austerity, has an eloquence of
its own. The first stage production took place in Berlin under Otto Klemperer
in February, 1928. It was outstandingly successful. No less successful have
been the many concert performances this work has received, many of them
under Stravinsky's direction.

Like the masterpieces he had written a decade earlier, *Oedipus* is profoundly influenced by Russian music. The "Gloria" with which the first
act closes, and which reappears at the opening of Act II, stems directly from
the choral music of the Russian Orthodox Church. Eric Walter White
further notes that the choral salutation to Creon "might be a literal quotation from Mussorgsky's *Boris*," while the air of the messenger has the "modal
rusticity of a Russian folksong."

APOLLON MUSAGÈTE (APOLLO, LEADER OF THE
MUSES), ballet (1927).

Unlike so many other Stravinsky ballets, *Apollon Musagète* has virtually no plot. The ballet consists of two tableaux. The first describes the birth of Apollo, while the second tells of his association with the Muses Calliope, Polyhymnia, and Terpsichore. "After a series of dances," the composer has explained, "treated in the traditional style of ballet (Pas d'Action, Pas de Deux, Coda), Apollo, in the apotheosis, leads the Muses, with Terpsichore at their head, to Parnassus, where they are to live afterwards."

Elizabeth Sprague Coolidge commissioned Stravinsky to write *Apollon Musagète* for a modern music festival held at the Library of Congress in Washington, D.C. The first performance took place on April 29, 1928, with choreography by Adolph Bohm and *décor* by Nicholas Remisoff.

In describing the style he assumed for this classical ballet, Stravinsky has said: "It seemed to me that diatonic composition was the most appropriate for this purpose, and the austerity of its style determined what my instrumental ensemble must be. I at once set aside the ordinary orchestra because of its heterogeneity, with its group of strings, woodwind, brass, and percussion instruments. I also discarded ensembles of wind and brass...and I chose strings."

CAPRICCIO, for piano and orchestra (1929). I. Presto. II. Andante rapsodico. III. Allegro capriccioso ma tempo giusto.

Stravinsky's ironic vein is evident in this work, introduced in Paris on December 6, 1929, with Ernest Ansermet conducting the Orchestre Symphonique, and the composer playing the piano part.

"I had in mind the definition of a capriccio given by Praetorius," explained the composer. "He regarded it as meaning a fantasia—a free form made up of fugato instrumental passages. This form enabled me to develop my music by the juxtaposition of episodes of various kinds which follow one another, and by their nature give the piece that aspect of caprice from which it takes its name."

The first and last movements project a light mood. The middle part, however, is rhapsodic music in a baroque style.

SYMPHONY OF PSALMS, for chorus and orchestra (1930).

An intensely religious man, Stravinsky has here produced his most reverent music. It was written "to the glory of God," and is permeated from the first bar to the last with profound spirituality, though on occasion the beauty is austere and remote. It has the primitivism of early Christian art, and it has reminded Paul Rosenfeld of "mosaics in a Byzantine church."

Stravinsky produced this work to commemorate the fiftieth anniversary of the Boston Symphony Orchestra. It was, however, not introduced in Boston but in Brussels, on December 13, 1930, Ernest Ansermet conducting the Brussels Philharmonic. One week later, Serge Koussevitzky conducted it in Boston.

For his text (sung in Latin), the composer went to the Vulgate: verses 13 and 14 of Psalm XXXVIII (Part I); verses 2, 3, and 4 of Psalm XXIX (Part II); and the entire Psalm CL (Part III).

The composer has written: "The juxtaposition of the three psalms is not fortuitous. The prayer of the sinner for divine pity (prelude), the recognition of grace received (double fugue), and the hymn of praise and glory are the basis of an evolutionary plan. The music which embodies these texts follows its development according to its own symphonic law. The order of the three movements presupposes a periodic scheme and in this sense realizes a 'symphony.' For a periodic scheme is what distinguished a 'symphony' from a collection of pieces with no scheme but one of succession, as in a suite."

In his orchestration, Stravinsky dispenses with violins and violas. His musical style leans heavily on polyphonic writing, equal prominence being given to orchestra and chorus.

CONCERTO IN D MAJOR FOR VIOLIN AND ORCHESTRA (1931). I. Toccata. II. Aria. III. Aria. IV. Capriccio.

Stravinsky wrote his violin concerto for Samuel Dushkin, who introduced it in Berlin on October 23, 1931, with the Berlin Radio Orchestra, the composer conducting.

The work is integrated by an introductory series of chords in the solo violin which (slightly varied) preface each of the four movements. The first section has three principal themes, which are subjected to considerable, often complicated, development. Two arias follow, the first being a spacious melody first heard in the solo violin, while the second is more ornamental. The closing section consists of two main themes and has much virtuoso writing for the solo instrument.

In 1940-41, the music of this concerto was adapted by the De Basil Ballet Company for a ballet entitled *Balustrade,* choreography by Balanchine.

PERSÉPHONE, melodrama (1933). I. Persephone Abducted. II. Persephone in the Underworld. III. Persephone Restored.

In 1933, the dancer Ida Rubinstein commissioned Stravinsky to set to music a poem which André Gide had written, a poem based on the Homeric *Hymn to Demeter.* In three parts, this poem describes Persephone's descent to the lower regions, following her breathing of the narcissus aroma, which gives her a vision of that world of which she is to be queen. She grows bored with that world and yields to nostalgia for the life she has deserted. At last she succumbs and returns to the upper regions.

This poem became the basis of a "melodrama," a veritable mélange of the arts, calling for music, singing, dancing, miming, and recitation. The score utilizes a speaking voice, tenor, chorus, and orchestra. The world première took place in Paris at the Opéra on April 30, 1934. Ida Rubinstein appeared in the title role. André Barascq designed the scenery, and Kurt Jooss prepared the choreography. Stravinsky conducted.

Hugh Ross noted that the most commendable feature of the score is its "undisguised ... melodies, such as those of the women's choral dance (Part I), the oboe solo at the beginning of Part II, and the seductive Scherzando of Eumolpe, the spring chorus, and the madrigal in Part III." Classical repose is another distinguishing trait of this music, as, for example, in the two opening choruses and in the chorus hailing Persephone's return to the upper world.

CARD GAME (JEU DE CARTES), ballet "in three deals" (1936).

In 1936, Stravinsky was commissioned by the American Ballet to write a new work for its repertory. The *Card Game* was introduced by that organization at the Metropolitan Opera House on April 27, 1937, the composer conducting. George Balanchine was in charge of the choreography.

The composer has thus summarized the action: "The characters in this ballet are the cards in a game of poker, disputed between several players on the green baize table of a gaming house. At each deal the situation is complicated by the endless guile of the perfidious Joker, who believes himself invincible because of his ability to become any desired card.

"During the first deal one of the players is beaten, but the other two remain with even 'straights,' although one of them holds the Joker.

"In the second deal, the hand which holds the Joker is victorious, thanks to four Aces, who easily beat four Queens.

"Now comes the third deal. The action grows more and more acute. This time it is a struggle between three 'flushes.' Although at first victorious over one adversary, the Joker, strutting at the head of a sequence of Spades, is beaten by a 'royal flush' in Hearts. This puts an end to his malice and knavery."

The three "deals" of the ballet are divided as follows:

I. Introduction; Pas d'Action; Dance of the Joker; Little Waltz.

II. Introduction; March; Variation of the Four Queens; Variation of the Jack of Hearts and Coda, March, and Ensemble.

III. Introduction; Waltz-Minuet; Presto (Combat between Spades and Hearts); Final Dance (Triumph of the Hearts).

The ballet score is sometimes heard as a concert piece, in which form it is performed without interruption and without appreciable alteration.

CONCERTO IN E-FLAT MAJOR ("DUMBARTON OAKS"), for fourteen instruments (1938).

Stravinsky wrote this composition for a Washington, D.C., music lover and named it after his patron's estate, which since that time has become famous as the scene of a celebrated international monetary conference. The style is contrapuntal, in the vein of the Bach *Brandenburg Concertos*. The three movements are performed without interruption. Fugal writing pre-dominates throughout, and becomes the climactic page of the first and third movements. A graceful and gentle melodic middle movement (Allegretto), classic in its objective beauty, provides a serene interlude for two robust movements (Tempo giusto and Con moto).

SYMPHONY IN C MAJOR (1940). I. Moderato alla breve. II. Lar-ghetto concertante. III. Allegretto. IV. Adagio; Tempo giusto.

There was a thirty-five-year hiatus between Stravinsky's First Sym-phony (E-flat major), and his Second, in C major. During these years Stravinsky passed from being an apprentice studying under Rimsky-Korsakov to being a composer in full mastery of his technique. Though the style of the Second Symphony is in Stravinsky's later vein, the form follows the First in its adherence to classical structures. The first movement is in strict sonata form, with two clearly stated themes developed in classical style and then recapitulated. A beautiful song, written simply, forms the second movement, appropriately described by its composer as an "aria." Two classical dances—the minuet and the passepied—form the third movement, which culminates in a grandiose fugue. The closing section begins with an impressive Adagio (bassoons and brasses) and continues with a robust section faintly suggesting the concerto grosso style.

This symphony was written, as the composer said, "to the glory of God," and was dedicated to the Chicago Symphony Orchestra to com-memorate its fiftieth anniversary. That orchestra, under the composer's direc-tion, introduced it in Chicago on November 7, 1940.

ODE, triptych for orchestra (1943). I. Eulogy. II. Eclogue. III. Epitaph.

Stravinsky was commissioned to write an orchestral work by the Koussevitzky Music Foundation. He decided on an ode—a eulogy to the late Natalie Koussevitzky, an appreciation of her "spiritual contribution to the art of the eminent conductor, her husband, Dr. Koussevitzky."

A chant in three parts, the ode opens with a song in sustained melody, treated fugally. A lively piece follows suggesting outdoor music; this was intended by the composer to be a tribute to Tanglewood, home of the Berk-shire Music Festival, where Koussevitzky officiates each summer. A serene theme introduces the final section which is melancholy throughout.

The *Ode* was introduced by the Boston Symphony Orchestra under Serge Koussevitzky on October 8, 1943.

SYMPHONY IN THREE MOVEMENTS (1945). I. (Tempo indi-cation not given.) II. Andante. III. Con moto.

Five years after he wrote his Second Symphony in C Major, Stravinsky produced a third work in the symphonic form. A radical change in the composer's approach to the symphonic style is here evident. The *Symphony in Three Movements* is completely independent of formal symphonic structure. There is no sonata form, no development, no recapitulation. The music is conceived, as Ingolf Dahl wrote in his definitive analysis, "as the succession of clearly outlined blocks, or planes, which are unified and related through the continuity of a steadily and logically evolving organic force."

The first movement is the most ambitious of the three. Though it has no marking other than metronomic, it is essentially an Allegro. It has been described as a toccata and is in three sections, the first and third being harmonic and the middle, polyphonic. A kind of "delicate intermezzo," with the concertino formed by harp and flutes, is heard in the second movement, which has a chamber-music texture. A majestic theme in full orchestra prefaces the closing movement, which, like the first, is in three sections—though here the sections may be regarded as variations of the original theme. A fugue, unusual for its rhythmic and intervallic construction, leads to a coda-like finale.

The symphony is dedicated to the New York Philharmonic-Symphony Orchestra, which introduced it in New York City on January 24, 1946, the composer conducting.

CONCERTO IN D MAJOR FOR STRINGS (1946). I. Vivace. II. Arioso. III. Rondo.

The twentieth anniversary of the Basel Chamber Orchestra led its conductor, Paul Sacher, to commission Stravinsky to write a new work to commemorate the event. The result was a chamber concerto modeled after the classical concerto grosso. It was introduced in Basel, Switzerland, on January 21, 1947.

With a comparatively simple tone language, and with transparent instrumentation, the concerto utilizes the concerto grosso style by setting solo instruments alternately with and against the rest of the orchestra. One of the fine moments in the work is in the lyrical middle movement, as the sustained melody is first heard dolce espressivo in the first violins and cellos. A brisk Vivace opens the concerto, and the closing movement is marked by striking instrumental effects.

MASS, for mixed chorus and ten wind instruments (1948).

Stravinsky composed this, his first major liturgical work, in 1948. It was introduced in Milan on October 27 of that year under the direction of Ernest Ansermet.

Stylistically, the music reaches back to the early contrapuntal Flemish school. But though the modal writing suggests the distant past, the dissonant counterpoint is primarily of our times. This is one of Stravinsky's most economically realized works. The texture is transparent; the writing, pure and refined; the mood, almost continually subdued. Effective use is made of the wind instruments, which are frequently heard alternating with the a cappella choruses.

When the Mass was introduced in the United States, on February 26, 1949 (it was heard twice on the same program, before and after the intermission), there was considerable difference of opinion among the critics regarding the success of the composer in producing religious music. Olin Downes wrote in the *New York Times* that, for the most part, the Mass "is singularly bereft of either spirituality or human feeling.... Nowhere, except in the few measures of the Hosanna, was there anything to imply that the music was intended for actual use in a religious service. Nothing could be further removed from the spiritual than the trivial march employed in the Christe Eleison."

On the other hand, Arthur V. Berger, critic of the *New York Herald-Tribune,* found the work to be of "uncommon purity and remarkably unforced religious sentiment.... This Mass, as a whole, is a work of beauty and has the simple directness of truth."

ORPHEUS, ballet (1948).

In his ballet, Stravinsky follows closely the classic and well-known story of Orpheus and Eurydice, treating it with simplicity and directness.

The published score contains the following summation of the ballet:

"Scene I: Orpheus weeps for Eurydice. He stands motionless with his back to the audience. Friends pass, bringing presents and offering sympathy. Air de Danse. Dance of the Angel of Death. Interlude (the Angel and Orpheus reappear in the gloom of Tartarus).

"Scene II: Pas des Furies (their agitation and their threats). Air de Danse (Orpheus). Interlude (the tormented souls in Tartarus stretch out their fettered arms towards Orpheus and implore him to continue his song of consolation. Air de Danse (Orpheus). Pas d'Action (Hades, moved by the song of Orpheus, grows calm. The Furies surround him, bind his eyes, and return Eurydice to him.) Pas de Deux (Orpheus and Eurydice before the veiled curtain). Interlude. Pas d'Action (the Bacchantes attack Orpheus, seize him, and tear him to pieces).

"Scene III: Apotheosis of Orpheus. Apollo appears. He wrests the lyre from Orpheus and raises his song heavenwards."

The score is almost continually in a subdued mood, written with simplicity, avoiding ornamentation of all kinds, and achieving a deeply affecting eloquence through spare writing. A high degree of expressiveness and an almost gentle melancholy bring to this music a human quality not often encountered in the later Stravinsky—these, and a truly classic repose. However, though it is generally quiet and serene, *Orpheus* has (as Alfred Frankenstein points out) "its share of those prickly, dynamic dances, as if the body of the music rested on a bed of fine steel springs, that are a Stravinsky specialty....

Orpheus indicates that Stravinsky has finally suffused his classic ideal with a rich and sensitive humanism."

Orpheus was introduced by the Ballet Society in New York on April 28, 1948. The dancers included Nicholas Magallanes and Maria Tallchief. George Balanchine prepared the choreography, and the scenery and costumes were designed by Noguchi. Stravinsky conducted the première performance.

Orpheus received a special citation from the New York Music Critics Circle in 1948 as "an outstanding work by an internationally famous composer."

When performed in the symphony hall, the score of *Orpheus* is utilized without any changes whatever. The first concert performance took place in Boston on February 11, 1949, with Stravinsky conducting the Boston Symphony Orchestra.

THE RAKE'S PROGRESS, opera (1951).

In 1922, Stravinsky had written the opera *Mavra*. It took him twenty-nine years to return to the operatic stage.

The libretto of *The Rake's Progress* was prepared by W. H. Auden and Chester Kallman and was based on the set of eight drawings of Hogarth. The plot is set in the eighteenth century, and revolves around Tom Rakewell. He abandons his sweet, Anne Trulove, squanders a recently inherited fortune on lust and carousing, and consigns his soul to Shadow (Mephisto). A last attempt to redeem himself makes him assume the futile role of a benefactor. He must now live up to his bargain and deliver his soul to Shadow, but he succeeds in convincing the devil to engage in a game of chance for it. Tom wins the gamble, but he loses his mind, and must wander in Bedlam. In the end, just before his death, his sweetheart Anne returns to him, and the lovers are finally reunited.

The première of *The Rake's Progress* was an event of international significance. It took place on September 11, 1951, in Venice, in conjunction with the Venice Festival, which was reputed to have paid $20,000 for the performance rights. Tickets were at a premium, as music lovers from all parts of Europe converged on Venice to attend the première. It was an immense success. Before a year had passed the new opera was performed in Paris, Copenhagen, Antwerp, Brussels, Cologne, Düsseldorf, Frankfurt, Hamburg, Milan, Monte Carlo, Munich, Stuttgart, and Zurich, and was accepted by the Metropolitan Opera of New York for the 1952-53 season.

The structure of the opera follows a traditional pattern, utilizing arias, recitatives, ensemble numbers, and choruses. "He has used for the most part the gallant, elegant style of the eighteenth century," wrote Howard Taubman in the *New York Times*. "He has composed music that has gaiety and tenderness, simplicity and brilliance, incisive wit and honest feeling."

KAROL SZYMANOWSKI   1883—1937

Szymanowski was the foremost composer of our time in Poland; Hugo Riemann goes so far as to consider him the greatest creative figure to emerge in Poland since Chopin.

Szymanowski found himself artistically when he began drawing his inspiration and material from native sources, producing a series of national works in which his land and its people are mirrored. But Szymanowski came to nationalism by a circuitous route. As a visitor to Berlin, in 1905, he was greatly affected by Germanic romanticism; his works from op. 1 to op. 10 are imitative of Bruckner, Mahler, and, most of all, Richard Strauss. He then freed himself of Germanic influences to produce music that was subjective, feverish in moods, filled with dramatic or tragic pronouncements (opp. 11-23). For a brief period, he turned to mysticism and oriental philosophy, an interest that was responsible for the writing of his *Love Songs of Hafiz,* op. 24, the opera *Hagith,* and the symphony, *The Song of the Night,* op. 27. After that came an interest in Debussy and Scriabin; the fingerprints of both these composers are discernible in such works for the piano or the violin as *Metopes,* op. 29, *Mythes,* op. 30, and *Masques,* op. 34.

Obviously he was groping for a personal idiom. He found it soon after a visit to Zakopane, in the Tatras mountains of Poland. He listened to the songs and dance music of this region, with its free use of melody and harmony, and felt as if he had suddenly stepped into a new world. "The music," he later wrote, "is enlivening by its proximity to Nature, by its force, by its directness of feeling, by its undisturbed racial purity." Back from this visit, he wrote his first mazurka. From that moment on, he was not only a composer from Poland but a *Polish* composer. "Each man must go back to the earth from which he derives," he wrote. "Today I have developed into a national composer, not only subconsciously, but with a thorough conviction, using the melodic treasures of the Polish folk." How overwhelming an experience this contact with native Polish music was, and how profoundly it affected his musical thinking, was soon demonstrated. Between 1926 and 1928, he produced two of his masterpieces—the ballet *Harnasie,* and the *Stabat Mater*—both of which are intensely national in feeling.

His music derives its rhythmic force and its rich harmonic colors, as well as its prevailing oriental sensuality, from Slavonic folk music; but to these qualities is often added a vein of mysticism.

Szymanowski was born in Tymoszowka, in the Ukraine (where his parents had an estate), on September 21, 1883. His was a cultured household where all the arts were appreciated; therefore, he early came into contact with good music. His first studies took place with local teachers. When he was seventeen he wrote his first pieces—preludes in the vein of Chopin. In 1903, he went to Warsaw for more intensive study, principally with Sigmund Noskowski, and before very long succeeded in winning prizes for several large piano works. In 1905, he went to Berlin to saturate himself with German music. While there he began writing for the orchestra; the influence of the German romantic composers predominates in these compositions. In Berlin he joined forces with several other gifted young Polish composers—Szeluto, Fitelberg, Rozycki. Calling themselves "Young Poland in Music," these composers expressed their devoted allegiance to Germanic romanticism. They sponsored a concert of their own music, which was received rather apathetically.

In 1908, Szymanowski left Berlin. The next six years were spent either on his paternal estate in the Ukraine or in extensive travels. During this period, his first two symphonies were introduced in Warsaw. The outbreak of war found him in Russia. Now unable to travel to Europe, he spent his time in the principal cities of Russia, becoming acquainted with its national music and with the works of Debussy and Scriabin. The Revolution left him destitute. Virtually penniless, Szymanowski settled in Warsaw in 1920. One year later he paid a brief visit to this country.

After discovering the national songs and dances of Poland in the Tatras mountains, Szymanowski not only became an outstanding national composer but one of Poland's most influential musicians. In 1926, he became director of the Warsaw Conservatory. Soon after assuming this post, Szymanowski began writing the works by which he was to achieve international fame, notably *Harnasie* and the *Stabat Mater*.

Always delicate in health, he suffered a physical breakdown in 1929 which necessitated his resigning as director of the Warsaw Conservatory. Strengthened by a stay in a sanitarium, Szymanowski returned to composition, producing several distinguished works, the most famous of which were the Second Violin Concerto and the *Symphonie Concertante,* for piano and orchestra.

Suffering a physical relapse, Szymanowski was advised by his physicians to take a holiday in France. There he attended an outstandingly successful performance of *Harnasie* at the Paris Opéra. His health now deteriorated so rapidly that he was confined to a sanitarium in Lausanne, Switzerland. He died there of laryngeal tuberculosis on March 28, 1937.

The following works by Szymanowski are discussed below: *Concerto No. 2 for Violin and Orchestra;* Études; *Harnasie; Metopes; Stabat Mater; Symphonie Concertante No. 2.*

METOPES, for piano, op. 29 (1915). I. The Island of Sirens. II. Calypso. III. Nausicaa.

Debussy's influence on Szymanowski is particularly evident in several piano works, of which *Metopes* is characteristic. It is a cycle of three sensitive tone-poems, evoking pages from the *Odyssey* with vivid harmonic writing and languorous melodies. Three different moods are created: the first, describing the island of the sirens, is sensual; a tender and wistful picture is etched in Calypso; and the final piece, telling of the games of maidens, is corybantic. (The word "metope" represents carved work on the Doric frieze.)

ÉTUDES, for piano, op. 33 (1917).

At different times in his early career, Szymanowski was influenced by different composers. The Études, written while Szymanowski was in Russia, stem not from Chopin but principally from Scriabin (though there are occasional suggestions of Debussy and Schoenberg). The Études, which the composer wished to be played in their entirety and without interruption, are not so much exercises in technique or virtuosity as they are brief impressions. Each is self-sufficient in its rhythmic or harmonic interest, yet gains in effect through contrast of mood or tempo, as the result of its juxtaposition to its neighbors. The often subtle interplay of rhythms, the refinement of speech, the involved chordal structures, are all derived from Scriabin.

STABAT MATER, for soloists, chorus, and orchestra, op. 53 (1925).

"For many years," Szymanowski has written, "I have thought of Polish religious music. I have tried to achieve first of all the direct emotional effect, in other words, the general intelligibility of the text and the fusion of the emotional substance of the word with its musical equivalent. I wanted the music to be as far as possible from the official liturgical music, from its elevated and former musty academicism."

The *Stabat Mater* was the composer's first venture into liturgical music. It is one of his finest works, and the first of his compositions to be acclaimed in his native land. Its première in Warsaw in 1928 was a tremendous success.

Within a highly flexible form, Szymanowski mingled religious and national feeling to produce a highly personal work: sixteenth-century polyphony (treated with freedom) is blended with Polish rhythm and melody. The result is music that is more pictorial and dramatic than spiritual. As the Italian critic, Guido Pannain, noted, "the drama of the Cross becomes a prophetic vision of a legendary epic.... It is not the heart of the believer that is wrung by emotion ... but the fancy of a poet that conjures up an epic vision."

HARNASIE, ballet (1926).

Soon after coming into contact with the life, music, and dance of the Tatras mountaineers, Szymanowski decided to interpret them in a national work for the stage. He wrote his ballet *Harnasie* in 1926, deriving his subject from legendary sources. The story is a simple and primitive one: a peasant bride is abducted from her wedding by the leader of the Harnasie, a wild mountain tribe; soon after this, love between them flowers. With the cogent rhythmic force, the coruscant harmonic colors, the exotic melodies and shifting tonalities of the peasant music of the Carpathian mountains, Szymanowski produced not only a score of immense power and originality, but also one of his most vital national creations.

In *Music and Letters*, H. H. Stuckenschmidt described *Harnasie* as follows:

"The music conjures up with the power of genius the wild and lonely landscape of the Carpathians. It is dominated by the thematic *idée fixe*, which is used in modified forms in nearly all the nine numbers of the score.... The peculiar orchestral texture, which gives preference to oboe or clarinet solos and avoids the thickness of earlier Szymanowski scores, contributes much to the impression of local color. Tenor solos and mixed choruses are added to the orchestral sound. Pieces like the march of the Harnasie, the Cossack-like drinking song, and the peasant dance (made famous by Paul Kochanski's violin arrangement even before the whole ballet was known) show Szymanowski as a masterly manipulator of nationalist melody and of intricate Slavonic rhythms."

SYMPHONIE CONCERTANTE NO. 2, for piano and orchestra, op. 60 (1932). I. Allegro moderato. II. Andante molto sostenuto. III. Allegro non troppo.

In calling his only work for piano and orchestra a *Symphonie Concertante* instead of a concerto, Szymanowski was emphasizing the equal importance enjoyed by both the solo instrument and the orchestra in projecting the music. In May, 1933, it was introduced with overwhelming success in Warsaw by the Warsaw Philharmonic under Fitelberg, with the composer at the piano. It has been performed extensively throughout the world of music, and has become one of the composer's most celebrated works.

In the first movement, the piano comes forth with the principal theme against quiet, syncopated chords in the strings. This theme is taken up by the orchestra, and is then developed. The second theme is heard in the flute against chromatic-scale passages in the strings—a whimsical idea which has been compared to an ancient Venetian dance. The flute opens the second movement with a feeling melody set against the piano and strings; the violas then join with a countermelody. The second theme, no less beautiful than the first, appears first in muted horns and then in the piano. A recall of the principal theme of the first movement serves as a transition to the third, which is vital with dance rhythms. The music develops with savage intensity until it erupts in a breath-taking climax, a "healthy liberation of energy," as Herbert Elwell described it.

CONCERTO NO. 2 FOR VIOLIN AND ORCHESTRA, op. 61 (1933).

One of Szymanowski's most intimate friends was the violinist Paul Kochanski, for whom he wrote many works, including two concertos. Kochanski introduced the Second Concerto in Warsaw on October 6, 1933, with the Warsaw Philharmonic, Georg Fitelberg conducting.

Though divided into two sections (separated by a cadenza), the concerto is in a single movement. In the first part, the principal theme is heard in the solo violin after a brief prelude. After this idea has been imitated by several different instruments of the orchestra, the solo violin returns with the second melody, which is also taken up by parts of the orchestra. The music grows in rhythmic and emotional force until an Appassionato section is reached. The intensity is relaxed. A cadenza leads into the second section, which begins rhythmically, but then proceeds into the statement of a beautiful lyrical theme. The principal subjects of the first and second sections are then developed, after which the music is built up into a forceful climax.

ALEXANDRE TANSMAN   1897—

Tansman has tried to reconcile modern techniques and styles with the identity of Polish national music. The dances of Poland have left their throb and rhythm in his works; but a strong and personal lyricism is equally evident. He indulges in extended melodic ideas that frequently assume the personality of a lied and which, after they are fully unfolded, are subjected to elaborate development. The setting for these melodies is a modern harmonic language, with frequent excursions into dissonance.

Tansman was born in Lodz, Poland, on June 12, 1897. He began his music study with local teachers and continued it in Warsaw with Pierre Rytel; at the same time he pursued the study of law at the University. He began composing early: he was only fifteen when he heard one of his own works performed in public, and only twenty-two when his compositions won the Grand Prize of Poland. In 1920, he established his home in Paris and became an integral part of its musical life. From there he traveled throughout the world of music, appearing as pianist and conductor in performances of his own works. His first visit to the United States took place in 1927. He settled in the United States in 1941, remaining here during the years of World War II. Soon after arriving here, he was awarded the Elizabeth Sprague Coolidge medal for distinguished services to chamber music. Besides composing many major works in this country, Tansman also produced music for Hollywood films. Soon after the end of World War II, Tansman returned to his home in Paris.

The following works by Tansman are discussed below: *Ricercari;* Symphony No. 5; Symphony No. 7; *Triptyque.*

TRIPTYQUE, for string quartet or string orchestra (1931). I. Allegro risoluto. II. Andante. III. Presto.

The *Triptyque*—or "three panels"—is one of Tansman's best works for chamber-music groups. It was introduced in 1931 in Paris by the Brosa String Quartet. Tansman also scored the work for string orchestra, in which version it was introduced by the St. Louis Symphony under Vladimir Golschmann on November 6, 1931.

The composer has analyzed the work as follows:

"I. A marked and energetic theme is given out by the second violins, with the rhythmic emphasis clearly punctuated in the violoncellos. This is repeated and seized upon by the first and second violins and, in harmonic and rhythmic development, leads into a second theme based upon a rhythmic play on the interval of the third. In a closely woven exposition the two themes are superimposed in dynamic and harmonic development, which leads to an incisively rhythmic close.

"II. The movement begins with a fugal development of a theme of calm and serene character which rises in lyrical ecstasy to a climax and then returns a little slowly to the pianissimo of the beginning....

"III. This movement develops in a sort of 'perpetual motion,' in which the rhythms are superimposed in a fashion sometimes playful, sometimes case-hardened and mechanistic. Into this rapid movement enters an interlude of grave character, but the whir of rhythms returns to develop into an interlacing of the several themes of the work, which finishes in a sort of Polish hymn."

SYMPHONY NO. 5 (1942). I. Lento—Allegro con moto. II. Intermezzo: andante sostenuto. III. Scherzo: vivo. IV. Finale: lento—Allegro con moto.

This is the first work written by Tansman in this country after he had settled here in 1941. On February 2, 1943, it was introduced in Baltimore by the National Symphony Orchestra (of Washington, D.C.), the composer conducting.

The symphony is classical in form, and is predominantly melodic. A slow introduction leads into the Allegro, in which the first theme is a lyric passage for strings; the second theme is also melodious. Both ideas are worked out polyphonically; in the stirring climax the two melodies are played simultaneously. The second movement is lyrical and introspective: the first theme is presented by the clarinet against divided violas, and the second is heard in the strings. The Scherzo, in song form, is particularly interesting for its frequent changes of meter and rhythm. A slow introduction ushers in the finale, in which the principal theme—fully projected and developed in the ensuing Allegro con moto section—is suggested.

SYMPHONY NO. 7 (1944).

Tansman's Seventh Symphony was heard for the first time on October 24, 1947, in St. Louis, with Vladimir Golschmann conducting the St. Louis Symphony Orchestra.

The work, which is played without interruption, is for the most part meditative. It opens with a slow introduction in which the principal themes are heard; the main part follows, built around two fast subjects. The second movement is quiet and contemplative. This is followed by a scherzo, one of whose themes has the character of a folksong. The finale is lively. Toward the close of this movement, strains of the first movement reappear gradually, and as the pace slackens, the symphony ends with a reiteration of the opening introduction.

RICERCARI, for orchestra (1949). I. Notturno. II. Scherzo—Danza. III. Intermezzo. IV. Toccata. V. Study in Boogie-Woogie.

Several modern composers have resurrected the form of the ricercare (the American, Norman Dello Joio, for example). The ricercare is a contrapuntal form—the instrumental counterpart of the vocal motet; it develops a basic idea (or several ideas) fugally. With different modern composers, the ricercare form has undergone different transformations. With Tansman it consists of five contrasting movements: the first is a placid melody, first heard in the oboe, and then repeated by the flute, trumpet, and clarinet; this is followed by a sprightly Scherzo, which develops into a mazurka-like dance; a brief Intermezzo for muted strings brings temporary repose; after a robust Toccata for full orchestra comes a glaring anachronism—a boogie-woogie treatment of an earthy idea.

This composition was commissioned by the St. Louis Symphony Orchestra to honor its seventieth anniversary. The orchestra, under Vladimir Golschmann, introduced it in St. Louis on December 22, 1949.

DEEMS TAYLOR

The music of Deems Taylor is not the kind to create new styles or influence new composers. Its function is to bring pleasure to the listener, which it usually does; and it brings pleasure through its logic, gracious wit and sentiment, suave sophistication, and graceful movement. Taylor has never paid even lip service to any single style or trend, nor has he ever attempted to join any school of musical thought. He must write as his heart, not his intellect, dictates. His works consequently are romantically conceived, generously filled with pleasing melodies, attractive in their settings of warm harmonies and apt instrumentation. His works—whether for the symphony hall or opera house—may never transport us into a new world; but they will bring a brighter glow to the present one.

Taylor was born in New York City on December 22, 1885, and received his education in public schools, the Ethical Culture School, and New York University. He began the study of the piano when he was fourteen, was a pupil of Oscar Coon in harmony and counterpoint, and learned what he could about composition and orchestration from textbooks. He began his professional musical career as a journalist, achieving a position of first importance among American music critics on the *New York World,* where he served from 1921 to 1925. For a period after that he was editor of the journal *Musical America.* Meanwhile he achieved note as a composer with his witty and delightful orchestral suite, *Through the Looking Glass,* in 1919. Commissions from the Metropolitan Opera Association for two operas, *The King's Henchman* and *Peter Ibbetson*—and their successful performances—made Taylor a nationally famous composer. Besides his achievements as a music critic and composer, Taylor has become famous as a musical commentator over the radio and as the author of several books on music.

The following works by Taylor are discussed below: *Elegy; The King's Henchman; Peter Ibbetson; Through the Looking Glass.*

THROUGH THE LOOKING GLASS, suite for orchestra (1919). I. Dedication; The Garden of Live Flowers. II. Jabberwocky. III. Looking Glass Insects. IV. The White Knight.

Though this suite is the earliest of Taylor's major works, it is also one of the best. Its spontaneity and wit assure it permanency in the literature of American orchestral music. Taylor wrote it between 1917 and 1919 as a three-movement work for flute, oboe, clarinet, bassoon, horn, piano, and strings; in this version it was heard for the first time in New York on February 18, 1919, in a performance by the New York Chamber Music Society. Two years after that Taylor scored this music for full orchestra and added two new movements. The orchestral adaptation—and the one by which this composition is now known—was introduced by the New York Symphony Society under Walter Damrosch in Brooklyn on October 10, 1923.

The suite is, of course, inspired by the delightfully nonsensical fairy tale of Lewis Carroll. Taylor has written his own program notes for the music:

"I. Carroll precedes the tale with a charming poetical foreword, the first stanza of which the music aims to express. It runs—

> Child of the pure, unclouded brow
> And dreaming eyes of wonder!
> Though time be fleet, and I and thou
> Art half a life asunder,
> Thy loving smile will surely hail
> The love-gift of a fairy-tale.

A simple song theme, briefly developed, leads to The Garden of Live Flowers. Shortly after Alice had entered the looking glass country, she came to a lovely garden in which the flowers were talking.... The music, therefore, reflects the brisk chatter of the swaying, bright-colored denizens of the garden.

"II. This is the poem that so puzzled Alice, and which Humpty-Dumpty finally explained to her. The theme of that frightful beast, the Jabberwock, is first announced by the full orchestra. The clarinet then begins the tale, recounting how, on a 'brillig' afternoon, the 'slithy toves did gyre and gimble in the wabe.' Muttered imprecations by the bassoon warn us to 'beware the Jabberwock, my son.' A miniature march signalizes the approach of our hero, taking 'his vorpal sword in hand.' Trouble starts among the trombones—the Jabberwock is upon us! The battle with the monster is recounted in a short and rather repellent fugue, the double-basses bringing up the subject and the hero fighting back in the interludes. Finally his vorpal sword (really a xylophone) goes 'snicker-snack' and the monster, impersonated by the solo bassoon, dies a lingering and convulsive death. The hero returns to the victorious strains of his own theme—'O frabjous day! Callooh! Callay!' The whole orchestra rejoices—the church bells are rung—alarums and excursions. Conclusion. Once more the slithy toves perform their pleasing evolutions, undisturbed by the uneasy ghost of the late Jabberwock.

"III. Here we find the vociferous *diptera* that made such an impression upon Alice—the Bee-elephant, the Gnat, the Rocking-horse-fly, the Snapdragon-fly, and the Bread-and-butter-fly....

"IV. The White Knight was a toy Don Quixote, mild, chivalrous, ridiculous, and rather touching. He carried a mousetrap on his saddle-bow, because 'if they *do* come, I don't choose to have them running all about.'... There are two themes; the first, a sort of instrumental prance, being the knight's own conception of himself as a slashing daredevil. The second is bland, mellifluous, a little sentimental—much more like the knight as he really was. The first theme starts off bravely, but falls out of the saddle before very long, and has to give way to the second. The two alternate, in various guises, until the end, when the knight rides off, with Alice waving her handkerchief—she thought it would encourage him if she did."

THE KING'S HENCHMAN, opera (1926).

Deems Taylor's first opera has known the fate of many another American opera. It was introduced with the loud fanfare of publicity bugles—so much so that its première assumed the proportions of a world-shaking artistic event; it was accorded the cheers of audiences and the extravagant praise of critics; it was the favored topic for parlor discussions; and then, after it had been around awhile, it was relegated to permanent obscurity.

The King's Henchman was not—as Lawrence Gilman said of it after the première performance—"the best American opera we have ever heard." Nor was its introduction at the Metropolitan as much of a red-letter day in musical history as the newspaper accounts at the time would lead us to believe. But it is also much better than its present neglect suggests. It is the work of a cultured musician who combines compositional skill with taste and refinement and a sensitive feeling for beauty. It may lack originality, with its frequent reminiscent echoes of Wagner and sometimes Debussy; it may lack an American personality; it may occasionally seem static in its movement. Yet the charm and freshness of its best pages make it a rewarding experience for the opera lover. There are many pages of fine music: the forest love scene; the simulation of English folksongs in the Bardic Song of Act I and the Incantation Song of Act II; and the prelude to the last act.

When an opera was commissioned from Taylor by the Metropolitan Opera Association, he called upon one of America's foremost poets for his libretto—Edna St. Vincent Millay. She produced a variation of the Tristan and Isolde theme. King Eadgar of tenth-century England is in love with Aelfrida, the Devon princess. To press his suit, the King sends his best friend, Aethelwold, to Devon. There Aethelwold goes to sleep in a forest at the same time that Aelfrida wanders through it, intoning an incantation that will bring her a lover. Because of the powers of this incantation, Aethelwold and Aelfrida fall in love with each other and get married; meanwhile, Aethelwold has dispatched to King Eadgar the news that Aelfrida is much too unattractive for him. The arrival of the King to Devon uncovers the fraud and sends Aethelwold to his death by his own hand.

PETER IBBETSON, opera (1930).

Taylor's second opera followed the first by four years, and—like its predecessor—was the result of a commission by the Metropolitan Opera Association. For his subject he selected the famous novel of Du Maurier which—in collaboration with Constance Collier—he adapted into a workable libretto. The story is, of course, familiar. Peter Ibbetson is the victim of a tyrannical uncle who has adopted him, and, to escape from the grimness of reality, he yields to dreams about his childhood in which he meets his little sweetheart, Mary. But dreams are not enough to relieve Peter of his misery: in a fit of fury, he murders his uncle. Sentenced to life imprisonment, Peter once again seeks solace in dreams, and once again evokes Mary out of the past. After thirty years of imprisonment, Peter learns that Mary has died. The will to live has now gone from him. As he dies, the walls of his prison disintegrate; Peter is young again; he rises from his couch and turns to Mary, who is waiting for him.

The tender vein of melody in the opera—made colorful by the effective interpolation of French folksongs for children—the delightful orchestration, and the warm sentiment were the qualities that endeared *Peter Ibbetson* to its audiences when it was introduced at the Metropolitan Opera on February 7, 1931. It was heard sixteen times during the next four seasons (including the opening night of the 1933-34 season). The critics did not like *Peter Ibbetson* as much as they had *The King's Henchman,* but they did single out several passages in the opera which were of great interest: the waltzes of Act I; the inn music of Act II; the dream music of Act III.

Taylor took the major orchestral passages of the opera and adapted them into two suites. The first includes two extended orchestral passages marked Molto allegro and Andante. This suite was heard for the first time on March 18, 1938, in Indianapolis, with the Indianapolis Symphony Orchestra conducted by Fabien Sevitzky. The second suite, comprising the waltzes, inn music, dream music, and finale, was introduced by the Baltimore Symphony Orchestra under Howard Barlow on January 7, 1940.

ELEGY, for orchestra (1946).

When the *Elegy* was introduced by the Indianapolis Symphony Orchestra under Fabien Sevitzky on December 6, 1946, the composer provided the following analysis:

"The first section, marked Lento, introduces a dirge-like main theme, heard as a horn solo. It is taken up by the strings and then by the full orchestra, which brings it to a climax. A long, descending subsidiary theme leads to the second section, marked Tranquillo. Its theme is simple and lyric in character, suggestive of youth and naiveté. It is developed at some length, but is interrupted by a grave reminder of the dirge theme. Then the lyric theme resumes, and is followed by two variants, one very lively and dance-like, the other, greatly augmented, intoned by the brass. The two variants alternate until they reach a climax that is cut across by the trumpets, playing a harsh reminder of the dirge. The music subsides, and the final section begins with the dirge theme, played by all the violins, on the G-string. After a last climax, the descending theme of the first section leads to a quiet close."

RANDALL THOMPSON 1899—

Thompson himself has said that his works fall into two distinct categories. Some of them utilize melodic ideas with a decided national character, stamping these works as native products and their creator as an indigenous composer. But Thompson has pointed out that a great many other works are eclectic, with a universal appeal; instead of being *American* music, these compositions are music by an American.

But in whichever of these two categories his works may fall, they are all characterized by economy and simplicity of means and nobility of expression. Thompson has always felt the necessity for a composer to write music "that will reach and move the hearts of his listeners in his own day." Consequently, he has never had any interest in esoteric styles or intricate techniques and forms; but he has always tried to write with sincerity, high purpose, and depth of feeling within traditional forms that are impressive for their sound construction and inexorable logic.

Randall Thompson was born in New York City on April 21, 1899, and was graduated from Harvard, where he took music courses with Spalding, Hill, and Davison. For a while, he studied music privately with Ernest Bloch. In 1922 he won a fellowship of the American Academy at Rome, enabling him to spend three years in Europe. After returning to this country, he filled several posts as conductor (Dessoff Choirs), professor of music (Wellesley College, University of California, University of Virginia, Princeton University, and Harvard University), and director (Curtis Institute). His earliest works followed romantic patterns with an occasional digression into jazz. Not until his Second Symphony did he arrive at a style of his own and emerge as a significant composer.

The following works by Randall Thompson are discussed below: *Alleluia; The Peaceable Kingdom;* Symphony No. 2; Symphony No. 3; *The Testament of Freedom.*

SYMPHONY NO. 2 (1931). I. Allegro. II. Largo. III. Vivace. IV. Andante moderato; Allegro con spirito; Largamente.

The Second Symphony was Thompson's first major work to stamp him as an outstanding American composer, and his first large work to achieve success. It was introduced in Rochester, New York, on March 24, 1932, by the Rochester Philharmonic, conducted by Howard Hanson. Since then, it has become one of the most frequently heard American symphonies.

The following is the composer's own analysis of the symphony: "I. The principal theme is announced immediately by the horns, forte, and answered by the trumpets. From this motive is derived a series of rhythmic figures which form the toccata-like background of the entire movement. The subsidiary theme is of a more reticent nature, but the violoncellos accompany it in persistent rhythm. The development section begins quietly and forms a gradual crescendo, at the apex of which the first theme returns in an ominous fortissimo against a counter-rhythm of the kettledrums. A more extended transition leads to a sinister presentation of the second theme. At the close, a major version of the second theme in augmentation is sounded fortissimo by the horns and trumpets against the continuous pulse of the strings. The movement subsides, apparently to end in the major. An abrupt minor chord brings it to a close.

"II. The violins play a warm, quiet melody against pizzicato chords in the violoncellos. A contrasting melody is sung by the oboe. The movement is not long, but its mood is concentrated. It ends simply." (The composer might have added that the main melody resembles a Negro spiritual.)

"III. Scherzo with trio. The first section begins in G Minor and ends in D Minor. The trio progresses from B Major to G Major. The first section returns transposed. Now, beginning in C Minor and ending in G Minor, it serves as a kind of extended 'subdominant answer' to its former presentation. There is a short coda, making intensified use of material from the trio.

"IV. The slow sections which begin and end this movement serve to frame the Allegro, a modified rondo. The theme of the Allegro is a diminution of the theme of the first and last sections. The Largamente employs for the first time the full sonorities of the orchestra in a sustained assertion of the principal melody."

THE PEACEABLE KINGDOM, for mixed chorus (1936).

A painting by Edward Hicks (in turn inspired by verses from Isaiah) was the motivation for this choral work, commissioned by the League of Composers for its twenty-fifth anniversary. It was first performed in Cambridge, Massachusetts, on March 3, 1936, at a concert of the Harvard Glee Club and the Radcliffe Choral Society, G. Wallace Davison directing.

There are seven choral sections, with the text taken from Isaiah:

"I. Say ye to the righteous, it shall be well with him; woe unto the wicked, it shall be ill with him.

"II. Woe unto them . . .

"III. The noise of a multitude in the mountain. . . . Everyone that is found shall be thrust through. . . . Their children also shall be dashed to pieces before their eyes. . . . Their faces shall be as the flames.

"IV. Howl ye, for the day of the Lord is at hand. Howl! O gate; cry! O city! Thou art delivered.

"V. The paper reeds by the brooks, and everything sown by the brooks, shall wither, be driven away, and be no more.

"VI. For ye shall go out with joy, and be led forth with peace.

"VII. Ye shall have a song, and gladness of heart, as when one goeth with a pipe to come into the mountain of the Lord."

ALLELUIA, for mixed chorus (1940).

This short and brilliant choral work—one of the finest in present-day American music—had an exciting, even breathless, origin. It was commissioned by Serge Koussevitzky for the opening-day ceremonies of the first session of the Berkshire Music Center; and the time allowed for the composition was only three weeks. Thompson chose as his text the single word *Alleluia*—and set to work. G. Wallace Davison tells the rest of the story:

"On Saturday, forty-eight hours before the formal opening, we had not heard from Thompson nor seen the music. Mr. Judd telephoned to Philadelphia; Thompson assured us that the score had just been printed, and that three hundred copies would arrive in Lenox Monday morning. . . . At two o'clock on Monday afternoon the students assembled for the first time. . . . In the corner of the barn I had secreted our collection of Bach chorales, for one mail after another had arrived at the Lenox post office during the morning without the package from Philadelphia. But at just five minutes before two, Mr. Judd came in with the music. I tried it over once on the piano, and the chorus of two hundred and fifty, assembled from all over our country for the first time, went to work. By 2:45 it was time to go to the Shed for the exercises, and at 3:30 we had given the first performance of a work which has been heard hundreds of times in choral concerts from Boston to San Francisco. So sure was Thompson's technique, so expert his craftsmanship, and so masterly his grasp of the true genius of choral singing, that despite a blueprint of unique limitations, he had created one of the noblest pieces of choral music in the twentieth century."

THE TESTAMENT OF FREEDOM, for men's chorus and orchestra (1942).

The *Testament*—written to honor the two-hundredth anniversary of the birth of Thomas Jefferson—sets four passages from Jefferson's writings. It opens with the following declaration: "The God who gave us life gave us liberty at the same time; the hand of force may destroy but cannot disjoin them" (from *A Summary View of the Rights of British America,*

1774). The next part, taken from *The Declaration of Causes and Necessity of Taking Up Arms* (July 6, 1775), begins with the following line: "We have counted the cost of the contest and find nothing so dreadful as voluntary slavery." The third section is also taken from this *Declaration,* beginning with: "We fight not for glory or for conquest." The fourth part comes from a letter to John Adams (September 21, 1821): "I shall not die without a hope that light and liberty are on steady advance." The *Testament* concludes with the declaration that opened it.

With the hope of reaching large masses with this paean to freedom and democracy, Thompson utilized the simplest possible resources for his musical setting. The chorus is often heard in unison; and when it is divided, the part-writing has the directness of an anthem. The orchestral background is subdued, built on conventional harmonic schemes to set off the voices. As Olin Downes wrote after the first New York performance, he "has ... written ... as a most thoughtful and modest artist, seeking for the right notes to communicate something profoundly of his people that was in his heart. His musical instincts and honesty protected him from all the notes but the right ones."

The *Testament* was introduced on April 13, 1943, at the University of Virginia (which had been founded by Jefferson, and where, at this time, Thompson was serving on the music faculty). The University Glee Club was directed by Stephen Tuttle, while the composer played the accompaniment on the piano. This performance was broadcast over the CBS network and was transmitted by short wave by the OWI to the armed forces. On April 14, 1945, the *Testament* was performed at Carnegie Hall by the Boston Symphony Orchestra under Koussevitzky, to honor the memory of the recently deceased President Roosevelt.

SYMPHONY NO. 3 IN A MINOR (1948). I. Largo elegiaco. II. Allegro appassionato; Calmato ma triste assai. III. Lento tranquillo. IV. Allegro vivace.

The Third Symphony, commissioned by the Alice M. Ditson Fund, was completed almost two decades after the second. It was begun in 1944, when the composer sketched the material for all four movements; but it took four years to complete the work. It was introduced by the CBS Symphony Orchestra under Thor Johnson in New York City on May 15, 1949, as part of the American Music Festival.

The following analysis of the symphony is by the composer: "The first movement is in sonata form, with only one principal theme and one principal rhythm. The prevailing mood is one of sadness. The second movement is full of action and defiance. The form is a modified rondo, in which the final statement of the principal theme is presented more slowly. Allusions to the theme of contrast, also greatly augmented, bring the movement to a desolate conclusion. The third movement is introduced by a phrase in the horn which later grows into a melody. The principal theme is song-like, and its three presentations are set off by plaintive passages in the woodwinds alone. The finale is in sonata form, and all the material is cheerful. There is no apotheosis of the themes nor any heroic peroration. The serious and even tragic elements of the earlier movements are dispelled in exuberance."

VIRGIL THOMSON   1896—

In the middle 1920's, when so many composers were helplessly sucked into the vortex of their theories and inextricably enmeshed in the labyrinth of their techniques, Thomson set out to write music as simply and as lucidly as he could. He wanted to produce good tunes and good-sounding harmonies within clearly defined forms. He wanted to write the kind of music that audiences could listen to and respond to with their hearts. He had no desire to be impressive for his skill or erudition or courage; he merely wanted his works to provide the hearer with a pleasurable esthetic experience.

Because he always tried to be entertaining and charming, Thomson was for a long time not taken very seriously by his fellow musicians. But as he produced one work after another, he achieved a considerable measure of success. Following the première of *Four Saints In Three Acts,* it became apparent that his simplicity was deceptive: that it required a consummate skill to arrive at the ease of expression and the precise logic found in Thomson's music; that because this music was so easy to listen to, it was not necessarily superficial or trite.

In whatever form he has chosen to write, Thomson has continued to write simply. He has wit and he has feeling. He has a pronounced American identity: many of his healthy melodies are shaped after old American hymns and folksongs. He has charm and sophistication. By being himself and writing as he feels, Thomson is, as Aaron Copland said of him, "about as original a personality as America can boast, in or out of the musical field."

Virgil Thomson was born in Kansas City, Missouri, on November 25, 1896, and was graduated from Harvard University, where he took courses in music with Davison and Hill. Further study took place in Paris with Nadia Boulanger. He remained in Paris for seven years. There his career as a composer was launched; but recognition did not come until the successful première of his provocative opera, *Four Saints in Three Acts,* in 1934. He also began writing about music in Paris, criticisms for the magazine *Modern Music,* and an engaging book entitled *The State of Music.* In 1940, he succeeded Lawrence Gilman as the music critic of the *New York Herald-Tribune.* He resigned from this post in 1954 to devote himself exclusively to composition.

The following works by Virgil Thomson are discussed below: *Four Saints in Three Acts; Louisana Story; The Mother of Us All.*

FOUR SAINTS IN THREE ACTS, opera (1928).

On February 8, 1934, a group that called itself "The Society of Friends and Enemies of Modern Music" presented an experiment in opera in Hartford, Connecticut. Called *Four Saints in Three Acts,* it boasted an undecipherable libretto (frequently consisting of unintelligible words and syllables, or intelligible phrases and words that had no seeming relation to their fellow phrases and words), the work of Gertude Stein, apostle of alogical writing. The music was by the then-unknown American composer, Virgil Thomson. An all-Negro cast was dressed in cellophane costumes.

So unorthodox an opera inevitably invited interest. Soon after the première performance, the opera was moved to New York—to Broadway. There it enjoyed a successful six-week run and attracted national attention. Later the same year, the opera was seen in Chicago. Since then, it has had several revivals in concert form, was produced on Broadway a second time by ANTA in 1952, and was seen the same year in Paris.

For all its unintelligibility, it proved to be a delightful opera—amusing, earthy, novel, piquant. What caused most surprise, however, was not the strange text, or the revolutionary staging and costuming, or even the unusual casting—but the very pleasing and melodious music that accompanied all these peculiar proceedings. The simplicity of the score (utilizing only the most elementary progressions and the most rudimentary harmonic language) had the naïve but robust quality of folk music, calling attention to the fact that Thomson derived the character of some of his writing from American folk and popular sources. But within that simplicity, Thomson gave expression to an infectious wit, charm, and even melodic beauty. It was, as Lawrence Gilman said of it, a truly "suave and charming score."

With *Four Saints in Three Acts,* Thomson realized his first major success; it lifted him out of obscurity into national prominence.

THE MOTHER OF US ALL, opera (1947).

When Virgil Thomson was commissioned by the Alice M. Ditson Fund to write a new opera, he decided to revive his collaboration with

Gertrude Stein, the librettist of his *Four Saints in Three Acts*. Stein agreed, and provided the composer with a somewhat more intelligible text than her first: a political fantasy based upon the career of Susan B. Anthony, pioneer in the woman suffrage movement, from her earliest struggles to her ultimate triumph after death. Somewhat obscure, rambling, and poetic, the play was full of anachronisms and digressions into discussions of marriage, politics, love, etc.; the thirty-one characters included Ulysses S. Grant, Lillian Russell, Daniel Webster, Andrew Jackson, Thaddeus Stevens, John Adams, and Anthony Comstock, as well as two other people thinly disguised as Gertrude S., and Virgil T.

The opera was introduced on May 7, 1947, at Columbia University in New York City, during the American Music Festival.

The program for that performance carried the following excellent summary of the Stein libretto:

"The opera opens in the home of Susan B. Anthony, where she discusses with her supporter, Anne, her purposes and her difficulties. Virgil T. and Gertrude S. supply comment and interpretation. The second scene depicts a political rally, ending with a formal debate between Susan B. Anthony and Daniel Webster.

"The second act takes place on a village green beside Miss Anthony's house. Andrew Jackson and Thaddeus Stevens quarrel. Constance Fletcher and John Adams fall in love. The second scene of this act represents a daydream in which the suffrage leader reflects upon Negro suffrage, political celebrity, and the mystery of wealth and poverty. The third scene shows the wedding of Jo the Loiterer to Indiana Elliot, which is variously interrupted but eventually performed.

"The first two scenes of the third act take place in the drawing room of Susan B. Anthony. A delegation of politicians wishes her to speak for them at a meeting. She at first refuses, but finally accedes. In the next scene she is again at home. She has spoken, been successful, and foresees the final triumph of her cause. The last scene is a sort of epilogue, ending with the unveiling of Miss Anthony's statue in the Congressional Library."

The text obviously called for tongue-in-cheek music, and Thomson produced a score that met the demands of the play felicitously. It was witty, entertaining, satiric, even popular. It was filled with folksy melodies (though there were no actual set arias), some of them reminiscent of old waltzes, ballads, and hymns.

In June, 1947, the New York Music Critics Circle voted a special citation to the opera; the regular award could not be given because Thomson was a member of the Circle.

After completing the opera, Thomson wrote three orchestral numbers based on thematic material from the opera. These three numbers—together with a fourth, transcribed from the opera—became an orchestral suite. The four movements were: I. Prelude (overture to the work as a whole). II. A Political Meeting (prelude to Scene Two). III. Cold Weather (prelude to Scene Three). IV. Wedding Hymn and Finale (transcription of the wedding hymn scene and the final song of the opera).

LOUISIANA STORY, suite for orchestra (1948). I. Pastoral—The Bayou and the Marsh Buggy. II. Chorale—The Derrick Arrives. III. Passacaglia—Robbing the Alligator's Nest. IV. Fugue—Boy Fights Alligator.

In 1948, Thomson was commissioned to write the music for a documentary film called *Louisiana Story,* produced by Robert Flaherty. The film told the story of an oil-development project in Louisiana and its impact on the life of a single French-speaking family—all seen through the eyes of a fourteen-year-old boy.

For this film, Thomson wrote a score that was influenced by the songs and dances of the Acadian region.

Thomson subsequently created two orchestral suites out of this music, the first of which has enjoyed great success. It was first introduced by the Philadelphia Orchestra under Eugene Ormandy on November 26, 1948, and six months later won the Pulitzer Prize in music.

Thomson has described the suite in the following way: "The orchestral suite...consists of four movements: the Pastoral, describing bayous, the boy in his rowboat, and the maneuvers of the 'marsh buggy,' an amphibious bulldozer which is part of the oil-prospecting machinery; a Chorale, which represents the boy playing in a tree with his pet racoon and his view from there of the drill barge's majestic approach; a Passacaglia, which recounts the boy's adventure in robbing an alligator's nest of its eggs, ending with the approach of the mother reptile; and a chromatic Fugue in four sections, which is used in the film to accompany the boy's fight to land an alligator that he has hooked with bait."

A second suite is called *Acadian Songs and Dances,* and is strongly influenced by the waltz and polka rhythms of Cajun folk tunes and dances.

ERNST TOCH   1887—

Though Ernest Toch shook off permanently a tendency to imitate the style and mannerisms of Brahms (to which he had succumbed up to about 1918), he never rejected Brahms' healthy respect for form. The structural logic of Toch's music is one of its outstanding qualities, revealing at all times the hand of a master. Within these forms, Toch has produced music that successfully reconciles classical traditions with modern thinking. Articulateness combines with craftsmanship to produce works that are usually lyrical, charged with feeling, original and forceful in the flowering of the ideas—ever satisfying both to the ear and to the mind.

Toch was born in Vienna on December 7, 1887. Though he was directed to a professional career and was entered in the University of Vienna for medical studies, he never renounced his passion for music. He devoted himself indefatigably to its study and to composition. He was only seventeen when his String Quartet was performed in public by the Rosé Quartet; by the time he was twenty-two he was the recipient of the Mozart Prize, enabling him to pursue the study of music at the Hoch Conservatory in Frankfurt-am-Main. From this time on, he rejected the idea of a medical career for the sake of music. He won several major music awards, and in 1913 began a long and successful career as a teacher of music. During World War I, he served in the Austrian Army. Following the war, he established his reputation as a composer with successful performances of several chamber-music works at the Donaueschingen and Baden-Baden festivals.

When Hitler came to power in Germany, where Toch had established himself both as teacher and as composer since the end of World War I, the composer exiled himself voluntarily, coming first to London and then to this country. Since 1936, he has lived in California, teaching composition at the University of Southern California, writing music for the movies, and producing many major works. His Symphony No. 3 (see Supplement) received the Pulitzer Prize in music in 1956.

The following works by Toch are discussed below: *Big Ben;* Concerto No. 2 for Piano and Orchestra; *Hyperion; Pinocchio, a Merry Overture.*

CONCERTO NO. 2 FOR PIANO AND ORCHESTRA, op. 61 (1933). I. Allegro. II. Scherzo. III. Adagio. IV. Zyklus Variabilis.

Toch's Second Piano Concerto is one of his finest works. It was written seven years after the First Piano Concerto, op. 38. The première performance took place in 1933 in London, with the composer playing the solo part and Sir Henry J. Wood conducting.

The work is classical in its form and gives such equal importance to both the solo instrument and the orchestra that it has at times been described as a "symphony for piano and orchestra." The first movement is in sonata form, with both principal themes stated early and developed soon after they make their appearance; the first theme is treated fugally between piano and orchestra, while the second theme gets a more harmonic setting. The second movement has a marked dance rhythm and consists of two ideas, one in a tarantella rhythm, the other in waltz time. The slow movement is brief; it is full of feeling and reaches a climax with a long and impressive section for unaccompanied piano. The composer himself described the final movement as "Changeable Cycle," by which he meant that it utilizes a free-variation form, the last part of which carries memories of melodic ideas first stated in the first two movements.

BIG BEN, variation-fantasy for orchestra (1934).

One foggy evening when Toch was in London, he crossed the Westminster bridge and heard the chiming of Big Ben. "The theme," the composer explained, "lingered in my imagination for a long while, and evolved into other forms, somehow still connected with the original one, until finally, like the chimes themselves, it seemed to disappear into the fog from which it emerged. I have sought to fix this impression in my variation-fantasy."

Toch did not write this work until he came to this country. He completed it in the fall of 1934, and on December 20 of the same year it was heard for the first time in Cambridge, with Richard Burgin conducting the Boston Symphony Orchestra.

The Big Ben theme is heard somewhat disguised in the opening of the work. The variations that follow are of changing moods, ranging, as Paul A. Pisk once wrote, "from the heavy, peasant-like, almost Russian dance to the pastel colorings of a London fog." The climax of the work is a fugue, after which there comes a transitional passage to the concluding sounds of the chiming clock.

PINOCCHIO, A MERRY OVERTURE, for orchestra (1936).

This gay and sprightly piece of music was written soon after Toch had become acquainted with the story of Pinocchio at the home of Alvin Johnson, then director of the New School for Social Research. It was introduced by the Los Angeles Philharmonic under Otto Klemperer on December 10, 1936.

The following verse appears on the title-page of the score:

Italian lore would have us know
That gay marionette Pinocchio!
With deviltry and gamin grace
He led them all a merry chase.

The score then carries the following description of the tale, which serves admirably as the program for Toch's music:

"Pinocchio is a figure in Italian folklore created by Carlo Collodi. According to the story, he was fashioned by old Gepetto, a wood-carver, from a curiously animated piece of wood. His rascally demeanor and mischievous escapades gave his creator many an anxious moment. His particular failing was fibbing, each lie prompting his already long nose to grow longer. He is a sort of brother-in-mischief to the German Till Eulenspiegel. To this day Italian children are warned by their elders that their noses will grow as long as Pinocchio's if they do not tell the truth."

HYPERION, dramatic prelude for orchestra, op. 71 (1947).

Toch wrote this dramatic prelude on a commission from the Kulas Fund in Cleveland. On January 8, 1948, it was introduced in Cleveland, with George Szell conducting the Cleveland Orchestra.

The composer provided the following description: It begins in a somber, subdued mood, and though based on close unity of its thematic material, rises to a mood of hopefulness and assurance—somehow perhaps reflecting the idea of the Latin proverb, *'Per aspera ad astra.'*"

The work opens slowly with a chromatic theme in the bassoons. The tempo then quickens, and a broad and spacious subject is heard in the bassoons and lower strings. The principal idea of the piece then arrives in the trumpets and trombones, derived from the opening bars of the work. The opening theme also serves as material for the climax, which is played by unison strings, bass, and bassoon.

VINCENZO TOMMASINI   1878—1950

Tommasini joined forces with such twentieth-century Italian composers as Respighi, Casella, Pizzetti, and Malipiero in creating an Italian school of instrumental composers. In his apprentice works, he imitated first the German romanticists, then the French impressionists. Gradually, however, he arrived at a nationalist style in which old Italian forms were stylized and old Italian songs and dances were simulated. Melody is the basis of Tommasini's works—but it is an *instrumental* melody as opposed to the operatic; the harmony, while never experimental, is allowed freedom of movement; the idea and form are inextricably synthesized so that it is often difficult to isolate one from the other.

Tommasini was born in Rome on September 17, 1878. His father, a well-known historian, insisted that he receive a comprehensive academic education as well as a musical one. While acquiring his musical training from Falchi, Pinelli, and Mazzarella, Tommasini attended the Liceo San Cecilia and the University of Rome, specializing in Greek language, literature, and philology. These studies completed, Tommasini undertook extensive travels, during which he came into contact with German and French musical thought. In 1910, he produced his first important work, the Quartet in F, for strings. In 1913, he won first prize, given by the city of Rome, for an opera, *Ugale*. When Arturo Toscanini introduced one of the nocturnes of *Chiari di Luna* in 1916, and the Diaghilev Ballet presented the ballet *The Good-Humored Ladies* (derived from the music of Domenico Scarlatti) in 1917, Tommasini's importance as a composer became internationally recognized. Tommasini died in Rome on December 24, 1950.

The following works by Tommasini are discussed below: *The Carnival of Venice; Prelude, Fanfare, and Fugue; Tuscan Landscapes.*

TUSCAN LANDSCAPES, rhapsody, for orchestra (1922).

Tuscan Landscapes (Paesaggi Toscani) is a rhapsody on popular Tuscan folk melodies. It was introduced by the Augusteo Orchestra in Rome under Bernardino Molinari in December, 1923. The work is in two sections, played without interruption. The first (Andante sostenuto) is grave and dreamy; out of a nebulous background rises a melancholy Tuscan folksong. The second part (Vivace) is, by contrast, vital and gay, built out of two Tuscan folk tunes.

PRELUDE, FANFARE, AND FUGUE, for orchestra (1927).

The three sections of this work are played without interruption. Two lyrical ideas comprise the first part, the Prelude: the first appears in muted strings and first horn in unison; the second in English horn and celli against the roll of tympani. A pianissimo passage for first and third horns against a roll of tympani and tremolo of low strings marks the beginning of the Fanfare. A flourish comes from the distance, growing into the Fanfare proper, which develops into a crashing fortissimo. A decrescendo follows, culminating in one trumpet sounding a long C. This note ties in with the first note of the ensuing fugue. The work ends with a dramatic climax for full orchestra.

The piece was introduced soon after its composition by the Augusteo Orchestra in Rome under Victor de Sabata.

THE CARNIVAL OF VENICE, variations for orchestra (1928).

Tommasini wrote these variations, "à la Paganini," in 1928, and they were introduced in New York by the New York Philharmonic-Symphony Orchestra under Arturo Toscanini on October 10, 1929.

Tommasini's description of this work is as follows:

"The composition is an evocation of the Carnival of Venice in the manner of Paganini. On the thrice-familiar theme, the celebrated violinist composed twenty bravura variations for the violin, and in these he tried, it would seem, to describe various episodes and scenes of the Venetian festival.

"The orchestral composition begins with an introduction that depicts nightfall on the canals in the city of lagoons. After the exposition of the theme there follow thirteen variations, the substance of which is drawn from just so many selected from the twenty written by Paganini. Suddenly one hears a prolonged blare of brass on the chord of C major. This interrupts, as if in a startling vision, the series of variations. Forthwith one hears the striking of midnight. Then a brief finale, describing the return of festivities even more animated than before."

JOAQUÍN TURINA   1882—1949

Turina belonged with the school of Spanish nationalist composers which came into being as a result of the inspiration and researches of Felipe Pedrell (see Albéniz). Like his celebrated compatriot and fellow nationalist, Manuel de Falla, Turina spent many years in Paris; and the impress of French music is even more noticeable on Turina's work than on those by Falla. As a pupil of Vincent d'Indy, Turina absorbed the influence of César Franck, whose stylistic traits (serenity and mysticism) and technique (the cyclic form) are evident in much of Turina's music. The delicate impressionistic writing of Debussy, whom Turina knew personally, is also one of Turina's attributes as a composer. To these French mannerisms Turina brought the rhythms, melodies, and personality of his native land, producing music that was distinctly his own.

Joaquín Turina y Perez was born in Seville on December 9, 1882. After preliminary study in music in Seville, and additional piano lessons with José Tragó in Madrid, he went to Paris in 1905. There he remained for more than a decade, studying at the Schola Cantorum—principally under Vincent d'Indy—and beginning composition. A quintet was successfully performed in Paris in 1907, marking Turina's official debut as a composer. Influenced by Albéniz to turn to the writing of national Spanish music, Turina composed his first important work in 1912, the *Procesión del Rocio*. In 1914, Turina returned to his native land to assume a position of major importance among its national composers. He also distinguished himself as professor at the National Conservatory of Madrid, as conductor, and as a pianist in the Quinteto de Madrid. He died in Madrid on January 14, 1949.

The following works by Turina are discussed below: *Danzas Fantasticas; L' Oración del Torero; La Procesión del Rocio.*

LA PROCESIÓN DEL ROCIO, for orchestra (1912).

Each season in June there takes place in Triana, a suburb of Seville, a colorful religious procession known as the "Procession of the Dew," in which the image of the Virgin is carried in a silver cart drawn by oxen. This procession is described in Turina's best-known orchestral work, written in 1912 and introduced by the Orquesta Sinfónica of Madrid in March of the following year. The orchestral piece is in two sections. The first describes festive Triana throbbing with song and dance and festivity. The second brings up the impressive procession. A religious melody appears and reappears throughout the work to solemnize the occasion. After a climax, in which the religious theme is prominent, songs and dances of Triana are heard anew, and then ebb away.

DANZAS FANTASTICAS, for orchestra. I. Exaltation. II. Musing. III. Orgy (1920).

Out of the storehouse of Andalusian dance rhythms Turina drew the materials for this set of three Spanish dances. The first, which begins somewhat placidly but develops frenetically, was inspired by the following quotation by José Más: "It was like the features of some incomparable picture, moving within the calyx of a blossom." The sinuous movement of the Andalusian folksong provides the character of the second dance, which is full of oriental languor. For this movement, the following quotation was utilized by the composer: "The strings of a guitar sounding laments of a nature that remind one of nothing so much as the weight of sorrow." An orgiastic outburst of energy marks the concluding dance, for which the composer provided this quotation: "The perfume of flowers is intermingled with the odor of the camomile, and the bouquet of tall chalices filled with incomparable wine. From this, like an incense, the dance rises."

Danzas Fantasticas was introduced in Madrid in March, 1911.

L' ORACIÓN DEL TORERO, for string quartet (1925).

The Bullfighter's Prayer is marked by a striking contrast of moods and colors. It opens quietly: after progressing with impulsive rhythms to moods of impetuous character, an expansive melody which dominates the composition is unfolded. A forceful climax then arrives. After this has been fully realized, the ideas stated in the beginning of the piece are repeated. The principal melody brings the work to a gentle conclusion.

RALPH VAUGHAN WILLIAMS 1872—1958

The debt that English folk music owes to Vaughan Williams is profound; and vice versa. There is no question but that his painstaking researches into the music of England's past, undertaken in the first years of the present century, and the tasteful adaptations he made of this music have helped to lift it out of its undeserved neglect. But it is also true that this service has not been without compensations. For not until Vaughan Williams came upon the carols, madrigals, folksongs, and dances of the Tudor period—came upon them and absorbed them so completely that they became a part of his musical thinking—did he arrive at his destiny as a composer. Identification with his country and its music gave Vaughan Williams the direction he needed; from them he drew strength and inspiration.

More than this: from the music of the Tudor period Vaughan Williams extracted and assimilated stylistic elements which gave shape and substance to his own music. The tendency toward modal writing, the robust rhythm, the transparent counterpoint, the serene melody, the restrained feelings are all qualities which Vaughan Williams' music acquired from folk sources. Not that there is a question of imitation or borrowing! The fusion of such traits with his own veins of mysticism, poetry, and introspection is so inextricable and complete that what we have in the works of Vaughan Williams is not the resurgence of an old style but the emergence of a highly personal one. That style may be ineluctably tied up with the past; but—like a relay runner—it takes up the stick from its predecessor and forges ahead on its own power.

Vaughan Williams was born in Down Ampney, in Gloucester, England, on October 12, 1872. His musical education took place at the Royal College of Music, where his teachers included Parry and Stanford; it continued in Germany with Max Bruch; and for eight months in 1908 it was concluded with Ravel. Not until his imagination was fired through contact with English folk music of the Tudor period did Vaughan Williams reveal importance as a composer; the first work in a national vein was the first *Norfolk Rhapsody*, written in 1906. In 1907 there took place the first public performance of one of his works when his *Towards an Unknown Region* was performed at the Leeds Festival.

The brief study with Ravel strengthened his technique, but did not alter his style, which remained national. With works like the song cycle

On Wenlock Edge and the *Fantasia on a Theme by Thomas Tallis,* written in 1908 and 1910 respectively, his style became crystallized.

During World War I, Vaughan Williams served first in the Military Corps, then at the front as an artillery lieutenant. The war ended, he joined the faculty of the Royal College of Music, where he taught until his death. In 1922, he visited the United States to conduct at the Norfolk Festival. His stature as a composer grew formidably after World War I. In 1935 he received the Order of Merit. He paid his third visit to the United States in 1954. He died in London on August 26, 1958.

The following works by Vaughan Williams are discussed below: *Fantasia on a Theme by Thomas Tallis; Fantasia on Christmas Carols; A London Symphony; Norfolk Rhapsody No. 1 in E Minor; Pastoral Symphony;* Symphony No. 4 in F Minor; Symphony No. 5 in D Major; Symphony No. 6 in E Minor.

For Symphony No. 2, see *A London Symphony;* for Symphony No. 3, see *Pastoral Symphony.*

NORFOLK RHAPSODY NO. 1 IN E MINOR, for orchestra (1906).

Many of Vaughan Williams' major works for orchestra are elaborate settings of English folksongs which he unearthed during his researches, collected, and then arranged.

Between 1905 and 1906, he wrote three orchestral rhapsodies based on some of the folk tunes he had gathered at Kings Lynn in Norfolk.

He had originally intended integrating the three rhapsodies into a folksong symphony, with each rhapsody serving as one of the movements. Dissatisfied with the quality of the second and third rhapsodies, he abandoned the symphony project. The first *Rhapsody*—and the most famous of the three—was introduced at the London Promenade concert on August 23, 1900; the second and third rhapsodies (D Minor; G Minor and G Major) were first heard at the Cardiff Festival on September 27, 1907.

The following songs appear in the first *Rhapsody:* "The Captain's Apprentice," "A Bold Young Sailor," "The Basket of Eggs," "On Board a '98," and "Ward the Pirate."

Vaughan Williams revised the first *Rhapsody* in 1914.

FANTASIA ON A THEME BY THOMAS TALLIS, for string quartet and double string orchestra (1910).

Thomas Tallis was an English composer of contrapuntal music who lived in the sixteenth century and who served as organist of the Chapel Royal during the reigns of Edward VI, Mary, and Elizabeth. In 1567, Tallis composed eight tunes, in eight modes, for the Metrical Psalter of Matthew Parker, Archbishop of Canterbury. The third of these tunes was adapted by Vaughan Williams for his *Fantasia,* introduced at the Three Choirs Festival in Gloucester on September 6, 1910.

To bring out the antiphonal character of sixteenth-century music, Vaughan Williams divided his strings into two orchestras and a quartet of solo instruments. The Tallis theme is first heard in the orchestra against the tremolo of first violins, following a short introduction. The first violins repeat the melody. The two orchestras (one muted) discourse on this idea, after which it is passed on to the solo instruments. The melody is developed and transformed; then a forceful climax emerges. The melody is then heard in the solo violin against a contrapuntal background of a solo viola. The music comes to a serene close.

FANTASIA ON CHRISTMAS CAROLS, for baritone, chorus, and orchestra (1912).

Vaughan Williams utilized four English Christmas carols in this elaborate fantasia: "Come, All You Worthy Gentlemen," from Somerset; "The Truth Sent from Above" and "There Is a Fountain," from Hereford; and "On Christmas Night" from Sussex.

The work opens with a solo for violoncello. The baritone then enters with "The Truth Sent from Above"; after the baritone has sung the second verse, the solo cello relinquishes the role of accompaniment to the chorus, which hums softly in the background. (Here, as in other parts of this work, the chorus is used more like a part of the orchestra than as a vocal supplement to it.) In the final stanza, the chorus joins with the baritone.

The second carol, "Come, All You Worthy Gentlemen," is sung by tenors and basses, with the entire chorus participating in the sixteenth measure; sopranos and altos render the second stanza, while the entire chorus is again heard in the final four lines.

Four measures for orchestra serve as a prelude to the third carol, "On Christmas Night," which is sung by the baritone to an accompaniment of strings. Five measures later the chorus enters, the sopranos singing the text, while the rest of the chorus chants the syllable *Ah*. A climax is reached with the expression of exultation, in which the music for chorus and orchestra grows in sonority until a formidable fortissimo is evolved. The chorus repeats the last line of the carol diminuendo, after which the baritone returns to sing the final stanza of the *second* carol to a choral counterpoint of the final stanza of the *third*. Chimes and full orchestra proclaim a New Year's greeting during which the fourth carol, "There Is a Fountain," is heard in the orchestra.

The *Fantasia* was introduced on Septemebr 12, 1912, at the Hereford Festival.

A LONDON SYMPHONY (1913). I. Lento; Allegro risoluto. II. Lento. III. Scherzo. IV. Andante con moto; Maestoso alla marcia; Andante sostenuto.

Vaughan Williams' first two symphonies are programmatic. The First,

the *Sea Symphony,* for chorus and orchestra (1910), has a text by Walt
Whitman. The Second, which was written in 1912-13, provides a clue to its
meaning in its title, *London Symphony.* Yet, notwithstanding this title,
Vaughan Williams never actually intended the work to be descriptive. As
he explained: "The title...may suggest to some hearers a descriptive piece,
but this is not the intention of the composer. A better title would perhaps
be *Symphony by a Londoner,* that is to say the life of London (including
its various sights and sounds) has suggested to the composer an attempt
at musical expression; but it would be no help to the hearer to describe
these in words. The music is intended to be self-impressive, and must stand
or fall as 'absolute' music. Therefore, if listeners recognize suggestions of
such things as the Westminster chimes or the *Lavender Cry,* they are asked
to consider these as accidents, not essentials of the music."

And yet the music of this symphony is so pictorial and, at moments,
so realistic, that the listener cannot help bringing up to mind definite pictures of London as he hears the music. The composer must have finally
recognized this fact, for he did not dissuade his friend, the conductor Albert
Coates, from providing an elaborate verbal description of the intent of the
music when the latter directed a revised version of the symphony in 1920.

The following has been accepted as the key to the meaning of this
music:

I. London sleeps. The Thames flows serenely through the city. The
city awakens. We get different glimpses of the city—its varied character—
its good humor—its activity.

II. Portrait of the region known as Bloomsbury. It is dusk—damp
and foggy twilight. There is poverty everywhere—poverty and tragedy. An
old musician outside a pub plays *Sweet Lavender.* The gloom deepens. The
movement ends with the musician still playing his sad tune.

III. Sitting late one Saturday evening at the Temple Embankment.
On one side of the river are the slums; on the other, the stately majesty of
the Houses of Parliament. The Thames River flows serenely.

IV. A picture of the crueler sides of the city: the unemployed; the
unfortunate. The music ends with chimes of Big Ben on Westminster
Tower. The Epilogue (Andante sostenuto) gives a picture of London as
a whole. The symphony ends as it began—with the Thames flowing silently,
serenely.

The first performance of *A London Symphony* took place in London
under the direction of Geoffrey Toye on March 27, 1914. After that the
composer twice revised the work, and in its final version the symphony was
first presented in London, Albert Coates conducting, on May 4, 1920.

PASTORAL SYMPHONY (1921). I. Molto moderato. II. Lento
moderato. III. Moderato pesante. IV. Lento; Moderato maestoso; Lento.

Though Vaughan Williams provided his Third Symphony with the sobriquet of "Pastoral," he once again emphasized (as he had done in the case of the *London Symphony*) that he wanted it to be listened to as pure music.

The symphony is not, as its name might indicate, a portrait of Nature; there are no descriptive passages of brooks or storms, such as one encounters in another *Pastoral Symphony*—that of Beethoven. Vaughan Williams' symphony is a contemplative work. All four movements are comparatively slow and melancholy and quiet, filled with the most personal musings. If there is little variety in either pace or feeling there is, as Guido Pannain pointed out, considerable variety, nevertheless, "in the inner movement of the music, in subtle changes of mood rather than in the external program of the work." Pannain further remarks that in the final movement a clue is given to the meaning of the entire symphony: Here a voice enters singing a wordless chant—a "vocal liturgy"—speaking of "nature purified of the senses, absorbed in a greater faith and contemplation of itself—the tenderness of affection and the poetry of unvoiced prayers."

The contemplative character of the first movement is set forth in the expressive opening theme for basses and harp, accompanied by woodwinds in consecutive triads. "You think you have had contemplation in the first movement," wrote Herbert Howells, the English composer. "But what Vaughan Williams means by 'contemplative mood' you will only know when the second is reached." Introduced by a song for solo horn, the movement has a remote character due to its modal writing, which helps it achieve a plane of calm and eloquent beauty unique even in Vaughan Williams. The composer has designated the third movement as a 'slow dance'; it consists of three ideas, one for trumpets and trombone, another for flute, and a third for trumpet (the last in the Mixolydian mode). The fourth movement—which features the wordless solo for voice—creates an unforgettable atmosphere of peace and the infinite.

On January 26, 1922, this symphony was introduced by the London Philharmonic Orchestra, Adrian Boult conducting.

SYMPHONY NO. 4 IN F MINOR (1932). I. Allegro. II. Andante moderato. III. Scherzo: allegro molto. IV. Finale con epilogo fugato: allegro molto.

Of Vaughan Williams' symphonies, that in F Minor, his fourth, is the only one in which he has experimented with a modern idiom. The romantic and introspective poet of the *London* and *Pastoral* symphonies now uses complicated rhythms, jarring melodic ideas, dissonance. The result is a work that one does not associate with the name of Vaughan Williams; but it is a work which, nevertheless, has forceful and original writing, wonderful integration of form, powerful momentum, skillful polyphony.

When this writer visited Vaughan Williams before World War II, he expressed amazement that a work like this symphony should have been written by that composer. Vaughan Williams shrugged his shoulders and remarked simply: "I wrote as I felt." He added that if he never wrote a work in a similar vein, he still had to write the F minor Symphony at the time he did and in the way he did. To another writer, he remarked at another time: "I don't even know if I like it—but that is what I meant when I wrote it."

The two themes of the first movement become the basic materials of the entire symphony and are heard throughout, though often transformed. The first is stated by full orchestra, and the second by brass alone. The slow movement begins with a development of the second theme, played by the first violins; after considerable polyphonic development, the flute enters with a transformation of the first theme. The next two movements utilize fugal writing extensively; the concluding movement is the climax of the entire work. In this last movement, the culmination comes with an elaborate fugal epilogue, the subject of which is the first theme (trombones) combined polyphonically with other ideas. With a reminiscence of the opening measures of the first movement, the symphony comes to a close.

This symphony was introduced on April 10, 1935, in London, by the B.B.C. Symphony under Sir Adrian Boult.

SYMPHONY NO. 5 IN D MAJOR (1942). I. Preludio. II. Scherzo. III. Romanza. IV. Passacaglia.

That it was only a temporary excursion into the realms of modernism that Vaughan Williams had made with the F Minor Symphony—and not a permanent visit—was proved with the Fifth Symphony, which came a decade later. Introspective moods, gentle serenity, sensitive balance between thinking and feeling—these and the predilection for modal harmony once again characterize Vaughan Williams' writing.

In this symphony, the composer incorporated ideas he had sketched for a subsequent opera, *Pilgrim's Progress;* but he took pains to explain that—with the exception of the slow movement—none of the music has any spiritual affinity with the Bunyan allegory.

The four movements have a unanimity of mood. It is one of tranquillity and inner peace (such as prevails in the Concerto for Oboe and Orchestra, written at about this time) incongruous with the period that produced it, the first harrowing years of World War II. This mood is projected in the opening of the first theme with a subject stated by two horns. The entire movement has a contemplative character. In the Scherzo that follows, another meditative idea is unfolded at some length in the strings. The connection between the third movement and Bunyan is emphasized by the following quotation from the allegory, which appears in the printed score: "Upon that place there stood a cross, and a little below, a sepulchre. Then he said: 'He hath given me rest by His sorrow, and life by His death.'" This is rhapsodic music, created out of two themes. The final movement is a passacaglia in which the cellos provide the ground bass. The music gains in power and exultation until, as A. E. F. Dickinson wrote in a review of this work, it "seems to fill the whole world with its song of good will."

The Fifth Symphony was introduced in London at a Promenade concert on June 24, 1943: the composer conducted the London Philharmonic. It is dedicated to Jan Sibelius.

SYMPHONY NO. 6 IN E MINOR (1947).

A product of Vaughan Williams' old age (completed in his seventy-fifth year), this symphony does not betray any weakening of the composer's creative powers. On the contrary, it shows them to be at their very height. It is one of Vaughan Williams' greatest works; and, perhaps as an inevitable corollary, it is one of the finest musical creations of our generation.

The turmoil of the war and the postwar period reverberates in this strong and powerfully felt music. The composer, who had managed to find escape from the realities of war in such earlier works as the Concerto for Oboe and the Fifth Symphony, could escape no more from the world around him. In the lamentation which rises from the strings in the opening and closing of the first movement, we have an expression of the mighty tragedy of our times. In the second movement, the anguish makes way for philosophic evaluations, and there is momentary calm. But the Scherzo brings back the turmoil and the terror. Then comes the much-discussed last movement (the longest of the four). This is the most serene music that the imagination can conjure, a whisper from beginning to end, ebbing away into infinite silence. The soul has found peace, at last, within itself.

The four movements (Allegro; Moderato; Scherzo: allegro vivace; Epilogue) are played without any interruption, with each of the first three movements having "its tail attached to the head of its neighbor," as the composer put it.

The first performance of the Sixth Symphony took place in London on April 21, 1948. Sir Adrian Boult conducted the London Philharmonic.

HEITOR VILLA-LOBOS   1887—

Variety is the spice of Villa-Lobos' music. It would be impossible to try to prejudge the kind of music one is likely to hear when one attends a première performance of one of his works. For there is hardly a composer anywhere who has written in so many different veins, in so many different forms, and for so many different combinations of instruments. He has been romantic, impressionistic, and decidedly modern. In different works he has been sardonic and witty or poignant and pathetic; grandiose and eloquent or introspective. He has been on occasion cerebral; and on other occasions popular. He has been entirely original; and he has utilized parody and quotation.

The common denominator of his amazing output—amazing not only for its variety but also for its quantity (he has written more than fifteen hundred works)—is its national feeling. From the music of his country, its popular tunes and ditties as well as its folksongs and dances, Villa-Lobos has assimilated rhythms, melodies, and instruments in the creation of music which, whatever its idiom may be, beats with the heart and pulse of his native Brazil. Since Brazilian music is for the most part highly rhythmic and syncopated (carrying within it the throb of the jungle), Villa-Lobos' music most often has vertiginous movement and momentum. Since Brazilian melodies are often tender, Villa-Lobos' lyricism is often filled with a pleasing sentimentality. Since Brazilian music is vivid with color, Villa-Lobos' music usually contains rich harmonic schemes and brilliant orchestral effects.

He is, in short, Brazil in music. More than any other composer, as Irving Schwerké once said of him, "he seems to be actuated by the interior flame of his race."

Villa-Lobos was born in Rio de Janeiro, and while the year of his birth has been in some doubt, it is now generally accepted as 1887, on the fifth day of March. He did not have much schooling. Compelled to make his own living when his father died, he played in restaurant and theatre orchestras, coming into direct contact with Brazilian popular music. For a brief period he attended the National Institute of Music in Rio de Janeiro, but he never took to studies. In 1912, he went on an expedition to uncover the folksongs and dances of his native land. He went throughout Brazil, writing down the melodies he heard. The study of this music had a far-reaching influence on his development as a composer: it was only after he had absorbed the native music of Brazil that he was able to arrive at his own personal style. The first concert of his works took place in Rio de Janeiro in 1915; but it was still some time before he was to receive recognition.

For four years, from 1922 on, he lived in Paris. It was upon his return to Brazil that he assumed a major role in the musical life of his country. As supervisor and director of music education, he revolutionized the methods of music teaching. As a conductor, he drew attention to the music of Brazilian composers. And as a composer of international importance, he gave inspiration and significance to a national movement.

In 1944, Villa-Lobos visited the United States for the first time, at which time the League of Composers set aside an entire week in his honor.

The following works by Villa-Lobos are discussed below: *Bachianas Brasileiras; Choros Nos. 1-13; Madona; Mandu-Carara;* Quartet No. 6; *Rudepoêma; Uirapurú (The Enchanted Bird).*

For *Brazilian Quartet No. 2,* see Quartet No. 6.

UIRAPURÚ (THE ENCHANTED BIRD), tone-poem for orchestra (1917).

This early work is one of Villa-Lobos' first successful attempts to build a musical structure out of folksong materials. He wrote it in 1917 and revised it extensively in 1948.

The published score contains the following program:

"This is the story of the legendary Uirapurú, who, according to the fetishists, was the King of Love and the most beautiful Cacique in the world. The Uirapurú's nightly song lured the Red Indians into the Brazilian wild woods to seek the magic singer. An ugly Indian played with his nose a flute in a peaceful and serene forest. Suddenly a gay group of natives appeared. They were the most handsome inhabitants of Para. The unsightly Indian attempted to conceal himself, but the natives found him and showed their displeasure at his invasion of their forest by driving him away, kicking and beating him mercilessly.

"They then continued their eager search for the Uirapurú, leaving no spot in the forest unexplored in their efforts to locate him. They were confident that they would be rewarded by finding a youth more handsome than any ever seen by human eyes. All the animal kingdom which reigns at night —glowworms, crickets, owls, bacarus, enchanted toads, bats—were witnesses to this harried search.

"An occasional sweet trill in the distance encouraged them and spurred them on in their search.

"Lured by the touching song of the Uirapurú, a beautiful and charming Indian maiden appeared. She held a bow and arrow and looked like a capable huntress. The Uirapurú was suddenly transformed into a handsome youth, to the amazement of all the Indians who had been so anxiously seeking him. They discussed this transformation among themselves, while they happily and with a sense of victory followed the huntress who had fascinated the Uirapurú.

"When their discussions ceased they heard the sharp, shrill tone of a flute made of bones. The Indians feared the revenge of the ugly Indian and quickly tried to hide the handsome youth. However, the bloodthirsty and vindictive Indian came upon the unsuspecting youth in his hiding place and aimed an arrow which struck its mark and instantly killed the boy. The Indian maidens immediately took him into their arms and carried him to the brink of a fountain where he suddenly changed into a bird, became invisible, and left the sad and impassioned maidens. They heard his beautiful song as it died down in the silence of the woods."

CHOROS NOS. 1-13.

The "choros" is a musical form of Villa-Lobos' invention. Nicolas Slonimsky explains that a "choros" is a street band which plays popular tunes; subsequently the term *choros* was applied to the kind of music such a band played. However, in his works written in the form, Villa-Lobos extended the meaning of the word. It became, as he himself explained, "a new form in which are synthesized the different modalities of Brazilian, Indian, and popular music, having for principal elements rhythm and any typical melody of popular character.... The word 'serenade' gives an approximate idea of the significance of the choros."

These compositions are written for a great variety of instruments. The first is for guitar solo; the fifth, for piano; choros *bis,* for violin and violoncello. The second, third, fourth, sixth, and seventh are for various combinations of instruments (the third includes a chorus). The eighth through the thirteenth are for full orchestra, usually supplemented by native instruments; the tenth is for chorus and orchestra; the eleventh and thirteenth are actually concertos for piano and orchestra.

Characteristic works in this form are the following:

No. 5, *"Alma Brasileira,"* for piano solo, one of Villa-Lobos' most famous compositions. It is in three-part song form, the two outer sections being rhythmic, while the middle part is lyrical, reminiscent of a Brazilian popular song.

No. 6, for orchestra, guitar, and native percussion instruments, was written between 1922 and 1926 and was introduced on July 18, 1942, in Rio de Janeiro, under the direction of the composer. This is music of melancholy character, opening with a plangent theme for flute. The work employs a polyphonic treatment of several folk melodies and occasionally quotes popular tunes heard in small Brazilian towns.

No. 10, for chorus and orchestra, was written in 1926 and introduced in Rio de Janeiro under the direction of the composer on December 15 of the same year. The composer described this work as follows in the published score: "This work represents the reaction of a civilized man to stark nature; his contemplation of the valleys of the Amazon and the land of Matto Grosso and Para. The vastness and majesty of the landscape enrapture and captivate him. The sky, the waters, the woods, the birds fascinate him. But little by little his humanity asserts itself; there are living people in this land, even though they are savages. Their music is full of nostalgia and of love; their dances are full of rhythm. The Brazilian song 'Rasgo o Coracao' is heard, and the Brazilian heart beats in unison with the Brazilian earth."

RUDEPOÊMA, for orchestra, also for piano solo (1932).

One of the fruits that grew out of the friendship of Villa-Lobos and the celebrated concert pianist, Artur Rubinstein, was a long and highly technical piece for the piano, written in 1926. Villa-Lobos intended it as a tonal portrait of Rubinstein's temperament—hence the title, which means "savage poem." Free in form and rhapsodic in character, the work has vertiginous rhythmic vitality and impetuous movement; it utilizes large sweeps of sound that tax the timbres and sonorities of the piano. Indeed, it is more orchestral than pianistic, a fact that must have occurred to the composer, since he orchestrated it in 1932. The orchestrated version was introduced in Rio de Janeiro, under the composer's baton, on July 15, 1942.

BACHIANAS BRASILEIRAS (1932-1945).

In his suites for various combinations of instruments which he entitled *Bachianas Brasileiras,* Villa-Lobos has attempted a fusion of Bach's style with the personality of Brazilian folk music. Frequently the composer utilizes alternate sets of titles for his movements to emphasize this duality; one set suggests Bach, the other, Brazilian lore.

The most characteristic works are the following:

No. 1, for eight celli, was written in 1932. It is in three movements: I. Introduction (Embolada). II. Prelude (Modhina). III. Fugue (Conversa). The first movement is essentially Brazilian in its rhythmic interest and in its evocation of popular tunes. The spiritual character of the melody for solo cello in the second movement, later carried on (often in unison) by the other celli, and the fugal counterpoint of the third movement recall Bach.

No. 2, for orchestra, is in four movements: I. Prelude (Song of the Hoodlum). II. Aria (Song of Our Country). III. Danza (Woodland Memory). IV. Toccata (The Little Train to Caipira). The second movement, with its beautiful and sentimental melody for solo cello, and the fourth movement, with its realistic picture of a little train puffing its way through Brazilian communities, are of particular interest.

The first movement (Aria) of No. 5, for soprano and eight celli, was written in 1938, and the second (Danza) seven years later. The Aria is one of Villa-Lobos' most famous creations. It is a three-part song, the first and third parts of which consist of a wordless chant to the syllable *Ah.* The middle section, which has a text, is in the manner of a folksong.

QUARTET NO. 6 IN E MAJOR (Brazilian Quartet No. 2), for strings (1938). I. Poco animato. II. Allegretto. III. Andante. IV. Allegro vivace.

Villa-Lobos has written two string quartets which he subtitled "Brazilian" to point up their debt to the folk music of that country. The second is the more famous. The work opens with a movement that is full of animation and good spirits. In the second movement the main theme is a broad and sensual melody. There follows an Andante which is a delicately atmospheric tone-painting, subtly impressionistic, quivering with the sounds of a Brazilian jungle on a summer's night. A staccato theme for violins opens the final movement, which is alive and colorful with Brazilian rhythms and melodies.

MADONA, tone-poem for orchestra (1945).

Madona was commissioned by the Koussevitzky Foundation. It was introduced in Rio de Janeiro under the composer's direction on October 8, 1946.

Dedicated to the memory of Natalie Koussevitzky, *Madona* was intended by its composer as a portrait of Mrs. Koussevitzky. Villa-Lobos wrote: "There was an indefinable expression in her features which at once inspired in me an intuitive and definite confidence, remaining as an inexplicable and enduring memory of a being possessed with rare gifts of kindness.... Since it would be impossible for me to describe her in a prolonged literary dissertation, objective, concrete or conventional, I depend upon the mystery of sounds, as embodied in the free songs of my country's birds and folk and natural surroundings by which my musical nature is inspired."

MANDU-CARARA, symphonic poem (or ballet) for two pianos, percussion, large chorus, and children's chorus (1946).

Hugh Ross, who conducted the world première of *Mandu-Carara* with the Schola Cantorum in New York on January 23, 1948, wrote the following illuminating description:

"*Mandu-Carara* is a legend of the Nheengatu people, a Brazilian Indian tribe. The work is named for a famous young Indian dancer, and the climax is a triumphal dance led by Mandu-Carara in celebration of the happy ending of the story.

"The legend concerns the adventures of two children, and parallels in a Brazilian setting the story of Hansel and Gretel. Two greedy children have been left by their poor father in the woods as he is unable to feed them any longer. In their wanderings they come upon an ogre, Currupira, who lures them to his hearth. They ask him the way home, but he detains them and his wife begins stuffing them with food.

"A musical interlude then describes how the children outwit Currupira, telling him how they had just seen two fat monkeys near his hut. He goes in search of them, and meanwhile the children kill his wife and run away.

"Currupira comes home and rushes madly about the wood, crying with fury. The children save themselves from him by swimming across a river and with the help of forest creatures find their way home. There they find Mandu-Carara with their father. This is the signal for a general celebration, culminating in the dance of Mandu-Carara.

"The story has elements both of symphony and ballet. The one-eyed Currupira with reversed ears and feet and his wicked Indian wife, the cotias and monkeys of the jungle, the children, Mandu-Carara and the Indians all find their musical embodiment in Villa-Lobos' score.

"The percussion instruments emphasize the rhythms of Mandu-Carara's dance. A heavy stumbling ostinato, soon after the entry of the chorus, represents the frightened children wandering in the jungle."

WILLIAM WALTON

1902—

Eric Blom has pointed out a salient trait that sets Walton apart from most living composers: his capacity "to create a musical work that is not only all of a piece, but remains unique and unrepeatable, for each time he tackles a new composition it turns out to be entirely different from the last."

However great is the stylistic difference between, say, *Façade* and *Belshazzar's Feast,* or *Belshazzar's Feast* and the Viola Concerto, or the Violin Concerto and the Symphony, certain individual mannerisms remain: the long, sinuous melodic line; the detailed harmonic and contrapuntal writing, which never appears cluttered because of the transparency of the texture; the rich and brilliant orchestration; the irresistible drive of the rhythms and cross-rhythms. His extraordinary craftsmanship and articulateness, revealed from the very first, have enabled Walton to blend form and content, idea and style, into an inextricable unity. Though his works are comparatively few in number, they are all distinguished by technical mastery and a wide gamut of expressiveness; and it is for these reasons that, ever since his early *Façade,* he has been one of the most significant and interesting composers in England.

Walton was born in Oldham, Lancashire, on March 29, 1902. His father, a church musician, gave him his first music lessons, after which he attended the Christ Cathedral Church School at Oxford. Following matriculation, he profited by contact with and advice from several eminent musicians, notably Edward J. Dent, Busoni, and Ansermet.

He first attracted attention as a composer when an early string quartet was performed in 1923 at the International Society for Contemporary Music Festival at Salzburg, and when, one year later, a piano quartet was published by the Carnegie Trust. Fame was not slow in coming, and it came with the first performance of his amusing and provocative *Façade*. *Portsmouth Point* scored a decided success at the International Society for Contemporary Music Festival in Zurich in 1926. From then on Walton's reputation was firmly established.

During World War II, Walton served in the British Army. He was knighted in 1951, and in 1953 he composed a *Te Deum* and a march for the coronation of Elizabeth II. His first opera, *Troilus and Cressida* (see Supplement), completed when he was fifty-two, was successfully introduced in London on December 3, 1954.

The following works by Walton are discussed below: *Belshazzar's Feast;* Concerto for Violin and Orchestra; *Façade; Portsmouth Point;* Quartet in A Minor; *Scapino; Sinfonia Concertante;* Symphony No. 1.

PORTSMOUTH POINT, overture for orchestra (1925).

Portsmouth Point, a British naval arsenal opposite the Isle of Wight, was the subject of a print by Thomas Rowlandson. A feverishly active and colorful water-front scene is depicted. On the left is a moneylender's shop, on the right a tavern, and at the dock several sailing vessels. Sailors are busily loading ships; loving couples are saying farewell; a lonely musician with a wooden leg is playing the violin.

This print inspired Walton to write his brisk English overture. It is filled with salty themes that suggest nautical tunes of the eighteenth century and the vigorous rhythms of sailor dances; but Constant Lambert also finds the influence of Catalonian sardanas in some of the material.

The overture had its première at the International Society for Contemporary Music Festival in Zurich on June 22, 1926, Volkmar Andrae conducting. It was outstandingly successful.

FAÇADE, melodrama for reciting voice and seven instruments (1926).

On April 27, 1926, there took place at the Chenil Galleries in London a unique entertainment. Twenty-one abstractionist poems by Edith Sitwell were recited by her; she herself was out of sight, her voice coming to the audience through a megaphone-shaped mouth of a face painted on the curtain. The instrumentalists (also concealed) provided a musical setting for the poems.

Sitwell described her poems (which frequently made very little sense) as "technical experiments—studies in the effect that texture has on rhythm, and the effect that varying and elaborate patterns of rhymes and assonances and dissonances have on rhythm."

There is, however, nothing either abstract or esoteric about the music that Walton wrote for these poems. With a down-to-earth sense of humor, he used burlesque, parody, mock seriousness, tongue-in-cheek sentimentality, and calculated clichés—producing a score that was not only great fun but also a tour de force of technical mastery. For all its irrepressible lightness, the score was, as Hubert Foss remarked, "accomplished stuff indeed, well wrought and beautifully written."

An earlier version of this *Façade* music had been heard in London at the Aeolian Hall on June 12, 1923. After the première of the more definitive, enlarged score, Walton took five of the sections, scored them for full orchestra, and collated them into *Façade Suite No. 1*. The sections of this suite are: I. Fanfare. II. Polka. III. Swiss Yodeling Song. IV. Waltz. V. Tango Pasodoble. A second orchestral suite came in 1928, with the following four parts: I. Popular Song. II. Country Dance. III. Scotch Rhapsody. IV. Tarantella Sevillana.

SINFONIA CONCERTANTE, for orchestra with piano obbligato (1927). I. Maestoso; Allegro spiritoso; Allegretto. II. Andante commodo. III. Allegro molto.

This composition was introduced in London by the London Philharmonic under Ernest Ansermet on January 5, 1928; York Bowen was the assisting artist.

After a slow introduction, the Allegro spiritoso movement arrives, built out of several ideas which appear consecutively. In the section that follows, development and recapitulation are telescoped into one. The brass is used sparingly in the second movement for music of devotional character; Walton's talent for writing sensual music of emotional impact is here evident. Gaiety comes in the concluding movement with several lusty themes.

BELSHAZZAR'S FEAST, cantata for baritone, chorus, and orchestra (1931).

The breadth of design and the majesty of style of the Handelian oratorio are combined with the violent surge and pulse of modern harmonic and rhythmic writing in this, Walton's first work for chorus. It was introduced with outstanding success at the Leeds Festival on October 10, 1931, Malcolm Sargent conducting. The text, written by Osbert Sitwell, is a poetic adaptation of passages from the Bible, beginning with the prophecy of Isaiah, and including passages from Psalms 81 and 137.

The cantata opens with a trumpet call, prefacing the words, "Thus Spake Isaiah." Isaiah's dire prophecy of Babylonian captivity follows. We then hear—quoting from Colin Mason's fine analysis of this work—"a short orchestral passage," succeeded by "a lament sung by chorus, 'By the Waters of Babylon We Sat Down and Wept,' which has often been praised as Walton's finest music. The magical change from the first mood to this, effected neither by a long transition nor by a distinct pause, takes place, it seems, inevitably, though we wonder afterwards how it was done. The passionate sorrow of the captives is expressed here as finely as the brutality of the prophecy, the repetition of words not being used in the classical ornamental way, but to give the impression of their echoing cries, lamenting for Jerusalem.

"From this point the intensity rises until the dramatic moment of Belshazzar's death, after which Walton gradually changes it into an exultant hymn, with some passages almost of the beauty of the prisoners' lament, and a massive, Handelian Alleluia."

SYMPHONY NO. 1 (1934). I. Allegro assai. II. Scherzo: presto, con malizia. III. Adagio con malincolia. IV. Maestoso; Brioso ed ardentemente; Vivacissimo; Maestoso.

It is perhaps indicative of the far-reaching interest of Walton's public in his music that the first performance of his First Symphony should have taken place even before it was completed. When the first three movements were finished in 1934, they were heard in a performance by the London Symphony Orchestra under Sir Hamilton Harty on December 3 of the same year—even though it was known that a fourth movement was being written. That fourth movement was completed the following summer; the entire symphony was then heard on November 6, 1935, in a performance by the B.B.C. Symphony under Harty.

The symphony is a complex work which employs elaborate harmonic and contrapuntal textures and a profusion of terse themes. The first movement is not in the usual sonata form but passes fluidly from one idea to the next, by-passing the usual development and recapitulation sections found in conventional symphonies. There is an undercurrent of malicious irony in the Scherzo, which is markedly rhythmic. But the slow movement that follows enters a world of contemplation and calm in which irony has no place; Walton's rich vein of lyricism is here tapped. The symphony ends in a broadly designed finale which is in four sections—the first and the closing parts being somewhat declamatory, while the middle portions are vigorous, with a climax reached in a fugal exposition.

QUARTET IN A MINOR, for strings (1937). I. Allegro. II. Presto. III. Lento. IV. Allegro molto.

This quartet is Walton's second, the first—an apprentice work—having been written in 1922. The Second Quartet came fifteen years later, and was first performed in London on May 4, 1947, by the Blech Quartet.

This is one of Walton's most compact and economical works. Intense in feeling, subdued in expression, its best pages reflect a restrained melancholy. The main theme of the first movement, heard in the upper register of the viola, is elegiac, as is the entire third movement, in which muted strings speak of intimate and tender thoughts. Only in the final movement is the spell of sad revery shattered; the music now becomes turbulent and passionate.

CONCERTO FOR VIOLIN AND ORCHESTRA (1939). I. Andante tranquillo. II. Presto capriccioso a la napolitana. III. Vivace.

Walton produced this work for Jascha Heifetz. The violinist introduced it in Cleveland on December 7, 1939, with the Cleveland Orchestra, Artur Rodzinski conducting. It was subsequently revised.

This concerto is music that is deeply felt and emotionally projected. It opens with a slow movement in which an atmosphere of tranquillity is evoked. A long, beautifully carved melody for the solo violin follows the introduction; subsidiary ideas are superimposed on this melody to provide contrapuntal interest. Later there appear some dramatic outbursts in the orchestra and assertive passages for the violin; but the initial mood is re-established both in the orchestra and solo instrument, and new material is introduced to heighten the serenity and eloquent beauty of the opening passage. The movement that follows has spirited movement and boisterous spirit: an impetuous dance appears in the violin after a one-bar introduction by the orchestra; a second brief orchestral exclamation leads into a Neapolitan song, also heard in the solo violin; a third orchestral outburst brings on an infectious waltz.

The main theme of the finale is heard first in the lower strings and bassoons, and becomes the matrix for several subsidiary ideas; a second theme appears in the woodwinds, with embellishments by the violin. The music of this movement passes from whimsy to melancholy, from sensitive moods to passionate ones.

SCAPINO, a comedy overture for orchestra (1940).

This infectious and gay little overture is in the vein of *Portsmouth Point*, full of spirited melodies and rhythms. Scapino is, of course, a familiar character in the Italian commedia dell'arte. For his inspiration, Walton went to two etchings of Callot, reproductions of which he pasted into the manuscript score. The overture opens with a delightful character study of Scapino (Molto vivace); after a relaxed theme is heard in the horns and violas and then in the violins, there comes an interlude which is described by the composer as a "serenata." A playful section, in which earlier material returns, closes the work.

Walton wrote this overture on a commission from the Chicago Symphony Orchestra to commemorate its fiftieth anniversary; at that time, the composer was serving in the British Army. The première took place in Chicago on April 3, 1941, with Frederick Stock conducting the Chicago Symphony.

ANTON WEBERN   1883—1945

A passionate disciple of Arnold Schoenberg, Anton Webern remained true to the twelve-tone technique. But he carried it beyond the boundaries set and established by his master. In some of his works, notably the Sinfonietta and the Symphony (for chamber orchestra), he not only adhered rigidly to the order of twelve different tones but also postulated a principle of twelve different tone colors: thus each of his instruments plays only a note at a time and is not heard again with another tone till the other instruments are, in turn, heard from.

What is surely the last word in musical expressionism has been spoken by Webern. The expressionist strives for brevity; there are certain pieces by Webern which are only a few seconds long, while some of his themes are only of a single tone. The musical expressionist strives for refinement; Webern's harmonic and contrapuntal texture usually consists only of a few isolated tones, while it pays little heed to sonority. The expressionist strives for delicate effects: Webern's music is frequently no more than a whispered suggestion of an effect—so much that it has sometimes been described as "pianissimo espressivo."

This is threadbare simplicity; yet its logic is highly complex. For there is little recognizable melody, rhythm, or harmony, and its effect is of the most elusive and subtle kind. Nicolas Slonimsky put it well when he said that in Webern's music "thought and sound come together," and it is often impossible to separate the one from the other.

Webern was born in Vienna on December 3, 1883. He attended the University of Vienna, where he studied musicology with Guido Adler and received a doctorate in philosophy. For a while he earned his living by conducting orchestras in small German theaters. At the same time he began composing. His opus 1 was a Passacaglia, written in 1908; it was conventional music following Germanic traditions. But his association with Arnold Schoenberg soon led him from traditional writing to atonalism. The *Six Orchestral Pieces* created a scandal when introduced in Vienna on March 31, 1913, at a concert in which the music of Schoenberg and his disciples was heard. From this time on, he was relentless in his fanatical adherence to Schoenberg's musical principles; and the music he wrote in the twelve-tone technique was all subject to abuse and denunciation.

Though Schoenberg abandoned the European scene soon after the rise

of Hitler in Germany, Webern remained in Vienna throughout the Anschluss and World War II. On the evening of September 15, 1945—while on
a visit to his daughter at Mittersill in Austria—he took a stroll to smoke a
cigarette. An American officer ordered him to stop short. Misunderstanding
the order, Webern approached him; he was instantly shot and killed.

The following works by Webern are discussed below: *Six Bagatelles;*
Symphony.

SIX BAGATELLES, for string quartet, op. 9 (1913).

In these miniatures, Webern strips music to its very bones. They are
the last word in brevity: the longest of them takes only a minute or so while
the shortest is of a few seconds' duration. A few unrelated tones—and a basic
idea is expressed. The harmony is as austere and impoverished as the melodies. In place of statement there is only the barest suggestion, which led
Schoenberg to say of these *Bagatelles* that "a whole novel" is expressed "in
a single sigh."

The *Bagatelles* were dedicated to Alban Berg.

SYMPHONY, for chamber orchestra, op. 21 (1925). I. Ruhig schrei-
tend. II. Variationen.

Even within the larger framework of the symphony, Webern remained the miniaturist for whom brevity and economy are basic elements.
The Symphony is written for a small ensemble: clarinet, bass clarinet, two
French horns, harp, and strings. It is a short work, taking only fifteen
minutes for the two movements. The thematic material is terse, frequently
consisting of isolated and unrelated tones. The instrumentation is gaunt and
naked, as, in the composer's attempt at nonrepetitive tone color, an instrument frequently plays no more than one or two notes before passing on the
theme to another instrument. The sounds appear disconnected, separated by
sudden pauses, as music is reduced to its very essentials.

The first movement is a double canon, with each instrument providing
only one or two tones of the theme. The second movement consists of a
theme and seven variations.

The Symphony was written on commission for the League of Composers, who introduced it in New York on December 8, 1929, under Alexander Smallens' direction. The response was hostile; nor has the antagonism
to this music relaxed.

KURT WEILL

In the period between the two world wars, there arose in Germany an esthetic cult in which Kurt Weill was a major force. That cult was called *Zeitkunst,* and it glorified all art that was vibrantly contemporary in theme and style, speaking for and interpreting twentieth-century experiences.

The operas Weill wrote during this period were admirable examples of this *Zeitkunst.* The librettos were usually as timely as the front pages of the newspapers. And the musical style was also a legitimate offspring of the times, borrowing rhythmic and melodic techniques from popular sources. In his fabulously successful adaptation of *The Beggar's Opera* (which he called *The Three-Penny Opera* and which had more than four thousand performances in about 120 German theaters after its première in 1928), and in his own provocative operas (*The Protagonist* and *The Rise and Fall of the City of Mahagonny,* written in 1927 and 1930, respectively) Weill evolved a song form which belonged more to the musical-comedy stage than to that of the opera house. Characteristic of this form was "The Alabama Song" from *Mahagonny,* which became a "hit" in Germany and in which the later composer for the Broadway theatre begins to emerge.

As a follower of *Zeitkunst,* Weill not only revealed his gift for writing in a popular vein, but also in producing functional works. In 1930, he wrote an opera called *Der Jasager,* the first German opera to be written directly for schools.

Thus it can be seen that, as one of the foremost composers for the Broadway theatre after 1935, and as the composer of the educational one-act folk opera, *Down in the Valley,* Weill had not entered upon any new creative phase but was continuing an old one. With his delightfully lyrical scores for a long chain of Broadway stage successes, he proved himself to be one of the most resourceful composers for the popular theatre; but that talent had already been strongly in evidence in his German operas. And what he had done in Germany with *Der Jasager* he repeated in this country with *Down In the Valley:* writing functional music for schools, music which had such freshness and originality that its interest transcended the school auditorium and successfully penetrated the opera house.

Weill was born in Dessau, Germany, on March 2, 1900. His music study took place at the Berlin Hochschule, principally with Humperdinck and Kasselt, following which he became a pupil of Busoni. His early works for string quartet and orchestra revealed a sound technique; but not until he turned to the writing of opera did his creative gift unfold completely. *The Protagonist,* produced in Dresden in 1927, was a great success, launching Weill not only as a major operatic figure in Germany but also as a spokesman for the then prevailing vogue for *Zeitkunst.*

When Hitler rose to power, Weill left Germany and for two years lived in Paris. He came to this country in 1935 and remained here for the rest of his life. His first score for the Broadway theatre was *Johnny Johnson,* a satire by Paul Green. It was not long before he became one of the most successful and inventive writers of theatre music. His long string of successes included *Knickerbocker Holiday* (libretto by Maxwell Anderson), *Lady in the Dark* (by Moss Hart), *One Touch of Venus* (by Ogden Nash and S. J. Perelman), *Street Scene* (by Elmer Rice), and *Lost in the Stars* (by Maxwell Anderson).

Kurt Weill died in New York City on April 3, 1950.

DOWN IN THE VALLEY, folk opera (1947).

In 1947, the dean of the School of Music of Indiana University turned to Weill for a student opera. At that time, Weill had in his drawer the score of a fifteen-minute radio opera, inspired by the American folksong *Down in the Valley,* the libretto of which had been prepared by Arnold Sundgaard; the opus had been turned down by prospective sponsors as too highbrow for public consumption. Weill decided to adapt and enlarge the radio piece into a musico-dramatic composition. Together with his librettist, he extended it into a forty-five-minute one-act opera and interpolated a great deal of new music.

This revised work was heard for the first time at Indiana University on July 15, 1948, Ernst Hoffman conducting. It proved to be so successful that one month later it was repeated at Ann Arbor by the University of Michigan, at which time it was broadcast over the NBC network. After that—and within a comparatively short period of time—the opera was presented by hundreds of organizations throughout the country, amateur and professional. It was featured at summer camps and festivals. It was televised and recorded. It was even incorporated into the repertories of several European opera houses.

It is not difficult to explain its immediate popularity. It is a charming opera, unpretentious in its simplicity and directness, at turns engagingly lyrical and dramatic. And it is as indigenous to the American scene as the folksong that inspired it. It calls for the most elementary forces: a small orchestra, or, failing that, two pianos; limited stagecraft and scenery; a small cast, on whom the vocal demands are not too exacting.

The tale is equally simple, succinctly summarized by the "Leader" in the following words sung at the opening of the work: "I'll sing of Brack Weaver, who died on the gallows one morning in May, he died for the

love of sweet Jennie Parsons, he died for the slaying of Thomas Bouche."
The story is then told in a series of flashbacks. Sentenced to death for the
murder of Bouche, Brack Weaver feels he cannot face the gallows without
seeing his beloved Jenny once more. He makes a break, and finds his loved
one sitting on her porch. With her he recalls how they met and fell in love;
how the villain, Bouche, tried to force his attentions on Jenny; how, at a
square dance, he killed Bouche in a brawl. Convinced that Jenny still loves
him, Brack can face his doom. He gives himself up to the posse that has
come to hunt him.

The opera is filled with lovely songs for the principal characters and
many dramatic passages for the chorus, which plays a prominent role both
as commentator on the drama and as an actual participant in it. Five American folksongs are interpolated in the score: *Down in the Valley; The Lone-
some Dove; The Little Black Train; Hop Up, My Ladies;* and *Sourwood
Mountain.*

JAROMIR WEINBERGER   1896—

The influences of three different countries have shaped the style of
Weinberger's music at different periods: France, Czechoslovakia, and the
United States. His apprentice works were written in the impressionist style
of Debussy. Recognizing that in these early pieces he was imitative rather
than creative, he destroyed them and set off in another direction. It was then
that he subjected himself to the principles of Smetana and Dvořák in the
writing of Czech music that had pronounced national traits. After coming
to this country and becoming a permanent resident, he abandoned the Czech
idiom permanently to write music inspired by the culture and backgrounds
of his new land: he wrote compositions inspired by Whitman, Lincoln, and
Washington Irving, and even adapted the song *Dixie* into an orchestral prelude and fugue.

His style may have changed at different periods in his life, but his
basic creative approach never has. The shaping of new idioms and techniques he has left to others. He has always been the romanticist who goes in
for well-shaped melodies and good-sounding harmonies within sound classical forms. A superb craftsman and an elegant orchestrator, his music is the
cultured speech of an artist who is not afraid to search the deepest recesses
of his heart and to express what he finds there.

Weinberger was born in Prague on January 8, 1896, and was a student at the Prague Conservatory. Later he was a pupil of Max Reger in Berlin. In 1922, he came to the United States to serve as professor of composition at the Ithaca Conservatory. When he returned to Europe in 1926, he was appointed director of opera at the National Theatre of Bratislava and director of the Eger School of Music.

Some recognition came to him with several orchestral works. But international fame did not come until 1927, when his most famous opera, *Schwanda, the Bagpipe Player,* was successfully introduced in Prague. Performances followed in practically every opera house in Europe and at the Metropolitan Opera House in New York.

Weinberger revisited the United States in 1933. When Nazi Germany occupied the Sudeten territory of Czechoslovakia, Weinberger abandoned his native land and settled in Paris. In 1939 he returned to the United States, this time to establish a permanent residence.

The following works by Weinberger are discussed below: *Christmas Overture; The Legend of Sleepy Hollow; Schwanda, The Bagpipe Player; Under the Spreading Chestnut Tree.*

SCHWANDA, THE BAGPIPE PLAYER, opera (1926).

Like its distinguished predecessor, Smetana's *Bartered Bride, Schwanda* went to Bohemian legend and folksong for text and music. The text, by Milos Kares, gracefully mingles fantasy with realism. The bandit Babinsky is hiding at Schwanda's farm, where he meets and falls in love with Schwanda's wife, Dorota. Schwanda, he feels, must be erased from the picture so that he, Babinsky, may have Dorota for himself. He tells Schwanda fabulous tales about the court of Queen Ice-Heart, where one can become rich and powerful; and Schwanda decides to go there with Babinsky. At the court, Schwanda plays his bagpipe, and with such eloquence that he wins the heart of the Queen, who desires to marry him. Dorota appears and frustrates the marriage—a fact which so infuriates the Queen that she orders Schwanda's death. Babinsky, however, saves Schwanda, who continues to delight the court with his wonderful music. But Dorota nags Schwanda about his affair with the Queen, while the bagpipe player protests his innocence. May he be consigned to the depths of Hell if the Queen ever even kissed him! Hardly have these words been spoken when the earth swallows Schwanda. But Dorota remains true to him, even though he has departed for other worlds. Babinsky recognizes that Dorota, after all, is not for him, and restores Schwanda to her—by winning him in a game of cards with the devil.

There can be no question that there are derivative echoes in the score Weinberger wrote for this merry tale. There are more than mere suggestions of Smetana and Rimsky-Korsakov in the music: on occasion there are even outright quotations. It is also true that the recitatives are often long and dull;

that the harmonic writing is not always original. But in spite of these flaws, the music is a delightful experience—gay, infectious, tuneful. The melodies assume the character of Bohemian folksongs; the best of them—such as the recurring farm song sung by Dorota—have a distinctly personal flavor. The orchestral pages, such as the overture, the intermezzi, the rousing polka with which Schwanda sets the court a-dancing, and the fugue, are brilliantly scored and ingenious in their rhythmic and contrapuntal writing.

Strange to say, when this opera was heard for the first time—in the National Theatre of Prague on April 27, 1927, it was not particularly successful. But the first German performance, which took place in Breslau on December 16, 1928 (in a translation into German by Max Brod), was a triumph. To the German audiences, *Schwanda* appeared as a delightful escape from the intellectualism with which so many German operas of the time were concerned; and they responded to it enthusiastically. That success set off the magnificent career of *Schwanda* in the opera houses of the world: within a four-year period it was heard more than two thousand times in Central Europe. It was introduced at the Metropolitan Opera in New York on November 7, 1931.

The deservedly famous and popular "Polka" and "Fugue" from *Schwanda* are frequently heard at orchestral concerts. The Polka has a rousing peasant vigor and healthy good spirits which make it everlastingly appealing. Within the classic structure of the "Fugue," the folk elements of the music are magically retained; at the climax, the melody of the "Polka" is effectively joined with the principal theme of the "Fugue."

CHRISTMAS OVERTURE, for orchestra and organ (1929).

This is one of Weinberger's most successful works for orchestra in the Czech idiom. It is a delightful potpourri of Czech Christmas songs inspired by old Czech folk tales. Up to the time of World War II it was heard everywhere in Europe; it was a tradition in Czechoslovakia to play this work over the radio each Christmas eve.

It utilizes three poignant Christmas songs of the festival of Epiphany (Koledy) and fuses them with what the composer describes as "old organ mixtures."

THE LEGEND OF SLEEPY HOLLOW, suite for orchestra (1939).
I. Sleepy Hollow. II. Katrina's Waltz. III. The Headless Horseman and Ichabod Crane. IV. Dutch Polka.

In 1939, Weinberger was commissioned by Nathaniel Shilkret to write this work, inspired by Washington Irving's famous story. On November 21, 1940, it was introduced in Detroit by the Detroit Symphony Orchestra, Victor Kolar conducting.

Quotations from Irving's *The Legend of Sleepy Hollow* preface each of the four movements in the published score and provide the programmatic clue to the music:

I. "Not far from the village of Tarrytown there is a little valley, or rather a lap of land, among high hills, which is one of the quietest places in the world. A small brook glides through it with just murmur enough to lull one to repose...."

II. "Old Baltus van Tassel moved about among his guests with a face dilated with content and good humor, round and jolly as the harvest moon.... Ichabod prided himself upon his dancing... the lady of his heart was his partner."

III. "It was the very witching time of the night that Ichabod... pursued his travel homewards along the sides of the hills. The night grew darker and darker.... He was approaching the place where many of the scenes of his ghost stories had been laid."

IV. "Brom Bones, shortly after his rival's disappearance, conducts the blooming Katrina in triumph to the altar."

UNDER THE SPREADING CHESTNUT TREE, variations and fugue on an old English tune, for orchestra (1939).

In the summer of 1938, Weinberger attended a cinema theatre in Juan les Pins, on the French Riviera, where he saw a newsreel of the King of England and a group of young people in a boys' camp, singing a popular song called *Under the Spreading Chestnut Tree*. The tune made a deep impression on the composer, who decided to write a major orchestral work based on it. It was not written, however, until early in 1939, after the composer had come to this country.

The published score carries a detailed analysis of the work by the composer himself. The melody is heard at the opening. After it has been stated, the piano creates a transition from the theme to the first variation (throughout the work the piano serves as a catalytic agent between the different parts of the work). Called "Her Majesty's Virginal," the first variation is a canon. In the second variation, "The Madrigalists," the composer pays tribute to the early English composers, while the third is entitled "The Dark Lady," after the heroine of the Shakespeare sonnets. The tune acquires a Scottish character in the fourth variation, "The Highlanders," as the orchestra simulates the quality of bagpipe music. In the "Pastorale" variation that follows, the composer attempts a description of the English countryside. The twenty-third chapter of Dickens' *Pickwick Papers* was the stimulation for the sixth variation, entitled "Mr. Weller, Senior, Discusses Widows With His Son, Samuel Weller, Esq." The concluding variation is a "Sarabande," for the Princess Elizabeth, Electress Palatine and Queen of Bohemia in the early seventeenth century, the unhappy daughter of James I, and the unhappy ruler of an unhappy country. A fugue, the theme of which has eight bars, brings the orchestral work to a culmination.

ERMANNO WOLF-FERRARI   1876—1948

Though one of his most successful operas, *The Jewels of the Madonna,* is tragic, the name of Wolf-Ferrari is almost always associated with the field of comic opera. He may often succumb to a conventional lyricism and artificiality of form. But Wolf-Ferrari also possesses those qualities which make for successful opera buffa: spontaneity and freshness and a talent for pointing up comic situations with a few swift strokes of the pen. *Le Donne Curiose* (1903) and his masterpiece *The Secret of Suzanne* rank with the finest creations of twentieth-century opera buffa, and give their composer a deserving place with those great men, from Pergolesi through Rossini and Donizetti, who originated and developed that form.

Wolf-Ferrari was born in Venice on January 12, 1876, the son of a German father and Italian mother. At first it was his intention to follow in the footsteps of his father by becoming a painter. But in his adolescence he decided to specialize in music, going to Munich to study with Rheinberger. During this period he heard a performance of Wagner's *Siegfried* which affected him so strongly that he became ill. In later years, adulation for Wagner's music dramas was displaced by outright revulsion; his own operatic writing was an attempt to negate everything for which Wagner stood.

After returning to Venice, he achieved his first successes as a composer in the field of the oratorio, with *La Sulamita* and *La Vita Nuova.* His first opera, *Cenerentola,* while none too successful when introduced in Venice in 1900, was exceptionally well received in Germany two years later. With *I Quattro Rusteghi,* adapted from Goldoni and introduced in Munich in 1906, Wolf-Ferrari hit his stride as a composer of comic opera.

For several years, he was director of the Liceo Benedetto Marcello in Venice. In 1912, he visited the United States to supervise the American première of *The Jewels of the Madonna* in Chicago. He died in Venice on January 12, 1948.

The following works by Wolf-Ferrari are discussed below: *Chamber Symphony; The Jewels of the Madonna; The Secret of Suzanne.*

CHAMBER SYMPHONY, for chamber orchestra, op. 8 (1901). I. Allegro moderato. II. Adagio. III. Vivace con spirito. IV. Adagio; Con fuoco.

Though Wolf-Ferrari's reputation rests almost exclusively on his works for the stage, he did produce a few creditable instrumental works, one of the best of which is a *Chamber Symphony*. Though his long, fully realized melodic lines remind us that he is essentially a composer for the voice, Wolf-Ferrari did possess a fine feeling for instrumental writing, a sound structural craftsmanship, and a highly developed harmonic sense.

The work opens with an introduction for the piano, following which the main theme is introduced by the clarinet; this and the secondary theme are broadly melodic. A bassoon solo, in an emotional theme, dominates the slow movement, which midway passes from a sentimental to a capricious mood. A majestic slow section opens the finale, yielding to a vigorous section; the moods alternate from the lyrical to the dramatic and back to the lyrical as contrapuntal writing and percussive effects are generously exploited.

THE SECRET OF SUZANNE, comic opera (1909).

The changing mores of society have reduced to absurdity the one-act libretto of *The Secret of Suzanne,* written by Enrico Golisciani. A jealous Count detects the smell of tobacco in his house, and forthwith suspects his wife of having a lover. Suzanne soothes her irate husband and sends him off to the club. But still unconvinced, the Count hides outside the window of his house to spy on his wife. What he discovers is that she does not harbor a secret lover, but rather a secret passion—for smoking. Delighted that his wife is faithful to him, he comes inside to join her in a smoke.

But so vivacious and infectious is the music for this rather silly story that the "intermezzo" (as Wolf-Ferrari aptly called it) remains a jewel in the literature of comic opera. Unpretentious in its artistic aims, it remains from beginning to end a delightful excursion into lighter moods. The effervescent overture and its best arias (*"Canzone dell'orso"* for tenor, and *"Gioio la nube leggiere"* for soprano) are truly in the best traditions of opera buffa—fresh, witty, vital, effervescent music which requires no familiarity or analysis to be fully appreciated, and which never seems to lose its appeal.

The Secret of Suzanne was heard for the first time at the Munich Opera on December 4, 1909.

THE JEWELS OF THE MADONNA, opera (1911).

The Jewels of the Madonna is Wolf-Ferrari's only opera in a serious vein. While it lacks the spontaneity and charm of his lighter works, it does generate considerable dramatic power. It is excellent theatre, even when the music on occasion appears commonplace in inspiration. A product of the *Verismo* school of operatic writing, it employs realistic effects (even in the orchestration), and frequently with fine dramatic effect.

The libretto is by E. Golisciani and C. Zangarini. In present-day Naples, Gennaro, a worker, and Rafaele, leader of the Camorra, are rivals for the love of Maliella. When Gennaro overhears Rafaele boast that he will steal the jewels of the Madonna for Maliella—jewels on the statue of the

Madonna which is carried throughout Naples in a religious ceremony—he decides to beat his rival to the game, even though the punishment for this crime is death. Eventually, when Maliella recognizes that she is an outcast because she is the possessor of the stolen jewels, she commits suicide by jumping into the sea. Gennaro, too, realizes the immensity of his crime: he atones for it by killing himself with a knife.

The Intermezzo between the first and second acts (which, it is interesting to note, was written after the opera had been completed, and almost as an afterthought) is perhaps the most famous single part of the work.

The Jewels of the Madonna was successfully introduced at the Berlin Opera on December 23, 1911.

Schools—Styles—Techniques—
Trends—Movements—and Tendencies
in 20th-Century Music

Arcueilists: A school of modern French composers founded by Satie, which included Henri Sauguet, Roger Désormière, Henri Cliquet-Pleyel, and Maxime Jacob, and which was dedicated to simplicity.
See Satie.

Atonality: The absence of a basic tonality or key.
See Schoenberg, Berg, Webern.

Dynamism: See Neo-Primitivism.

Expressionism: The seeking of the very essence or inner soul-state of a subject through abstraction.
See Schoenberg, Berg, Webern.

Formalism (or *"Decadent" Formalism*): The charge of cerebralism leveled against leading Soviet composers by the Central Committee of the Communist Party of the U.S.S.R., on February 10, 1948.
See Prokofiev, Shostakovich.

(The) French Six (Les Six): A school of modern French composers that included Auric, Durey, Tailleferre, Honegger, Milhaud, and Poulenc.
See Honegger, Milhaud, Poulenc.

Gebrauchsmusik: Functional music.
See Hindemith, Weill.

Impressionism: The escape from realism in which emphasis is placed more on the impression or sensation aroused by a subject than on the subject itself, more on light, color, and mood than on form and substance.
See Debussy.

Italian Manifesto against Cerebral Music: A manifesto signed by several leading Italian composers (Pizzetti, Zandonai, Pick-Mangiagalli, etc.) on December 17, 1932, condemning those composers who wrote cerebral music.
See Respighi.

Jazz: Jazz techniques and styles have been exploited by many composers in works of serious artistic intent.
See Gershwin, Carpenter, Copland, Gould, Grofé.

(La) Jeune France: A school of contemporary French composers that includes Daniel-Lesur, Jolivet, and Olivier Messiaen.
See Messiaen.

Linear Music: Contrapuntal music in which the voices move independently of harmonic relationships.
See Hindemith.

Mystery: A metaphysical concept of Scriabin which was to be a synthesis of all the arts and which would embrace the whole history of mankind.
See Scriabin.

Nationalism in Music: The reflection in music of the rise of nationalism in Europe in the late nineteenth century. Composers made a conscious attempt to express national feeling in their music by banding into schools whose mission was to express their countries' backgrounds, history, culture, and people in music, and to exploit idioms derived from folk (and sometimes popular) sources.

LEADING NATIONAL SCHOOLS

Armenia. *See* Khatchaturian.
Bohemia. *See* Weinberger.
Brazil. *See* Villa-Lobos, Mignone.
Finland. *See* Sibelius.
Hungary. *See* Bartók, Kodály.
Italy. *See* Casella.
Mexico. *See* Chávez, Revueltas.
Moravia. *See* Janáček.
Poland. *See* Szymanowski.
Rumania. *See* Enesco.
Soviet Union. *See* Shostakovich.
Spain. *See* Albéniz, Falla, Turina.
Sweden. *See* Atterberg.
United States. *See* Copland, Cowell, Ives, Siegmeister.

Naturalism: See Realism, Verismo.

Neo-Baroque Music: The reversion to the contrapuntal style of the sixteenth and seventeenth centuries.
See Hindemith.

Neo-Classicism: The reversion to old classical forms and styles.
See Hindemith, Stravinsky.

Neo-Mysticism: The imposition of religious implications into music that is romantic in its expression and usually Wagnerian in idiom.
See Scriabin, Messiaen.

Neo-Primitivism: The transfer of the dynamic and elemental force of primitive music into sophisticated musical forms. (Also called "Dynamism.")
See Prokofiev, Stravinsky.

Neo-Romanticism: The reversion to the romantic ideals of the middle nineteenth century: gargantuan forms, frequently elaborate programs, and, just as frequently, philosophic or metaphysical implications
See Mahler, Busoni.

New England School of Composers: A group of New England composers who were conservative in their outlook. These included Foote, Chadwick, Gilbert, and Parker.
See Foote, Gilbert.

Political Music: Music serving to propagandize political or social dogmas.
See Blitzstein.

Polymeters: Simultaneous use of different rhythms. (Also called "Polyrhythm.")
See Stravinsky.

Polytonality: Simultaneous use of different tonalities.
See Milhaud.

"Prepared Piano": The "preparation" of a piano is an innovation of John Cage in which dampers of metal, wood, rubber, felt, etc., are stuffed between the strings of a piano, in carefully measured positions, to produce unusual percussive effects.
See Introduction.

Proletarian Music: Soviet music written for mass consumption which reflects the interests and ideologies of the people and is easily assimilable.
See Shostakovich.

Realism (or *Naturalism*): The simulation of realistic effects in music (see also *Verismo*).
See Richard Strauss.

Society for the Advancement of Proletarian Music: A society founded in the Soviet Union in 1925 to promote the principles of proletarian music (*q.v.*)
    See Shostakovich.

Soviet Musical Policies: See Formalism, Proletarian Music.

Tone Clusters: The extension of harmonic writing through the extensive use of simultaneous seconds produced on the piano keyboard by the use of fists, forearms, and the palms of the hands (or, as in the case of Ives, a ruler).
    See Cowell, Ives.

Triton: A group of French composers seeking moderation in style, including Barraud and Rivier.
    See Rivier.

Twelve-Tone System (or *Technique*): The construction of a musical work out of a set row of tones, twelve in number, according to definitely set laws.
    See Schoenberg, Berg, Webern.

Verismo: Realism or naturalism in opera, as realized by such Italian composers as Mascagni, Leoncavallo, and Puccini.
    See Puccini.

Whole-Tone Scale: A scale created out of whole tones, the octave being divided into six equal intervals.
    See Debussy.

Zeitkunst: Art that deals with contemporary themes and interprets contemporary life.
    See Weill.

Supplement

SAMUEL BARBER

VANESSA, opera (1958).

Vanessa is Samuel Barber's first opera. Fruit of his full maturity it is one of the most significant American operas of our time. Its successful première took place at the Metropolitan Opera in New York on January 15, 1958. Later the same year it received the Pulitzer Prize in music, and became the first American opera to be performed at the Salzburg Festival in Austria.

Another distinguished opera composer was responsible for the somber but always compellingly dramatic libretto: Gian-Carlo Menotti. (Menotti also served as producer of the opera in New York and Salzburg.) The setting is a Scandinavian city in 1905. In her funereal baronial manor, Vanessa has waited twenty years for the return of her lover. He is dead; but his son, Anatol, returns. Anatol seduces Vanessa's niece, Erika, offers to marry her, but is turned down because Erika knows he does not love her. Anatol finally marries Vanessa and takes her away with him. Now it is Erika's turn to inhabit the gloomy baronial manor and wait for her lover.

To his music, Barber brought not only his earlier command of writing for the voice and the breadth and dimension of his symphonic writing, but also a remarkable dramatic strength and a rare gift at projecting atmosphere and subtle moods. His style is eclectic, ranging from the sentimentality of a Puccini aria to the dissonances and atonality of an avant-garde composer; from the lilting music of the waltz and a country dance to the symphonic grandeur of a Wagner or Richard Strauss music drama. But the music always meets the demands of the text; and the result is an opera that has profound emotional impact without sacrificing the melodic and emotional values of Romantic opera.

ERNEST BLOCH

QUARTET NO. 3, for strings (1951). I. Allegro deciso. II. Adagio. III. Allegro molto. IV. Allegro.

Bloch's third string quartet was dedicated to and introduced by the Griller String Quartet in New York on January 4, 1953. In the same year it received the New York Music Critics' Circle Award. Unlike the composer's first two string quartets—which are rhapsodic in style, spacious in form, and alternate between spiritual and dynamic statements—the third quartet is for Bloch a singularly compact work making use of economical materials. While the Adagio movement finds Bloch in a recognizably introspective and poetic mood, the ensuing third movement has a light, whimsical feeling not often encountered in Bloch.

The same tendency towards terseness of expression, economy of thematic materials, and modest proportions of form prevails in Bloch's next two string quartets. The fourth and fifth string quartets were both introduced by the Griller Quartet, in 1954 and 1956 respectively.

CONCERTO GROSSO NO. 2, for string orchestra (1952). I. Maestoso; Allegro; Maestoso. II. Andante. III. Allegro. IV. Tema con variazioni.

Bloch's second concerto grosso was introduced in London by the BBC Symphony under Sir Malcom Sargent on April 11, 1953. It received the New York Music Critics' Circle Award. As in all traditional concerto-grosso writing, the technique of alternating and combining a smaller group of instruments with a larger one is followed. In the first movement an expressive Maestoso precedes and follows a dramatic fugal section. A lyrical slow movement follows without interruption. In the third movement the solo quartet is briefly separated from the main string section. The finale consists of a descending chromatic theme subjected to four variations. Bloch planned a third concerto grosso but finally expended it to symphonic dimensions and called it *Sinfonia breve* (1953).

BENJAMIN BRITTEN

TURN OF THE SCREW, opera (1954).

Henry James' eerie and at times gruesome horror story, adapted into an opera libretto by Myfanwy Piper, is the source of one of Britten's most powerful operas, a work of extraordinary musical invention and dramatic impact. Britten wrote this opera for the Venice Festival, where it was introduced on September 14, 1954. Its première in the United States took place in New York on March 19, 1958.

James' strange tale has been followed here with only minor and unimportant deviations. A curse of evil has descended upon two children, protected by a neurotic governess, and abetted by the presence of two ghosts of former servants. All efforts to protect the children result only in arousing the morbid terror of the little girl and in bringing the little boy to his death. Thus a theme familiar in so many of Britten's operas—the struggle between good and evil—is here translated into a life-and-death clash between innocence and guilt, with innocence finally sacrificed.

One of the original procedures in this opera is the preface of an orchestral sequence before each of the sixteen scenes. These interludes are actually variations on a twelve-note theme arranged in fourths and thirds, and serve the dramatic purpose of commenting orchestrally on what is transpiring on the stage. "Frequent ostinato, ingenious percussive effects and the tendency to polarize round easily recognizable chords," wrote Cynthia Jolly, "produce an almost hypnotic effect of terrifying persistence."

Turn of the Screw—like the composer's *Rape of Lucretia*—is a chamber opera of small dimensions. There are only six in the cast; and the orchestra numbers just fifteen. But economy and the reduction of all musical materials to their essentials make no sacrifice of dramatic values. In few of his operas has Britten written such high-tensioned music, so vivid in atmosphere and characterization; in few of his operas does he reveal such remarkable inventiveness of melodic and harmonic writing and such extraordinary variety of orchestral effects.

PAUL CRESTON

SYMPHONY NO. 5, op. 64 (1955). I. Con Moto. II. Largo. III. Maestoso; Allegro.

Creston's fifth symphony was written for the twenty-fifth anniversary of the National Symphony Orchestra of Washington, D.C., which introduced it on April 4, 1956, Howard Mitchell conducting. "The keynote of the emotional basis of this symphony," explains the composer, "is intensity, and the feeling is generally one of spiritual conflicts which are not resolved until the final movement." The composer goes on to explain the construction as follows: "All the thematic material stems from the series of tones presented at the very beginning by cellos and basses, evenly measured, but irregularly grouped. From these tones three definite, rhythmically patterned themes evolve: the first, aggressive and defiant; the second, lyric and impassioned (an inversion of the first theme); and the third, tender and poignant (played by the flute)."

NORMAN DELLO JOIO

MEDITATION ON ECCLESIASTES, for string orchestra (1957).

In its original version, this work was intended to be accompanied by dance. It was written for José Limon on a commission from the Juilliard School of Music. He introduced it with his own choreography in New York on April 6, 1957, Frederick Prausnitz conducting. This composition has subsequently been performed by symphony orchestras without choreography. In 1957 it received the Pulitzer Prize in music.

The music interprets verses from the opening of Chapter 3 of The Book of Ecclesiastes. The composition has twelve sections, each in one of the twelve tonalities; structurally it consists of a theme and variations. The twelve sections are: I. Introduction (Largo), "to everything there is a season and a time to every purpose under the heaven"; II. Theme (Adagio con sentimento), "a time to be born"; III. Variation I (Solenne), "and a time to die"; IV. Variation II (Soave e leggiero), "a time to plant and a time to pluck up that which is planted"; V. Variation III (Grave), "a time to kill"; VI. Variation IV (Larghetto), "and a time to heal"; VII. Variation V (Animato), "a time to break down and a time to build up"; VIII. Variation VI (Adagio), "a time to weep and mourn"; IX. Variation VII (Spumante), "a time to dance and laugh"; X. Variation VIII (Adagio liberamente), "a time to embrace and a time to refrain from embracing"; XI. Variation IX (Con brio, deciso), "a time of hate and of war"; XII. Variation X (Semplice), "a time to live and a time of peace."

DAVID DIAMOND

SYMPHONY NO. 6 (1954). I. Introduzione: Adagio interrotto; Allegro, fortemente mosso. II. Adagio interrotto. III. Deciso; Poco allegro.

Diamond's sixth symphony received its world première in Boston, Charles Munch conducting the Boston Symphony, on March 8, 1957. The most dramatic of the composer's symphonic compositions, this one utilizes the cyclic form in that all themes of all movements are related to the two themes of the first movement. The first theme, slow and stately, is heard at the very opening in oboe and English horn; the second appears in cellos and is faster and more sharply accented. The second movement is unusual in that it continually alternates slow and fast sections, its thematic material closely related to that of the introduction of the first movement. The third movement is in the form of an introduction, passacaglia and fugue. The fugato subject in the finale is based on the opening theme of the first movement, and so is its countersubject.

CARLISLE FLOYD   1926—

Carlisle Floyd has described his principles and attitudes as a composer of opera in *Musical America*: "My first consideration in attempting an opera is whether or not the subject is one in which the emotional, psychological, and philosophical concepts of the story can be externalized through action and visible situation and style retain absorbing, multi-dimensional characters. For the very reason that opera must be primarily externalized, we have erred too often, I feel, in favor of situation, leaving character development in a rather primitive, elementary state.... Also I feel it is time that we who write operas attempt to make some commentary on timeless human problems in a contemporary way, and that it is not inappropriate that an opera have a 'theme' so long as it is not tiresomely didactic."

Carlisle Floyd was born in Latta, South Carolina, on June 11, 1926. After studying piano with private teachers he received in his sixteenth year a scholarship in piano for Converse College. There he was a pupil of Ernst Bacon, with whom he continued his music study while attending Syracuse University. He also studied piano privately with Rudolf Firkusny. In 1947 he became a member of the music faculty of Florida State University in Tallahassee, where he has remained since. He wrote two operas—*Slow Dusk* in 1949 and *Fugitives* in 1951—before achieving fame with *Susannah*. Since *Susannah* he has written *Wuthering Heights,* which received its world première in Santa Fe, New Mexico, in the summer of 1958.

SUSANNAH, musical drama (1954).
Susannah, the opera with which its composer achieved nationwide success, was introduced by the Florida State University in Tallahassee, Florida on February 24, 1955. A year and a half later, on September 27, 1956, it was produced by the New York City Opera with tremendous success, receiving soon thereafter the New York Music Critics' Circle Award. In the summer of 1958, it was given at the Brussels Exposition in Belgium.

The composer wrote his own libretto. The central theme is, as the composer explains, "persecution and the concomitant psychological ramifications." The setting is a farm in New Hope Valley, in the mountains of Tennessee, in the present day. The heroine lives with her brother, Sam. She is held in suspect by her townspeople because she is so seductively beautiful, and because one day she is caught bathing nude in a nearby creek. Susannah thus is victimized by merciless gossip until it begins to destroy her spirit. Concerned over her soul, Reverend Blitch calls on her. Relieved at being able to pour out her grievances and bitterness to the Reverend, Susannah becomes sympathetic to his suddenly bold advances. When Susannah's brother, Sam, learns what has happened he kills the preacher, even as the latter is praying for Susannah's understanding and forgiveness. The crowd advances menacingly on Susannah to destroy her with its hatred, but is kept in check by Susannah with a shotgun. As the final curtain descends, Susannah is left alone, standing in the doorway of her farm, a forlorn and tragic figure.

Through the consistent use of hymn tunes, arias with a folk-song identity, and square dances, Floyd endowed his score with a rich American flavor, which is perhaps its main appeal. The opera opens with a hoedown; the first appearance of Reverend Blitch is greeted with a four-part American hymn; Sam's "Jaybird Song" is in the recognizable idiom of an American folk song. But Floyd's operatic style is also often rooted in the more traditional style of Puccini and Wagner: Puccini in some of the arias (as in Susannah's moving refrain, "Ain't it a Pretty Sight," for example), Wagner in the exploitation of the *Leitmotiv* technique. Floyd also owes a debt to the moderns, in his skillful use of the *Sprechstimme,* in his use of sung dialogue against a persistent musical background by the orchestra, and in his equally effective employment of polytonality and dissonance to heighten the dramatic impact of some of the more tragic episodes of his opera. "The story as I conceived it," said the composer, "seemed to me to be explosive with theatrical potential and forseeable situations which would lend themselves to musical treatment and exploitation." The strength of Floyd's opera, and the reason for its immense popularity, is that he always found the proper musical treatment and exploitation for the demands of his play and its characters and situations.

HOWARD HANSON

SYMPHONY NO. 5, "SINFONIA SACRA" (1954).

In his fifth symphony, Hanson interprets musically the story of the first Easter as told in The Gospel According to St. John. The composer, however, does not tell this story programmatically, but, as he explains, attempts "to invoke some of the atmosphere of tragedy and triumph, mysticism and affirmation of this story which is the essential symbol of the Christian faith." In a single movement, this symphony is in the style of the Gregorian chant, but no chants are quoted directly. "Mr. Hanson," explained Olin Downes in the *New York Times,* "is not trying to go archaic.... He has himself invented his themes, integrating them, technically speaking, in a more or less contrapuntal style throughout." The symphony was introduced in New York on February 22, 1955, Eugene Ormandy conducting the Philadelphia Orchestra.

ROY HARRIS

SYMPHONY NO. 7 (1955).

The first version of Harris' seventh Symphony was introduced in the summer of 1952, when it received the Naumburg Prize. In 1955, Harris revised it extensively, a definitive version in which it received its world première in Copenhagen, on September 15, 1955, Eugene Ormandy conducting. In a single movement, the symphony employs an idiom based on the twelve-tone technique. The composer goes on to explain: "in one sense it is a dance symphony; in another sense it is a study in harmonic and melodic rhythmic variation. The first half is a passacaglia with five variations. The second half is divided into three sections—contrapuntal variations in assymetrical rhythms; contrapuntal variations in symmetrical meter, and further statement and development of the preceding two sections, wherein the original passacaglia theme is restated in large augmentation and orchestration, while ornamentation develops the melodic and rhythmic materials of the second section. A final variation of the rhythmic materials of the work serves as a coda.... The first half of the work is contemplative and traditional, predominantly harmonic in technique; however with each successive variation, the mood becomes more dynamic and rhythmically free.... The second half of the work is an expression of merry-making America, predominantly contrapuntal in technique; however, the return of the passacaglia subject in the third section brings back the mood of contemplation which is absorbed in the vigorous coda. In this work I have hoped to communicate the spirit of affirmation as a declaration of faith in Mankind."

PAUL HINDEMITH

DIE HARMONIE DER WELT, symphony (1950). I. Musica Instrumentalis. II. Musica Humana. III. Musica Mundane.

Hindemith's symphony was derived from his score to an opera of the same name, introduced in Munich on August 11, 1957. The setting of the opera is the Thirty Years' War, and its principal character is the renowned astronomer and mathematician, Johannes Kepler. "This is ... no opera in the usual sense," wrote Everett Helm, "but rather a pageant of events and conditions.... Kepler is treated almost symbolically, as are other figures as well. A strong philosophical speculative and ethical tendency underlies and motivates the work. It is in a sense a grandiose essay in music on the subject of cosmic order."

The symphony was first heard in Basel, Switzerland, on January 24, 1952, Paul Sacher conducting. The first movement describes Kepler's unhappy childhood; the second discourses on his spiritual evolution; and the third, a passacaglia, treats of his mundane existence.

DMITRI KABALEVSKY

SYMPHONY NO. 4 (1956). I. Lento; Allegro molto e fuoco. II. Largo. III. Scherzo. IV. Lento; Allegro.

Kabalevsky's fourth symphony is a work of consistently dramatic character. The composer has hinted that it is autobiographical but he has failed to assign specific programmatic interpretations for the music. The symphony received its American première on October 31, 1957, Dimitri Mitropoulos conducting the New York Philharmonic, soon after its world première in the Soviet Union. The work is well integrated; material from the first movement recurs in one guise or another in succeeding movements, and is used to bring the symphony to a rousing culmination in the concluding Allegro.

BOHUSLAV MARTINU

PARABLES, for orchestra (1958). I. The Parable of Sculpture. II. The Parable of a Garden. III. The Parable of a Labyrinth.

Martinu dedicated *Parables* to Charles Munch, who presented its world première with the Boston Symphony in February 1959. The first two parables were inspired by Antoine de St. Exupéry's *Citadella;* the third by Georges Neveux' *Voyage de Thesée.* In the first parable the composer speaks of the way in which sculpture arouses in the observer the impulse that led to the creation of a work of art. The second is atmospheric impressionistic writing explaining that the cycle from fruit to seed and rebirth as part of life's plan. The third speaks for the strength of man to conquer a monster and also of his softness before a woman.

GIAN-CARLO MENOTTI

THE SAINT OF BLEECKER STREET, opera (1954).

The Saint of Bleecker Street was introduced at the Broadway Theater, New York, on December 27, 1954, Thomas Schippers conducting. It was acclaimed by the critics both for the tense drama of the libretto (as usual with Menotti, his own) and the effective musical setting. Brooks Atkinson called it "the most powerful drama of the season," and Olin Downes reported that the music "dexterously underscores every word of dialogue, and every instant of action." *The Saint of Bleecker Street* received the Drama Critics' Award as the best play of the year, the Music Critics' Circle Award as the best opera, and the Pulitzer Prize in music.

The setting is the Italian quarter of New York City; the time, the present. Annina, who lives on Bleecker Street, is a sickly girl who is a religious mystic. When she receives the stigmata on her palms, she inspires the religious devotion of all her Catholic neighbors. But her brother, Michele, is an agnostic who regards all religious dogma as superstition. Devoted to Annina, he tries vainly to convert her to his irreligious ways. His sweetheart, Desideria, is jealous of Michele's attachment to his sister. In a bitter fight that ensues between them Michele kills Desideria and is forced to go into hiding. But he cannot resist the temptation of returning to Bleecker Street to attend the festive ceremonies in which Annina is accepted by the Church as the Bride of Christ. Thus he is a witness when Annina, overwhelmed by the emotional experience and joy during the ceremony, falls dead.

As in his earlier musical dramas, Menotti skilfully combines contemporary techniques and idioms—with which he projects the tensions and the gripping dramatic climaxes of his play—with a lyricism that often has the sentiment and the tenderness of Puccini. Together with vividly realistic writing, the score embraces florid songs that mingle humor with emotion (the three wedding songs in the second act), humorous ditties (Corona's tune in the third act), dance tunes (the juke-box melody in the second act), gripping recitatives (the Saint's stirring narrative in the opening scene) and religious chants (the San Gennaro procession in the first act).

THE UNICORN, THE GORGON, AND THE MANTICORE, chamber opera (1956).

Subtitled "The Three Sundays of a Poet," and described as a "madrigal fable," this intimate and charming chamber opera represents a radical departure in technique and style from the more grim and realistic dramas for which the composer has become famous. The work requires a chorus, ten dancers and nine instruments; and the score embraces an introduction, twelve madrigals almost in the style of Monteverdi and often a cappella, and six orchestral interludes.

The central character is a lonely, retiring poet who is looked upon with suspicion by his neighbors. One day he emerges from his solitary castle retreat to lead a pet unicorn in a Sunday promenade. The women of the town now demand of their husbands pet unicorns of their own. But on another Sunday the poet emerges with a pet manticore, and after that with a pet gorgon, always to the envy of the women who want similar pets. The three pets are at the poet's death bed—symbolizing, in turn, the poet's youth, middle age, and old age—as the poet, with his last dying words, upbraids his neighbors for their foolishness in trying to feel what other men have suffered and who are the destroyers of the poet's dreams.

The chamber opera was introduced at the Coolidge Foundation Festival in Washington, D.C., on October 21, 1956.

MARIA GOLOVIN, musical drama (1958).

In *Maria Golovin* we once again find those ingredients for which the composer has long been famous and which add up to compelling theater: melodrama and suspense; a principal character who is physically afflicted, and who with the others is subjected to violent emotional torment; penetrating psychological insight; an eclectic style that wanders freely from enchanting Italian-like lyricism (such as the love music of the third act and the trio in the second) and formal arias and ensemble numbers, to realistic tone painting, programmatic writing, and dramatic recitatives. The setting is a town near a European frontier; the time, a few years after "a recent war." Maria Golovin, a wealthy and attractive woman, is the wife of a man who for four years has been a prisoner of war. She has found a home with her son in an apartment in a villa owned by Donato, a blind maker of bird cages. Since both she and Donato are emotionally starved, they fall in love. The affair fills the blind man with an all-consuming apprehension for the future, and with self doubts. When Maria's husband is released from prison, she informs Donato she is leaving him to reestablish a home with her husband for the sake of their son. As she leaves, Donato fires a shot at her, but misses aim. However, he is deluded into believing he has killed her and that no other man will ever possess her.

Maria Golovin was commissioned by NBC for the Brussels Exposition in Belgium, where it was introduced on August 20, 1958. On November 5, 1958 it received its American première at the Martin Beck Theater but was able to survive only five performances. Nevertheless, early in 1959 it was presented over television by NBC and shortly thereafter revived by the New York City Opera Company.

DARIUS MILHAUD

SYMPHONY NO. 6 (1955). I. Calme et tendre. II. Tumultueux. III. Lent et doux. IV. Joyeux et robuste.

Milhaud was commissioned to write this symphony by the Koussevitzky Foundation for the 75th anniversary of the Boston Symphony. That orchestra, under Charles Munch, introduced it in Boston on October 7, 1955. The first movement, in 6/4 time, has two ingratiating lyric ideas. The first appears immediately in the strings, while the second is heard in a fuller orchestra. A lively movement follows, mainly in full orchestra, but it ends in a subdued vein to prepare the emotional climate for the third movement. That movement is a highly lyrical section in traditional three-part song form; its middle section is dominated by a chromatic subject in 3/4 time. Vigor returns in the finale with a stout, joyous theme for full orchestra in 12/8 time and continues in this energetic fashion until the conclusion of the symphony.

DOUGLAS MOORE

THE BALLAD OF BABY DOE, opera (1957).

This American folk opera was commissioned by the Koussevitzky Foundation in honor of the centennial of Columbia University. The world première took place at Central City, Colorado, on July 7, 1957, with Emerson Buckley conducting. The following April 3 it was successfully introduced in New York by the New York City Opera Company.

The libretto, by John Latouche, is based on historical fact. The setting is Leadville, Colorado, during the gold-rush days of the late 19th century. Two central characters are Horatio Tabor and his wife, Augusta, who came to Colorado to prospect for gold and who for many years have suffered the direst poverty. Finally, Horatio becomes a partner in a rich silver mine and becomes a millionaire and a powerful political figure. It is at this point that he deserts his wife to marry a blond beauty from Wisconsin, Baby Doe. Towards the end of the century, Tabor loses all his wealth and power when government legislation impoverishes all the silver-mine owners of Colorado. But Baby Doe sticks with him faithfully and uncomplainingly until his death in 1899. For thirty-six years after that she lives alone in a shack at the worthless silver mine left her by her husband. There she froze to death in 1935.

"The score," wrote Howard Taubman in the *New York Times,* "makes no attempt to pursue advanced techniques. It is full of tunes; it seeks to sing at all times.... In jubilation or sorrow it scales no heights. But it provides scenes of atmosphere and feeling. It serves the story well enough to cause it to hold the interest firmly." And in a later review, Mr. Taubman added: "At its liveliest it is just as gay as a musical comedy, and it has the advantage of dealing sympathetically with characters one can believe in. Since it is an opera, it does not hesitate to probe as deeply as it can into the emotions of its people."

CARL ORFF

Orff is one of the most original, forceful and inventive composers for the contemporary stage. He believes that music, in the long-accepted classical or romantic traditions, has come to the end of its development; that the contemporary composer must seek out new forms, new avenues of expression. He also feels that the stage is the only fruitful medium of artistic self-expression left to the present-day composer. Therefore since 1935—when he completely disowned and withdrew everything he had written up to then—he has dedicated himself exclusively to the stage. His most significant operas are almost elementary in technique, style, approaches and idioms, in a conscious effort to reduce the stage and its appurtenances to their barest essentials. His musical writing is equally bare and primitive, consisting mainly of a rhythmic declamation (often unaccompanied) that utilizes rapidly repeated notes and a primary melodic, harmonic, and rhythmic vocabulary.

Orff was born in Munich, Germany, on July 10, 1895. He was graduated from the Munich Academy of Music in 1914, and several years later continued his study of composition with Heinrich Kaminski. In 1925 he founded the Gunther School of Music in Munich and became conductor of the Bavarian Theater Orchestra. Between 1925 and 1935 he wrote some instrumental and vocal music which in 1935 he discarded completely to embark upon a new direction in his writing; this new direction took place with *Carmina Burana,* the first of a trilogy of operas collectively entitled *Trionfi.* Since then Orff has relentlessly pursued his goal with a passionate single-mindedness. His later operas have been *Antigone* (1949) and *Astututli* (1953).

TRIONFI, a trilogy of operas including "Carmina Burana," "Catulli Carmina" and "Trionfo di Afrodite" (1937-1951).

Trionfi is made up of three works. The first is *Carmina Burana,* a scenic oratorio based on 13th-century medieval poems of unknown authorship found in a Bavarian monastery. The text—by the composer in medieval Latin, and partly in medieval German—concerns the activities of itinerant students as jesters. It is made up of three parts: "Springtime," "In the Tavern" and "The Court of Love." Scored for soprano and baritone solos, small chorus, and a large orchestra, this work is the last word in simplicity and economy, both in text and music. Orff did not specify in his score the precise nature of the scenery, costuming or staging required, leaving such matters entirely in the hands of producers. *Carmina Burana* was first performed in Frankfort, Germany, on June 8, 1937.

Catulli Carmina, the second work in this trilogy, is a dramatic ballet accompanied entirely by a cappella choruses, with the exception of an instrumental prelude and postlude by four pianos and percussion. The text is based on poems by Catullus and is entirely in classic Latin. This work was introduced in Leipzig on November 6, 1943.

Trionfo di Afrodite, the concluding work, is a scenic cantata that was given its world première in Milan on February 13, 1953. The text, in Latin and Greek, was derived from a Latin poem by Catullus and Greek poems by Sappho and Euripides.

In discussing Orff's unorthodox musical style, Henry Pleasants wrote: "Orff has retreated to the Middle Ages and even to the Greeks, turning his back on the entire fund of harmonic, polyphonic, rhythmic and instrumental resources inherited by the contemporary composer.... He confines himself to the simplest melodic and rhythmic patterns, often reminiscent of Gregorian chants. There is no thematic development in any conventional sense, no counterpoint, no polyphony, and nothing but the barest diatonic and modal harmonies."

GOFFREDO PETRASSI   1904—

Petrassi's earlier works were in a neo-classical idiom. Eventually he turned to the twelve-tone technique with which he has become one of Italy's most vital musical creators. He uses this system not dogmatically but freely, always keeping in mind musical rather than orthodox values.

He was born in Zagarolo, Italy, on July 16, 1904. In his twenty-first year he entered the Santa Cecilia Academy, where his formal musical training began. He first attracted interest with a work in neo-classical style, a Partita for orchestra, heard at the International Society for Contemporary Music Festival in 1933. His major works after that were in the twelve-tone technique and included numerous orchestral, chamber-music, and piano compositions. In 1939 he became professor of composition at the Santa Cecilia Academy; from 1947 to 1950 he was director of the Accademia Filarmonic Romana; and since 1950 he has served as superintendent of the Teatro La Fenice in Venice. He paid his first visit to the United States in 1955.

CONCERTO NO. 5, for orchestra (1955). I. Molto moderato; Presto. II. Andante tranquillo; Mosso con vivicita; Lento e grave.

This work was commissioned by the Koussevitzky Foundation for the 75th anniversary of the Boston Symphony, which introduced it in Boston on December 2, 1955, Charles Munch conducting. In writing works for orchestra Petrassi has shunned the symphonic form, preferring to write orchestral concertos. But unlike the classical concerto grosso, these works contain no solo or concertino passages; and the style is in the twelve-tone technique. The first two movements are based on two fundamental themes comprising the twelve-tone series. The first theme is heard in a six-note sequence in the opening of the first movement, in violas *ponticello;* the remaining six-note sequence occurs in muted trumpet. The second theme is derived from the composer's own *Coro di Morti.* The second movement uses the second six-note sequence. The concerto ends serenely.

WALTER PISTON

SYMPHONY NO. 6 (1955). I. Fluendo espressivo. II. Leggerissimo vivace. III. Adagio sereno. IV. Allegro energico.

Piston's sixth symphony was commissioned by the Koussevitzky Foundation for the 75th anniversary of the Boston Symphony. That orchestra, under Charles Munch, introduced it in Boston on November 25, 1955. The composer provides the following succinct description of his music: "The first movement is flowing and expressive in sonata form; the second, a scherzo, is light and fast; the third, a serene adagio, has theme one played by solo cello and theme two by flute; and the fourth is an energetic finale with two contrasting themes."

ILDEBRANDO PIZZETTI

ASSASSINIO NELLA CATTEDRALE (MURDER IN THE CATHEDRAL), opera (1958).

This is Pizzetti's most important opera since *Fra Gherardo*. Its première took place at La Scala in Milan on March 1, 1958, and was a success of major proportions. The American première took place at Carnegie Hall, New York, on September 17, 1958. The text is the famous poetical drama of T. S. Eliot, adapted into Italian by Alberto Castelli. The central character is the 12th-century Archbishop, Thomas à Becket, who was assassinated in Canterbury Cathedral. While the action of the opera often proves static, and dramatic interest sometimes tends to lag, Pizzetti's musical writing achieves such power and poetic eloquence that the opera remains throughout a compelling emotional experience.

Most of the opera is written in a skilful accompanied recitative style which succeeds magically in capturing the mystical mood of the play. But the melodic element is not altogether absent, and is found particularly in the moving arias of the Archbishop at the end of the first act, and of the First Corifea at the beginning of the second. But as in Pizzetti's earlier operas, the most significant music is reserved for the chorus, for the moving choruses of the priests and of the Canterbury women. "It may be doubted," wrote Francis Toye, "whether he has ever done anything better.... The fear, the misery and the horror of the women are reflected to perfection in their music."

QUINCY PORTER

CONCERTO FOR TWO PIANOS AND ORCHESTRA (1953).

This concerto, with which Porter won the Pulitzer Prize in music in 1954, was commissioned by the Louisville Orchestra in Kentucky, which introduced it on March 17, 1954, Robert Whitney conducting, with Dorothea Adkins and Ann Monks as soloists. The work is a unified one-movement composition which, as Howard Boatwright has written, "maintains tensions and variety by juxtaposition of expressive and lyrical elements and dance-like or energetic rhythmic elements." Mr. Boatwright goes on to explain: "Its pattern, in the broader sense, consists of a series of interruptions—the energetic elements interrupt the lyrical elements, and the lyrical element suddenly appears as the energetic sections come to abrupt endings.... But the real organization of this work is not a series of contrasting and thematically unrelated sectional blocks. It is ... a fluidly conceived, subtly interrelated construction on the basis of a few simple motives. These motives appeared in varied disguises and forms throughout the whole piece—fast and slow, loud and soft, tender and wild." The tempo markings of the various sections are: Lento; Poco allegro; Lento; Allegro; Lento; Allegro.

FRANCIS POULENC

LES DIALOGUES DES CARMÉLITES, opera (1957).

The Dialogues of the Carmélites is Poulenc's first full-length tragic opera, and it is one of his unqualified masterworks. This is music of exalted character, an opera suffused with religious ardor and spiritual exaltation. Utilizing a continuous lyric line which reaches heights in the "Ave Maria" of the second act and the "Salve Regina" of the closing scene—and which makes ample use of fully developed arias—Poulenc has produced a drama touched with radiance and which progresses towards a shattering conclusion with unrelenting dramatic force.

The libretto by Georges Bernanos was inspired by a novel by Gertrud von Le Fort and a motion-picture scenario by Philippe Agostini and the Rev. F. P. Bruckberger. With the French Revolution as the setting, the opera concerns the tragic fate of sixteen nuns who prefer to meet death rather than dissolve their order. These are dedicated women, to be sure, but women with weaknesses as well as strength, and with doubts as well as faith. One of the main characters is the Mother Superior who succumbs to paralyzing fear when she must meet her death; by contrast, a noblewoman, who has become a nun because of her distaste for the outside world, proves herself a heroine at the guillotine.

The opera received a triumphant world première at La Scala in Milan on January 26, 1957, and soon thereafter was performed throughout the world of music. The American première took place in San Francisco in a performance by the San Francisco Opera on September 22, 1957. In 1958, the opera was telecast by NBC, and it received the New York Music Critics' Circle Award as the best new opera of the year. Howard Taubman in the *New York Times* described it as "one of the most impressive pieces for the lyric theater in our time.... One is bound to admire the delicacy and taste of Poulenc's music. In its finest moments it sings with radiance."

WILLIAM SCHUMAN

CREDENDUM, for orchestra (1955).

Commissioned by the United States National Commission for UNESCO, *Credendum* received its world première in Cincinnati, with Thor Johnson conducting the Cincinnati Symphony, on November 4, 1955. The composition opens with a majestic statement (a prelude which the composer designated as a "Declaration"). This leads into an equally impressive chorale. This material is developed dramatically and carried to a powerful climax. The work ends with a forceful scherzo section.

NEW ENGLAND TRIPTYCH, suite for orchestra (1956).

On several occasions Schuman has utilized material from the music of William Billings, the famous American 18th-century composer of psalms and fuguing tunes and of "Chester," often described as the *Marseillaise* of the American Revolution. The *New England Triptych* utilizes Billings' melodies most freely, merely as a point of departure for Schuman's own musical thinking; and, consequently, it is more Schuman than Billings that we find in this work. The first part of the triptych utilizes Billings' anthem, "Be Glad America," and reaches an impressive climax. This is followed by music based on Billings' "When Jesus Wept," and on "Chester." Since "Chester" had started out as a religious hymn and was only later adapted by Billings into a war song with new lyrics, Schuman makes a point in his own elaboration to emphasize both the religious and the martial character of this music.

This work was commissioned by André Kostelanetz, who directed its world première in Miami, Florida, on October 28, 1956.

DMITRI SHOSTAKOVICH

SYMPHONY NO. 10 IN E MINOR (1953). I. Moderato. II. Allegro. III. Allegretto; Lento; Allegretto. IV. Andante; Allegro.

SYMPHONY NO. 11 IN G MINOR, "1905" (1957). I. Palace Square (Adagio). II. January 9 (Allegro). III. Eternal Memory (Adagio). IV. Alarm (Allegro non troppo).

Shostakovich's tenth symphony was his first new work in that form in almost eight years. It was introduced in Leningrad on December 17, 1953, Eugene Mravinsky conducting, and in 1954 received the New York Music Critics' Circle Award. The composer has explained he hoped to make his music express the "thoughts and aspirations of our contemporaries," and specifically their thoughts about and aspirations for peace. But he did not provide a specific program. The work opens with a slow introduction in which a six-note theme is prominent in cellos and basses; this subject recurs several times throughout the symphony. After fifty measures, the pace quickens and a lyric thought is projected by the clarinets. A more rhythmic idea, in flutes, but equally lyrical, is still another important subject in this movement. The brief scherzo that follows as a second movement is brisk, rhythmic and charged with motor energy. Then comes the slow movement, opening with a folk-song like melody in strings in imitation. A solo horn is later answered by the strings in a new version of the six-note opening theme. There then ensues a poetic nocturne in which a horn solo over plucked strings is prominent. This is followed by an English horn giving important treatment to the opening material of the movement. The finale opens leisurely and meditatively with an oboe solo of Oriental character. The main theme that follows is a martial melody. There then take place a brief recall of material from the scherzo and slow movements, and a final repetition of the six-note motive, after which the work rushes on towards an exciting conclusion.

In his eleventh symphony, descriptive titles for each of the four movements provide a clue to the music's intent. In writing the symphony in commemoration of the Russian Revolution of 1905, for whose fiftieth anniversary this work was commissioned, Shostakovich placed considerable emphasis on virile, martial-like melodies, brass fanfares, and percussion effects imitating the marching of men and the firing of shots. The symphony comes to a theatrical conclusion with a finale dramatized by the pealing of chimes. For his melodic material, the composer drew from folk songs and the songs of the Revolution; also from two themes expropriated from his own earlier works written to honor the same revolution. This symphony was introduced in Moscow on October 30, 1957, Nathan Rakhin conducting.

CONCERTO IN A MINOR, for violin and orchestra, op. 99 (1955). I. Nocturne (Moderato). II. Scherzo (Allegro). III. Passacaglia (Andante). IV. Burlesca (Allegro con brio).

Shostakovich wrote this violin concerto for David Oistrakh who introduced it in Leningrad on October 29, 1955, Eugene Mravinsky conducting. One of the unusual features of this work is its four movements; another, its sensitive and transparent scoring, through the omission of heavy brass and emphasis on such instruments as the celesta, harp and xylophone.

The main thought of the first movement comes after a Moderato opening when the violin presents a flowing melody in shifting meters against a contrapuntal background of a bassoon. In the scherzo, a light subject for flute and bass clarinet, with interpolations by the solo violin, provides the first main subject. A change of key brings on a dynamic and dramatic episode, after which the earlier graceful material is brought back by the solo violin. The third movement, a passacaglia, is built from an ostinato subject in cellos and basses answered by horns. The violin appears with a sustained song. In the cadenza considerable prominence is given to the ostinato figure. The finale enters without pause. A gay dance-like tune in orchestra, in the composer's identifiable vein of mockery, appears in the orchestra. From then on, the music progresses with numerous brilliant virtuoso passages for the violin and dramatic episodes for the orchestra.

IGOR STRAVINSKY

CANTICUM SACRUM, cantata (1956).

Stravinsky was commissioned to write his cantata by the Venice Festival in honor of St. Mark, patron saint of Venice. The world première took place in Venice on April 11, 1956, the composer conducting. The *Canticum Sacrum ad Honorem Sancti Marci Nominis* (as the full title reads) is an economically conceived work, transparent in instrumentation, spare in material, and in the "serial technique" to which the composer had now become partial. It is scored for tenor, baritone, choirs, organ, and an unorthodox orchestra made up of flute, three oboes, three bassoons, four trumpets, four trombones, harp, violas and basses. The text is in Latin and was chosen by the composer from the Vulgate. "The work," wrote a reviewer in *Musical America,* "continually exploits different combinations of solo sonorities—the instruments and voices almost never being scored in tutti.... The dedication, sung in duet by tenor and baritone with two trombones, as well as the monumental opening and closing choirs, are diatonic. The first choir, which opens in typical Stravinskian fashion, is reflected in retrograde by the final one, the work ending on a low note from the bassoon. These two solid bastions, invoking the command to teach the Gospel, flank the three more mystical inner sections, written in the twelve-tone technique, which are concerned with spiritual faith.... The beautiful tenor solo, 'Surge Aquillo'...and the introspective baritone solo...ending in 'Credo, Credo'...surround the central section for choirs and instruments—itself subdivided into three parts extolling Charity, Hope and Faith. Here are short organ interludes in passacaglia form ...which make effective, beautiful points of repose in the intricate choral counterpoint."

AGON, ballet (1957).

Agon is a classic ballet on the subject of a Greek dance competition, the word "Agon" being a Greek term for contest or struggle. The ballet, however, is devoid of any further plot or program, and is presented without decor or costumes. The music has also been reduced to barest melodic and harmonic essentials. It is based upon classic dance melodies uncovered by the composer in a 17th-century French dance manual, including the Sarabande, Galliard, and Bransle. The idiom is in the "serial technique." The ballet was commissioned by the Rockefeller Foundation, and received its first performance in New York on December 1, 1957, by the New York City Ballet. When the ballet-suite is given at symphony concerts, the entire eighteen-minute ballet score is used, and not merely excerpts.

ERNST TOCH

SYMPHONY NO. 3, op. 75 (1955).

One of the unusual features of this unusual symphony is its instrumentation. Two instruments never before used in a symphonic work are required to produce sounds never before heard in a concert hall. One of these is a tank of carbon dioxide that produces a hissing sound through a valve; the other, a wooden box in which croquet balls are set into motion to create a percussion sound by a rotating crank. Both these "instruments" are used backstage. In addition the score calls for a Hammond organ, a pipe organ, an Armonicon (glass harmonica), and tuned glass bells, besides the usual orchestra.

The mood of the music is suggested by a quotation from Goethe's *The Sorrows of Werther* appended to the score: "Indeed am I but a wanderer, a pilgrim on earth—what else are you?" Two sections of the symphony are lyrical, one is dramatic. The composer explains his structure as a kind of "ballistic curve with an initial impulse, a steady line, and then a decline," found in each of the three sections.

The symphony was introduced by the Pittsburgh Symphony, William Steinberg conducting, on December 2, 1955. In 1956 it received the Pulitzer Prize in music.

RALPH VAUGHAN WILLIAMS

SINFONIA ANTARTICA (1952). I. Prelude. II. Scherzo. III. Landscape. IV. Intermezzo. V. Epilogue.

SYMPHONY NO. 8 IN D MINOR (1956). I. Fantasia. II. Scherzo alla marcia. III. Cavatina. IV. Toccata.

SYMPHONY NO. 9 IN E MINOR (1957). I. Moderato maestoso. II. Andante sostenuto. III. Scherzo: allegro pesante. IV. Andante tranquillo.

In 1949, Vaughan Williams wrote the music for *Scott of the Antarctic,* a motion picture based on the ill-fated expedition of Sir Robert Scott to the South Pole in 1911-1912. The music was intended specifically to reflect the unspoken thoughts of the men as they made the journey, and symbolically to voice the spiritual qualities of man which enable him to "defy power which seems omnipotent." Much of the effect of the music came from its capacity to project the mood and atmosphere of the frozen landscape through austere tone colors and sounds produced by a large orchestra supplemented by a piano, organ, celesta, vibraphone, xylophone, glockenspiel, and wind machine. Vaughan Williams adapted this film music into a symphony, his seventh, utilizing a wordless soprano solo and a female voice choir as well as the large orchestra. It was introduced in Manchester on January 15, 1953, Sir John Barbirolli conducting. The opposition of man and Nature is portrayed in the opening Prelude and concluding Epilogue. The Scherzo and Intermezzo represent pictures of animals found in the Antarctic regions, including the lumbering whales and the cumbersome penguins. The Landscape movement is a picture of the icy regions.

The eighth symphony, introduced in Manchester on May 2, 1956, is unusual in structure. The first movement represents a series of variations, not on any given theme, but on isolated figures. After a rhythmic, airy scherzo, scored entirely for winds, comes a slow movement outstanding for lyric expressiveness and scored for strings. The finale is remarkable for its dramatic impact, heightened through the elaborate use of percussion, including gongs and bells.

The Ninth was Vaughan Williams' last symphony; it received its world première in London on April 2, 1958, Sir Malcolm Sargent conducting the Royal Philharmonic. The scoring here requires three saxophones and a fluegel-horn in B-flat (a kind of keyed bugle) besides the usual large orchestra. This symphony is a personal utterance, sometimes described as the composer's summation of his artistic faith and principles. This is not music of faith or optimism, but music of brooding despair. A haunting melody in the first movement recurs in various guises throughout the work. In the slow and eloquent finale there is sounded most strongly the voice of despair, and almost as if aware of this pessimism the composer added after the final bar the single word "niente" ("nothing").

HEITOR VILLA-LOBOS

CONCERTO NO. 2 IN A MINOR, for cello and orchestra (1955). I. Allegro non troppo. II. Molto andante cantabile. III. Vivace. IV. Allegro energico.

In the twelve-measure introduction to the first movement the woodwind and strings suggest a subject that is amplified into a dramatic statement by the solo cello. After an extended development, the solo cello also presents the second theme, a lyric idea contrasting the mood of the first theme. In the second movement, flutes, clarinets, muted strings and brass create the proper mood with which to introduce a beautiful folk-song-like melody of rhapsodic character in the solo cello. A light and capricious scherzo that culminates in a cadenza leads without pause to the finale in which principal material from the first and second movements are recalled. A powerful momentum is then built up through varied rhythms, contrasting meters and expanding sonorities.

The concerto received its world première in New York on February

5, 1955. Aldo Parisot was the soloist and Walter Hendl conducted the New York Philharmonic.

SYMPHONY NO. 11 (1955). I. Allegro moderato. II. Largo. III. Scherzo: molto vivace. IV. Molto allegro.

This work was commissioned by the Koussevitzky Foundation for the 75th anniversary of the Boston Symphony, which introduced it in Boston on March 2, 1956, the composer conducting. A stately subject for full orchestra leads to the main theme of the first movement in strings. The second main theme comes later in horns and trumpets over ostinato figures in strings and harp. The melody of the second movement is assigned to the flutes; a second section then begins with a subject in bass clarinet which is soon taken over by various woodwind instruments, a violin solo, and brass. The scherzo movement is made up of a succession of woodwind solo passages. The finale consists mainly of a vigorous, strongly accented subject developed with considerable force by the full orchestra.

WILLIAM WALTON

TROILUS AND CRESSIDA, opera (1954).

It took Sir William Walton seven years to complete his first opera. The libretto by Christopher Hassall was based on Chaucer's adaptation of the medieval romance. Though Troilus and Cressida are in love, Cressida goes against her will into the enemy camp to become the queen of the Greek commander. All efforts by the lovers to reunite are frustrated, and in the end Troilus is killed by Cressida's father, who has defected to the enemy, and Cressida commits suicide.

Though the dramatic element is pronounced in the text, and is heightened in the music through orchestral and vocal devices and an expert use of the *Leitmotiv* technique, the lyric element is the one the composer has exploited most fully. "It is not afraid to sing," reported Howard Taubman of the opera. "The roles of Troilus and Cressida have sustained lyric passages integrated in such a way that they cannot be called set arias. These passages have a restrained sweetness and are noble in character." Thus perhaps the most moving and eloquent moment in the opera is the love scene in the second act, with its impassioned orchestral interlude to provide an appropriate commentary.

The opera was introduced in London on December 3, 1954. The American première took place at the San Francisco Opera on October 7, 1955.

CONCERTO FOR CELLO AND ORCHESTRA (1956). I. Moderato. II. Allegro appassionato. III. Lento; Allegro molto; Adagio.

Walton wrote his cello concerto for Gregor Piatigorsky, who introduced it in Boston with the Boston Symphony on January 25, 1957, Charles Munch conducting. The composer described the first movement as "lyrical and melodic." The soloist projects a lengthy lyrical discourse over divided strings and a harp chord. The tempo then quickens and the mood becomes dramatized, but the lyrical element is soon reassertive. About the second movement the composer has said that it is "technically more spectacular," based as it is on a perpetual-motion kind of rhythmic theme in the solo cello. The finale incorporates within itself the slow movement of the concerto, with an expressive melody for the solo instrument over a transparent accompaniment in an opening Lento section. An ascending passage in the solo instrument brings on the full orchestra with a section consisting of a theme and four improvisations. The second and fourth improvisations are for the solo cello alone. The fourth leads to an epilogue based on ideas from the first and third movements. The concerto ends quietly and majestically.

PARTITA, for orchestra (1957).

This work was commissioned by the Cleveland Orchestra for its fortieth anniversary, and it was introduced in Cleveland on January 30, 1958, George Szell conducting. This is virtuoso music for orchestra made up of three sections: Toccata, Pastorale Siciliana, and Giga Burlesca. Dazzling writing for orchestral forces is combined with witty statements in the flanking sections, with a welcome contrast provided by the romantic Siciliana in which is highlighted a beautiful melody for oboe and viola solo.

Index